INTRODUCTION TO SOCIAL PROBLEMS

INTRODUCTION TO SOCIAL PROBLEMS

Leonard Glick
Daniel E. Hebding

COMMUNITY COLLEGE OF PHILADELPHIA

▲ ADDISON-WESLEY PUBLISHING COMPANY

Reading, Massachusetts   Menlo Park, California   London   Amsterdam   Don Mills, Ontario   Sydney

This book is in the

ADDISON-WESLEY SERIES IN SOCIOLOGY

Library of Congress Cataloging in Publication Data

Glick, Leonard.
    Introduction to social problems.

    Includes index.
    1. Sociology. 2. Social problems. 3. United
States–Social conditions. I. Hebding, Daniel E.,
joint author. II. Title.
HM51.G6   362'.042   78–67953
ISBN 0–201–02600–7

Preface

This book is for students enrolled in social problems courses within both two- and four-year colleges. In writing this text we have pursued and hopefully achieved certain basic goals. Our utmost priorities have been to present our readers with a comprehensive and up-to-date analysis of the nature and origins of, and the possible solutions to, many of our major contemporary social problems. At the same time, we have recognized the necessity of writing a book that is interesting and enjoyable as well as pedagogically sound.

In order to maximize the achievement of these goals, we have constantly endeavored to incorporate various characteristics and qualities into this text. The desire to write a book that is truly readable has been foremost. We have made a conscientious attempt to present all materials and information with clarity and in a straightforward manner, without diminishing the importance of the conceptual and theoretical framework of sociology and other scientific disciplines. Our approach to the analysis of social problems is an eclectic one; we do not adopt a single theoretical stance on any particular problem. Rather, we have endeavored to present a variety of competing ideological points of view on the same problems. Although our approach places heavy emphasis upon a distinct sociological way of evaluating social problems, we frequently draw upon the evidence and theoretical perspectives of other fields, such as history, psychology, biology, and anthropology. It is our belief that eclecticism is very helpful in providing a fuller understanding of many of our current social problems. In addition, we have made an all-out effort to provide a highly up-to-date and thoroughly researched book. In some instances we have also attempted to make general interpretations and summary statements of relatively larger quantities of current research literature rather than present massive amounts of detailed facts, which students sometimes find burdensome to master.

From the standpoint of organization, we have attempted to incorporate both structure and flexibility into our text. Our introductory chapter begins with a discussion of the nature of social problems, sociological inquiry, and the scientific approach. Of major importance here is our section on the sociologist's role in the study of social problems. Next, we establish the distinct sociological frame of reference for this study, outlining many of the most fundamental notions that sociologists often employ in analysis. Various aspects of this frame of reference and theoretical orientation are also applied in later chapters. Finally, three major theoretical approaches to the study of social problems—social disorganization, deviance, and conflict—are discussed in detail.

The remaining chapters of the book are devoted to the discussion of specific problem areas. These chapters are logically and systematically structured to facilitate study. Each chapter begins with a discussion of the nature, extent, and scope of the problem. This is followed by an analysis of various historical and contemporary explanations of its causes. Sociological explanations are given particular emphasis in this section. The final section of each chapter is concerned with responses to the problem. Here we evaluate past and present efforts to deal with the problem and their probable future consequences. New proposals are similarly discussed. In contrast to the structure of the individual chapters, the overall organization of the book is open and flexible. Our arrangement of the chapters is just one way in which they can be assigned. The chapters have been written and constructed as distinct units, and the professor may assign them in virtually any order.

This book is both a text and a reader in the fullest sense of the words. The readings have been very carefully selected and integrated into the text and are not employed simply as "filler" material. The readings not only support various points mentioned in the text but also add other important dimensions to the reader's knowledge. Thus it is crucial that the reader see these readings as vital portions of each chapter. Each reading, selected for presentation, scholarship, and ability to hold interest, is prefaced with its own introduction and is placed at the point we feel is most advantageous for comprehension.

Finally, many specific learning aids are also in the text, including learning objectives and introductory sections for each chapter and reading, chapter summaries, margin notes, an extensive glossary, very carefully selected photographs, and many clear charts and graphs. These devices, along with the lucid presentation of text materials, have been utilized to aid the student in developing an increased understanding of all materials presented in the book.

We would like to express our appreciation to those people at Addison-Wesley who made vital contributions to this text. Very special gratitude must also go to our wives, Marie and Nevie, for their support, patience, suggestions, critical comments, and the many hours of brute physical labor that they gave toward the preparation of this book. Sincere thanks also to our children, Sonia, Gretchen, and Leonard, Jr., for their understanding, patience, and cooperation during the many months spent on our book.

Daniel E. Hebding
Drexel Hill, Pennsylvania

Leonard Glick
Cinnaminson, New Jersey
August, 1979

Contents

3
SEXISM AND RACISM

4
AGISM

5
CRIME AND DELINQUENCY

6
DRUGS AND ALCOHOL

7
FAMILY PROBLEMS

8

PHYSICAL AND MENTAL HEALTH

9

POPULATION

10
ENVIRONMENT

Marshall Henrichs

1
Introduction

Chapter Objectives

1. To give a clear and concise definition of the term "social problem."

2. To define and give two examples of what is meant by the objective and subjective components in the definition of social problems.

3. To identify and discuss the guidelines of the scientific approach to the study of social problems.

4. To identify the major reasons why sociology cannot be totally value-free in the study of social problems and to contrast by means of essay the arguments as to whether sociology should be value-free.

5. To list and describe the four major roles that sociologists perform in the study of social problems.

6. To discuss in an essay the basic sociological principle that social problems are often related to the "way of life" of a society, to value conflicts, to flaws in the basic social structure, or to social change.

7. To define what is meant by social disorganization, listing its five major potential sources.

8. To define what is meant by deviant behavior and to identify the three major perspectives for explaining the phenomenon of deviance.

9. To compare by means of essay the conflict approach to explaining social problems with the functionalist approach.

10. To compare by means of essay the conflict approach to explaining social problems with the deviance theory.

SOCIOLOGY AND SOCIAL PROBLEMS

SOCIAL PROBLEMS: CONTRASTING VIEWS

By nature people are social and live in groups. Being social animals, we are dependent upon groups to help us cope with problems related to meeting our needs. Today, throughout our society, the needs of people are not being met. Within our communities, towns, and cities, we are all being confronted with many problems that threaten the quality of our life.

To many and no doubt the vast majority of Americans, the term "social problem" is commonplace. We listen to the news on television or radio or glance at a newspaper or weekly newsmagazine and are instantly informed of a number of situations or occurrences that in one way or another spell out misery or trouble. Examples of these occurrences are endless: the robbery of a liquor store, the high rate of unemployment and high living costs, the greater likelihood of being victimized by violent crime, a community threatened with industrial pollution of its air and water supplies, a new escalation of conflict between nations, the need for organized governmental efforts to deal with the growing population crisis, a neighborhood attempting to cope with a crisis of drug abuse, the chronic inequalities of sex and race, the growing specter of alienation and indifference toward life situations.

In some respects, these occurrences share something in common: They arise within or are a product of group life. They also occur frequently enough to affect relatively large numbers of people. In this sense, a single person out of work, a single violent crime, a single death or instance of drug abuse does not signify the existence of a social problem. As we shall see, for a social problem to exist several conditions must be met, including the fact that significant numbers of people must be affected—i.e., a high rate of unemployment, drug abuse, crime, and so forth must exist.

In this sense, when sociologists speak of social problems, we are concerned with conditions or situations that in one way or another affect group life. It is important to note, however, that in a complex society like our own, different types of people will tend to view various conditions of group life in different ways. Thus while certain people may define a condition as one type of problem, others may view the situation as another problem or perhaps as no problem at all! To some people, population increase and its effect upon world resources constitute a major social problem. Many such people may be insistent that governments take a much more active role in creating and implementing nationwide population control programs in the areas of sterilization, birth control, and legalized abortion. Others may feel that population increase constitutes little, if any, problem. To these people, population *limitation*, particularly by means of governmental control programs, may constitute the real problem. Again, the owner of a particular factory may view pollution quite differently from the un-

Social problems are familiar to everybody

Problems affect many people

People define problems in different ways

fortunate nearby residents, who must contend with an environment of smoke-filled air or tainted water. To the factory owner, pollution may constitute a problem to the degree that he or she is forced to lay out expenditures and make adjustments in the manufacturing processes in order to conform to increased federal antipollution legislation.

Likewise, many people may be aware of major problems within our society, yet, as a result of their own individual life circumstances, they may conceive of these problems in quite different ways. People who have directly experienced the conditions of unemployment, discrimination, and poverty are very likely to view these problems in ways quite distinct from those who have not. Similarly, a self-employed businessperson's conception of the daily problems and dissatisfactions of blue-collar assembly line workers will probably vary from the workers' own ideas.

Examples such as these serve to illustrate important points regarding social problems that sociologists have longed recognized.[2] The first point relates to the fact that within society we do not always have a consensus on just what the specific problems of group life are. Thus conditions that are defined by some people as problems may not be recognized as problems by others. The second point is that, even when we consider a number of conditions that *do* tend to be widely recognized as problems of group life (such as those examined in this text), different people will interpret these problems in varying ways. Differences in the way people view social problems ultimately result from the fact that people frequently hold diverse positions and roles within the society. Thus, people of different ages, religions, ethnic memberships, and social class positions will tend to view their society (and its problems) in distinct ways. Third, people holding different positions in society will often advocate widely divergent ways of coping with social problems. To give an example, when it comes to the matter of tax reform, it is the middle-income tax payers, not the superrich or corporate power blocs, who are much more likely to advocate the closing of vast tax loopholes. Likewise, divorce as a possible response to marital problems is approved or accepted by many Protestant religious groups, whereas the Catholic church has been steadfast in its opposition to divorce on any grounds. Finally, certain people within various structural positions in the society may be somewhat ambivalent toward *any* proposed remedies for specific problems since such solutions may damage their own social, political, or economic interests. Sociologist Herbert Gans clearly points out that poverty has some beneficial consequences to many nonpoor groups in our society. For example, poverty helps to guarantee that "society's dirty work" will be done. Gans asserts that "the poor also aid in the upward mobility of groups just above them . . . many Americans have entered the middle class through the profits earned from the provision of goods and services in the slums."[1]

Consensus on problems does not always exist

Social problems do not always harm everyone

WHAT IS A SOCIAL PROBLEM?

The above analysis has introduced a number of ideas that are highly useful in defining just what sociologists mean by social problems. We have seen, first, that social problems are related to situations or conditions of group life; second, that social problems affect significant numbers of people; and finally, that the judgments and values that people have toward these situations appear to play an important role in determining which situations are defined as problematic and what should be done about them.

It should be noted that sociologists define the term social problem in various ways, some of which we will examine later. For now, based upon our above discussion, we will define a social problem as a group condition or situation that significant numbers of people consider undesirable and in need of remedy through group action. It should be pointed out that this definition contains both an *objective* component—i.e., the actual situation or group condition (a particular rate of crime or incidence of drug abuse, for instance)—as well as a *subjective* (value) aspect. This latter dimension refers to the idea that a social problem exists when people view the condition as undesirable and feel that something can and should be done to remedy it.

It should be noted at this point that sociologists will sometimes disagree on the relative importance of objective and subjective factors in defining social problems. Some sociologists prefer to define social problems primarily in terms of their objective aspects—the actual conditions in and of themselves. They argue that certain conditions constitute hazards to group life even though people may not be aware of their existence. Sociologists holding this position feel that it is sociology's role and responsibility to identify the problems and inform the public of the ways in which these conditions may endanger group needs, standards of living, and avowed interests. Other sociologists prefer to view social problems primarily and at times exclusively in terms of their subjective aspects—how people feel toward conditions of group life. Sociologists holding this view would emphasize that *any* condition of group life, regardless of its nature, is not a social problem unless and until people define it as one—i.e., view it as being undesirable and feel that it can and should be remedied.

Based upon our definition of social problems, it is our view that *both* objective and subjective components are indispensable elements in determining their existence. Insofar as sociologists can determine reality in terms of the values and needs that people consider important for their way of life and of the actual conditions that conflict with and have an adverse effect upon those values and needs, situations such as these must not be ignored, especially when large numbers of people are involved. On the other hand, as we have seen in our definitions, people's awareness of conditions as undesirable and in need of change is also an indispensable factor in determining the existence of social problems. In these terms, we cannot say that

Social problem defined

Social problems have objective and subjective dimensions

Objective and subjective elements are both important

a particular condition constitutes a problem, in the fullest sense of our definition, unless people are disturbed about the condition and feel that it can and should be remedied.

Given the existence of certain conditions of group life, it is the people, particularly those who have power in society, who determine which conditions or situations are disturbing. The intensity and extent of concern over a particular condition can vary within a society from one time to another. For example, in the late nineteenth century thousands of young children worked twelve-hour days in the dangerously poor conditions that existed in our nation's mining and textile industries. For many years this situation was not considered to be a social problem. Many people accepted it as a natural, inevitable aspect of American industrialization. Young children working under subhuman conditions did not cause concern among significant numbers of Americans and there was no belief that a remedy was needed. People were not concerned and it was therefore not considered to be a social problem. In the early twentieth century, when the condition began to cause concern, there developed a call for its remedy and it became a social problem. Through this social concern, which led to the formation of interest groups that were directed toward correcting the problem, and through ensuing legislation, the problem of child labor was corrected. In terms of our definition of a social problem, there no longer existed an objective condition or situation—i.e., children no longer worked in the mines and mills—and there was therefore no longer a need for corrective group action.

It becomes quite obvious to even a casual observer of American society that there are many social groups for which a variety of conditions could be considered social problems. Therefore, any particular text in this area must be selective. In this text, we will limit our focus to an examination of those conditions or situations that influence, and are held to be undesirable by, vast numbers of Americans. How do we determine those conditions that are of widespread significance within society? We may begin to answer this question by examining many of the resources within society that are able to provide us with information.

One such resource is the public opinion poll. Public opinion polls conducted by social science researchers or private polling organizations provide data on those social conditions that are considered to be important social problems by many Americans. In polling people's attitudes and opinions, sociologists have made extensive use of the sample interview survey (in which the interviewer and respondent meet) to obtain data about the conditions that are felt to be social problems. Over the past several years, the sample interview survey has developed into an economically efficient instrument for gathering valid and reliable information on people's values, attitudes, and opinions concerning social issues and problems. Also, ques-

Concern over conditions varies from time to time

Estimating undesirable conditions

Public opinion polls and mass media

tionnaires filled out by a sample of people that is statistically representative of the larger population have provided sociologists with a relatively fast and inexpensive method of obtaining information about social conditions. Poll taking, through a wide variety of statistical methods and sampling techniques, has become quite sophisticated and accurate within the social sciences. By using these techniques and by asking people to identify the social conditions that are of significant concern to them, we can establish a list of conditions that influence and are held to be undesirable by vast numbers of Americans.[3]

The mass media is an important additional resource available within society that is able to provide sociologists with information on social conditions. Television, radio, newspapers, and weekly newsmagazines are important resources that the sociologist can carefully analyze in order to measure people's ideas about existing social conditions.

SOCIAL PROBLEMS AND SOCIOLOGICAL INQUIRY

During previous ages, people's knowledge and interpretations of the nature of their social world were derived largely from their beliefs in an unchanging natural law, the inevitability of certain conditions, and even divine will. Famine and disease were believed to be natural facts of life. Widespread poverty was felt to be inevitable. In many instances, religious or moralistic answers were given to account for the tragic conditions of human existence. Many people argued that famine, poverty, and war were actually God's punishments, which people had to accept and endure in attonement for their evil and sinful natures. It was only through prayer, personal sacrifice, and a renewed commitment to moral principles that any hope for improvement of the human condition was possible.

Interpretations of social problems: Past and present

Today, although some of these philosophical, religious, and social reformist views are still present, information about and interpretations of social problems come from a wide variety of additional sources. For example, scores of contemporary journalists and novelists have often been the first to call attention to a variety of social conditions that stand in need of amelioration. Likewise, members of the legal, medical, and social work professions continuously deal with various aspects of social problems within their respective fields. Many of these professionals have taken an active role, proposing new approaches and alternatives to the treatment of problems that affect countless individuals within our society. Also, many social sciences, such as anthropology, political science, psychology, and history, have in their own specific ways contributed to a scientific understanding of social problems. Today, more than in any other period of human history, these explanations and solutions have become widely accepted and utilized.

Of all the social sciences, sociology has no doubt been most involved with the study of social problems. Sociology can be defined as the scientific study of human interaction. Thus sociology is thought of as a *general* social science because it focuses upon the study of all aspects of human social life, group behavior, and social organization. From this perspective, the study of social problems is important, but it is nevertheless only one major area of sociological inquiry. Although sociologists sometimes find it important to utilize the findings of disciplines such as biology, anthropology, and psychology in the study of social problems, it is important to recognize that sociologists view social problems in ways somewhat distinct from these other sciences. From the sociological point of view, social problems arise within and can be linked to the patterns of human relationships and social organization found within society.[2] Thus problems such as crime, poverty, and discrimination have social or human-made origins. Further, the sociologist feels that long-range answers as to the causes and remedies for social problems can best be achieved by examining and evaluating just how well human groups function to meet the needs of their members.

Sociology: The scientific study of human interaction

THE SCIENTIFIC APPROACH TO SOCIAL PROBLEMS

Sociology can also be distinguished from many other approaches to understanding social problems, such as the literary, religious, and philosophical, in that sociology attempts to employ the *scientific method* in its investigations.[3] In using the scientific approach in the study of social problems, the sociologist uses certain guidelines in doing research and developing conclusions. What are some of these guidelines and characteristics of the scientific point of view?

For one thing, the sociologist insists that research be based upon factual data. Factual information is not based upon personal beliefs, idle speculation, or commonsense notions. For example, some people may believe that crime in general is greater among the lower social classes than in the higher classes. Likewise, other people may believe that if juvenile delinquents receive counseling their delinquent behaviors will be eliminated. The sociologist would not accept these beliefs, in and of themselves, as constituting factual or observable *evidence* on these topics. Rather, the sociologist would insist that valid data on these subjects be obtained by means of scientific research.

Scientific research is based on factual data

As we shall see, scientific research dealing with social problems covers a variety of areas: the precise definition and description of the major social problems existing within society, the development of explanations as to possible causes of these problems, the evaluation of the success of past and present efforts to deal with or alleviate numerous social problems, and the analysis of various future treatment possibilities and their likely consequences.

Another major characteristic of the scientific method is that of objectivity. Objectivity refers to the ability and willingness to study the subject matter of a given field without prejudice. Thus in being objective, the social scientist attempts to conduct research and draw conclusions without personal bias, preconceptions, or personal feelings. A sociologist may believe, for instance, that divorce represents a feasible and beneficial way of alleviating marital conflict and unhappiness for many people; but, in being objective, he or she must not allow such personal feelings to interfere with the research or the conclusions on the subject.[3]

It is important to understand that objectivity is something that can never be fully achieved within any science. This does not imply, however, that personal biases or preconceptions on the part of the scientist should not or cannot be reduced and held to a minimum. Quite the contrary, social scientists constantly attempt to do this when doing research within their field of study. In order to maximize objectivity in scientific research, sociologists must constantly be aware of, and guard against the imposition of, their own values and feelings. They must also receive adequate training in the scientific approach. As indicated above, the researcher trained in the scientific method will be very much aware that data on a particular social problem or on another sociological question must be based upon factual evidence. Such evidence must be derived from scientific research, not from mere speculation or commonsense notions.[3]

A third guideline of the scientific approach is the fact that the scientific method demands precision in all its facets of operation. Thus, the researcher must maintain a high degree of accuracy in the collection and analysis of data from the research on a particular question or problem. In order to ensure precision, the scientist is required to develop a research design prior to the investigation of a particular question or problem. The research design precisely defines the specific kinds of data to be collected and the sources to be utilized in gathering this data, for example, official crime reports, labor department statistics, and court records. The research design also specifies the time period during which the data will be gathered and gives a thorough description of the methods to be employed in the data gathering, such as using questionnaire or interview surveys or developing and conducting a particular set of experiments. Finally, the research design will also specify the methods by which the data, once gathered, will be classified and analyzed and the procedures used in the development of conclusions.

A final major element of the scientific approach is that of critical appraisal and verification of the research by an audience of competent peers. These people will evaluate the research in terms of the degree to which it adheres to the above-mentioned scientific guidelines. Evaluation and verification on the part of professional peers is a vital element in the scientific approach and is of great importance in ensuring that objectivity as much as possible.[3]

Objectivity is important in studying social problems

Full objectivity cannot be achieved

Precision is important in science

Research must be checked by others

SOCIOLOGY AND VALUES

An important issue that is frequently raised by many people, including sociologists themselves, is whether sociology can be, and for that matter *should* be, totally objective or value-free in its methods of investigating society's problems. As we pointed out earlier, objectivity is a most difficult quality to acquire within any science and in fact can never be fully achieved. This is particularly true when it comes to the study of social problems. When the sociologist investigates a social problem, the goal, as in all other areas of sociological inquiry, is to be as objective as possible. The sociologist, however, cannot simply block out or suspend all his or her values and preferences when judging whether the research has potential for alleviating human problems. Behind many studies of social problems is the hope that the research might be of some use in improving peoples' lives. Objectivity is difficult to achieve, but the sociologist must try to look at society in a detached, value-free way. In so doing, the sociologist must be willing to recognize that society itself, with its many inconsistencies, conflicts, and inequalities, may frequently constitute the *source* of many major social problems. Looking at society in such an extremely detached manner is far more difficult than most people realize.

Difficulties in attaining objectivity

In a much larger but related sense, sociological inquiry is not and in fact cannot be totally value-free. As sociologist Robert Merton points out, implicit sets of values underlie and surround the entire sociological enterprise. According to Merton, values play a role in sociological research at a number of crucial points. For example, values implicitly underlie the problems that the sociologist will select for study, such as when certain sociologists object to studying a problem connected with military defense out of fear that such study may at least indirectly contribute to the nuclear arms race. Values will also influence the way in which the social scientist will formulate a problem for research. In other words, the sociologist may often design and conduct research in such a way that the results of the investigations may be more useful for one group than for another. For example, a sociologist may decide to do research on a problem of police and community relations within a particular city. Obviously, however, what the "problem" will turn out to be, including possible solutions for it, will ultimately depend on to whose complaints—those of the police or of the citizens at large—the researcher decided to listen.[2]

Finally, as Merton notes, the scientific approach can never be totally value-free since science itself has a number of explicit values and norms that help to define the proper conduct for scientific research. Many of these values and norms, however, help to ensure objectivity! One such value is specified in the norm of "organized skepticism" mentioned above, which refers to the requirement that research and conclusions be subject to critical evaluation and verification by professional peers.[2]

Organized skepticism can help ensure objectivity

Today, virtually all sociologists agree that sociology cannot be totally value-free. This is not to say, however, that sociology as a social science should not and cannot strive to maximize objectivity. We have seen that objectivity is an important element of the scientific approach, and we have indicated various characteristics of the scientific method that help to ensure that objectivity is maintained as fully as possible.

It is also important to understand that objectivity has various implications for the kinds of questions that sociologists can ask as well as for the kinds of answers that sociologists are able to give regarding different questions, issues, and problems. For example, objectivity requires that science remain *neutral* with respect to human values. The sociologist can identify the values that people have and determine the ways in which certain values conflict with others and the many consequences of such conflicts. However, the sociologist *as a scientist* cannot tell people what values they *should* have. Thus the sociologist does not make any personal value judgments regarding the morality of the values or beliefs that he or she is studying. Science can be used to supply us with much factual knowledge concerning the values that people hold, but science cannot prove that one value is better or more worthwhile than another. For example, the sociologist may discover that many people in our society disapprove of capital punishment, divorce, or gun control, but the sociologist as a scientist cannot conclude that these people are right or wrong in their opinions. Answers to questions concerning the merits of values cannot be determined by science.[3]

Neutrality and human values

Objectivity also requires that scientists adopt a position of neutrality with respect to determining the *uses* of scientific knowledge. For example, science may develop new methods for artificial birth control or provide us with insight into ways of reducing or eliminating poverty or pollution, but science in and of itself cannot decide for us whether or in what ways this knowledge *should* be used. Questions concerning the uses of scientific knowledge call for political as well as value judgments and decisions, and thus cannot be settled scientifically. Science can identify values and goals that people have, and scientific knowledge can also be used to help people reach the goals that they prefer. Scientific knowledge in itself, however, cannot be used in determining for people what they *should* want or how they *should* live.[3]

While virtually all sociologists recognize that sociology *cannot* be totally objective, it is important to note that sociologists do not always agree as to whether or not sociology *should* be value-free. Sociologists such as George Lundberg and Robert Bierstedt have taken the position that sociology *must* be totally value-free. This position was advanced by a number of sociologists many years ago and reflected a need to complete sociology's separation from social philosophy and gain increased respectability as a

Lundberg and Bierstedt: Should sociology be value-free?

social science. Bierstedt has noted that many of our social problems may be solved using sociological knowledge. He notes, however, that it is not the job of social scientists to apply this knowledge. For him, the "immediate goal of sociology is the acquisition of knowledge about human society, not the utilization of that knowledge."[6]

Today, as in the past, sociologists will sometimes debate as to just what their role should be, particularly as this relates to the area of social problems. Many sociologists adopt the position of neutrality, as outlined above, when it comes to matters of value judgments and the uses of scientific knowledge. They are of the opinion that sociology should limit itself primarily to the analysis of social problems and to the evaluation of various treatment possibilities and their likely consequences.

Other sociologists will seriously question the limitations of this role. From their point of view, social sciences in general and sociology in particular have an important responsibility to take an active role in formulating and publicly advocating policy decisions and reform measures aimed at alleviating society's problems. They are of the opinion that sociologists have an obligation to publicly prescribe what society *ought* to do about its social problems. Sociologists such as Alvin Gouldner and C. Wright Mills have rigorously criticized the neutrality position with respect to the study of society and social problems.[7] They believe that a value-free sociology is a myth and that values are very much a part of the research process. They feel that the sociologist in his or her investigations cannot and should not refrain from making value judgments on issues and problems within today's society. Gerald Berreman agrees with this position, noting that "to do nothing in today's world is as political in its effect as to do something."[8] Obviously, there are no simple solutions to this issue. But the reader should at least be aware that this controversy exists today.

Gouldner and Mills on the question of neutrality

THE SOCIOLOGIST'S ROLE

As we have seen above, sociologists will sometimes disagree as to what their role should be in the analysis of social problems; however, sociologists will generally agree that they have made many important contributions in their role as social scientists. Sociologists contribute to the study of social problems mainly through the use of scientific research, which enables them to obtain facts and develop questions and conclusions concerning various problematic areas of social life. At this point it is important to examine the types of questions that sociologists attempt to answer in their role as scientific researchers.

Sociologists study social problems through scientific research

One of the most fundamental questions that sociologists attempt to answer through research is "What are the major social problems that exist within a particular group or society?" The attempt to identify, define, and measure the extent of social problems is far more complex than might appear at first glance. First of all, as we have seen, each social problem has

Cary Wolinsky, Stock, Boston

The impact of an ever-increasing world population is one of the problems being studied by sociologists and others today.

a subjective or value aspect. Problems are *undesirable* conditions that contradict some particular value that people feel is important. Thus, in defining social problems, the sociologist must first attempt to identify the actual values that people hold. Identifying values is a difficult task for social scientists. This task is made more complicated because American society contains many subgroups that have different types of values and norms. Sociologists use various research methods for identifying people's values. These include large-scale interview and questionnaire surveys and in-depth studies of the value preferences of people residing within a number of American cities and towns as well as the analysis of various newspapers, magazines, and speeches and interviews given by a variety of political leaders.

Identification of social problems

In addition to identifying people's values, the sociologist must also determine what people consider to be the major social problems of group life. In other words, from the standpoint of public opinion, what conditions conflict with major social values? Here, the sociologist is involved in identifying major issues of public concern, which can be documented in a variety of ways. These include: the use of public opinion polls asking people to name conditions that they feel are problematic and in need of remedy; the analysis of mass media content as it indicates issues of public concern; and the review of governmental activities and legislation.

Identification of social problems: Public concerns

Once the sociologist has identified people's values and determined issues of public concern, he or she must then attempt to measure the *actual extent* of problematic conditions of group life. Given the fact that people view crime, discrimination, and poverty as undesirable conditions in need of remedy, sociologists must still determine the actual extent of these conditions within society. In addition, sociologists must also determine the degree to which these conditions vary in terms of factors such as age, sex, religion, and social class. Data on the extent and variation of social problems are obtained from a variety of sources. For example, information concerning the extent of crime is available from official crime statistics published by the FBI, statistics published by the U.S. Department of Health, Education, and Welfare, and independent sociological studies on the incidence of crime based upon reports provided by actual victims.

In brief, then, the sociologist defines and describes the many social problems that exist in the society and provides us with factual data on a variety of them. The student should understand, however, that the sociologist's role is not merely to identify social problems and list various facts and figures, but also to analyze, interpret, and organize this information within a systematic framework in order to provide a clearer understanding of the problems' dimensions and scope. Prior to any understanding of how social problems develop or why they exist, we must have organized all the valid data on various social phenomena. First, as we have seen, people's values must be defined; second, issues of public concern must be defined; and third, measures of the actual extent of problematic conditions of group life must be obtained. A description of the important facts and dimensions of social problems is a necessary prerequisite to any analysis and understanding of social problems.

Analyzing and interpreting information on problems is important

In addition to identifying social problems, a second major goal of the sociologist is to attempt to explain their existence. Simply stated, the sociologist is interested in explaining how and why conditions that have been defined as social problems originate: What are their causes?

Explaining social problems' origins

Many of the social problems in America are the inevitable products of existing social conditions and social structures. As we have noted earlier, social problems arise within and can be linked to the many patterns of human relationships and social organization found within society.[2] The sociologist helps us to recognize many of the conditions and structural characteristics within society that may account for and contribute to the existence of social problems. The explanation of social problems is not that simple, however. American society is complex, and the explanations that account for the causes of social problems are as complex as the society. The sociologist attempts to explore the many conditions and causes of social problems and to examine those factors in society that contribute to their continued existence. Sociological knowledge can help students develop an understanding of the connections between social problems and various existing values and social structures.

Social problems are highly complex

In order to explain how and why social problems arise, the sociologist adopts the roles of both *theoretician* and *researcher*. In the role of theoretician, sociologists and other social scientists develop theories (tentative explanations) for the causes of certain phenomena. For example, theoretical explanations for drug addiction, alcoholism, and crime currently stress a number of causal factors, including physiological characteristics and personality traits within the psychological makeup of the individual. Other explanations, more sociological in nature, stress the importance of social learning. In addition, other sociologists note the influence that social and economic inequalities have on the creation of personal frustrations and conflicts, which may in turn induce people to engage in various forms of deviant behavior. The sociologist is keenly aware of the important relationship between theory and scientific research. For the sociologist, simply getting the facts about a particular problem (i.e., whether crime is increasing or which particular groups in society are most affected by poverty) is not enough: The causes must be discovered as well. In order to do this, the sociologist must develop theories and then test their adequacy by means of scientific research.

The sociologist as theoretician

The sociologist thus provides the student with a wide variety of theories regarding social problems, contributing to the student's understanding of such problems. In addition, as we will see below, theories provide a framework within which the student can examine (a) current policies and proposals and (b) past and present treatment efforts that have been established to deal with or alleviate social problems. The sociologist clearly recognizes that theories are important for the development of social policies and treatment programs for dealing with social problems and those who are affected by them. The fact is that any proposed social policy or treatment program for dealing with social problems is based upon some type of theory, regardless of whether the authors of the proposal are aware of it. For instance, many different proposals have been advanced to deal with the problem of drug addiction. Some have recommended giving the addict free drugs; others have recommended treatment in a therapeutic community; still others have recommended imprisonment. Underlying all these proposals, however, are distinct theories on the causes of addiction and the potential possibilities, if any, for its cure. Thus, the question is not whether we should have theory or whether we need theory; rather, the important

Sociological information can help in evaluating social policies and treatment efforts

question is how adequate the theories are in helping us to understand the causes of social problems and to best deal with them. It is in this area that the sociologist can make important contributions in the two roles of theoretician and researcher. In performing these roles, the sociologist develops theoretical explanations for social problems and then tests the validity of these theories by means of scientific research.

Because of a unique understanding of social problems, the sociologist may be engaged in a number of additional roles related to the field of social problems. For example, many sociologists engage in the role of *social critic*, presenting opinions and knowledge for the purpose of assessing the adequacy of current philosophies and policies on many of society's major social problems. As we have previously indicated, while acting in the role of social critic, some sociologists have also attempted to take an active part in formulating and advocating the adoption of policy decisions and social, economic, and legal reform measures aimed at the alleviation of society's problems.

The sociologist as social critic

Finally, sociologists also employ their theoretical knowledge and research skills as *evaluators*, testing the adequacy of specific programs for treating various social problems. It should be emphasized that, in addition to identifying social problems and developing theories aimed at explaining their causes, the analysis and evaluation of current treatment programs represents a major area of sociological inquiry. Sociologists and other social scientists have amassed a great deal of evidence on the adequacy of a variety of treatment programs, including: the influence of counseling on delinquent behavior; the effectiveness of psychotherapy programs for treating alcoholism and other forms of drug addiction; the adequacy of the current welfare and public assistance programs for dealing with various facets of poverty in American society; and the influence of imprisonment upon subsequent criminal behavior. In the role of evaluator, the sociologist analyzes a wide variety of existing programs for dealing with social problems, recommends needed changes, if any, and suggests the direction that new programs should take.

The sociologist as evaluator

In summary, we have seen that in the study of social problems, sociologists have a number of important goals: first, to identify, define, and describe the major problems of society; second, to analyze, interpret, and organize reliable data about these problems; and third, to develop theoretical explanations for their causes. The information that the sociologist develops may then be helpful in evaluating current and future treatment programs designed to alleviate the problems.

A SOCIOLOGICAL FRAME OF REFERENCE

As we pointed out in the beginning of this chapter, when sociologists examine social problems they tend to focus upon those conditions that are society-wide in their effects. Due to the fact that social problems are very complex, sociologists do not generally agree upon a single overall theory that would help us to explain their existence, but they do share certain ideas or notions about the nature of social life and the ways in which social problems arise. In this section, we will examine some of these ideas and identify a few of the characteristics of group life that generate social problems.

A framework for social problems

SOCIAL PROBLEMS ARE RELATED TO SOCIETY'S "WAY OF LIFE"

One very important idea that sociologists often employ as a starting point in their analysis of social problems is the notion that social problems are often a result of the culture or "way of life" of a society. Perhaps this idea is most clearly seen in the fact that different societies have social problems specific to their own patterns and standards of living.[24] For example, our society places high emphasis upon the values of individualism, contractural relationships, and personal satisfaction and happiness. Consequently, if individuals do not find fulfillment and happiness in their unions with others, opportunities for dissolving the relationships are available to them. Obviously, values such as these have many beneficial consequences and are important to our way of life. Yet on the other hand, they are partial contributors to some of our current social problems, as evidenced by our vastly increasing rates of separation and divorce. Likewise, our growing problems of excessive drinking and alcoholism must be seen in large measure as a consequence of the social importance placed upon the use of alcohol. In fact, our current emphasis upon the use of alcohol has reached the point where the *nondrinker* is often considered strange or deviant.

Our social problems are often related to our culture

Again for instance, the well-publicized population crisis that is currently being experienced in several nonindustrial and industrial societies results in large part from the fact that many people have continued to follow more traditional values and norms, which specify the importance of having large families. During previous centuries, high birth rates and large families were important since many children did not survive and adults frequently died at relatively young ages. Today, however, recent medical advances have had the effect of lowering death rates within many societies. The net result is that many societies now face the problem of trying to feed and otherwise provide for an increasing population.

Many other examples illustrate the fundamental principle that social problems are often related to or a direct result of the culture or way of life of a society. For instance, we can characterize the United States as a highly industrialized society whose population tends to be geographically mobile and urbanized. Many problems specific to our society result from these patterns of living. Examples would include the industrial and automobile pollution of our air and water supplies, the dense overcrowding in many sections of our cities, and the congested and often clogged highway systems, which do not meet the needs of our population.

In stressing the principle that social problems are basically a by-product of a society's way of life, sociologists also tend to emphasize two important related ideas. The first is the fundamental notion that social problems are not caused by "evil people" doing "evil things." This idea is difficult for many people to accept because we have been socialized to view things in terms of their being right or wrong or good or bad. However, sociologists stress the principle that many social problems are simply a normal and, in a sense, an inevitable consequence of average people acting in typical and generally approved ways. In this sense, there is nothing wrong in and of itself with wanting to be geographically mobile, taking a drink, having children, or desiring personal fulfillment and happiness.

Tied to this is our second basic idea, that social problems are often unforeseen results of human activity. A review of the examples above should show the reader that most people are often not in a position to recognize or understand many of the larger social consequences of their day-to-day behavior. Rather noteworthy examples of this principle are the passage of the Prohibition Amendment in the early 1920s and the more recent enactment of various drug laws on the part of legislators. Obviously, such legislation had a significant effect upon alcohol and other drug use. However, this legislation also had the unintended and largely unforeseen result of creating and sustaining the contemporary large-scale problem of organized crime in the United States.

VALUE CONFLICTS AND SOCIAL PROBLEMS

Aside from the general principle that social problems are often the result of the way of life of a particular society, sociologists have also identified a number of features or conditions of group life that often tend to generate or contribute to the rise of social problems. One such general condition is the existence of value conflicts. The student will remember that when sociologists speak of values, we are referring to people's judgments of the worth or desirability of objects, events, or conditions of group life. Earlier in our discussion, we indicated that for a social problem to exist, people must view a condition as undesirable, in that it contradicts some value they feel is important. However, it is often the case, particularly in complex societies, that many values, even dominant ones, may tend to be incompatible and may even conflict. In this situation, the attainment of one value may place the attainment of other important values in a certain degree of jeopardy. Many sociologists view such value conflicts as a major source of various social problems. For example, most Americans place a great deal of emphasis upon personal achievement and individuality. However, these values may conflict with more humanitarian values and ideals that are also considered important in our society.[25]

In addition to generating social problems, value conflicts also encourage their continuation. For instance, many Americans advocate racial integration of our schools because they view educational equality to be an important social goal. On the other hand, many other Americans believe that racial

Social problems may be caused by people acting in approved ways

Problems as unforeseen results of human behavior

Values defined

Value conflicts occur frequently in complex societies

integration within schools, particularly by means of bussing, is undesirable because it may threaten the quality of education for their children.

A frequently asked question is "Why are value conflicts so common within American society?" In answering this question, sociologists often point out that we live in a highly complex and heterogeneous society, containing many different groups and types of people. Many of these groups will tend to learn and share some of the dominant values and norms (group standards for acceptable behavior) that are characteristic of the general culture. However, they will often maintain a number of their own distinctive values, some of which may conflict to a certain degree with those of other groups as well as with those of the larger society. Sociologists term these various groups or categories of people *subcultures*. Thus we can identify a variety of religious, ethnic, racial, social class (in so far as they represent occupational, income, and prestige differentials), age, and regional subcultures. In addition, other groups within the society are frequently referred to as *deviant* subcultures because they share a number of values (and norms) that tend to be in opposition to those of the larger society. For example, we can note the existence of many delinquent, homosexual, prostitution, and drug-using subcultures.[3]

Value conflicts: Subcultural dimensions

The wide variety of cultural and subcultural differences within the United States means, in effect, that we do not always have a consensus on which values should receive priority within our society. Thus, value conflicts are frequently present. These conflicts in turn are often the source of many disagreements: Which situations should be defined as social problems? Should they be changed or completely eliminated? What is the best method to effect this?

SOCIAL STRUCTURE AND SOCIAL PROBLEMS

In addition to examining the role that value conflicts can play in the development of social problems, sociologists also recognize that the actual structure or organization of society itself can create problems. A major advocate of this principle is the well-known sociologist Robert Merton. According to Merton, American society assigns much importance to the attainment of certain goals, such as acquiring economic success and material goods. In addition, the society defines certain approved, "legitimate" means for attaining these goals, such as a well-paying job or higher education. However, our society is organized in a way that often places severe limitations on the opportunities of certain people (the lower classes and various racial and ethnic groups) to acquire and use the legitimate means for goal attainment. As a result, these people are likely to experience pressures, strains, and frustrations that are often severe enough to lead them to commit various forms of deviant (nonconforming) behavior. For example, in this situation some people might reject the legitimate means for goal attainment and turn to

Ways in which social structure can create social problems

various types of crime, such as robbery, burglary, or forgery. Others might decide to reject both the legitimate cultural goals and the means to obtain them and retreat into a life of excessive alcohol or other drug consumption. Thus from this perspective, many of our major social problems, such as chronic alcoholism, various types of crime, drug addiction, and even some forms of mental illness, often arise from and are perpetuated by the inconsistencies found within the organization or structure of society itself.[3,4]

SOCIAL CHANGE AND SOCIAL PROBLEMS

Finally, another important feature of group life that frequently tends to generate the rise of many major social problems is the presence of social change. Although sociologists have different theories on social change and why it occurs, most agree on two points. First, modern industrial societies are characterized by rapid social change; second, this change is often the result of technological inventions. Countless examples of technological inventions can be easily called to mind: the airplane, synthetic fabrics, many laborsaving devices within the home and industry, television, and the automobile. Obviously, each of these devices has yielded many advantages to our way of life. On the other hand, they have often been the source of many concerns for people within our society. Television, for example, has greatly expanded our avenues for communication, knowledge, and entertainment. Yet according to many people, it has resulted in the "TV addict" and has exposed children in particular to excessive amounts of violence. Likewise, the automobile has been very useful, but has been the source of such current problems as urban traffic congestion and air pollution.

Social change is often a source of social problems

Some years ago, well-known sociologist William Ogburn developed the theory of *culture lag,* which has many implications for the ways in which change can bring about social problems. According to Ogburn, technological changes (changes within the material culture of the society) tend to occur prior to and more rapidly than changes in the society's nonmaterial culture—i.e., in its values, customs, and life patterns. These technological changes necessitate attendant changes in the nonmaterial culture, but there is generally a gap, or culture lag, between the technological advancements and the development of new values, norms, beliefs, and life patterns necessary to adapt to them. This lag inevitably brings about certain social problems. For example, improvements in medical technology have resulted in an increased life expectancy for Americans, but medical benefits to care for the needs of our senior citizens have only recently been instituted.[3,5]

Technological change and social problems

As we have seen from these examples, technological change has benefited our way of life, but it has also led to the rise of a number of human problems. The solutions to these problems require adjustments in many of our values, customs, beliefs, and life patterns.

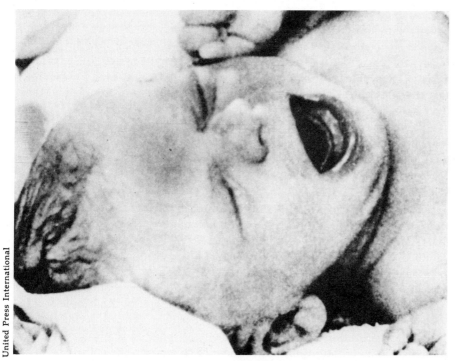

United Press International

The birth of Louise Brown, the first "test-tube" baby, was "a miracle" to her parents, but raised new moral and ethical questions for the larger society.

THEORETICAL APPROACHES TO THE STUDY OF SOCIAL PROBLEMS

There is a wide variety of sociological theories that attempts to explain social problems and provides the student with a framework within which social problems can be analyzed. Obviously, we can select only a few of the theories for examination. Accordingly, we have selected the following major theoretical orientations, which dominate the study of social problems in American sociology: the *social disorganization* approach; the *deviance* approach; and the *conflict* approach.

> There are various theoretical approaches to the study of social problems

These theories provide important insights into the nature of social problems and should be examined carefully. However, the student should be aware of the fact that these theories are complex and have their limitations. No single theory is the only correct approach. Each is useful and

Each theoretical approach is important, yet has limitations

focuses upon different aspects of reality. In our analysis of social problems in the following chapters, elements of each of these theories will be employed, since no single approach can adequately explain all the various social problems. At times one or more theories may be better able to explain a particular problem or some aspect of it. Perhaps we may find, for example, that the social disorganization or the conflict approach is more useful than the deviance approach in an examination of social change and racial conflict in America. However, the deviance approach may be better able to account for the social problems of drug addiction and juvenile delinquency. The first theoretical approach to be examined is social disorganization.

SOCIAL DISORGANIZATION

Social disorganization as a theoretical approach to the study of social problems has its roots in the process of social change and is related to the fact that Americans live in a society characterized by heterogeneity, various value conflicts, and many subcultures. As noted earlier, societies are characterized by different aspects of social change. Some societies are characterized by extensive change. No society, however, is free from social change. It is present in all societies and is manifested by alterations in people's social relationships. In societies that experience periods of rapid social change, social disorganization may develop as new attitudes and norms evolve. For some people and institutions, adjustment to changes in the culture or social structure is not difficult. For others, change may mean many difficulties. When people in the society resort to using traditional guidelines in order to cope with new social conditions and then experience frustration and confusion because the traditional rules were no longer effective (they no longer applied), we have what sociologists term social disorganization. This theoretical approach examines social problems by analyzing the social disorganization that develops with social change.

Social disorganization theory stresses the influence of social change

Before examining this approach further, the student must have a clear conception of what the sociologist means by social *organization*. Much of what the sociologist terms social organization consists of social norms and expectations that guide human behavior. In all societies, people depend upon one another for their survival and for the attainment of goals. People develop social organization to regulate their own conduct, the conduct of others, and the use of various resources to meet their needs. Reciprocal expectations are developed as people come to depend on one another. In other words, people learn what to expect from themselves, what to expect from others, and what others expect from them. Then cultural traditions, customs, and complex systems of rules and regulations, which guide people in their various actions and activities, are developed. Society's laws, which are the codified rules of the culture, define which forms of social behavior are desirable and which are not. The customs, rules, and laws of the society embody social expectations and, to an extent, govern the behavior of so-

Social organization involves social norms and expectations that guide behavior

ciety's members. It is in this manner that society "becomes organized around behaviors that contribute to survival, maintenance, and the fulfillment of other culturally prescribed values."[9]

In all societies, then, there are standards of expected behavior, or what sociologists term *social norms*, which guide people in the roles they play. When these norms are functioning efficiently, they go largely unnoticed by most people living in the society. According to the social disorganization approach, people internalize the social expectations and rules, which then facilitates the smooth operation of society. With social change, however, many of society's norms are unable to function effectively. As noted above, when people use traditional guidelines that are no longer appropriate for new social conditions, we have social disorganization. When there is a decline in group unity due to the ineffectiveness of institutionalized patterns of behavior there is social disorganization.

Thomas and Znaniecki have defined social disorganization as a decrease in the influence of existing rules upon individual members of the group.[10] With social change, in many cases, there is a breakdown among people in the consensus of social rules, which results in the fragmentation of the social order. When people's actions are not oriented by social values, social disorganization develops. As noted by Antonio, people do not know what kind of behavior to expect from others and they are not sure what others expect from them. When this happens, "cooperative activity diminishes, conflict intensifies, and the very existence of the group may be imperiled. . . . social disorganization generates feelings of uncertainty and fear that are sometimes expressed in self-destructive, maladjusted, or anti-social behaviors."[8] Social disorganization, in other words, creates *personal disorganization*.

In addition to social change, there are many other important sources of social disorganization in a society. Robert Merton, for example, has identified four major sources of social disorganization.[2] The first is *conflicting interests and values*. The potential for social disorganization, according to Merton, "comes partly from the basic structural fact that social groups and social strata have some interests and values in common and also some different, sometimes conflicting, interests and values." The second source of social disorganization is *conflicting status and role obligations*. People occupy many different statuses in the community and society. According to Merton, the statuses of parent, carpenter, and labor union member, for example, can pull a person in different directions by requiring various, sometimes opposite, behaviors. He states that "when the social system fails to provide a widely shared set of priorities among these competing obligations, the individuals subject to them experience strains. Their behavior becomes unpredictable and socially disruptive, which may be judged 'good' or 'bad,' but in either case remains disorganizing."[2] *Faulty socialization*, the third major source of social disorganization, refers to the idea that there can be defects in the socialization process. Lastly, *faulty communication* refers

Social change renders many traditional guidelines ineffective

Other sources of social disorganization

to the idea that social disorganization may be the result of inadequate communication or "partial breakdowns in channels of communication between people in a social system."[2]

Assumptions of the social disorganization approach

At this point, the student may be curious as to how current social problems develop, according to the social disorganization approach. Using this theoretical approach, many sociologists would probably first assume that at some point in time a current social problem was either nonexistent or not yet defined as problematic. Second, they would assume that the community or society was then stable—that there was agreement between social behavior and the values of the community. The third assumption would be that a social change or series of changes then affected this agreement, and old forms of social behavior and practices were no longer effective in dealing with the new social conditions and changes. That is, there occurred a breakdown of traditional norms of social behavior. The fourth assumption: no new rules of social behavior have yet developed, and confusion exists. Thus we have social disorganization. From this state, people develop a new system of behavior, which leads once again to a stable social condition. At this point, the entire process may repeat, as some new social change disrupts the agreement, just developed, between people's behavior and the new values of the society.[12]

Other views on social disorganization

Sociologists such as Horton and Leslie, in their examination of social disorganization, note that there are few, if any, periods of time when there is total social stability or total instability in any society. The social processes of change, disorganization, and reorganization occur simultaneously in most societies.[12] Other sociologists, such as Dentler, believe that the idea of social disorganization itself is inadequate because it puts a high value on the status quo—i.e., it "presupposes a type of social organization that is *de facto* [in reality or fact] functional, in which value consensus within and between groups is deep and widespread."[9] Johnson has noted that social disorganization is relative, in that it is "one of the *stages of transition*, from organization through disorganization to reorganization, through which a society proceeds."[13] He states that in the organization stage some social groups become dissatisfied with social or cultural developments. They grow alienated and restless because of social inequalities, frustrations, and insecurities. They become discontented and protest, then propose actions that will relieve the unsatisfactory conditions in the social order. On the other hand, those groups that are satisfied with the organization and functioning of society attempt to keep the social order from disintegrating. In the disorganization stage, however, "recognition spreads that social problems exist, and some remedial or reform efforts are undertaken." In the reorganization state, "some new social order is established to prepare the way for a new cycle."[13]

Social disorganization, a stage of transition

Social disorganization as a theoretical approach to the study of social problems, then, focuses upon the social norms of the community that have broken down, the social changes that have occurred, and the new rules that develop in response to this disorganization.

DEVIANCE

The second major theoretical approach to the study of social problems is *deviance*. This approach attempts to explain the phenomena of social problems in terms of people's behavior. Sociologists have defined deviance as behavior that does not conform to social norms. It is behavior that in some way does not meet with the expectations of a group or the society as a whole.[3] To better understand what the sociologist means by deviance and how it relates to the study of social problems, we must first examine what sociologists mean by *conformity*.

Built into every society are many mechanisms of control that bring about conformity to the social values and norms. Through socialization, members of societies learn systems of values that are, to an extent, internalized and conformity can result. In addition, conformity can be induced through external controls. Every day in their interpersonal relationships, people experience pressures in meeting the expectations of others. Many people think of these expectations as obligations owed to others in return for things they have done. Sociologists have indicated that many of these social expectations become standardized as a result of being linked to roles that are played in society. Failing to meet these expectations as people play their respective roles usually results in a wide variety of sanctions, from ridicule in small primary groups such as the family or play group to being suspended from a job or school. The state is another external mechanism for maintaining conformity and order within society. Being the final authority, the state has the right and power to apply a variety of penalties, from fines to death, for behavior that violates society's laws.[3]

Even with these internal and external control mechanisms for maintaining conformity, it is evident that a certain amount of deviance can be found within every society. The student should be aware that conformity and deviance are matters of social definition—i.e., which human acts are considered deviant and which people are called deviants is always relative to the values and norms of the particular society. Behavior that is generally considered deviant in one society, geographic area, or subculture may be considered normal in others. For example, men carrying around large knives are not considered deviant in the Appalachian regions of the eastern United States—the knives are useful for killing snakes that crawl up onto front porches. However, when many of the Appalachian men migrated to midwestern cities, such as Detroit, the act of carrying knives was defined as deviant and also as violating the criminal code. Moreover, behavior defined as deviant from the standpoint of the norms of society may also vary from one period of time to another. After the Prohibition Amendment was passed, manufacturing and selling intoxicating beverages were defined as

Deviant behavior can cause social problems

Conformity can result from internal as well as external sources

Deviance is relative to the values and norms of society

Considered indecent and outrageous in the twenties, this flapper's "abbreviated" bathing costume was also illegal.

The Bettmann Archive, Inc.

deviant as well as criminal acts. However, they were no longer considered to be either deviant or criminal with the repeal of the Amendment in 1933. Norms that define behavior as deviant, then, show variation with respect to society, geographic area, subculture, and time.[3] As noted by Akens in his study of deviant behavior, this variation according to place and time does "not mean that there are no regularities or patterns." He says that there are "some actions which most societies have defined and continue to consider deviant. . . . there are some actions which seem always and everywhere to be considered deviant by most people." He then gives an example of this type of action—unprovoked and capricious violence against an innocent victim—but notes that even this type of behavior has been tolerated by a few sub-groups in the society.[15]

Sociologists who explain social problems on the basis of this theoretical approach emphasize a number of perspectives, or reasons for deviance.

Three of these are the *learning perspective,* the *opportunity structure perspective,* and the *social reactions perspective.*

Three perspectives on deviance in explaining social problems

Learning Perspective. Many sociologists who employ a deviance approach in the study of social problems emphasize the idea that deviant behavior is *learned*—i.e., acquired by people in the course of their interactions with others. The criminologist E. H. Sutherland employed this perspective and developed the theory of *differential association* to explain deviance—in particular, criminal behavior. He notes that criminal behavior is learned through interaction with people during the communication process. He gives particular attention to a person's group affiliations, especially to primary groups within which people "prefer and practice various forms of deviant behavior."[2,16] Sociologists who emphasize the idea that much deviant behavior is learned believe that it is learned through participation in deviant subcultures. These sociologists, in a study of the social problem of drug addiction, would probably direct their attention to the drug addict's group affiliations and take into consideration the various norms of those different groups. Also, they might explain that the majority of people engaged in deviant drug use are not "sick" or "abnormal" but are actually conforming to the deviant norms of the subculture to which they have been socialized. This learning perspective indicates, then, that much deviance is a product of deviant subcultures and that the primary factor determining whether a person *becomes* deviant is the degree of his or her "differential association," or differential exposure to persons within the deviant subculture.[3]

Deviant behavior is learned in association with others

Opportunity Structures Perspective. Another perspective to the deviance approach for explaining social problems stresses the idea that our society places considerable pressure upon people to be materially successful in life. However, the society also either limits or denies certain people the means to achieve that goal. Deviance, in this case, develops from the discrepancy between society's goals, such as success, and the absence of institutional means to achieve them. Many people who have limited or no access to the goals approved by society become alienated and have a greater tendency to deviate from the conventional social goals and norms. In discussing his perspective of *anomie-and-opportunity-structures* (as he defines it), Merton states that "rates of various kinds of deviant behavior are highest where people have little access to socially legitimate means for achieving culturally induced goals."[2] That is, where people are greatly restricted from legitimate means for attaining goals, there are high rates of deviance. Using this perspective, the social problem of drug addiction may be explained in terms of "giving up," or rejecting both the culturally approved goals and the culturally approved means. The person, in a sense, "retreats" to drug use as a way of withdrawing from society.

Deviant behavior and the absence of means to achieve culturally approved goals

Social Reactions Perspective. Still another perspective to the deviance approach in studying social problems emphasizes the analysis of *social reactions* to deviance and the implications of these reactions for individuals who come to be identified and labeled as deviant. This social reactions, or *labeling*, perspective stresses the process by which the label of deviant is applied. The focus of attention is shifted from the exclusive concern with the deviants themselves. Here, sociologists are concerned with deviant behavior as a product of social definitions—i.e., deviance is created by the definitions and reactions of groups. Here the social problem of drug addiction would be examined in terms of the basic idea that this form of deviance is relative to group norms and, therefore, is not inherently characteristic of certain humans or their acts. Drug addiction, in other words, is not *in itself* a deviant act, but the way that society defines drug addiction makes it a deviant behavior. H. S. Becker concisely states this perspective as follows: "Social groups create deviance by making rules whose infraction constitutes deviance, and by applying those rules to particular people and labeling them as outsiders."[17]

> **Deviant behavior: A product of social definitions**

As stated by Merton and others, these theoretical perspectives on deviance complement one another; they are not contradictory. Merton notes that "each has its own theoretical thrust . . . its own key questions, focused on selected aspects of the complex social phenomena of deviance."[2] Becker's theory, however, has been criticized on several counts. First, it must not be assumed that a person once labeled as deviant will necessarily continue to commit deviant acts and progress toward a deviant career. Second, Becker's theory deals almost entirely with reactions to acts labeled as deviant but does not really explain why some people commit deviant acts to begin with while others refrain from such behaviors. In spite of these and other criticisms, Becker's theory allows significant insight both into the nature of social response to behavior and, in a sense, into the implications of such factors for the actual creation of deviance.[3]

> **Theoretical perspectives complement one another**

CONFLICT

Conflict theory is the third major theoretical approach that sociologists employ in the study of social problems. Unlike the social disorganization approach, which views society as having an overall unity that is impaired by conflict, the conflict approach has as its *starting point* "the heterogeneity, diversity, and lack of uniformity in modern society."[15] Unlike the deviant approach, the conflict approach does *not* focus upon the deviant, stress the social and psychological background of people considered to be deviants, or emphasize the people with whom they interact. The conflict approach is, moreover, critical of the deviant approach, emphasizing that focusing upon the individual deviant is only locating the symptoms, not the causes, of social problems. Deviants, according to conflict theory, are the manifestations of the "failure of society to meet the needs of individuals . . . . the

> **Conflict theory: Society has failed to meet individuals' needs**

sources of crime, poverty, drug addiction, and racism, are found in the laws, customs, and distribution of wealth and power."[18] Advocates of this approach believe, for example, that the quality of life in America is the social problem, not mental illness. The unequal distribution of wealth is the social problem, not poverty.

Conflict theory is based in the idea that many social values conflict with each other and that these value conflicts are the root of many of our social problems. Advocates of the conflict approach believe that various segments of society compete for such things as power, wealth, high social status, and scarce resources. The conflict approach assumes that the basic form of social interaction is competition. That is, we must examine the relationships between the competing values and interests of business, labor, government, agriculture, etc., in order to understand society's problems, since this competitive form of interaction can and does lead to conflict and social problems.

Many conflict theorists consider such factors as economics, vested interests, and power to be important variables in explaining many of our social problems. They argue that many of our problems exist and are difficult to control because some people socially, politically, or economically gain by them. Karl Marx, an early conflict theorist, wrote that our social reality must be understood in terms of the class struggle for the underlying mode of production. Marx believed that the basic cause of social problems is conflict between the owners of productive property and the workers.[3] In general, the conflict approach to social problems stresses that "societies and social organization are shaped by diversity, coercion, and change . . . . society is held together by force and constraint and is characterized by ubiquitous conflicts that result in continuous change."[19]

Conflict theorists view social conflict as having many positive societal functions rather than being socially disorganizing. Lewis Coser, in an analysis of the views of Georg Simmel (another early conflict theorist), notes that Simmel viewed conflict as the very essence of social life:

> Simmel never dreamed of a frictionless universe, a society from which clashes and contentions among individuals and groups would be forever banned. For him, conflict is the very essence of social life, an ineradicable component of social living. The good society—far from conflict free—is, on the contrary, "sewn together" by a variety of criss-cross conflicts among its component parts.[20]

In an analysis of Simmel and Gluckman, Coser also has indicated that conflict may be a precondition for the orderly functioning of society. He states that conflict theorists view

> stability as a temporary balance of conflicting forces; they contend that conflict, far from being a sign of disease of the body social, has

Many social values conflict with one another

Marx stressed the importance of class conflict in generating social problems

indeed many positive functions in society, not the least of which may be to bring about increased social solidarity of group members.[21]

The positive functions of conflict

Many conflict theorists, then, believe that society's organization and continuity depend upon the social process of conflict. Society is viewed as a "congeries of groups held together in a shifting but dynamic equilibrium of opposing interests and efforts."[15,22] Conflict theorists see society as characterized by competing elements, with social institutions continually in a state of dissension and redefinition. The tensions produced by these processes are not an indication that society's organization is weakened; rather, conflict theorists feel that these tensions "encourage viability, growth, and creative change rather than unyielding adherence to traditional values and arrangements."[23]

The conflict approach and its assumptions are the opposite of what has been termed the *functionalist* approach in American sociology, and the conflict approach in the study of social problems is quite critical of the functionalist position. Functionalism emphasizes the theory of social disorganization, which we have discussed above, in explaining social problems. Basically, functionalists view society as being made up of a set of interdependent and related units. Society is seen as a system of interrelationships between actors and the various social institutions. The most fundamental relationship between those parts is characterized by harmony and cooperation. As long as people (the actors) in the society are appropriately socialized—i.e., bound by consensus to society's common values—the system will function smoothly. This highly integrated society, in which social change is gradual and adjustive, is quite stable, according to the functionalists. Social problems are viewed as dysfunctional, or as consequences that "result from a behavior, belief, or group activity that interferes with the functional requirements of the social system." A basic requirement of all social systems is that people conform to the rules of society. Widespread or "systematic violation of these rules is disruptive and dysfunctional since it serves to undermine the order and consensus that perpetuates the system."[11]

The functionalist viewpoint: Social problems are dysfunctional

The conflict approach does not conceptualize social problems as "breakdowns" in the social order, as does the functional approach, and functionalists have been criticized for failing to "capture the value and conflict factors that are inherent in social problems."[11] Nor does the conflict approach view the fundamental relationship among segments of society as cooperative and harmonious. Conflict theorists assume that there is no basic consensus on society's norms. The society is loosely integrated, and social change is not gradual, but abrupt.

The conflict vs. the functionalist view of social problems

The conflict approach to the study of social problems, then, stresses the idea that our society is characterized by competition, divisiveness, and change, as opposed to harmony, integration, and stability. It states that the established social system is not "sacred"; if, as presently organized, the society does not meet people's needs and causes social problems, it needs to be restructured. In conclusion, conflict theorists stress that dominant groups, through their constraint, maintain that impaired society for their own benefit. Social problems are explained as the "failure of the current order to meet changing needs as a product of the exploitive practices of the dominant group."[13]

As we have seen, there are many sociological theories that attempt to explain social problems and provide students with important insights into their nature. The social disorganization approach focuses upon change and the use of society's traditional guidelines, which are no longer applicable to new social conditions. This approach is highly applicable to the problems of overpopulation and environmental deterioration. As we shall see in the chapters on those topics, the increase in technological, scientific, and medical knowledge during the twentieth century has resulted in vast population and industrial expansion. In turn, this has led to world shortages in food and other basic resources. The traditional values of many people, however, continue to favor this growth.

Social disorganization

Deviance, on the other hand, explains social problems in terms of people's behavior deviating from the norms of society. This theoretical approach emphasizes the facts that: (1) deviant behavior is learned in the course of interactions with others; (2) deviance develops from a discrepancy between society's goals and the absence of institutionalized means to achieve them; and (3) deviant behavior is also a product of social definitions. This approach is highly applicable to such problems as criminal and delinquent behavior. As we will see in the appropriate chapter, this behavior violates society's codified rules, which are termed laws. Deviance, of course, is a matter of social definition, and is always relative to the people or groups that do the defining.

Deviance

The conflict approach to the study of social problems stresses that many values conflict, and this conflict is at the root of social problems. Competition, a basic form of social interaction, particularly in a capitalist society, is viewed as leading to conflict and social problems. As we shall see in the chapter on racial and sexual inequalities, this approach is applicable to these areas. Many people suffer, yet many others economically, socially, and/or politically gain from the perpetuation of these inequities.

Conflict

All of these theoretical approaches are useful in the analysis of social problems. No single approach is the correct approach or is able, by itself, to adequately explain all social problems, although some of them are more adequately explained by certain individual theoretical approaches. America's social problems are complex phenomena that require students to use a variety of theories, each of which emphasizes different factors.

All approaches are useful

SUMMARY

This chapter has focused upon a general discussion of the sociological approach to understanding social problems. Sociologists define a social problem as a group condition or situation that significant numbers of people consider undesirable and in need of remedy through group action. This definition contains an objective component—i.e., the actual condition, such as a particular rate of crime or incidence of drug abuse. In addition, the definition also contains a subjective component, which means that for a social problem to exist, people must view the condition as undesirable and feel that something can and should be done to alter it. Based upon this definition, we can see that social problems are related to situations or conditions of group life, and that the judgments people make about these situations play an important part in determining just what specific conditions are defined as problematic. People, however, will not always agree on what the specific problems of group life are, nor will they always agree on what steps should be taken to remedy them.

Distinct from the literary, philosophical, and religious approaches, sociology attempts to employ the scientific method in its investigations into social problems. The scientific point of view stresses that: (1) research be based upon factual data; (2) objectivity be maintained as fully as possible throughout all phases of the research; (3) precision be maximized; and (4) the research be subject to evaluation and verification by professional peers. While there is a general consensus that sociology cannot be totally objective or value-free, sociologists will often debate as to whether sociology should be value-free. Some argue that sociology should strive toward complete objectivity and neutrality in the analysis of social problems. Others argue that sociology has a responsibility to propose and advocate policy decisions and reform measures that will alleviate society's problems.

Sociologists perform a number of roles in their inquiries. As scientific researchers, sociologists attempt to identify, define, and measure the extent of social problems within society. To this end, they must identify people's values, determine issues of public concern, and attempt to measure the actual extent of problematic conditions. In addition, sociologists attempt to explain the origins of social problems. In order to do this, they must adopt an additional role, that of theoretician. In this role they develop theories, which are tentative explanations, for the causes of social problems. Many sociologists also engage in the role of social critic, presenting opinions and knowledge that are useful in assessing the adequacy of current policies on contemporary problems. As social critics, certain sociologists have also taken an active role in formulating and advocating the adoption of new policies to deal with social problems. Sociologists will also sometimes play the role of evaluator, analyzing the effectiveness of specific programs for treating various social problems.

Although sociologists do not generally agree upon a single overall theory for explaining the existence of social problems, they do tend to share similar ideas and notions concerning their nature. This perspective emphasizes the basic principle that social problems are often related to, or a product of, the way of life of a society. Employing this frame of reference, sociologists have identified certain features of group life that tend to contribute to the rise and perpetuation of social problems. Some of these conditions include widespread value conflicts, restrictions within the structure of the society itself, and the presence of social change.

Finally, three major theoretical approaches to the study of social problems were examined in detail: social disorganization, deviance, and conflict. Social disorganization stresses the role of social change in bringing about problems, since change often necessitates difficult adjustments to new social conditions and life situations. The theory of deviance explains the phenomena of social problems in terms of people's behavior deviating from the norms of society. Deviance itself can be explained by the learning, opportunity structures, or social reactions perspectives. Finally, conflict theory is based on the ideas that many social values inevitably conflict and that these value conflicts are at the root of many of our social problems. Many sociologists trace the origins of social conflicts to the existence within modern societies of various basic inequalities, such as vast inequalities in the distribution of power, wealth, and status.

KEY TERMS

Competition
Conflict theory
Conformity
Culture
Culture lag
Deviance
Deviance theory
Differential association
Evaluator
External social controls
Functionalist theory
Heterogeneous society
Internal social controls
Labeling perspective
Learning perspective
Material culture
Neutrality
Nonmaterial culture
Objective aspects of social problems
Objectivity

Opportunity structure perspective
Organized skepticism
Precision
Scientific method
Social change
Social critic
Social disorganization
Social disorganization theory
Social norms
Social organization
Social problem
Social reactions perspective
Society
Sociology
Subcultures
Subjective aspects of social problems
Theory
Value conflict
Value-free
Verification process

2
Poverty

Chapter Objectives

1. To compare the absolute and relative definitions of poverty.

2. To list the characteristics of those Americans in poverty today, according to the Census Bureau, and to describe the different problems encountered by the poor who are young and the poor who are old.

3. To list at least six of the basic characteristics of the "culture of poverty" perspective.

4. To differentiate between the situationalist and the "culture of poverty" approaches.

5. To define Rodman's concept of "value stretch."

6. To list three statements that indicate an understanding of the conflict approach to poverty.

7. To describe, by essay, the concept of individualism, its relation to social Darwinism, and its implications for helping the poor.

8. To define Feagin's three different explanations of poverty and to discuss today's most prevalent attitude, according to his research.

9. To critique in an essay three major governmental programs that have been established to ameliorate some of the effects of American poverty.

10. To list four of the misconceptions Americans have about welfare programs and welfare recipients.

11. To detail in an essay four abuses of the welfare system that were common during the 1950s and 1960s.

12. To discuss President Carter's proposals for welfare reform.

HISTORICAL PERSPECTIVE OF POVERTY IN AMERICA

Rediscovered during the Kennedy and Johnson administrations, poverty remains today a major social problem in America. From twenty-five to fifty million Americans are victims of poverty. Inflation, high unemployment, and many other factors are reminders that poverty is not a thing of the past. As we shall see, poverty has always been a part of American society. Throughout our history, Americans have responded to this problem in a wide variety of ways. We will begin our analysis of poverty with an examination of its historical roots. Afterward, we will examine how it is measured and defined, and how we have responded to this serious social problem.

History indicates that many people have made fortunes in America. Others have risen economically to comfortable levels of living. As people moved up the class ladder, other groups of poor, mainly immigrants from abroad, replaced them. However, for many other groups in society, primarily for blacks, Indians, and other minority groups, there has been a more-or-less permanent poverty.

COLONIAL AMERICA

Poverty is nothing new in the United States. In colonial America, most of the labor was recruited at first from the ranks of England's poor, who were told that gold and silver could be had in America "just for the asking." Some poor were able to pay for their passage to the New World; for thousands of others, however, passage was obtained by selling themselves into bondage. Still others came unwillingly—they were kidnapped from the streets of England or were criminals sent to America as seven-year slaves. An estimate of more than 400,000, or half the immigrants during America's colonial period, were poor white slaves. Thousands died while sailing to America; thousands of others, as with African black slaves, had their families broken up, "children going to one master, the wife to another, and the husband to a third."[1] Many of these poor newcomers were beaten, given inadequate food, and forbidden to marry or to buy or sell anything.

The American black population also grew during this period. With the growing labor needs of the colonies, Africa became another important source for free labor. From a total of about two million blacks brutally torn from their families and cultures, more than a quarter of a million ended up in America between 1686 and 1786. The oppressing difference between white and black slavery was that the whites could work out of it, whereas blacks remained in slavery and passed it to their children. According to historian Sidney Lens, slavery—white and black—was "the worst form of poverty in colonial times."[1]

Little was done in colonial times to ameliorate poverty among slaves, farmers, and tenants. Only the *helpless* poor—the blind, sick, or aged—

Margin notes:

Poverty is nothing new in America

White slavery

Black slavery

Few poor were helped during colonial times

were given some relief. Large landholders and merchants became wealthy and small farmers and poor tenants were squeezed by high taxes, prices, and credit. Many of the poor spent most of their time in jails and workhouses, where they were forced to work to pay off their debts.

Quakers attempt to
help the poor

In the late seventeenth and early eighteenth centuries, various individuals and religious groups, such as William Penn and the Quakers in Pennsylvania, attempted to deal with the problems of the poor. The Quakers believed that by encouraging the poor the real benefit of the public was promoted. With food, shelter, and fuel, they aided those who were "the hands and feet of the rich"; poor black slaves were bought for the sole purpose of freeing them. However, the Quaker attempt to build the "virtuous society" failed as time passed and the Quakers, like other Americans, became interested in profit-making endeavors.

REVOLUTIONARY PERIOD AND INDUSTRIALIZATION

The American Revolution and rapidly increasing inflation caused tens of thousands of Americans to become "saddled with debts" and plunged them into the depths of poverty. History notes, for example, that "if the laws for imprisonment for debt had been enforced in New Hampshire, in 1785, almost two-thirds of the people would have been in jail."[1] The American Revolution did allow some landless people to take over Tory properties, but the most significant result of the American Revolution for the poor was the opening of the lands west of the Appalachians for homesteading.

The American Revolution and the opening of western lands

The urban poor

The Industrial Revolution, the growth of cities, and the several depressions of the 1800s affected thousands of poor urban workers. Unlike farm workers, the urban worker starved if unable to find work. Hunger, tenement housing, disease, and many other problems were commonplace for the urban poor of the nineteenth century. Many men and women of this period formed trade unions to improve their wages and working conditions. Through collective action, many of the poor improved their situation by obtaining the right to vote, better educational opportunities, and a change in the penal code that ended imprisonment for debt.

TWENTIETH CENTURY AND THE PROGRESSIVE ERA

With the growth of urban areas, poverty grew much worse. Hunter, a sociologist at the turn of the century, described the plight of the millions of people in city tenements: The poor were packed seven and eight to a small room, and heat, flies, garbage, and manure boxes were common.[2]

Hunter: Housing and the poor

Basic necessities were unobtainable

Even those who held regular jobs and earned an income were poor, since basic necessities were, to a great extent, unobtainable. Badly fed, clad, and sheltered, the poor had no opportunity to improve their status. They were not, as many people believed at the time, lazy or unfit. Hunter noted that at least ten and perhaps as many as fifteen or twenty million people (almost a quarter of the population) were poverty stricken. In 1900, a quarter of the labor force had been unemployed at one time or another during the year.[1]

At the end of the nineteenth century, in what was termed the Progressive Era, attempts were made by many individuals and organizations to improve the plight of the poor. Intellectuals, labor leaders, the socialist party, and political progressives waged an attack against many injustices plaguing the poor. Writers such as Jack London and Upton Sinclair exposed the many problems encountered by the working poor. Jane Addams fought against vice and corruption in the political relm. Prior to her work for women's suffrage, she fought for workmen's compensation, prison reform, and child labor laws.

> **The Progressive Era and poverty**

Historians such as Schlesinger and Lens have noted that more social reforms were enacted in the first fifteen years of this century than in all of our prior history. These reforms largely resulted from the government's assuming a little more responsibility for the public welfare.[1] Urban slums were, to some extent, made more tolerable through the development of a network of schools, parks, playgrounds, roads, and sewage systems. Wages of the poor no longer plunged downward, and some actually increased to an extent. However, the progressive package of regulatory and welfare measures of this era "neither checked the advance of unbridled wealth nor gave the poor a cushion against economic insecurity."[1]

> **Social reforms**

> **Some improvements for the poor**

THE GREAT DEPRESSION AND THE NEW DEAL

In 1929, soon after a brief period of unprecedented prosperity led many to believe that poverty would very shortly cease to exist, our country began to experience the worse depression in its history. Poverty wasn't experienced by only a few million people—it was a poverty of the majority. Several thousand banks failed, and thousands of families lost all their savings. Poverty was no longer just the plight of laborers, immigrants, and farmers. Poverty struck everyone: many professional people suddenly found themselves unemployed and selling apples on streetcorners.

With the establishment of Franklin D. Roosevelt's New Deal, however, massive efforts were developed to feed the hungry and relieve the widespread poverty. The political forces that developed from the depression forced the government to act on behalf of the poor, through the formation of federally subsidized public assistance programs, or welfare. The Federal Emergency Relief Administration spent millions in dealing with poverty in our counties and cities. The national relief costs of almost thirty million people were paid for by the FERA. In addition, the Civil Works Administration developed almost 200,000 programs and projects for improving our roads, schools, parks, and public buildings, which offered work to several million people who had been unemployed. President Roosevelt was criticized by conservatives and liberals alike for establishing these and other

The Bettmann Archive, Inc.

During the Great Depression, high levels of unemployment made breadlines a common sight.

The New Deal did not end poverty

programs designed to ameliorate the plight of the poor in America. Conservatives believed he was upsetting the free enterprise system; liberals and radicals of the time believed he had not done enough. Many of the New Deal programs helped several million poor by providing jobs, but poverty in America was not eliminated. An estimated ten to eleven million people were unemployed at the end of 1938.

WORLD WAR II AND THE POSTWAR ERA

WW II: Poverty no longer a social problem

The Second World War ended poverty for millions of people. The war effort pumped up the economy: New jobs were made available and the number of unemployed dropped sharply, from eight million in 1940 to 670,000 in 1944. For several years poverty was not a social problem, but war spending, not planning or reform, eliminated much of it.[1]

Avoiding another depression

Many Americans believed that after the war we would again return to a depression-level poverty, but this was avoided through an increase in consumer spending (from accumulated savings), which stimulated the economy. In general, the postwar period was one of unprecedented prosperity. Wages and benefits increased, and the New Deal reforms helped ease many problems of unemployment and old age. In the period between 1946 and 1960 it was widely believed that the "affluent society" had arrived, and there was relatively little public concern for the poor. In the 1950s, according to John K. Galbraith, the United States actually achieved the status of an affluent society—i.e., poverty was an afterthought, not a major affliction.[3] Yet even in the midst of all this prosperity, many millions of Americans were still hopelessly poor.

Prosperity and poverty

REDISCOVERING POVERTY

Many Americans doubt the true extent of poverty in this country because of the continual growth of affluent communities and because of poverty's invisibility. Michael Harrington, in his book *The Other America*, which greatly contributed to our country's rediscovery of the problem, explains this quality. Poverty exists primarily in out-of-the-way places, such as urban ghettos and Appalachian mining towns, which middle-class America avoids. Also, a large percentage of the poor consists of the aged and the very young, who generally stay close to home. Finally, the poor do not, on the whole, join political parties, trade unions, or fraternal organizations, which keeps them politically silent. Besides these explanations, there's the simple fact that the poor can't be recognized on the street by any particular characteristics, such as clothing or manner.[4]

Michael Harrington: The poor are invisible

Through the works of writers such as Harrington and the public appeals of civil rights leaders such as Martin Luther King, Jr., Americans were made more aware of the fact that millions were still painfully poor. Using this increase in the public awareness, Presidents John F. Kennedy and Lyndon B. Johnson both attacked poverty. President Kennedy developed service- and work-oriented counseling programs for the poor. He stressed noneconomic factors and called for solutions that would help the poor to help themselves.[5] President Johnson, in his "War on Poverty," advocated greater opportunities for the poor. Through his "Great Society" plan, billions of dollars were allotted for programs dealing with jobs, education, and community problems, but the war in Vietnam eventually superseded the "War on Poverty."

Martin Luther King

Later, President Richard M. Nixon also expressed concern for the poor, particularly for the disabled, the aged, and mothers of small children. Innovative reform programs for the poor were suggested in his administration; however, due to the programs' own shortcomings and much criticism, the actual proposals were never implemented.

President Jimmy Carter has introduced what he considers to be a sweeping change in our country's poverty programs. Whether his efforts will effectively contain or reduce our nation's poverty remains to be seen.

HOW POVERTY IS DEFINED AND MEASURED

Now that the historical background of poverty has been given, we will examine the ways in which poverty is currently measured and defined in America.

How many poor people are there in America today? The number varies depending on the means used to measure and define poverty. Most people agree that low income is an important part of any definition; however, social scientists debate whether poverty should be viewed in terms of a low *absolute* income or a low *relative* income.

LOW ABSOLUTE INCOME LEVEL

When determining poverty in terms of a low absolute level, a poverty line based upon family budget needs for minimum subsistence tends to be used. The Social Security Administration developed the most frequently used absolute poverty line, which is for a nonfarm family of four and stood at $5815 per annum in 1976.[6,15] The Census Bureau classifies people as being below or above the poverty level using the Federal Interagency Committee Poverty Index of 1969. This index is based on the Economy Food Plan of the Department of Agriculture. According to the Department of Commerce, this plan reflects the "different consumption requirements of families based on their size and composition, sex and age of the family head, and farm-nonfarm residence."*

Using this poverty line, which is based on estimates of income necessary to provide a nutritonally adequate diet (assuming that one-third of total family income is spent on food), there were about 25.0 million poor people in 1976. This represented 11.8 percent of the national population and was higher than the Commerce Department's revised 1974 figure of 23.4 percent. Also in 1976, there were 35.5 million people earning less than $7269, which is just 25 percent more than the poverty level of $5815.[6,15]

Some sociologists indicate that because an absolute poverty measure is based on the cost of a nutritionally adequate diet, it is believed to be an "objective and nonarbitrary measure of poverty."[7] However, critics note that there *is* an arbitrariness to poverty lines based upon nutrition—that there "is no sharp line above which people have no nutrition-related health problems and below which they die of starvation. . . . The measure tells us

---

* The Census Bureau notes that this plan was derived from a Department of Agriculture survey of food consumption, which found "that families of three or more persons spend approximately one-third of their income on food; the poverty level for these families was, therefore, set at three times the cost of the economy food plan." Adjustments were made for family size. For example, for "smaller families and persons living alone, the cost of the economy food plan was multiplied by factors that were slightly higher in order to compensate for the relatively larger fixed expenses of these smaller households."[6,15]

Margin notes:

Poverty: Low income

Poverty: An absolute level of income

Nutritional poverty lines are arbitrary

how many fall below the specified poverty line, but tells us nothing about the difference in degree of poverty between families below the line." [7] Rose Friedman notes that only three-quarters of the people living at the absolute poverty line have nutritionally adequate diets.[8]

Using an absolute poverty line to determine the exact number of American poor is complicated by the fact that the money necessary to buy basic needs in one community may not be sufficient in another. Food and rent are more costly in Chicago than in rural Mississippi. In addition, it is estimated that several million people are not counted in the annual census. Most of these are poor people: migrant workers, who are never in one place long enough to be counted; people jammed into urban slum housing; and people in remote rural areas, such as the Appalachian region.

Money needs vary and some poor are never counted

One more criticism of an absolute poverty line is that it fails to consider changes in customary definitions of an "acceptable minimal standard of life"—i.e., it fails to consider increases in living standards.[7,9,10,11] For many Americans who earn less than the poverty level, such items as televisions, telephones, and even cars are becoming indispensable. One could say, therefore, that poverty is relative to time. Many of the people who are poor today—who have running water, toilets in their homes, telephones, and televisions—would not be considered poor if judged by standards of the turn of the century.

LOW RELATIVE INCOME LEVEL

Poverty may also be viewed in terms of a low relative income, which *does* take into consideration increases in the nation's standard of living. Williamson and Hyer, in their study of the measurement of poverty, indicate that people who prefer relative income lines (such as Fuch's poverty line, equal to 50 percent of the median family income)* argue that poverty is due to relative deprivation.[7,12] This concept suggests that "it is the comparison which an individual makes between his own situation and the situation of others† which is critical in determining satisfaction, rather than the objective situation in which he finds himself."[14]

An example of relative deprivation is the situation in which a family with an income of $40,000 a year feels poor because the other families in the community earn $100,000 a year. Some sociologists have even made a

Poverty is due to relative deprivation

---

* Median income is the value that divides the income distribution into two equal parts—one half of the income falling below this value and one half exceeding it.

† According to Glazer and Creedon, the "others with whom he compares himself are 'reference groups' (with whom the self may or may not interact, and with whom the self may or may not be similar in social status or social category). Satisfaction is a function, then, of relative deprivation and relative reward rather than of an absolute level."[13]

"distinction between the 'objective' relative deprivation indicated by the actual income of poor families and the 'subjective' relative deprivation indicated by their feelings about the inadequacy of this income."[7,11]

According to Miller and Matza, poverty is not a permanent specification or a fixed position.[16] They note that as a society "changes in the quantity and kind of production and in the 'prevailing standards' of life, the definition of poverty changes. . . . it is relative to the possibilities of society and the 'average' standard of life in a society, although we can have sharp disagreements about the level of the relationship."[16]

Sociologists favoring a relative definition of poverty note that poverty in America is quite different from poverty in other societies. Basically, most of our poor are not on near-starvation diets or living on the streets. Rather, the American poor have simply "fallen far behind the rest of society. This is the meaning of poverty in the affluent society . . . not that individuals are facing starvation and physical destruction—although some of our poor do —but that they are not full members of society."[16]

This relative conception of poverty notes that families in the lowest one-fifth of the nation's income distribution "will feel deprived irrespective of their level of income."[9] Matza and Miller, in their analysis of poverty, state that an important question to consider when using a relative definiton is "whether important shifts have occurred in the percentage of aggregate income going to the poorest one-fifth."[9]

Table 2.1 indicates the percent of aggregate income received by each ranked category of families from 1950 to 1976. The percentage of aggregate income earned by the lowest one-fifth has changed very little in that period.[15] According to some sociologists, a major improvement in the relative position of the lowest one-fifth—"the poorest category of the popula-

People are poor because they have fallen behind

Little relative change

Table 2.1. Percent of aggregate income received by each one-fifth and highest 5 percent of families: 1950–1976

FAMILIES, BY INCOME RANK	1950	1955	1960	1965	1970	1973	1974	1975	1976
All families	100%	100%	100%	100%	100%	100%	100%	100%	100%
Lowest one-fifth	4.5	4.8	4.8	5.2	5.4	5.5	5.5	5.4	5.4
Second one-fifth	11.9	12.2	12.2	12.2	12.2	11.9	12.0	11.8	11.8
Middle one-fifth	17.4	17.4	17.8	17.8	17.6	17.5	17.5	17.6	17.6
Fourth one-fifth	23.6	23.4	24.0	23.9	23.8	24.0	24.0	24.1	24.1
Highest one-fifth	42.7	41.8	41.3	40.9	40.9	41.1	41.0	41.1	41.1
Highest 5 percent	17.3	16.8	15.5	15.5	15.6	15.5	15.5	15.5	15.6

Source: U.S. Bureau of the Census, *Statistical Abstract of the United States: 1977*, 98th edition, Washington, D.C., 1977, p. 443, Table 713; *Current Population Reports*, Series P-60, No. 114.

Table 2.2. Persons below poverty level: 1959–1976

YEAR	NUMBER (MILLIONS)	PERCENT OF TOTAL POPULATION
1959	39.5	22.4
1960	39.9	22.2
1965	33.2	17.3
1967	27.8	14.2
1968	25.4	12.8
1969*	24.1	12.1
1970	25.4	12.6
1971	25.6	12.5
1972	24.5	11.9
1973	23.0	11.1
1974	24.3	11.6
1974†	23.4	11.2
1975†	25.9	12.3
1976†	25.0	11.8

* Beginning with March 1970 survey, the data are based on 1970 census.

†Not strictly comparable with earlier years due to revised procedures.

Source: U.S. Bureau of the Census, *Statistical Abstract of the United States: 1977*, Washington, D.C., p. 453, Table 733; *Current Population Reports*, Series P-60, No. 107.

tion"—would be a "doubling of [this category's] share of aggregate income" over a 25-year period.[9] Fuchs has also indicated in his research that the proportion of America's population that earns less than 50 percent of the national median income remains constant (20 percent of the total).[12]

These relative measures of poverty give the impression that there has been little, if any, decrease in the number of poor. On the other hand, when an absolute measure of poverty is employed, a marked decrease can be seen.

Table 2.2 indicates that the population of American poor decreased from 22.4 percent of the total to 11.8 percent in the period covered.[15] Therefore, the choice of either a relative or an absolute poverty line has major implications for measuring the size of the poor population.[7]

The choice of measurement also has implications for the *types* of people who are poor. Williamson, Hyer, Miller, and others have noted that when an absolute measure is employed, the evidence indicates that "poor families increasingly tend to be female-headed, aged, black, and physically

Size of poor population varies

disabled. But when the relative measure is used, the evidence suggests little change [deviation from national characteristics] in the composition of the poor."[7,17] Relative and absolute income measures are not, however, the only ways to measure poverty. Sociologists have employed indexes of socio-economic status that used such factors as occupation, education, and community.[18,19] Still others stress resources such as capital assets, community services, and occupational fringe benefits.[20]

Other measures of poverty

In any event, measuring poverty is not an easy task. In our complex industrialized, pluralistic, and ever-changing society no one standard of poverty can be universally applicable or acceptable. By one method, people who should be counted among the poor are left out; by another, many people who should not be counted among the poor are included. Various indicators of poverty are not necessarily equivalent, and caution must be exercised when comparing studies that use different measures. For example, many studies have used public dependence, or welfare assistance, as an indicator of poverty. However, a study using that measure could not compare with a study based on an absolute income measure, since the welfare population "is not representative of the poor more generally." As stated by Williamson and Hyer, "among the most obvious differences, the welfare population includes a disproportionately large number of female-headed families, families with an aged head, and families with a disabled head."[7] Keeping these points in mind, we will examine some characteristics of the poor in America.

Measuring poverty is not an easy task

CHARACTERISTICS OF THE POOR
The makeup of the poor as a class and any observable changes in this population are recorded to a certain extent in the Census Bureau's 1976 Advance Report on Consumer Income. Various characteristics of the poor, and some significant changes that have occurred among their population between 1974 and 1975, can be seen in Table 2.3.

The data in Table 2.3 indicate that the number of poor increased by 2.5 million, or 10.7 percent, in that single year. In 1975 there were 25.9 million people below the poverty level,* comprising 12 percent of the total population.[6] This represented the largest increase in a one-year period since 1959, which was the first year for which poverty data were available. This increase, according to the report, was "quite pervasive, occurring for both black and white persons, for persons of Spanish origin, and for the young as well as for the elderly."†

Number of poor increased

* The 1975 poverty level is $5500 for a nonfarm family of four.

† The increase in the number of poor aged 65 years and older was significant at the 90 percent level. Unless otherwise qualified, all other comparisons are significant at the 95 percent confidence level.

Table 2.3. Changes in the number of poor persons and families between 1974 and 1975

CHARACTERISTICS	1975	1974	CHANGE NUMBER (THOUSANDS)	PERCENT
Total individuals	25,877	23,370	2,507*	10.7
Spanish origin	2,991	2,575	416*	16.2
White	17,770	15,736	2,034*	12.9
Black	7,545	7,182	363*	5.1
Younger than 65 years	22,560	20,285	2,275*	11.2
65 years and older	3,317	3,085	232	7.5
Total families	5,450	4,922	528*	10.7
Male head	3,020	2,598	422*	16.2
Female head	2,430	2,324	106	4.6

* The 1975 figure is significantly different from the 1974 figure at the 95 percent confidence level.

Source: *Current Population Reports*, Series P-60, No. 103, "Money, Income, and Poverty Status of Families and Persons in the United States: 1975 and 1974 Revisions," (Advanced Report), Washington, D.C., September 1976, p. 3.

The percentage of low-income whites increased by about 13 percent in that year, to a total of 17.8 million in 1975. The percentage of low-income blacks increased by about 5 percent in the same period, totaling 7.5 million. There was a 16 percent increase in the number of low-income people of Spanish origin, but the census report indicates that because of the small sample size of this group, it cannot be "reliably determined whether this increase was greater than the increase . . . for whites and blacks."[6]

With respect to the age characteristic, there was an 11 percent increase in the number of low-income people younger than 65, and a 7.5 percent increase in the number of people older than 65 living in poverty, or a total of 3.3 million people.

The 10.7 percent increase to 5.5 million families in poverty reflected in part a high unemployment rate during 1975.* The number of poverty-level

* The increase was from 2.3 to 2.4 million and was significant at the 93 percent confidence level, according to the Census Bureau. The Bureau notes that this increase also reflected the fact that more people exhausted their unemployment benefits in 1975 than in previous years: about "42 percent of the 528,000 increase in the number of poor families between 1974 and 1975 was associated with those in which the head was 'unable to find work during the entire year' or was a part year worker 'unemployed 15 weeks or more' during the year."

families with a male head rose by 15 percent (the greatest increase), growing from 2.6 to three million. The number of poverty-level families headed by women increased by 5 percent.[6]

MEASURING POVERTY NOW

Keeping in mind the variations in amount and composition of the poor with respect to choice of measure, what is the most important factor for determining whether a family is poor? Is it, as many people believe, employment? Is it education? Do the "hard-core" poor remain in poverty year after year, or is it a temporary situation? Also, what is the relationship between family disorganization and poverty? Does living in the country or city make a difference? What does the racial variable have to do with the likelihood of becoming poor? These and many other questions are addressed in the following longitudinal study of several thousand families conducted by the Institute for Social Research at the University of Michigan. This reading, entitled "A Surprising Profile of America's Poor," challenges many of the more popular American stereotypes of poverty.

U.S. NEWS & WORLD REPORT READING——OBJECTIVES

1. List five of the major findings about poverty described by the University of Michigan Institute for Social Research.

2. In an essay, compare the importance to poverty of education and employment.

3. Describe in an essay the importance of city living and being poor.

A Surprising Profile of America's Poor

Some surprising conclusions about the poor in the United States emerge from a study of more than 5,000 families conducted over a seven-year period by the University of Michigan's Institute for Social Research.

Among major findings:

Institute's major findings

• Education—not jobs—is the single most important factor in determining whether a family is poor.

• Disintegration of families is a major contributor to the movement of people into poverty.

• Rural residents run a bigger risk of being poor than do city dwellers.

• Blacks are many more times likely than whites to drop into the poverty category.

Reprinted from *U.S. NEWS & WORLD REPORT*, November 8, 1976. Copyright © 1976 U.S. News & World Report, Inc.

• Relatively few "hard-core poor" stay in the poverty class year after year.

The study, supported by the government and conducted annually since 1968, is analyzed by a staff led by James N. Morgan at the institute's headquarters in Ann Arbor, Mich.

By keeping track of the same people over a long period, experts hope to learn more about how Americans drop into poverty and how they get out.

Poverty for most people is a temporary situation, according to the study. Results show that more than half of the poor families are poor only for limited periods. Over a five-year span, their incomes average well above the poverty threshold.

Reason: People keep moving into poverty—often by getting divorced or leaving a parental home. At the same time, others are climbing out of the poor class by getting married, changing occupations or getting more schooling.

The upshot is that while 1 out of every 11 American families may be rated as poor in any single year, only a fourth of them are likely to stay poor every year over a five-year period. These are the persistently poor.

In addition, researchers found "no significant evidence" that children from welfare families are themselves more likely to go on welfare.

As the institute puts it: "Thus, the stereotype of large numbers of families living from generation to generation on welfare is not borne out by these data."

Education often is the key to determining whether a family enters or remains in a poverty category. Experts conclude that having at least six grades of schooling drops a person's chances of being persistently poor—beyond a year—from about 40 to 20 per cent.

Importance of a basic education

Additional education beyond the sixth grade further insures escaping poverty, although to a lesser degree.

EDUCATION'S IMPACT

Whites benefit more than blacks from schooling, the survey indicates. While six grades of education cuts a white family's chance of being persistently poor to about 1 in 5, it takes at least some college training to do the same for blacks.

Lack of education not only handicaps adults but rubs off on their children. The study found that in the case of a father who had less than six years of schooling, his youngsters ran a much higher than normal risk of growing up in long-range poverty. If a parent finished high school, the proportion of his children in poverty dropped perceptibly.

Completing high school pays off in other ways as well. Workers who did not hold high-school diplomas lost about 400 hours of work in the five years studied, compared with only a third of that work loss for high-school graduates.

Illogical as it may seem, the survey concludes that unemployment is not a major cause of the poverty problem.

Over a five-year period, male heads of families being studied averaged only 5½ weeks of unemployment. Those hit by serious job problems—out of work for 30 weeks or longer during the period—ranged from 25 per cent of the poorest families to less than 5 per cent at median-income levels and above.

Unemployment: Not a major cause of poverty

Joblessness, the experts decided, "emerges as a problem which compounds but is not the root cause of the economic difficulties of low-income workers."

The scholars added: "Even if it were possible to devise a policy which utterly eliminates unemployment but which leaves relative wage rates unchanged, only 1 in 4 of the very poor male workers and 1 in 8 of the near poor would gain more than 12 per cent in work time over a five-year period."

If jobs are not a major factor in poverty, breakups of families do contribute greatly to enlarging the numbers of those classed as poor.

The survey shows that a family headed by a female is more than twice as likely to be poor and stay poor as one led by a male—28 per cent versus 12 per cent. And the family with children is about twice as likely to be persistently poor as couples without offspring, regardless of whether the breadwinner is male or female.

Families of seven or more disclosed the highest disruption rates, and people living in large cities were more likely to split up than those in small towns.

The lower a husband's income-education level and occupational status, the more probable it is that his family will be disrupted.

About 20 per cent of women in poor families work at least part time for wages and thus make a major contribution to the family's income.

Marriage: A way out of poverty

Observing this fact, the study comments: "A major way to climb out of poverty is to get married, and a major way to fall into it is to get divorced."

In general, the study found, women who are widowed, separated or divorced have a "better than 50-50 chance" of dropping into the poverty category.

Behind those conclusions lies the fact that women as job seekers usually have fewer qualifications and less work experience than men and they must settle for more menial jobs. Even when they perform the same duties as males, chances are that women will be paid less despite laws that prohibit sex discrimination.

Women also are more commonly found on welfare rolls than men. Once a woman goes on welfare, the study shows, "she has a high probability of staying on until her children grow up or until she marries."

Divorce appears to compound the problem. The survey found that divorced women who are heads of families are worse off financially than any other family leaders and much more likely to live below the poverty line.

IMPACT OF CITY LIVING

Whether the family lives in a large metropolitan area or on a farm also makes a big difference in the odds against being poor.

People living within 30 miles of a big city, says the report, "have a considerably smaller chance of being persistently poor than those in more rural areas."

Size of the city appears to make little difference for whites. But researchers note: "For blacks, however, larger cities clearly decrease the chance of being persistently poor, perhaps by widening job opportunities."

The survey found that blacks in the U.S. tend to be poor to an "extraordinary" degree, both in the short run and over the long term.

Race and poverty

The finding: Even when their average lower education and occupational levels are discounted, black families are many more times as likely as white ones to fall into poverty and stay there.

Table 2.4. Who are today's poor?
(based on official poverty definition)

AGE: MOSTLY CHILDREN, ELDERLY

	Number	% of all poor
Under age 18	11,104,000	42.9%
Aged 18–64	11,456,000	44.3%
Over age 64	3,317,000	12.8%

HOME: MORE IN CENTRAL CITIES, RURAL AREAS

	Number	% of all poor
In central cities	9,090,000	35.1%
In suburbs	6,259,000	24.2%
Outside metropolitan areas	10,529,000	40.7%

REGION: LARGEST NUMBER IN SOUTH

	Number of families	% of all poor
South	2,343,000	43.0%
North Central	1,152,000	21.1%
Northeast	1,014,000	18.6%
West	941,000	17.3%

RACE: WHITES, 2 OUT OF 3

	Number	% of all poor
Whites	17,770,000	68.7%
Nonwhites	8,107,000	31.3%

EDUCATION: MAINLY THOSE WITH LESS SCHOOLING

Among heads of households over age 25 with—	% of poor families	% of families above poverty line
1 to 8 years of schooling	41.8%	18.6%
9 to 11 years of schooling	24.3%	14.4%
High-school diploma	23.7%	34.5%
College—1 year or more	10.2%	32.5%

Source: U.S. Census Bureau

Over a five-year period, the number of white families in poverty fell from 4.1 to 2.8 per cent. But the number of poor black families increased from 19.4 to 22.1 per cent.

Besides being less educated and earning less than whites as a group, blacks more often are poverty-stricken because they tend to have more children and more families headed by women, according to the study.

The impact of this is especially noticeable on black children. More than one fifth of the young blacks studied—21.9 per cent—were in poverty all five years of the cycle, compared with only 1.3 per cent of the white children.

Viewed from another angle, only 38.4 per cent of the black children were able to avoid poverty in each of the five years, while 85.4 per cent of the white youngsters never were poor in that time.

DIFFERENT VIEW

Poverty in America, then, under this close examination seems to be far different from most of the popular stereotypes. The study finds:

Many slip into and out of poverty

Few poor families, if any, are starving. Thousands slip into and out of the poor class every year. Even lack of a job is not of itself responsible for much of today's poverty. Only undereducated blacks appear to be condemned to a lifetime of being poor.

And how do poor people climb out of poverty? The Michigan Institute offers this advice:

"What individuals can change that matters is their family and living arrangements, the number of earners and, over the longer run, their job mobility and the education and occupational entrance of their children."

PERSONAL ASPECTS OF POVERTY

Statistics do not reflect personal aspects of poverty

Examining these statistics on the poor in America cannot yield the full scope of the problem, because the statistics do not reflect the personal aspects and consequences of poverty for the various groups. To be young and poor means one thing; to be old and poor means something else. Add to this a minority group status—being female, for example—and an altogether new dimension has been created. In the 1970s, Harrington stated that "the very same groups which were poor in the early 1960s (when *The Other America* was written) are poor today."[4] These groups are people of depressed regions (such as Appalachia), blacks, Spanish-speaking people, the unemployed and underemployed, the aged, and Indians.[4] Space does not permit us to view the wide variety of poor groups in America; therefore, we will focus upon the young and old poor, at times stressing various other characteristics, such as minority status.

POVERTY AND THE YOUNG

Millions of children live in poverty

Millions of poor people are children. Many of these, because they live in slums and ghettos, also have a greater probability of becoming victims of violence, whether on the street or in the home. Even though child abuse occurs at all levels of society, the bias against the poor may be related to that group's inability to hide the abuse. Most reported cases are concentrated among the poor, where the pressures of "ignorance, powerlessness, and most other social ills are felt more strongly."[21]

With respect to education, poor school-age children are one or more years behind national scholastic achievement norms. Dropout rates for this decade are also much higher for the poor than they are for the nonpoor,

even though more than half of the dropouts participated in federal programs in which they received financial assistance for vocational training.[22]

Many poor children of minority groups, such as Chinese, Chicanos, and
Indians, have problems regarding their native language and culture. For
example, many poor Indian children are forced to attend government boarding schools that employ teachers who often have little, if any, knowledge
of the children's background, customs, or language.

Poor children of migrant workers in America experience particularly
stressful situations. Hundreds of thousands of these children work from
twelve to fourteen hours a day, seven days a week, harvesting crops all
across our nation. Being shifted from community to community causes
many of them to become apathetic, depressed, and confused. The constant
exposure to pesticides generates many complex physical diseases, and the
children's mortality rate is very high.[23] These rootless children, transported
by crew leaders from one part of the country to another, from one school
to another (if they attend school), experience little success. In our society
their future is very bleak.

The rootless poor

Hundreds of thousands of poor children are still concentrated in the
Appalachian regions of this country, where many get very little, if any,
welfare assistance. Consequently, many are malnourished and are slowly
starving to death. Senate subcommittees found children in Mississippi with
all types of severe skin, ear, and eye diseases brought on by lack of food.
Many poor children in Louisiana, Texas, and the Carolinas also suffer from
severe malnutrition and vitamin and protein deficiencies.[24]

Poverty and malnutrition

Citizen's boards of inquiry and various reports and investigations of the
past decade on the problem of hunger describe the following problems for
poor children in America:

> Two words unfamiliar to many Americans are increasingly being used
> to describe the effects of malnutrition on growing children. They are
> *marasmus* and *kwashiorkor*. Marasmus is a condition of severe protein
> deficiency associated with an overall deficiency of caloric intake.
> Kwashiorkor, a Ghanaian word, is a condition of protein deficiency
> generally associated with an excess of other calories; it is marked by
> distended belly, weight loss, and listlessness, sometimes vomiting and
> diarrhea.

> Marasmus and kwashiorkor were believed to be absent in the United
> States. But cases have been found among Navajo Indians and Mexican
> Americans in the Southwest, Negro migrant workers in Florida, and
> Puerto Ricans in New York City. . . .

> Kwashiorkor has also been reported in Beaufort County, South
> Carolina, along with other diseases resulting from inadequate diets
> long endemic to the region—pellagra, scurvy, and rickets. Parasitic

Arthur Grace, Stock, Boston

Poverty in America knows no age limit; the young, middle-aged, and elderly are all its victims.

Worms compete with the child for food

infestation associated with hunger ravages the poor, and substantial numbers of children have intestinal worms, both round-worms and whipworms. The former may grow to a foot in length, and a child may have from 100 to 200 in his digestive tract. At infestation levels of this magnitude, the worms compete with the child for the food he eats. For a child with a low caloric intake, say 800 calories per day, there are hardly enough calories to support the child and "rarely enough to support the worms." Children with this level of infestation have low resistance against other diseases, particularly pneumonia and diarrhea. According to some medical experts, parasitism in Beaufort County ranks in level of incidence with Egypt and several countries in South America.[25]

These citings of marasmus and kwashiorkor were discovered in America during the 1960s. However, Dr. Chase discovered more cases among the children of migrant workers in the 1970s.[26] He found malnutrition among them as serious as many cases found in Nigeria during the Biafra war.

As we shall see later, many poor children with these problems have been helped by several federal programs; unfortunately, too many others have not. The future of poor young Americans appears to be a dim one.

Harrington, in a discussion of poverty in this decade, notes that, "since half of the poor are young people destined to enter a sophisticated economy at enormous disadvantage, unless countermeasures are taken, the children of this generation's impoverished will become the parents of an even larger generation of the other America."[4]

POVERTY AND THE AGED

Poverty is particularly brutal for the aged. Harrington, in the revised edition of his book *The Other America*, speaks of the aged as being particularly invisible since they are often sick and unable to get about. Isolated in rented rooms or in neighborhoods whose populations are no longer familiar to them, they are literally "out of sight and out of mind, and alone."[4]

Many of them are plagued by ill heath (despite Medicaid) and by social rejection. Inflation has also had a profound effect upon their fixed incomes, such as Social Security. As stated by a retiree to a *Washington Post* reporter, "you simply can't imagine the feeling of helplessness that comes over you from time to time now, about what you'd do if the furnace conks out or the plumbing goes. There's no reserve money for a replacement or repairs."[27]

Americans are no longer surprised when they hear of the aged eating dog or cat food or freezing to death when their heat is turned off. Perry, in an analysis of agism, noted that "all too often, old people are trapped by illness, lack of transportation, physical limitations and lack of knowledge of where to go, so they cannot seek help in the early stages of need. They become depressed, fail to eat, and may become confused. When they finally reach treatment, they may be diagnosed as senile or [as having] chronic brain syndrome, instead of undernourished."[27]

As we have seen, the consequences of poverty are manifold. Social class position is related to many aspects of social behavior, such as religious preferences, voting behavior, early socialization, marital status, and size of family. In turn, it influences what Max Weber termed "life chances." As a result, the poorer strata of American society (who have the lowest class position), have a decreased level of education and life expectancy and an increased rate of infant mortality and disease.[28]

AMERICA'S MIGRANT POOR

The following reading, entitled "Working with Migrants," reports on many of the fears, frustrations, and problems of migrant workers. A group of students from Duke University in North Carolina set out to see how migrant workers live in an attempt to understand the social, economic, political, and racial struggles that are related to migrant poverty, and to see what measures could be taken to relieve their situation. The poor hous-

(margin notes)
Half the poor are young

The aged are the "invisible" poor

Social class position influences "life chances"

ing and health conditions among migrant workers today are basically the same as they have been in the past. Earning low wages and being exploited and harassed by crew leaders, migrant workers and their families are among the poorest people in our nation.

COLES AND DAVEY READING——OBJECTIVES

1. Examine in a brief essay the reasons for the students' decision.
2. List and describe four of the problems confronting migrant workers.
3. List and examine three major changes that you believe are needed to eliminate some of the migrant workers' problems.

Working with Migrants
ROBERT COLES & TOM DAVEY

Thousands of acres of rich farmland stretch between North Carolina's industrial Piedmont and its Atlantic coast beaches. In county after county—the names evoke the old South: Johnston, Lenoir, Beaufort—farmers grow table vegetables—cucumbers, bell peppers, corn, sweet potatoes—and, very important, a major share of this nation's tobacco, which is harvested in July, sent on to Durham or Winston-Salem and turned into millions of carcinogenic, highly profitable cigarettes. It is a land of relatively small farms, most about 100 acres, often passed down from generation to generation. It is the old South—rural, conservative, strong on patriotism. It is the South of winding dusty roads, lined by red clay, and just beyond that, the crops—everywhere the promise of growth—and here and there a weathered tobacco storage shed that tells of a farmer's vulnerability.

Farther back (out of sight, usually) are the other buildings—similarly old and "functional"—the camps. Over 400 migrant labor camps accommodate the approximately 10,000 migrant workers who make their way into North Carolina during the first part of June, when cucumbers are ripening, and stay until late November, when the last of the sweet potatoes get harvested. Actually, there is no accurate information on how many migrants come into the state or where and how they live. State officials admit they keep an eye on only one-half, at most, of the camps in the state.

No accurate information about migrants exists

This past summer a group of Duke University students tried to see for themselves how migrants live in North Carolina; tried to find out what, if anything, they could do to help; tried, also, to become familiar with the larger struggles—social, economic, political and not least, racial—that are very much connected to each migrant worker's grim condition. The students had read articles and books on the subject of "farm labor," particularly migrant labor. They almost inadvertently began to realize that migrants were at their very back door—a county or two away from Durham. "We didn't want to stop reading," one of them pointed out, as she thought back to the origins of the project. "Why do professors and deans say that we're at college to *learn*—as if you don't learn by going out to see how people live, what kind of jobs they have, what working conditions are like? We took books with us. We read a lot of articles and books before we left the neo-Gothic buildings of Duke. We interviewed state and federal officials—even a professor or two. We learned that way—*learned* that economics or sociology or political science can be taught at a major university without the students learning how thousands of people live a few miles away, and what their problems are, and what needs to be done if they are to live half-decent lives. We thought that rather than take a year to 'study in Europe,' we'd stay here and *learn*—from the people in North Carolina; and maybe in some way be of service to a few of them. We organized what we hope will be the start of a tradition here, and in other universities. The migrants go all over America. They're never far away from a college."

Migrants work through-out America

The students first had to obtain access to migrant labor camps. Growers are suspicious, and not impressed one bit by the academic credentials of students who knock on their doors. Growers do, however, respond, loud and clear, when asked their side of things. They respond often as the aggrieved one. Farming is no easy matter, they kept insisting; migrants get undue attention from "do-gooders." "And no one ever bothers to ask the farmer what he feels," one grower in Sampson County added, after getting a lot off his chest. Then he got off some more: "We're like anyone else working hard to make a living, so as to have a comfortable life. All those 'do-gooders' blame us for mistreating the migrants. Do the 'do-gooders' know that half of the migrants are alcoholics and the other half of them are running from the law? A lot are mental incompetents. They have different standards than we do. We give them a place to live and the crew leader feeds them, and that's better than being out on the streets. If we didn't have migrants, the nation would go hungry. We'd do all right down here; we can plant a garden, and survive. But the rest of the country would starve. People ought to think about their stomachs before they jump on us farmers. People ought to ask if they want to pay more for their food. If we pay the migrants more, we have to get more for our produce."

Argue with him; remind or show him that the "costs" of migrant labor are nothing compared to those of machinery, fertilizers, pesticides, not to mention the enormous take of various middle-men—the wholesalers and supermarket operators who really set food prices. He knows only his own precarious situation —that of the small, independent farmer, in constant jeopardy, himself exploited by the distant manipulations and more than occasional irregularities of "the system." In a candid moment he mixes self-pity and fierce self-justification with discerning social analysis: "All right, I live good, and the migrants live bad. There's no denying that. But what about the people who criticize us—the college types, the liberals, the 'do-gooders,' we call them? Isn't everyone profiting from someone? Here it's out in the open. What about the guy who collects his stock dividends, or the college that lives off those dividends—from the agribusinesses, that really run the Department of Agriculture in Washington?

"It's easy to pick on me, and call me no good. I'm a little guy; I'm nothing. Why don't you people go checking into oil companies and mining companies?

How about the textile companies over there in Greensboro, or the tobacco companies? You think they're in business for fun? You think they're giving all their money away to the workers? You don't even see unions down here, not many of them. Do they teach you why in college? Do they teach you the truth—that the little farmer is in the same boat as the migrants? We're both small-fry. The bigger you get, the less is known about the way you make your money—and keep it, the tax laws see to that. If you get big enough, you even get to be a trustee of a college."

The stuff of populism and of class consciousness—from a man who voted for and still supports the unqualified, unrelenting conservative Senator Jesse Helms. As for that farmer's camp, it is like the others, as the students on the Duke Migrant Project soon enough learned. One of them, in a journal, described what he saw: "The camps lack facilities and conveniences I've just taken for granted, I guess, as every American's. There aren't screens to keep out flies and mosquitoes; there aren't adequate shower facilities, so that lines of people wait to wash themselves after working 10 to 12 hours in a hot, dusty field; there aren't decent toilet facilities, and sometimes it's a choice between a dirty outhouse or the field. There's no privacy; bedrooms are crowded and the rooms poorly ventilated. According to figures provided by the Migrant and Seasonal Farmworkers Association [an agency set up in 1965 to provide essential services to migrants] way over half of the migrants in the state have 'serious' to 'critical' problems, so far as housing goes. They live in houses that are unsafe, unsanitary, dangerous; and a lot of times, even condemned—for all the good it's done. The sheriffs know which laws to enforce and which ones to forget about."

Unsafe conditions

The students then sought out officials of the Occupational Safety and Health Administration (OSHA), a division of the Department of Labor charged with the responsibility of inspecting migrant housing and keeping standards. In almost every camp the standards were not met; one OSHA official acknowledged that 95 percent of the known camps were "in violation." And the agency is, at best, ineffectual. Of the 400 known labor camps, only 30 percent are inspected, and only 15 percent of those camps are inspected a second or third time at a later date—an utterly necessary follow-up. For every officially registered camp there is another that no one ever inspects; only 1.5 to 2.25 percent of the total number of labor camps in North Carolina are given more than a single, and sometimes all too cursory, once-over.

Moreover, as the students emphasized in their reports, the so-called "gravity factors," designed to register the seriousness of a violation, are based on industrial safety hazards rather than health hazards created by inadequate housing. The migrant laborers must be protected not only from positive danger; they must also be protected from living conditions that are so adverse that they are unhealthy and inhumane. The regulations ought be designed to compel growers to provide migrant laborers with decent housing. If the Labor Department continues to regard migrant housing as a network of factories, then labor camps will, at best, become "injury proof" tenements—places without poison gas, or exposed electrical circuits. Unfortunately, some migrant housing lacks *any* electricity or gas, so there is no chance of *that* kind of danger. As for cases in which violations have been recorded, compliance with regulations is voluntary, no less—left to the grower's discretion. Why? The astonishing answer from federal officials does make a certain kind of sense: "To offset the limited number of inspectors as compared with the large number of inspections they must perform."

With such facts and statements in mind, the students testified at the Labor Department OSHA public hearings held in Raleigh in mid-July. Two undergraduates, in particular, described the camps they and others had visited and insisted that all of the known camps at a minimum be inspected; that camps cited for violations be inspected, repeatedly; that the "gravity system" determining the seriousness of violations be reconsidered. They ended their appeal this way: "We have been shocked by substandard living conditions we have found in the migrant camps in North Carolina. And we have begun asking why these conditions are present, why they are being allowed to continue, and what can be done to alleviate them. The OSHA standards can provide some protection for the migrants, some limited guarantee against wretched conditions. But our findings make it clear that this can be done only if the requirements are specific, detailed, and made the basis for action on the part of the federal government."

There is a need for protection and regulation

And only the federal government. It is all very nice, and these days quite the rage, to talk about the weaknesses or excesses of the central government as compared with the virtues of "the local level." But what goes on at that level in the rural South, in Appalachia, in the Southwest or Alaska? What have blacks, Kentucky and West Virginia yeomen, Indians and Chicanos and Eskimos experienced at the hands of "local" officials—sheriffs and deputy sheriffs, and welfare investigators and agricultural agents, and not least, voting registrars—the whole lot of bureaucrats who fill up those courthouses the breadth of the land? To whom, exactly, are such people "responsive"? Whose interests do they serve? One student in the Duke Migrant Project, headed for law school as a result of his work with migrants, made this observation in a final report: "The old problem of political patronage determines the way migrants are treated. They are viewed as aliens and criminals on the local level. Most of the programs designed to deal with migrants are locally administered—even if federally financed. But justice and relief from the problems that afflict migrants are not forthcoming at 'the local level.' For example, in Johnston County, North Carolina, the health inspector is the son of a grower, the sheriff is the brother of a grower, as is another county commissioner. How else, except for *mandatory* federal standards and enforcement procedures, to get around such 'coincidences?' "

Poor health and pay

Then, there is the matter of health—a devastating spectacle for the students to witness. In many camps the students saw small children with ugly sores on their arms and legs, with a variety of untreated, chronic illnesses, and in almost every case, badly infested with parasitic worms. Often those children are left to themselves, while both parents try to make as much money as they can in a brief harvest time. The students brought the children and their parents to local health clinics—created especially to deal with migrants, but sorely in need of funds. (Many migrants have never heard of the clinics, and have no way to get to them if they had.) As for "dental hygiene," rotten teeth are the rule. The only service local dentists could offer was to pull teeth, often done without benefit

Grant Heilman Photography

Even an abundant harvest does not guarantee migrant workers an adequate income.

of anesthesia. The students kept finding among county health officials—again that "local level"—a sadly condescending, indifferent or contemptuous attitude: the migrants are ignorant, a burden, "different."

They are indeed different. The average annual income of a migrant farm worker is a little over $2500. He or she is lucky to keep one-third of that. It is the crew leader who brings migrants north, south, east, west. It is the crew leader who all too often controls almost every facet of their lives—treats grown men and women as peons. Even when obviously in pain and seriously ill, a migrant must ask for the crew leader's permission to look for help. The crew leader has the car, the money, the power, as a woman told one of us: "You don't see a doctor when you need to. The crew leader won't take you. He'd rather see you in the fields, even if you're going to drop dead—because he's making money off you, and if you have to leave to see a doctor, that's less money in the pocket of the crew leader. He watches you when you're well to see that you're working fast. And he keep his eye on you when you're sick—to make sure you get out in the fields. A lot of people in this camp need to see a doctor, but they're not even going to admit they're in pain. Here you just cry and cry—and show up when the crew leader's truck shows up. And you have no choice. You pay that $35 each week."

The pay supposedly covers the cost of cheap, starchy meals—often prepared by the crew leader's wife. The arrangement not only means a tidy profit for the crew leader, but is another guarantee that the migrant is virtually indentured. In many states only those who prepare their own food are eligible for food stamps. Even when a migrant is sick, without work because of the weather, on the road or idle, he pays the crew leader for food, transportation and all sorts of odds and ends. And he pays through the nose: "Before I can collect my pay each week, this crew leader has already taken $35 for food, even if I haven't eaten every meal—and you should see the meals, and you should see what happens if you complain. He'll pull a gun on you. He'll threaten you with the grower, who'll threaten you with the sheriff. They'll lock you up; they'll call you a drunk, or say you're in debt, and you won't get out until you pay up. Who's ever heard of going to a lawyer?"

He was asked why he didn't go to a lawyer. After his anger subsided, he continued his story of fear and sadness and pain and constant, illegal personal abuse: "He charges us 75 cents for a pack of cigarettes (and we're the ones picking the tobacco for those cigarettes), and in this state they only cost 35 cents in a store; he charges 25 cents for a cup of coffee—and what coffee!—and over a dollar for every drink, and it's no good wine. How can a man have any money left, with expenses like that? My first two weeks here I didn't make any money— not one penny! On payday I found out that I owed money to the crew leader. I work all week long, and who do I end up working for? Everyone but myself! Last week I finally got paid—$4.20. Four dollars and 20 cents! I came up here thinking I would make some money, and instead I'm going into debt faster than I can get out! And who's keeping the books! He sits there and tells us what we owe, and that's it! That's freedom for you! Is there any difference between now and when there was slavery?"

Some migrants have it a little better; in some counties of North Carolina and other states, there is a little evidence of concern. One of the Duke students, upset and outraged by what she had seen, went to the Health Department of Nash County, North Carolina, in search of a job—any job that would allow her to help migrants. She was hired and became responsible for approximately 1000 migrants in the county. She spends her days driving to camps, seeing migrants and driving them to doctors when necessary. She has become a bit weary, reflective: "The medical and dental needs of migrants are overwhelming. We could keep the Duke Medical Center busy for a long time. But there's no money, no doctors—not for migrants. I am responsible for the county's entire population of migrants, but I don't have the time to see all of them. And what can I do without funds? And then there's the harrassment. One day it's a crew leader who beats up 'his' migrants—and sells them rotgut at champagne prices, and keeps a prostitute or two around, also for sale. The next day it's one migrant after another who's sick, so sick they all belong in hospitals—vomiting blood, or coughing their lungs up or complaining of bad pain someplace; and I don't know what to do, except complain and try to tell the county people what I'm seeing. They know, in the back of their heads, what I'm seeing; but they don't want to be told."

After two months of working with migrants the Duke students were thoroughly demoralized, but also full of ideas and plans. No people in America are more vulnerable or exploited than migrant farm workers. They are treated unfavorably or ignored outright by federal laws that regulate the minimum wage and protect the right of workers to organize into unions and bargain collectively. College students cannot in one summer's time change these economic facts in the

Some have it a little better

slightest. In the South, especially, migrants are very much on their own—deprived, even, of the large, sympathetic liberal constituency a state like California gave Cesar Chavez and his co-workers. Political organizers have insisted in recent years that outsiders who come and go don't help the poor in ghettoes or rural areas much, and maybe even cause harm: they are just slumming as *noblesse oblige*, or as a privileged (and self-congratulatory) exercise in "field work." And it can indeed be confusing for a community when well-to-do, university people arrive, so full of *their* plans and ideas—and often enough, implicitly, if not outspokenly condescending, arrogant, contemptuous of the hopes, fears, worries of various benighted "victims."

On the other hand, among some poor people, and especially among migrants, the issue is not only indifference, apathy and ignorance, but a strong, paralyzing and quite intelligent fear: one protests, one tries to persuade others to protest, and one promptly ends up in jail. Anyone who has seen what those county jails are like in eastern North Carolina (or central Florida, where many thousands of migrants spend their version of the winter under a warm sun) knows what a sheriff meant when he told one Duke student this summer to "watch out." The point was not to intimidate the student personally; the sheriff was smart enough to avoid doing that. The point was to remind a sensitive youth that she could always leave, but that others were not so free.

The student was not intimidated, however. She had learned a few things—as students are supposed to do. She had begun to understand, after 10 weeks of hard work—as migrants do, sunup to sundown—that the sheriff and the growers of a particular county were also frightened, hence their constant threats and insults. The one friendly grower she had met told her why: "Even the textile workers can't organize in this state. How do you expect migrants to do anything for themselves without being slapped down? No one here gets worried too much about what the state officials say, or even those federal inspectors. They're not backed up; they don't have tough laws behind them. But when a lot of students come here, people get nervous. You don't just arrest students. No telling who the person is you're arresting, and what will come of it. They go poking around, making friends with the migrants, teaching their kids, helping them get food stamps or taking them to a doctor or a dentist—and what will they do next? That's what the sheriff and his cronies (the meanest growers in the world, some of them) begin to wonder about. If there was a group of students—it doesn't have to be a large one—hanging around growers in every state, we'd probably behave better. We'd shout a lot; but we'd watch ourselves, too."

Some improvements made

Dozens of migrant children are at least a little better educated because of the efforts of a group of Duke students. Dozens of migrants are in better health, too. (A government-supported survey found that about half of the state's migrants suffer "serious" or "critical" nutritional deficiencies, and almost *all* are in medical jeopardy for one reason or another.) Likewise, further documentation—for example, on problems of housing and sanitation—has been done, made public, reported by the press. Nevertheless, a long tradition of muckraking journalism, not to mention fat books, scholarly and reportorial, have done little for hundreds of thousands of wandering and ostracized people.

"Their Eyes Were Watching God," said Zora Huston in her neglected, powerful novel about migrant life of the 1930s. Theirs are "The Grapes of Wrath," said

John Steinbeck in his much better-known story of the same decade. Now, almost half a century later, the same outrageous conditions prevail.

EXPLANATIONS OF POVERTY

Poverty has been explained in many ways. No one theory or perspective can adequately deal with it, however, because it has different origins and takes a variety of forms. We cannot examine all the theoretical explanations of poverty, but we will present some of the major theories and perspectives that have been developed.

THE "CULTURE OF POVERTY" PERSPECTIVE

Without doubt, a major sociological perspective on the poor, which was popularized by the well-known social scientist, Oscar Lewis, is denoted by the phrase "culture of poverty." During the past decade, there has been much debate in the field of sociology as to whether such a "culture of poverty" exists among the poor in America. This perspective stresses the idea that various social strata manifest distinct cultures and that the values of the poor are substantially different from the values of people in the mainstream of society.[29] Lewis states that his purpose in developing this perspective was to form a conceptual model in terms of a set of interrelated traits, poverty being the crucial one.[29,30]

> Oscar Lewis on the "culture of poverty"

There are, according to Lewis, seventy traits that characterize the "culture of poverty." Examples are powerless and helpless feelings, unemployment, an inability to defer gratification, the lack of privacy, gregariousness, and a predisposition to authoritarianism. Many of these traits inhibit the poor from the adjustment to a success-oriented middle-class society and from upward mobility in that society. In fact, the "culture of poverty" viewpoint stresses that the poor do not even value upward mobility. This is indicated by a "general lack of commitment to any endeavor requiring sustained effort, self-discipline, and renunciation of present for future gratification."[29] According to Lewis, severe material deprivation and poverty are not in themselves sufficient to generate a "culture of poverty." It "emerges only as a concomitant of poverty within a competitive, open-class type of society, one that possesses a highly individualistic ideology."[29]

> Characteristics of the "culture of poverty" inhibit upward mobility

Proponents of this viewpoint argue that the poor "do not share the middle-class abhorrence of consensual unions, sexual promiscuity, illegitimacy, and violence in interpersonal relations" and that, "many of the poor value a life free of binding entanglements, which permits relatively free expression and gratification of impulses. . . . they do not seem to value participation in the larger society, but instead prefer to restrict their relationships to members of their own families."[29] From this perspective, the values of the poor reflect a lack of desire to be a part of or advance in society's social institutions. Instead, they reflect a desire to condone behavior re-

> The poor value a "free life"

garded by the middle-class as being deviant. According to Lewis, the "culture of poverty" is, for the poor, a series of reactions and adaptations to their marginal position in American society. He believes America's poor could not continue to carry on without this "culture of poverty" and its structure, rationale, and defense mechanisms. It is a stable and persistent way of life, transmitted from generation to generation in the family.[30] Lewis states that the "culture of poverty has its own modalities and distinctive social and psychological consequences for its members. It is a dynamic factor which affects participation in the large national culture and becomes a subculture of its own."[30]

When the poor in America realize how highly improbable it is that they will achieve success and the "American Dream," the "culture of poverty" enables them to cope with their feelings of hopelessness and despair. It should also be noted that once the "culture of poverty" is developed and transmitted from one generation to the next, the younger generation is motivationally and culturally unready to achieve, even if opportunities are present.

In addition to Lewis, Daniel P. Moynihan is another proponent of the "culture of poverty" perspective. Poverty has been explained by Moynihan in terms of a "poverty cycle."[31] This idea states that low income results in poverty, creating a cultural environment that in turn, acts as a barrier to motivation, aspiration, and the capacity to achieve. Not being motivated, the poor are unable to acquire an adequate education, which results in a low degree of mobility and a limited earning potential. A low earning potential combined with poor health results in limited income opportunities. Poverty becomes inevitable. It should be noted that Moynihan's theory has been criticized for underemphasizing the broader, deep-seated cultural and institutional forces that perpetuate poverty, within which his "poverty cycle" operates.[32,33]

Walter Miller and Nathan Glazer are also proponents of the "culture of poverty" persepective, although each emphasizes different points. However, according to Richard Fave, a sociologist who has analyzed this perspective, they both stress the following premises:

1. A set of values exists that is unique to the poor.
2. These values develop from the experience of living in poverty.
3. They greatly influence the day-to-day behavior of the poor.
4. Some of this behavior is considered "deviant" by middle-class standards.
5. Much of this behavior is dysfunctional for the poor because it works against their moving up and out of poverty.
6. The values of the poor are transmitted from one generation to the next and remain largely intact.

The "culture of poverty" as a defense mechanism

The "culture of poverty" helps the poor cope with reality

Moynihan: The "poverty cycle"

Premises of the "culture of poverty" perspective

7. Due to the self-perpetuating nature of these values, the poor will continually fail to take advantage of opportunities for upward mobility, even if these opportunities were greatly expanded.[29]

The "culture of poverty" concept summarizes a view of poverty that is shared by consensus theorists. The *consensus* approach believes a major cause of poverty to be the ongoing creation, by the poor, of a "consensus pattern at odds with the dominant culture." Consensus theorists believe that the poor adapt to poverty through illegal activities legitimated by their subculture.[34]

"Culture of poverty" is shared by consensus theorists

Another related theory is the *functional* approach. Functionalists, who believe that our society has a class-differentiated value system, see poverty as a form of deviance, and the behavior of those in poverty is "the reverse of what is adaptive or functional" in society.* Functionalists believe the poor are deficient in personality traits (such as impulse control, achievement, and planning drives), role skills (such as manners and punctuality), and mental functioning (due to inadequate socialization). They also have a "restricted role repertory limiting their ability to adapt to changing work opportunities."[34]

Functionalist: Poverty is deviance

In their analysis of the "culture of poverty" debate, Coward, Feagin, and Williams noted that the federal government has played a significant role in making this perspective a legitimate and popular approach.[35] Some studies supporting the "culture of poverty" perspective resulted in an emphasis on remedial strategies focusing on the removal of pathological cultural traits assumed to be typical of the poor. The "culture of poverty" issue, then, is not just an abstract theory analyzed by social scientists, but is a "critical notion" with "serious policy implications."[35]

"Culture of poverty" and the government

Because in their study they found little to support Lewis' "culture of poverty" argument, Coward and her associates question the federal government's use of the "culture of poverty" perspective as a basis for policy decisions.[35] Their research indicates that few studies have attempted to compare the poor with the nonpoor on the basis of a number of Lewis' poverty traits. The research also fails to support a "culture of poverty" perspective because this viewpoint stresses that all the poor everywhere are culturally different from the more affluent in society.

"Culture of poverty" and policy implications

THE SITUATIONALIST PERSPECTIVE

Another major sociological perspective in the literature on the poor is the *situationalist* perspective. Situationalists in general are any who have reacted negatively to and criticized the "culture of poverty" approach. In particular, however, they study patterns of behavior among the poor and

* Talcott Parsons is considered to be a functionalist.

explain these patterns as a means of adapting to the environment. Situationalists such as Lee Rainwater, Elliot Liebow, Hylan Lewis, and Charles Valentine reject the point of view that the poor have a unique set of values. They do not deny, however, that among the poor there exist distinctive life-styles. They claim that life-styles among the poor are not mechanically transmitted from one generation to the next, but that each generation of poor recreates particularly distinctive life-styles, ways of thinking, and behaviors as a reaction and an adjustment to living in poverty.

Situationalists recognize that there are several areas in which behavior of the poor differs from that of the middle class. However, they believe that "such differences in behavior are *not* attributable to differences in *values*;" rather, the differences "result from the efforts of the poor to devise behavior patterns that enable them to *cope* with the exigencies of poverty."[29]

Liebow believes that the values of the middle class *are* subscribed to by the poor and are transmitted to each succeeding generation. Poor people begin their lives with high ambitions that remain strong through adolescence and until repeated failures destroy hope. The poor then adapt to reality by striving for more modest satisfactions in life. Fear of failure inhibits any further attempts at previously held ambitions.[29,36]

Valentine has criticized much of the research on the poor, urging researchers to discern those cultural features that are shared by different subsystems, specifically, those shared by the poor and the middle class, or by all strata of society.[37] Valentine believes that unemployment, unskilled work, poor wages, poor housing, and poor education are *not* ingrained patterns of social response, but are "conditions of poverty." Other sociologists' research supports Valentine by suggesting that the majority of traits that lent support to Lewis' perspective might be "better classified as situational conditions of poverty rather than a bonafide 'culture' of poverty."[35] Traits that are distinctive by class do not indicate cultural patterns. Low expectations and low levels of aspiration are, according to Valentine, consistent with the poor's situation; however, they should not be viewed as ingrained subcultural values, but as "inevitable emotional responses to the actual conditions of poverty." He also believes that government programs criticize the poor for their cultural inadequacies, such as low achievement motivation, instead of dealing with problems of income distribution, which are the basis of our nation's poverty.[37]

THE "VALUE STRETCH" PERSPECTIVE

Hyman Rodman, a critic of both the "culture of poverty" and situationalist approaches, has examined the relationship between values and social class in America in an attempt to determine whether our society has a class-differentiated value system or a common value system. He believes that both viewpoints are (a) correct, (b) incomplete by themselves, and (c) complementary. He notes that people in poverty share with other poor certain

The poor do not have unique values

Behavior is a method of adaptation

The poor share middle-class values

Valentine: What traits are shared?

Traits are situational conditions of poverty

Rodman: The relationship between values and social-class

values unique to themselves and they also share society's basic values with the nonpoor—i.e., "those who hold that the basic values of society are common to all classes are correct. . . . those who hold that the values differ from class to class are correct." According to Rodman and his concept of "value stretch," people in poverty react to their situation by adjusting some aspects of their values, letting other aspects remain the same; they develop an alternative set of values, but do not drop society's general standards. "Without abandoning the values placed on success," the poor stretch the values so that "lesser degrees of success also become desirable. . . ." The result is that they have a much wider range of values than do the nonpoor.[38]

Rodman states that values among the poor become "stretched" when they fail to attain middle-class goals by encountering socioeconomic barriers. He notes that the poor

> maintain a strong commitment to middle-class values that they cannot attain. . . . a change takes place. . . . they come to tolerate and eventually to evaluate favorably certain deviations from the middle-class values. In this way they need not be continually frustrated by their failure to live up to unattainable values. The resultant is a stretched value system. . . .[38]

America's poor do desire achievement and success; however, these desires are modified as the poor attempt to cope with their social and economic circumstances.

Fave, in his analysis and critique of the "value stretch" concept of poverty, states that both proponents and critics of the "culture of poverty" concept are partially correct. He feels that the values of the poor resemble those of the middle class in terms of *preferences*; however, they "differ most noticeably from middle-class values in terms of *expectation* and *tolerance*. . . . the poor display the most severely stretched values of any class."[29] Fave notes that the expectation level indicates those values that a person actually expects to realize; the preference level, those values that a person prefers to realize. He also notes that "tolerance is defined as the minimal level of acceptability. Thus, if an individual has a high level of tolerance, it means that only the highest levels of values are acceptable to him. In conventional usage such an individual would be considered intolerant." There is a "wide variety of values to which these predictions can be applied, e.g., educational, occupational and income aspirations. . . ."[29]

Gans, a critic of various perspectives on poverty and, as we shall see further on, an advocate of the conflict approach to poverty, has also argued that both the "culture of poverty" and the situationalist perspectives are able to explain America's heterogeneous poor. For particular times and places, both approaches are valid for different groups of poor. In America the poor are as varied as the affluent.[39] Then criticizing both viewpoints,

---

The poor "stretch" their values and modify their goals

Fave: Value preference, expectation, and tolerance

Gans: Both approaches can be accurate

he stresses the multidimensional nature of poverty. According to Gans, some people have been poor for generations, others, only periodically. Likewise, many poor share middle-class values, others share working-class values.[40]

THE CONFLICT PERSPECTIVE

The basic assumptions, goals, and solutions of a fourth perspective on poverty—the *conflict* perpsective—are somewhat different from those just examined. The conflict approach to poverty stresses that the social, economic, and political structures of America deprive the poor from a decent living standard. Some conflict theorists, most notably Marx, view the problem as a product of capitalism.[42] In a market economy, those in poverty are exploited by the few who continually amass privileges and power. Class being the significant fact of social life, the poor become merely a tool for those in power. The social problem of poverty develops out of the dynamics of class struggle and is the product of capitalistic power relations and economic structure.[41]

Many other conflict-oriented writers note that poverty and other social problems in America exist because the powerful in society do not want them corrected. According to David Caplovitz, the poor provide a market for poorly-made products. They also provide profits for slum supermarkets, tenement landlords, and unscrupulous salespeople.[42,43]

These ideas are also explored by Gans, who believes that people in power profit from the poor. Even though he maintains a conflict perspective, Gans has examined and explained poverty from the standpoint of its uses and positive functions.[44] Unlike those who believe that poverty is harmful to our entire society, Gans indicates that, although it is harmful to some people, for other individuals and groups it is economically, socially, and politically beneficial. For example, it ensures the completion of society's "dirty work"—dangerous, dirty, dead-end, and menial jobs. The poor also create and support professions that service the poor—without the poor, where would the welfare department be? The poor function as "human garbage cans," consuming day-old bread and buying old cars. They guarantee the status of the nonpoor (someone has to be at the bottom). The poor are the ones who suffer the displacement caused by progress.

It should be noted that Gans does not intend to suggest that because poverty is functional in society it *should* or *must* exist. He does examine several functional alternatives to poverty, but indicates that implementation of such alternatives would create many additional problems for America's affluent. Gans makes the point that if America is sincerely interested in eliminating poverty, changes in our social structure have to be made.

Other conflict, or "alienation," theorists view problems of poverty as being social, political, and personal conditions in which the poor are short-

---

Marx: Social, economic, and political structures exploit the poor

The powerful profit from the poor

Gans: The positive functions of poverty

Changes have to be made to eliminate poverty

changed on such things as opportunity for education, social mobility, participation in decision-making, and self-respect. They are not merely short on cash and basic services, they have few, if any, assets such as housing, savings, and wealth. Many who maintain this approach believe not only that poverty is problematic, but also that stratification in general is a serious social problem.[45,46]

Stratification itself is the problem

In his analysis of poverty, Amitai Etzioni, a well-known sociologist, notes that other approaches, to both poverty and social problems in general, have recently been gaining prominence. These approaches are *neoconservatism, symbolic interactionism,* and *ethnomethodology.**

Other approaches to poverty

Basically, neoconservatives believe that poverty is simply a greatly exaggerated problem. In contrast, symbolic interactionists and ethnomethodologists see poverty merely as a label placed on some members of society by others. In general, concern focuses on labeling and the way it "stigmatizes the individuals who are its object and affects their life."[34] Etzioni states,

> The definiton of the situation projected upon them by those with whom the poor come into contact forces the impoverished person to engage in degrading but expected forms of behavior. The stigmatization is not an automatic result of low income, but is related to an imputation of moral character.[47]

These and other explanations of poverty are complex and contain weaknesses and, at times, contradictions. In spite of the work that has already been accomplished, there is still a great need for research on the interpretation of poverty. The theories examined here, however, have provided important insights, and some are already the basis of governmental policies. As we shall see in the following section, they are also important in determining possible solutions, although the solutions will vary according to the perspective maintained.

RESPONSES TO POVERTY

In this section we will first examine the relationships among the ideology of individualism, the poor, and the government's concern for the poor. We

---

* For Etzioni, the stress among the symbolic-interactionists and ethnomethodologists is the "immediate context of the behavior that is considered problematic." Symbolic interactionists are concerned with the interactions in forming or shaping meaning. Ethnomethodologists stress asocial, individual meanings and are "interested in uncovering the commonsense rules used by persons in everyday life and by their somewhat more formalized counterparts in agencies of social control, whereby persons are assigned to one or another category of poverty."

will then examine several major programs that constitute much of our welfare system. Lastly, we will study several myths and realities concerning welfare programs and recipients, and examine welfare reform.

INDIVIDUALISM AND SOCIAL DARWINISM

As noted earlier, poverty has always been a part of the American scene. Relief for the poor has also been a part of our history, but has often caused controversy because factors such as fear of revolt, low-cost labor needs, and humanitarian impulses influenced its various dimensions.[48] Historically, welfare was defined as charity and was considered to be a community matter, especially in colonial America. Only the most deserving could qualify, and the circumstances under which relief was given were so unpleasant that the poor would often prefer any alternative.

Welfare historically defined as charity

Until the depression of 1929, very little was done at a federal level to significantly improve the plight of the poor. This lack of involvement on the part of the government had its roots in the individualistic and work-oriented ideologies of the Reformation and ascetic Protestantism in the fifteenth and sixteenth centuries. In the seventeenth century, poverty—both cause and cure—was still considered to be an individual problem. Reforms of this notion were few, being greatly influenced by the prevailing individualistic and religious environment, which legitimated negative attitudes toward relief. Poverty and social inequality were believed to be divinely ordained and necessary proofs of the variations in virtue among people. The structure of society as a causal factor was "not to be probed."[49]

Poverty as an individual problem

This strong individualism stressed that "individuals were to be free from constraint in pursuing success in the land of opportunity."[48] However, it also accounted for the slow development of humanitarian reform through the late nineteenth century. During this period of economic and industrial expansion, individualism was further strengthened by the doctrines of social Darwinism.

Charles Darwin's work influenced such social thinkers as Herbert Spencer and William Sumner, who in turn contributed to the development of individualism.[50,51] The social Darwinists believed that poverty was inevitable and that society would be better off if the poor and disabled were not helped by private and governmental means. Spencer and Sumner felt that the rich advanced society, while the poor contributed to a regression in its evolutionary development. In social and economic processes, social Darwinists opposed governmental interference; relief, or any other programs for the poor, were out of the question.[49]

The poor would be better off unhelped

Darwin's evolutionary theory, as applied to human society by social Darwinists, maintained two themes, the "struggle for survival" and the "survival of the fittest." According to Feagin, an authority in the field,

Social and economic life was considered to be by nature a life-and-death struggle in which the best individual competitors both should and would win out over others. Moreover, the hierarchical structure of society and its socioeconomic or class divisions, including distinctions between rich and the poor, were also thought to be the result of the operation of basic laws of nature. Closely linked to these beliefs was the further idea that the competitive struggle should not be tampered with by government, lest all manner of social and economic ills result.[49]

This philosophical perspective had serious implications for the poor, because sanction from the social Darwinists reinforced earlier justifications for inequality and poverty.[49] Governmental programs for the poor were remote and were viewed as destroyers of progress. Not until the depression of 1929 would our government seriously question the tenets of both social Darwinism and individualism or consider significant involvement in poverty relief.

The Great Depression caused a sharp reversal in that attitude because of the extremely bad economic conditions. Relief to the poor expanded to all levels of government, especially to the federal level. Welfare in America changed with the institution of the Federal Emergency Relief Administration: for the first time, the federal government directly intervened in state and local welfare activities.[48] The 1935 Social Security Act, which developed out of the depression, recognized some of the structural forces behind our nation's poverty and formed the basis for today's welfare system. Providing unemployment insurance and old-age pensions, it established "the basic structure of the federal government's future intervention in welfare."[48]

Governmental expansion of relief

CURRENT INDIVIDUALISTIC ATTITUDES IN AMERICA

Before examining various welfare programs established to deal with poverty, we will first discuss whether individualism is still prevalent in American attitudes and beliefs. In his study of the welfare system, Feagin also examined the beliefs of Americans regarding the causes of poverty. Through a nationwide survey, he established three basic belief categories explaining why there are poor in America: (1) the *individualistic* explanation places responsibility for poverty on the poor themselves; (2) the *structural* explanation blames social and economic forces; and (3) the *fatalistic* explanation stresses factors such as bad luck and illness. As the research predicted, the individualistic explanation "received the greatest emphasis. About half . . . evaluated lack of thrift, laziness, and loose morals—individualistic factors—as very important reasons for poverty. Significantly less emphasis . . . was given to structural factors . . . . fatalistic explanations varied. . . ."[49]

Individualistic interpretations are still strong

It appears then, that an individualistic interpretation of the cause of and cure for poverty is still common among many Americans, despite the recent emergence of the structural interpretation. The social and economic sources of these views indicated that particular groups in America are more likely to rely on individualistic explanations of poverty, particularly the middle-socioeconomic group, the elderly, whites, and Southerners. Strongholds of structuralism were found to be the lower-socioeconomic group and Jewish Americans. Both rich and poor emphasized individualistic factors.[49]

Therefore, we see that: the ideology of individualism has greatly influenced the attitudes of the people and the government regarding the plight of the poor; throughout early American history, the government's involvement in relief was indirect at best; and relief, as charity, remained for many years a community function.[48] Keeping these facts in mind, we will examine America's current welfare system.

AMERICA'S WELFARE "SYSTEM"

Before examining several of the major programs that constitute the bulk of our national relief plan, the student should be aware of a major criticism of America's welfare system—that it is not a system at all. According to Casper W. Weinberger, former Secretary of HEW, "it is a whole array of programs enacted at different times, with different goals and characteristics, unguided by any conscious, consistent philosophy or even actual necessity."[52] He believes, for example, that a particular family might be interviewed separately by agency officials from different governmental levels. Since there is very little interaction among these officials, the family will probably not be viewed as "a whole considering 'all' the aid it may be receiving or could receive."[52]

The welfare system is not a system

The American welfare system is a maze of almost 170 antipoverty programs found in multilayered federal, state, and local agencies. The major federal agency dealing with poverty is the Department of Health, Education and Welfare (HEW), although many other agencies, federal and local, are responsible for a variety of programs.

Aid for children without parental support

AID FOR FAMILIES WITH DEPENDENT CHILDREN
Created by the Social Security Act Amendments, Aid to Families with Dependent Children (AFDC) is one of the largest public assistance programs. In 1975, $8.6 billion was received by several million families with dependent children; in 1977, total benefits under the program are expected to exceed $11 billion for more than 11.3 million people.[53] Eligibility for AFDC is not based only on financial need. Payments under this program go to particular family categories "where there is a dependent child deprived of parental support," and "usually only to a so-called one-parent family," where the male head is absent from the household.[52] (This last stipulation

has been criticized, because for many years aid could not be obtained unless the male head of the family was absent. This led many unemployed males to desert their families in order to make the children eligible to receive welfare monies.) Each individual state establishes a needs standard for determining a family's eligibility for benefits. AFDC is a completely subjective system requiring social workers to interview and intrusively question the "most intimate details of the applicant's life.[52]

FOOD STAMP PROGRAM

For many years, surplus commodities (such as powdered milk, beans, flour, peanut butter, and lard) were offered by the Department of Agriculture to help feed millions of poor Americans. The Food Stamp program was developed in 1962 as a small program (it originally cost $35 million and served only 400,000 people) to remove surplus commodities from the market while still helping the hungry. About 40 percent of all poor families (using the Department of Commerce poverty line) purchase food stamps. According to the Bureau of Census, in 1975 the total number of households using food stamps rose to almost 4.5 billion.[54] The annual cost of the program is between $5.5 billion and $6 billion. Households receiving AFDC are automatically eligible for food stamps. If a household is not receiving other types of public assistance, it is able to qualify for food stamps after the family is reviewed to determine its size, income, and assets. Only half of those who are eligible for food stamps actually receive them. Also, almost half of those who do receive food stamps have incomes *above* the poverty line. It is also interesting to note that as "family income rises, food stamp 'income' diminishes, so there is an incentive *not* to work."[52]

Rising food stamp costs

Only half of those eligible for food stamps actually receive them.

Mark Antman, Stock, Boston

MEDICAID AND HOUSING SUBSIDIES

By paying the medical bills of many poor, Medicaid helps many of those who are in need of medical care. This program provides federal matching funds, from the 1975 figure of $6.8 billion to the 1977 requested amount of $9.2 billion. Unlike Medicaid, the Medicare program, which will be discussed in the chapter on aging, pays the medical costs for Americans older than 65. In 1977, almost $22 billion will be spent on Medicare.[52]

The government is also engaged in the production of housing and offers locally administered subsidies for rent payments and home purchases. Eligibility depends on income, and those who qualify are charged at rates below the market value of the housing units. Unfortunately, only a small proportion of those who qualify actually receive the needed housing.

THE FEDERAL OASDHI AND SSI PROGRAMS

Established by the Social Security Act, social insurance programs provide against wage loss resulting from old age, prolonged disability, death, or unemployment and against the cost of medical care during old age and disability (through Medicare). The federal Old-Age, Survivors, Disability, and Health Insurance (OASDHI) program provides cash benefits to disabled or retired insured workers, and provides for their dependents and survivors. In 1975, the federal government spent $78.5 billion in OASDHI payments— more than twice the amount spent in 1970.[53,57] Unfortunately, one serious problem with OASDHI, especially for the poor, is that benefits are proportionate to pre-retirement earnings. In other words, the poorer you are at the time of retirement, the less retirement pay you will receive.

Through the Supplemental Security Income (SSI) program, which began in 1974, the federalization of aid to the aged, blind, and permanently and totally disabled was established. According to the Department of Commerce,

> Until 1974, money payments and social services financed in part from Federal funds granted to States under the Social Security Act were provided to the aged, blind, the permanently and totally disabled, and families with dependent children (AFDC). Federal grants also assisted States in providing medical assistance (Medicaid) . . . . Beginning 1974, the SSI Program replaced Federal grants to States for aid to the aged, blind, and disabled . . . . The SSI program provides a minimum income for the aged, blind, and disabled, and establishes uniform national basic eligibility requirements and payment standards.[53]

Many confusing changes have been made in the SSI program, and according to a former Secretary of HEW, instead of having "one simplified, unified program to supplement the income of the blind and disabled we have wide diversity between states, and within states, reflecting primarily the strength of various lobbies rather than actual need."[52]

These programs are only a few of those developed to aid the poor. Public social welfare expenditures cost $287 billion in 1975. In 1977, the federal cost for the Income Security program alone already exceeds $177 billion.[53]

Welfare costs have risen greatly in the past several years, and with them have grown many misconceptions and myths about welfare programs and their recipients. In the following section, we will briefly examine and attempt to correct these misunderstandings.

MISUNDERSTANDINGS ABOUT WELFARE

The majority of Americans believe that too many people, who are readily employable and should be working, are on welfare rolls. The fact is that there are not. A very small percentage of our nation's welfare recipients are physically able to work. In fact, most people on welfare are AFDC children (49 percent), the elderly (19 percent), and the disabled.[49]

Many Americans believe that the poor, especially those receiving welfare, do not want to work. However, studies indicate that public assistance is "a place of last resort" for the poor who either cannot find work or cannot work. Research also indicates that the typical attitude of a welfare recipient is not "anti-work or oriented toward laziness and delight with welfare living."[49] In most states, the usual welfare payments are so small (still below established poverty levels) that they generate little "delight."

Some Americans also believe that many people receive welfare dishonestly by lying about their needs and their financial status. The fact is, studies of welfare recipients across the country indicate that only 5 or 6 percent of them are actually ineligible, and it should be noted that among these there was very little intentional fraud. Most were granted benefits through "agency error." Any errors made are, for the most part, not intentional or premeditated but are honest mistakes. Very few (less than 1 percent) welfare cases are prosecuted for fraud.

Some Americans believe that most women receiving welfare have illegitimate children in order to obtain more money, or that most of the children in welfare families are illegitimate. In fact, almost 70 percent of children receiving AFDC are legitimate, and most families receiving aid have only one or two children. Other research indicates that the great majority of children born to unmarried women do not receive public assistance, and that the majority of children receiving aid "were conceived or born before the family applied for assistance."[49] These and many other myths are still very much alive in America. Welfare recipients and the welfare system are the subjects of much criticism.

Programs do not reflect need

People on welfare are not readily employable

Welfare is a place of last resort

Welfare recipients are not dishonest

Welfare children are legitimate

EXPLODING THE "CADILLAC MYTH"

The following reading, entitled "The Real Welfare Chiselers," explores the popular "Cadillac myth" about the welfare poor and examines the "welfare chiseler" as an American "folk-villain." It discusses the general belief that the poor are themselves responsible for their plight, a belief that enables Americans to live with the fact that millions of citizens live in desperate poverty. The article then examines the reason why taxpayers have turned against the poor and indicates where the actual chiseling and waste occur.

SHEAHEN READING——OBJECTIVES

1. List and discuss in a brief essay two reasons why the "welfare chiseler" has become a kind of "folk-villain."

2. Explore in an essay three ways in which people may be manipulated into believing that welfare fraud is rampant in America.

3. Examine in an essay the costs of welfare compared to other factors that increase American taxes.

The Real Welfare Chiselers
AL SHEAHEN

Which is worse? A welfare chiseler, or a rich man who uses legal loopholes to pay little or no taxes? In a recent Lou Harris poll, 58 percent felt that the rich man was worse. 28 percent voted for the welfare chiseler.

The vote was surprising, since millions of sincere Americans still seem to believe that the welfare system is loaded with able-bodied but lazy loafers who get rich and drive Cadillacs while the rest of us work and pay taxes to support them.

Richard Nixon once requested the song "Welfare Cadillac" at a formal White House event:

"We get peanut butter and cheese and, man,
They give us flour by the sack.
'Course them welfare checks, they meet
The payments on this new Cadillac."

The 1971 Grammy-award winning country and western song, "When You're Hot, You're Hot" has the lyric:

"I gotta go down and pick up my welfare check.
So I can make the payment on my Cadillac."

A Texas University survey found that 84 percent of people believe "too many people who should be working are on welfare." The idea of welfare recipients driving around in Cadillacs is a peculiar myth, but obviously a popular one. The truth is that the average monthly payment to a welfare recipient is only $65.52.

Twenty-four million Americans still live in the depths of poverty in the richest nation in the history of the world.

Only half of America's poor receive any welfare at all. For those who do, welfare payments can be described as guaranteed annual poverty. Welfare is the "good life" only to those who have never experienced trying to live on 18-cent lunches.

Yet the "welfare chiseler" has become a kind of "folk-villain" in America today. While the traditional American folk-hero has been the self-made, rags-to-riches man, as deeply ingrained into the American system is the belief in a folk-villain, the self-made poor man, lazy, immoral and irresponsible.

The "welfare chiseler" as a folk-hero

The work ethic is one reason why. Teamster official Nicholas Kisburg says "one reason why blue-collar guys hate welfare so much is that they feel, psychologically, that it theatens them. Working, bringing home the check each week, is one way of establishing their supremacy, to themselves and their families. Work is the one thing they have. When they see a guy getting a check for doing nothing, they go crazy."

Another reason is guilt. Years ago the American people really didn't know the extent of poverty in this country. Now we know, but we don't seem to be able to do anything about it. And that bothers us.

Melvin Lerner, in *Psychology Today*, writes: "If we can help a victim, we are inclined to do so. But God help the victim if we can't—we're likely to decide that he richly deserves everything that is happening to him."

In a series of experiments, Lerner found that most people get emotionally upset whenever they see innocent suffering, and any sense of responsibility for the suffering increases our pain. Most people are not indifferent to the suffering of others. In fact, just the reverse is probably true—we are extremely vulnerable to the suffering of others.

"But," says Lerner, "we feel miserable and under stress when the hero—the good person—suffers. Yet we are indifferent or even pleased when the villain finally gets his just desserts. We all have a need to believe that our world is just . . . that the good are rewarded and the bad are punished. We care deeply about justice for ourselves and others. This need to see justice done causes us unbearable stress if the victim is beyond help, or if the person inflicting the suffering is too powerful to resist."

Dr. Bruno Bettleheim noticed this process in the way many Germans living under the Nazis first reacted to the concentration camps. If the people seized by the Nazi police and put into camps were truly innocent, as they appeared to be, then their government was extremely unjust. This conclusion was too frightening for most Germans to accept, in spite of what they saw directly. They wanted to believe that they lived in a world governed by law and order.

To maintain their sense of justice, if not their sanity, Germans convinced themselves that those who were sent to the concentration camps must have really deserved their fate. They were criminals of some kind and the government was merely protecting all good Germans from this criminal element. The average German citizen could then go about his daily life secure in the belief that his government, his world, was just.

To some degree, the same process is at work in America today. Most Americans believe the poor are themselves responsible for their plight and society is

Are the poor themselves responsible for their plight?

not to blame. We have convinced ourselves that the typical welfare recipient is dishonest, lazy, untrustworthy. We are thus able to live with the fact that millions of our fellow Americans are living and, indeed, dying in squalor. We can tell ourselves that they deserve what they're getting.

BEHIND THE MYTH

The facts, of course, are different.

A government investigation of fraud determined that 0.4 percent—4 out of every 1,000—of all welfare cases were fraudulent. Another government survey showed that only 0.7 percent of welfare recipients were even suspected of cheating, and that only 0.06 percent—6 out of every 10,000—were ever prosecuted by law enforcement agencies. Government surveys also show that less than one percent of welfare recipients are able-bodied, unemployed males. Most beneficiaries are children, the aged, the disabled and mothers. But a lot of people are unaware of, or don't want to believe, the figures. So the myth of the "welfare chiseler" persists.

It's not only psychological. It's orchestrated at the highest levels of government. One of the oldest, yet most effective, political tricks is to blame a country's problems on one segment of the population; to find a sacrificial lamb; to direct the anger of the many against a few, so as to divert people's attention from the real problem. Hitler did it in the 1930s against the Jews. To a lesser degree, the U.S. government has done it with the poor. They're the most vulnerable. They have no money . . . no prestige . . . no political clout. So it's become the old story of turning one group—the taxpayers—against another group—the poor; the workingman against the downtrodden.

The poor: A sacrificial lamb

How is this done? How do you manipulate people to believe that welfare fraud is rampant when, in fact, it is 0.4 percent? It's not difficult.

If you're then-President Richard Nixon, you go on national television and you tell the American people: "The thing that is demeaning is for a man to refuse work and then ask someone else who works to pay taxes to keep him on welfare." (Applause).

If you're the State Welfare Director of Nevada, you make the front page by charging that: "50% OF WELFARE RECIPIENTS CAUGHT CHEATING." Later you are found to be "running roughshod over the rights of welfare recipients" and your charges totally unfounded by the Federal District Court in Las Vegas. But the truth never quite catches up with the headline.

If you run a San Diego newspaper, you devote a 5-column, 50-inch story to then-Governor of California Ronald Reagan's blast at rising welfare costs, while in the same issue, you put the latest poverty figures on an inside page in a two-inch story.

If you run the Los Angeles Times, you headline: "WELFARE COSTS SKY-ROCKET," citing the annual welfare cost rise to $16.3 billion. But a few days later you virtually ignore the U.S. Senate's voting of $21 billion for military procurements. You bury the story on the inside pages. Then when the government announces its latest survey showing that welfare fraud is less than 1 percent, you ignore the story completely. You don't even print it.

So it's not difficult to see how the public is regularly deluded into believing that welfare costs and welfare chiselers are the cause of rising taxes, and that the poor of America are richly getting what they deserve. The truth is that since the total annual welfare costs—federal, state and local combined—are $16.3 billion, and the fraud rate is 0.4 percent, we can calculate that welfare fraud costs the U.S. $65 million annually, or $1.03 per family per year, or two cents a week.

By comparison, farm subsidies cost the U.S. $4.2 billion a year, or $66 per family. Oil import quotas cost Americans $7.2 billion a year, or $114 per family. The national interest on government debt, mostly war-created, will cost $24.7 billion in 1974, or $389 out of the pocket of the average American taxpaying family. Defense spending will cost each family $1,230 this year. Defense cost overruns in the past few years cost each of us $527. Tax loopholes are plugged by the rest of us to the tune of $907 per year.

Welfare for the rich

Welfare fraud is a tiny fraction of the massive, calculated chiseling which goes on daily in this country. Politicians who angle for headlines and votes by blaming "welfare chiselers" for rising taxes are lying and they know they are lying. They know there is a thousand times more chiseling and sheer waste in government and business than in the entire welfare program. They know that this country could easily provide a guaranteed adequate income to all the people simply by cutting the defense budget by only 25 percent, or by closing a third of the tax loopholes.

For us to worry about some poor guy on welfare, who can't make it through life, chiseling us out of a few nickels and dimes, seems ludicrous. Given the temptation, given that a few dollars more or less welfare money may be a matter of survival, the prevailing honesty of welfare recipients—their fidelity to the rules of the very system which keeps them poor—is, to say the least, remarkable.

WELFARE ABUSE

It should also be noted that welfare myths have been aggravated by many abuses from the agencies themselves with which the poor have had to contend. From World War II to the 1960s, state and local administrative policies of welfare bureaus denied aid to several million needy poor. In some cases, these abuses were deliberately employed to keep people off the welfare rolls.

Aid denied to many in need

Based on the research of Turner and Starnes, the most widespread and abusive practices in this period were the following:

1. Unlike the Veteran's Administration and Social Security, welfare bureaus never provided the public with information on available benefits. Not knowing their benefits, almost half of those who could have qualified for welfare never even applied.

2. Many welfare officials deliberately subjected poor applicants to a variety of practices used to discourage applications. Long waits, aggressive

clerks, and hostile questions were typical assaults on the applicant's self-esteem and dignity.

3. Welfare applicants were often arbitrarily rejected even when eligible. Also, many who received benefits suddenly found them discontinued without explanation.

4. In many cases, recipients received less than they were legally entitled to receive because relief payments were underbudgeted by the state bureaus.

5. Invasions of recipients' privacy by investigators were typical. To check for men in the house, the homes of AFDC mothers were subjected to midnight raids, because the sexual behavior and morals of these women were always open to investigation.[48]

Widespread abuse of the poor

Very little could be done by the welfare applicant or recipient to stop these practices because prior to 1960 no formal appeal channels existed. Turner and Starnes note also that these practices were developed to keep people in the job market as well as off the welfare rolls. It wasn't that the welfare workers did not care about the needs of the poor; many were concerned and worked conscientiously to meet their needs. However, abuse was widespread, and it deterred many from applying for help.[48] In some of the cases

> welfare administrators were simply responding to political and economic pressure for an inexpensive and seasonal labor supply; in other cases, administrators were reacting to public pressure to enforce the work ethic for "people's own good"; and in still other cases workers were simply imposing their own versions of morality on their clients.[48]

The correction of abuse

The NWRO

During a "welfare explosion" between 1960 and 1975, when the number of people on the welfare rolls increased dramatically, many abusive practices ended. Court challenges, political pressure, and welfare rights organizations all worked successfully to eliminate them. In the late 1960s and early 1970s recipients could appeal the suspension or curtailment of benefits and deny entry into their homes to welfare agents. Also, women receiving AFDC were allowed to have a "man in the house." Through the dispersal of both rights information and money (from dues), the National Welfare Rights Organization has protected many welfare recipients from other abuse. Some social scientists have interpreted this relaxation of welfare restrictions or "cooling out," as a way of avoiding "major structural changes in patterns of urban government, school segregation, union exclusion, and housing discrimination."[48]

According to Feagin, author of *Subordinating the Poor*, this decade is a time of criticism, when moderate and conservative leaders continue to be the "most likely to articulate publicly their critical views of welfare programs and recipients, and to support work-oriented cures for welfare ills."[49] There is still concern for the poor, but much of it appears automatic. Most of the time this concern evokes the old stereotypes of the poor, which emphasize their "lack of effort, their low ambitions, or their need for stimulus to work, rather than the issues of low relief payments or the lack of jobs indicated by high unemployment rates."[49]

Some social scientists have questioned whether our welfare system actually promotes the poor's well-being. Turner and Starnes believe it is misleading to use the term "welfare" because it implies the existence of a system that assumes people "fare well" in society. They feel that the welfare programs in America often help perpetuate poverty, and they indicate that the poor are unable to exert the necessary power to improve their condition. In other words, the welfare system is not just an expression of humanitarian values but also represents upper-class interest in maintaining an inexpensive labor pool. They state that "by inducing and forcing the poor to work in jobs for low wages and few fringe benefits, the wealthy can enjoy certain privileges at low cost."[48]

Criticism of welfare programs

WELFARE REFORM

Because welfare programs are multiple and complex, because many of them do not meet the needs of the poor, which is their purpose, and because they can often deny equal access to their benefits, there has been much interest in welfare reform. The many alternative programs that have been suggested are well beyond the scope of this chapter. However, one likely alternative to our current welfare system is, according to some sociologists, a guaranteed annual income.

Guaranteed annual income

Sometimes referred to as a negative income tax, the guaranteed income would "set an income floor for all families and individuals."[48] The difference between income actually earned and this hypothetical income floor would be subsidized by the federal government and would ensure a livable income for the poor. With this alternative, state welfare bureaucracies would be eliminated and their workers could then perform other community services. Additional advantages include the reduction of recipient abuse and the establishment of an auditing system. Providing the "income floor were set at an adequate level" and adjustments were made for inflation, the primary advantage is that "abject poverty would be eliminated."[48]

There are disadvantages to a guaranteed income. The high cost of the program (at least $30 billion per year) and the accompanying inflation, caused by increased federal expenditures, are unpopular dividends. And should the program be developed through the tax agencies, "all of the problems associated with tax expenditures would apply to the guaranteed income."[48]

Turner and Starnes, in their analysis of the guaranteed income, note that perhaps the greatest disadvantage "cannot be easily overcome" because it is part of and "built into the cultural, political, and economic realities of American sociey."[48] They state,

> It is likely that Congress . . . would make the guaranteed annual income so low that it would not provide an adequate standard of living for the poor. . . . Congress would legislate work requirements for some categories of recipients, to keep them from violating the work ethic.

President Carter on welfare reform

At the time of this writing, President Carter has announced the outline of a welfare reform program that would guarantee jobs for those who can work and cash assistance for those who cannot. His review of the welfare system concluded that "the present welfare programs should be scrapped." His new program, which will not be fully implemented until 1981, basically calls for guaranteed jobs. Every family "with a child and a member able to work" would be guaranteed a publicly financed job if a private job was unavailable. For the poor who cannot work, a "decent income" in the form of a single cash payment would be provided. This goal would be achieved through the consolidation of AFDC, SSI, and Food Stamp benefits. With adjustments for geographical cost-of-living differences, the payments to recipients would be basically the same nationwide. The working poor would be helped through earned income tax credits. The program would also include incentives for taking jobs in the private sector and keeping families together.[56]

Many differences exist beween various segments of the government that will affect the preparation and implementation of any new welfare system. HEW, for example, stresses cash assistance, while the Department of Labor naturally emphasizes the creation of public service jobs.[56]

SUMMARY

Poverty has always existed in America, and has been rediscovered by the public many times in our history. In colonial America only the helpless poor were given some relief. Throughout the American Revolution and the later period of rapid industrialization and urbanization, the ranks of the poor swelled. Some improvements for the poor occurred during the Progressive Era, at the turn of this century. Just when many Americans believed that poverty would shortly no longer exist, however, the 1929 depression made poverty a major social problem. The American government then took a major step in helping the poor, through massive federally-subsidized New Deal programs.

Because of low unemployment levels during World War II, much of our nation's poverty was eliminated, and the postwar period brought prosperity to millions. However, this affluence merely hid the poverty that still existed, and poverty was again rediscovered in the early 1960s. Today it continues to exist as an important social problem in America.

There is disagreement over the definition of poverty and over its true extent in this country. An absolute definition sets a specific income level below which is the poverty classification. A relative definition takes into consideration increases in the standards of living—i.e., poverty is viewed in terms of a low *relative* income. Measurement choice has implications for determining the composition and numbers of the poor. The personal aspects and consequences of poverty are overwhelming, especially for the young and the aged.

Earlier in this examination of poverty we noted that solutions to the problem vary according to the explanatory perspective maintained. Governmental programs, such as various civil rights projects, the old Job Corps, and President Carter's proposals for a reformed welfare system, maintain a situationalist perspective. In other words, they focus upon job opportunities, income guarantees, and other economic subsidies that would enable the poor to leave poverty situations. This varies from the "culture of poverty" approach, which dominated many of the "War on Poverty" programs during the Johnson administration. These programs attempted to prevent the poverty life-styles and "culture" from being transmitted from one generation to the next by resocializing the poor—i.e., effecting changes in their personalities. Finally, both the "War on Poverty" and President Carter's proposals differ from a conflict perspective, which basically states that no welfare or work program for the poor—cultural *or* situational—will be effective in our society because the causal and alienating conditions have not been corrected.

Poverty is explained in a variety of ways. Some perspectives stress that social strata manifest distinct cultures and there is among the poor a "culture of poverty." Others explain the behavior of the poor as a way of adapting to their situation. Still other perspectives, such as the "value stretch" and conflict approaches, have been developed to account for poverty in its various forms. In addition to explaining poverty, the various perspectives are important for determining solutions since the solution will vary according to the approach taken.

The responses to poverty in America have been greatly influenced by the ideologies of individualism and social Darwinism. Individualistic attitudes in America continue to remain strong, although the Great Depression and the ensuing vast network of government relief programs reversed that trend of thought. Today, in addition to other programs, the AFDC, Food Stamp, Medicaid, OASDHI, and SSI programs help million of Americans in poverty. Unfortunately, still more millions of poor have not been helped.

There have been and still are misunderstandings about the programs and the recipients. Welfare abuses, however, are no longer as widespread and frequent as they once were. Interest in welfare reform has grown recently, but whether current efforts will help the American poor remains to be seen.

KEY TERMS

Absolute poverty line
AFDC
CWA
Conflict perspective
Consensus approach
Culture of poverty perspective
Fatalistic explanations
FERA
Food stamps
Functional approach
The Great Depression
Guaranteed annual income
Individualism
Individualist explanations
Industrialization and urbanization
Malnutrition
Medicaid
NWRO

The New Deal
OASDHI
Poverty
Poverty cycle
Poverty traits
Preferences
The Progressive Era
Relative poverty line
Situationalist perspective
Social Darwinism
Structural explanations
SSI
Tolerance
Value stretch perspective
The War on Poverty
Welfare abuse
Welfare myths
Welfare reform

Rick Smolan

3

Sexism
and
Racism

Chapter Objectives

1. To define prejudice and discrimination.

2. To explain the traditional view of women in American culture in terms of behavior, temperament, intelligence, and creativity.

3. To examine prejudice and discrimination in relation to women's jobs, salaries, and education.

4. To list three conditions that must be met in order to establish a relationship between race and intelligence.

5. To examine by brief essay three areas in which blacks have experienced prejudice and discrimination in the past decade.

6. To evaluate the importance of socialization in the sociocultural explanation of prejudice and discrimination.

7. To briefly contrast Cox's exploitation theory of prejudice with Blumer's vested interest theory.

8. To compare the three feminist explanations of sexism.

9. To detail five major ways in which minority groups respond to their subordinate positions.

10. To compare by essay the feminism of today with the feminism of the past, briefly describing the history of the women's movement.

11. To examine at least four reasons for both supporting and opposing the Equal Rights Amendment.

12. To examine in an essay the growth of the Civil Rights Movement as a response to black subordination.

DEFINING THE PROBLEMS

In every society, some people are set apart from others for a variety of reasons, such as physical features or behavior patterns. On the basis of skin color, religion, sex, age, physical handicap, or cultural characteristics, people are prevented from participating equally and fully in many aspects of social life.

Women, the aged, racial groups, and other minorities experience a limited range of life choices and alternatives and encounter more prejudice, restrictions, and discrimination than do the dominant groups in our society. These groups are all minorities since they are people who, "because of their physical or cultural characteristics, are singled out from the others in the society in which they live for differential and unequal treatment, and who, therefore, regard themselves as objects of collective discrimination." This minority status carries with it the "exclusion from full participation in the life of the society."[1]

Most minority groups suffer greatly from prejudice and discrimination. Three groups—women, blacks, and the aged—are the largest minorities. Many of the problems they encounter parallel the inequalities encountered by other minority groups. Our primary focus in this chapter will be on prejudice and the unequal treatment that women and blacks in particular experience in American society; the following chapter will focus on the problems of the aged.

SEXISM AND RACISM DEFINED

Sexism and racism are widespread in American society. They are the systems of social, economic, political, and psychological practices and pressures that suppress these minorities on the basis of certain biologically predetermined characteristics. Comments such as "You are qualified for the job, but you won't work out because you might get pregnant," or "This is a white community; if you move in, everyone else will leave," are typical statements expressing sexual and racial prejudice.

Understandably, blacks and women do not experience prejudice and discrimination in the same ways. However, they share many similar experiences, and the alleged biological basis for their respective roles in society provides the justification for examining them together.

When sexism and racism are combined the results are compounded. In view of the fact that among all major social groups, poverty is most likely to occur among nonwhite families headed by women, the disadvantages of being female and black are considerable.[2] In fact, any combination of two or three characteristics (the third being old age) carries with it severe consequences. For example, being black and old in America has its own particular problems. While recognizing the fact that all old black people are not alike, Jacqueline Jackson notes that race is a common reality we cannot

Many minorities exist in America

Sexism and racism defined

Blacks and women have many similar experiences

deny. She says, "We should not now begin to treat them as if they were the same as old white people. They are not. Racism has adversely affected their preparation for old age."[3]

To prove the existence of racism or sexism, the suppression must be contrary to, or extended beyond, the normal divisions of social class. For example, an unskilled black laborer may be suppressed and exploited, but this can be termed racism only "if his vulnerability and suffering [are] greater than . . . that of his white co-worker."[4] In American society, race and sex are subordinate to social class as determinates of life chances and opportunities. It is a sociological fact that class position is a critically powerful factor in the determination of inequality. However, when the factor of class is held constant, the variables of sex and race (and age, as we shall see later) operate freely as bases for unequal treatment. A person within a society who is a target of the "isms" is "systematically relegated to a substrata within the major strata he or she belongs to by occupational and educational achievement."[5]

The "isms" are not just in people's minds, they are also institutionalized. There is a strong relationship between the basic cultural values of our society and its various patterns of structured social inequality. That is, sex and race reflect various conditions and inequities that are part of our society's basic institutional structure.

Unequal treatment because of race or sex

PREJUDICE AND DISCRIMINATION DEFINED

Before we examine the various elements of sex- and race-based inequities in our society, it is important for us to understand the key concepts of prejudice and discrimination. Prejudice is an emotional and rigid attitude or belief, a "predisposition to respond to a certain stimulus in a certain way toward a group of people."[6] It is a state of mind, a "system of negative conceptions, feelings, and action-orientations, regarding the members of a particular group."[6] Prejudices are learned, not genetically inherited. They are learned as individuals are socialized to the values, attitudes, beliefs, and behavior patterns of their culture by family, friends, schools, and the mass media.

Prejudice: A learned attitude

Discrimination, on the other hand, is an act or actual response. It is not just an attitude or predisposition to act. Discrimination involves action and can be defined as the practice of according negative treatment on the basis of sex, race, age, religion, or ethnic background. Minority group members have been excluded from certain types of employment, educational and recreational opportunities, political rights, housing, hospitals, and churches. This institutionalized form of discrimination, enforced by law or by custom, is termed segregation.[7]

Discrimination involves action

Discrimination can be the result of prejudice. As Gordon Allport, a noted social scientist, has noted, prejudices have the tendency to somehow, somewhere express themselves in action, such as orally expressing antagonism, avoiding members of the disliked group, or discriminating against the group in question. He states that, if the negative attitudes are strong enough and there are conditions of heightened emotion, prejudice can lead to violence and extermination.

In America the prejudice against women and ethnic minority groups is used as a criterion for discrimination. However, the reverse is also true—i.e., prejudice can result from discrimination. It can develop as a result of rationalizing the feelings of guilt that may arise after discriminating against someone. Both prejudice and discrimination can exist independently; both can exist together. Usually they are mutually reinforcing.[8]

Needless to say, discrimination on any basis is expressly prohibited by our Constitution and by a variety of American statutes. However, various studies consistently note that many Americans still experience this discrimination.[9] We will begin an examination of the various elements of sex- and race-based inequities in our society with a discussion of the ways in which women have experienced inequality in America.

Usually prejudice and discrimination are mutually reinforcing

SEXISM

The Census Bureau reports that the female population of the United States is about 109.4 million. This represents over 51 percent of the population. Projections indicate that women will outnumber men by almost eight million at the end of the century.[10] Numerically speaking, women are the larger group in society. They are a minority group because a majority-minority situation is a pattern of relationships or a distribution of power, not necessarily a relationship of numbers. As a minority group, women in America experience discrimination and prejudice in many areas of their lives. They experience discrimination in housing, public accommodations, Social Security and other benefits, marriage, birth control, child care services, and various state laws that prohibit everything from being a natural guardian of minor children to establishing a legal domicile.[11]

Women are a minority group

Because of space limitations, we cannot examine all or even most of the social, economic, or civil issues involving discrimination and prejudice against women. This discussion will focus on the inequities concerning women's jobs, salaries, and educational opportunities. It is first necessary, however, to understand the historical role of women in American culture.

THE TRADITIONAL VIEWS OF WOMEN

Our society has many traditional views about women. Many of these are stereotypes that characterize women in negative terms and account for much of their discrimination. A central theme running through many of these views is that women are still considered to be less socially valuable than men.

Women considered less socially valuable

TEMPERAMENT AND BEHAVIOR

A major traditional view of women in American culture is based on the idea that the female temperament (and therefore behavior) is innately different from that of the male. Experiments on various animals suggest that sex hormones can account for variations in behavior and temperament. Even though it is quite obvious that men and women differ physically, we are not certain how these biological differences affect behavior and temperament, if at all. Sylvia Feldman has questioned whether the results of animal experiments concerning female behavior are applicable to humans. The cultural dimensions must also be considered before determining which behaviors are acquired and which are biologically inherited.[12]

All societies make cultural distinctions between sex and age categories. These cultural distinctions have various implications for prestige, identity, social and psychological characteristics, temperament, and behavior. Of course, the specific content of these distinctions varies from society to society. For example, old women receive very little respect and prestige in our society. They are even considered to be a problem.[13] In other cultures, however, they are highly valued and respected, since age signifies wisdom, authority, and knowledge.[14]

The effect of biological differences upon the temperament and behavior of women must be questioned after examining the studies of Margaret Mead, the famous cultural anthropologist. Her analysis of three primitive societies of New Guinea introduced an awareness of the cultural variations that exist between the sexes. Responsive and cooperative, both sexes among the Arapesh people behave in ways that would be defined by Americans as feminine or maternal. The personalities and activities of males and females are very similar and center on family life and child rearing.[15] Among the Mundugumors, females and males are aggressive and violent, and both sexes devalue family life and child rearing. Americans would label their behavior as masculine. The sharpest distinction between the sexes is made among the Tchambuli people. Their sex roles, temperaments, and behaviors are basically just the opposite of ours. The personalities of men are more submissive, passive, and dependent. Women, on the other hand, are aggressive and dominant and play what would be defined by Americans as "breadwinning" roles.

The link between sex, behavior, and temperament is critically questioned by Mead. She states that personality traits, "which we have called masculine or feminine are as lightly linked to sex as are the clothing [and] the manners . . . that a society at a given period assigns to either sex . . . . the differences between individuals who are members of different cultures, like the differences between individuals within a culture, are almost entirely to be laid to differences in conditioning, especially during early childhood, and the form of conditioning is culturally determined."[16]

Cultural dimensions are important

Mead: Behavior and temperament culturally determined

SEX AND INTELLIGENCE

Another traditional view about women in American culture concerns the relationship between sex and intelligence. It was once believed that brain size indicated amount of intelligence. Since it was also believed that female brains were smaller than male brains, women were considered to be less intelligent. There is still a tendency to believe that women cannot deal with abstract thought, or that they cannot think as clearly as men. Some people believe that women have a different type of intelligence, one linked to their emotions.[17] And, according to Kenneth Lanott, biological evidence indicates that the brains of women and men are specialized for somewhat different functions, that they are not identical.[18]

Years ago, John Stuart Mill noted no differences in basic intelligence between the sexes; what differences did exist were due to environmental factors, such as education. Anthropologist Ashley Montagu noted that scientific research refutes the theory linking intelligence and brain size. In fact, in relation to the size of the body, "the female brain is at least as large as, and in general larger than, that of the male."[19] Today, it is widely believed that the commonly observed differences in the intellectual capabilities of women and men are determined not by biology but by social conditioning. There appears to be virtually no concrete evidence of a biological explanation for any differences in intellectual capabilities. Sociologists explain that the very attempt to uncover basic intelligence differences between men and women reflects cultural biases that make the research invalid. Today, the great majority of scientists believe that our intellectual capabilities are distributed by nature without regard to sex. Small numbers of female scientists and doctors therefore reflect a lack of opportunity and encouragement, not a lack of innate ability.

Differences in intelligence determined by social conditioning

The differences that do exist can probably be best explained in terms of cultural conditioning. Woman, according to Feldman, "is taught to emphasize her emotions and is often discouraged from developing her mind."[20] What, if any, intellectual differences exist between men and women are difficult to detect because of our prejudices and unwillingness to treat men and women as equals.[20]

SEX AND CREATIVITY

Traditionally, women have been viewed as less creative than men. For example, there have been few women playwrights, inventors, and composers; however, women have also had much less opportunity to realize their creative potential. Women have faced discrimination whenever they have attempted to enter fields dominated by men. The traditional idea of woman's proper role in society was that of wife and mother. Only the female can bear children and naturally feed them; the child-care role is primarily an extension of a female's biological function beyond pregnancy,

Woman as wife and mother

and a woman was considered to be naturally fulfilled and content in these roles.

The perspective that rejects the traditional view of woman as wife and mother rejects the idea that child rearing is a full-time job. Proponents of this perspective believe that restricting women to the roles of wife and mother tends to "diminish human beings and harm society."[21] No longer considered justifiable, these traditional roles "create unhappy, dissatisfied, and angry women who resent their husbands and children and who, as a result, often hinder them from achieving their potential."[21] They feel that viewing women in the traditional way contributes to the growth of a dehumanized society, for which, "unless sexual roles disappear and sexual equality is realized, there is no hope for more humane relationships between people for a more humane world."[21]

SEXIST MYTHS

These traditional views of women form the basis for most of the inequalities they have experienced. To understand the discrimination women encounter concerning employment, income, and education, we must first examine the various myths about women and the world of work, which are the basis for much of the discrimination against women. Needless to say, a review of data from the Department of Labor, the Census Bureau, and other resources reveals these myths to be false and misleading, since they lead people to believe women are economically less valuable than men.

WOMEN AND THE PAID LABOR FORCE

One myth is that many women in America are spoiled and pampered—that they watch television soap operas all day and "don't really work hard." The fact is that women work very hard in our society, either as wives and mothers or as members of the paid work force. However, most people do not view housekeeping and child rearing as work. Husbands and children say "My wife (mother) doesn't work, she just stays home"; even a woman herself will tell a person "I don't work, I'm just a housewife." Housewives do not draw salaries, and the value of their work is not figured into the gross national product of the United States. Yet, economists at the Chase Manhattan Bank determined that the "average full-time housewife works a total of 99.6 hours a week, or an average of more than 14 hours a day, 7 days a week." The different jobs a woman performs as homemaker include maid, housekeeper, cook, dishwasher, laundress, seamstress, practical nurse, and tutor. If women were paid for this work, they would receive salaries of well over $350 a week.[22] Housewives receive only the money their husbands give them, however, and their work is excluded from Social Security. Discrimination here takes the form of being underpaid and overworked with little, if any, financial security.

Myths are basis for discrimination

Women work hard in society

Abigail Heyman, Magnum Photos, Inc.

While women have made great strides toward job parity, this female firefighter remains the exception, rather than the rule.

American women also work in the paid labor force, and almost all who do are homemakers as well. Today, over 90 percent of all American women do paid work during some part of their lives. Thirty-nine million women in the United States—48 percent of all the women in the nation—hold jobs or are actively looking for work.[23]

Women in the paid labor force

According to the Census Bureau, between 1950 and 1976 the number of working women greatly increased. The change in the ratio of women to men who were year-round, full-time workers reflects a significant change in the female work force. The ratio changed from 29.6 women per 100 men in 1950 to 46 women per 100 men in 1976. That is, there were 46 women for every 100 men working in year-round, full-time jobs.[24]

WHY WOMEN WORK
Why do women work in our society today? Some people still believe they work for a few extra dollars or for pleasure. The fact is that women work out of necessity. Millions of women work in the paid labor force because high rates of inflation have considerably eroded disposable earnings and have forced many families to rely on two incomes in order to maintain their

Women work out of necessity

standard of living. Because of divorce, widowhood, and other reasons, many women work because they are the sole support of their families. Although a quarter of the women who work are single, more than 60 percent are married. Married women with preschool children and husbands in the households make up 36.6 percent of the female labor force, up from 11.9 percent in 1950. Almost 20 percent of working women are separated, divorced, or widowed.[25]

Some social scientists have explained the increase of women in the paid work force in terms of industries' growing demands. This is especially true in the service industries (a major job market for women) because service jobs have expanded at a greater rate than factory jobs in the past several years. The increase has also been explained in terms of smaller families, which free mothers at an earlier age from caring for their children. Technological advances, which have simplified work at home, have also freed women's time for paid work in the labor market.

Economic factors, however, appear to be the major reason for the great increase in the women's labor force. Unemployment among adult males has remained high for the past several years, and millions of families now count on the earnings of mothers and wives.

WOMEN AND INCOME DISTRIBUTION

Income gap between men and women

Another myth many Americans believe is that women today earn almost as much or the same as men. The fact is that women today earn only 59 percent as much as men, and this gap is wider now than it was twenty years ago. Many people believe that women have less education and training than men and should therefore receive lower wages, because people are paid what they are worth.[26] The fact is that women have basically the same amount of education as men, an average of almost twelve and one-half years.[27]

The Census Bureau statistics on median income for year-round, full-time workers in 1976 indicated that a man with only eight years of education is paid more than a woman with one to three years of college. Table 3.1 shows that, even with four years or more of college, the average female earns only $12,109, while the average male earns $19,338. That amounts to $7,229 more a year in earnings simply for being male.[28]

As we shall see, the major reason for the income gap is the difference in the types of jobs that the different sexes hold. For example, most women work in service, sales, clerical, and other low-paying jobs. Men work largely in the professional, managerial, and other high-paying fields. These facts explain the income gap but do not excuse it. According to Kirsten Amundsen, in her book *The Silenced Majority*, the question that must be answered is why women end up in low-paying jobs. She states that in order to justify the types of jobs now held by women, it would have to be shown that they "either do not have the capabilities for any other work and/or have no desire for it."[29] The first proposition can be rejected on the grounds that

Table 3.1. Median income for year-round full-time workers 25 years old and older by educational attainment and sex: 1976

EDUCATION	WOMEN	MEN	RATIO: WOMEN TO MEN
Elementary: 8 years	$ 6,433.	$11,312.	.55
High school: 1–3 years	$ 6,800.	$12,301.	.55
College: 1–3 years	$ 9,475.	$15,514.	.59
College: 4 years or more	$12,109.	$19,338.	.63

Source: U.S. Bureau of the Census, *Current Population Reports,* Series P-60, Nos. 37, 80, and 114; *Statistical Abstract of the United States: 1977,* 98th edition, Washington D.C., 1977, Table 730, p. 452.

significant numbers of women have already filled jobs that are supposedly "better suited to men." Women have proved their abilities as engineers, doctors, architects, scientists, and skilled technicians. The number of law suits filed by women who were denied "men's" jobs in the past several years reflects women's interest in the high-paying jobs, which rejects the second proposition. The only conclusion is that women have low-paying jobs because these are the jobs "considered 'fitting' for women—this is the only rank to which they are welcomed."[29] Amundsen says that this prejudice— shared by both men and women—is not a natural one, and the fact that it has been "wholly or significantly overcome in other societies is sufficient proof of that."[29]

WOMEN AND JOB SEGREGATION

The next myth, which is closely related, is that there is little, if any, segregation of women in the working world, and that many women are now employed in jobs that were once performed solely by men. Some women are now in jobs that were "men's jobs" in the past. Women now climb telephone poles for AT&T, trade stocks on Wall Street, and are members of corporate boards. Sociologists note, however, that these jobs are the exception; most women, as noted earlier, are still in the "employment ghetto," working as seamstresses, waitresses, secretaries, bookkeepers, and teachers. Patterns of segregation in employment are still quite apparent.[30]

One social scientist, Barbara Deckard, notes that occupational segregation is defended as being natural—i.e., "biological and mental differences supposedly determine that some jobs are 'obviously' for women and some [for] men." She says "there are no such differences that would disqualify

Segregation in employment still exists

men or women from any job—except that semen donors must be men, and wet nurses must be women."[31] Indeed, jobs that one country considers suitable for only one sex may be and often are performed by the opposite sex in another country. In the United States, for example, "being a doctor is considered too unpleasant or difficult for women," but in the Soviet Union it is considered to be a nurturing and, therefore, a woman's job.[31]

A common argument is that men are not absent from work or do not quit as often as women; therefore, women's low pay and poor jobs are justified. According to a Department of Labor study, however, women workers "have favorable records of attendance and labor turnover when compared with men at similar job levels and under similar circumstances."[32]

Segregation causes income gap

Segregation in employment still exists, then, in spite of antidiscrimination laws. Occupational segregation, as noted previously, is the main reason why men earn more than women. It stems from cultural conditioning, discrimination, and, as some research indicates, the "personal desires of women themselves," to some extent. There are also gross differences in pay in many cases, with men earning more than their female counterparts, even when the women have the same education and training and are doing the very same jobs. The pattern of women in "employment ghettos," where wages are held down, is supported by the view that men must be paid more because they are the major wage earners in the family. For millions of American families, however, this is not true. The number of women who are heads of households constitutes a high percentage of major wage earners.[33]

WOMEN AND EDUCATION

Inequality in education

The final myth we will examine concerns education. The myth is that women have achieved educational equality with men. Since 1950, the college enrollment rates for women have been rising more rapidly than the rates for men. However, in the mid-1970s, women still made up less than 45 percent of all college students. Today, in comparison to the 1960s, women attending college are moving into the traditionally "male" majors, such as engineering, business, law, and the sciences. However, women still constitute a very small proportion of students in those majors. According to 1976 federal reports,

> The percentage of engineering majors who were women rose from 2 per cent in 1966 to 7 per cent in 1974. The comparable figures for agriculture and forestry were 3 per cent in 1966 and 14 per cent in 1974. Female college students in 1974 remain a large proportion of traditional female majors, such as education (73 per cent), English or journalism (59 per cent), and health or medical professions (64 per cent).[34]

Economic improvement is difficult for working women to achieve because they are, to an extent, newcomers to the world of education and paid work. Because of the sociocultural and familial roles that have been associated with or imposed on their sex, the economic value of educated women and their jobs has "tended to be downgraded, underrated, and undercompensated."[35] The economic position of women in our society can improve only through educational and employment opportunities. Unless women are provided with these opportunities, they will not achieve their legally guaranteed rights.

RACISM AND BLACK MYTHS

It is easy to recognize many parallels between blacks and women in terms of the prejudice and discrimination experienced by both groups.* For example, both blacks and women share common myths that have developed about them. Racial prejudice, discrimination, and inequality are among America's oldest social problems. Blacks have experienced progress in the past several decades but have also had many setbacks. In this section we will discuss many of the attitudes that have persisted about blacks, along with the advancements and setbacks they have experienced in our society.

Racial prejudice is an old social problem

Myths and stereotypes are the basis for much of the prejudice and discrimination against blacks and for institutionalized racism that affects almost every area of black life. Stereotyped traits such as being lazy, happy-go-lucky, and superstitious (supposedly products of the black's genetic properties) are the typical justification for keeping blacks in low-paying jobs and in the poorer strata of society in general. For example, blacks are very underrepresented in professional and management positions, and are still segregated in the schools and in the better residential areas.

RACE AND INTELLIGENCE
Some people believe that there are innate differences in intelligence between blacks and whites. Today, this area still attracts much attention, even though the great majority of social scientists indicate that environmental factors "account for large differences in measured intelligence performance," and also that "minority groups are usually disadvantaged in terms of favoring environmental conditions."[36]

Vander Zanden, in an analysis of American minority relations, has noted that any claims regarding innate intelligence differences between whites and blacks cannot be substantiated unless the following conditions are met: (1) Adequate, valid, and reliable tests of native intelligence, uncontaminated by environmental influences, must be developed; (2) The social and cultural backgrounds (the environment) of the blacks and whites being tested must be fully equal; (3) The distinctive genetic homogeneity of the black and white groups being tested must be demonstrated, not merely assumed. Since these

Race and intelligence

---

* In this section, including the census data, the term "black" is used for all non-white minorities. Blacks constitute more than 90 percent of this group.

Table 3.2. Median income in constant 1975 dollars of families by race: 1947, 1965, 1975, and 1976.

YEAR	WHITE FAMILIES	MINORITY FAMILIES	RATIO: MINORITY TO WHITE	ABSOLUTE DIFFERENCE
1947	$ 7,608	$3,888	0.51	−$3,720
1965	$12,370	$6,812	0.55	−$5,558
1975	$14,268	$9,321	0.65	−$4,947
1976*	$15,537	$9,821	0.63	−$5,716

Source: U.S. Bureau of the Census, *Current Population Reports*, Series P-60, No. 105; *Statistical Abstract of the United States: 1976*, 97th edition, Washington, D.C., 1976, Table 650, p. 405.
* U.S. Bureau of the Census, *Current Population Reports*, Series P-60, No. 114, and unpublished data; *Statistical Abstract of the United States: 1977*, 98th edition, Washington, D.C., 1977, Table 708, p. 440.

conditions have never before been met, we cannot definitively assert that there are native differences in intelligence. Studies substantiating racial intellectual inferiority have yet to demonstrate that they met all of these conditions.[37]

Unlike sexism and agism, racial inequality is not a relatively new subject for scientific investigation. A long history and much documented evidence of prejudice and discrimination against blacks has made them more aware of their social, political, economic, and civil rights. This awareness is reflected in escalating legal encounters originated by blacks to achieve these rights. At this point we will examine some of the documented evidence in order to better understand the extent and impact of prejudice and discrimination against blacks.

BLACKS AND INCOME

Although blacks have made advances in certain areas, such as education, health, and election to public office, some problems still remain in the areas of income and employment. In 1976, black families had a median annual income of $9,821, whereas white families had a median income of $15,537. This represents a median income ratio of .63—i.e., black families earn only 63 percent as much as white families.

As can be seen in Table 3.2, the gap between family incomes of blacks and whites is no longer as great as it was in 1947, when it was 51 percent. The 1976 ratio of 63 percent also represents a significant improvement on the ratio of 55 percent in 1965. However, the general income disparity that exists between the races is still very great.[38]

Table 3.3. Employment distribution by occupation and race: 1960 and 1976.

OCCUPATION	WHITE		MINORITY	
	1960	1976	1960	1976
TOTAL EMPLOYED (× 1,000)	58,850	78,021	6,927	9,464
PERCENTAGES				
White-collar workers	46.6	51.8	16.1	34.7
Blue-collar workers	36.2	32.6	40.1	37.6
Service industries workers	9.9	12.3	31.7	25.4
Farm workers	7.4	3.3	12.1	2.3

Source: U.S. Department of Labor Statistics, *Employment and Earnings,* monthly; U.S. Bureau of the Census, *Statistical Abstract of the United States: 1977,* 98th edition, Washington, D.C., 1977, Table 661, p. 407.

This disparity between blacks and whites can be accounted for in terms of the types of jobs that each group holds. Basically, the same explanations that were presented for the differences between men and women apply to whites and blacks. To an extent, many blacks are in the low-paying occupations because of the myths that blacks have no desire for better jobs, that they are happier in jobs that are more fitting and in which they are more welcome, and that they are not able to perform certain jobs as well as whites.

Income differences because of race

BLACKS AND EMPLOYMENT

There have been changes in black employment patterns during the past decade. Whites are still overrepresented in the more advantaged occupational categories, but blacks have experienced an occupational upgrading in the past fifteen years. In fact, between 1960 and 1975 more occupational upgrading occurred among blacks and other races than among whites.

As can be seen in Table 3.3, from 1960 to 1976 the proportion of blacks who were employed in white-collar jobs more than doubled, from 16.1 to 34.7 percent. (This white-collar grouping includes high-level professional and managerial jobs and administrative, sales, and clerical positions.) The number of blacks in blue-collar jobs dropped from 40.1 to 37.6 percent. White workers also dropped in this category, from 36.2 to 32.6 percent. In the service industries, the proportion of black workers decreased from 31.7 to 25.4 percent, whereas whites increased from 9.9 to 12.3 percent. Both groups experienced a sharp decrease in the farm workers category. In general, however, there was an occupational upgrading for blacks in that period,

Occupational upgrading for blacks

Increased educational and career opportunities have enabled blacks to attain positions unthinkable a generation ago.

Blacks confined to low-paying, low-status jobs

but they still lag behind the white population in the proportion holding high-paying, more skilled jobs.[39]

The impediment to blacks' progress in the employment and income areas has resulted, in part, from a combination of various social and economic factors. Inflation, the downswing in the American economy in the 1970s, changing family composition, and the work experience patterns of family members have all had negative effects on black employment.[40]

The differences that still exist between whites and blacks in the job market indicate that racism continues. It should be noted again that suppression has to go beyond or be contrary to the normal divisions of class for racism to exist. As Amundsen notes, a black unskilled laborer "may be suppressed and exploited, but it is a case of racist oppression only if his vulnerability and suffering [are] greater than . . . that of his white co-worker. As a black, he (or she) must be shown to have been made a member of a class within a class. A victim of racism will thus be systematically relegated to a substrata within the major strata he or she belongs to by occupation and educational achievement."[41] Sociological research indicates that blacks are still discriminated against solely on the basis of race. Blacks are still basically confined to low-paying, low-prestige positions and specific job classifications.

Black unemployment rates have consistently exceeded those of whites for many years. The jobless rate for blacks and other minorities was almost 14 percent in 1975. Relative to their proportion in the labor force, a 2 to 1 ratio—i.e., two black workers unemployed for every white worker unemployed—has generally held true ever since the Korean War. In 1976 the minority unemployment rate was 13.6 percent; for whites it was 7.5 percent.[42]

BLACKS AND EDUCATION

Research indicates that, for blacks in America, jobs and the education necessary to get them are the major factors in the achievement of a better life. Of all the forces of discrimination affecting their life, blacks themselves consider these to be the most important.[43] As recent census data indicate, some improvement in the employment situation has occurred. There has also been progress in the area of education for young blacks. This improvement is critical, since no area of discrimination is as damaging as this starting point.[44]

Statistics indicate an increase in the enrollment levels for young black children and in the proportion of blacks completing high school, which generally results in rising educational levels. The proportion of blacks in their early twenties who graduated from high school reached 71 percent.* From 1970 to 1975 college enrollment increased more rapidly for blacks than for whites. There were 56 percent more black enrollments and only 15 percent more for whites. However, the proportion of blacks aged 18 to 24 enrolled in college (18 percent) was lower than the comparable proportion of young whites (25 percent).[46]

Educational level of blacks has risen

HEALTH AND MINORITY STATUS

The general problems of health and America's health-care delivery system are discussed in a later chapter. However, it is appropriate here to at least note that the health conditions for blacks and Spanish-speaking minorities are so poor that these people suffer high incidences of illness and early death.

High risk of disease and death

There has been a narrowing of the gap in death rates for whites and blacks since 1900. In that year the rate of white deaths per 1000 was 17 percent, compared to the black rate of 25 percent. By 1970, both death rates had dropped, to 9.4 percent for whites and to 9.5 percent for blacks.[47] More blacks than whites die of diseases that have been medically controlled,

---

* However, the educational gap between blacks and whites remains in that 85 percent of whites in their early 20s had completed high school.[45]

however. Black people are also four times more likely to die of cancer, cardio-vascular disease, and hypertension than are whites. Kidney diseases, diabetes, tuberculosis, syphillis, influenza, and pneumonia are three times more likely to be the cause of death for blacks than for whites. Black females are six times more likely to die in childbirth than are white females.[48] Black children, in the first month of life, have a greater chance of dying than white children of the same age; between the first month and first year of life, about three times as many black children die.[49]

Black women are more likely to die in childbirth

There are many consequences of the inadequate and insufficient medical care for blacks and other ethnic minorities. The absence of adequate medical care means a higher frequency of illness and, therefore, a special difficulty in obtaining and maintaining jobs. It also means that minorities see doctors only when their health is so poor that it is considered to be an emergency. Minority parents "encounter special difficulties in meeting their responsibility of providing adequate health care for their children."[50]

These data also yield the conclusion that blacks continue to be discriminated against in many areas of their lives. Their color differentiates them from dominant groups in America, and they are prevented from being equal participants in many of the various phases of social life. In spite of certain improvements in such areas as income, employment, and education, blacks still occupy a distinct position in the American stratification system.

THE BLACK CASTE

Blacks constitute a caste

Duberman, in her analysis of minority groups as caste groups, notes that, because of economic and political deprivation, blacks constitute a class. They also, however, constitute a caste—a form of stratification based exclusively on factors of birth. Even though blacks are in all social classes, they constitute a caste because "the reactions of whites are more often based on racial characteristics than on economic status." When speaking of blacks, Duberman believes that "caste is a more salient classification than class."[51]

Pinkney, in his review of black history, agrees with the caste theory. He notes that, from the time of the slaves' first arrival at Jamestown in 1619 to the 1954 Supreme Court decision to end public school segregation, there developed a caste system in America that still "continues to relegate the former slaves and their descendents to a subordinate position in society."[52] At birth, blacks are assigned to a racial group. Largely because of high visibility, escape is difficult and rare. Every aspect of their lives is affected by their low status, of which they are acutely aware. There is still only limited access to avenues of social mobility, such as education. In terms of housing, jobs, and personal interaction, relations with whites are still restricted. Although they are not legalized, these rules of segregation are entrenched in American culture by customs and mores.

Many years may have to pass before any significant progress is made. As noted by Duberman,

> Black Americans are not and never have been an integral part of white American society. Some progress has been made, but it is slow, with the result that decades may pass before blacks lose their caste-like status.[53]

POVERTY WITHIN PROSPERITY

Racial and ethnic groups span the range of lower and higher positions in the class structure of American society. Minorities, however, constitute a disproportionately large segment of the lower strata and occupy a distinct position in the American stratification system. The following reading, "The American Underclass," examines the many problems encountered by members of the lower strata who comprise that "underclass." All races and ethnic groups make up this strata; however, the majority are poor, urban blacks.

The article notes that the "underclass" has been virtually unhelped by the many gains in civil rights and federal programs of the past two decades. Riots, unemployment, poor housing, and dissolution of the family structure are common.

TIME READING——OBJECTIVE

1. To define in an essay the meaning of the term "American underclass."

The American Underclass

The barricades are seen only fleetingly by most middle-class Americans as they rush by in their cars or commuter trains—doors locked, windows closed, moving fast. But out there is a different world, a place of pock-marked streets, gutted tenements and broken hopes. Affluent people know little about this world, except when despair makes it erupt explosively onto Page One or the 7 o'clock news. Behind its crumbling walls lives a large group of people who are more intractable, more socially alien and more hostile than almost anyone had imagined. They are the unreachables: the American underclass.

The term itself is shocking to striving, mobile America. Long used in class-ridden Europe, then applied to the U.S. by Swedish Economist Gunnar Myrdal and other intellectuals in the 1960s, it has become a rather common description of people who are seen to be stuck more or less permanently at the bottom, removed from the American dream. Though its members come from all races and live in many places, the underclass is made up mostly of impoverished urban blacks, who still suffer from the heritage of slavery and discrimination. The universe of the underclass is often a junk heap of rotting housing, broken furniture, crummy food, alcohol and drugs. The underclass has been doubly left behind: by the well-to-do majority and by the many blacks and Hispanics who have struggled up to the middle class, or who remain poor but can see a better day for themselves or their children. Its members are victims and victimizers in the culture of the street hustle, the quick fix, the rip-off and, not least, violent crime.

Their bleak environment nurtures values that are often at radical odds with those of the majority—even the majority of the poor. Thus the underclass minority produces a highly disproportionate number of the nation's juvenile delinquents, school dropouts, drug addicts and welfare mothers, and much of the adult crime, family disruption, urban decay and demand for social expenditures. Says Monsignor Geno Baroni, an assistant secretary of Housing and Urban Development: "The underclass presents our most dangerous crisis, more dangerous than the Depression of 1929, and more complex."

Rampaging members of the underclass carried out much of the orgy of looting and burning that swept New York's ghettos during the July blackout. (In all, 55% of the arrested looters were unemployed and 64% had been previously arrested for other offenses.) They are responsible for most of the youth crime that has spread like an epidemic through the nation (Time cover, July 11). Certainly, most members of this subculture are not looters or arsonists or violent criminals. But the underclass is so totally disaffected from the system that many who would not themselves steal or burn or mug stand by while others do so, sometimes cheering them on. The underclass, says Vernon Jordan, executive director of the National Urban League, "in a crisis feels no compulsion to abide by the rules of the game because they find that the normal rules do not apply to them."

That disaffection is doubly distressing because the nation is in its third year of a strong economic recovery, an advance that has created 6 million new jobs since the end of the 1973-75 recession. No fewer than 90.5 million Americans are now at work. The underclass remains a nucleus of psychological and material destitution despite 20 years of civil rights gains and 13 years of antipoverty programs that were only temporarily slowed, but never really hobbled, during the Nixon era. Tens of billions of dollars are spent every year by the Federal Government, states and cities to eliminate drastic poverty. In addition, special hiring drives, private job-training programs, university scholarships and affirmative-action programs are aimed at aiding the motivated poor. Yet by most of society's measures—job prospects, housing, education, physical security—the underclass is hardly better off, and in some cases worse off, than before the War on Poverty.

The war, of course, has not been lost. The proportion of the nation officially listed as living in poverty has dropped since 1959 from 22% to 12%. One of America's great success sagas has been the rise of many blacks to the secure middle class. Today 44% of black families earn $10,000 or more a year. More than 45% of black high school graduates now go on to college. Though some

The underclass is doubly left behind

A total dissatisfaction with the system

discrimination persists, more and more nonwhites are seen in at least the junior management ranks of banks and corporations and government, where they are moving up.

But the new opportunities have splintered the nonwhite population. The brightest and most ambitious have rapidly risen, leaving the underclass farther and farther behind—and more and more angry. While the number of blacks earning more than $10,000 is expanding and the number earning $5,500 to $10,000 is shrinking, almost a third of all black families are still below the poverty line, defined as $5,500 for an urban family of four (only 8.9% of white families are below the line). Says Harvard Sociologist David Riesman: "The awareness that many blacks have been successful means that the underclass is more resentful and more defiant because its alibi isn't there."

Others echo those sentiments in gutsier language. Says Naomi Chambers, a Detroit social worker, who is black: "Now that some black people have cars, dresses and shoes, there is jealousy. Jealousy can make me hate you and take what you have." Indeed, the blacks who looted during the New York blackout were totally nondiscriminatory, emptying out stores owned by blacks and whites alike. There is a strong feeling among social experts and politicians, both black and white, that much the same rampage could have struck any U.S. city in similar circumstances—and that next time it will be worse.

Concerned officials from the White House to the humblest city hall are grappling with questions about the underclass. How big is it? Who is in it? What motivates its members? Most important, how can this minority within a minority be reduced?

For many of the deprived, poverty is a transitory condition that can—and will—be overcome by education, ambition or the sheer refusal to stay down. Similarly, most of the unemployed are only temporarily out of jobs; more than 86% have been unemployed for less than 26 weeks. But the underclass is made up of people who lack the schooling, skills and discipline to advance, and who have succumbed to helplessness—a feeling of being beaten.

Long-term unemployment is a factor in that. Many members of the underclass come from the ranks of the 1,061,000 workers who are listed as "discouraged" because they have given up even looking for jobs. To that number can be added the entrenched welfare mothers: at least 2.4 million have been enrolled for one year or longer. Then there are their many children, a few million kids who are growing up without a heritage of working skills or of employed society's values. In addition, many of the chronically unemployed in the 18-to-21 age group have had—and will have—a desperate time landing and keeping their first regular jobs. A portion of the 4.4 million disabled who are receiving welfare also belong. Allowing for the overlaps in those groups, the underclass must number at least 7 million to 8 million Americans—perhaps even 10 million.

Though this subculture is predominantly black, many Hispanics and more than a few poor whites belong to the underclass. Among the most glaring subgroups: the Appalachian migrants to dilapidated neighborhoods of some cities, the Chicanos of the Los Angeles slums, the Puerto Ricans of Spanish Harlem. But the Hispanics appear to be moving ahead somewhat faster: 55% of the nation's blacks, v. 49% of the Spanish-speaking minorities, still live in the mostly depressed areas of central cities. The black concentration in the cities seems

New opportunities have splintered the nonwhite population

Many minority groups constitute the underclass

fated to increase because the birth rate among blacks is 51% higher than among whites. There are other reasons for this continuing concentration: lingering discrimination on the part of the white majority, a crippling absence of education, training and opportunity among the black minority. Says Randolph Taylor, a Presbyterian minister who works among the underclass in Charlotte, N.C.: "How one feels about society depends on whether one thinks that door may some day open. The whites are generally staying with the system on the basis of hope."

It is the weakness of family structure, the presence of competing street values, and the lack of hope amidst affluence all around that make the American underclass unique among the world's poor peoples. Reports TIME Atlanta Bureau Chief Rudolph Rauch, who until recently was stationed in Latin America: "Almost anyone who has lived in or near the crowded *barrios* of South America knows that looting on the scale that occurred in New York could almost never happen there—and not because the army would be standing by to shoot looters. Family structure has not broken down in South America. Nor has the idea of a neighborhood. A child usually feels that he lives in both in a Latin American city. In a U.S. urban ghetto, he often belongs to neither."

TIME Chicago Correspondent Robert Wurmstedt, once a Peace Corps volunteer, reports: "The poverty in the black and Puerto Rican neighborhoods on the West Side of Chicago is worse than any poverty I saw in West Africa. The people there are guided by strong traditional values. They do not live in constant fear of violence, vermin and fire. You don't find the same sense of desperation and hopelessness you find in the American ghetto."

Hopelessness and despair prevail

Hopelessness is a home in a fetid ghetto flat, where children make morbid sport of chasing cockroaches or dodging rats. There may never be hot water for bathing or a working bathtub to put it in—or any other functioning plumbing. Under these conditions, afflictions such as lead poisoning (from eating flaking paint) and severe influenza are common. Siblings often sleep together in the same bed, separated by a thin wall or a blanket from parents (though frequently there is no man around). Streets are unsafe to walk at night—and, often, so are halls. Nobody starves, but many people are malnourished on a diet of hot dogs, Twinkies, Fritos, soda pop and, in rare cases, whatever can be fished out of the garbage can. Alcoholism abounds; heroin is a favorite route of escape. Another road to fantasy is the TV set. On it dance the images of the good life in middle-class America, visions that inspire envy and frustration.

Strutting pimps and pushers, cutting a sharp swath with their broad brims and custom-made suits, are often the local heroes and the successful role models for the kids. Schooling is frequently a sick joke: teachers conduct holding operations in the classroom, while gang leaders instruct. Inordinate numbers of the black young drop out of school before graduation, landing on the street corners unskilled, undisciplined and barely literate. Those who finish high school are not much better off. Says Richard McNish, director of a manpower training program in Los Angeles' Watts neighborhood: "Kids aren't required to produce to get a diploma. Nothing is required except to be cool and not try to kill the teacher. They don't know how to read and write."

Portraits from a gallery of despair: In Brooklyn's grimy Bedford-Stuyvesant ghetto, a welfare mother surveys her $195-a-month tenement apartment, an unheated, vermin-ridden urban swamp. The bathroom ceiling and sink drip water on the cracked linoleum floor. There are no lights, no locks on the doors. Disheveled and 35, the woman has been on welfare ever since her five-year-old son was born. She joined in the looting during July's traumatic blackout, and calls the episode "convenient. We saw our chance and we took it." Now she also worries: "We don't have any place to shop any more."

In Boston, Ana C., a Hispanic and a mother of seven, speaks no English and has no marketable skills. She draws $294 monthly from welfare. To this she adds the profits from selling heroin at $30 a "spoon" (dose). Ana disapproves of the drug, realizes that it is a major cause of street crime. Yet she rationalizes: "I didn't know how to put food on my table, buy clothes for the children and still pay my $95 rent and the gas bills."

In Watts, a wine-sipping ex-con in his 30s keeps vigil on his doorstep, staring at a cluster of shabby apartments across the street. "I've been looking for a job since I got out of the penitentiary in 1974," he says in a monotone. "I tried to get a job in the CETA [federal Comprehensive Employment and Training Act] program. They told me that if I don't have a telephone, I can't get one." He points at a chain-link fence around the neighboring apartments. "They put up those fences to show the people what they're getting ready for. They have two fences around the penitentiary."

In Harlem, Donald Williams, 29, an ex-junkie, scuffs the streets of New York City as a panhandler. A former student at North Carolina Central University, he says that he was thrown out because he took part in a student demonstration. Williams' lament: "My values are gone. You're looking at a weird dude, a dude on the borderline of insanity. Every day, it doesn't seem to get better—only worse."

In Chicago, hundreds of unemployed young blacks mill on the street where Albirtha Young, 29, lives with her welfare-supported family—twelve people in all. "I didn't want to pick cotton all my life," she says, explaining her move to the city's West Side from Mississippi nine years ago. She brought two children North, now has four more—along with two left to her care by an aunt, plus two younger brothers and a sister to tend. The extended family lives in a two-story frame house bracketed by vacant lots, gutted houses and apartment buildings. Albirtha has not held a job since 1968. One reason: her wage would be less than her $420.60 monthly welfare payment plus the $298.80 she receives in Social Security survivors' benefits—and she would have to pay the cost of a baby sitter besides. Says she: "It's no easy job just sitting here from one year to the next doing nothing."

· From everywhere in the ghetto comes the cry for more jobs. The unemployment rate among blacks is 13.2% v. 6.1% among whites. The rate for black teenagers is 39% v. 14.3% for whites. A generation of young people is moving into its 20s—the family-forming years—without knowing how to work, since many have never held jobs.

A cry for more jobs

EXPLANATIONS OF SEXISM AND RACISM

There is a wide variety of theoretical explanations for prejudice, discrimination, and other inequities experienced by women and blacks. This is because various inequities are of many types and have different origins. In this section, we will present several of these major theories, which are based on observations of and ideas about our society and have been examined and tested by many different social scientists. The social phenomena of sexism and racism are complex; these theoretical explanations help us understand their complexity by organizing in a conceptual framework selected significant aspects of the empirical world. The theories also explain the existence and continuation of prejudice, discrimination, and the inequities of sexism and racism.

Explanations help us to understand the "isms"

SOCIOCULTURAL EXPLANATION

The *sociocultural explanation* of prejudice and discrimination is based on the belief that human attitudes and behavior are, to a great extent, patterned by culture. Social norms, which are rules or standards of expected behavior, are part of culture and are learned by people as they are socialized into their respective cultures. These norms also inform people of the socially appropriate behavior and guide them in their intergroup relations.[54]

Cultural norms inform dominant and minority group members alike how they are expected to think, act, and feel toward one another. A fairly rigid example of this exists in South Africa, where the culture specifies through its normative structure—i.e., its laws, customs, and traditions—how whites and blacks are expected to act toward each other. Cultural norms may also, notes Vander Zanden, spell out the "proper" racial etiquette. A black in some southern rural areas of America, he notes, is still

> "supposed" to go to the back door of the white's home, to knock on the door, to retreat down the steps to the ground level, and, with the appearance of the white, to remove his hat. He is "expected" to speak with deference, attempting to please the white, and to intersperse his speech with frequent expressions of "sir," "yes, boss," and "sho 'nuff." The white is "expected" to call the Negro by his first name, to avoid the use of "Mr." in reference to the Negro, and to tell, not ask, the Negro what to do.[55]

Prejudices are part of the folkways

In other words, in the sociocultural explanation prejudices are part of the folkways and mores of the society. They are among the learned responses that have been acquired as part of the standard cultural equipment through the socialization process. During socialization, an individual internalizes most if not all of the culturally appropriate values, attitudes, beliefs, and behavior patterns—i.e., the human culture becomes a part of the individual. This process gets multiply reinforced by family, friends, schools, and the mass media, so that eventually most children develop as expected. These children will grow up prejudiced to the same extent that they were exposed to prejudiced traditions and beliefs by their reference groups during the socialization process.[56] One way of understanding the importance of culture and socialization to the explanation of our society's prejudice and discrimination is to examine the relationship between race and sex roles and this socialization process.

Socialization: Sex Roles. Sociologists have long been concerned with socialization into race and sex roles. In the past decade, however, sex roles have become a burning issue as a result of the many questions raised by the Women's Liberation Movement. A significant theme in sex role analysis that developed from the movement is that our society "demands the socialization of both men and women into fixed social roles, at great cost to the individual needs of members of both sexes."[57]

Sex roles appear to be basic to all societies because sex is such an apparent differentiating characteristic. For women and men, all societies prescribe different attitudes and activities; women and men are expected to think and act differently. The physical and reproductive differences between them are used to rationalize role prescriptions. Studies indicate that these factors might have been starting points for a division between males and females, but the actual ascriptions are basically determined by culture.[58]

American society places great importance on sexual differences, and our culture defines certain behaviors as appropriate or inappropriate for each particular sex. (To a great extent, this is also applicable to racial or age groups.) Sex is an ascribed status, assigned at birth and based on factors beyond the individual's control. In all cultures there are social roles or patterns of behavior that are expected of individuals who occupy particular positions or statuses.

The belief and therefore social expectation that men and women are quite different has the tendency to be a self-fulfilling prophecy. Believing a condition (for example, that men and women differ in mathematical ability) to be true when it is not can create that very condition. The process of socialization guarantees that as long as the belief that women and men differ in abilities exists, male and female children will grow up to be different in culturally expected ways.[59]

Early socialization of females is very important for maintaining sexual inequality in our culture, so socialization of sex roles begins in infancy, when we are first dressed in either blue or pink clothing. The earliest social categories that members of society learn are those of sex, age, and race. As children, we learn to differentiate between mother and father, child and parent, black and white. Because they are learned at such an early time in life, these role expectations are very resistant to change. During close primary relationships with family and friends, young females will learn to accept authority from males and the older generation. Rossi has noted that by the time girls become adults, they are well socialized "to seek and to find gratification in an intimate dependence on men, and in responsible authority over children." She notes that women may be dominant or assertive in the role of mother or teacher but be submissive in the role of wife.[60]

Margin notes:

Socially expected responses

Sex roles are basic to all societies

A self-fulfilling prophecy

Socialization begins at birth

Leonard Glick (both pictures)

Our culture has defined certain activities and interests as appropriate for a particular sex.

Nursery schools reinforce sex roles

The learning and reinforcing of behavior that is sex-role appropriate continues at school. Serbin and O'Leary have indicated that nursery school teachers unwittingly maintain an environment in which children will learn that boys can be aggressive and have the ability to solve problems, while girls are to be passive and submissive. Teachers react differently to boys and girls, thereby limiting the children's freedom to develop psychologically and intellectually. With almost no exception, nursery school teachers are much less likely to react to a girl's appropriate *or* inappropriate behavior than to a boy's. In terms of adult responses and reactions, the actions of girls have much less effect on their environment than the actions of boys. Serbin and O'Leary state that "coupled with portrayals of the ineffectual female on television and in books, benign neglect in the classroom rapidly becomes malignant."[61]

In other school studies, boys were taught to be, and rewarded for being, assertive, inquisitive and independent; being shy, passive, and fearful was strongly disapproved. For girls, being cooperative, flexible, and willing to take directions was positively reinforced by teacher and parental approval, while being assertive and quarrelsome was not condoned.[62]

Parents reinforce sex-role-appropriate behavior

The ideas that girls are timid and dependent and that boys are naturally brave, resourceful, and independent tends to be a self-fulfilling prophecy, according to Recker, in her analysis of sex roles. She writes that parents will base their child-rearing practices on this idea and, therefore, boys, more than girls, are given their independence at an earlier age. Boys are "allowed to play away from home, to walk to school alone, to pick their own activities, movies and books earlier than their sisters." Boys are also given more personal privacy than girls, "to pick friends and girlfriends and to come and go as they please without parental consent being required."[63] According to noted sociologist Mirra Komarovsky, parents will retard the emancipation of the girl from the family, while they tend to speed it up in the case of her brother.[64]

The family and school are not the only agents of socialization. The child's peer group, which consists of the many groups of children in which the child participates, is also an important agent of socialization. Notions of feminine, masculine, and racial attitudes and behaviors are also part of a peer subculture governed by children's rituals, rules, interests, and logic.

The mass media (television, movies, radio, books, and comic books) is also important in transmitting to individuals the cultural beliefs, values, and traditions regarding sex roles. Children, especially in our society, spend many hours each week viewing, and therefore being socialized by, television programs, which generally reinforce the notion that girls are less capable than boys, that blacks are less capable than whites, and that the aged are less capable than the young.

Elementary school texts convey to children that males are more interesting and important than females and that characteristics such as passivity, dependence, fearfulness, and incompetence prevail among girls. Dozens of textbooks portray girls as continually crying, baking cookies, washing dishes, and deriving much satisfaction from this behavior. Not only are girls portrayed as dependent and domestic, much of the time "they are just plain stupid."[65]

The transmission of various cultural values, attitudes, and beliefs through the socialization process, then, trains boys and girls in our society for their respective sexual roles. Beginning at birth, children continually learn about their sexual roles from parents, teachers, and peers. The following nursery rhyme is an excellent example of those qualities considered for many decades to be important for girls to have in our culture.[66]

My Little Wife

I had a little wife,
the prettiest ever seen;
She washed up the dishes,
and kept the house clean.
She went to the mill
to fetch me some flour
And always got home
in less than an hour.
She baked me my bread
She brewed me my ale,
She sat by the fire
And told many a fine tale.

The media as a source of prejudice

Socialization: Race Roles. The learning and reinforcing of behavior that is race-role appropriate occurs in equally direct and subtle ways. According to Vander Zanden, learning that we are black or white is part of the process by which we acquire self-identity. As we learn other social roles, we learn our racial role. The child acquires the "symbols and expectations appropriate to his or her racial role, and in the process is achieving the answer to the question 'Who am I?'" Society provides the answer, which is defined in terms of a variety of situations that quite clearly spell out what being black or white means.[67]

Learning racial roles

Richard Wright, in his book *Black Boy*, relates an experience he had as a youth, while applying for a job in a white woman's home:

"Do you want this job?" the woman asked.
"Yes, ma'am," I said, afraid to trust my own judgment.
"Now, boy, I want to ask you one question and I want you to tell me the truth," she said.
"Yes, ma'am," I said, all attention.
"Do you steal?" she asked me seriously.
I burst into a laugh, then checked myself.
"What's so damn funny about that?" she asked.
"Lady, if I was a thief, I'd never tell anybody."
"What do you mean?" she blazed with a red face.
I had made a mistake during my first five minutes in the white world. I hung my head.
"No, ma'am," I mumbled. "I don't steal."
She stared at me, trying to make up her mind.
"Now, look, we don't want a sassy nigger around here," she said.
"No, ma'am," I assured her. "I'm not sassy."
Promising to report the next morning at six o'clock, I walked home and pondered on what could possibly have been in the woman's mind to have made her ask me point-blank if I stole. Then I recalled hearing that white people looked upon Negroes as a variety of children, and it was only in the light of that that her question made any sense. If I had been planning to murder her, I certainly would not have told her and, rationally, she no doubt realized it. Yet habit had overcome her rationality and had made her ask me: "Boy, do you steal?" Only an idiot would have answered: "Yes, ma'am. I steal."[68]

Limitations to the socio-cultural approach

At this point, it should be noted that the sociocultural explanation has a weakness: social norms, themselves, are unable to explain the source of prejudicial traditions in a society. In other words, the theory fails to explain why a particular minority is chosen to be on the receiving end of prejudice and discrimination.

The importance of the sociocultural factor should not be underestimated, however, as is evidenced by this analysis of sex and race roles and the socialization process. The sociocultural explanation provides answers to the question of why prejudice against a particular minority remains, even though the causes of the prejudice are no longer present. For example, prejudices still exist against the Japanese on the west coast of America. They exist because they are part of the cultural value system of that area's dominant group, even though the cause of the prejudice—job competition from the Japanese—is not present any longer.

Despite its critics, the sociocultural perspective is an important explanation of prejudice and the many inequities in our society. People's attitudes and behavior are patterned by social norms, which are part of culture. These norms inform people of the socially appropriate behavior and guide them in intergroup relations. The norms guide both dominant and minority group members and "inform them how they are expected to think, feel, and act toward one another."[69]

Exposure to prejudiced traditions

ECONOMIC EXPLANATIONS

Economic factors play an important role in the explanation of prejudice and discrimination. In fact, power, vested interests, and economics are considered by many theorists to be the most important factors in explaining dominant-minority relations. Prejudice, discrimination, sexism, and racism exist partly because some individuals in society gain politically, socially, or economically by them. For Marxists, the basic cause of prejudice and discrimination is class conflict. According to Pierre L. Van den Berghe,

> Vulgar Marxism has a monocausal theory on the origin of racism: racism is part of the bourgeois ideology designed especially to rationalize the exploitation of nonwhite peoples of the world during the imperialistic phase of capitalism. Racist ideology thus becomes simply an epiphenomenon symptomatic of slavery and colonial exploitation. In the modern American context, vulgar Marxists have interpreted racism as a capitalistic device to divide the working class into two hostile segments for better control.[70]

A proponent of Marxist views, Oliver Cox believes that racial prejudice and exploitation of blacks "developed among Europeans with the rise of capitalism and nationalism," and that "all racial antagonisms can be traced to the policies and attitudes of the leading capitalistic people, the white people of Europe and North America." Cox also notes that racial prejudice in America is the "socio-attitudinal matrix supporting a calculated and determined effort of a white ruling class to keep some people or peoples of color and their resources exploitable."[71] Many economic theories stress the exploitation of minorities, emphasizing the functional nature of prejudice and discrimination in maintaining an exploited minority group for resources or labor. A minority group's persecution is justified in the interests of those in power.

Capitalism causes racism

Socialist Feminism. The origin and persistence of women's inferior status has also been accounted for by economic factors. Many socialist feminists have their ideological roots in the writings of Marx and Engels, and they believe that women's oppression stems from the class system. Some socialist feminists also believe that in primitive cultures women were recognized by men as equals. This equality was lost when a class-divided society, with its private property, state power, and patriarchal family, replaced the matriarchal clan commune.[72] Women became breeders and possessions of their husbands because of the institutions of private property, the family, and the class-divided society. They are oppressed by a subordinate role in both the family and the work world. Sexism is viewed by socialist feminists as functional for the capitalist system. Corporations make higher profits from poorly paid women workers. The work force is also maintained by women's work at home, which is also "for the reproduction and maintenance of the work force."[73]

Basically then, the socialist feminist explanation of oppression places major emphasis on the economic factors. The persistence of sexist ideology and the institution of the family, which maintain the inferior status of women, are explained in terms of their being an important part of, and performing an important function for, capitalism. According to these feminists, women can only be free through a socialist revolution, because their oppression is useful to a capitalist system.[74]

VESTED INTEREST AND COMPETITION EXPLANATIONS
Related to the economic explanation are the *vested interest* and *competition explanations.* Dominant groups in society have vested interests in maintaining the subordination of minority groups. Through prejudice and discrimination, economic and social advantages are preserved. The dominant groups believe that they are entitled to such things as incomes, occupations, social position, and property. Prejudices and discrimination then develop among these groups in response to the fear that minorities will challenge their dominant position.[75]

Herbert Blumer states that prejudice is a defensive reaction, which functions to protect and "preserve the position of the dominant group."[76] The vested interest explanation views the dominant group as "having a vested interest in another group's subordination ... a stake in preserving an order characterized by privilege and advantage. Prejudice becomes an instrument for defending this privilege and advantage."[77]

Vander Zanden, in his analysis of the sources of racism as they relate to vested interests, notes that various writers emphasize the economic factors in relation to slavery. He states,

> The emergence and elaboration of racist ideas were closely associated in time with the advent and development of Black slavery. An integral

Oppression stems from the class system

Prejudice is a defensive device

aspect of slavery was the economic gain realized by White slave-owners. Accordingly, it too has been concluded by some and implicitly implied by others that the racist dogma evolved primarily as a means to excuse and sanction the institution of slavery in general and the economic exploitation of slaves in particular.[78]

The vested interest approach, then, maintains that when a group has an advantage over another group, such as wealth, power, or status, the advantaged group will use prejudice and discrimination to maintain its privileged position.

Prejudice and discrimination can often develop between groups that are in competition for scarce commodities, such as jobs and housing. Every society has such values and commodities, rare and divisible, but considered very desirable. Wealth, power, and status are examples. When different groups in the society claim to be entitled to these desirable values, the groups' interrelationships will be characterized by competition and, at times, by conflict. Vander Zanden, in his analysis of minority relations, notes that where "relations between two groups are perceived as competitive, negative attitudes—prejudice—will be generated toward the out group."[79]

The racial riots prior to and during the 1940s in cities such as Chicago, Detroit, and Atlanta focused upon such economic factors as job competition from blacks, the depreciation of property values, and competition with whites for housing accommodations. Grimshaw, in research on racial violence, noted that the incidence of violence tended to be greater where blacks and whites competed directly for housing and other accommodations.[80] Several other studies indicate that prejudice is "most likely at the point of greatest sensed threat from social and economic competition."[81] Prejudice and discrimination against the Japanese on the west coast of the United States was greatly increased when they competed with whites for jobs.

Just as there are limitations to the other explanations, the economic competition and vested interests explanations also have limitations. For example, competition may explain the appearance of a particular prejudice or discriminatory pattern, but it does not explain the continuation of the prejudices when the economic factor, such as job competition, was ended.[82]

Competition for socio-economic status breeds prejudice

Racial violence increases with competition

Limitation of economic explanations

PERSONALITY EXPLANATIONS

In addition to cultural and economic explanations, there are a variety of *individual* and *psychological explanations* for prejudice and discrimination. Some personality explanations stress the idea that certain personality types are prone to prejudice; others stress the importance of frustration.

Scapegoat Theory of Prejudice. One personality theory of prejudice, for example, is termed the *frustration-aggression*, or *scapegoat*, theory. This explanation is based upon the fact that people have needs that at times are

Scapegoat theory of prejudice

not met because goals established to meet the needs are blocked. This blockage may create frustration and anger, which in turn can cause people to vent their hostility in aggressive behavior. The aggression produced may be directed toward the source of the frustration; however, if the source is too powerful (the government or an employer) or is unknown, minority groups become the targets (scapegoats) for hostility. There is a displacement from the source of the frustration to the scapegoat. The scapegoat can be "a group, or someone or something which is forced to bear the blame for others."[83] Jews were the scapegoats for Hitler in World War II. Southern blacks were the scapegoats for white southerners after the Civil War.

Limitations of the scape-goat theory

The scapegoat theory has limitations also. It fails to explain why a particular minority group is chosen as the scapegoat. Also, frustration does not necessarily result in aggression. One may respond to frustration by becoming apathetic, by seeking substitute goals, or by raising or lowering efforts to achieve a goal.

Radical Feminism. Radical feminism is another major theory of women's liberation. Radical feminists believe that the "oppression of women is the first and most basic case of domination by one group over the other."[84] Racism and oppression of women are extensions of male supremacy. Radical feminists explain that sexism's function is psychological as well as economic. Based upon their sex, women are categorized as an inferior class.[85]

Radical feminists: Sexism is functional for men

Firestone, a radical feminist, says that women's biologically determined reproductive roles—i.e., the bearing and nursing of children—are the roots of America's sex-class system, which developed from the basic biological differences. Until reliable birth control methods were developed, women were at the mercy of their biology and therefore did not enjoy the same privileges as men.[86] Women are kept in their place and oppressed by such institutions as marriage, motherhood, and love. For women to be free, these institutions and sexist ideology in general must be destroyed by revolution, and a total restructuring of society must take place.[87]

Moderate feminism: Sexism is dysfunctional for society

Moderate Feminism. A less abstract and less theorizing ideological explanation of sexism is moderate feminism, or women's-rights feminism. Its roots lie in the beliefs that all people are created equal and all should have equal opportunity. These principles have not been but should be applied to women. The moderate feminist explanation believes in the necessity of a liberation movement to remove the institutionalized secondary status of women. Moderates view sexism as "dysfunctional for society—it deprives society of the talents of half its members."[88] Moderates do not view sexism as being helpful to a particular segment of society. They believe false consciousness from sexist socialization, not from self-interest, precipitates opposition to feminist demands. Deckard, in her analysis of moderates, says that even though moderates use the term "revolution," they do not mean it literally. Moderates believe they can eliminate a sexist society through the current system. Reform, not radical restructuring, will change society.[88]

The socialist, radical, and moderate feminist explanations of sexism are ideologically distinct but differ much less in terms of strategies and tactics. Many similar actions and techniques are employed by all three segments of the women's liberation movement.

Women's groups have similar strategies

The explanations examined thus far emphasize a variety of factors, cultural, economic, and psychological. Other theoretical explanations emphasize other factors. For example, concerning racial prejudice in America, some theories emphasize an historical approach, regarding slavery and reconstruction as important variables in an explanation of black-white relations. Daniels and Kitano in their explanation of racial prejudice state,

A case may be made for urbanization, for industrialization, for the effects of materialism, depersonalization, and the mass culture; another point of view . . . emphasizes mobility in our society. . . . Broader theories . . . find the roots of prejudice in the unsavory nature of man himself.[89]

After centuries of trying to blend into a white culture that downgraded their tribal customs, American Indians now take pride in their heritage.

Jill Freedman, Magnum Photos, Inc.

SEXISM AND RACISM: RESPONSES

Women and blacks have responded in a variety of ways to their subordinate positions in America. Their responses have varied according to the degree to which they have been made the targets of prejudice and discrimination. Their responses have also varied according to time and to the extent that their values, norms, and customs differ from those of the dominant group's. Several important response patterns have developed. They are *submissive acceptance, aggressive rejection, evasive avoidance, integration, assimilation,* and *passing.*

SUBMISSIVE ACCEPTANCE

Some minority groups have submissively accepted the subordinate status that has been imposed on them by those in power. Occasionally, accommodation is viewed as a necessary prerequisite for survival. Blacks and other minorities have, at times, responded with submissive acceptance in order to survive hostile intergroup situations. For many women, however, submission is simply conformity to cultural traditions that have developed about them; their acceptance is a conditioned reaction in a society characterized by much prejudice.

AGGRESSIVE REJECTION

Responding with aggression, the minority group rejects the dominant group's negative image that has been imposed on them. The minority's response can take the forms of direct aggression (race riots) or protest (organizations such as the National Urban League and the National Organization of Women).

EVASIVE AVOIDANCE

The response of evasive avoidance occurs when minority group members avoid situations in which a high probability of experiencing prejudice and discrimination exists. Many women and blacks in America will, at times, shy away from situations that could develop into a humiliating or debasing experience. Some blacks, Jews, and other minorities have responded to their positions by seceding from the larger society.

Separatism occurs through the effort of a minority to realize or maintain "a separate group identity that is usually linked with efforts to achieve territorial separation from the dominant group." [90] Separatist movements such as Jewish Zionism and black Garveyism are not simple avoidance, they are more appropriately termed aggressive avoidance.[90] Minority groups have also avoided disadvantageous conditions through the process of emigration.

Many blacks have migrated from undesirable conditions to more favorable situations in communities far from home. For example, hundreds of thousands of blacks, for economic reasons, migrated to the north during the 1940s. Today, for a variety of political, economic, and social reasons, black migration rates in the reverse direction are increasing.

INTEGRATION, ASSIMILATION, AND PASSING

With integration, members of the minority group reject the idea that they are inferior. Rather than attempting to avoid contact with the dominant group, they attempt to integrate with, and stand alongside, members of the dominant group. There will be times, however, when the minority group desires to become culturally and socially fused with the dominant group. This is assimilation. The minority group wants to lose its identity, because the members basically accept the bad image that the dominant group has given them. Other times, because of expediency or self-hatred, an individual of a minority group will withdraw from that group and may, if able, pass into the dominant group. This "leaving the minority group and 'passing' as a member of the dominant group" is one of the most complete forms of assimilation.[91] It is not, however, an alternative for all minority group members. It is a "feasible alternative for those minority group members who physically and culturally resemble the dominant group."[91] Many minority group members who have masked or do not possess identifying ethnic or racial characteristics have passed into the dominant environment, which "would reject them out of hand if their true identity were to be revealed."[92]

Passing is not open to all

OTHER RESPONSES

It is important to note that these are only a few of the many responses to dominance. Vander Zanden, in an analysis of several studies, distinguishes a number of other responses, such as *obsessive sensitivity, ego enhancement, self-hatred,* and *flight from reality.*[93]

Vander Zanden's models of response

If a minority group's members become preoccupied with identifying manifestations of prejudice, to the point that all members of the dominant group are "viewed with suspicion and relentlessly scrutinized for 'telltale signs of bigotry'," this is termed obsessive sensitivity.[94]

Ego enhancement occurs when minority group members seek to "inflate their feelings of self-worth through compensatory behavior" as a response to the constant abuse of their self-respect. Exaggerated ethnic or social pride, enhanced status striving, or symbolic striving may be the result.[95]

Self-hatred, according to social psychologist Lewin, is a tendency that exists within every minority group. It is an attitude "toward one's own group characterized by aversion and dislike.[96] Flight from reality is a way of withdrawing from the frustrations of minority group status, by submerging into a world of drugs, alcohol, and/or fantasy. Those who feel defeated escape from feelings of insecurity and inadequacy.[97]

The use of one exclusive response pattern is never followed by any minority. "Intergroup relations are much too complex for any one pattern to be operative at all times . . . frequently some combination may predominate."[98] This will become evident as we now specifically examine the responses of women and blacks.

THE RESPONSE TO SEXISM

Women have both accepted and rejected status

Today, as in the past, millions of American women have responded to their subordinate position in society with submissive acceptance. Their acquiescence is one of conformity to the cultural traditions that have developed over the years concerning the female role. It is a conditioned reaction enabling women to survive in a society characterized by sexual prejudice and discrimination.

However, beginning slowly in the mid-nineteenth century and growing in strength during the past several decades, the women's movement in America has reflected a response pattern characterized by the rejection of the dominant group's negative image of women. The primary focus in this section is on that rejection response.

Throughout our history, especially during the past century or so, a variety of women's protest organizations at the community and national levels have reflected significant changes in the response patterns of both women and society regarding sexism. Women have rejected the social, economic, and political inequalities in their fight against sexism. Many women still accept their traditional place in society; however, these women are becoming fewer in number through increasing awareness of their subordinate position. Millions of American women who are not members of protest organizations have still indicated their dissatisfaction with woman's subordinate status and have assertively rejected this image. This response is evidenced by the various women's movements that have existed through much of our history, which we will now examine.

Prerevolutionary conditions: "Free" women had few rights

Most people are aware of the fact that women fought many years for their right to vote. However, the history of women for over 125 years reflects a fight for full social, economic, and political equality, in response to very unpleasant and unequal conditions. Many of the women who came to America before the Revolution had no rights, and their lives were characterized by a continuous struggle for freedom. For example, in prerevolutionary America, many women came to this country from England as indentured servants. They were kidnapped from the streets or sold from London prisons. These women eventually gained their freedom, after serving seven years as virtual slaves, but had no money. Black women were kidnapped from their families in Africa, shipped as cargo to America, and were enslaved for their entire lives. But even free women in early America had few, if any, rights. Married women's property and inheritance belonged to their husbands, and if separated, so did their children. Women could not

sign contracts or testify in court, and for most of them there was no education until 1820.[99] Few rights were gained after the Revolution.

WOMEN'S MOVEMENTS OF THE PAST

The fight against sexism grew in magnitude in the nineteenth century when
women who had participated in the abolitionist movement came to realize
that they themselves did not have the very same rights they were demanding for slaves. Their involvement with the abolitionists enabled them to
learn the dynamics of politics and made it possible for women to develop an
ideology concerning their own rightful place in America. This was the most
important factor in the growth and development, during the 1830s and
1840s, of the women's movement.[100]

Women gain experience

Also contributing to this growth was a significant increase in the number of educated women and in the number of women working outside their
homes. Poor pay, discrimination, and other factors, combined with the militant unionism in which some women participated, gave added impetus to
the growth of the movement.

Established by Lucretia Mott and Elizabeth Stanton, the first major
meeting of women to discuss women's rights was held at Seneca Falls, New
York in 1848. This marks the point at which the collective discontent of
women had finally been "translated into an organizational effort to improve
the status of women."[101] It was at this meeting that women declared, "We
hold these truths to be self evident: that all men and women are created
equal."[102] They also listed the various forms of discrimination experienced
by women and pledged to use all available means to eliminate it. They
fought for the right to control their own lives and property, the reform of
divorce and custody laws, and the right to vote.

First women's meeting

Some years later, in 1869, Susan B. Anthony and Elizabeth Stanton
founded the National Woman Suffrage Association (NWSA). Members of
the NWSA and other women were upset by the fact that the Fourteenth
and Fifteenth Amendments, introduced in 1866, still restricted the right to
vote to male citizens. By applying pressure to the government, they attempted to gain a wide variety of rights for women. They excluded men's
admission to the NWSA and focused on and worked militantly for suffrage.

The NWSA

A more moderate middle- and upper-class organization, The American
Woman Suffrage Association (AWSA), was founded by Julia Ward (Howe)
and Lucy Stone in 1869. Its first president was a man, and men were permitted to become members. They focused only on suffrage and attempted to
obtain the vote by instituting change in each state. In 1890 the NWSA and
AWSA merged into the National American Woman Suffrage Association
(NAWSA). The goal of NAWSA was to obtain the right to vote and, therefore, obtain a position to affect other issues.

The AWSA

From the early 1870s to the early 1900s, suffragists were not successful
in their efforts because of their own conservative and alienating tactics and
because of opposition from those who feared women's votes. In 1920, how-

1920: The right to vote

ever, the Nineteenth Amendment, which gave women the right to vote, was ratified. Suffrage was won through the support of trade unions, socialists, and the Progressive Movement.[103]

However, because they had focused on one issue—suffrage—women in the early 1920s found it difficult and at times impossible to unite on other issues. After obtaining the right to vote, the suffrage movement began to split, and different segments focused on such nonliberation issues as prohibition and children's labor reform. Discrimination did not end after the victory in 1920; it continued to be a problem in many occupational areas, in education, and in pay differentials. In the mid-1920s, a conservative reaction that was rooted in America's economic progress of the period resulted in antiprogressive legislation, which in turn helped eliminate any vestiges of the women's movement.

With little exception, between 1920 and 1960 there was no significant organized women's movement in America. This was primarily because the suffragists operated from an elite class base and a limited ideology. So strongly had they "emphasized the vote," Deckard notes, "and only the vote, that their successors—like the League of Women Voters—could declare in the 1920s that there was no more discrimination against women and that liberal women should merely fight for general reforms for all people."[104]

WWII: Breaking the sexist image

During World War II, many women were employed in traditionally male occupations. It was at this time that women began again "their own long march toward liberation," by moving in great numbers into the American economy and breaking the sexist image.[107] Polls taken then indicated that it was acceptable for married women to work, reflecting a major shift in American attitudes.

Suburbs and women's roles

However, after the war attitudes toward women again reversed. Slowly, the growth of the American suburb and the return of men to college under the GI education bill contributed to a redefinition of women's roles. The homemaker and mother images grew with the middle-class suburbs, because significant segments of women's days were spent shopping, cleaning, and chauffering children to and from their activities.

Development of the Women's Liberation Movement

This middle-class role, characterized by a loss of self-esteem, helped form the roots of middle-class women's participation in the current Women's Liberation Movement. These women were joined by women from the paid labor force who were denied the same wages and advancement opportunities offered to working men. Female students who were denied equal participation in the decision-making processes of major educational institutions also joined.

In the early 1960s, a number of events occurred that influenced the development of today's Women's Liberation Movement. In 1963 the first official governmental study on the status of women was issued. The President's Commission on the Status of Women Report recommended equal opportunity for women in employment and the political arena, the elimination of property law restrictions, and a greater availability of child care services. In the same year, after eighteen years of deliberation, Congress finally passed the Equal Pay Act. It required equivalent salaries for men and women doing the same work, for those jobs covered by the act. Also in 1963, *The Feminine Mystique* by Betty Friedan was published.[105] It criticized the traditional societal roles for women and examined the psychological costs of the limited homemaker role. Other events, such as passing the 1964 Civil Rights Act and establishing the Equal Employment Opportunity Commission, also influenced the movement's development.

Title VII of the 1964 Civil Rights Act afforded protection against sex discrimination. As amended in 1972, the act prohibits discrimination in employment based on sex, race, religion, color, or national origin. The act makes it against the law for

Title VII: Protection against sex discrimination

> employers, labor unions, or employment agencies to discriminate in hiring or firing; wages; fringe benefits; classifying, referring, assigning, or promoting employees; extending or assigning facilities; training, retraining, or apprenticeships; or any other terms, conditions, or privileges of employment.[106]

The Equal Employment Opportunity Commission (EEOC) was established to enforce Title VII. The EEOC issued guidelines that bar

> stereotyped characterization of the sexes, classification of labeling of 'men's jobs' and 'women's jobs,' or advertising under male or female headings and preference in the content of the advertising based on sex.[107]

These laws, plus other events and conditions, influenced the development of the contemporary Women's Liberation Movement. At this point, we will examine that movement and note any differences from women's previous responses to discrimination and prejudice.

WOMEN'S MOVEMENT TODAY

Feminism today is different from feminism in the past. According to Chafe, a social scientist, today's feminism has roots and is moving in a direction taken by other social trends in American society. The movement operates from a decentralized, diverse organizational base, and seeks those objectives that will contend with the basic causes of sexual inequality.[108]

Today's feminism is different

Unlike the Seneca Falls Declaration of 1848, which maintained feminist objectives that were outside the people's daily experience, the programs and goals of the current feminist movement directly address today's social realities and concerns.

Obtaining the right to vote was a symbolic victory because the prevailing social conditions of that period were not conducive to the achievement of full equality. As noted earlier, authority patterns, the division of

The right to vote was a symbolic victory

labor between men and women, and many other traditional roles were not modified by women's suffrage. In the early part of the twentieth century, women experienced an expansion of sexual freedom but did not achieve gains in jobs, households, or politics. Nineteenth and twentieth century suffragists were not in contact with the underlying forces in the society.

The earlier feminists underestimated the extent of sexual inequality's roots through the socialization process, and they overestimated the importance of the ballot. As Chafe notes, the "problem of inequality was imbedded in the day-to-day routine of men and women, and until those began to alter, there was little chance of a popular base for feminism."[109]

Feminism is in touch with prevailing social trends

The feminist drive of the 1970s is in touch with prevailing social trends.[110] Work and activities common to both men and women, current cultural values, and smaller families have not produced equality, but they have provided a foundation for a strong feminist movement. An example of the interplay between social trends and feminism's revival is the previously examined change in women's employment.

The volume of women in the work force disturbed the status quo of traditional sex roles. A greater sense of power, independence, and confidence developed from their having jobs. These and other experiences "provided the basis for the development of new attitudes toward women's 'place'," and the daily experiences of women were now addressed by feminist programs.[111]

The current movement is different in structure

The current feminist movement can also be distinguished from previous movements in terms of organization and structure. Wherever women's values and attitudes are changing, there is the women's movement. Finding strength in local communities, the movement today is both diverse and decentralized.[111]

The organizational base is broad. The majority of the movement's membership is from the middle class, but it is not as elitist as it was in the past. Responding to feminist ideas are women from various economic, social, and ethnic backgrounds. Conscious of class and racial issues, the movement's demands reflect the special needs of these members. The special interests of black women and female workers have been asserted by the National Black Feminist Organization and the Coalition of Labor Union Women.[112]

NATIONAL ORGANIZATION OF WOMEN

NOW: A significant force in the movement

The National Organization of Women (NOW) is also a significant force in the Women's Liberation Movement. Founded in 1966, it basically reflected middle-class women's interest in legal, political, and occupational rights. Its early activities focused upon women's civil rights, discrimination, and EEOC's enforcement of Title VII. NOW is to the women's movement what the NAACP is to the black movement in America, in that both have concentrated their efforts in a legal fight against discrimination.

NOW is considered to be a moderate, "establishment" women's organization, in contrast to the radical wing of the movement. Women's rights as perceived by radicals are part of a more complex and broader effort to restructure society as a whole. This position is reflected in the New York Radical Feminists' Manifesto:

> Radical Feminism recognizes the oppression of women as a fundamental political oppression wherein women are categorized as an inferior class based upon their sex. It is the aim of radical feminism to organize politically to destroy this sex class system. We believe that the purpose of male chauvinism is primarily to obtain psychological ego satisfaction, and that only secondarily does this manifest itself in economic relationships. For this reason we do not believe that capitalism, or any other economic system, is the cause of female oppression, nor do we believe that female oppression will disappear as a result of a purely economic revolution.[113]

Unlike the radical feminist organizations, which emphasize the family and personal oppression of women, the socialist feminists emphasize women's economic oppression. They feel that the cause of women's subordination is rooted in the institutions of slavery and private property and stress the necessity of a socialist revolution as a prerequisite to women's complete liberation.

NOW, which maintains a moderate position, has worked with both radical wings of the movement, but their differences have not made regular joint activities possible. Still, the Women's Liberation Movement has grown and has significantly affected the "attitudes of many women who are not members of any group."[114]

Organized at the national level, NOW and other women's organizations have grown in the 1970s. An example is the National Women's Political Caucus, whose basic goal is to "awaken, organize, and assert the vast political power represented by women."[115] However, at present, Deckard notes, the variety and number of groups in the Women's Liberation Movement have increased to the point where it is no longer possible to isolate vanguards. The thrust of feminism does not come from national organizations such as NOW. Today, the decentralized women's movement operates primarily from small, local, and informal community groups. In communities throughout the United States, women meet in various groups to raise their levels of consciousness concerning sexism and their minority status.[116] The direction of the movement is derived from local conditions close to the daily lives of involved women. Many liberationists believe that decisions can be made collectively, and that " 'leaders' are unnecessary."[117]

The Women's Liberation Movement has been criticized for its lack of a national structure and leadership. The local informal group structure,

The thrust of feminism comes from local, informal groups

United Press International

Supporters of the Equal Rights Amendment marched in the nation's capital to urge extension of the ratification period.

however, does not mean that feminists lack a sense of participation in a national movement. Chafe has stated that "a profound feeling of community unites the diverse women working in disparate local settings."[118]

Finally, the current women's movement differs from previous women's movements in that the newly developed objectives for striking at the causes of sexual inequality have a greater latitude. As we have seen, social and political factors in the past greatly influenced a single-answer approach to the problem. In the nineteenth and early twentieth centuries, liberationist organizations focused on either suffrage or an Equal Rights Amendment as *the* solution to their problems. No such simple solutions are sought today; a variety of approaches are necessary to deal with the broadbased, pervasive problem of sexual inequality. There is, for example, the realization that success with today's Equal Rights Amendment means even more work ahead. These attitudes are based on the fact that racism in America did not end when the Civil Rights Act was passed.

The current movement's objective has a wider latitude

EQUAL RIGHTS: JOBS AND PAY

The Women's Liberation Movement is involved in a variety of issues, such as abortion, rape, child care, and abuse. Birth control, marriage, housing, public accommodations, and poverty are also serious concerns. Three issues for which major goals have been established by most women in the movement are equal job opportunity, equal pay for equal work, and the Equal Rights Amendment to the United States Constitution.

Major goals of the movement

Liberation in other areas of life is a difficult, if not impossible, goal to achieve if women are unable to support themselves economically. The passing of new laws, such as the Equal Pay Act and Title VII of the Civil Rights Act, and women's victories in some sex discrimination court battles, indicate that progress has begun in the critical areas of jobs and equal pay. Problems, however, still exist in the enforcement of these laws.

NOW and other women's groups have been concerned with the EEOC's sex discrimination guidelines and enforcement procedures. Starting in the late 1960s, great pressure was placed on EEOC for favorable guidelines and positions. With an extension of powers, EEOC has directly sued many employers who have violated civil rights laws. Under Title VII, various women's groups have also brought legal suits to the United States Federal Courts. In the 1970s, sex discrimination suits were brought against large corporations, airlines, and universities. Women and other minority workers won a $50-million back pay settlement from American Telephone and Telegraph in 1973, after sex discrimination complaints were filed by the EEOC, women, and black organizations.

Court decisions and various EEOC rulings have benefited many women. The enforcement of rulings and laws, however, has not been as satisfactory, and many segments of the women's movement have continued to increase their pressure.

THE EQUAL RIGHTS AMENDMENT

An additional goal of the Women's Liberation Movement is the passage of the Equal Rights Amendment (ERA). The major focus of the ERA is the removal of all employment barriers as well as other types of sexual discrimination. The amendment's passage would mean that sexual equality will be guaranteed by the Constitution and would discourage further discrimination against women. It will affect the entire range of laws and social institutions that serve to differentiate women and men in our society. For example, it would be much more difficult for organizations and companies to stereotype jobs by sex, and there would be more uniformity in the criminal code concerning women.

The fight for the ERA

Basically, the first section of the ERA notes that "equality of rights under the law should not be denied or abridged by the United States or by any state on account of sex." The second section gives Congress the power

Table 3.4. The Equal Rights Amendment

REASONS FOR OPPOSING ERA	REASONS FOR SUPPORTING ERA
1. It is unnecessary because the 14th Amendment's Equal Rights Clause covers most areas of discrimination.	The 14th Amendment is inadequate with respect to discrimination against women.
2. State courts and legislatures should change inequitable laws.	Changes through state courts and legislatures are slow and uncertain. There is progress in some states and none in others. Without ERA, the burden in the courts would be on each woman plaintiff to show that the sex discrimination is "unreasonable."
3. Some discrimination is beneficial to women, such as laws limiting working hours and the amount of weight women can lift.	Discrimination is often more detrimental than beneficial. Laws that exist to "protect" women usually keep them from achieving equal opportunities.
4. The differences in criminal laws that benefit women would be abolished.	The law will punish offenders not on the basis of sex but on the basis of the nature of the crime. ERA will not invalidate sex crimes such as rape.
5. Women will become eligible for military service and combat.	Women will be able to volunteer for military services, as men are. Men and women will probably be treated equally, if there is a draft.
6. Marriage laws will be altered and the traditional structure of the family will be endangered.	The ERA eliminates marriage laws that discriminate on the basis of sex.
7. ERA threatens our social structure because it ignores biological differences between the sexes.	ERA improves our social structure because it requires equal treatment for each citizen, male and female, as an individual. It does not affect private action or purely social relationships between men and women.

Source: This table is based upon S. Feldman, *The Rights of Women*, Rochelle Park, N.J.: Hayden Book Co., 1974, pp. 68–71.

Ratification is still required

to enforce, through legislation, "the provisions of this article." The third section states that the amendment "shall take effect two years after the date of ratification."[119] In 1972, the House of Representatives passed the ERA by a vote of 354 to 23. In that same year, the Senate passed the ERA 84 to 8. However, ratification by three-fourths of the states is still required.

After Congress passed the Amendment, many states quickly ratified it. In the mid-1970s, however, various opposition groups developed. Conservative groups have interpreted the ERA as degrading women in their traditional roles of homemaker and mother.[120] The ERA has also been opposed by such conservative organizations as the National States Rights Party, The Christian Crusade, the John Birch Society, and the Ku Klux Klan. Some labor groups fear the ERA will nullify certain work laws that were established to protect women. Leftists also have opposed the ERA. The Socialist Worker and the Communist Parties "partly base their argument on the protective laws issue."[121] One nationwide organization, STOP ERA, makes use of half-truths and misstatements to achieve its point of view. Phyllis Schlafley, spokeswoman for STOP ERA, believes that "rest rooms and prisons will be desegregated; unwilling mothers will be forced to go to work; women will be sent into combat."[122] Table 3.4 examines several of the arguments for and against the ERA.

Opponents of ERA

The Equal Rights Amendment needs to be ratified by thirty-eight states in order to be law. If it is not ratified by June 1982, it will not take effect. If the ERA fails to become part of the Constitution, a serious barrier to feminism's success will remain. The success of the movement can also be seriously impeded if internal dissension grows; there is currently disagreement between factions over the goals, methods and procedures of the movement.

The success of the current movement is also blocked by the extent to which our sociocultural identities, which were developed through socialization, are being threatened. As discussed earlier, we are all socialized into sets of personality traits labeled masculine or feminine. Our identities, emotions, and reactions are very much defined by our sex roles. Deviations from these culturally set prescriptions and proscriptions cause much consternation for people. Much of the Women's Liberation Movement stresses the necessity of having people overcome their commitment to the traditional sex roles and institutions of society—and therefore to the *values* of society, as well. For example, movement supporters desire to alter such basic cultural institutions as the family and marriage. In conclusion, it is important to note that the more people are made aware of this deeply rooted cultural aspect of the problem, the greater this obstacle becomes.[123]

RACISM: THE RESPONSE TO SLAVERY

Racism, in particular the prejudice and discrimination experienced by blacks in America today, has its roots in slavery. In Africa, the ancestors of most American blacks were hunted down, chained, and, treated worse than cargo, transported to America in slave ships. Most of those who survived the dehumanizing voyage were sold, separated from their families, and subjected to inhumane working conditions. They were ill-fed, ill-clothed, and beaten.

The variety of slavery experienced by the blacks was one of the harshest in the world. Neither the church nor state interfered with the arbitrary power of the slave master.[124]

Other systems of slavery, such as many in South America, did not break up the slave's family. In these systems, slaves were often permitted to be educated and to work their way to freedom. This was not true in North America. According to Van den Berghe, plantation life in the United States was rigidly stratified, with a complex etiquette system regulating the interaction between slaves and their masters. Slaves were "expected to behave submissively through self-deprecatory gestures and speech, the frequent use of terms of respect toward whites, self-debasing clowning, and general fulfillment of their role expectation as incompetent and backward grown-up children."[125]

The agony of poor treatment and overwork made the slaves respond by feigning illness or by committing desperate acts of violence against themselves. To avoid being overworked or auctioned off, slaves "chopped off fingers and toes. They plied themselves with herbs that induced vomiting and with drugs that induced miscarriage." William Cheek, in an analysis of black resistance (which took the form of aggressive rejection) prior to the Civil War, notes that this response to the plight of blacks was deeply rooted in the past and began with the slave trade itself. He states,

> When black people were torn from their homes in the African interior or along the coastal waters, they resisted. When black people were torturously transported to the New World, they resisted. When subsequently black people were enslaved and forced to toil for Northern and Southern masters, they resisted. And when black people were compelled to live out their lives under the severe discrimination that obtained across the pre-Civil War North, they resisted.[126]

Rebellion is another form of aggressive rejection, and Herbert Aptheker cites 250 slave conspiracies and insurrections in American history. However, others such as Winthrop Jordan cite no more than a dozen. Of those revolts authenticated, none succeeded; all were localized and very limited in scope. They were never even temporarily successful.[127] In fact, there was never any real danger of a slave uprising, a fact understood by the majority of blacks who considered the possibility. Slavery was too dehumanizing, and blacks were "too atomized and too geographically isolated on the various plantations" for a concerted collective action. Considering the power of the slaveholders, any collective effort to destroy the slave system was a suicide mission.[128]

This inability to rebel, however, did not keep blacks from fleeing. The number of runaway slave advertisements in southern papers reflected the

Submissive acceptance of slavery

Slave revolts were limited

fact that flight was a fairly common response. However, of the many thousands who attempted to reach freedom, only a fraction were able to achieve that goal.

Prior to the Civil War, blacks did not encounter problems in the south only. In the "free" north, they were subjected to discrimination and segregation, enforced by common custom. Blacks were relegated to menial jobs such as dish washers, rivermen, and cooks.

During slavery, then, many blacks in the south and north responded to their plight with resistance, but submissive acceptance was a more common pattern of survival. There was, among the majority of slaves, a sense of futility about changing their status. Many resigned themselves to their fate and attempted to maintain feelings of individual worth and dignity. Others internalized the "attitudes associated with this status." Many accepted the existing order, "neither questioning it nor doing anything about it."[129] Significant numbers of blacks, in many parts of the United States, still follow this pattern of submissive acceptance and are resigned to their status.

Slavery: Response of flight

END OF SLAVERY

Just prior to the Civil War, however, black leaders, wanting their people's suffering to end, became more aggressive and used all constitutional means to abolish slavery and gain equal rights for blacks. In addition to editing and publishing a variety of black newspapers, black conventions and protest meetings were held. Eventually, with the Civil War and the Emancipation Proclamation, the American slave system ended.

End of slavery

The Emancipation Proclamation of 1863 was largely a tactical maneuver, however. It was issued in spite of President Lincoln's "considerable misgivings and as a result of considerable pressure from Union Army generals who felt that it would deal the Confederacy a serious blow."[130] The Emancipation Proclamation was

The Emancipation Proclamation

> carefully designed not to emancipate, in fact, a single slave; it excluded not only the slave-owning border states who fought on the Union side but also those districts of the Confederacy under Union Army occupation. Thus the Proclamation applied only to those areas in which it patently could not be enforced.[131]

Despite its intentions, the Proclamation *did* end slavery and, along with the Reconstruction Period that lasted into the late 1870s, change the south. Blacks were no longer just a piece of property with no rights. They had finally attained the status of human beings in this country; however, they were severely underprivileged. Vander Zanden notes that the Emancipation

Proclamation was not able to eradicate "the heritage of slavery."[136] After the Civil War,

> the ex-slave's illiteracy, his lack of capital and prosperity, his habituation to the past, and the continuing authority and power of the whites created new conditions for the continuance of dependence . . . and for adjustments based upon acceptance of, and accommodation to, minority status.[132]

During the post-Reconstruction counter revolution of the 1880s and 1890s, blacks were deprived of the right to vote through the use of poll taxes and literacy tests. This disenfranchisement and "Jim Crowism" (the physical segregation by race) relegated blacks to second-class citizenship. There was also an increase in terrorist tactics and in the growth of organizations such as the Ku Klux Klan.

Significant changes in American race relations and in the black response to their minority status began to occur in the early 1900s. These changes occurred in response to labor demands, to northern industrial expansion, and to the Civil Rights Movement. In response to labor demands and the industrial expansion, black "emigration from the South accelerated, thereby scattering the nonwhite minority more and more widely over the nation . . . to populate the widely dispersed urban ghettos of large metropolitan centers where they displaced as unskilled workers the European immigrants."[133]

THE CIVIL RIGHTS MOVEMENT

The Civil Rights Movement was and is a powerful force for change in America's black-white relations. It also represents a more aggressive rejection of the dominant group's negative image. After an analysis of social movements and change in America, the Civil Rights Movement directed its efforts on the legal and social inequalities experienced by blacks. The three objectives of the movement were: (1) to realize basic civil liberties for black people; (2) "to make separate facilities genuinely equal" (specific for the first forty years of this century); and (3) to pose a "legal challenge to the idea that separate facilities could be equal" (specific for the post-World War II period).[134]

THE NAACP

The aggressive rejection of minority status and racism took the form of the many civil rights organizations of the past several decades. One of the oldest organizations to fight racism is the National Association for the Advancement of Colored People (NAACP).

The NAACP was established in 1910, when many blacks were not protected by the law and were even victimized by it on occasion. The orga-

"Jim Crowism" (margin)

Civil Rights objectives (margin)

nization's purpose was not to overthrow the system but to change it. Founded by black intellectuals (who came primarily from the middle class) and white liberals, the NAACP focused on discriminatory laws against blacks. In 1915, they won an important victory against the "grandfather" clauses that kept blacks from voting. They also focused on anti-lynching campaigns.

The NAACP's preferred tactics of change were litigation and dissemination of information through publications such as *The Crisis,* edited by W. E. B. Du Bois. Not only did they seek to change laws through court review and legislation, but also to change administrative policies through executive order. The NAACP reacted to the inability of blacks to change their status through conventional interest-group politics. They fought in the courts to help ensure that the "separate but equal" facilities (*Plessy* vs. *Ferguson* decision of 1896) were in fact equal. The NAACP also fought in its early years for black access to public accommodations and transportation and for equal educational opportunities. They sought to change old customs, behavior patterns, and beliefs through demonstrations.

The NAACP: Change through law

A major institution of society, education, was changed by the efforts of blacks through the nation's legal system. The NAACP's well-developed legalistic approach eventually culminated in the landmark Supreme Court decisions of 1954, *Brown* vs. *the Board of Education* and *Bolling* vs. *Sharp,* which outlawed public school segregation at all levels of education. Basically, then, the NAACP attempted to "achieve a situation where blacks enjoyed at least minimal human rights where there was some minimal respect for their basic humanity."[135]

1954 Supreme Court decisions

Taking a stronger form of aggressive rejection, black protest of the 1960s differed from earlier activities, such as those of the NAACP. First of all, there was a shift to direct action, such as sit-ins, boycotts, and demonstrations, rather than the indirect educational and legal means of protest. Second, there was a shift in initiative to average blacks, who were ready and willing to deal with segregation or institutionalized discrimination through direct action. No longer did only a few black professional leaders or intellectuals have the initiative in black protest. Third, protest of the 1960s was directed against the entire segregated social order, not just against a particular public facility or school. Fourth, the black movement cut across class and other divisions in the black community and spread throughout the country.[136]

Shift to aggressive rejection

THE SCLC AND THE URBAN LEAGUE

In the 1960s, Rev. Martin Luther King, Jr. and the Southern Christian Leadership Conference (SCLC) led an aggressive series of demonstrations and sit-ins in an attempt to secure remedial legislation on a variety of segregational barriers. The SCLC had its roots in Mahatma Gandhi's philosophy of nonviolent resistance. Through sit-ins and boycotts, Rev. King focused the SCLC's attack primarily on the registration of black voters and the desegregation of public transit systems. The demonstrators went to the streets nonviolently to exercise their constitutional rights. Violence was the usual response from racists, which led to a nationwide call for decency and, thus, for federal intervention. Under pressure, the federal government then initiated measures of immediate intervention and remedial legislation.[137] These were the intentions, methods, and goals of the SCLC and, in many respects, they were successful.

In the early part of the twentieth century, there were many other organizations involved in reform activities that helped blacks in a variety of ways. One such organization was the National Urban League, founded in 1910 but still working today. Originally the League helped rural blacks find jobs and housing when they moved to northern cities. The League employed the strategy of negotiation rather than confrontation in response to segregation and discrimination. They continue to emphasize equality in government, industry, and business today.

THE BLACK PANTHERS

The late 1960s and early 1970s saw the development of even more aggressive black organizations, such as the revolutionary Black Panther Party. Their goal was originally the destruction of capitalism by oppressed communities of blacks through revolutionary intercommunalism. Its members were to be totally committed to the goal of a communist society full of kindness and free of oppression. Reformers were viewed as enemies because they only attempted to make life a little more tolerable under an existing system unable to respond adequately to black needs.

However, there was a shift in the response of the Black Panther Party when a split in leadership occurred between Eldridge Clever and Huey Newton. Today, instead of stressing the destruction of capitalism through disruption and violence, the Panthers are much less aggressive and much more involved in community organization and politics. This shift indicates how, at particular times, revolutionary organizations and their leaders can moderate their objectives and change into reformist organizations.

Even though there have been revolutionary organizations such as the Black Panthers, authorities in the field of minority relations believe that there has not been a black revolution in America. In particular, Van den Berghe says that the major civil rights organizations (the NAACP, the Urban League, the SCLC, etc.) are reform movements and that, "far from questioning the underlying values and premises of American society, they seek legitimacy in the American creed and Christian ethics and plead for a change of practices in line with the dominant group ideology."[138]

RIOTS

Not only has black reponse to racism taken the form of protest organizations, it has also taken the form of direct aggression, in the form of racial rioting. Riots based on racial, ethnic, or religious background are part of American history. In the middle of the nineteenth century there were anti-Catholic and anti-Irish riots. Near the turn of this century, there were many instances of anti-Chinese riots, especially on the West Coast.

In this century, there have been many black-white riots, some of which were person-oriented while others were oriented more toward the destruction of property. The 1943 race riots of Detroit, Michigan left more than thirty people dead and several hundred injured after black and white mobs attacked each other. On the other hand, the 1964 Philadelphia riots, which were similar to other city riots of the mid-1960s, were directed more toward destroying buildings and looting stores rather than attacking people.

There are many factors that influence the manifestation of black aggression in the form of rioting. One such factor has been termed the *social disorganization* thesis. This attributes black riots to a breakdown of society's consensual norms and to the social control agencies' inability or unwillingness to effect normative restoration. These conditions develop from such processes of social change as urbanization, industrialization, and cybernation.

Concurrent with these changes, people feel alienated and anomic—i.e., they feel detached from the existing social order. Vander Zanden states,

> When large numbers of people experience frustration and stress over an extended period of time, they become susceptible to courses of action not otherwise considered. As the Black population migrated to urban centers, the traditional structure of race relations, characterized by Black subordination and adapted to a feudal, rural environment, was no longer appropriate. Black rioting, then, may be viewed as an attack upon the traditional accommodative pattern of race relations.[139]

The *group conflict* thesis views rioting as a "product of a struggle for power among various groups within society" for scarce and divisible things defined as good and worth having.[144] Looting of furniture, liquor, and food shops is perceived as a "bid for a redistribution of property" and as "a message that certain deprived sectors of the population want what they consider their fair share—and that they will resort to violence to get it."[140]

A *riot ideology* thesis views civil violence as a "legitimate and productive mode of protest" as well as a response to "frustrations experienced within a racist society and to shared interpretations of such frustration."[141] A *psychology of violence* thesis, on the other hand, views violence as a "cleansing force" at the individual level. In other words, violence is a personal and political necessity for black colonial peoples striving to be independent and "to be men." For Frantz Fanon, a black psychoanalyst, violence "frees the native from his inferiority complex and from his despair and inaction; it makes him fearless and restores his self-respect."[142]

Explanations of rioting

Finally, the *relative deprivation* thesis focuses on the gap that exists between what people have and what they come to expect as their due.[143] This view, which will be further examined in the reading, feels that the riots are rooted in the discrepancy between black expectations and their actual attainments.

Many factors have contributed to the violent response of rioting. Social scientists do not consider any particular one to be more important than the others. All the factors are important and should be considered in any analysis of black-white riots.

THE SHIFTING BLACK RESPONSE

The following reading, by William J. Wilson, examines the shift among blacks in America from a response pattern characterized by litigation, through a pattern of passive resistance, to a new response characterized by violence. Wilson notes the way in which the nonviolent resistance strategy proved to be effective in the creation and implementation of civil rights laws. He also notes the reasons for the federal government's favorable reaction to the demands of nonviolent protest. The dynamics of violence as a response are then examined in terms of an intolerable widening of the gap between blacks' expectations and gratifications. White violence, black militancy, ghetto rebellions, and the Black Power Movement are also examined before ending with a discussion of cultural nationalism.

WILSON READING——OBJECTIVES

1. To list five reasons why the federal government responded favorably to the demands of the nonviolent protest movements of the 1960s.
2. To examine in an essay the shift among blacks in America from a response pattern of litigation to one of violence.

Power and the Changing Character of Black Protest
WILLIAM J. WILSON

One pattern of behavior
seems to emerge

Throughout the discussion of black social thought and protest in the United States, one pattern of behavior seems to emerge: *the changing goals of black advancement tend to be associated with the changing definition of black despair, and both the defined problem and the conceived goal are ultimately associated with the choice of possible pressure or constraint resources that blacks can mobilize in pressing for the desired solution.* However, it should be noted that despite the definition of the problem and the conception of the goal, the choice of pressure resources is influenced or determined by the extent to which blacks find themselves in competitive relations with whites. The now more conservative black protest movements, such as the NAACP and the National Urban League, developed and gained momentum when racial accommodations were undergoing change but when the dominant-group controls were so strong that the pressure tactics of the mid-twentieth century activist movements would not have been tolerated.[1]

Before the emergence of the activist black protest movements, the drive for civil rights was therefore in the hands of a few professionals competent to work through controlling legal and educational channels.[2] The NAACP achieved great success through these agencies, and its definition of the problem facing black people signified its planned strategy. Specifically, prior to 1960 the NAACP tended to define the racial problem as legal segregation in the South, and its major goal, popularized by the slogan "free by 1963," was the elimination of all state-enforced segregation. Although the officials of the NAACP have lacked a power orientation, the mobilization of their legal machinery has represented a display of power—the power of litigation—in this instance, a power resource of high liquidity. Working through prevailing institutional channels, the NAACP was able to win an overwhelming number of cases in the Supreme Court and thus helped to produced laws designed to improve racial conditions in America, although white Southerners ingeniously circumvented the new laws and thus usually prevented their implementation. Lewis M. Killian has discussed this matter:

> It is ironic that the white South was extremely successful in minimizing the impact of the desegregation decision of the federal court without arousing the indignation of the rest of the nation. As much as the White Citizens Council and the Ku Klux Klan are invoked as symbols of the southern resistance, they and their extra-legal tactics did not make this possible. Far more effective were the legal stratagems, evasions, and delays that led Negroes to realize that although they had won a new statement of principle they had not won the power to cause this principle to be implemented.[3]

White procrastination made it apparent to many black leaders that both the goal and the problem had been too narrowly defined. A new definition of the problem thus emerged—token compliance to the newly created laws—and a corresponding new goal—the elimination of both de facto and de jure segregation. Litigation, no longer an effective pressure resource in the face of white procrastination, was replaced by passive or nonviolent resistance. The fact that the power balance between blacks and whites had undergone some alteration also helped bring about the shift to nonviolent direct-action protest. As blacks increased their political and economic resources, as the Supreme Court rendered decisions in favor of desegregation, and as the United States government became increasingly sensitive to world opinion of its racial situation, black expectations were heightened, continued white resistance became more frustrating, and consequently support for direct-action (albeit nonviolent) protests quickly mushroomed. Although some writers have identified the successful Montgomery bus boycott of 1955–1956 as the beginning of the black revolt,[4] Meier and Rudwick have maintained that "the really decisive break with the pre-eminence of legalistic techniques came with the college student sit-ins that swept the South in the Spring of 1960."[5] These demon-

A new definition of the problem

strations set a chain of nonviolent resistance movements to desegregation into motion that subsequently swept the country from 1960 to 1965. Even though the initial emphasis was on persuasion resources rather than constraint resources, the technique of nonviolence was in reality an aggressive manifestation of pressure. Its twofold goal was to create and to implement civil rights laws. Even though many of the nonviolent protests were not specifically directed at the federal government, they were in many cases intended to apply indirect pressure on it. Black leaders recognized that because of their political and pressure resources and because of the United States' concern for world opinion, the government was not in a position to ignore their stepped-up drive for civil rights.

Reasons for favorable federal response

For a brief period of time, the nonviolent resistance strategy proved to be highly effective. In addition to forcing local governments and private agencies to integrate facilities in numerous Southern cities and towns, the nonviolent demonstrations pressed the federal government into passage of civil rights legislation in 1964 and voting rights legislation in 1965—acts that satisfied many of the black demands of the early 1960s. There are several reasons why the federal government responded favorably to many of the demands emanating from the nonviolent protest movement: (1) the demands that accompanied the protests tended to be fairly specific, e.g., "end discrimination in voting," and hence the government was able to provide "remedies" that clearly approximated the specifications in the demands; (2) the attempt to satisfy these demands did not call for major sacrifices on the part of whites, and hence there was little likelihood that a significant political backlash against the government would occur in sections of the country other than the South; (3) the demands were consistent with prevailing ideals of democracy and freedom of choice, and hence they could not be easily labeled "extreme" either by the white citizens or by governmental authorities; (4) the more blacks pressed their demands and carried out their protests, the more violent was the Southern response, and because these developments were receiving international attention, the government became increasingly concerned; (5) the government was sensitive to the political resources blacks had developed and became cognizant of the growing army of Northern whites sympathetic to the black cause; (6) blacks' political strength seemed to be magnified by the united front they presented, as groups ranging from the relatively conservative NAACP to the radical Student Nonviolent Coordinating Committee all joined in nonviolent protests to effect change.

To understand why many blacks shifted away from nonviolence both as a philosophy of life and as a technique to achieve racial equality, it is necessary to understand the dynamics of minority protest: if an extended period of increased expectations and gratification is followed by a brief period in which the gap between expectations and gratifications suddenly widens and becomes intolerable, the possibility of violent protests is greatly increased. Davies applies this analysis to the black rebellion of the 1960s:

> In short—starting in the mid-1950's and increasing more or less steadily into the early 1960's—white violence grew against the now lawful and protected efforts of Negroes to gain integration. And so did direct action and later violence undertaken by blacks, in a reciprocal process that moved into the substantial violence of 1965–67. That 3 year period may be considered a peak, possibly the peak of the violence that constituted the black rebellion.

It merits reemphasis that during this era of increased hostility progress intensified both the white reaction to it and the black counteraction to the reaction, because everytime a reaction impeded the progress, the apparent gap widened between expectations and gratification.[6]

Even though there was no sudden or sharp increase in black unemployment and no sudden reversal in the material gains blacks had accumulated during the prosperous 1960s, "there was, starting notably in 1963, not the first instance of violence against blacks but a sudden increase in it. This resurgence of violence came after, and interrupted, the slow but steady progress since 1940. It quickly frustrated rising expectations."[7] For the first time, there was a real sense of apprehension among blacks that, not only would conditions stop improving, but gains already achieved could very well be lost unless steps were taken to counteract mounting white violence.

Birmingham, Alabama, in 1963 was the scene of this initial wave of white violence and black counterreaction. In April, Birmingham police used high-pressure water hoses and dogs to attack civil rights marchers, and blacks retaliated by throwing rocks and bottles at the police; in May, segregationists bombed the homes of black leaders, and blacks retaliated by rioting, setting two white-owned stores on fire and stoning police and firemen; on September 15, whites enraged by school desegregation bombed a black church, killing four small girls and injuring twenty-three other adults and children, and blacks angrily responded by stoning police.[8]

However, racial violence was not retricted to Birmingham, Alabama, in 1963. Medger Evers, an NAACP official in Jackson, Mississippi, was shot to death in front of his home on May 28, 1963. Whites and blacks in Cambridge, Maryland, engaged in a gun battle after blacks had stormed a restaurant to rescue sit-in demonstrators beaten by whites; the black quarter in Lexington, North Carolina, was attacked by a white mob after blacks had attempted to obtain service at white restaurants, and in the ensuing gun battle a white man was killed; mounted police at Plaquemine, Louisiana, galloped into a group of civil rights demonstrators and dispersed them with electric cattle prods—fifteen demonstrators were injured; police used tear gas, shotguns, and high-pressure water hoses in Savannah, Georgia, to break up a protest demonstration that turned into a riot—at least ten whites and thirteen blacks were injured; and mass arrests of civil rights activists took place in Athens, Georgia; Selma, Alabama; Greensboro, North Carolina; Orangeburg, South Carolina and several other Southern towns.[9]

The gap between expectations and emotional gratifications[10] increased black support for violent protest and was reflected, not only in the way blacks responded to white attacks beginning with the Birmingham incident in 1963, but also in the changing philosophy of younger civil rights activists. In the early months of 1964, members of the Student Nonviolent Coordinating Committee (SNCC) and the Congress of Racial Equality (CORE) openly challenged the philosophy of nonviolence and called for more belligerent forms of protest.[11] It was during this same period that Malcolm X, shortly after he resigned from the Nation of Islam, called for blacks to arm themselves and abandon nonviolence and that the Brooklyn chapter of CORE attempted to tie up New York traffic (on April 22, the opening of the World's Fair) by emptying the fuel tanks of 2000 automobiles and abandon-

The gap between expectation and gratification

ing them on the freeways leading to the fairgrounds (lacking support, the strategy failed).[12] Continued white violent acts such as the murder of civil rights workers by white terrorists in Mississippi in 1964, Ku Klux Klan terrorism in Mississippi and Alabama in 1965, attacks against CORE organizers in Bogalusa, Louisiana, in 1965, the beating and murder of civil rights activists in Selma, Alabama, in 1965, and police brutality that precipitated rioting in Northern ghettoes in 1964 deepened the militant mood in the black community and widened the gap between expectations and emotional gratification.

In the face of these developments, the call by some black leaders for greater militancy was based on the optimistic belief that the larger society was more likely to respond properly to black demands backed by belligerent and violent protests than to those reinforced by nonviolent resistance. Theoretical analysis suggests either that blacks believed they possessed sufficient resources not only to disrupt the larger society but also to prevent an all-out repressive reaction by whites, or that they felt that by the mid-1960s, the system had developed a high tolerance for minority protests.[13] However, it was lower-class urban blacks who dramatically demonstrated that a more belligerent mood had gripped the black community when they rocked the nation with a proliferation of ghetto revolts from 1964 to 1968. In the early 1960s, nonviolent protests were heavily populated by middle-class or higher-educated blacks, who were far more likely at this period to participate in a drive for social justice that was disciplined and sustained.[14] Ghetto blacks for the most part were not directly involved in the nonviolent resistance movement of the early 1960s, and many of the gains achieved did not materially benefit them (the civil rights movement up to 1965 produced laws primarily relevant to privileged blacks with competitive resources such as special talents or steady income);[15] nevertheless, the victories of the nonviolent movement increased expectations among all segments of the black population.[16] In the age of mass communication, Northern ghetto blacks, like blacks throughout the country, were very much aware of and identified with the efforts of Martin Luther King, Jr., and other civil rights activists. By the same token, they were also cognizant of the white violence that threatened to halt the gradual but steady progress toward racial equality.

Accordingly, ghetto rebellions cannot be fully explained in isolation or independently of the increasingly militant mood of the black community. However, what made the situation of ghetto blacks unique was the fact that the gap between expectations and emotional gratification was combined with concrete grievances over police brutality, inferior education, unemployment, underemployment, and inadequate housing. It is true that these conditions have always existed in ghetto life and did not suddenly emerge during the 1960s, but the important point is that increased expectations and greater awareness of racial oppression made these conditions all the more intolerable.[17] Charles Silberman was essentially correct when he stated that "it is only when men sense the possibility of improvement, in fact, that they become dissatisfied with their situation and rebel against it. And 'with rebelling' as Albert Camus put it 'awareness is born,' and with awareness, an impatience 'which can extend to everything that [men] had previously accepted, and which is almost always retroactive.' "[18] Likewise, as the number and intensity of ghetto revolts increased, black complaints about human suffering became more explicit and focused.

The Harlem revolt in 1964 actually marked the beginning of ghetto uprisings of the 1960s (where groups of blacks looted stores, burned buildings, and attacked firemen and police in the black community), but the most serious revolts occurred in 1965 in Watts (resulting in 34 deaths, 900 injuries, 4000 arrests, and an estimated property damage of $100,000,000), in 1967 in Detroit (43 deaths, 1500 injuries, 5000 arrests, and $200,000,000 in property damage), and Newark (26 deaths, 1200 injuries, 1600 arrests, and $47,000,000 in property damage). The assassination of Dr. Martin Luther King, Jr., precipitated the final series of ghetto rebellions in the spring of 1968. During that four-year period (1964–1968) of intense racial violence, thousands of persons, mostly black, were killed or injured, and the property damage was estimated in the billions of dollars.

Ghetto revolts

In addition to these manifestations of greater black militancy, the emergence of the Black Power Movement in 1966, with its shift in emphasis to racial solidarity and its explicit repudiation of nonviolence as a strategy of protest and way of life, can also be associated with the sudden gap between rising expectations and emotional gratification. In a fundamental sense, however, the Black Power Movement represented a return to the self-help philosophy and emphasis on black solidarity that usually occurs "when the Negroes' status has declined or when they experienced intense disillusionment following a period of heightened but unfulfilled expectations."[19]

The Black Power Movement

Unlike the self-help nationalistic philosophies that developed in the 1850s following increased repression in the free states, in the Booker T. Washington era as response to the growth of biological racism and resurgence of white supremacy, and in the post World War I period as a reaction to white violence perpetrated against black urban immigrants in the North, the Black Power Movement developed during a period when blacks had achieved a real sense of power.

Killian has commented on this new feeling of power:

> The nonviolent demonstrations of SCLC, CORE, and SNCC . . . had not solved the bitter problems of the Negro masses, but they had shown that the Negro minority could strike terror into the hearts of the white majority. They had produced concessions from white people, even though the triumph of winning these concessions had soon turned to despair because they were never enough. Watts and other riots reflected no clearly formulated demand for new concessions. They did reflect the basic truth that Negroes, mobilized in ghettoes to an extent never before experienced and made confident by earlier victories, were no longer afraid of white power. Within a few months after Watts, they would begin to proclaim their faith in Black Power.[20]

This new sense of power was reflected not so much in the programs actually introduced under the banner of Black Power as in the revolutionary rhetoric used to articulate Black Power philosophy. That certain black radicals dared, through national media, to call openly for the use of violence to overthrow racial oppression was a clear indication that blacks felt secure enough to threaten the very stability of the larger society. In actual fact, however, although Black Power advocates often disagreed about the aims and purposes of the movement, their various demands and programs were more reformist in nature than revolutionary[21] (e.g., programs emphasizing black capitalism, the running of black candidates for political office, self-help in the area of jobs and housing, black studies in high schools and colleges, and black culture and identity). Some of the programs introduced by Black Power spokesmen were an extension of the conservative separatism advocated by the Nation of Islam (Black Muslims) under the leadership of Elijah Muhammad. From the 1950s to the first half of the 1960s, when black social thought continued to be overwhelmingly supportive of integration,[22] the Nation of Islam served as the major medium for a black nationalist philosophy.[23] Commenting on Muslim philosophy, Cruse wrote that the

> Nation of Islam was nothing but a form of Booker T. Washington economic self-help, black unity, bourgeois hard work, law abiding, vocational training, stay-out-of-the-civil-rights-struggle agitation, separate-from-the-white-man, etc., etc. morality. The only difference was that Elijah Muhammad added the potent factor of the Muslim religion to race, economic, and social philosophy of which the first prophet was none other than Booker T. Washington. Elijah Muhammad also added an element of "hate Whitey" ideology which Washington, of course, would never have accepted.[24]

Muhammad and Malcolm X

The most significant influence on the radical flank of the Black Power Movement was ex-Muslim minister Malcolm X. Because of differences with Elijah Muhammad, Malcolm X resigned from the Muslim organization and moved beyond its program of territorial separation and bourgeois economic nationalism. Shortly before he was assassinated in 1965, he had begun to formulate a philosophy of revolutionary nationalism (that "views the overthrow of existing political and economic institutions as a prerequisite for the liberation of black Americans, and does not exclude the use of violence[25]) subsequently adopted by militant Black Power leaders such as Stokely Carmichael and H. Rap Brown and incorporated into the philosophy of the newly emerging Black Panther Party in the late 1960s.

Yet, of all the philosophies of nationalism or racial solidarity that emerged under the banner of Black Power, none has received as much support from black citizens as has cultural nationalism.[26] Cultural nationalism is concerned mainly with positive race identity, including the development and/or elaboration of black culture and history. One of the most illustrative statements of this theme has come from Blauner:

> In their communities across the nation, Afro-Americans are discussing "black culture." The mystique of "soul" is only the most focused example of this trend in consciousness. What is and what should be the black man's attitude toward American society and American culture has become a central division in the Negro protest movement. The spokesmen for black power celebrate black culture and Negro distinctiveness; the integrationists base their strategy and their appeal on the fundamental "American-ness" of the black man. There are nationalist leaders who see culture building today as equal or more important than political organization. From Harlem to Watts there has been a proliferation of black theater, art, and literary groups; the recent ghetto riots (or revolts, as they are viewed from the nationalistic perspective) are the favored materials of these cultural endeavors.[27]

But certainly we must not lose sight of the fact that cultural nationalism, like other forms of nationalism has become popular during certain periods in history—periods when black disillusionment follows a brief interval of black optimism and commitment to integration. It is not so important that structural assimilation,[28] especially for middle-class blacks, is occurring at a greater rate than ever before; what is important is the black perception of the racial changes that are occurring. Black awareness has been heightened by the efforts of both the civil rights and the Black Power activists, and impatience and frustration with the pace of racial equality have become more intense. Whereas the cultural nationalism of the 1850s and of the Harlem Renaissance period was largely confined to segments of the black intelligentsia,[29] the cultural nationalism of the late 1960s and early 1970s has transcended class lines. Awareness of the evils of racial oppression and of white resistance to racial equality is characteristic of all segments of the black population; support for racial solidarity with emphasis on black culture and racial identity has reached unprecedented heights.

NOTES

1. See Clarence E. Glick, "Collective Behavior in Race Relations," *American Sociological Review*, 13:287–293 (June 1947).

2. James H. Laue, "The Changing Character of Negro Protest," *Annals of the American Academy of Political and Social Science*, 357:120 (Jan. 1965).

3. Lewis M. Killian, *The Impossible Revolution?: Black Power and the American Dream* (New York: Random House, 1968), p. 70.

4. See, for example, Louis Lomax, *The Negro Revolt* (New York: Signet, 1962).

5. August Meier and Elliot Rudwick, *From Plantation to Ghetto: The Interpretative History of American Negroes*, rev. ed. (New York: Hill and Wang, 1970), p. 227.

6. James C. Davies, "The J-Curve of Rising and Declining Satisfactions as a Cause of Some Great Revolutions and a Contained Rebellion," in *Violence in America: Historical and Comparative Perspectives*, ed. Hugh Davis Graham and Ted Robert Gurr (New York: Bantam Books, 1969), p. 721.

7. Davies, op. cit., p. 723.

8. Keesing's Research Report, *Race Relations in the USA, 1954–68* (New York: Scribner's, 1970), pp. 152–153.

9. Ibid., pp. 154–155.

10. A number of writers have not made full use of Davies' "J-curve" theory because they have restricted the notion of "gratification" to material gains or physical gratification and have ignored the factor of "emotional gratification." See, for example, James A. Geschwender, "Social Structure and the Negro Revolt: An Examination of Some Hypotheses," *Social Forces*, 43:248–256 (Dec. 1964), and Thomas F. Pettigrew, *Racially Separate or Together?* (New York: McGraw-Hill, 1971), chap. 7.

11. Keesing's Research Report, op. cit., pp. 164–165.

12. Ibid., p. 164.

13. For a discussion of this latter point, see L. H. Massotti and D. R. Bowen, eds., *Riots and Rebellion: Racial Violence in the Urban Community* (Beverly Hills, Calif.: Sage, 1968), and Pettigrew, op. cit., chap. 7.

14. As M. Elaine Burgess observed in 1965, "Neither the lower class nor the upper class could have mounted the resistance movement we are now witnessing throughout the South. The former does not possess the resources, either internal or external,

essential for such a movement, and the latter is much too small and, very frequently, too far removed from the masses to do so. Such activity had to wait the development of an ample middle class that was motivated to push for validation of hard-won position, thus far denied by the white power structure. The question of unequal distribution of status and power between Negroes and whites would consequently appear as a special case of the more basic problems of order and change. By no means are we saying that all challenges to established social structures or power distributions are class oriented, or directly concerned with relative social position. Nevertheless, it is true that one of the major sources of tension and therefore of change and potential change in the South, as in the broader society, stems from the new middle-class Negro's disbelief in past rationales for inequality and the desire for substitution of new rationales." M. Elaine Burgess, "Race Relations and Social Change," in *The South in Continuity and Change*, ed. by John C. McKinney and Edgar T. Thompson (Durham, N.C.: Duke U.P., 1965), p. 352.

15. As Martin Luther King, Jr., once observed, "What good is it to be allowed to eat in a restaurant if you can't afford a hamburger?"

16. See, for example, William Brink and Louis Harris, *Black and White: A Study of U.S. Racial Attitudes Today* (New York: Simon & Schuster, 1966), p. 42; H. Cantrell, *The Pattern of Human Concerns* (New Brunswick, N.J.: Rutgers U.P., 1965), p. 43; and Pettigrew, op. cit., chap. 7.

17. See *Report of the National Advisory Commission on Civil Disorders* (New York: Bantam, 1968), and Nathan S. Caplan and Jeffrey Paige, "A Study of Ghetto Rioters," *Scientific American*, 219:15–21 (Aug. 1968).

18. Charles Silberman, *Crisis in the Classroom* (New York: Random House, 1970), pp. 19–20.

19. John H. Bracey, August Meier, and Elliot Rudwick, eds., *Black Nationalism in America* (Indianapolis: Bobbs-Merrill, 1970), p. xxvi. It is true, as John Bracey has argued, that black nationalist philosophy has always existed among some segments of the black population (see "John Bracey Sketches His Interpretation of Black Nationalism," *Ibid.*, pp. lvi-lix), but what available research there is clearly establishes the fact that support for this philosophy increases and declines during certain periods in history.

20. Killian, op. cit., pp. 105–106.

21. Harold Cruse, *Rebellion or Revolution* (New York: Apollo, 1968), chap. 13, and *The Crisis of the Negro Intellectual* (New York: Morrow, 1967), pp. 554–565.

22. According to Bracey et al., "The proliferation of nationalist ideologies and organizations that reached a climax during the 1920's was followed by a thirty year period in which nationalism as a significant theme in black thought was virtually nonexistent. From the thirties until the sixties, with few exceptions, leading Negro organizations stressed interracial cooperation, civil rights, and racial integration. Among the chief reasons for the temporary demise of nationalism were the effects of the Depression and the consequent necessity of relying on the New Deal for survival, and the influx of trade Unionists and Communists into the black community preaching and practicing racial equality and brotherhood. The principal ideological concerns of articulate blacks during the Depression decade focused on very practical aspects of the Negro's relationship to New Deal agencies and the Roosevelt Administration, on the role of industrial unions in the advancement of the race, and on the relevance of Marxist doctrines of the Negro's problem." Bracey et al., op. cit., p. xiv.

23. Founded in the early 1930s, the Nation of Islam became a viable institution around 1950. It achieved its greatest popularity after the late Malcolm X became a convert to the Muslim sect and one of its most influential ministers until he resigned in 1964.

24. Cruse, *Rebellion or Revolution,* op cit., p. 211.

25. Bracey et al., op. cit., p. xxviii. Also see *The Autobiography of Malcolm X* (New York: Grove, 1964).

26. For example, the Opinion Research Corporation survey in 1968 revealed that 86 per cent of the blacks in their sample felt that black people should be taught subjects in school that added to their feeling of pride in being black. In their study of black attitudes in fifteen American cities, Angus Campbell and Howard Schuman have found that "There is a strong trend in the data that is related to, but different from and much stronger than 'separation.' It concerns the positive cultural identity and achievements of Negroes, rather than their political separation from whites. The finding appears most strikingly in the endorsement by 42 percent of the Negro sample of the statement 'Negro school children should study an African Language.' Two out of five Negroes thus subscribe to an emphasis on 'black consciousness' that was almost unthought of a few years ago." Angus Campbell and Howard Schuman, "Racial Attitudes in Fifteen American Cities," in *The National Advisory Commission on Civil Disorders, Supplemental Studies* (Washington, D.C.: G.P.O., 1968), p. 6.

Despite the strong sentiment for cultural nationalism in the black community, institutional nationalism—i.e., the efforts of black citizens to gain control of the political, economic, and social institutions in their community and/or establish separate institutions free of control by the dominant white society—although increasing in popularity, still receive support from only a minority of blacks. See, for example, Brink and Harris, op. cit.; *Report of the National Advisory Commission on Civil Disorders,* op cit.; Campbell and Schuman, op. cit.; Caplan and Paige, op. cit.; and Gary T. Marx, *Protest and Prejudice: A Study of Belief in the Black Community,* rev. ed. (New York: Harper, 1970).

27. Robert Blauner, "Black Culture: Myth or Reality?" in *Americans from Africa: Old Memories, New Moods,* ed. by Peter I. Rose (New York: Atherton, 1970), pp. 417–418.

28. Following Milton M. Gordon, "structural assimilation" is defined as "large scale entrance into cliques, clubs, and institutions of host society on primary group level." Milton M. Gordon, *Assimilation in American Life* (New York: Oxford U.P., 1964), p. 71.

29. As Robert A. Bone has noted, "Even at the peak of Renaissance nationalism the middle-class writers could never muster more than token enthusiasm for a distinctive Negro culture." Robert A. Bone, "The Negro Novel in America" in *America's Black Past,* ed. by Eric Foner (New York: Harper, 1970), p. 385.

SUMMARY

This chapter focused on the prejudice and unequal treatment that women and blacks encounter in American society. Sex and race operate freely as bases for unequal treatment, and sexism and racism are widespread. The basic concepts of prejudice and discrimination were first examined.

Women were viewed as a minority group in terms of power distribution. The traditional roles and views of women, along with their implications, were then examined, in addition to the many myths about women with respect to income, employment, and education.

Racial prejudice and discrimination are among America's oldest social problems. There is much documentary proof of the unequal treatment accorded blacks in the areas of income, employment, education, and health. In spite of some improvements, blacks still occupy a distinct position in the American stratification system. The reading explained that all races and communities make up the "American underclass"; however, it consists primarily of poor urban blacks.

There are, of course, many sociological explanations for racism and sexism. We have presented what are considered to be the leading explanations for prejudice, discrimination, and inequality. All of these theories can be supported, to some extent, with a respectable and reliable body of research. It must be remembered, however, that no one approach can adequately explain all prejudice or all discrimination. Racism and sexism are complex phenomena consisting of sociocultural, economic, and individual personality elements. An understanding of these elements, however, provides a basis for understanding the existence of various inequalities, prejudices, and discriminatory patterns in society. Taken together, the explanations examined in this section provide a great deal of insight into and a better understanding of the many problems encountered by two of the largest minority groups in America.

In this section, the wide variety of response patterns were examined. Concerning sexism, our primary focus was women's rejection of the social, economic, and political inequalities in society. Women's movements of the past and present were examined and compared. The major issues of equal job opportunity, equal pay, and the Equal Rights Amendment were examined.

Regarding racism, our primary focus was on blacks' responses of acceptance and rejection of their subordinate status in society. The effects of slavery and the major organizations in the American Civil Rights Movement were examined. The reading "Power and the Changing Character of Black Protest" examined the shift among blacks from a response pattern characterized by litigation to one of violence.

KEY TERMS

Aggressive rejection
The American underclass
Assimilation
Black Panther Party
Discrimination
Economic explanations
Equal Rights Amendment
Evasive avoidance
Group conflict thesis
Integration
Minority group
NAACP
National Urban League
NOW
NWSA, AWSA, NAWSA
Passing
Personality explanations
Prejudice

Psychology of violence thesis
Racism
Radical feminism
Relative deprivation thesis
Riot ideology thesis
Scapegoat theory
SCLC
Segregation
Self-fulfilling prophecy
Sexism
Social disorganization thesis
Socialist feminism
Sociocultural explanations
Submissive acceptance
Vested interests and competition
    explanations
Women's Liberation Movement

4
Agism

Chapter Objectives

1. To list and briefly describe three major trends that are the basis of the situation facing the aged today.

2. To briefly analyze at least three of the major health problems encountered by the aged.

3. To examine at least three explanations of agism.

4. To compare by brief essay the 1971 White House Conference on Aging to earlier conferences on the subject.

5. To briefly examine two federal programs designed to help the aged.

6. To describe the federal response to the aged's health problems.

7. To discuss at least two arguments both for and against mandatory retirement.

8. To compare the problems of the aged with those of women and blacks in America.

PROBLEMS OF THE AGED

Through advancements in medicine and technology, we have created a situation in which the people of our society live much longer lives. Yet we are socially ill-equipped to deal with this situation.

According to the National Council on Aging and the Harris poll, the aged in America believe that they share many common problems. Older people in America are concerned about the problems of health, money, loneliness, and being victimized by criminals. The aged fear being unable to cope with illness. They also fear that money saved or received from Social Security will be inadequate for basic needs. In addition, the elderly fear being isolated from others in their community and from society in general.

The aged have many fears

Millions of our older people—in fact the majority—depend on Social Security as their basic source of income, and the adjustment of Social Security payments to the cost of living has helped to an extent.[1] Unfortunately, too many elderly receive amounts that are still insufficient to secure basic needs. Medicaid and Medicare have helped millions of older people overcome many fears about depleting their assets because of sickness. However, health care for the aged in America is still very inadequate.

In our society, jobs give people much of their social status and self-esteem; therefore, when the aged retire, most of them lose their status and self-esteem. Feeling forgotten, and caught up in a continuous search for something to do, the elderly develop various emotional and physical problems.

The aged are shelved

Agism is widespread in America. Systems of social, economic, political and psychological activities and pressures suppress the aged because they exhibit certain biological characteristics. Many points that were made in the previous chapter on sexism and racism are also applicable to the aged. For example, there is a strong relationship between the basic cultural values of our society and the various patterns of structured social inequality based on age. That is, age reflects various conditions and inequities that are part of our society's basic normative and institutional structure. Prejudice against old age is used as a criterion for discrimination.

Age discrimination in America is expressly prohibited by our Constitution and by a variety of statutes. Yet studies have consistently shown that many Americans still experience discrimination because of age. In this chapter we will examine the complex problems encountered by the aged.[2]

SOCIAL GERONTOLOGY

Much of our knowledge about the aged comes from the field of social gerontology, which studies the nonphysical aspects of growing old. Gerontologists have noted that, while there are individual variations, most people in their 60s and 70s are greatly aware of aging and have difficulty becoming future-oriented. The combination of retirement (with its usual reduction in

The nonphysical aspects of aging

income), failing energy, vision, and hearing, and poor health reduces the personal contacts of the elderly. Their social environment becomes limited also by children moving away and deaths of friends and relatives. The later stages of old age mark the "beginning of the end." In many cases, there is extreme frailty and disability. Restricted activity, loneliness, and boredom are common characteristics of this very unpleasant time.[3]

These stages do not necessarily correspond with chronological aging. Gerontologist Robert Atchley, in an examination of social forces in later life, notes that categories such as "later maturity" and "old age" are "based on characteristics other than chronological age." While in most cases chronological age is related to life cycle phases (adolescence, middle age, old age, etc.), the relationship is not necessary. Atchley says the important point "is whether one has the characteristics of old age, not whether one has reached a certain age."[4] In other words, one person can be considered old at age 50, while another can be physically and socially active, vibrant, and very much alive at age 85.

TRENDS ARE THE BASIS OF PROBLEMS

Four major trends

There are four major trends that form the basis for the situation in which the aged of America find themselves today: (1) the direction of the current population growth; (2) increased urbanization; (3) the rapid pace of social change; and (4) detachment from the extended kinship network.[5]

The aged population is growing

The first major trend can be understood by examining recent Census Bureau data. The percentage of elderly people* has been growing. In fact, it's rate of increase is twice that of the total population. Since 1900 the American population has almost tripled, from seventy-six million to 217 million people (1977). The aged population has increased from three million (in 1900) to twenty-four million, or 11 percent of the 1977 population.[6]

The median age of Americans has also risen, from 16 years old in 1790 (i.e., half the population was 16 years old or younger) to almost 30 years old today. In twenty years, 35 will be our median age. By the year 2030, it is estimated that one out of every six, or fifty-two million people, will be older than 65.[7]

Increased urbanization

The second major trend is the process of urbanization. With increased urbanization came changes in the cities and in their neighborhoods. These changes, and the large turnover of people in the neighborhoods, have separated older people from the community.

The third major trend, the fast pace of social change, has contributed to the elderly's inability to keep up with what is expected of them. The social norms learned in earlier life are no longer appropriate for unprecedented situations and positions. The position of "retired person," for ex-

---

* Age 65 and older is a widely accepted operational definition of "elderly."

ample, has no set norms, because they are still being developed. This makes it difficult for the aged to see themselves clearly and for others to respond to them easily.

Along with the fast pace of social change, there has been a breakdown in the extended kinship network. Because of this, the elderly are often detached from their families. In the past, several generations often lived together in the same home; today elderly people "expect and are expected to maintain a household separate from their married children." The difficulty in adjusting to these changes has partly contributed to the aged's problems.[8]

SOCIAL CONCERN, PREJUDICE, AND STEREOTYPES

There exists much social concern about the problems of the elderly in America. Various state governments and the federal government maintain administrative departments that deal with these problems. However, many people ask "Why is aging considered to be a social problem?" It seems logical to them to consider the longevity of larger numbers of people to be a great social achievement. Unfortunately, those who, through technological and scientific development, live longer lives have many fears and apprehensions about old age. These fears are not unfounded, because there is in America much prejudice and discrimination against the aged.

Prejudice against old age is, to an extent, the result of the unearned and unjust stereotypes that many Americans hold. Just as women and blacks are subject to sex- and race-role stereotyping and discrimination, the aged are also recipients of discrimination and stereotyped attitudes. For example, the attitudes that old people are rigid in their ways, sexless, constantly sick, and devoid of useful skills are typical stereotypes. These attitudes are clearly illustrated in the research of Payne and Whittington, which examined some of the popular stereotypes about older women in society.[9]

Noting that in this culture men are considered more socially valuable than women, and that the young are considered more valuable than the old, the elderly woman is viewed as socially unimportant and is the recipient of more negative stereotypes than any other age-sex group. Older women are viewed as "weak, ineffective, inactive, asexual old maids or widows . . . . older people and women . . . are groups which have traditionally faired quite badly in this country's social and economic marketplace and which continue to suffer discrimination motivated, at least in part, by such negative stereotypical images."[10]

However, research evidence indicates that these women are not significantly more sick or weak than men of the same age. The elderly woman "is not devoid of either sexual feeling or satisfaction . . . . widowhood is not necessarily a social or emotional grave . . . . leisure time is not always spent inactively or in lonely solitude." These stereotypes affect what the aged think of themselves as well as what others think about them.[11]

One point, however, must be noted. Compared to racial and even to sexual inequality, agism is a relatively new topic of scientific investigation. Kasschau states that, although agism is a common feature of society and both young and old share stereotypes about the aged, "older persons do not typically report a great deal of discrimination." Also, when problems were reported in the past, they were seldom attributed to age by the elderly respondents. Unlike blacks or other ethnic groups, the aged are probably far less likely to see and report conditions as being discriminatory because of the age factor. Reasons for this situation are described by Kasschau:[12]

> Factors including the individual's ambiguous personal response to his own aging, the ambiguous legal definition of the older American's civil rights, and the relatively low public visibility of the nature and magnitude of age discrimination, all militate against the older person's developing a definition of any particular situation as discriminatory and therefore, unjust and intolerable.

Because of these factors, discrimination on the basis of age appears to be more subtle and elusive than racism or sexism. Therefore it could be more difficult to control or eliminate. It should also be noted that age discrimination depends on the visibility of the undesirable trait. Ethnic minority group members who do not look as if they belong to their respective minority groups escape the effects of discrimination. Likewise, the elderly who "do not look their age" escape the consequences of age discrimination.[13]

ROLE SOCIALIZATION

Americans have been socialized to devalue the capabilities of the aged, and this devaluation is reflected in the operation of our social institutions. Restrictions of various kinds are placed on the opportunities available to older persons, for example, the necessity to retire at a certain age or the inability to procure a mortgage. All of these political, legal, and economic barriers have had the result of underutilizing the skills, talents, and capabilities of the aged.

Before we examine some of the major role changes experienced by people in later life, it should be pointed out that the elderly population is not a homogeneous mass with little differences between its members. This group is highly heterogeneous. As we have seen, elderly black women, for example, contend with situations that are quite different from those experienced by elderly white men. However, despite their many differences in sex, race, etc., the aged as a group play particular roles in society.

Just as societies prescribe particular roles for women and blacks, they also prescribe particular rights, duties, obligations, and roles for people solely on the basis of age. The ascribed role of "older person" is generally not associated with such characteristics as prestige, status, wealth, or power. This does not mean that no elderly people have these characteristics, it means that "when an older person has wealth or prestige or influence, it is because he simultaneously occupies some other position to which these benefits are attached."[14] Margaret Mead had much prestige in our society, not because she was old, but because she was a famous social scientist. In some cultures old age, per se, can be prestigious, but not in ours.

In any event, the society's expectations of a person and that person's behavior are closely related to the position he or she occupies in society. The roles associated with becoming old are negatively valued in America, and there are very few, if any, desirable rewards for obtaining the position of "old person." Yet, all people, if they live to old age, experience various role changes, which we will briefly examine in the next section, that accompany later life.[15]

Elderly roles are negatively valued in America

THE DEPENDENCE ROLE

One new role the aged in America experience is characterized by dependence. Many older people fear becoming physically or financially dependent on others after being self-sufficient and independent for many years. In the family, it can mean role reversals between parent and child. With the parent now having to depend on the child, anger, frustration, and guilt may develop on the part of both. The parent "may feel guilty because he feels he shouldn't be dependent. The child, now an adult, may also resent having to provide for both his own children and his parent, yet, he may feel guilty for having this resentment. And . . . the child's spouse may not willingly accept the diversion of family resources to the aged parent."[16]

Fear of becoming dependent

The dependence role, especially financial dependence, is played by millions of American aged. Various authorities have indicated that income is a major problem of the elderly in America.[16] In 1976, according to the Census Bureau, 15 percent (more than 3.3 million people) of the elderly population were living below the poverty level. This represents a drop in the number of elderly poor from the 1959 figure of 5.5 million, or 35 percent. Of course, there are a number of problems with these governmental statistics, as noted in the chapter on poverty. However, it is accurate to state that in 1976 the average income for households with a head 65 years of age or older was $8,708. This is a considerably lower figure than the one for households with heads 55 to 64 years old, which was $16,115 in 1976.[17]

Income can drop 40 to 50 percent or more at retirement. As the elderly become even older, income continues to decline. Very few of the aged have significant income from assets such as rents, interests, and dividends from investments. Since only a few million elderly are in the paid labor force (less than three million, or 14.1 percent of the aged), few of them draw money from earnings. Where then do the elderly get their money? For the great majority of aged Americans, Social Security is the major source of income.[18]

Income declines with age

Social Security is a major
source of income

Over 9.4 million men received average monthly retirement benefits of $248 through OASDHI. Over 7.7 million women received monthly payments of $197. Social Security benefits have been increasing and now contain cost-of-living provisions, but they still do not keep up with inflation. The payments for those elderly who have no other source of income do little more than keep them at subsistence levels. Besides, although incomes for the aged have increased, when compared to those of the general population, the incomes of the aged have basically remained the same. Census data also indicate that retirement incomes are still out of line with pre-retirement levels. This leads to one of the most important role changes accompanying old age, the shift from the role of worker to the role of retiree.[19]

THE RETIREMENT ROLE AND PENSIONS

The shift from worker
to retiree

The institution of mandatory retirement affects other aspects of a person's life. With retirement, there is also the loss of occupational identity, which for many provides the "social substance by which other identities are maintained, various roles are coordinated, and the appropriateness of social activity is substantiated." Every year thousands of Americans are forced or choose to retire from the labor force. For many elderly Americans, the retirement period they have been anticipating becomes a serious problem.[20]

Many cultures have institutionalized roles for the elderly; America does not, and each retiree must create a new life style. For those who can afford it, there are the leisure communities, with golf courses, swimming pools, and horse trails. Many wealthy older Americans make the adjustment to this leisurely life. However, for others the swimming and golfing routine becomes monotonous. A *Newsweek* article on "Growing Old Happy" quotes a restless retiree as follows: "If you play golf or pool five times a week for a couple of months, it becomes a pain in the neck." For those who cannot afford the costs or for those who are unable to move from their old neighborhoods because of friends, relatives, or a poor housing market, joining a leisure retirement community in Florida or California is not an alternative.

According to the Census Bureau, almost two-thirds of the aged live in metropolitan areas. Many of the aged poor live in highly concentrated urban communities. These high concentrations of elderly urban poor can turn into

"Geriatric ghettos"

"geriatric ghettos."[21] One report notes that,

> In New York City . . . apartment rentals are so high (37 per cent above the national average) that fully one-third of the over-60 population lives in the city's 26 poorest neighborhoods, where the risk of mugging, rape and murder is a constant worry. In Miami Beach, Fla., where a majority of the 90,000 residents are over-65 pensioners, some of the elderly have become a public nuisance. Though actual crime runs mainly to jay-walking and shoplifting, police find that they must maintain lists of senile residents who stray from home, unable to remember who they are or where they live.[22]

Obviously then, the life-style of the retiree is related to income.

Prior to retirement, many elderly believe that the pension plans provided by their employers will provide them with sufficient income to live comfortably. However, because private pensions are a relatively new development in America, and because most retired elderly did not work under pension plans (or work long enough under the plans) very little income is received by the aged from this source. Pension plans developed out of a need for money beyond what was available through Social Security. Unfortunately, many pension plans fail for those who retire, because the old **Many pension plans fail** employers go out of business. Also, there is the problem of nontransferability, which means that retirement credits cannot be transferred from one pension plan to another. In other words, if the worker changes jobs, all earned retirement credits are lost.[23] The Department of Labor summarizes the problem as follows: "In all too many cases the pension promise shrinks **The pension promise** to this: 'If you remain in good health and stay with the same company until you are sixty-five years old, and if the company is still in business, and if your department has not been abolished, and if you haven't been laid off for too long a period, and if there is enough money in the fund, and if that money has been prudently managed, you will get a pension.' "[24] The integrity of employer pension plans is further addressed in the Califano reading.

Until the recent trend to eliminate the mandatory age-65 retirement policy, it appeared that early retirement would continue. If it lasts, the trend to abolish forced retirement may increase the number of elderly in the work force and therefore increase their aggregate income, which has been on the decline.

As people grow old, then, their income drops sharply, especially at retirement. The only significant income the majority of our aged receive comes from Social Security, and this means that several million of our elderly are living at or near poverty levels. For those aged who have limited economic resources, there is poor housing, inadequate food and clothing, little, if any, travel or entertainment, and most important, poor health care.

HEALTH CARE AND INSTITUTIONALIZATION
Health is an important factor in all of our lives, although many of us take it for granted. When we are not in good health, it is difficult to perform our various social roles and to have a satisfying, successful life.

Gerontologists note that as old age advances, health becomes an impor- **The influence of health** tant influence on participation in the community, in the family, and on the job. Health needs "absorb a larger amount and proportion of a person's income as he grows older."[25] It is obvious that health is a major influence on the elderly's situation, just as it is for all ages. At this point, we will note some of the health problems of the aged, keeping in mind that the broader health care problems and programs for health improvement are examined in the chapter dealing with health care in America.

Most of the aged have what are termed chronic conditions. These long-term permanent conditions "leave residual disability, or require special training for rehabilitation, or may be expected to require a long period of supervision, observation, or care."[26] Examples of chronic problems are heart disease, high blood pressure, diabetes, and arthritis. More than 80 percent of all men and women between 65 and 74 years of age have at least one chronic condition. For people younger than 45, the figure drops to 35 percent.[27] In addition, about 3.5 million people 65 and older have some type of mobility limitation, caused by a chronic condition. About one-third of these people must be confined to the house and need the assistance of another person or a wheelchair.[28]

The duration of health problems increases with age so that those older than 65 report twice as many "time restricted" periods than do people 45 to 64 years old. "Time restricted" periods are those times when a person cannot perform the most necessary activities and work.[29] This restriction of a major activity is called disability. Disability and impairment are often the result of chronic conditions. Rates of impairments on sight, hearing, speech, etc., per 1000 increased from 212 for those between 45 and 64 to over 615 for those people older than 75. It should be noted, however, that old age does not automatically mean illness and disability. Many older people are in good health. On the other hand, chronic illness, impairments, and disability increase steadily with age and constitute serious problems for older people.[30]

Activity limitations of the aged

People 65 years old and older are much more likely to have limitation of activity because of a physical or health condition. They have a higher average number of restricted activity days and bed disability days. Of the total national population, only 13 percent have activity limitations; that rate jumps to 43 percent of the elderly population.[31] Because of the activity limitations of the elderly, and because many of the elderly do not have people around who can care for their needs, many older people must turn to nursing homes.

Few aged live in institutions

Occasionally, news programs, investigating committees, and governmental leaders will report the many problems and negative aspects of America's nursing homes and institutions for the aged. However, 96 percent of the aged do not live in institutionalized settings. In fact, more than 85 percent of the aged *older* than 85 are not institutionalized. Many who are in nursing and personal care homes have, of course, physical and mental impairments. However, impairment is not necessarily related to institutionalization.[32]

Studies indicate that institutionalization rates present an inaccurate account of the elderly's overall health status, because those rates include the nonimpaired, nondisabled, and healthy aged who live in homes. Gerontologists note that in nursing homes, "about half of the older patients are ambulatory and continent; while in mental hospitals, the proportion reaches upwards of 80 percent."[33]

While many older people continue to lead active lives, others suffer physical or mental deterioration and spend their final years in nursing homes.

Abigail Heyman, Magnum Photos, Inc.

This low percentage of older people in nursing homes in no way denies the negative effects those institutions have on the several hundred thousand aged who are confined in them. Many in the homes believe them to be places where you go to die. And, in fact, that is what often happens. This is especially true during the first year, when mortality rates are much higher in nursing homes than they are in private residences. This is at least partially due to the fact that older people are often encouraged to go to the home because of sickness. If they do survive, there is a severe loss of personal control and little, if any, privacy. Restrictive rules control most of the daily routine, such as when to eat, sleep, and bathe.

The physical facilities are generally inadequate and few have provisions for activities. Staffing of homes is poor, and those staff members who are there are poorly trained. Cut off from the community in this "last place to go," the aged find that dehumanization is common and excused "on the grounds of administrative and medical necessity."[34]

Nursing homes are "where you go to die"

Whether older people are institutionalized depends on the family system and the residential setting. Residential setting refers to the living situation prior to institutionalization, and is important since there is a tendency for those who lived alone to be placed in homes. If there is financial ability, and if relatives are willing to help care for their aged kin, many elderly are able to stay out of nursing and personal care homes.

The aged in nursing and personal care homes, then, tend not to have children, or a spouse. It is the breakdown in the family support system that "appears to be the primary cause of institutionalization among older people."[35]

THE PROBLEMS OF BEING OLD AND FEMALE

In the reading, "The Double Standard of Aging," Susan Sontag examines the problems of being old and female in American society. The variables of sex and age, as we have seen, are important factors in our social relationships. Sontag examines the reasons why our society offers few rewards to women who are aging. In fact, for a majority of women, aging means a "humiliating process of gradual disqualification," because they were taught as children to view the process of aging as objectionable. This, in turn, has major consequences in their lives.

SONTAG READING——OBJECTIVES:

1. To examine in an essay at least three of the problems experienced by elderly women in American society.
2. To discuss in an essay whether older men and women experience the same kinds of problems.

The Double Standard of Aging
SUSAN SONTAG

"How old are you?" The person asking the question is anybody. The respondent is a woman, a woman "of a certain age," as the French say discreetly. That age might be anywhere from her early twenties to her late fifties. If the question is impersonal—routine information requested when she applies for a driver's license, a credit card, a passport—she will probably force herself to answer truthfully. Filling out a marriage license application, if her future husband is even slightly her junior, she may long to subtract a few years; probably she won't. Competing for a job, her chances often partly depend on being the "right age," and if hers isn't right, she will lie if she thinks she can get away with it. Making her first

Reprinted by permission of *Saturday Review*, September 23, 1972. Copyright ©
1972 Saturday Review, Inc.

visit to a new doctor, perhaps feeling particularly vulnerable at the moment she's asked, she will probably hurry through the correct answer. But if the question is only what people call personal—if she's asked by a new friend, a casual acquaintance, a neighbor's child, a co-worker in an office, store, factory—her response is harder to predict. She may side-step the question with a joke or refuse it with playful indignation. "Don't you know you're not supposed to ask a woman her age?" Or, hesitating a moment, embarrassed but defiant, she may tell the truth. Or she may lie. But neither truth, evasion, nor lie relieves the unpleasantness of that question. For a woman to be obliged to state her age, after "a certain age," is always a miniature ordeal.

If the question comes from a woman, she will feel less threatened than if it comes from a man. Other women are, after all, comrades in sharing the same potential for humiliation. She will be less arch, less coy. But she probably still dislikes answering and may not tell the truth. Bureaucratic formalities excepted, whoever asks a woman this question—after "a certain age"—is ignoring a taboo and possibly being impolite or downright hostile. Almost everyone acknowledges that once she passes an age that is, actually, quite young, a woman's exact age ceases to be a legitimate target of curiosity. After childhood the year of a woman's birth becomes her secret, her private property. It is something of a dirty secret. To answer truthfully is always indiscreet.

The discomfort a woman feels each time she tells her age is quite independent of the anxious awareness of human mortality that everyone has, from time to time. There is a normal sense in which nobody, men and women alike, relishes growing older. After thirty-five any mention of one's age carries with it the reminder that one is probably closer to the end of one's life than to the beginning. There is nothing unreasonable in that anxiety. Nor is there any abnormality in the anguish and anger that people who are really old, in their seventies and eighties, feel about the implacable waning of their powers, physical and mental. Advanced age is undeniably a trial, however stoically it may be endured. It is a shipwreck, no matter with what courage elderly people insist on continuing the voyage. But the objective, sacred pain of old age is of another order than the subjective, profane pain of aging. Old age is a genuine ordeal, one that men and women undergo in a similar way. Growing older is mainly an ordeal of the imagination—a moral disease, a social pathology—intrinsic to which is the fact that it afflicts women much more than men. It is particularly women who experience growing older (everything that comes *before* one is actually old) with such distaste and even shame.

The emotional privileges this society confers upon youth stir up some anxiety about getting older in everybody. All modern urbanized societies—unlike tribal, rural societies—condescend to the values of maturity and heap honors on the joys of youth. This revaluation of the life cycle in favor of the young brilliantly serves a secular society whose idols are ever-increasing industrial productivity and the unlimited cannibalization of nature. Such a society must create a new sense of the rhythms of life in order to incite people to buy more, to consume and throw away faster. People let the direct awareness they have of their needs, of what really gives them pleasure, be overruled by commercialized *images* of happiness and personal well-being; and, in this imagery designed to stimulate ever more avid levels of consumption, the most popular metaphor for happiness is "youth." (I would

> Old age is a genuine ordeal

insist that it is a metaphor, not a literal description. Youth is a metaphor for energy, restless mobility, appetite: for the state of "wanting.") This equating of well-being with youth makes everyone naggingly aware of exact age—one's own and that of other people. In primitive and premodern societies people attach much less importance to dates. When lives are divided into long periods with stable responsibilities and steady ideals (and hypocrisies), the exact number of years someone has lived becomes a trivial fact; there is hardly any reason to mention, even to know, the year in which one was born. Most people in nonindustrial societies are not sure exactly how old they are. People in industrial societies are haunted by numbers. They take an almost obsessional interest in keeping the score card of aging, convinced that anything above a low total is some kind of bad news. In an era in which people actually live longer and longer, what now amounts to the latter *two-thirds* of everyone's life is shadowed by a poignant apprehension of unremitting loss.

The prestige of youth afflicts everyone in this society to some degree. Men, too, are prone to periodic bouts of depression about aging—for instance, when feeling insecure or unfulfilled or insufficiently rewarded in their jobs. But men rarely panic about aging in the way women often do. Getting older is less profoundly wounding for a man, for in addition to the propaganda for youth that puts both men and women on the defensive as they age, there is a double standard about aging that denounces women with special severity. Society is much more permissive about aging in men, as it is more tolerant of the sexual infidelities of husbands. Men are "allowed" to age, without penalty, in several ways that women are not.

American society offers few rewards to aging women

This society offers even fewer rewards for aging to women than it does to men. Being physically attractive counts much more in a woman's life than in a man's, but beauty, identified, as it is for women, with youthfulness, does not stand up well to age. Exceptional mental powers can increase with age, but women are rarely encouraged to develop their minds above dilettante standards. Because the wisdom considered the special province of women is "eternal," an age-old, intuitive knowledge about the emotions to which a repertoire of facts, worldly experience, and the methods of rational analysis have nothing to contribute, living a long time does not promise women an increase in wisdom either. The private skills expected of women are exercised early and, with the exception of a talent for making love, are not the kind that enlarge with experience. "Masculinity" is identified with competence, autonomy, self-control—qualities which the disappearance of youth does not threaten. Competence in most of the activities expected from men, physical sports excepted, increases with age. "Femininity" is identified with incompetence, helplessness, passivity, noncompetitiveness, being nice. Age does not improve these qualities.

Middle-class men feel diminished by aging, even while still young, if they have not yet shown distinction in their careers or made a lot of money. (And any tendencies they have toward hypochondria will get worse in middle age, focusing with particular nervousness on the specter of heart attacks and the loss of virility.) Their aging crisis is linked to that terrible pressure on men to be "successful" that precisely defines their membership in the middle class. Women rarely feel anxious about their age because they haven't succeeded at something. The work that women do outside the home rarely counts as a form of achievement, only as a way of earning money; most employment available to women mainly exploits the training they have been receiving since early childhood to be servile, to be both supportive and parasitical, to be unadventurous. They can have menial, low-skilled jobs in light industries, which offer as feeble a criterion of success as housekeeping. They can be secretaries, clerks, sales personnel, maids, research assistants, waitresses, social workers, prostitutes, nurses, teachers, telephone operators—public transcriptions of the servicing and nurturing roles that women have in family life. Women fill very few executive posts, are rarely found suitable for large corporate or political responsibilities, and form only a tiny contingent in the liberal professions (apart from teaching). They are virtually barred from jobs that involve an expert, intimate relation with machines or an aggressive use of the body, or that carry any physical risk or sense of adventure. The jobs this society deems appropriate to women are auxiliary, "calm" activities that do not compete with, but aid, what men do. Besides being less well paid, most work women do has a lower ceiling of advancement and gives meager outlet to normal wishes to be powerful. All outstanding work by women in this society is voluntary; most women are too inhibited by the social disapproval attached to their being ambitious and aggressive. Inevitably, women are exempted from the dreary panic of middle-aged men whose "achievements" seem paltry, who feel stuck on the job ladder or fear being pushed off it by someone younger. But they are also denied most of the real satisfactions that men derive from work—satisfactions that often do increase with age.

The double standard about aging shows up most brutally in the conventions of sexual feeling, which presuppose a disparity between men and women that operates permanently to women's disadvantage. In the accepted course of events a woman anywhere from her late teens through her middle twenties can expect to attract a man more or less her own age. (Ideally, he should be at least slightly older.) They marry and raise a family. But if her husband starts an affair after some years of marriage, he customarily does so with a woman much younger than his wife. Suppose, when both husband and wife are already in their late forties or early fifties, they divorce. The husband has an excellent chance of getting married again, probably to a younger woman. His ex-wife finds it difficult to remarry. Attracting a second husband younger than herself is improbable; even to find someone her own age she has to be lucky, and she will probably have to settle for a man considerably older than herself, in his sixties or seventies. Women become sexually ineligible much earlier than men do. A man, even an ugly man, can remain eligible well into old age. He is an acceptable mate for a young, attractive woman. Women, even good-looking women, become ineligible (except as partners of very old men) at a much younger age.

Thus, for most women, aging means a humiliating process of gradual sexual disqualification. Since women are considered maximally eligible in early youth, after which their sexual value drops steadily, even young women feel themselves in a desperate race against the calendar. They are old as soon as they are no longer very young. In late adolescence some girls are already worrying about getting married. Boys and young men have little reason to anticipate trouble because of aging. What makes men desirable to women is by no means tied to youth. On the contrary, getting older tends (for several decades) to operate in men's favor, since their value as lovers and husbands is set more by what they do than how

Aging means sexual disqualification

they look. Many men have more success romantically at forty than they did at twenty or twenty-five; fame, money, and, above all, power are sexually enhancing. (A woman who has won power in a competitive profession or business career is considered less, rather than more, desirable. Most men confess themselves intimidated or turned off sexually by such a woman, obviously because she is harder to treat as just a sexual "object.") As they age, men may start feeling anxious about actual sexual performance, worrying about a loss of sexual vigor or even impotence, but their sexual eligibility is not abridged simply by getting older. Men stay sexually possible as long as they can make love. Women are at a disadvantage because their sexual candidacy depends on meeting certain much stricter "conditions" related to looks and age.

Since women are imagined to have much more limited sexual lives than men do, a woman who has never married is pitied. She was not found acceptable, and it is assumed that her life continues to confirm her unacceptability. Her presumed lack of sexual opportunity is embarrassing. A man who remains a bachelor is judged much less crudely. It is assumed that he, at any age, still has a sexual life —or the chance of one. For men there is no destiny equivalent to the humiliating condition of being an old maid, a spinster. "Mr.," a cover from infancy to senility, precisely exempts men from the stigma that attaches to any woman, no longer young, who is still "Miss." (That women are divided into "Miss" and "Mrs.," which calls unrelenting attention to the situation of each woman with respect to marriage, reflects the belief that being single or married is much more decisive for a woman than it is for a man.)

Men do not experience spinsterhood

For a woman who is no longer very young, there is certainly some relief when she has finally been able to marry. Marriage soothes the sharpest pain she feels about the passing years. But her anxiety never subsides completely, for she knows that should she re-enter the sexual market at a later date—because of divorce, or the death of her husband, or the need for erotic adventure—she must do so under a handicap far greater than any man of her age (*whatever* her age may be) and regardless of how good-looking she is. Her achievements, if she has a career, are no asset. The calendar is the final arbiter.

To be sure, the calendar is subject to some variations from country to country. In Spain, Portugal, and the Latin American countries, the age at which most women are ruled physically undesirable comes earlier than in the United States. In France it is somewhat later. French conventions of sexual feeling make a quasi-official place for the woman between thirty-five and forty-five. Her role is to initiate an inexperienced or timid young man, after which she is, of course, replaced by a young girl. (Colette's novella *Chéri* is the best-known account in fiction of such a love affair; biographies of Balzac relate a well-documented example from real life.) This sexual myth does make turning forty somewhat easier for French women. But there is no difference in any of these countries in the basic attitudes that disqualify women sexually much earlier than men.

Aging varies with social class

Aging also varies according to social class. Poor people look old much earlier in their lives than do rich people. But anxiety about aging is certainly more common, and more acute, among middle-class and rich women than among working-class women. Economically disadvantaged women in this society are more fatalistic about aging; they can't afford to fight the cosmetic battle as long or as tenaciously. Indeed, nothing so clearly indicates the fictional nature of this crisis than the fact that women who keep their youthful appearance the longest—women who lead unstrenuous, physically sheltered lives, who eat balanced meals, who can afford good medical care, who have few or no children—are those who feel the defeat of age most keenly. Aging is much more a social judgment than a biological eventuality. Far more extensive than the hard sense of loss suffered during menopause (which, with increased longevity, tends to arrive later and later) is the depression about aging, which may not be set off by any real event in a woman's life, but is a recurrent state of "possession" of her imagination, ordained by society—that is, ordained by the way this society limits how women feel free to imagine themselves.

There is a model account of the aging crisis in Richard Strauss's sentimental-ironic opera *Der Rosenkavalier*, whose heroine is a wealthy and glamorous married woman who decides to renounce romance. After a night with her adoring young lover, the Marschallin has a sudden, unexpected confrontation with herself. It is toward the end of Act I; Octavian has just left. Alone in her bedroom she sits at her dressing table, as she does every morning. It is the daily ritual of self-appraisal practiced by every woman. She looks at herself and, appalled, begins to weep. Her youth is over. Note that the Marschallin does not discover, looking in the mirror, that she is ugly. She is as beautiful as ever. The Marschallin's discovery is moral—that is, it is a discovery of her imagination; it is nothing she actually *sees*. Nevertheless, her discovery is no less devastating. Bravely, she makes her painful, gallant decision. She will arrange for her beloved Octavian to fall in love with a girl his own age. She must be realistic. She is no longer eligible. She is now "the old Marschallin."

Strauss wrote the opera in 1910. Contemporary operagoers are rather shocked when they discover that the libretto indicates that the Marschallin is all of thirty-four years old; today the role is generally sung by a soprano well into her forties or in her fifties. Acted by an attractive singer of thirty-four, the Marschallin's sorrow would seem merely neurotic, or even ridiculous. Few women today think of themselves as old, wholly disqualified from romance, at thirty-four. The age of retirement has moved up, in line with the sharp rise in life expectancy for everybody in the last few generations. The *form* in which women experience their lives remains unchanged. A moment approaches inexorably when they must resign themselves to being "too old." And that moment is invariably—objectively—premature.

In earlier generations the renunciation came even sooner. Fifty years ago a woman of forty was not just aging but old, finished. No struggle was even possible. Today, the surrender to aging no longer has a fixed date. The aging crisis (I am speaking only of women in affluent countries) starts earlier but lasts longer; it is diffused over most of a woman's life. A woman hardly has to be anything like what would reasonably be considered old to worry about her age, to start lying (or being tempted to lie).

The crisis can come at any time. Their schedule depends on a blend of personal ("neurotic") vulnerability and the swing of social mores. Some women don't have their first crisis until thirty. No one escapes a sickening shock upon turning forty. Each birthday, but especially those ushering in a new decade—for round numbers have a special authority—sounds a new defeat. There is almost as much pain in the anticipation as in the reality. Twenty-nine has become a queasy age

The crisis can come at any time

ever since the official end of youth crept forward, about a generation ago, to thirty. Being thirty-nine is also hard; a whole year in which to meditate in glum astonishment that one stands on the threshold of middle age. The frontiers are arbitrary, but not any less vivid for that. Although a woman on her fortieth birthday is hardly different from what she was when she was still thirty-nine, the day seems like a turning point. But long before actually becoming a woman of forty, she has been steeling herself against the depression she will feel. One of the greatest tragedies of each woman's life is simply getting older; it is certainly the *longest* tragedy.

Aging is a movable doom

Aging is a movable doom. It is a crisis that never exhausts itself, because the anxiety is never really used up. Being a crisis of the imagination rather than of "real life," it has the habit of repeating itself again and again. The territory of aging (as opposed to actual old age) has no fixed boundaries. Up to a point it can be defined as one wants. Entering each decade—after the initial shock is absorbed—an endearing, desperate impulse of survival helps many women to stretch the boundaries to the decade following. In late adolescence thirty seems the end of life. At thirty, one pushes the sentence forward to forty. At forty, one still gives oneself ten more years.

EXPLANATIONS OF AGISM

There is a broad variety of explanations attempting to account for the various inequities experienced by the aged in America. Many of the explanations examined in the previous chapter on racism and sexism, such as the sociocultural and economic, can help account for some inequities. For example, the sociocultural explanation accounts for age prejudice in terms of the folkways and mores of society. Prejudices are among the learned ways of responding, which have been acquired as part of the standard cultural equipment through socialization. In the field of social gerontology, however, several other theoretical explanations have been developed in an effort to explain many of the problems experienced by the aged.

Minority group theory

"MINORITY GROUP" THEORY

One important explanation to consider has been termed "minority group" theory.[36] This explanation states that the elderly experience discrimination because they share the common biological characteristics of old age, just as blacks share the same race and women share the same sex.

Prejudice and stereotypes are the basis for discrimination

The "minority group" approach notes that the undesired trait (being old, for example) must be visible for discrimination to occur. Blacks who are able to pass for whites escape racial discrimination, and aged people who do not appear to be old avoid age discrimination.[37] This approach also indicates that the prejudices and stereotypes of the aged function as a basis for discrimination against them. There are differences in individual situations, but the aged in America experience many of the same problems experienced by other minority groups, such as low social status, unequal opportunities in the work world, and low income.

The "minority group" explanation is closely related to the subcultural theory of social gerontology. This theory explains the aged as a subculture whose members share being old, being categorically responded to in a negative manner, and in many respects, being forced to interact only with other older people.[38] However, the three most prevalent explanations of agism in the field of social gerontology are *disengagement, activity,* and *continuity*.

Subcultural theory of gerontology

DISENGAGEMENT, ACTIVITY, AND CONTINUITY THEORIES

Disengagement is defined as a gradual and inevitable process in which people reduce the number of new interpersonal relationships and make changes in the remaining relationships. In addition, they also become separated from their social roles. This explanation is based on people's mortality. Society, in order to continue and survive, must find a way to accomplish the transfer of power from the old to the young. The disengagement process fills this need. The probability of death increases with aging, and the disengagement approach indicates that "at some point it no longer pays society to rely on the services of those who are about to die. For this reason it is profitable for society to phase out those whose possible contributions are outweighed by the possible disruption their deaths would cause to the smooth operation of society."[39]

Disengagement: An inevitable process

Gerontologists indicate that this theory is actually two theories, one applying to the individual, the other to society. Both are held to be mutually desirable and inevitable. The elderly disengage from society out of a desire to turn their attention inward; society disengages "from older people in order to replace its inefficient members and avoid disruption as the probability of death increases." Although this theory has generated much research, it is limited because the norms of societal disengagement are inoperative in some social institutions, such as American politics. Also, individual disengagement is often quite selective; people frequently withdraw only from certain roles. Another complaint is that it is simplistic and needs more complex explanatory models.[40]

A separation from social roles

Activity theory states that the norms for both middle and old age are the same, and that the elderly should be evaluated by middle-aged standards.[41] This theory is based on the idea that the elderly deny old age as long as possible and believe themselves to be successful if they act and function as do middle-aged people. A primary assumption of activity theory is that the process of aging is a continual battle to stay middle-aged. Research indicates that the great majority of the aged believe themselves to be middle-aged, not old.[42] However, a problem with this theory is that it does not deal with those elderly who cannot maintain middle-aged standards.

Activity: Denial of old age

Continuity theory is based on the idea that experiences people have in life create the predisposition to maintain, if possible, those same experiences, such as having particular friends, living in a certain neighborhood, and shopping and working in one place. In other words, as people become old,

Continuity theory

they are predisposed to maintaining continuity in the preferences, habits, and associations that have developed over the years.[43] The theory's basic premise is that "people will stay the same unless there is a reason for change." Advocates of this theory note that the reasons for change "should be sought in the relationships among the individual's biological and psychological capabilities, his personal habits, preferences, and associations, his experiences, and his situational opportunities."[44]

RESPONSES TO AGISM

Many problems are social

In the past decade, America's aged have come to realize that many of the problems they experience are social rather than individual in nature. Therefore, these problems are in need of social remedies.

For many years, the aged have been rarely visible and only occasionally heard in our society. Many aged still accept youth and middle-aged domination in order to survive. Their acceptance is a conditioned reaction to our society's age prejudice. Many aged Americans still avoid situations in which they might experience prejudice and discrimination. They will often shy away from potentially humiliating or debasing situations. Others, instead of avoiding contact with younger people, will attempt to integrate with them.

The aged's response has shifted

Recently, however, the elderly's response to agism has shifted, from accep-

No longer willing to tolerate discrimination against the elderly, Maggie Kuhn and the Gray Panthers use some tactics of other civil rights groups to fight agism.

tance, avoidance, and assimilation to aggressive action. The aged in the 1970s have begun to agitate for legislative changes and a variety of other social actions. As they become a more vocal, visible, and larger group, the aged will become an increasingly powerful force.

Because of their many years' experience in dealing with society, the aged have learned how to effectively organize. The American Association of Retired Persons (AARP) alone has more than twelve million members. Other such organizations, when combining their efforts and strength, can forcefully make their needs and concerns known to bureaucrats, political leaders, and businesspeople. There are also more political organizations, such as the Gray Panthers and Senior Power. These have aggressively lobbied many government legislatures for the passage of bills, covering housing and tax relief needs, the right to work, and the use of generic drugs in prescription filling.

FEDERAL INTERVENTION

The federal government's intervention in the many problems of the aged began with the passage of the Social Security Act in 1935. This act established old age and survivor's insurance. It was significant also because it bypassed state and local governments and dealt directly with individual citizens. According to social scientist Fred Cottrell, Social Security was treated from the beginning as "something outside politics, not to be administered in the same way as other Federal programs."[45] The program gained a reputation for reliability and provided security that was never before known to aged Americans. Social Security's efforts to raise the aged's living standards were based on a political rationale that "maintained that society had a responsibility to those members least able to help themselves."[46]

The Railroad Retirement system was initiated at about the same time as Social Security. The Civil Service also initiated pensions for the government's civilian employees. Military pensions, like Social Security, also represented a direct government service to a particular class of aged. Together, these systems represent the federal government's major efforts to deal directly with the aged's problems. Cottrell says that "the rest is done by programs that are joint national and state efforts, or they result from programs, like Housing or Health, which serve people regardless of their age."[47]

WHITE HOUSE CONFERENCES

The federal government has also responded to the problems of the aged in the form of three major White House conferences. Such meetings provided the setting for various "widely divergent organizations to combine their experience, knowledge, and influence for the resolution of a single problem."[48] The first conference, called by President Truman in 1950, studied the elderly's problems and made recommendations that functioned as guide-

The Social Security Act

lines for future programs and actions. However, the problems of the aged were not resolved then and became even worse. In 1961, the White House Conference on Aging was held at the request of President Eisenhower.* This conference also made a series of recommendations, which became guidelines for increases in Social Security benefits and for the establishment of Medicare. Also from these recommendations, the Older Americans Act (OAA) established in 1965 the Administration on Aging in Washington, D.C.

The Administration on Aging

During the 1960s various research projects were developed to further study the aged's problems. Other programs trained manpower to serve the aged and provided health care and related social services. Many aged were helped by these programs. More insistent problems developed, however. The diminishing value of the elderly's income due to inflation, the increasing costs of medical services (which forced Medicare to pay for less), and the steady increase in taxes, particularly on property, have drastically reduced the elderly's fixed incomes. These problems, combined with a downgrading of the Commission on Aging, a reorganization of the Department of Health, Education, and Welfare, and a diversion of OAA research to nonaging purposes, led to a demand for another conference.[49]

The 1971 conference

Unlike the previous meetings, the 1971 White House Conference on Aging reflects the desires and needs of the aged themselves, who participated through local and community forums. Its theme was "Toward a National Policy on Aging." The issues and problems discussed reflected a consensus on the "needed changes in planning and policy that derive from the present status of older people in American Society."[50] Specific needs of the aged, as reported by them, were discussed, the means necessary to achieve these ends were examined, and recommendations were made.

Many issues and recommendations developed from the 1971 conference.[51] With respect to income and work, the conference recommended that the aged be given tax relief and a cash income at a respectable standard of living. It was also recommended that they be allowed to have increased earnings without penalty under Social Security. The necessity of increased efforts in order to eliminate age discrimination in jobs and to utilize the aged's talents in public jobs was also stressed.

Recommendations of the 1971 conference

Pertaining to retirement, the conference recommended that retirement ages be flexible and that the elderly be given a free choice between continuing to work, if able, and retiring on an adequate income with opportunity for meaningful activity. The conference also emphasized the need for private pension plans that are solvent and provide for survivor benefits. In the areas of physical and mental health, the conference called for the expansion of the present health care delivery systems to include long-term health care, preventive medicine, rehabilitation services, and special needs (such as

* Requested prior to his leaving office.

optical services). It also recommended the development of adequate and appropriate alternatives to institutional care.[52]

Recommendations were also made in other important areas, such as housing, education, spiritual well-being, nutrition, and transportation. Much concern was also voiced in the areas of planning, research, training, and the interest of government and nongovernment organizations.

All the results of this White House Conference on Aging are too complex and numerous to list. Cottrell notes, however, that the thrust of what was brought up "would result in greatly increased centralization and demand increased funding." He also notes that in the "Year of action"—provided by the Conference—in 1972, materials and information were collected which indicated that the conference had influenced all levels of government: Social Security payments were substantially increased (by 20 percent); the Administration on Aging was appropriately restored in the office of the Secretary; and appropriations larger than those originally proposed by the Administration on Aging (although still relatively small) were passed.[53]

Political leaders, decision makers, and planners are aware of the aged's problems in America. Implementation of the White House conference recommendations, however, is a matter of politics. The aged and their supporters still have to develop and exert sufficient political pressure on political leaders in order to obtain the desired results. The question we might ask is, "How do social scientists view the political power of the aged in America?"

The aged and political power

There is a variety of views concerning this matter. Some people view the aged as a category that is developing into a subculture.[54] Others view the aged as a pressure group influencing legislators. Still others consider the "problems of aging as the central focus for the formation of a social movement that involves not only older people but people of all ages in an attempt to solve these problems." Atchley believes that action on behalf of the aged depends on political support from organizations, such as unions and political parties, that are not based on age. "The role of old age interest groups is to make the need for action highly visible." He notes also that "if, once the need is visible, the cause is not picked up by a broad-based organization, little action is likely to result." He concludes that the aged "have little genuine political power of their own."[55]

At this point, we will examine some of the activity that has taken place on behalf of the aged as a result of their becoming more vocal and visible and of their having received more political support.

FEDERAL PROGRAMS

During the past several years, there has been an increase in activities and efforts on behalf of the aged. Private, educational, and government organizations and institutions have developed many advocacy, research, and participatory programs. Some researchers note that the challenge facing plan-

The challenge facing planners

ners concerned with the aged's problems can be viewed from *socioeconomic*, *psychosocial*, and *community* perspectives.[56] The socioeconomic perspective asks how the society will meet the financial, medical, housing, and social service needs of the aged. The psychosocial perspective asks what programs, policies, and attitudes will be required in order for the aged to play social roles and engage in activities that meet their social needs. The community perspective asks how the skills and knowledge of the aged will best be used to benefit the community; it also asks for the aged to become producers, not just consumers, of service.

The Foster Grandparent Program (FGP), the Senior Companion Program (SCP), and the Retired Senior Volunteer Program (RSVP) are all administered under the Older American's Volunteer Programs (OAVP) of ACTION, the Federal Volunteer Agency established in 1971 under the authority of the Older Americans Act. Bowles states that FGP, SCP, and RSVP are "all designed to provide meaningful work roles for older persons during their retirement years, to relieve the effects of poverty, and improve human services, using the skills, experience and talents of older persons as a resource to meet community needs and to enable them to enjoy the self-respect and satisfaction that comes from being needed and serving others."[57]

FGP: The aged help children; SCP: The aged help the aged

Under the Foster Grandparent Program, the aged poor work with children in such places as hospitals, correctional homes, and day care centers. They provide concern, guidance, support, and love for children with special needs. FGP has been shown to benefit both the aged and the children involved in the program.[58] The Senior Companion Program utilizes the services of poor older people to provide help to other aged in need. Senior companions provide companionship and help to other elderly people at home, in hospitals, at senior citizen organizations, and in nursing homes. Volunteers in both FGP and SCP receive a nontaxable stipend for their work. Under the Retired Senior Volunteer Program, aged volunteers provide activities for residents in housing projects and nursing homes, shut-ins, and post-stroke victims. There is no stipend available in this program.

Programs help provider and recipient

All of these programs were developed and established to meet provider and recipient needs. Research indicates that the aged volunteers (the providers) are the major beneficiaries. This has been termed by Riessman as the "helper-therapy principle," which maintains that "in a helper-helpee relationship those who help may benefit more." Bowles believes these programs provide support for the further development and utilization of the aged's skills for the benefit of society and for themselves.[59]

In many other respects, as the aged make their needs known and felt, business, private organizations, and the government are making changes in goals to meet these needs. For example, one community service program at Duke University, The Older American Resources and Services Program (OARS), provides legal and medical help and at-home nursing care. OARS

Both "grandchild" and "grandparent" benefit
from the Foster Grandparents Program.

The Boston Globe

"arranges for 'chore workers' who cook and do odd jobs in the house, 'meals
on wheels' to provide shut-ins with home-delivered meals, and a volunteer
corps of drivers who take the disabled on trips."[60]

The Department of Elder Affairs in Massachusetts has experimented
with "alternate-living" arrangements. They established several day care centers instead of "purely social Golden Age Centers." In the day care centers,
they experimented with "boarding houses and communes, where small
groups of residents can care for each other, and an 'adoption center'
through which old people can live with young families."[61]

HEALTH CARE

Social Security, as noted earlier, has responded to the needs of the aged in terms of financial help. Congress has also responded with action linking Social Security payments to the cost of living, a response greatly welcomed by those elderly who depend on Social Security as their only source of income. Because many families living on Social Security alone were economically destroyed when chronic disease or medical emergency struck, the federal government established the Medicare program in 1965.

Medicare and Medicaid help the aged

Medicare and Medicaid have also somewhat lessened the financial burden of health care for the aged. All aged eligible for Social Security have the right to join Medicare, which pays for some of their medical costs. The Medicare program has helped many aged, but because of coinsurance provisions and the exclusion from coverage of many services (which are then charged to the patients), Medicare in some years has paid less than half of the aged's medical bills.[62]

Health costs are still high

In 1966, Medicare patients were charged $40 for the first sixty days of hospitalization; as of January 1, 1978, patients will now have to pay $144 for a stay of sixty days or less.[63] For many these costs are difficult, if not impossible, to meet. Under Medicare, fees charged to the aged are adjusted annually on the basis of hospital costs. Since Medicare's inception, these costs have risen at rates exceeding those of all other health services. Political leaders concerned about the lack of controls for the added charges have called for legislation limiting hospital fee increases.

Cottrell notes that in response to the medical bill problems of the aged, organizations such as labor unions now place great stress on protection against medical catastrophe. Through bargaining, some unions have excellent medical coverage for their members. The unions have actively supported universal medical insurance under a national plan. Cottrell states that with the support of unions and with "that of a growing number of older people disillusioned with respect to Medicare coverage, such a national plan may emerge."[64]

The medical profession, in the past, has been largely unresponsive to the problems of the aged. Less than half of the medical schools offer relevant courses. Medical school professors who specialize in the aged are virtually nonexistent. However, a shift in attitude toward a more positive response appears to be developing. Some hospitals are showing interest in starting geriatric residency training programs. Also, the number of physicians who are members of the American Geriatrics Society has dramatically risen in the past several years.

The response to the health needs of millions of aged is still inadequate. This lack of adequate response may be based in the fact that health care in America is primarily a private matter, arranged between provider organizations and the individual receiving care. Atchley notes that from prolonged research of health care in America two conclusions have developed.

One is that a method of payment has yet to be found that will adequately open up health care for the poor, especially the aged poor. The second is that health care in the United States is "so poorly organized that genuinely adequate care is both scarce and expensive . . . this is because health is still considered to be an institution that communities are responsible for setting-up and supporting; while control is considered to be largely a matter for private enterprise or private nonprofit organizations." [65] The result is a situation in which the planning and coordination that are needed in order to get the most out of community health care resources are difficult to achieve. This situation hits the aged the hardest, because so many are poor and have a very great need for health care.[66]

Health care and planning are needed

THE RIGHT TO WORK

For years older workers have been unfairly treated and discriminated against in the work and business world. Finally, in 1967, the Age Discrimination in Employment Act was passed. This act banned job-related bias against older workers, but only for those between the ages of 40 and 65. Early in the 1970s Congress responded to the problems of workers older than 65 with efforts to raise or eliminate the age ceiling by law. At the same time, various elderly pressure groups, such as the National Council on Aging, The Gray Panthers, and the National Council of Senior Citizens, began to push for the right to work beyond the age of 65.

Discrimination in work

The desire for a more flexible retirement system is evidenced in the National Council on Aging's Harris survey:

> . . . the public at large is strongly opposed to an inflexible mandatory retirement system. Those older people who want to continue work into their 60's, 70's and 80's and who are still able to do their jobs (a majority of the public feel most older people are still able) should not be retired against their will. These results represent a strong public mandate for the rollback of mandatory retirement guidelines and practices.[67]

The public wants a flexible retirement system

According to this poll, 86 percent of the population that was surveyed agreed that "nobody should be forced to retire because of age if he wants to continue working and is still able to do a good job."[68]

Late in 1977, the House of Representatives passed by an overwhelming majority the Pepper Bill, which extends the mandatory retirement age from 65 to 70 in private industry and removes it altogether for federal workers. Proponents of the bill (those against mandatory retirement) argued that a "man or woman should not be forced out of work at a given age unless they are not able to continue further."[69] In testimony during hearings by The Select Committee on Aging of the House, one representative noted that,

The Pepper Bill

besides the humanitarian reasons for the abolition of mandatory retirement, there are

economic factors which indicate that a favorable cost-benefit ratio would be derived from it. As older workers are forced to retire, they tax an already strained Social Security System. Social Security benefits are financed by payroll taxes contributed by employees, employers, and the self-employed. Declining birth rates, coupled with increasing retirement rates, have resulted in fewer workers supporting the system. A few years ago the ratio of workers to Social Security Beneficiaries was 4 to 1; today, the ratio is 3.2 to 1; by the year 2030, the ratio will approach 2 to 1. The abolishment of mandatory retirement would alleviate this lopsided ratio and help insure continuous retirement benefits.[70]

Opponents of the bill (those in favor of mandatory retirement) argue that mandatory retirement "eliminates unequal treatment stemming from individual judgments as to who should and who should not continue to work after a certain age. . . . It opens up promotional opportunities . . . for young people."[71] Other supporters of mandatory retirement argued that passing the bill "would increase the number of individuals age 65 and over in the work force; it may simply shift the tax burden from Social Security to unemployment and other social-welfare programs."[72]

In the spring of 1978, President Carter signed into law a bill that extended the mandatory retirement age from 65 to 70. The law covers businesses and organizations that employ twenty or more workers, which encompasses about 70 percent of the nation's labor force. Workers still retain the option of retiring at age 65 or earlier. If workers want to continue working, and are able to do the job, they may now remain.

ESTABLISHING EFFECTIVE BROAD-BASED PROGRAMS

In this next reading by Amitai Etzioni, "Old People and Public Policy," the author stresses the fact that public policies should move from a relatively rigid reliance on ascribed status to more reliance on achieved status. However, he notes that this principle, if applied to retirement, would prove costly. Etzioni believes also that the aged will benefit in the long run from programs and policies that are based on the needs of all citizens in society. Viewing the aged as a status group with special needs has the tendency to "set up a dysfunctional tension" between the aged and others in society.

ETZIONI READING——OBJECTIVE

1. Examine in an essay Etzioni's argument that the aged, in the long run, will benefit from programs based on the needs of all people in society.

Old People and Public Policy
AMITAI ETZIONI

UNIVERSALISTIC POLICIES

My view is that in general older persons can be expected to benefit, in terms of their self-view and the image of them held by others, the more their problems are handled via broad-based "universalistic" social policies aimed at coping with social problems as they affect all citizens and the society at large rather than via "particularistic" old-age-oriented policies, although these latter are necessary where more universalistic approaches are not available for one reason or another.

The view of older persons as a status group with unique specialized needs tends to set up a dysfunctional tension between older Americans and the rest of society. The tension is created by an implicit invoking or reinforcing of negative stereotypic images of older persons (in their own minds as well as in the minds of others). They tend to type them as victims of social segregation, physical isolation, and discriminatory attitudes and perhaps also serve to incur resentment toward them as a social albatross that must be borne by the rest of society.

This tension would be much reduced if more general, societywide policies replaced categorical programs in taking care of older persons' special needs. Needless to say, such policies are also more likely to have wide and lasting public support than policies which seek to benefit a subgroup, however sizable, powerful, and well organized.

There is a need for more general societywide policies

ECONOMIC POLICY

Older persons are economically disadvantaged because being increasingly phased out of the labor force their real income is declining, often sharply, especially during periods of inflation. Attempts to deal with this problem follow two principal strategic courses: general, universalistic correctives or particularistic, older-person-specialized ones, although of course many mixes exist and others have been suggested.

The best example of a general corrective which is *not* older-person-related is the suggested policy of income maintenance. It defines a given level of income as the right of every American and supplements the income of those whose income falls below this standard. It encompasses young people (especially mothers) and children now on welfare, as well as the handicapped, in addition to older persons and provides a form of antipoverty insurance for the middle class should prolonged unemployment or catastrophic illness strike. It thus meets the needs of a far wider segment of society than a policy of increasing Social Security benefits to persons 65 or older.

Similarly, from the viewpoint of encouraging a less age-graded society, one which is less prone to adversely labeling those over 65, income maintenance is a more suitable policy than continuously increasing Social Security benefits. This is especially so as higher Social Security benefits continuously increase payroll taxes. These tax raises are more and more viewed by those who work not as payment into *their* retirement fund but transfer payments to those currently over 65. Of course income maintenance might well also be viewed as a transfer pay-

Policy of income maintenance

ment (and hence, if sizable, generate resentment and opposition), but it would not single out older persons as the target for resentment because not all older persons would receive it and younger persons would also be its beneficiaries. Above all, it is a need-related and not a status-bound policy.

A general policy focused on reducing inflation would likely prove the most effective, because it would benefit an even wider segment of society than either income maintenance or increased Social Security payments. Those concerned both with serving the economic needs of older persons and the undesirable segregation of the aged as a separate status group should find this policy especially compelling because, just as a high rate of inflation in the long run harms practically all segments of society, but especially persons who are retired and living off savings, pension funds, Social Security, and other sources of fixed income, so a reduction of inflation especially benefits these groups. Indeed, if inflation could be held to, say, a 4 percent (or lower) yearly average over the next 20 years, an even larger segment of older persons would be able to maintain a decent standard of living *without* special supplements, and increased Social Security taxes could be wholly or largely avoided. (To explore this matter fully, one must address the question of whether the reduction of inflation is better achieved through a depressed, slow-growth economy or through one of substantial growth but some form of price and wage control. The advantages for older persons hold in either case, albeit more so under the second set of conditions.) In conclusion, the implications for the issue of whether to emphasize universalistic or older-person-specific policies is illustrated by the inverse relationship between success in curbing inflation and the need for special income supplements for older persons.

Reduction of inflation

HEALTH CARE

In the area of health care the same points are illustrated by the relationship between national health insurance and Medicare. Medicare singles out older persons as recipients of special help. Again, efforts to lobby for minimizing the cost charged to its beneficiary, i.e., older persons (thereby asking society as a whole to bear the added cost), set up a tension between older persons and the rest of society, reinforcing the image of the aged as a separate status group. The introduction of a national health insurance to cover all persons according to their health needs would both serve to meet the health needs of older persons and eliminate older persons as a distinct service group.

National health insurance

Partial national health insurance, e.g., coverage of catastrophic illness, would have only a limited impact in this direction; it would not eliminate Medicare and older persons as specialized recipients. Indeed catastrophic illness provisions might well so inflate health costs by encouraging expensive forms of hospital care to obtain reimbursement that further cutbacks in regular Medicare coverage would be demanded, thereby decreasing the actual benefits to the elderly while fueling possible societal resentment against their "special privileges."

INDEPENDENCE AND COMMUNITY SERVICES

Older persons will tend to benefit the more their needs are met through reliance on self, kin, peers, and community, in contrast to government and/or institutions (e.g., nursing homes). However, older persons should not be pressured to act more independently than they are able to, and services by and in institutions should be available for those who will require them either temporarily or for a longer term.

Too frequently we assume that independence, capacity to function autonomously, and self-help are unquestionable virtues while dependency, especially on the government or on institutional care as opposed to one's self or kin or peers, is a matter to be embarrassed about or ashamed of or a sign of weakness and deficiency. For example, the 1971 White House Conference on Aging and the 1973 report "Towards a New Attitude on Aging" depict independence as of unquestionable preferability to dependence and associated with dignity, while dependence is not. Aside from such beliefs in the community at large, many behavioral science textbooks describe the capacity to function autonomously as *the* earmark of the "mature person" while the inability to so function is viewed as the attribute of the immature child, the mentally ill, "disturbed," people on welfare, etc.—all negative associations.

Such a strong emphasis on independence is excessive; it establishes a norm many older persons, and quite a few others, cannot live up to and should not be overbearingly pressured to try to live up to, just as those who are or can be independent should not be pushed to become dependent.

Sociopsychologically the issue is as follows: the society, through its dominant value structure, rewards independence and sanctions dependence, although, it seems, somewhat less than it used to in previous generations. One principal mechanism for negative sanctioning of dependency is social stigma. This means that, as when any other attribute is defined as highly desirable, be it sexual activity or a trim waistline, whoever does not or cannot live up to it is made to feel guilty, ashamed, undignified, incompetent. Reactions to such feelings on the part of individual older persons may give rise to desperate attempts to act independently when the person is unable, may delay her or his use of institutions when use is appropriate, and so on.

> Society rewards independence and sanctions dependence

It might be argued that a *mild* societal pressure to be independent is necessary to curb excessive dependency, but the existing pressure seems to me too strong and public policy ought to endeavor to ease it rather than to exacerbate it. The basic principle of public policy in this area should be that persons be free to feed their needs and not a mechanical universal dictum. Thus for an 80-year-old person afflicted with several illnesses that require frequent medical service and administration of drugs, and suffering from impaired mobility, a nursing home might well be the best place, just as for others home health services might be best suited, while still others will require none.

Second, the institutional policies should be brought in line with the images which public values and public policy espouse. Presently they are frequently at odds. Thus, despite the high nominal value placed on keeping older persons out of institutions and providing services to them in the community, it is still *much* easier to provide services for older persons in nursing homes than through home health service or in community centers. A significant expansion of home health services and community centers, combined with a possible leveling off of the nursing home growth rate, would go a long way to correct the current imbalance between the manifest values we profess and the latent values our policies at present convey. Such a shift toward community-based services has often been recommended—albeit on rather different grounds—but for the most part has not been implemented.

It should also be noted that when it comes to deinstitutionalization, several alternatives, not one, stand out. Moreover, the policy approach sociological insight might tend to favor is not necessarily the one most compatible with the way independence is, at least usually, perceived. Usually independence brings to mind self-reliance. The autonomously acting person the value system depicts is not excessively dependent on any one, even spouse, as well as children, parents, or other kin, or peers. Actually, a strong individual may well be a person well integrated into a rich and diversified social fabric, while a "self-reliant" individual may well oscillate between dependency-breakdown and obsessive independence (e.g., refusal to be treated). A person well integrated into a family and a community is hence the one probably best able to function independently, both psychologically and otherwise, in obtaining help, some nursing, a small loan, etc., without a governmental program. The trouble is that many older persons are widowed, divorced, or separated from their spouses, isolated from their children and other kin, and not integrated into a community. To help them function autonomously—in the sense of remaining independent of government and institutions—it may well be necessary to help them (though of course not force them) to relate more to one another. Group living (two or more older persons per apartment or residential unit) and peer socializing (e.g., at older persons centers) are two main avenues.

Last but not least, economic independence is a major source of psychic independence. Obviously, if welfare in one's home provides for much less than Medicaid in a nursing home, as happens to be the case, then for those who are poor nursing homes become more of a necessity than they would be if there were more adequate income supplementation prior to institutionalization. Even more to the point are reforms of pension funds and Social Security. Recent legislative reforms, which have made deferring income to retirement more attractive, improved the accountability of pension managers, and lessened the chance of losing pension rights (e.g., due to transfer from one place of employment to another), are steps in the right direction toward more economic security for older persons without either federal financing or institutionalization. If Social Security were reformed to improve its investment policies (e.g., allow it to invest in high-quality corporate bonds), if inflation were further curbed (as discussed above), and Social Security not be used to service other needs beyond financing retirement, it could go a long way to allow older persons to be economically independent, which in turn makes psychic independence easier.

FROM ASCRIPTION TO ACHIEVEMENT

Public policies should move from relatively rigid reliance on ascribed status to greater reliance on achieved status, although one must realize that such a transition entails considerable human and economic cost. These, in turn, can be much curtailed if the transition goes "most of the way" but not all the way, and several accommodating mechanisms are provided.

Older persons correctly protest ageist policies which imply that when a person reaches a specific chronological age he or she is too old to perform certain

Economic independence is a source of psychic independence

Public policies: From reliance on ascribed status to reliance on achieved status

activities or is generally incapacitated. They hold that a person should be judged by his or her functional age, i.e., ability to perform. This entails evaluating a person's capacities on an individual basis rather than in terms of an impersonal biological clock.

From a civil rights, humanitarian perspective the demand to be treated as an individual rather than according to one's ascribed status has wide appeal; it has been legitimated in other areas from the rights of racial and ethnic minorities to those of women. It also finds no objection in fact: indeed many an older person will be able to perform a task more effectively than many a younger (though not necessarily "young") person, even if statistically it is correct that the average of older persons' functional capacities in some areas will be lower than the average of younger persons'. Moreover, the prevalent view that persons a few years older than 65 differ significantly in their functional capacities from younger, especially middle-aged, persons is being progressively invalidated by improvements in the overall health status of older persons due to socioeconomic factors as well as medical advances.

The area of sexual conduct may serve to illustrate the point. Two decades ago the view was widely held that older persons, say 65 or older, for the most part could not and should not be sexually active. Since then much has been written, both in professional literature and popular media, on behalf of the view that older persons can and should engage in sexual activities. The facts, again, are not at issue. While there may well be statistical differences across the groups (if one were to compare 55 to 66 year olds with 65 to 75 year olds), the main point is that many individuals in the 65 to 75 group may "outperform" many in the 55 to 65 group. The conclusion is *not* to expect, and in this sense demand, that all older persons engage in sexual activity, but to stress that for all persons, whatever their age, whether they do or don't, no stigma will be attached, nor will expectations be tailored to their age but rather to their individuality.

Unfortunately, the social scientist must point to the costs attached to these often stated views, *not* to urge that the price not be paid but to prevent a backlash when it is exacted. Economic and psychic costs are generated by a transition from public policies which rely on ascription to those which rely on achievement. Retirement provides a pivotal case in point. Many civil service agencies, corporations, colleges, etc., maintain an age-specific retirement policy. These rules often include some leeway, allowing for some earlier retirement with little or no penalty and some measure of deferment. However, while this flexibility in the rules serves to accommodate individual differences and needs, these two are defined by chronological age: say, 62 for "early" retirement and, say, 71 for "late" retirement. What are the costs of a public policy which would abolish all age-specific retirement rules, judge all personnel individually, and retire those no longer "up to snuff" whatever their age?

There are high costs to achievement-based public policies

The preceding arguments in favor of achievement-based public policies provide the reasons such an approach should be favored. However, one should not disregard that an application of this principle to retirement would likely prove costly. First, such a change in policy would require assessment of matters rather difficult to measure reliably, from mental agility to energy level. It is enough to recall the difficulties entailed by IQ tests to recognize how technically troublesome and controversial such a procedure would be. Second, extensive reliance on an individual's fitness for continued work on the part of his or her superiors or colleagues could result in paternalism and favoritism rather than a safeguarding of employees' rights. Third, even more significant from the viewpoint of the self-image and image others hold of older persons, such achievement-based retirement would tend to label the retired person as less competent or incompetent. In contrast, under the present status-based, ascribed, "arbitrary" retirement policies, a retired older person may well feel (and others feel about him or her) that he or she is still in his/her prime but was retired because of ascribed rules. Judgment about competence is not necessarily involved.

To a considerable extent one can seek to reap the benefits of the achievement-based system without incurring the high costs entailed by complete abandonment of the ascribed rules. This can be accomplished by widening the range of retirement age, and by allowing continued part-time work, consulting, relations, etc., after these stages. This, if the age range were to reach from 59 (or after x years of service) to 71 or more, and if after that age there were room for part-time work, much of the rigidity of current policies would be eliminated, opening opportunities to accommodate differences in achievement without making the achievement criterion the dominant and socially visible one.

Another human cost should be mentioned: delaying the mandatory retirement age would tend to generate pressure on people to stay and work to earn larger incomes and benefits and not opt for or accept an "unproductive" life-style before they need to. This is compatible with the Protestant ethic but not with a transition to a more relaxed society. Also, such a policy might be suitable to a growth economy where there is enough work to go around and opportunities for young persons to move up, even if older persons do not retire early. In a slow economy the opposite holds. Here again, greater flexibility rather than a radical shift to a purely achievement-based employment policy seems to be the preferred public policy.

Similarly, age-specific discounts for persons 65 and older (in transportation, movies, etc.) have the undesirable attribute of being based on ascribed (age) rather than achieved (income) status. While it would be better to grant these discounts to poor people whatever their age, such an approach would tend to label people as poor on their identity cards, coupons, or stamps needed for discounts, a rather unattractive idea to say the least, as the stigma attached to the use of food stamps shows. The problem can be reduced if, as I recommend, all discounts were to be treated as income to the recipients which would be taxed back at progressive rates. Since this rate of "tax-back" would be confidential between the person and the Internal Revenue Service, no stigma would be attached to discounts, although they would still benefit the lower-income older person more than economically well-off members of his or her cohort. This would bring the policy closer in line with need and away from age status. I would recommend a similar policy with respect to Medicare benefits for the same reasons.

The precedent for such an approach, suggesting that it is both legitimate and workable, is found in the provision calling for Social Security benefits for older persons to be reduced by 50 cents for each one dollar they earn above a specific amount. Now this particular example might well represent much too low a ceiling, and too high a tax-back rate, but it serves to illustrate the public acceptability of the principle involved. Indeed, if all benefits were taxed back in this manner it would be more readily possible to have a much higher ceiling for exempt amounts and much slower slope of tax-back percentages. The basic point is, however, that there is no apparent reason for allowing rich and well-off people the full range of benefits free of charge simply because they are over a certain age; yet one need not abolish discounts to those who are old and in need or less well off.

KINSHIP WITHOUT PREJUDICE

Public policies should encourage nuclear, extended, and intergenerational families, but not penalize those who seek other alternatives.

The public policies concerning the nuclear family may be the most controversial. A growing variety of arguments are being advanced to suggest that it is obsolescent and that single living or living together without marriage are just as socially functional, or more so, than the two-partner nuclear family. The issue is much less important for older persons than for young ones, because even those who do favor the "traditional" nuclear family are concerned first and foremost with the character formation of young children (aged 0 to 6); very few older persons have children that young.

What is relevant is, to a limited extent, role modeling, and to a larger extent, the proper alignment of public policy vis-à-vis individual roles, rights, feelings. Regarding role modeling: to the extent that it is desirable (which I hold it is for reasons given elsewhere) that the nuclear family be sociologically shored up rather than further undermined, I suggest that the more older persons live together without marriage, the more difficult it is to expect young persons to believe in the importance of marriage. True, in our society grandparental figures serve less as role models than in most other societies, but nevertheless they do perform such a function.

Much more important is the fact that older persons are now under pressure from public policy *not* to marry, which means that public policies exact penalties from those who do in the form of reduced Social Security benefits. While I certainly would not favor penalties on those who stay single or live together without marriage, penalties on the most legitimate and, in my judgment, personally and socially functional form of cohabitation, is a poor public policy and should be modified.

The aged are under pressure not to marry

Income policies such as Social Security should provide all persons with the same benefits and not reduce them if they marry. (It might be said that this provides a hidden reward for marriage because of the greater economies possible in a merged household; however, the same economies are achieved by living together unmarried or even more so by a group of singles residing together.)

Even more important are matters which concern the intergenerational family. While it is not easy to document, many policy makers in Washington (for instance, on the staff of the National Institute of Mental Health), significant segments of the media, as well as a sizable portion of the intellectual community have come in recent years to look with favor on the extended family, especially the intergenerational one (specifically, grandparents, parents, and children). Researchers and commentators dealing with minority families have pointed out that grandparents can act as a partial replacement for the often absent or come-and-go father or working mother, making up, they claim, for the suggested ill effects of higher incidences of common-law marriage and male turnover. Similarly, students of immigrants point to the value of the extended family (or clan) in providing its members with various services from loans to providing day care for children and ministering to the health needs of the elderly. Indeed, there are proportionately few Blacks and Puerto Ricans in nursing homes. Anthropologists also extol the emotional significance of extended families, for example in India, where children are said to benefit from a large variety of emotional contacts instead of being limited to attachments to parents or siblings. Some church groups have felt that where natural extended families are lost, artificial extended families should be created through several nuclear families joining together.

While there are merits in these arguments, it should be considered, *not* as refutation but as a means of balancing them, that American society is, relative to many other European and Latin, Asian, and African societies (although not as compared to some preliterate tribes) a highly age-segregated society. Values, social habits, residential arrangements, all point to at least a two-way, often three-way generational split. This is illustrated by the fact that each generation will tend to spend more of its leisure time with its peers than in intergenerational situations, although of course situations of both kinds abound. The deeper reasons are rooted in the economic structure of the nation, which requires a high rate of continentwide mobility of employees, which in turn allows transfer of the nuclear but not extended family as a rule; the youth-oriented nature of the society (which puts a negative value on association with older persons); and others. While these factors may be both normatively undesirable and factually less significant than they once were, they are still quite powerful and public policy could not be expected to turn them about. Moreover, in attempting to do so it would have to counter not only powerful historically rooted forces but the personal preferences of many persons.

Public policy should ease intergenerational families

In conclusion, I therefore suggest that public policy should ease rather than hinder intergenerational families (e.g., zoning regulations which limit buildings to single family residences should be changed to allow two families where the second is one of kin; expansion of home health services would reduce need for institutionalization of older persons and help maintain intergenerational contacts where they exist, etc.). However, no pressure should be placed nor implicit penalties exacted from those who wish to lead an age-segregated life, which may well continue to appeal to a majority of mainstream Americans of both the older and the younger generations. Just as grandparents should not be pressured away from their children and grandchildren to retirement communities, so they should not be, even indirectly, pushed into an intergenerational situation if they prefer age-segregated living.

Aside from the general psychological rationale that the most effective and normatively preferable policies try not to make people behave in ways they do not wish to behave unless there are compelling human or public interest reasons (as in antismoking efforts) there are serious economic considerations. These stem from current residential and service patterns. The existing residential patterns are complex and far from fully known. It is clear, though, that any significant shift from existing patterns to accommodate greater intergenerational living, unless very gradually introduced, would entail major capital expenditure, as where there is now no intergenerational living the existing dwelling units and community layouts tend not to be suited for it. For instance, older persons typically need smaller apartments than those needed by other persons to make maintenance easier, as well as fewer staircases, more elevators, wider doors (for wheelchairs), railings, and so on. In communities deliberately designed for intergenerational living, especially in Great Britain and Sweden, buildings contain living quarters especially suited to the needs of older and younger persons, deliberately mixed together. Such a strategy could of course be followed with respect to new public buildings in the United States and in private ones to the extent there were a demonstrable demand for it. But to adapt existing structures on a large scale seems a relatively poor investment of public funds in view of the uncertain appeal of intergenerational life and the huge amounts involved.

Regarding services, especially health services, more and better research is badly needed to determine under what conditions they can be rendered in a less costly manner. It is quite possible that concentration of older persons in their own communities is by far the most economical way to serve them, allowing for special transportation (e.g., minibuses to bring older persons to day centers, either for treatment or social life), ready availability of day hospitals, and health centers staffed with specialists in medical gerontology, specialists in rehabilitation, and specialized nurses.

On the other hand, greater economy might possibly be achieved through integration of older persons into other social service networks through "exchange" of child care and elderly care in intergenerational families, or—for fees —among families not related. Still other alternatives must be explored, such as subcommunities for older persons within larger integrated communities, which might allow them to have the benefits of both approaches as long as the distances were not too large.

Such analyses must be careful not to confuse operating budgets with capital expenditures. Where new communities are being designed, the alternatives are relatively open, but under most circumstances where existing facilities must be used, large-scale reconstruction to suit a public policy is not a realistic approach, at least for the near future.

My interest is not so much in the economic aspects per se but in the articulation between economic factors and the preceding discussion of desired patterns for social living. What is necessary is to put price tags on the various policies designed because of their social and psychic implications. Not that these price tags will decide the question of which policy is to be followed, but as they will affect their workability as well as other factors, they are best taken into account from the outset.

CURE AND CARE

The balance between care and cure in public policy should be modified to admit openly the need to *care,* for long periods, for many older Americans, rather than pretend that they are about to be *cured,* fully rehabilitated, weaned from the need for service rather quickly.

Current health-care policy for older Americans under Medicare is almost exclusively oriented toward meeting the need for treatment of serious acute conditions. Hospitalization is generously covered, while ambulatory and drug costs, especially long-term out-of-hospital drug costs, are provided for much less generously, with much more reliance on recipient cost-sharing provisions. Nursing home benefits under Medicare are virtually nonexistent; the limited financing of services provided for in "extended care facilities" is intended to cover the costs of posthospital convalescence and rehabilitation only. While home health benefits are theoretically available, they are hedged with so many limitations and restrictions that few persons are found eligible and few home health agencies can support themselves on Medicare payments. In sum, then, Medicare policy is heavily oriented toward cure rather than care. Older Americans with chronic disease and disability conditions (such as crippling arthritis or arteriosclerosis) that often require long-term care in an institution are generally forced to turn to Medicaid. However, unlike Medicare which is available to all older Americans regardless of income, Medicaid is exclusively for the poor. Hence an older person who needs the expensive services Medicaid finances and who is not already a public assistance recipient or deemed "medically indigent" must impoverish himself or herself in order to become eligible. Moreover, once having spent-down to indigent status, elderly persons in institutions covered by Medicaid become in effect de facto prisoners of these institutions and of the state since they often no longer have autonomous means to control what institution they are placed in or of protesting poor care by threatening to go elsewhere, especially not the option of returning to the community even if their health permits it. Thus, Medicaid retains, with respect to chronic care for older Americans, the negative features of Kerr-Mills which Medicare was intended to overcome. The policy issue thus is whether some adaptations in either Medicare or Medicaid or both should not be made to prevent or at least mitigate enforced pauperization of older Americans in need of long-term, especially long-term institutional, care for chronic illness and disability. In terms of messages public policy emits to older Americans' self-view or the image of them held by others, it should not stress so much that being incapacitated in varying degrees for longer periods is bad, and so-called proper illnesses are of short duration and curable; but it should serve to increase understanding and support for many older Americans who have no realistic hope of full recovery, nor are they terminally ill; they will have to live for years with some supportive care, without shame or guilt.

Medicare: Oriented toward cure rather than care

OLDER PERSONS AND PUBLIC SAFETY

The aged are viewed as more helpless than others

Older persons are typically viewed by others and by themselves as more helpless than most other persons. This view has its source in part in intrapsychic factors, but in part in institutional factors as well. To the extent that the latter are at work, policies which would improve the protection of older persons would benefit them three ways: (1) lower the incidences of specific abuse; (2) counter the view that older persons are vulnerable and hence deter those who seek to prey on them; (3) improve the self-image of older persons.

Areas in which special efforts are necessary include: (1) crime (not only by muggers who prey on their physical weakness but by con artists and white-collar financial and professional criminals, who prey on their loneliness and isolation);

(2) exploitation by nursing home owners, Medicaid mills, etc. (older persons in institutions are abused in many ways, from bilking their personal accounts to neglect of health care and nutrition); (3) consumer fraud (of which older persons are disproportionately victimized).

Modes of protection vary. Again, strengthening policy approaches which benefit all are probably best suited. Thus, older persons would be the beneficiaries of improved police work, better systems to regulate quality and prevent fraud and abuse in nursing homes and other health facilities, and greater efforts in the area of consumer protection along with, though comparatively more than, the rest of society.

Second, in the case of those older persons who are partially impaired, special assistance seems appropriate; for example, consumer counseling services attached to senior citizen centers, special communication devices (to allow older persons in their homes to mobilize security or health aides), etc. In addition, protective legislation should be drafted on behalf of older persons who are highly impaired: where there are no active next-of-kin to safeguard their best interests, public interest guardians would be appointed to look after their finances and health decisions so that such decisions would not be made by providers who have a vested interest in these matters.

Finally, the recently formulated patients' bill of rights (or a modified stronger version) should serve as more than a statement of intent but be required by law to protect older persons in health facilities. Also, the right to refuse treatment and the legal status of the "living will" deserve additional attention. Present tradition in this area may leave too much power in the hands of physicians, who may then choose to deal with all older persons as if they were impaired or infantile.

POLITICAL ACTIVISM

Older persons have become increasingly politically as well as socially and physically active over the past two decades and such political activism on the part of those over 65 has gained in legitimacy, it seems. Moreover, older persons increasingly perceive themselves as entitled to public participation as a group and as individuals, although they do not appear to have as yet developed a political self-image akin to politically organized ethnic groups. The question is to what extent public policy should encourage, discourage, or ignore these tendencies toward increased political activism on the part of older Americans.

At stake is a conception of what is to be deemed appropriate, democratically legitimate participation in public affairs. Thus, it has been stated about practically all active groups that they are not a "proper" base for public action. Behind this suggestion often is a textbook image of the democratic process: the government is run by elected representatives and the legitimate way to influence them is by casting one's vote as a citizen and not as a member of any partisan group. Likewise, it is thought voting preferences should be based on considerations of a the nation's needs rather than on the needs or desire for special privileges of a particular subgroup.

The elderly are more active

While it is quite true that, in part, the democratic process does work this way, it also proceeds by a large variety of groups each looking after its own set of concerns—not just "lobbies" or private interest groups, such as farm, labor, or business groups, but groups promoting the civil rights of particular constituencies, such as the NAACP and CORE, Italian American Association, American Jewish Congress, as well as groups representing the public interest, such as the American Civil Liberties Union, the Sierra Club, Nader's Raiders, etc. Indeed, to the extent that the government does attend to the people's needs it works at least as much by responding to these groups, which among them encompass most Americans, as to general voters. It also follows that needs not so represented or weakly represented will tend to be undeserved.

One might argue that the processes of government would be more rational and more ethical if there were no such groupings, but they exist in all politics, especially in democratic ones, and it is unrealistic to assume their demise although one may seek to reduce their influence. Hence, for older persons, or any other group, to forgo collective action and participation in the competition for public awareness of and attention to their needs is basically to allow other groups to gain a larger share of the government attention and resources.

The question might be raised whether older persons have not already gained an excessive share of publicly allocated resources. This is perhaps the case where their "clout" is compared to some much weaker groups, such as the poor, the handicapped, the mentally ill, but compared to the main power groups this seems hardly the case. Hence a greater political mobilization of older persons on behalf of the rights and needs of older persons is both quite legitimate and will serve to better balance the scale of allocative justice rather than bias it.

It also follows that when we look for methods to improve the responsiveness of government and its capacities to guide social processes in desired directions, it might be futile to look for ways to "reform" government only from within, e.g., through new civil service regulations, more and better trained personnel, and so on. Without proper "outside" attention, the policy directions of government in general or of specific agencies will tend to be skewed toward mobilized groups. One example should suffice: state nursing home administrators are leaning toward the providers because nursing home clients, chiefly older persons, are not organized and active, nor as a rule the focus of attention of older American activist groups.

As noted at the beginning of this discussion, however, insistence on the special and unique needs of older Americans and efforts to gain special programs just for them tends to set up a tension between older persons and the rest of society. Thus politically organized older Americans might be best advised to support policies and social services needed by or favorable to the aged in the

There is a need to support more universalistic approaches

context of supporting more universalistic approaches. Other mobilized groups have enhanced how the rest of society views them by following such a strategy, e.g., labor union support for Social Security and national health insurance. In addition, coalition building is one way of building support for one's own special aims; thus, older American groups might do well to work more closely together with other groups seeking the needed changes in public policy. Public policy in a pluralistic society reflects the political energy the various active groups generate and leans toward those who pull together, away from those who go it on their own.

SUMMARY

In this chapter, we have seen that the aged in America are the recipients of much prejudice and discrimination. Aged Americans are to a great extent shelved and forgotten, and must cope with many problems alone. Major trends forming the basis of this situation have been examined, as have the elderly's dependence and retirement roles. The aged have many problems in the areas of income, pensions, and health. The reading, "The Double Standard of Aging," has indicated how important the variables of sex and age are concerning social relationships. There are few rewards for elderly women in America.

As we have seen, there are various explanations for agism, and we have briefly presented some of the most popular. All can be supported, to some extent, with a respectable and reliable body of research. It must be remembered, however, that no single theoretical approach can adequately explain all the inequities experienced by the aged, because these problems are complex. Taken together, however, the theoretical explanations presented in this section provide a great deal of insight into, and a better understanding of, the many problems encountered by the aged in America.

Concerning people's responses to agism, our focus was on the recent shift among the aged from a response pattern characterized by acceptance to one characterized by aggressive action. The federal government's responses to the problems of the aged were also examined, along with a review of the White House conferences and the various federal programs for the aged. The health care response and the right to work issue were also discussed. The reading by Etzioni suggests that the aged will benefit in the long run from programs designed to meet the needs of all Americans.

KEY TERMS

Acceptance
Activity theory
Aggressive action
Agism
Assimilation
Avoidance
Continuity theory
Dependence role
Disengagement theory
FGP
Geriatrics
The Grey Panthers
Medicaid

Medicare
Minority group theory
Nontransferability
OAVP
Pensions
Retirement role
Right to work
RSVP
SCP
Social gerontology
Social Security
Stereotypes
White House conferences

Danny Lyon, Magnum Photos, Inc.

5

Crime and Delinquency

Chapter Objectives

1. To define "crime" and "juvenile delinquency."

2. To give four examples of the ways in which law and crime are relative to time, place, and subculture.

3. To discuss recent trends in the growth of crime as indicated by official crime statistics.

4. To describe in a brief essay the major findings of victimization studies regarding the extent of unreported crime.

5. To list the basic assumptions of the classical school of criminology.

6. To compare the biological, sociological, and psychological explanations for criminal behavior.

7. To evaluate the contributions of the labeling, differential association, anomie, and subcultural theories to the understanding of criminal behavior.

8. To discuss by essay the nature and history of the public's retribution-deterrence response to crime.

9. To contrast the rehabilitative philosophy underlying imprisonment with the reality of contemporary prison life.

10. To statistically substantiate the statement "Punishment in and of itself does not provide an effective deterrent to crime."

11. To list some of the advantages of community-based rehabilitation programs over those in institutions.

12. To briefly contrast probation and parole, and to compare through statistical analysis their relative rehabilitative effectiveness with that of imprisonment.

13. To identify the major reasons for the contemporary shift from institutionalization of offenders to the use of community-based correctional programs.

THE NATURE OF CRIME AND DELINQUENCY

Crime, whether on the part of juveniles or adults, is considered to be a major social problem today. Virtually all Americans are to some degree aware of the magnitude of crime in our society. Many of us have been victims of crime or know others who have been victims. In addition, the mass media keeps us constantly aware of crime. Newspapers, for instance, run a daily account of various forms of criminal activity: the robbery of a local store, the conviction of a bank official for embezzlement, the gang mugging of an area resident, the rape of a young woman.

From the standpoint of sociology, crime represents a major form of what is termed deviant behavior. In discussing the concept of deviant behavior, sociologists initially point out that all human groups and societies set up systems of norms or rules that specify how people are expected to act in their relationships with others. In this sense, norms bring about a certain degree of stability and order within society, thus helping to ensure the fulfillment of many basic needs and social values. When sociologists speak of deviant behavior we are referring to behavior that does not conform to norms, i.e., behavior that does not meet the expectations of a group or perhaps of the society as a whole.[1]

Crime: A major form of deviance

SOCIETY'S ROLES

It should be obvious that all human groups develop various techniques to ensure that social control and conformity to norms are maintained. Chief among these mechanisms is the socialization process itself. Socialization results in the development of *internal* self-controls, since within this process children learn and internalize the values of those around them. In contrast, conformity to social norms is also induced through a variety of *external* control mechanisms. For example, many social groups, particularly small societies, rely on systems of *informal* control. Individuals who violate community norms are subject to the censure of others and perhaps of the community as a whole in the form of public ridicule and ostracism. Typically, however, as societies grow in size and complexity, these informal social control mechanisms become increasingly ineffective and tend to be replaced by *formal* varieties. These would include systems of formal written law and legislative and judicial bodies as well as various specific agencies of law enforcement.[2]

Social control: Internal and external sources

DEFINING CRIME

Even though there is a variety of mechanisms for maintaining social control and conformity, it is evident that these mechanisms are never totally effective. Thus deviance, like conformity, can be found throughout human history and within all groups and societies.[3] Deviance can be manifested in a variety of ways. Some individuals may violate codes of etiquette or stan-

Deviance can take many forms

Crime violates norms termed laws

dards of dress for certain occasions. Others may be negligent in fulfilling their responsibilities at work or at home. Still others may be deviant because they engage in behaviors that are defined as criminal. When sociologists speak of crime, we are referring to behaviors that violate specific types of norms called laws. Laws are frequently referred to as "formal norms," since they are formally written rules that govern behavior considered to be offenses against the state. Thus the state has the authority to establish laws that define certain actions as illegal, since such acts are seen to threaten the interests and general welfare of the society. The state also prescribes certain punishments for these violations, which can be in the form of fines, imprisonment, and even death. Violation of certain laws, such as those prohibiting criminal homicide, aggravated assault, and robbery, are legally termed *felonies* and involve substantial penalties, such as heavy fines and/or a minimum of one year's imprisonment. Other less serious offenses, such as petty theft and vagrancy, are termed *misdemeanors* and carry penalties such as limited fines or jail sentences of less than one year.[4]

Felonies are more serious offenses; misdemeanors, less serious offenses

Civil law deals with noncriminal offenses

In addition to criminal law, there is another vast body of legal regulation termed civil law. *Civil* (or *tort*) law deals with noncriminal offenses, which are handled by civil rather than criminal courts. Civil offenses, although they may cause suffering, harm, or injury, to a person or persons, are not considered to be offenses against the state or the general welfare of the society at large. Thus the civil court does not defend the interests of society, but rather merely functions as an arbitrator between particular individuals. Civil law typically deals with matters such as libel suits or automobile accidents, in which one party brings a civil suit against another.[5]

JUVENILE DELINQUENCY

An important area of law violation, which does not come under the area of criminal law nor under the jurisdiction of criminal courts, is termed juvenile delinquency. Delinquency cases involve a separate area of law and are specifically dealt with by juvenile courts. Delinquency refers to illegal acts on the part of young people, usually 16 to 18 years of age. From the standpoint of the law, delinquency can pertain to all behaviors that, if committed by an adult, would be considered crimes plus a variety of other offenses applying specifically to youths, such as incorrigibility, truancy, and running away.[6]

Juvenile law stresses guidance, protection, and rehabilitation

Distinct from the adult criminal code, the juvenile laws and court system emphasize the notions of protection, guidance, and rehabilitation of juveniles rather than their punishment and incarceration. This philosophy is based on the idea that, in general, juveniles are too young to be capable of having the *criminal intent* necessary to commit malicious crime.[7] The philosophy also accentuates the notion that youth can be helped and redirected from a life of crime. This philosophy was first expounded by a nineteenth-century American social movement known as "child saving."

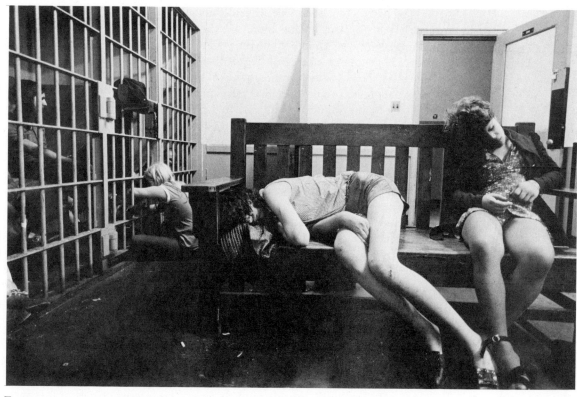

Leonard Freed, Magnum Photos, Inc.

Teenage runaways arrested for prostitution. Theirs are "victimless" crimes.

"Child saving" origins of juvenile justice

This movement was spearheaded by a number of people who were committed to the idea of saving "wayward youth" from the effects of a "poor home" and a "bad environment." The child savers argued that youths were basically good rather than bad, and therefore a revised system of juvenile justice and corrections was needed, in which the state would act as parent to the young offender. If necessary, removal of the child from the home or community should be undertaken for the youth's protection and reform rather than for punishment and incarceration with hardened adult criminals. The child savers movement was largely responsible for the passage of the Juvenile Court Act of 1899, which paved the way for the establishment of the first juvenile court in Illinois in the same year. The Juvenile Court Act of 1899 laid the foundation for the juvenile court system present within the United States today. In addition, the child savers movement was also partly responsible for the development of new types of correctional institutions for handling young offenders.[8]

Today, the philosophy of juvenile law still emphasizes the ideas of protection and guidance rather than punishment. The young offender receives a "hearing" rather than a trial. Judges are permitted rather wide discretion in deciding upon a course of action that would be most beneficial for the youngster. Thus in theory, the young offender is not "tried" or "sentenced." Often, however, actual practice falls quite short of this philosophy, with juveniles being handled as adults. In some measure, this situation has resulted from the fact that delinquency encompasses a much wider range of behaviors than the adult criminal code, and the number of judicial and correctional personnel are inadequate to deal with the large number of juvenile offenders.[9] However, a recent Supreme Court decision in the 1967 Gault case has helped to ensure the legal rights of the juvenile offender. According to this decision, juveniles who are likely to be committed to state correctional institutions are granted the same legal rights to "due process under the law" as adults. In spite of the special judicial and correctional procedures designed to handle the juvenile offender, it is obvious to both professionals and the general public that delinquency remains a very serious problem today. As we shall see later in this chapter, statistics indicate that arrests of juveniles have increased substantially over the last decade, that delinquency often involves very serious types of crime, and that many delinquents often have repeated contacts with the police and juvenile court systems.

As we have indicated earlier, crime, whether committed by adults or by youths, refers to behaviors that violate specific types of norms, which we term laws. Legally speaking, acts cannot be termed crimes unless there are laws that prohibit them. It should be evident, therefore, that crime is relative, since the content of criminal law will vary with time and place.[10] At one time or another, for example, such acts as printing certain books, singing obscene songs, giving alms to unemployed but ablebodied persons, selling beverages containing more than .50 percent alcohol, and kissing a woman in public were all considered crimes since they were against the law, and the state or other political authority could impose punishments on the offenders. No doubt most people would find these examples to be humorous, since laws such as these often prohibited essentially harmless behavior. We should understand, however, that laws still exist in our society that define many essentially harmless acts as criminal. On the other hand, there are acts that can injure others that are not called crimes because they are not prohibited by criminal law.

There is a wide variation in the law and also in the behaviors that people define as harmful and harmless. Often these spheres may conflict. Today, for example, many of the Puritan blue laws remain on the books within many states. Some people view these as important and worthwhile forms of legislation; others strongly disagree. Morals laws dealing with "victimless crime," such as homosexuality, prostitution, and gambling, are still strongly enforced in a number of our states and not in others. Conflicts

Juvenile justice: Theory and practice

Delinquency remains a serious problem today

Crime is relative, since laws are relative

Laws sometimes define harmless behaviors as crimes

among different groups as to the harmfulness of these practices and therefore the value of laws prohibiting them tend to be very severe.[11] Again, powerful corporations may be able to surround themselves with protective legislation; whether such legislation is in everyone's better interests is another matter. We should understand, therefore, that law is basically derived through the political decision-making process. Thus, while it is no doubt true that much of our law protects society against behaviors that are socially injurious to the general welfare, there are certain laws that tend to support the values and interests of more dominant and powerful groups within our society.[12]

Legislation does not always protect everyone's "better interests"

THE MOVE TO DECRIMINALIZE VICTIMLESS OFFENSES

For many years, sociologists and others have recognized the many negative consequences of attempting to enforce morals laws, which control many forms of "victimless crimes," such as drunkenness, gambling, prostitution, drug abuse, and homosexuality. Professors Alexander Smith and Harriet Pollack have contended, for example, that the existence and attempted enforcement of morals laws threaten the civil liberties of people whose "crimes" do not have victims and also contribute to the pervasiveness of organized crime within the United States. Smith and Pollack also feel that the morals laws are counterproductive to an effective criminal justice system, since the attempt to enforce these laws actually creates more crime than the laws prevent. The drug addict for example, frequently engages in serious crime in order to support an illegal habit.[13] The following reading examines what appears to be a new trend within our criminal justice system—the movement to decriminalize victimless crimes. Behind this movement lies the practical advantage of freeing law enforcement personnel and judicial officials to fight the rising numbers of serious violent crimes, such as murder, robbery, and rape, that *do* have victims.

U.S. NEWS & WORLD REPORT READING——OBJECTIVES

1. To identify the various factors that are responsible for the recent trend to decriminalize victimless crimes.
2. To discuss in an essay the initial effects of decriminalizing certain victimless crimes, such as public drunkenness, marijuana use, gambling, and prostitution.

Behind the Trend To Go Easy on "Victimless Crimes"

A new approach to the crime crisis is spreading rapidly across the U.S.

The idea is to spend less time and money prosecuting so-called victimless crimes, such as drunkenness, gambling, prostitution, marijuana use and homosexuality.

By doing this, officials and lawmakers hope that more law-enforcement resources can be freed to fight the rising tide of serious crimes that are aimed directly against victims—such as murder, robbery and rape.

More and more States and cities are "decriminalizing" victimless acts by outright repeal of laws that made the acts illegal or by substituting civil penalties, usually fines, for the jail and prison terms exacted in the past.

Eight States, for example, have eliminated criminal penalties for possessing small amounts of marijuana. Seven have taken that step since mid-1975.

Half of the 50 States have decriminalized public drunkenness, many in the last two years.

San Francisco recently stopped prosecuting prostitutes. Maine eliminated prison terms for prostitution. Several Nevada counties have legalized it.

More than a third of the States have removed bans against homosexual practices and other commonly outlawed sexual acts if they involve only consenting adults.

Certain forms of gambling have been legalized in 34 States, and 13 States have even set up their own betting operations. On November 2, New Jersey voters approved casino-style gambling for Atlantic City. Other States and cities are studying similar moves.

SPARKING THE TREND

What's behind this trend toward acceptance of acts that once were viewed as criminal and sternly prosecuted?

Norval Morris, dean of the University of Chicago Law School and an expert on victimless crimes, says a principal factor is the shortage of law-enforcement resources at a time of rising crime. It's estimated that about one third of the 9.3 million arrests made by police in 1975 were for victimless crimes.

"Many States have come to realize," says Mr. Morris, "it's difficult if not impossible to fight serious crime and still enforce laws on pot smoking and drunkenness."

Arrests for public drunkenness alone have run between 1 and 2 million a year, according to the Federal Bureau of Investigation. Marijuana arrests, most for simple possession, exceed 400,000 annually.

Such arrests take up a considerable part of police time and resources which many officials feel could be spent to better advantage on more serious crimes.

The lure of new sources of revenue prompted States to get into the gambling business. The National Gambling Commission, in a report released October 15, estimated that Americans now gamble 17.7 billion dollars legally each year. Estimates of illegal gambling range from 5 to 39 billion dollars. The idea is to tap this huge illegal business to produce income for State or local governments.

Gilbert Geis, author of a Government study on victimless crimes, cites these added factors behind decriminalization:

- Attempts to discourage gambling, prostitution and the like by making such acts a crime have failed.

Reprinted from *U.S. News & World Report*, November 15, 1976. Copyright ©
1976, U.S. News & World Report, Inc.

Indicators of a new approach to victimless crimes

Enforcement of morals laws hinders efforts to deal with more serious crimes

- Prosecution of victimless crime is "selective," with some such crimes widely ignored by officials while others are prosecuted, a situation that leads to disrespect for the law and corruption among police.
- Police must engage in degrading activity to enforce laws against victimless crimes, often posing as prostitutes or drug users.
- Prosecution of victimless crimes may lead to further crime. For example, drug addicts often steal or rob to support their habits because the illegality of drugs makes drug prices high.
- Decriminalization has become a "respectable" idea, having been endorsed by several prominent persons, including President-elect Jimmy Carter, as well as by the American Bar Association, the National Council of Churches and several presidential commissions.
- It has become politically unpopular to prosecute certain victimless crimes— marijuana use, for example—because they have become pervasive among the suburban middle class.

Additional factors behind decriminalization

A 1972 survey by a presidential commission indicated that about 8 million Americans then were using marijuana regularly, while 26 million had tried it at least once.

THE INITIAL IMPACT

What has been the effect of decriminalizing victimless crimes? The most obvious result has been a drop in the number of arrests police have had to make. Arrests for public drunkenness and marijuana use, for example, have decreased significantly as more and more States have eliminated penalties for such acts.

Decriminalization has the immediate effect of lowering the number of arrests

A look at some of the decriminalization approaches gives an idea of how they've worked out in other ways.

In the 25 States that have decriminalized public drunkenness, the focus now is on treating drunks rather than jailing them. One of the first of these efforts took place in St. Louis. Begun in 1966, that city's program now treats about 2,500 persons annually in a 40-bed detoxification center. In most cases, police still pick up drunks on the street. But instead of being hauled to the local jail's "drunk tank," the drunks are taken to the center.

In practical terms, the St. Louis program is regarded as a success. City police say it saves them the bother of booking, jailing and testifying against the drunks. Says Larry Pattison of the St. Louis police planning and development department: "The program is working well because we're taking the drunk off the street and getting him into a medical and counseling situation. It saves time for police because we can get back on the street quicker and the drunks seem to stay off the street longer this way."

George Friesen, director of the St. Louis comprehensive alcoholism and drug-abuse program, adds: "We're also saving lives. And that's important. I know a lot of drunks we've taken through detoxification who would be dead today if they had been thrown into a drunk tank at the jail."

Lifting the criminal stigma of drunkenness has also increased the number of voluntary admissions to the center.

Illinois has one of the most recent experiments with decriminalization of drunkenness. It began July 1. The program experienced some start-up snags in Chicago when not enough detoxification centers were ready to accommodate drunks. But city officials are optimistic about the way the program is operating now.

COST IN BILLIONS

Already, it is estimated, relapses among Chicago's alcoholics have been cut by 15 per cent, says Dr. Lee Gladstone, a psychiatrist who established one of the four detoxification centers in the Chicago area. Dr. Gladstone stresses that treating, rather than jailing, drunks increases their productivity by restoring them to working health, and thus increases their usefulness to society.

"What a lot of people don't realize," he says, "is that all those drunks are not unproductive hoboes. We work with alcoholic lawyers, doctors and businessmen. The cost to the country from alcoholism is in the billions of dollars."

In Massachusetts, which decriminalized drunkenness in 1974, it is estimated that police handling of drunks has been cut by 40 to 65 per cent, according to Edward Blacker, director of the Massachusetts division of alcoholism.

"I consider the detoxification centers a success," he says. He adds that only 35 per cent of those admitted to the centers are repeaters and that membership in Alcoholics Anonymous has increased as a result of the program.

A program in King County (Seattle) in Washington State has also cut the number of repeat drunks.

MARIJUANA USE

Oregon was the first State to decriminalize minor marijuana use. In 1973, it made possession of a small amount of "grass" punishable by fine only, much like a parking violation. Some people predicted that the State would be overrun with "potheads" and "hippies." But this forecast apparently has not proved accurate.

Surveys by the Drug Abuse Council in 1974 and 1975 indicated that there was no significant increase in marijuana use in those years.

According to State Police Lt. H. D. Watson, the number of reported arrests for simple possession of marijuana jumped 22 per cent while the number of persons arrested for trafficking in the drug or cultivating it fell substantially in the first year after Oregon decriminalized its use.

Lieutenant Watson added that police are saved time and energy under the new setup because they can simply issue citations rather than having to go through normal arrest procedures.

In addition to Oregon, seven States—California, Alaska, Maine, Colorado, Ohio, South Dakota and Minnesota—have stopped arresting people for smoking marijuana or possessing small amounts of the drug.

California's new law has stirred controversy. Technically, possession of a small amount of marijuana is still treated as a minor crime, a misdemeanor. But it is punishable by a fine only. And violators are issued citations, not arrested. Many law-enforcement officers have expressed concern that the new law will lead to increased smoking, smuggling and trafficking. A few police departments, such

Alcoholics: Treatment vs. jail

Oregon: The first state to decriminalize minor marijuana use

California's trend: Easing up on arrests for marijuana use

as the one in Los Angeles, have continued zealously arresting marijuana users, even though penalties have been reduced. But relaxed enforcement is the rule in most cities.

In San Francisco, for example, police issued only 12 citations for possession in January, the first month of decriminalization. During the previous year, police had averaged 128 arrests a month for the same offense.

Despite the criticism, it appears California may liberalize its marijuana law even more. State Attorney General Evelle Younger says he thinks "the votes to eliminate all penalties for marijuana exist in the legislature, and I would anticipate that would be the way they'll go next year."

GAMBLING

Of all types of victimless crimes, gambling appears to have the widest social and governmental approval.

Thirteen States now operate some form of lottery. Thirty-two have some form of legal pari-mutuel wagering, mostly on dog racing or horse racing. Thirty-four States allow bingo playing. Three States—Connecticut, Florida and Nevada—allow bets on jai-alai games.

Three States—Connecticut, Nevada and New York—have off-track betting operations for horse racing, and the city of Chicago is considering following suit.

New York's off-track betting (OTB) is one of the most successful and publicized State-run gambling operations. Begun in 1971, it handled a record 780 million dollars in bets in the fiscal year that ended June 30. It has distributed more than 300 million dollars in profits to the State and city governments.

Gambling is receiving wide social and governmental approval

One aim of New York's OTB was to cut into the illegal gambling run by organized crime. OTB officials say they have hurt the small bookmakers. But they acknowledge that the big "bookies" haven't been affected much. In fact, big bookies often refer small bettors to one of OTB's 154 offices, because they don't want to be bothered with small wagers. One reason big bookies haven't been hurt is that they take bets on events other than horse racing—bets the State does not accept. "The Monday-night football game is probably the biggest piece of action in town," says one gambling official. Unlike the State, the big bookies give credit to bettors and don't tax winnings.

Some New Yorkers have complained that OTB has had a side effect of increasing the number of persons who gamble, because it has made such activity legal.

Says Monsignor Joseph A. Dunne, president and executive director of the National Council on Compulsive Gambling: "Off-track betting brings gambling into the neighborhoods where it never existed before."

Some complain that off-track betting encourages more people to gamble

Gamblers Anonymous, an organization that helps compulsive gamblers, reports a surge in membership since OTB began.

Maryland's "numbers game" is another State-run operation that has become very popular. Begun last summer, it was designed to resemble the illegal numbers racket of organized crime, paying off bettors who select correctly the number on a given day.

The operation has been taking in as much as 2 million dollars a week, of which 35 percent goes to the State.

Sgt. Sidney Lightfoot of the Baltimore police department's vice squad says the State lottery "has made inroads into the illegal numbers racket by an estimated 15 or 20 per cent."

SEX CRIMES

Homosexual acts and prostitution have been major targets of those who would legalize victimless sex acts. Illinois and Connecticut were the first States to eliminate laws banning consensual sodomy and homosexual acts. Since the early 1970s, 16 other States have followed suit.

Ginny Vida, media director of the National Gay Task Force, says many of the recent repeals of sodomy and homosexual laws were achieved because:

- Lawmakers were made aware that the laws applied to certain acts practiced by heterosexuals as well as homosexuals.

Factors behind the repeal of sodomy and homosexuality laws

- As courts and legislatures recognized new civil rights for homosexuals in the areas of jobs and housing, the political atmosphere for repealing sodomy-type laws became more tolerant.

- More authorities began to argue openly that it is futile to send homosexuals to jail as punishment because homosexuality is rampant in penal institutions.

The impact of these repeals has not been marked, Ms. Vida says, because many busy police departments had already backed off on prosecuting homosexuality as a crime. Removing criminal sanctions has, however, eliminated much police harassment of "gays," she adds, because police can't threaten arrest.

Prostitution, along with some other victimless crimes, has, in effect, been decriminalized in San Francisco. When District Attorney Joseph Freitas, Jr., took office in January, he announced this policy: "If it's a nonviolent, noncoercive activity between adults and it doesn't involve any other crime, my office will not bother with it."

He was criticized initially by those who predicted San Francisco would become an "open city," a haven for prostitution. Some hotel owners have since complained that his policy has hurt business because of the proliferation of prostitutes. But local authorities say there are no reliable statistics to show what has actually happened.

What is known is that, in the first six months after Mr. Freitas switched attention and resources from victimless to violent crimes, the number of serious felony offenders sent to prison doubled compared with a similar period in the previous year.

Those who back the idea of decriminalizing victimless crimes predict that it will spread even more widely in 1977, an off year for elections.

Many Americans feel it is wrong to decriminalize victimless crimes

Opposition remains strong in large areas of the country, however. Many Americans still believe that the acts being decriminalized are wrong—and should be punished.

MEASURING THE EXTENT OF CRIME

Although there are many different types of crime in our society, our analysis will deal primarily with certain serious crimes, which are usually termed *common (street) crimes.* These crimes typically involve serious offenses against persons or property and therefore elicit much public interest and concern. Such offenses include acts of criminal homicide, rape, aggravated assault, robbery, burglary, larceny, and auto theft. The FBI terms these offenses *major* or *index crimes,* and they are typically used to estimate the seriousness of the crime problem in this country. As we shall see in the sections to come, all available statistics indicate that there has been substantial growth in crime, particularly in major crime, in the United States during the last several decades. There is also much evidence indicating that the general public views crime and delinquency as major social problems, and that public concern over crime has long existed and has, in fact, increased in more recent years.

Examples of common crimes

PUBLIC CONCERN

The existence of widespread concern over crime is evidenced in a number of ways.[14] These include, for example, the development and growth of a number of voluntary organizations that deal with crime and delinquency. No doubt the most famous of these has been the National Council on Crime and Delinquency, which was founded in 1907. Today, the NCCD has an active membership of thousands of professional and nonprofessional people, who form citizens' and community "councils" active in eighteen states. Along with sponsoring research into crime and delinquency, the NCCD also provides guidance and consultation to law enforcement, judicial, and correctional personnel throughout the United States.

Voluntary organizations dealing with crime and delinquency

The establishment of various types of federal crime control legislation, such as the Juvenile Delinquency Prevention and Control Act of 1968, the Organized Crime Control Act of 1970, and the Omnibus Crime Control and Safe Streets Act of 1968, serves as another indicator of concern about the crime problem. The Omnibus Crime Control and Safe Streets Act effected the establishment of the Law Enforcement Assistance Administration (LEAA). In 1969 the LEAA budget was $63 million, and by 1976 this figure had increased to $770 million. A large share of this money is allocated to state governments as "block grants" for crime-fighting purposes. The states then reallocate specific monies to their county and municipal governments for upgrading law enforcement, improving the education of law enforcement personnel, and developing and applying systems analysis techniques to law enforcement, for example.[15]

Special types of crime control legislation

Further evidence of concern over crime is manifested in the establishment of a number of national commissions for ascertaining the pervasiveness, and investigating the causes, of crime.[16] Such commissions include the National Commission on Law Observance and Enforcement (the Wickersham Commission), the National Advisory Commission on Civil Disorders, and the National Commission on the Causes and Prevention of Violence. Another agency, the President's Commission on Law Enforcement and Administration of Justice (established by President Johnson in the 1960s), con-

The establishment of national commissions

ducted the most highly comprehensive federal government inquiry to date into the nature, extent, growth, and effects of crime in American society. Its findings were published in the volume "The Challenge of Crime in a Free Society."[17] The commission included in its 1967 report a list of over 200 specific recommendations for crime prevention and control, as well as for improvements in the criminal justice system. In its introductory comments, dealing with the extent of crime in American society and its effects on the general public, the President's Commission observed:

The President's Commission on Law Enforcement and Administration of Justice

There is much crime in America, more than ever is reported, far more than ever is solved, far too much for the health of the Nation. Every American knows that. Every American is, in a sense, a victim of crime. Violence and theft have not only injured, often irreparably, hundreds of thousands of citizens, but have directly affected everyone. Some people have been impelled to uproot themselves and find new homes. Some have been made afraid to use public streets and parks. Some have come to doubt the worth of a society in which so many people behave so badly. Some have become distrustful of the Government's ability, or even desire, to protect them. Some have lapsed into the attitude that criminal behavior is normal human behavior and consequently have become indifferent to it, or have adopted it as a good way to get ahead in life. Some have become suspicious of those they conceive to be responsible for crime: adolescents or Negroes or drug addicts or college students or demonstrators; policemen who fail to solve crimes; judges who pass lenient sentences or write decisions restricting the activities of the police; parole boards that release prisoners who resume their criminal activities. . . . The existence of crime, the talk about crime, the reports of crime and the fear of crime have eroded the basic quality of life for many Americans.[18]

Findings of public opinion surveys regarding crime

Finally, the existence of widespread public concern and fear over crime has been carefully documented by a variety of national public opinion surveys undertaken in recent years. A nationwide survey conducted by the National Opinion Research Center (NORC) for the President's Commission found that, with the exception of race relations, Americans tended to view crime as the most serious of all nationwide problems.[19] In more recent years, problems of inflation, unemployment, and energy are most often viewed as the major problems facing the nation, yet many people are concerned over crime. A Gallup poll published in December 1977 indicated, for example, that 43 percent of the American population said they thought crime had increased in their neighborhood within the last year. This survey also indicated that close to one-half (45 percent) are fearful of walking at night in their own neighborhoods, and approximately one-sixth (15 percent) are fearful within their own homes at night. Some of these figures have declined somewhat since 1975, when 50 percent of the population said they thought crime had increased in their neighborhoods and 19 percent said they were fearful in their homes.[20]

While public concern over crime continues to remain relatively high, certain people are more apprehensive than others. The 1977 Gallup poll indicated that women were more likely than men to say that crime has increased in their area during the last year. The same held true for non-whites compared to whites. Also, residents of rural areas and smaller cities were more likely to say that crime has increased in their areas compared to residents of medium (50,000–499,999 people) and large (500,000 or more) cities. Likewise, both nonwhites and women were more likely than whites and men to report that they are fearful in their own homes and afraid to walk in their neighborhoods alone at night. There were no significant differences by size of community with regard to whether people felt fear in their own homes at night. According to the 1977 Gallup poll, however, those living in medium and large cities were more fearful of walking in their neighborhoods at night than were residents of small towns and rural areas.[21]

Other recent studies indicate that the elderly are particularly fearful of crime. A survey conducted by the Chicago Planning Council on Aging indicated that 41 percent of the city's residents older than 60 feel "that crime is their most serious concern."[22] The elderly, especially those living in large cities, are especially fearful of being victimized by young juvenile gangs. There is some evidence that crimes against the urban elderly, particularly those perpetrated by youth, are in fact increasing. More important, however, crime and the increased fear of crime is beginning to have a significant impairment upon the life-styles of many of our older citizens.[23] In general, national public opinion surveys consistently indicate that people tend to view crime as a serious domestic social problem, that many Americans are apprehensive and fearful about crime on the street and in their own neighborhoods, and that some even feel unsafe in their own homes.

Fear of crime has affected the elderly

REPORTED CRIME
The most extensive statistics on crime are those published by the FBI in a yearly bulletin entitled *Uniform Crime Reports*.[24] The statistical data on crime found within these bulletins are based upon reports submitted to the FBI from local police departments throughout the United States. Each police department submits data on the number and kinds of crime reported in its specific jurisdiction. Within the last few years, the FBI has assisted in the development of state Uniform Crime Reporting Programs, for providing increased accuracy in the recording of crime data supplied by local police departments within each state. Under this new program, many states have now developed their own data collection agencies, and local police departments are required to submit data to state collection agencies rather than

Uniform Crime Reports

The new State Uniform Crime Reporting Programs

directly to the FBI. This information is then forwarded to the FBI's national Uniform Crime Reporting Program by the state collection agency.

Based upon the reports supplied by local police and state collection agencies, data are compiled and published within the *Uniform Crime Reports* with respect to the FBI's list of seven major crimes. These include criminal homicide, rape, aggravated assault, robbery, burglary, larceny, and auto theft. These seven offenses are termed major crimes, or *crime index offenses*, since they are used as an estimate or index of crime trends throughout the United States. The offenses of criminal homicide, rape, robbery, and aggravated assault are collectively termed crimes of violence; burglary, larceny, and auto theft are termed crimes against property.

The *Uniform Crime Reports* indicate that in 1977 there were 10,935,800 index offenses reported throughout the United States, and the reports indicated an increase of 21.7 percent in the rate of reported major crimes for the period between 1973 and 1977. The rate of major crimes of violence (murder, forcible rape, robbery, and aggravated assault) increased 11.8 percent, and the rate of major property crimes (burglary, larceny, and auto theft) increased 22.8 percent within this five-year period. The rate of increase for all major crimes was 50 percent during the 1968 to 1977 period.[25]

Closer examination of the *Uniform Crime Reports* reveals a number of features in the incidence and distribution of crime. For instance, in any given year there are always far more crimes against property than crimes of violence. In 1977 violent crimes accounted for 9 percent of all index crimes, while crimes against property accounted for the remaining 91 percent. Still, violent crimes as a whole in 1977 increased 2.3 percent in volume from 1976, while the number of property crimes decreased 3.8 percent in volume during the same period. Comparison of the 1977 data with data from the previous year also indicates some recent decreases in the volume of certain

The types of crime index offenses

Major crimes have increased

Property crimes far exceeded crimes against persons

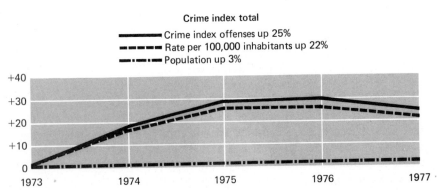

Crime index total
———— Crime index offenses up 25%
–––––– Rate per 100,000 inhabitants up 22%
—·—·— Population up 3%

+40
+30
+20
+10
0

1973   1974   1975   1976   1977

Fig. 5.1 The rising rate of crime. Source: *Uniform Crime Reports: 1977, 1978,* p. 35.

Joseph Schuyler, Stock, Boston

Crimes against property far exceed crimes of violence.

index offenses, notably robbery, burglary, and larceny-theft. Larceny-theft showed the largest decrease of all major crimes, declining 5.8 percent in volume over 1976.

With respect to the geographic distribution of crime, the *Uniform Crime Reports* data indicate that crime continues to occur more frequently in the cities—particularly in the metropolitan areas—than in rural areas. Still, in 1977, cities with a population in excess of 1,000,000 reported a 6.0 percent decrease in reported major crime over 1976. Suburban areas reported a decrease (3.3 percent), and rural areas reported a slight decrease (.9 percent) in reported major crimes for the same period.[26]

In spite of the comprehensiveness of the *Uniform Crime Report* data, it is difficult to use this information as a basis for making accurate interpretations of the true amount, distribution, and growth of crime in the United States. The *Uniform Crime Reports* are subject to a number of limitations and sources of error.[27] For one thing, not all police departments report their data on crime. For example, in 1977 reports were received from police departments that covered 98 percent of the national population. More specifically, these reports covered 99 percent of the population of standard metropolitan statistical areas, 96 percent of the population of other urban areas, and 92 percent of the rural population.[28] Second, in spite of some recent improvements in the procedures for collecting crime data, there still remains a certain lack of consistency in the methods of data classification

Uniform Crime Reports:
Limitations and errors

and tabulation by the various local law enforcement agencies. Third, the nature of reported data is such that we cannot always identify the characteristics of the offenders. For example, data on certain crime will not tell us whether the offender was male or female, a youth or an adult. Such information can be obtained only when and if the offender is arrested. Fourth, there are a number of offenses that are difficult to detect and are therefore not included within the reported index offenses. These include activities on the part of organized crime and various white-collar crimes, such as embezzlement, false advertising, corporate antitrust violation, and environmental pollution violations. Finally, perhaps the most important limitation of the *Uniform Crime Reports* is the fact that they can give us information only on reported crime—i.e., crimes reported to the police by citizens. To what degree this data represents the true spectrum of crime is difficult to tell. In many cases, crimes are not reported and thus never come to official attention.

Uniform Crime Reports reveal only "offenses known"

JUVENILE COURT STATISTICS

An important indicator of the amount of delinquency can be obtained through examination of the official records of juvenile courts. In 1975, the most recent year for which information is available, more than 1,800 juvenile courts (covering approximately 80 percent of the total U.S. population) submitted data on delinquency and other juvenile court cases. Primary responsibility for the collection of juvenile court information was transferred in 1974 from the Department of Health, Education, and Welfare to the Law Enforcement Assistance Administration (LEAA). LEAA in turn authorized the National Center for Juvenile Justice to gather and prepare national juvenile court statistical information.[29]

Measuring delinquency: The juvenile courts

Analysis of this data shows that in 1975 the juvenile courts handled 1,317,000 delinquency cases for youths 10 to 17 years of age. This represents a 5.1 percent increase in delinquency cases from the previous year and is particularly significant because the number of children in the total population aged 10 to 17 years decreased 1 percent during this time. Long-term trend data indicate that the number of delinquency cases in the period from 1960 to 1975 increased by approximately 158 percent, while the number of children 10 to 17 years of age increased by only approximately 30 percent during the same time. Moreover, from 1960 to 1975 the rate of delinquency cases almost doubled, increasing from 20.1 to 39.9 cases per 1,000 juveniles aged 10 to 17 in the general population. Statistics on the geographical distribution of delinquency cases indicate that, from 1974 to 1975, cases handled by urban courts decreased by 3.9 percent, compared to a 13.8 percent increase in semiurban court cases and a 2.3 percent increase in rural cases. Finally, even though there are more boys' than girls' delinquency cases, the number of girls' cases increased faster than the boys' during the period 1965–1974. The ratio of boys' to girls' delinquency cases decreased from 4

Delinquency has increased substantially

to 1 in the early 1970s to 3 to 1 by 1974. That ratio of three boys' cases to one girl's case remained constant during 1975.[30]

A NEW APPROACH TO HANDLING VIOLENT DELINQUENTS

Juvenile court statistics as well as arrest data clearly indicate the awesome growth in juvenile crime over the last decade. In fact, some authorities feel that adult crime represents only the "tip of the iceberg" in terms of our current crime problem. Not only has juvenile crime soared, but youth involvement in major violent crime has increased faster than youth involvement in major property crime. During the period 1968 to 1977, arrests of persons under 18 years of age increased 59.4 percent for major violent crime, compared to a 24.8 percent increase in juvenile arrests for property crimes. There is growing pressure to institute a number of reforms within the juvenile court and juvenile justice system which, if instituted, would bring about a tougher approach in the handling of violent juvenile criminals.

The Juvenile Justice Standards Commission, made up of leading psychiatrists, sociologists, penologists, youth workers, judges, and lawyers, recently completed a six year study of juvenile crime and punishment. The study resulted in twenty-three volumes of reform recommendations, which will eventually be proposed as models for new state legislation.

Citing the failure of the traditional juvenile justice system, the Commission recommends focusing on the misdeeds of juveniles who commit major crimes, rather than on what may be conceived of as their social needs. It suggests that the courts should "let the punishment fit the crime."

Specifically, the Commission urges:

- Juveniles aged 16 and 17 who commit violent crimes could be processed as adults, subject to the longer sentences now reserved for adults.
- Definite and, in some cases, longer prison terms should replace "indeterminate sentences," which have been criticized for being too lenient for violent offenders, too strict for nonviolent juveniles and unevenly applied to offenders committing similar crimes.
- The juvenile-justice process should be changed from a quasi-civil, secret, nonadversary proceeding, in which reform of the child is the main goal, to a public, adversary trial process in which punishment plays a greater role. As part of this change, juvenile defendants would be provided with lawyers.

At the same time, the Commission calls for more lenient treatment of some juveniles. Most importantly, it calls for removing "status offenders" from court jurisdiction, urging that they be handled instead by social agencies or by the family, free of the stigma of being certified "delinquent."

Status offenses, such as incorrigibility, immoral conduct, and running away from home account for about half of the one million cases that juvenile courts handle each year.[31]

ARREST DATA

In addition to providing information on the dimensions of reported crime, the *Uniform Crime Reports* also supply information on nationwide arrests for crime. In 1977 there were 10,935,800 major index offenses reported to the police. However, the *Uniform Crime Reports* data indicate that only 2,226,500 (approximately 21 percent) of these crimes were cleared by arrest. Generally, violent crimes against persons are cleared by arrest far more frequently than crimes against property. Often this is because police tend to place more effort into solving violent crimes and also because witnesses (including victims) are present who can later identify the offender.

It is important to stress that arrest data can give only a clue as to the characteristics of all violators. Many people who commit crimes are never arrested, while others who are arrested are never convicted of the offense. In addition, it is likely that law enforcement officers tend to react differently in their contacts with various types of people.[32] For these reasons, arrest data should be viewed primarily as a measure of police activity; at best it can give us only a rough indication of the types of people who violate laws.[33]

Over the years, statistics have consistently indicated that many of those arrested for crime are young. The *Uniform Crime Reports* indicate, for example, that nationwide in 1977, people under 15 years of age accounted for 8 percent, and persons under 18 accounted for 24 percent, of all arrests. Also, persons under 21 comprised 40 percent, and those under 25 accounted for 56 percent, of all arrests.[33] In addition, statistics show that persons under 18 years of age are far more frequently arrested for major property crimes than for crimes of violence. In 1977 the *Uniform Crime Reports* indicated that the under-18-year-old age group comprised 46.2 percent of arrests for major property crimes and only 21 percent of arrests for major violent crimes.[34] It is difficult to ascertain the specific circumstances under which youth crime occurs, but a recent LEAA study of the largest cities in the nation shows that youth crime, particularly violent crime, has become increasingly gang-related. Based on this study, it was estimated that 2,700 youth gangs, with a total of 81,500 members, can be found within the nation's six largest cities alone, and that increased amounts of violence are being directed against ordinary citizens rather than against other gangs' members.[35]

In addition to indicating differences in age, statistics also show that most persons who are arrested for crimes are male. With respect to all arrests in 1977, males were arrested five times more frequently than females.

Few major crimes are cleared by arrest

Youths are disproportionately arrested for crime

Young people are often arrested for property crimes

Males are more frequently arrested than females

Females accounted for 16 percent of the total arrests and for 20.1 percent of arrests for major index crimes during that year. Approximately 22 percent of arrests for major property crimes and 10 percent of arrests for major violent crimes were of females, and they accounted for 22.7 percent of the embezzlement arrests, 12.8 percent of the aggravated assault arrests, and 13.9 percent of the arrests for drug abuse violations. Of the major index crimes, female involvement was primarily in the area of larceny, which comprised 22.1 percent of all female arrests.

During the period 1973 to 1977, male arrests increased by 1.7 percent for all crimes and by 15.9 percent for serious crimes. On the other hand, during the same five-year period, female arrests increased by 17.3 percent for all crimes and by 32.8 percent for serious crimes. Long-term trend data also indicate that, in general, female arrests have been increasing faster than male arrests. During the period 1968 to 1977, male arrests increased by 13.4 percent for all crimes and by 36.4 percent for only the serious crimes, whereas female arrests increased by 57.6 percent for all crimes and by 115.5 percent for serious crimes.[36]

Differences in arrests are also very significant with respect to race. The 1977 data indicate that whites accounted for 71.7 percent of all arrests, compared to 25.7 percent for blacks and 2.7 percent for all other races, including Indians, Chinese, and Japanese Americans. With respect to arrests for the major index offenses only, the 1977 data show that whites accounted for 64.2 percent of arrests for these crimes, compared to 33.5 percent for blacks and 2.3 percent for all other races. Whites comprised 52.2 percent of arrests for major violent crimes and 67.1 percent of arrests for major property crimes. On the other hand, blacks accounted for 45.7 percent of arrests for major violent crimes and 30.6 percent of arrests for major property crimes. Blacks were arrested more frequently than whites for the major index offenses of murder, nonnegligent manslaughter, and robbery.[37]

Black-white arrest differentials become even more significant when the information on arrests is compared with the proportion of each race in the total population. In 1976, whites comprised 87 percent, and blacks comprised 11.5 percent, of the total population of the United States.[38] When this data is compared with arrest figures, we can see that whites are underrepresented in arrest figures, while blacks are overrepresented, by two or three times more than their proportion in the population. In large measure, it would appear that the higher crime rate among blacks can best be accounted for in terms of their lower socioeconomic status and also the likelihood of their receiving differential treatment from law enforcement and judicial agencies.

In addition to age, sex, and race, crime is also related to the factor of social class. The *Uniform Crime Reports* do not give any indication of the social class position of offenders reported or arrested for crime. Some independent studies based upon official statistics have indicated that those involved in crime, particularly index or street crime, come primarily from the lower socioeconomic status levels within our society. We must caution,

Racial variations in arrests

Blacks are overrepresented in arrest data

Crimes of certain classes often miss official attention

however, that even these studies may not give a full picture of crime's true distribution across class lines. There is much evidence suggesting that there is a great deal of crime, particularly middle- and upper-class white-collar and other property crime, that never comes to official attention.[39] Along these lines, sociologist Walter Reckless uses the concept of "categoric risks," which refers to the fact that the lower the socioeconomic status of an offender, the greater the risk of being arrested and ultimately imprisoned.[40] In part, the greater likelihood of the lower classes to become part of the official crime statistics can be explained by their greater lack of technical and legal knowledge as well as by their lack of financial resources, which are all necessary for coping with and, in a sense, "handling" our legal and judicial machinery.

VICTIMIZATION STUDIES

Many crimes go unreported to official sources

As we indicated above, one of the major weaknesses of the official statistics on crime is that at best they give information on offenses known to the police. For quite some time, sociologists and others have recognized that there is a tremendous amount of crime that is never reported to the police or to other official agencies. In order to obtain more comprehensive information on the true extent of crime and on its victims, the President's Commission on Law Enforcement and Administration of Justice enlisted the National Opinion Research Center (NORC) of the University of Chicago to conduct a nationwide survey on crime victimization. The survey sampled a total of 10,000 households, asking if people had been victims of crime during the past year. Based on the findings of this survey, the President's commission concluded that "the actual amount of crime in the United States today is several times that reported in the Uniform Crime Reports."

Victimization studies: An important source of information on crime

As Table 5.1 shows, the NORC survey found that the rates of personal injury crimes were approximately twice as high as the *Uniform Crime Reports* figures and that the rate of property crimes actually exceeded twice the amount indicated by the reports. Forcible rapes were over 3.5 times the reported rate. Burglaries, aggravated assaults, and larcenies were also two or three times higher than that of the official reported rates. Only in the cases of murder and auto theft were the NORC survey rates similar to the *Uniform Crime Reports* rates.[41] The survey also found that males are far more likely than females to be victims, that nonwhites are far more likely than whites to be victims of crime except for larceny, and that people with lower incomes are much more likely than persons with higher incomes to be victims of rape, robbery, and burglary.[42] The President's commission also cited the results of victimization surveys undertaken by the Bureau of Social Science Research (BSSR) in several Washington, D.C. precincts. These findings indicated that the rates for major crimes reported to the survey ranged from three to ten times higher (depending on the offense) than rates reported to the local police.[43]

NORC and BSSR surveys

**Table 5.1 Comparison of survey and UCR rates
(per 100,000 population)**

INDEX CRIMES	NORC SURVEY, 1965–66	UCR RATE FOR INDIVIDUALS, 1965*	UCR RATE FOR INDIVIDUALS AND ORGANIZA-TIONS, 1965*
Willful homicide	3.0	5.1	5.1
Forcible rape	42.5	11.6	11.6
Robbery	94.0	61.4	61.4
Aggravated assault	218.3	106.6	106.6
Burglary	949.1	299.6	605.3
Larceny ($50 and over)	606.5	267.4	393.3
Motor vehicle theft	206.2	226.0	251.0
Total violence	357.8	184.7	184.7
Total property	1,761.8	793.0	1,249.6

* *Uniform Crime Reports*, 1965, p. 51. The UCR national totals do not distinguish crimes committed against individuals or households from those committed against businesses or other organizations. The UCR rate for individuals is the published national rate adjusted to eliminate burglaries, larcenies, and vehicle thefts not committed against individuals or households. No adjustment was made for robbery.

Source: The President's Commission on Law Enforcement and Administration of Justice, *The Challenge of Crime in a Free Society*, New York: E.P. Dutton, 1968, p. 97.

In addition to the studies conducted for the President's commission, a number of major and more recent victimization studies were undertaken in 1972 and 1973 by the Law Enforcement Assistance Administration and the Census Bureau. The 1972 LEAA study of the nation's five largest cities indicated that only one-half of the crimes committed were actually reported to the local police agencies. Property crimes such as burglary were more frequently reported to the police than were crimes of violence against persons. The 1972 study also found that adult males and younger persons were more likely to be victims of crime than were females and older persons. The study also indicated that nonwhites were more likely to be victims of crimes such as robbery and burglary than were whites, and that people with lower incomes were much more likely to be victims of robbery and larceny than were those with higher incomes. In short, many of the LEAA study findings on victim characteristics are fairly consistent with those reported earlier by the President's commission. Finally, there is also some consistency between these findings and data supplied by a 1977 nationwide Gallup poll, which indicate that lower income groups and nonwhites are more likely to be victims of crimes, particularly crimes against the person, than are upper income persons and whites. That same poll also indicated that one household in five was "hit by crime at least once" during the twelve-month period ending in November 1977.[44]

Studies of crime in the five largest cities

Sociologists, psychologists, and others have a variety of theories for criminal behavior such as the bizarre murders by the Manson "family."

EXPLANATIONS FOR CRIMINAL BEHAVIOR

THE CLASSICAL SCHOOL

Attempts to explain crime date back through many centuries of recorded history. During the sixteenth and seventeenth centuries, for example, people who engaged in crime and other forms of deviant behavior were thought to be possessed by demons and evil spirits. During the eighteenth century, however, explanations for criminal behavior began to change radically with the emergence of the classical school of criminology, founded by Cesare Beccaria and Jeremy Bentham.[45] The classical school viewed human behavior as essentially rational in nature and felt that people had the ability to choose right from wrong. It was felt that the major element governing a person's choice of action were the basic human desires to obtain pleasure and avoid pain. Leaders of the classical school proposed a number of legal and judicial reforms along these lines to curb the problem of crime. These included the imposition of penalties and deterrents severe enough to outweigh any pleasures encountered through the commission of a criminal act.

The classical school and rationality

Under these circumstances, it was thought, people would willingly refrain from crime, once they had calculated that the penalties attached to the commission of a criminal act would exceed the pleasure involved in the act itself. Needless to say, proposals such as these had little effect on the crime problem.

Statistical improvements in crime measurement began to show the existence of certain patterns in the manifestation of crime. It was discovered that crime varied by age, race, sex, and geographic area. It became obvious that factors far beyond personal calculation and motivation were involved in the manifestation of crime. With the development of various scientific disciplines during the nineteenth century, attention drew away from notions of rationalism and punishment, moving toward an investigation of the causes of crime and stressing in particular the influence of hereditary, psychological, and social factors.[46]

BIOLOGICAL EXPLANATIONS

During the late nineteenth century, Cesare Lombroso attempted to explain crime on the basis of biological characteristics and heredity.[47] On the basis of various physiological and cranial measurements of known criminals, Lombroso developed the theory that certain persons who engaged in crime were "born criminals." Criminals could be recognized from noncriminals by various physical "stigmata," such as a long lower jaw, flattened nose, and long ape-like arms. He was careful to point out that the stigmata themselves did not cause crime. Rather, they were simply visible indicators of a personality type that was in essence a primitive throwback on the Darwinian scale of human evolution.[48]

The specific theories of Lombroso were eventually disproved, but research into the hereditary and constitutional factors of crime has continued. The more recent studies of William Sheldon and Ernest Kretschmer, for example, have attempted to demonstrate a relationship between certain body types or builds and various aspects of personality.[49] In turn, attempts have been made to demonstrate that certain of these "body-mind" types are particularly prone to crime and delinquency. Sheldon, for instance, identified three major types of physiques: endomorphs (soft, round people), mesomorphs (muscular, athletic people), and ectomorphs (tall, thin people). He claimed that mesomorphic persons were the most likely to engage in criminal and delinquent behavior. Present research into hereditary and biological factors of crime has attempted to demonstrate that the existence of an extra Y-chromosome in the male (the XYY pattern) leads to excessively aggressive behavior. In turn, it is theorized that such aggressiveness leads to the predisposition to various antisocial behaviors, particularly to crime against persons. To date, research into this area has been very inconclusive and offers little possibility for explaining the phenomena of crime and delinquency.[50]

Penalties would deter crime

Lombroso and biological explanations

The research of Sheldon and Kretschmer

PSYCHOLOGICAL EXPLANATIONS

Personality factors in crime

In contrast to hereditary and biological theories, there are also various psychological explanations, which emphasize the importance of personality factors and their role in deviant behavior. From this point of view, personality is acquired and developed *after* birth as a result of socialization and interpersonal relations with others. Thus abnormal personalities are developed, not biologically inherited, and are characteristic of persons who have been inadequately socialized to the norms and demands of others and of society in general. Personality explanations thus stress the influence of certain psychological disorders (psychosis and psychopathy) as a basis for explaining many other types of deviant behavior, such as crime and delinquency.[51]

Crime and psychological disorders are not often associated

In general, however, personality theories have been found to provide rather inadequate explanations for crime and delinquency. It is more than evident that most people who commit crimes do not suffer from psychological disorders, especially serious disorders. For example, a number of studies have consistently shown that relatively few persons (5 percent or less) imprisoned for crimes have been diagnosed as psychotic. Certain people with psychosis may commit crimes, but this in itself is not proof that the behavior resulted from the psychosis.[52]

SOCIOLOGICAL EXPLANATIONS

As we have seen above, biological and psychological theories tend to explain crime on the basis of the individual's physical or mental defects or abnormalities. In contrast, sociologists assume that individuals who engage in crime and delinquency do not represent a special class of abnormal or inferior people, either mentally or physically. Sociological theories tend to focus upon the influence of environmental and social factors in explaining the phenomena of crime and delinquency. Thus, in attempting to discover the causes of crime, sociologists stress the importance of looking at the general society and at the impact of social and group factors upon individual behavior.[53] Some sociologists argue, for example, that crime and delinquency are simply an inevitable result of the continuing social and economic inequalities found within the society itself. Furthermore, they contend that the law is inherently biased toward the interests of society's dominant or ruling groups and classes. Other sociologists argue that crime represents a natural fact of social life and is a sign of a healthy society. From their point of view, crime actually helps to ensure the stability of the society by identifying and clarifying social standards for acceptable and unacceptable behavior. Rather than disrupting society, crime actually serves to strengthen group solidarity by uniting people in disapproval against the deviant.[54]

Sociologists do not see criminals as "special types"

Crime may be the result of social and economic inequality

In general, sociological theories of crime and delinquency attempt to provide explanations for two interrelated yet analytically distinct questions.[55] First, they attempt to account for the specific causal processes by which individuals become criminals and delinquents: "How and why does a person become a criminal?" Second, they attempt to explain variations in the crime rates: "Why do different groups and categories of people within society manifest different rates of crime and delinquency?" There are a substantial number of sociological theories aimed at providing answers to these and other related questions. Of the leading theories, *labeling, differential association*, the *theory of anomie*, and the *subcultural theories* offer the most adequate explanations for the causes and varying rates of deviant behavior, particularly crime and delinquency.

The Individual and Labeling. This was recently advanced and popularized by sociologist Howard Becker. Labeling theory starts with the basic idea that we mentioned earlier, namely that deviance (criminality) is relative, since group norms and laws are relative. Thus what is deviant depends not on the act itself nor on a specific attribute of the person who commits the act. What is deviant is always dependent upon, and in a sense created by, group norms and social reactions to human acts. In this sense, deviance results from social judgments (which are relative to group norms) that are applied to certain forms of behavior. Becker states: "Social groups create deviance by making the rules whose infraction constitutes deviance, and by applying the rules to particular people and labeling them as outsiders." Thus, "deviance is not a quality of the act the person commits, but rather a consequence of the application by others of rules and sanctions to an 'offender.' The deviant is one to whom that label has successfully been applied; deviant behavior is behavior that people so label."[56]

From this perspective, many persons may be involved occasionally or regularly in various forms of deviant behavior without other people's knowledge. However if their deviance becomes known, they become labeled by others as deviant. In a sense, this situation generates a type of "self-fulfilling prophecy." The stigma of the deviant label renders them "outsiders" and they are inevitably excluded from participation in more conventional relationships and groups.[57] Thus their relationships with family and friends are likely to become strained and severed, and they may be forced into illegitimate types of work and activity, since a respectable employer may prefer not to hire them. All of this leads to the greater probability that they may be forced to associate with other "outsiders." Moreover, the deviant label increases the chances that others will become suspicious and keep a close "eye" upon their behavior, and sooner or later, the others are likely to find something that will confirm their suspicions. Finally, the ongoing process of labeling, stigmatizing, and ostracising is also bound to deeply influence their self-image to the point where they truly come to identify with and accept the view that others have of them. This deviant self-image ensures the likelihood that they will continue in their deviant activities, perhaps even as members of an organized deviant group.[58]

Why do people commit crimes? Why do crime rates vary among different groups?

The label of "deviant" has a powerful influence on behavior

Labeling creates a "self-fulfilling prophecy"

Labeling theory represents a somewhat new approach to understanding deviant behavior. However, the theory has been criticized on several counts. First of all, the initial labeling of an individual as a deviant (or criminal) does not automatically necessitate the person's continuing in the deviant behavior. For example, many individuals who are actually convicted of crime do not repeat their offenses nor do they adopt criminal life-styles or careers. Second, the theory deals mainly with the role of social reactions to deviance, particularly the long-range consequences of labeling and stigmatization on the individual. It should be clear, however, that this still leaves unanswered the question of why the individual committed the deviant act in the first place. Other theories provide much more adequate answers to this latter question. One such theory is that of differential association.[59]

The Individual and Differential Association. This theory was developed by Professor Edwin H. Sutherland, who proposed that criminal behavior, like all other social behavior, is learned. This learning occurs through interaction with others and, for the most part, occurs within intimate personal groups. In addition, this learning includes acquiring the techniques as well as the motives, attitudes, and rationalizations for committing crimes. The core element of the theory is Sutherland's statement that "a person becomes delinquent because of an excess of definitions favorable to violation of law over definitions unfavorable to violation of law."[60] In terms of this last statement, Sutherland would argue that everyone has contact with or exposure to both criminal and noncriminal behavior patterns, values, and attitudes. However, as a result of associations, a person becomes a criminal because he or she is exposed to (learns) more definitions favorable to or encouraging violation of law than definitions unfavorable to law violation. Thus, as Sutherland states, "When persons become criminal, they do so because of contacts with criminal patterns and also because of isolation from anticriminal patterns." The opposite would hold true for explaining why persons conform to legal codes. Sutherland also made clear that the greater the duration, frequency, and intensity of "associations with criminal behavior," the greater the likelihood that the person will violate the law. Using this theory, it would not be difficult to explain how and why a youth in a high delinquency neighborhood may turn to crime, since there is a likelihood that delinquent juveniles are already present to provide the youth with both example and encouragement. Likewise, adult white-collar corporate employees may learn from other employees the standardized techniques and rationalizations for padding expense accounts and for other forms of corporate theft.[61]

In formulating the theory of differential association, Sutherland was attempting to explain a wide variety of crime, particularly what is termed white-collar or *occupational* crime. Sutherland defined this phenomenon as "a crime committed by a person of respectability and high social status in the course of his occupation." Sutherland's study of officially recorded cor-

Labeling: A new approach to understanding deviance

The influence of learning on crime

People are exposed to criminal as well as noncriminal influences

porate violations of law in the 1940s constitutes one of the most widely known and comprehensive studies of white-collar crime to date. Sutherland examined the corporate dealings of seventy of the largest mining, manufacturing, and mercantile corporations in the United States and noted that the pattern of corporate white-collar crime was extensive. Included were 222 cases of patent infringement, 307 cases of restraint of trade, 158 cases of unfair labor practices, 97 cases of false advertising, 66 cases of illegal rebates, and 130 cases of miscellaneous corporate offenses.[62]

Since the time of Sutherland's initial writings, the definition of white-collar crime has expanded to include a variety of additional occupational crimes within the business world, the government, and the professions.[63] These include embezzlement, numerous types of fraud, kickbacks for political favors, illegal corporate campaign contributions, illegal acts of high political officials, fee splitting, padding expense accounts, price fixing, antitrust violations, employee theft, and more.

No one knows the true extent or the actual economic cost to society of today's white-collar crime. Frequently, these crimes are never officially reported or recorded and the offenders are often never prosecuted. There are a number of reasons for the infrequent prosecutions of white-collar offenders. These include the facts that occupational offenses are not highly publicized, that many white-collar criminals have a relatively high social status, and that the public tends to view these offenders as essentially respectable people rather than as criminals. In addition, since corporations are regarded as legal entities under federal law, it is more common for criminal actions to be handled by administrative agencies, such as the Federal Trade Commission or the Internal Revenue Service, than by the criminal courts.[64] Still, without doubt, the economic cost to society of white-collar crime is far greater than that of property index crime.[65]

Over the years, differential association theory has undergone a substantial amount of empirical testing and criticism. According to some researchers (Melvin DeFleur and Richard Quinney, for example), the principal problem with the theory is that some of its concepts are vaguely worded and phrased at such a high level of abstraction that precise mathematical testing of the theory is extremely difficult.[66] There have been several recent attempts to overcome this problem by reformulating the theory in more empirically measurable and precise terms. One such attempt was made by Robert Burgess and Ronald Akers. Their *differential association reinforcement* theory is essentially a reformulation that links differential association with many of the modern concepts and principles found within operant conditioning or reinforcement theory.[67] On the other hand, several other studies have indicated that in some cases the influence of associates in the learning of criminal behavior patterns appears to be minimal. Donald Cressey, in his study of embezzlers imprisoned in Illinois and California, found that the offenders did not necessarily learn the required criminal techniques from

Evaluation of differential association theory

Are one's associates always important?

their associates. Rather, their previously learned general business skills were sufficient to enable them to commit their crimes.[68] In addition, Travis Hirschi found that, although delinquent boys do tend to associate with other delinquents, they do not generally develop a strong identification with them or hold much respect for their opinions. He feels that often delinquent boys have delinquent associations only because they manifest similar delinquent backgrounds in the first place.[69]

Research tends to support differential association

In spite of these criticisms, the theory of differential association has been and continues to be held in high regard by sociologists. The theory has been subjected to extensive amounts of empirical testing and research, and most of the evidence thus derived tends to lend support to its validity. In general, the theory has proved to be an important aid in explaining a wide variety of juvenile and adult criminal behavior.

Explaining Rates of Crime—Anomie. As we mentioned above, a number of sociological theories have also attempted to explain the variations in the rates of crime and delinquency manifested by different groups and categories of people within society. Explanations for these variations require moving to broader levels of theoretical explanation. Two such theories would be the anomie and subcultural theories.

Durkheim's use of anomie

The well-known sociologist Emile Durkheim was the first to develop the concept of anomie (meaning normlessness) to explain increased rates of suicide produced by rapid social change within society. Durkheim used the term "anomic suicide" to refer to acts of self-destruction resulting from an abrupt breakdown of society's norms, which often occurs during periods of political crisis or economic depression.[70] In turn, sociologist Merton has modified the concept of anomie for explaining other forms of deviant behavior, particularly crime and delinquency.[71]

Anomie: A lack of integration between goals and means

According to Merton, anomie results from a lack of integration between culturally prescribed goals and the availability of legitimate or institutionalized means (norms) for goal attainment. He contends that American society places a great deal of emphasis upon the attainment of material and economic success. However, as a result of their structural positions within society, certain groups (the lower classes and certain racial and ethnic groups) have limited opportunities for, and are often denied access to, the legitimate means (a good job or a good education) to achieve this success. Given this situation, the members of these disadvantaged groups tend to experience many pressures and frustrations, which are often severe enough to cause them to deviate from the legitimate goals and/or means (norms) of the society. From Merton's point of view, individuals who are restricted in or denied access to the use of these legitimate means tend to become anomic,

Anomic individuals are more likely to deviate

or alienated from the society, and thus have a greater tendency to engage in various forms of deviant behavior.

Some individuals who find themselves blocked in goal attainment may simply decide to give up on the conventional goals as well as on the legitimate means. These people reject both and withdraw from the situation. Drug addiction, alcoholism, and suicide represent contemporary forms of this deviant response. Others may not only reject but actually rebel against the social order, attempting to introduce new goals and means for the society as a whole. Various radicals and revolutionary groups represent this form of deviant response.[72]

Merton stresses, however, that individuals who encounter limited access to the use of legitimate means frequently adopt a form of anomic or deviant response that he terms *innovation*. The innovator rejects only the legitimate means, not the goals, and substitutes instead illegitimate (criminal) means to achieve the goals. Merton contends that much crime (property crime, organized crime, robbery, drug pushing, and so forth) can be viewed as a form of anomic response that results when conventional or legitimate means for goal attainment are blocked. Thus the higher rates of crime characteristic of certain groups in our society are merely symptomatic of a disjunction between culturally approved goals and opportunities to use culturally approved means to attain them.[73]

> Crime rates are symptomatic of anomie

The theory of anomie provides important insights into the nature and origins of various forms of deviant behavior, particularly crime and delinquency. In general, however, the theory is more useful for explaining crimes against property than certain violent crimes against persons, such as murder, forcible rape, or aggravated assault. In addition, the theory gives a much better explanation for crime committed by the lower classes of our society than for crime committed by the more affluent classes, which by and large are neither deprived nor denied the use of the legitimate means for goal attainment.

> Anomie is useful for explaining property crimes

Explaining Rates of Crime—Subcultural Theory. In addition to anomie, subcultural theories have also attempted to provide explanations for variations in rates of crime and delinquency. When sociologists speak of subcultures, we refer to the fact that, in complex societies like our own, there are a variety of subgroups that, for the most part, are similar to or share the general culture. Nevertheless, they also maintain some unique norms that distinguish them from the wider culture. For example, there is a wide variety of religious, ethnic, and occupational subcultures within American society. The subcultural explanation of deviance stresses the fact that, given a multitude of subcultures, some will invariably contain norms that will be deviant from and in actual conflict with those of the general society. Conformity to these norms therefore involves deviance from those of the society at large. In this sense, deviance (rates of crime and delinquency) is simply a product of deviant subcultures. Obviously, subcultural theorists

> Deviance as a product of deviant subcultures

would assume that on the individual level, deviant (criminal) behavior is learned in association with others, but this is a different matter from that of attempting to account for variations in the rates of crime and delinquency. According to subcultural theories, these rates reflect the existence of deviant subcultural norms that are learned, shared, and perpetuated over time.[74]

Varieties of deviant
subcultures

Sociologists have noted the existence of many types of criminal subcultures, such as those related to professional theft, racketeering, organized crime, prostitution, and drug pushing. However, much sociological attention has been focused upon analyzing the nature and origins of delinquent subcultures. It is within these subcultures that youths, through participation and gradual absorption into group life, become socialized to a variety of norms, beliefs, and skills necessary to the commission of delinquent acts.

The delinquent gang

Albert Cohen, noting relatively high rates of delinquency on the part of working- (lower) class youths, developed a widely respected subcultural theory on delinquency.[75] According to Cohen, the delinquent subculture is most clearly manifested by the delinquent gang. For Cohen, the delinquent subculture exists because it offers a solution to the status problems and frustrations experienced by working-class boys in their efforts to achieve middle-class success. Although these boys typically aspire to middle-class life-styles and goals, their early life experiences leave them unprepared to successfully compete in school and other areas necessary for upward mobility. Working-class boys are constantly evaluated in terms of "middle-class measuring rods," as Cohen phrases it, yet their working-class background does not adequately equip them for the practice of middle-class standards necessary for success, such as suppression of aggression, deferment of gratification, self-reliance and self-discipline, ambition, and academic achievement. Given this discrepancy, the boys often experience status frustration.

Delinquency as rejection
of middle-class stan-
dards and goals

In order to deal with this frustration, working-class youths may develop what Cohen terms a "delinquent response": The youths reject middle-class standards and turn to the delinquent subculture of the gang. This subculture provides them with new forms of status, which are achieved through gang membership. Cohen describes this delinquent subculture as malicious, non-utilitarian, and negativistic. It is organized around the need to openly renounce anything suggesting middle-class values because such life-styles are largely beyond hope of attainment.[76]

Over the years, Cohen's analysis has been subject to a number of criticisms and modifications. Although agreeing that gang membership is often rooted in status problems, Gresham Sykes and David Matza argue that the delinquent subculture does not totally reject middle-class standards.[77] Instead, delinquent boys tend to have ambivalent attitudes toward middle-class standards and conformity to law. According to Sykes and Matza, the delinquent subculture solves this dilemma through its use of "techniques of neutralization," which permit youths to neutralize, or rationalize, their delinquent acts. Thus the youth may deny that their acts really

Delinquents "neutralize"
their acts

caused anyone harm, or claim that they only "borrowed" rather than stole a car, or assert that the victim of an attack actually deserved it.

Richard Cloward and Lloyd Ohlin have noted the existence of three distinct types of delinquent subcultures, the *criminal, conflict,* and *retreatist* subcultures.[78] In their view, not even illegitimate means (let alone legitimate means) are always available to lower-class youths. Thus, the particular type of delinquent subculture that forms depends in large part on whether the youths have access to deviant (criminal) opportunities and to adult criminal role models within their neighborhoods. Criminal subcultures develop in areas where opportunities for exposure to adult criminal models are present. It is likely that youths within this subculture will learn a variety of criminal roles and progress to adult criminal careers. Conflict (gang fighting) subcultures arise when access to both illegitimate opportunities and criminal role models is not available. Finally, the retreatist (drug using) subculture exists for those who are "double failures"—they cannot adapt to legitimate conventional means or to illegitimate means and criminal role models.[79]

As we have seen, sociological explanations for crime and delinquency are quite numerous and diverse. Some of these theories address the questions of how and why certain persons become criminals. Others attempt to explain variations in the rates of criminal and delinquent activity among the different categories of people within society. It is important to note that these theories help to explain some but obviously not all crime and delinquency. Ideally, future sociologists will provide more comprehensive theories, which will aid in the development of programs aimed at large-scale reduction of crime in American society.

> **Types of delinquent subcultures**

RESPONSES TO CRIME

RETRIBUTION—DETERRENCE

Throughout history, one dominant societal response to crime has been retribution, which involves the notion that a wrongdoer should be punished in order to "pay back" or compensate for his or her criminal acts. Retributive forms of punishment can be traced to ancient times. The famous Code of Hammurabi, for example, stressed the doctrine of *lex taliones*, "an eye for an eye." This brutal penal practice was based on the motive of revenge for crime: murderers were to be murdered themselves; those who caused physical injury to others were to be harmed in like manner. During the feudal period, trial by "ordeal" was common. In the "ordeal by water," for example, the accused were bound and cast into a stream; those who remained afloat were considered guilty. This period witnessed an increase in the severity of retributive punishments and a growth in the number of offenses to which such punishments applied. Punishment by death was frequent, followed by mutilation, corporal punishment, and banishment. In addition, a number of lesser offenses were punishable by fines, and it was

> **Retribution involves "paying back" society**

common practice to levy severe fines against fraudulent businessmen and unscrupulous landlords.[80]

Beccaria's and Bentham's penal reforms

It was not until the late eighteenth century that Beccaria and Bentham advocated a new philosophy and a new system of legal and penal reform. They argued that the proper objective of punishment should be to protect society and its laws. It was their view that punishment should not be inflicted for vengeance; rather, the primary purpose of punishment should be the reduction or deterrence of crime. They advocated that the excessively brutal punishments of death, mutilation, etc. be abolished and that penal reforms be introduced so that "the punishment fit the crime." Thus, it was

Can crime be deterred by threat of punishment?

their belief that crime in general could actually be deterred through the responsible and rational utilization of punishment. The punishments inflicted should be just severe enough to outweigh any pleasures, either contemplated or actually experienced, that could be derived from the commission of a criminal act. In this way, the threat of punishment would deter most people from committing crimes in the first place, and the actual infliction of punishment would deter the offender from committing additional criminal acts. Beccaria also presented convincing arguments for imprisonment as a form of punishment, saying it would be the most effective and efficient method for carrying out these new penal reforms. As it happened, a more than adequate number of jails and prisons were already conveniently available throughout Europe. Prior to this time, these buildings were used for the temporary confinement of minor offenders and those awaiting trial, and they were easily adapted for use in implementing Beccaria's programs.[81]

American society: The origins of imprisonment

By the turn of the nineteenth century, imprisonment had become a major form of punishment. In America, the Quakers of Pennsylvania spearheaded the movement to have imprisonment take the place of other forms of punishment. The Quakers emphasized that imprisonment should have a deterrence function, but more important, that is should also serve the purpose of reforming and rehabilitating the inmate. The Quakers were also very concerned with the potential detrimental effects of prisoner contact and association. Therefore, the two major penitentiaries built in Pennsylvania utilized what has come to be known as the "solitary system." Under this

The "solitary system"

system, each prisoner had a personal prison cell and exercise area. In effect, each prisoner was required to live and work in solitary confinement throughout the entire sentence. This system solved the problem of prisoner contact, provided prisoners more time and opportunity to learn a trade, and also gave them more time to think over their evil ways and practice penitence (hence the name penitentiary).[82]

The Quakers were more than satisfied with this system, but others were concerned with the detrimental effects that were likely to result from the prisoners' extended periods of physical and social isolation. Hence, in the decades that followed, few states adopted the "Pennsylvania system." In-

Steve Hansen, Stock, Boston

Dehumanizing and regimenting of prisoners has long been a part of our penal system.

stead, most states opted for an alternative plan of prison administration. This plan came to be known as the "silent system" or the "Auburn system," first introduced at the penitentiary in Auburn, New York, in 1823. Under this system prisoners were permitted to work side by side, but at no time were they allowed to speak or even glance at one another. When passing one another outside their cells, prisoners had to keep their eyes downcast. When moving about in the company of others, prisoners were required to walk in "lock step" formation (i.e., in single file, facing the back of the person immediately ahead). Infraction of these rules brought swift and severe disciplinary action.[83]

The "silent system"

During the late nineteenth and early twentieth centuries, many of these repressive disciplinary measures began to fade. Eventually, new regulations allowed prisoners to talk and associate with one another in a comfortable, open manner in all spheres of activity. We should note, however, that even during the twentieth century, prisons in themselves have not led the move for correctional innovations. Change within the prison system has occurred only slowly and, as we shall see, some of the older, more repressive methods are still being used in many institutions.[84]

Prisons still represent repression

CONTEMPORARY PRISONS: THEORY AND PRACTICE

Rehabilitation: The object of imprisonment

During the last several decades, rehabilitation of offenders, at least in theory, has been the dominant goal of imprisonment and other forms of correction. The aim has been to help the offender become a useful and productive member of society, instilling the appropriate standards, attitudes, and skills necessary for the offender to live a more acceptable life upon release. This philosophy is clearly emphasized by the National Advisory Commission on Criminal Justice Standards and Goals. The Commission states:

> A rehabilitative purpose is or ought to be implicit in every sentence of an offender unless ordered otherwise by a sentencing court. The correctional authority . . . should give first priority to implementation of statutory specifications or statements of purpose on rehabilitative services. A correctional authority's rehabilitation program should include a mixture of educational, vocational, counseling, and other services appropriate to offender needs. Correctional authorities regularly should advise courts and sentencing judges of the extent and availability of rehabilitative services and programs within the correctional system to permit proper sentencing decisions and realistic evaluation of treatment alternatives.[85]

The reality of prison life

Prisons: Punitive, de-humanizing, and hostility-breeding

In spite of these purposes and goals, the reality of the prison experience is quite different. In actuality, the prison atmosphere has remained punitive and oppressive, and prisoners are still subjected to harsh discipline and highly repressive regulations. Elaborate systems of regulations circumscribe the entire range of the prisoner's daily behavior: how and when to eat, work, sleep, etc. Violence is also often a way of life within many prisons, and prisoners are exposed to much verbal abuse and physical brutality, from guards as well as other inmates. Prison life exposes the offenders to a wide range of physically and psychologically degrading experiences, such as the strip search, regulation haircuts, and numbered uniforms. Ultimately, prisons punish offenders in many ways other than simply depriving them of their freedom. Prison is a punitive, dehumanizing, hostility-building experience, which for many serves only to reinforce criminal behavior patterns and attitudes. This experience provides offenders little chance to develop respect for themselves, for others, or for society, and it gives them little opportunity to deal with the problems responsible for their commitment in the first place. The system segregates the offenders from the society to which they are ultimately expected to adapt. Meanwhile, that society frequently offers little constructive assistance to help the offenders function effectively and acceptably in society when they are released. Additional indicators of the oppressive and debilitating atmosphere of many present correctional institutions within the United States can be obtained by examining the quality of the prisoners' living facilities within these institutions.

According to the Law Enforcement Assistance Administration (1977), there were a total of 265,674 prisoners serving sentences of more than one year as of December, 1976—240,862 within state institutions and the remaining 24,812 within federal institutions.[86] Recent data supplied by the Law Enforcement Assistance Administration (1977) on the characteristics of state correctional institutions throughout the nation indicate that 205 had living quarters with one-inmate cells, fifty-eight had quarters with two-inmate cells, twenty-eight had quarters with three- or four-inmate cells, and 503 had "other quarters" (including dormitories and cells for five or more inmates). Any institution may have more than one type of living facility. Approximately one-half of the one-inmate cells within state correctional institutions lacked a desk, a chair, reading lamps, seating space (except beds), windows, and fans. Furthermore, approximately one-half of all state prisons lacked medical equipment comparable to that found in a doctor's office, approximately two-thirds lacked medical equipment comparable to that found in an emergency room, and over 80 percent lacked medical equipment comparable to that of an operating room.[87]

In 1972 (the latest date for which nationwide data—LEAA, 1977—are available), there were 141,600 inmates confined within local jails. Approximately 67,000 of these inmates were actually serving their sentences (with and without appeal) within these institutions.[88] Recent nationwide data comparable to that on prison living facilities are not available for local jails. It seems reasonable to assume, however, that living conditions within many of the nation's jails are just as inadequate as those found within the nation's state correctional institutions, if not more so.

Jails: Additional repression and punishment

Of course, many people feel that the primary purpose of imprisonment should be to punish the offender. They argue that, by depriving individuals of their freedom and subjecting them to the punitive and debilitating conditions of prison life, the offenders will realize that "crime doesn't pay." Moreover, the threat of such punitive treatment will also aid in ensuring that other potential offenders refrain from crime. However, there is little if any evidence to indicate that punishment actually constitutes an effective deterrent to crime. For example, people sometimes call for the use of capital punishment in order to deter more serious forms of crime, such as murder. However, in his 1967 study, Sellin compared the homicide rates of those states that have capital punishment with the rates of those states that do not have it. The difference under these two conditions was negligible. He concluded that "the presence of the death penalty—in law or practice—does not influence homicide death rates."[89]

Punishment rarely deters crime

If punishment stands as a deterrent to crime, we would expect an increased use of punishment to result in a decline in the general crime rate.

Punishment and the crime rate

However, recent evidence indicates that this is not the case. During the last few years the rate of imprisonment has increased significantly, but so has the rate of crime within the United States. In 1972, the rate of incarcerated offenders within state and federal institutions was 94.6 per 100,000 general population.[90] By the end of 1975, this rate had increased to 113.0 per 100,000.[91] Moreover, the state and federal prison populations rose 11 and 17 percent, respectively, between December 31, 1975, and December 31, 1976.[92] Yet, as we have seen, the rate of major crimes throughout the nation has also increased, by 21.7 percent between 1973 and 1977.[93]

Those punished frequently repeat crimes

Furthermore, if punishment does in fact deter crime, we would expect those who were once imprisoned to refrain from additional criminal acts. Evidence indicates, however, that many prisoners are recidivists. For example, a follow-up study conducted by the FBI of 78,000 offenders released in 1972 indicated that 74 percent of those released from prisons under pardon or mandatory release were rearrested within four years.[94]

VIOLENCE AND OPPRESSION

What happens to people when they are labeled as "outsiders," "worthless animals," and "criminals," and are placed in a situation where they have to live with these labels? What happens to those who are placed in a situation where they are given virtually total power over the actions and lives of those "outsiders?" What happens when both groups are told that it is only an experiment—that they are only playing roles? What all too frequently actually happens within the American prison system? The following selection examines the results of a terrifying experiment at Stanford University, which had to be abruptly halted because of its frightening consequences and implications.

ZIMBARDO READING——OBJECTIVES

1. To write a brief essay describing the quality of the inmate-guard relationship within this experimental situation.
2. To analyze in an essay why, after only a short period of time, "prisoners" and "guards" were not able to differentiate between role-playing and reality.

Pathology of Imprisonment
PHILIP G. ZIMBARDO

I was recently released from solitary confinement after being held therein for 37 months [months!]. A silent system was imposed upon me and to even whisper to

Reprinted by permission of Transaction Inc. from *Society*, Vol. 9, April 1972. Copyright © 1972 by Transaction Inc.

the man in the next cell resulted in being beaten by guards, sprayed with chemical mace, blackjacked, stomped and thrown into a strip-cell naked to sleep on a concrete floor without bedding, covering, wash basin or even a toilet. The floor served as toilet and bed, and even there the silent system was enforced. To let a moan escape your lips because of the pain and discomfort . . . resulted in another beating. I spent not days, but months there during my 37 months in solitary. . . . I have filed every writ possible against the administrative acts of brutality. The state courts have all denied the petitions. Because of my refusal to let the things die down and forget all that happened during my 37 months in solitary . . . I am the most hated prisoner in [this] penitentiary, and called a "hard-core incorrigible."

Letter from a prisoner

Maybe I am an incorrigible, but if true, it's because I would rather die than to accept being treated as less than a human being. I have never complained of my prison sentence as being unjustified except through legal means of appeals. I have never put a knife on a guard's throat and demanded my release. I know that thieves must be punished and I don't justify stealing, even though I am a thief myself. But now I don't think I will be a thief when I am released. No, I'm not rehabilitated. It's just that I no longer think of becoming wealthy by stealing. I now only think of killing—killing those who have beaten me and treated me as if I were a dog. I hope and pray for the sake of my own soul and future life of freedom that I am able to overcome the bitterness and hatred which eats daily at my soul, but I know to overcome it will not be easy.

This eloquent plea for prison reform—for humane treatment of human beings, for the basic dignity that is the right of every American—came to me secretly in a letter from a prisoner who cannot be identified because he is still in a state correctional institution. He sent it to me because he read of an experiment I recently conducted at Stanford University. In an attempt to understand just what it means psychologically to be a prisoner or a prison guard, Craig Haney, Curt Banks, Dave Jaffe and I created our own prison. We carefully screened over 70 volunteers who answered an ad in a Palo Alto city newspaper and ended up with about two dozen young men who were selected to be part of this study. They were mature, emotionally stable, normal, intelligent college students from middle-class homes throughout the United States and Canada. They appeared to represent the cream of the crop of this generation. None had any criminal record and all were relatively homogeneous on many dimensions initially.

The design of the experiment

Half were arbitrarily designated as prisoners by a flip of a coin, the others as guards. These were the roles they were to play in our simulated prison. The guards were made aware of the potential seriousness and danger of the situation and their own vulnerability. They made up their own formal rules for maintaining law, order and respect, and were generally free to improvise new ones during their eight-hour, three-man shifts. The prisoners were unexpectedly picked up at their homes by a city policeman in a squad car, searched, handcuffed, fingerprinted, booked at the Palo Alto station house and taken blindfolded to our jail. There they were stripped, deloused, put into a uniform, given a number and put into a cell with two other prisoners where they expected to live for the next two weeks. The pay was good ($15 a day) and their motivation was to make money.

We observed and recorded on videotape the events that occurred in the prison, and we interviewed and tested the prisoners and guards at various points throughout the study. Some of the videotapes of the actual encounters between the prisoners and guards were seen on the NBC News feature "Chronolog" on November 26, 1971.

At the end of only six days we had to close down our mock prison because what we saw was frightening. It was no longer apparent to most of the subjects (or to us) where reality ended and their roles began. The majority had indeed become prisoners or guards, no longer able to clearly differentiate between role playing and self. There were dramatic changes in virtually every aspect of their behavior, thinking and feeling. In less than a week the experience of imprisonment undid (temporarily) a lifetime of learning; human values were suspended, self-concepts were challenged and the ugliest, most base, pathological side of human nature surfaced. We were horrified because we saw some boys (guards) treat others as if they were despicable animals, taking pleasure in cruelty, while other boys (prisoners) became servile, dehumanized robots who thought only of escape, of their own individual survival and of their mounting hatred for the guards.

We had to release three prisoners in the first four days because they had such acute situational traumatic reactions as hysterical crying, confusion in thinking and severe depression. Others begged to be paroled, and all but three were willing to forfeit all the money they had earned if they could be paroled. By then (the fifth day) they had been so programmed to think of themselves as prisoners that when their request for parole was denied, they returned docilely to their cells. Now, had they been thinking as college students acting in an oppressive experiment, they would have quit once they no longer wanted the $15 a day we used as our only incentive. However, the reality was not quitting an experiment but "being paroled by the parole board from the Stanford County Jail." By the last days, the earlier solidarity among the prisoners (systematically broken by the guards) dissolved into "each man for himself." Finally, when one of their fellows was put in solitary confinement (a small closet) for refusing to eat, the prisoners were given a choice by one of the guards: give up their blankets and the incorrigible prisoner would be let out, or keep their blankets and he would be kept in all night. They voted to keep their blankets and to abandon their brother.

About a third of the guards became tyrannical in their arbitrary use of power, in enjoying their control over other people. They were corrupted by the power of their roles and became quite inventive in their techniques of breaking the spirit of the prisoners and making them feel they were worthless. Some of the guards merely did their jobs as tough but fair correctional officers, and several were good guards from the prisoners' point of view since they did them small favors and were friendly. However, no good guard ever interfered with a command by any of the bad guards; they never intervened on the side of the prisoners, they never told the others to ease off because it was only an experiment, and they never even came to me as prison superintendent or experimenter in charge to complain. In part, they were good because the others were bad; they needed the others to help establish their own egos in a positive light. In a sense, the good guards perpetuated the prison more than the other guards because their own

---

In less than one week, most could not differentiate between role playing and reality

"Each man for himself" became the rule

Characteristics of the inmate-guard relationship

needs to be liked prevented them from disobeying or violating the implicit guards' code. At the same time, the act of befriending the prisoners created a social reality which made the prisoners less likely to rebel.

By the end of the week the experiment had become a reality, as if it were a Pirandello play directed by Kafka that just keeps going after the audience has left. The consultant for our prison, Carlo Prescott, an ex-convict with 16 years of imprisonment in California's jails, would get so depressed and furious each time he visited our prison, because of its psychological similarity to his experiences, that he would have to leave. A Catholic priest who was a former prison chaplain in Washington, D. C. talked to our prisoners after four days and said they were just like the other first-timers he had seen.

But in the end, I called off the experiment not because of the horror I saw out there in the prison yard, but because of the horror of realizing that *I* could have easily traded places with the most brutal guard or become the weakest prisoner full of hatred at being so powerless that I could not eat, sleep or go to the toilet without permission of the authorities. *I* could have become Calley at My Lai, George Jackson at San Quentin, one of the men at Attica or the prisoner quoted at the beginning of this article.

REHABILITATION WITHIN THE PRISON

There has been a growing awareness that punishment in and of itself does not provide an effective deterrent to crime. As a result, there have been recent attempts to develop rehabilitation programs within prisons. These include individual counseling, group therapy, and general education as well as occupational and vocational training. In addition to these, various work-release programs have been increasingly utilized during the last two or three decades. Under work-release programs, the prisoner is allowed to leave the prison for a certain number of hours each day for work or training within the community. Various types of work-release programs have been in existence for many years. Through the passage of the Prisoner Rehabilitation Act of 1965, these programs have recently been extended to cover those confined within federal prisons.

Utilization of work-release programs

Although the vast majority of prisons currently offer some form of rehabilitation program, the fact is that most prisons primarily provide mere custodial services rather than rehabilitation for offenders. For example, the Law Enforcement Assistance Administration (1977) reported that over one-half of all state prisons within the United States did not employ any full-time academic and vocational teachers or social workers. In addition, approximately 90 percent of these institutions did not provide for a full-time psychiatrist or a full-time counselor on the staff.[95] Even where meaningful rehabilitation programs do exist, they are often not very effective. Obviously, rehabilitation within a punitive and custodial atmosphere tends to be rather difficult to accomplish. In addition, vocational work-training programs found within prisons often fail to develop the knowledge and skills

Prisons provide a custodial environment

that would be useful to the offenders upon their release from the institution.[96] It is unfortunate that in many cases rehabilitation fails to progress beyond the point of menial tasks. Work-release programs have proved to be fairly successful, however, and they do provide valuable assistance in attempting to reintegrate the individual with the larger society.[97]

REHABILITATION WITHIN THE COMMUNITY

The growing awareness of the debilitating effects of prison life upon offenders and of the overall ineffectiveness of institutional rehabilitation programs has led to an increased utilization of community-based rehabilitation programs, particularly those of probation and parole. Not only are such programs far less costly than imprisonment, but they also provide a somewhat greater potential for reintegrating the offender with society.

Probation. Probation is the suspension of a sentence conditional upon good behavior, with community supervision imposed for a certain period of time. The origins of probation go back to English common law, which allowed clergymen to be released from criminal courts and to be dealt with by the church. In the United States, probation dates back to 1841, when John Augustus (a Boston shoemaker) was successful in obtaining court releases for offenders to whom he provided rehabilitative assistance. Probation as a formal correctional system, however, did not develop here until the twentieth century. Since early in this century, there has been rapid growth in its use. In 1907 there were only 795 probation officers; by 1970 there were approximately 25,000 officers (probation and parole) throughout the United States.[98] According to 1977 LEAA data, in 1975 more than 36,000 persons were received for supervision by the Federal Probation System alone.[99] The terms or conditions of probation usually include obeying all laws, keeping good habits, associating with noncriminals, maintaining regular employment, supporting one's family, and avoiding drugs and excessive alcohol use. In addition, the probationer must often obtain permission to change residence, marry, or divorce. Probation has proved to be a viable alternative to the incarceration of offenders.[100] For example, the previously mentioned follow-up study conducted by the FBI found that only 57 percent of those offenders who were placed on probation in 1972 were rearrested within the next four years.[101] This figure compares favorably to the 74 percent of those offenders released from prison (under mandatory release and pardons) who were subsequently rearrested during the same period.

Parole. Parole refers to the release of the offender from a correctional institution after part of the sentence has been served, under the condition

Some advantages of community rehabilitation

The history of probation

The conditions of probation

that the offender remain under the custody and supervision of the institution or other state-approved agency until granted a final discharge.[102] Although the terms of parole and probation are similar, they are different in that parole involves the release of an offender who has already served some of the sentence. In addition, granting parole is an "administrative decision," whereas the utilization of probation is exclusively a function of the criminal courts. In the United States, parole was initially adopted as a formal release system in 1876, with the creation of the Elmira Reformatory in New York State. The Elmira system employed indeterminate sentences and early supervised release for good behavior. The system of combining parole and the indeterminate sentence spread rather quickly: By 1922, no less than forty-five states had enacted parole laws, and by 1944 all states had developed such legislation.[103]

Today, most persons released from correctional institutions are released on parole. A parole board typically has the exclusive responsibility for determining when an offender may be released, and the board specifies the conditions under which the parole will remain in force. When making a decision on a release, most members of parole boards are primarily concerned with evaluating the likelihood of the offender's committing a serious crime while on parole, whether the person would benefit from a continued period of confinement, and finally whether the offender would "become a worse risk if confined longer."[104] The use of parole has met with some success in the treatment of offenders. The FBI's follow-up study of 78,000 offenders released in 1972 shows that 71 percent of those granted parole were rearrested within four years.[105] It is likely, however, that many repeating offenders are not rearrested for major crimes. In 1975 the National Council on Crime and Delinquency, National Probation and Parole Institutes conducted a three-year follow-up study of over 17,000 male offenders paroled from state institutions in 1970. The findings of this study (released by the LEAA in 1977) revealed that less than 10 percent of the parolees were recommitted to prison for a new major conviction.[106]

Most imprisoned offenders are released on parole

Evaluating the success of parole

CORRECTIONS: PRESENT AND FUTURE

During recent years, one of the most significant changes in the field of corrections has been the development and increased utilization of community-based correctional projects, such as probation, parole, and work-release programs. The shift from the mere institutionalization of offenders has occurred for a number of reasons. One of these is simply that institutionalization is far more costly than any type of community corrections program. Second, there has been increased realization that imprisonment often has a detrimental, not a rehabilitating, effect upon inmates. The inadequacy of the institutional approach to corrections has been emphasized

The increased use of community corrections

by the National Advisory Commission on Criminal Justice Standards and Goals. This Commission stated:

> The prison, the reformatory, and the jail have achieved only a shock-ing record of failure. There is overwhelming evidence that these institutions create crime rather than prevent it. Their very nature ensures it. . . . These isolated and closed societies are incompatible with the world outside. . . . The blame for this insufferable system cannot be placed on the shoulders of corrections alone. Correctional personnel have decried, at great length and in vain, public apathy and decades of formal neglect. The state of corrections today reflects in no small part society's past expectations as well as its respon-sibilities.[107]

Community rehabilita-tion requires public involvement

The recent shift toward community-based corrections represents, at least to some degree, changes in public attitudes. It reflects more willingness on the part of the public to become involved in and take on more responsi-bility for the correctional process. The importance of public involvement is emphasized by the National Advisory Commission on Criminal Justice Standards and Goals: "Implementation of community corrections requires citizen involvement on an unprecedented scale. In fact, the degree of citizen acceptance, involvement, and participation in community-based corrections will decide not only the swiftness of its implementation but also its ultimate success or failure."[108]

Despite some fairly recent trends that emphasize rehabilitation within an institutional and/or community setting, it is difficult to judge for certain whether rehabilitation of offenders will remain as a dominant correctional goal within our society. There is a growing body of evidence that indicates, as far as some experts are concerned, that rehabilitation programs, regard-less of their nature, simply do not work.[109] Again, even though the strategy of reintegrating the offender through community-based programs such as probation has proved to be somewhat successful, the fact still remains that most offenders (57 percent) are rearrested within four years after their release.

The growing amount of evidence on the relative ineffectiveness of re-habilitation and the fear of crime on the streets have brought about a change in the opinion of many experts, as well as of some of the public, to the effect that punishment for retribution, rather than rehabilitation, should once more be the approach to handling the offender. A number of experts within the corrections field are now calling for the introduc-tion of longer mandatory, or "fixed," sentencing policies in place of the intermediate sentence structure currently in use. As we have also seen, recent evidence indicates that many citizens are now urging that the courts get tougher on violent juvenile offenders, and a recent Gallup poll (1976) indicates that there has been a substantial increase in the number of Americans who now favor the death penalty for convicted murderers.[110] In addition, the Supreme Court recently voted to uphold the constitutionality of the death penalty.[111] Thus it would appear that, for the future, the issue is not likely to center on whether rehabilitation should be institutional or community-based; rather, the issue is more likely to focus upon the question of whether the primary purpose of corrections should be deterrence and punishment or rehabilitation. There are no easy answers to the questions of how to reduce crime in our society and how best to deal with offenders. Regardless of which alternatives are eventually chosen, it is clear that the public must be willing to take the responsibility and pay the price.

SUMMARY

Sociologists view crime and delinquency as major forms of deviant behavior. Crime refers to those acts that violate formal norms, which we call laws. Distinct from adult crime, juvenile delinquency refers to illegal acts on the part of youths 16 to 18 years of age. There are obviously many different varieties of crime present within our society. In this chapter we have been concerned with the analysis of certain major crimes, which are usually termed common or street crimes. These include criminal homicide, rape, aggravated assault, robbery, burglary, larceny, and auto theft.

There is much evidence to indicate that the general public is highly concerned about crime and delinquency and tends to view these phenomena as major social problems. This concern is evidenced in a number of specific ways, including: the development and growth of voluntary organizations to deal with crime and delinquency, the establishment of federal crime control legislation, the establishment of national commissions to investigate crime, and the utilization of various national public opinion surveys, which indicate widespread public outrage and fear.

Virtually all available statistics indicate that there have been substantial increases in the growth of crime within the last several decades. In this chapter we have examined the major sources of crime statistics, from the *Uniform Crime Reports* to victimization studies.

Biological and psychological theories for crime were briefly examined before giving attention to sociological explanations. Both labeling theory and the theory of differential association attempt to explain how and why a person becomes a criminal. In contrast, the anomie and subcultural theories attempt to account for variations in the rates of crime and delinquency manifested by different groups and categories of people in our society.

Public responses to crime and delinquency have included retribution and deterrence at one extreme and rehabilitation at the other. During the twentieth century, imprisonment has been the dominant method for dealing with criminal offenders; however, it has proved to be costly and largely ineffective. During recent years, one of the most significant changes in American corrections has been the development of community-based programs. Such programs are far less costly than imprisonment and, more important, provide more potential for rehabilitating offenders and reintegrating them with the larger society. However, the actual effectiveness of rehabilitation efforts, whether in an institutional or a community setting, has been called into question within very recent years. At present there is a growing movement in our society to decrease the emphasis placed upon rehabilitative goals and to institute instead a correctional philosophy based upon retribution and deterrence, particularly for serious offenders.

KEY TERMS

Anomic suicide
Anomie (Merton)
Categoric risks
Child savers
Civil law
Classical school of criminology
Conflict subculture
Crime
Criminal subculture
Delinquent subculture
Deviant behavior
Differential association
Differential association reinforcement
Ectomorphs
Endomorphs
Felonies
Innovation

Juvenile delinquency
Labeling theory
Laws
Mesomorphs
Misdemeanors
Norms
Parole
Probation
Retreatist subculture
Retribution-deterrence
Silent system
Social control
Solitary system
Subcultural theory
Subcultures
Techniques of neutralization
Victimization studies

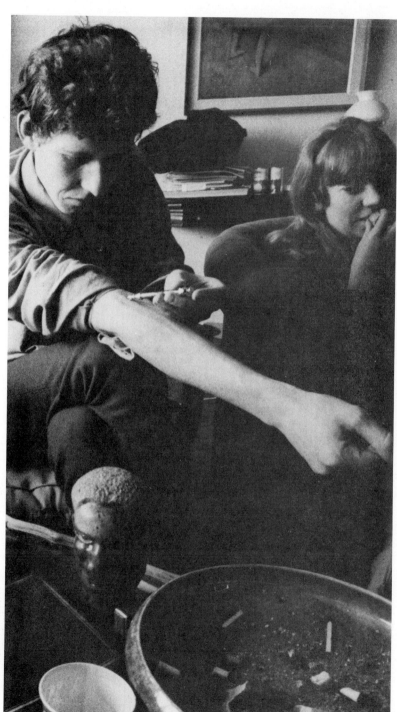

6

Drugs
and
Alcohol

Chapter Objectives

1. To document by way of statistics the degree of American involvement with drugs, and to identify the various factors related to the acceptability of certain drugs and drug uses in our society.

2. To define the term "drug" from a pharmacological, social, and social scientific point of view, and to distinguish between drug abuse and drug addiction.

3. To compare in an essay the effects of amphetamines and barbiturates upon the user and the differences in current use patterns of these psychoactive substances.

4. To briefly analyze the historical and contemporary patterns of opiate (heroin) use in American society.

5. To contrast the effects of light to moderate drinking with those of long-term, frequent, and excessive alcohol consumption.

6. To discuss the difference between problem drinking and alcoholism and to detail their various social and economic costs.

7. To describe the variations in drinking patterns and alcoholism by age, sex, socioeconomic status, religious affiliation, and ethnic background, citing those factors that are conducive to low alcoholism rates.

8. To briefly contrast the reinforcement and personality theories and the social learning and subcultural theories of drug use and drug addiction.

9. To discuss the dominant societal reaction in America to drug use, addiction, and alcoholism, citing the historical origins of public policies and their consequences.

10. To describe the essential characteristics of the AA program for the treatment of alcoholism.

11. To compare the methadone maintenance and the therapeutic community approaches to the drug addiction problem.

THE EXTENT OF DRUG AND ALCOHOL USE

American society is highly involved in the consumption of drugs. Nearly seventy-five million people smoke cigarettes, over 100 million drink alcoholic beverages, and even more regularly drink coffee and cola drinks (both of which contain stimulants). In addition, thirteen million people are regular users of marijuana, and millions of others have tried it at least once. Roughly 650,000 people are addicted to heroin and 89,000 people regularly use methadone as a substitute.[1] Americans also consume millions of pounds of aspirin each year. Another indicator of the degree of American involvement with drugs is the $9+ billion that is annually spent on prescription drugs, many of which are psychoactive compounds such as amphetamines or barbiturates and milder tranquilizers.[2] In addition, many more millions of dollars are spent annually on over-the-counter nonprescription drugs for countless ailments, such as coughs, backaches, indigestion, irregularity, and sleeplessness. The prescription and nonprescription drug market is vast but does not satisfy the American appetite: we annually spend an additional $2 billion for illegal drugs, $12 billion for cigarettes and cigars, and $33 billion for various alcoholic beverages.[3]

It is important to stress that much of the drug use present within our society is viewed by the majority to be acceptable behavior. Many people feel that there is nothing wrong with taking certain drugs in order to lose weight, drinking several cups of coffee each day, having one or two cocktails before or after dinner, smoking cigarettes, or using a prescription or brand-name drug to get rid of a headache. This kind of drug use tends to be seen as acceptable and legitimate—it is simply a matter of individual freedom of choice. In fact, the use of many drugs in our society is so common that large numbers of these substances are simply not often thought of as drugs.[4]

Although many drugs and many reasons for taking drugs are socially approved and even encouraged within our society, the use of heroin and other substances that society terms "hard drugs" or "street drugs" meets with much social disapproval. Although we often tend to define our drug problem exclusively in terms of the use of these disapproved substances, it is important to recognize that the use and abuse of many socially acceptable and legal drugs can be just as dangerous to the individual and society as the use of the so-called "hard" or illicit drugs.[5] Why do we tend to define our drug problem only in terms of specific drugs? Why are certain other drugs (and certain reasons for drug use) viewed as acceptable? There are a number of factors underlying this selective acceptability. One factor is surely that of tradition. Drugs such as tobacco, caffeine, and alcohol have a long history of use in our society. Still other drugs have been given the stamp of approval because they are legal, because they are broadly defined as medicines, or because they are prescribed by physicians. In addition, millions of dollars are spent each year by the tobacco, alcohol, and pharma-

Virtually all Americans use drugs

The American "drug appetite" costs billions

Much but not all drug use is viewed as acceptable in our society

Factors related to the acceptability of drugs

ceutical industries on the effort to market, and convince the public of the legitimacy of, their various products.[6]

In brief then, the acceptability of drug use is related to the way in which drugs are acquired, the reasons for their use, and the kinds of people who take them.[7] In many instances, drugs with a tradition of widespread use by dominant groups within our society tend to be both legal and acceptable. On the other hand, "certain drugs have become part of a life style that flouts such conventional middle-class values as the pursuit of wealth and occupational success." Many people tend to define this form of drug use as unacceptable and problematic.[8] The Commission on Marijuana and Drug Abuse state the issue in a somewhat similar way:

This society is not opposed to all drug taking but only to certain forms of drug use by certain persons. Self-medication by a housewife or a businessman with amphetamines or tranquilizers, for example, is generally viewed as a personal judgment of little concern to the larger society. On the other hand, use of such drugs by a college student or other young person to stay awake for studying or simply to experience the effect of such drugs is ordinarily considered a matter of intense community concern extending even to legal intervention.[9]

WHAT ARE DRUGS?

The term "drug" can be used in various ways. In a strict scientific sense, "a drug is any substance other than food which by its chemical nature affects the structure or function of the living organism."[10] Obviously, this is an extremely broad definition, under which could be included hundreds and no doubt thousands of substances. From a medical point of view, a drug refers to any substance prescribed by a physician to treat and cure illness. The term is also subject to social or popular definition, which frequently operates quite independently of the pharmacological and medical contexts. In a social sense, a drug is any substance that has been "arbitrarily defined by certain segments of society as a drug." Thus "society defines what a drug is and the social definition shapes our attitudes toward the class of substances so described."[11] Although we cannot ignore the importance of this social definition or the real consequences it has for shaping the public opinion on drugs, we must be aware that the popular labeling (or social definitions) of drugs typically involves certain prejudgments and stereotypes. In effect, social definitions tend to label only those chemical substances that are socially disapproved and illicit as drugs. Other substances, which in reality are also drugs, may not be labeled as such since their use is socially accepted. As the National Commission on Marijuana and Drug Abuse pointed out, the vast majority of people in our society regard

The users and their motives determine acceptability

The pharmacological and social definitions of drugs

heroin and cocaine as drugs, substantially fewer regard barbiturates and amphetamines as drugs, and few regard alcohol and tobacco as drugs.[12]

Using specific terminology, which is more adequate for our purposes, social scientists call these substances *psychoactive drugs*. This term emphasizes the fact that there is a wide range of chemical substances capable of affecting the user's central nervous system and thus influencing thought processes, perceptions, behavior, and emotions. Psychoactive drugs are typically divided into three very general categories: *stimulants*, *depressants*, and *hallucinogens*.

Psychoactive drugs influence behavior, perceptions, and emotions

Stimulants increase the functioning of the central nervous system. These psychoactive drugs tend to decrease appetite and fatigue and heighten mood, alertness, and general motor activity. Stimulants of the natural variety include nicotine (found in tobacco), caffeine (found in tea and coffee), and cocaine. Synthetic stimulants are termed *amphetamines*, examples of which would be benzedrine, dexedrine, and methedrine.

Stimulants excite the central nervous system

Depressants decrease or depress the functioning of the central nervous system, easing tension and anxiety. Some of these drugs also tend to produce euphoria. Examples include a wide variety of chemical substances, such as narcotics or opiates (opium, heroin, morphine, and codeine) and sedatives, including barbiturates and tranquilizers. In spite of popular notions, alcohol is also classified as a depressant, since its overall effect is to depress activities of the central nervous system, decreasing motor activity, inhibitions, and alertness.

Depressants slow down the system

As a whole, hallucinogens and marijuana are hard to classify since their effects on the user vary widely depending on the hallucinogen used and the dose taken. Generally, hallucinogens cause a mild to intense distortion of visual and auditory functions. Users tend to experience changes in mood and stepped-up thought processes. Long-term regular or heavy use often results in impaired judgment, delusions, and even acute psychosis. Well-known examples of hallucinogens would be LSD (lysergic acid diethylamide), psilocybin, and mescaline. Marijuana, on the other hand, can either stimulate or depress a person. Although the effects of marijuana are highly subjective and variable, in most cases the user tends to experience mild euphoria, relaxation, decreased alertness, and some confusion in time perspective.[13]

Hallucinogens have a wide range of effects upon the user

It is important to point out that in spite of these general categories and descriptions, the actual effect of a drug upon a user is not always so fixed. Users have been known to have widely different responses and reactions, even when using the same drug. Thus, while the type of drug taken and the frequency and size of the dose are key factors, other elements are also important. Factors such as the user's personality and prior drug involvement and the conditions under which the drug is used also help determine the full effects of drug use.[14]

The chemical properties of drugs are not the only determinants of their effects

DRUG USE AND ABUSE: NATURE AND CONSEQUENCES

Many people equate drug abuse with using the various socially disapproved and typically illegal psychoactive substances, such as the opiates or narcotics (particularly heroin), cocaine, and hallucinogens (such as LSD). In our society, patterns of drug abuse include but are surely not limited to the use of these socially disapproved substances. We will define drug abuse as the excessive and/or compulsive use of a drug to the degree that it is harmful to the user's health or social functioning or that it can result in harmful consequences to others.[15] In terms of this definition we can see that any drug, even common aspirin, has the potential for being abused. The drug itself may be socially acceptable and legal, such as caffeine or nicotine, or the drug may be socially unacceptable and illegal, such as heroin. Drugs such as alcohol, the barbiturates, and the narcotics run a high risk for abuse since their regular and continued use results in addiction. With addiction, the individual becomes *physically dependent* upon a drug and so will go through *withdrawal* if drug use ceases. Drugs such as the milder tranquilizers, antidepressants, and possibly the amphetamines do not create a physical dependence. However, the potential for abuse is still present since their constant use or overuse can lead to as well as result from a state of *psychological dependence* (habituation).[16]

Given the confines of a single chapter, it would be impossible to even briefly analyze the nature and consequences of drug use for all the different known psychoactive substances. Instead, we will focus upon four widely known psychoactive drugs: amphetamines, barbiturates, narcotics (particularly heroin), and alcohol. The individual and social costs of abuse of both narcotics and alcohol are extensive and tend to be matters of much concern for many people. On the other hand, as we shall see, the use of amphetamines and barbiturates has become widespread, particularly during the last decade or so. The excessive use of these substances is also becoming a matter of concern for many people within our society.

Amphetamines. These are synthetic stimulants that include a wide range of substances, such as methedrine (speed), dexedrine, and benzedrine. Amphetamines were initially developed in the 1920s, and their use began to increase rapidly during the 1930s and 1940s. Physicians began to prescribe these substances for a number of health problems, such as depression and various respiratory ailments. During World War II, amphetamines were frequently used by members of the military to reduce fatigue and stay awake for long periods of time.[17] From the 1950s to the present, the availability and use (both legal and illegal) of amphetamines has grown substantially. People take amphetamines for various reasons, including to reduce fatigue and to alleviate depression. Truck drivers often take amphetamines to stay awake during long-distance driving; students may take them to remain awake and alert for long periods of study. Amphetamines are

---

Any drug can be abused

Dependence can be physical (addiction) and/or psychological (habituation)

Use of amphetamines has grown substantially in recent decades

also widely used for weight reduction and control. Under many of these circumstances, people will frequently (but not always) obtain amphetamines by prescription, and they will generally take small to moderate doses. Doses of these sizes tend to produce a number of mental and physical changes, including increased alertness, lessened fatigue, enhanced feelings of confidence, mild euphoria, decreased appetite, insomnia, and increased heartbeat, respiratory functioning, and blood pressure.[18]

The effects of long-term or high-dose amphetamine use tend to be far more hazardous to the user's health. Among the effects of excessive use are malnutrition, susceptibility to disease resulting from severe appetite loss, extreme sleeplessness, irritability, and delusions. The most potent method of amphetamine use is intravenous injection, and those who practice this form of self-administration are termed "speeders" or "speed freaks." As with many heroin addicts, it is typical for "speeders" to become extensively involved in a subcultural pattern of drug use that becomes the dominant theme of their everyday lives. Amphetamines have the quality of producing *tolerance* fairly rapidly, even when moderate or small doses are taken. Thus the user requires more and more of the substance in order to get the same desired effect. The "speeder" typically winds up injecting massive doses and runs the risk of contracting serum hepatitis as well as amphetamine psychoses—paranoia and hallucinations.[19]

The use of amphetamines poses recognizable health risks for the individual. Even moderate amphetamine use, obtained by prescription, involves the clear danger of psychological dependence (or habituation) for the user. In addition, some evidence indicates that long-term, high-dose amphetamine use may lead to physical dependence.[20] Precise figures are not available, but virtually all estimates indicate that the use and abuse of amphetamines is widespread within our society today. Of particular significance is the finding that amphetamines and other stimulants are frequently used by high school and college students.[21] Although amphetamines are used throughout our society, recent evidence tends to indicate a slight nationwide decline in their use.[22] Much of this decline no doubt simply reflects recent reductions in the prescription use of amphetamines, resulting from tightened controls on the part of the Food and Drug Administration. The illegal use of amphetamines, however, remains a major social problem. In 1976 alone, U.S. customs inspectors confiscated over 200 million units of amphetamines (and barbiturates).[23] Such seizures can give us only a slight indication of the true spectrum of illicit use. There is little doubt that illicit amphetamine use is far more pervasive than that of heroin or other narcotics.

Barbiturates. These are depressant drugs and include such commonly used substances as phenobarbital, nembutal, and seconal. Barbiturates have a wide range of medical uses, including the treatment of mental disorders, epilepsy, tension, and insomnia. The first barbiturate, called veronal, was

The effects of amphetamine use

Amphetamines produce rapid tolerance

Young people have also acquired the amphetamine habit

Barbiturates: A major form of depressant drug

created in 1903. Since that time about 2,500 different barbiturates have been manufactured, although roughly only a dozen are frequently used today.[24]

When taken in small to moderate doses, barbiturates have an effect on the individual similar to that of other depressants, such as alcohol. Under these circumstances, the user typically experiences a mild euphoria, a slight impairment of reflexes, and a lessening of tension, anxiety, and inhibitions. With larger doses, the user experiences slurred speech, a noticeable loss of physical coordination, drowsiness, and sleep. Heavy or long-term use causes severely impaired coordination and a slowing of many bodily functions, such as respiration and heart action. It can also ultimately lead to coma and death.[25]

The effects of long-term barbiturate use

The long-term effects of heavy barbiturate use are very hazardous to the individual. Similar to alcohol, the frequent use of barbiturates will produce tolerance as well as psychological and physical dependence (i.e., addiction). In fact, the effects of barbiturates resemble alcohol so closely that Joel Fort refers to barbiturates as "solid alcohol."[26] Physical addiction to barbiturates is induced when excessive doses are taken over a period of several weeks. Withdrawal from barbiturates, particularly under conditions of long-term use, can be as acute as withdrawal from heroin, and sometimes even worse. Withdrawal symptoms typically include nausea, anxiety, intense physical pain, hallucinations, delusions, and severe convulsions. Death is also more likely to result from barbiturate withdrawal than from heroin withdrawal. There is no question about the fact that barbiturates have high potential for abuse. Barbiturate addiction is more common in our society than heroin addiction, and barbiturates are the primary cause of deaths resulting from drug overdoses. Some of these deaths are the result of accidental overdoses; others come about through the combined use of barbiturates and alcohol; still others represent deliberate barbiturate suicides.[27]

Withdrawal from barbiturates can be very severe

Although the National Institute on Drug Abuse has recently indicated a slight nationwide decline in the use of barbiturates, the fact is that barbiturate use is extensive in our society today.[28] Hundreds of tons, totaling billions of barbiturate units, are produced in the United States annually. The National Commission on Marijuana and Drug Abuse indicated that approximately 29 percent of medical prescriptions fall within the barbiturate category and that "the incidence of barbiturate use outside the medical system has increased significantly in recent years."[29] Finally, although barbiturates are most frequently obtained by prescription, the Domestic Council Drug Abuse Task Force has noted that barbiturates "are much more readily available in the illicit market than are wholly illicit drugs such as cocaine and heroin."[30]

The nonmedical use of barbiturates has grown substantially in recent years

Narcotics (Heroin). These depressant drugs are similar to barbiturates and alcohol. Narcotics have many medical uses and are widely known as pain relievers. They are divided into two broad classes: (1) the opiates, such as

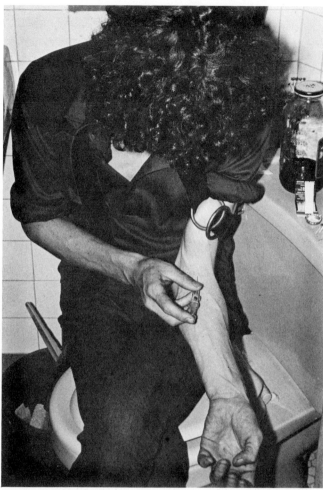

For the heroin addict, failure to "shoot up" at regular intervals brings on an agonizing withdrawal.

Peter Menzel, Stock, Boston

opium, morphine, heroin and codeine; and (2) synthetic narcotics such as methadone and demerol. When used in small to moderate doses, narcotics elicit drowsiness, a reduction of pain, mild euphoria, and a lessening of inhibitions, general alertness, and appetite. Occasionally, nausea and vomiting can also occur. Heavy narcotics use over an extended time period brings about sharp decreases in appetite, weight loss that frequently leads to malnutrition, temporary impotence in males, sterility, and the increased possibility of overdose, which may lead to death. Many of these latter effects result from physical addiction. Narcotics (particularly opiates) are highly addictive, and the narcotics user develops a tolerance for them rather quickly. With frequent use, the user may become addicted within a short time. With-

Varieties of narcotics

Narcotics are highly addictive

drawal symptoms vary depending on the specific narcotic, but nevertheless tend to produce great discomfort. Narcotic withdrawal resembles withdrawal from some other depressants, such as barbiturates and alcohol, but tends to be less acute. Symptoms include tension, anxiety, restlessness, headache, body cramps, chills, and continuous twitching of the body.

Opiates were available without prescription

The American involvement with opiates actually began prior to the discovery of heroin, which occurred in the late 1800s. In the nineteenth and early twentieth centuries, opium or its derivatives were widely available, in "over the counter" patent medicines or in prescriptions, and opiates were used to treat all kinds of ills, ranging from headaches to insomnia. The opium derivative morphine was used in many patent medicines, and its administration to injured soldiers during the Civil War resulted in the addiction of thousands of military personnel.[31] As Erich Goode notes, at the begining of the 1900s addiction to opium and its derivatives was widespread in America. Estimates of the addict population ranged from hundreds of thousands to several millions. Many of these people had become inadvertently addicted through medical use and, although addicts came from every walk of life, they tended to be white, middle-aged women who were likely to reside in rural as well as urban areas.[32]

The criminalization of addiction began with the Harrison Act

Around the turn of this century two changes occurred that had momentous consequences for the scope of opiate addiction. One was the development of heroin in 1898. Heroin, a substance far more powerful than morphine, became *the* opiate of addiction in the twentieth century—today, heroin is the most widely used illicit narcotic. The second involved the beginnings of an American recognition of a growing "opiate problem" and the passage of restrictive legislation, beginning with the Harrison Act of 1914, which prohibited the sale and use of opiate substances. Thus the process of defining addiction as *criminal* began.

Changes in the opiate-user population

The restrictive opiate legislation, however, also brought about changes in the addict population. In comparisons of the addict population of the early 1900s with that of the early 1970s, it has been noted that addicts tend to be younger, male, and more often residents of urban areas. There has also been a growth of users who are minority group members. Figures supplied by the Bureau of Narcotics indicate that there was a reduction in narcotics addiction during the period from 1920 to the early 1960s, but these figures have been disputed by a number of experts in the field of drug research.[33] However, from the late 1960s to the present, heroin use and addiction has increased and there has been a tendency for it to spread to new population groups—"the campus and the suburb."[34] In 1970 there were as many as 600,000 heroin addicts in the United States. With the reduction of heroin supply from the Turkish market, this figure decreased substantially by 1974, only to sharply rise again with the materialization of new heroin supplies—notably "Heroin B" or Mexican Brown.[35] Recent estimates indicate that there are approximately 650,000 heroin addicts throughout the

United States.[36] Still, it should be noted that the prevalence of heroin use and addiction in our society is relatively small compared to that of alcohol and barbiturates. Moreover, the majority of heroin users take the drug only a very few times and thus do not become physically dependent on it.[37]

The use of heroin results in a number of seriously detrimental effects upon the body. For example, it accounts for several thousand deaths each year. We should note that most of these deaths do not result from the chemical properties of the drug itself; rather, they are related to the conditions under which the drug is taken. Neither heroin nor the other opiates produce any long-range or irreversible damage to body organs or tissues.[38] Most heroin deaths are due to overdose, malnutrition, hepatitis, or other infections resulting from unsterilized needles, all of which are related to the haphazard conditions of "street" use.

Studies have also consistently indicated a strong relationship between heroin use and crime. However, the vast majority of crimes committed by addicts are property offenses rather than violent crimes. Many estimates indicate that addicts steal hundreds of millions of dollars in goods each year in order to support a habit that can cost $100 or more per day. The chemical properties of heroin in itself do not lead people to commit crimes. The relationship between heroin use and crime is explained by the fact that the drug is illegal and therefore expensive to obtain.[39]

Alcohol. This, like barbiturates and narcotics, is a depressant and functions mainly to decrease the activities of the central nervous system. People, however, often think of alcohol as a stimulant since, in limited quantities, it tends to make them more sociable, lively, and talkative. Actually, these mild effects are only by-products of its depressant action; the drug depresses areas in the brain that normally control inhibitions. Although the effects of alcohol upon the user will vary to some degree depending upon the user's personality, present expectations, and prior involvement with alcohol, the drug's effects upon the person's body are largely determined by the amount of alcohol absorbed and concentrated in the blood. In turn, the level of blood-alcohol concentration is affected by many other factors, such as body size and weight, the beverage drunk, the speed of consumption, and the presence of food in the stomach.

Thus if a 160-lb man consumed two or three ounces of whiskey, the effects of the drug would be almost unnoticeable since the blood-alcohol level would be only about 0.04 percent. If the same person consumed about six ounces of whiskey, the blood-alcohol concentration would rise to approximately 0.10 percent, and the person would experience slurred speech, decreased alertness, a reduction of motor and sensory functions, and a noticeable lack of coordination. At a .20 percent level of alcohol concentration the individual experiences such a huge loss of coordination that he or she becomes physically incapacitated. With continued increases in the level

Many hazards are related to the conditions under which heroin is used

The heroin addict usually commits property crimes

Alcohol is a depressant

The immediate effects of alcohol use are related to the level of blood-alcohol concentration

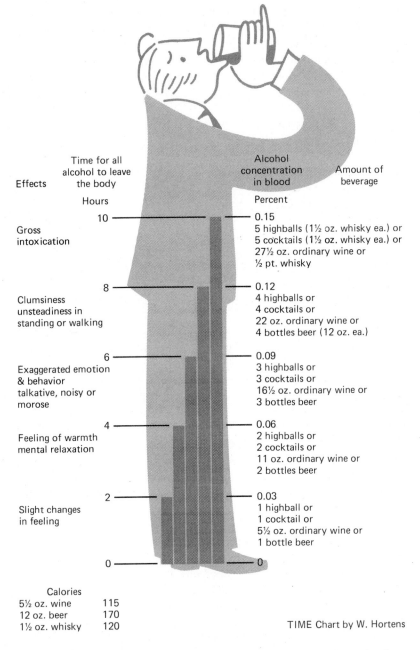

Alcohol levels in the blood

After drinks taken on an empty stomach by a 150-lb. person

Effects	Time for all alcohol to leave the body Hours	Alcohol concentration in blood Percent	Amount of beverage
Gross intoxication	10	0.15	5 highballs (1½ oz. whisky ea.) or 5 cocktails (1½ oz. whisky ea.) or 27½ oz. ordinary wine or ½ pt. whisky
Clumsiness unsteadiness in standing or walking	8	0.12	4 highballs or 4 cocktails or 22 oz. ordinary wine or 4 bottles beer (12 oz. ea.)
Exaggerated emotion & behavior talkative, noisy or morose	6	0.09	3 highballs or 3 cocktails or 16½ oz. ordinary wine or 3 bottles beer
Feeling of warmth mental relaxation	4	0.06	2 highballs or 2 cocktails or 11 oz. ordinary wine or 2 bottles beer
Slight changes in feeling	2	0.03	1 highball or 1 cocktail or 5½ oz. ordinary wine or 1 bottle beer
	0	0	

Calories	
5½ oz. wine	115
12 oz. beer	170
1½ oz. whisky	120

TIME Chart by W. Hortens

Fig. 6.1 Effects of alcohol: A little goes a long way. Source: *Time*, April 22, 1974. Copyright 1974, Time, Inc. Reprinted by permission.

of blood-alcohol concentration, the user experiences stupor, coma, the loss of breathing and heartbeat, and death.

It is interesting to note that in most cases light to moderate drinking apparently produces no damaging or pathological effects upon the user. However, alcohol abuse—the pattern of frequent and excessive alcohol consumption—leads to many devastating long-term consequences, both physical and mental. These include impairment of learning, loss of memory, impotency and testosterone deficiency in men, loss of appetite leading to malnutrition and increased susceptibility to disease, mental disorders, heart disease, cirrhosis of the liver, irreversible neurological and brain damage, and a lower life expectancy.[40]

Long-term effects of excessive alcohol consumption

The long-term consequences of frequent and excessive use of alcohol are usually associated with (and in fact are typically interpreted as signs of) problem drinking and alcoholism. What do we mean by the terms "problem drinking" and "alcoholism?" Unfortunately, there are no universal definitions of these concepts and the distinction between them is often blurred. Without doubt, problem drinking is more difficult to define; conceivably, it could refer to drinking of any kind, depending on people's attitudes toward the use of alcohol. Alcoholism is likewise subject to various interpretations. Some definitions stress the amount of alcohol consumed, others emphasize that alcoholics "are people with a desire that can be defined in medical terms and requires a proper regime of treatment."[41] Sociologist Richard Strauss has developed a widely accepted distinction between these terms. According to Strauss, problem drinkers are "all individuals who *repeatedly* use alcohol to an extent that exceeds customary dietary use or prevailing socially accepted customs or in amounts that, for them, cause problems of physical health, interfere with interpersonal relations, or disrupt the fulfillment of family, economic, or community expectations." Strauss also notes that, "among problem drinkers, alcoholics can be defined as those whose persistent abuse of alcohol is associated with a state of physical or psychological dependence involving often unbearable stress or discomfort or tension."[42] According to Strauss, the term problem drinker is the broader, encompassing alcoholics as well as those who incur difficulties with alcohol. On the other hand, alcoholics are those who have developed a true physical and psychological dependence upon alcohol.

Problem drinking vs. alcoholism

The alcoholic: The true alcohol addict

Although there are cases in which individuals may develop rapid dependence upon alcohol, the typical process of becoming an alcoholic extends over a considerable length of time, usually several years. This is because the development of tolerance to and physical dependence on alcohol takes place slowly, particularly compared to opiates. As Kessel and Walton see it, alcoholism goes beyond the stages of light or even moderate drinking. The process involves drinking to the point where tolerance increases dramatically. Continued excessive drinking in turn leads to the development of physical dependence (addiction) and the individual's loss of control over the

Chronic alcoholism: The most severe stage of alcohol addiction

drinking. At this point, cutting off the liquor supply would result in severe withdrawal symptoms. Finally, chronic alcoholism sets in and is accompanied by the many serious mental and physical illnesses described above.[43]

DRINKING AND PROBLEM DRINKING

Alcohol is one of the most widely used and widely abused drugs in American society. We estimate that approximately 108 million Americans aged 18 and older drink alcoholic beverages. One out of every twenty adults is an alcoholic, and millions of others are problem drinkers.[44] By any standards of measurement, the economic and social costs resulting from problem drinking and alcoholism are astronomically high. In 1974, the National Institute on Alcohol Abuse and Alcoholism (NIAAA) gave an estimate of more than $25 billion as the annual economic cost of alcohol-related problems.[45] This total included $9.35 billion in lost business and industrial production, $8.29 billion in health and medical costs, $6.44 billion in motor vehicle accident costs, $0.64 billion for alcohol programs and research, $0.51 billion in criminal justice system costs, and $0.14 billion in social welfare system costs.[46] Moreover, much personal and social harm associated with problem drinking, such as family strain and instability and serious injury or the loss of life resulting from motor vehicle accidents, are truly beyond dollar and cents value.

Surveys taken during the mid-1960s reported that 53 percent of the adult population drink at least once a month. Harris surveys during the mid-1970s reported a 5 percent increase in this figure, and other recent Gallup surveys showed that 71 percent of the adult population drink alcoholic beverages.[47] Whether and to what extent a person drinks are related to several sociocultural variables, including ethnic background, religious affiliation, socioeconomic status, age, and sex.[48]

With regard to ethnic background, studies indicate that, among groups in which drinking is well integrated with and regulated by group customs, rates of alcoholism tend to be low. Among groups lacking such integration patterns, rates tend to be high. The classic example is that of the earlier generation Italian and Irish Americans. Italians have particularly strong sanctions opposing drunkenness. Therefore, drinking tends to be moderate yet frequent and is well integrated with home and family, particularly in conjunction with meals. Low rates of alcoholism result. In contrast, the Irish drink to excess more often and drink outside the context of home and family life. Their drinking is less likely to be regulated by or integrated with many of the broader institutional aspects of their group life. High rates of alcoholism have been the result. However, some studies indicate that the rate of alcoholism is decreasing among later generation Irish Americans, while the incidence of alcoholism and heavy drinking is rising among second and third generation Italian Americans.

Some costs of alcohol addiction

Integration of drinking behaviors yields low rates of alcoholism

Religion is related to the presence as well as the amount of drinking. It is often the case that frequent church attenders are more likely not to drink at all or at least less frequently than people who do not attend church. Studies of the major religious groups in the United States note the following: A relatively large proportion of Catholics tend to drink and drink heavily. Although very few Jews are abstainers, they have a very small proportion of heavy drinkers and a very high proportion of light drinkers. Other recent studies indicate some increases in moderate and light drinking among Catholics and Jews. Drinking patterns among liberal Protestants resemble those of Catholics, except that liberal Protestants have fewer heavy drinkers. Conservative Protestants have the highest proportion of abstainers and the smallest proportion of heavy drinkers of all these groups.

Religious variations in alcohol consumption

With respect to socioeconomic status and drinking, research consistently indicates that proportionately more abstainers are found at the lower social class levels than at the higher levels. Moderate to heavy drinking is also more common within the higher social classes. In spite of popular stereotypes, people in skid row comprise less than 5 percent of the total population of alcoholics and problem drinkers.

Most alcoholics do not live on skid row

The social acceptability of drinking can help alcoholics hide their illness—even from themselves—for years.

Thomas Masci and Daniel Hebding

Over one million pre-
teens and teenagers
have serious drinking
problems

Age is also an important factor with regard to drinking patterns. Although increasingly large numbers of drinkers tend to be found among
young adults (21 to 24 years old), a large proportion of heavy drinkers are
men 18 to 20 years of age. In comparison, the largest proportion of abstainers is found among older persons. Recent studies also indicate that substantial proportions of teenagers drink. A 1978 Gallup poll indicated, for
example, that approximately one teenager in four (37 percent) drinks some
form of alcohol at least occasionally.[49] Moreover, most recent statistics
show that young people are starting to drink—often excessively—at
younger ages. According to an NIAAA study, there are 1.3 million preteens
and teenagers in the United States who have "serious drinking problems,"
and the number of high school drinkers "who have become intoxicated
doubled in the last twenty years."[50]

As we have seen, there have been a number of changes in American
drinking practices within recent years. One of the most important changes
concerns new drinking patterns among women. Statistics show that more
men than women drink and that men are more likely to be heavy drinkers.
However, the proportion of women who drink has been growing since
World War II. During the 1950s, one out of every five or six alcoholics was
a woman; today it is close to one out of every three. Recent studies also
indicate some important similarities in the drinking behaviors and motives
between the sexes.[51] The fact that drinking is now a widely accepted practice for women and that more women are experiencing isolation as a result
of family breakups are two possible reasons for the growth of female drinking and alcoholism. It has even been suggested that drinking helps women
feel more feminine just as it helps men feel more masculine. Regardless of
the underlying reasons for the rise in female alcoholism, women face a
number of special obstacles in attempting to get help with their drinking
problem. Many women simply try to hide their problem any way they can.
Even when women admit to their problem, doctors may be reluctant to
diagnose and effectively treat it and family and friends may be unwilling
to recognize the problem. At any rate, a "conspiracy of silence" surely
exists when it comes to female alcoholism.[52]

EXPLANATIONS FOR DRUG ADDICTION AND ALCOHOLISM

The reasons for alco-
holism and addiction
are complex

Ever since excessive drinking and drug addiction became recognized as
social problems, people have raised the basic question: Why do individuals
become involved with (and perhaps addicted to) drugs and alcohol? As one
might expect, there is no simple answer. Surely physiological explanations
dealing with the effects upon the body of alcohol and other drugs cannot be
ignored. On the other hand, scientific research has shown that neither the
chemical attributes of drugs nor the physiological response of the human
organism to drugs can sufficiently explain the process and patterns of ad-

diction. In order to fully explain how drugs influence people's behavior and why people become addicted to drugs, we must recognize that many social, situational, and psychological factors are also involved.

PHYSIOLOGICAL EXPLANATIONS

Many physiological theories for alcoholism make the assumption that alcoholism results from some physical or biological characteristic of the person. Some physiological explanations emphasize a genetic theory, namely that alcoholism is inherited and passed directly from parents to children. Other explanations stress genetotrophic origins of alcoholism, i.e., the theory that alcoholism comes about through an hereditary flaw that necessitates an exceptionally high need for a number of basic vitamins. Persons with this defect develop vitamin and nutritional deficiencies, which in turn bring about an insatiable desire for alcohol.[53] Still other physiological explanations emphasize the theory that alcoholism is caused by certain hormone imbalances caused by glandular problems. In general, it appears that these theories have some but only a limited potential for explaining alcoholism and its sociocultural variations. It is true that alcoholism is often found in the children of alcoholics, but it is found in the children of nonalcoholics as well. Likewise, the nutritional deficiencies and hormone imbalances often observed among alcoholics may well be effects of drinking rather than causes of it.[54]

> **Physiological theories give limited explanations for alcoholism and addiction**

During the early 1900s, purely physiological interpretations of the effects of drugs upon the human organism were extremely popular. This view is similar to what Goode terms the "chemicalistic" fallacy—"the view that drug A causes behavior X, that what we see as behavior and effects associated with a given drug are solely a function of the biochemical properties of that drug."[55] In this view, the person played a purely passive role; behavior, including whether the user became addicted, was entirely dependent upon the influence of the specific drug upon that person's body. In recent times, this view has come under serious attack by many medical experts and other authorities in the drug field. Still, large numbers of the public tend to view drug and alcohol use solely in terms of their effects upon the human organism. In many cases, the popular beliefs still hold that if people use drugs they will inevitably become addicted, that once in the "clutches of addiction" one is powerless to control the situation, and that a single dose of certain drugs will automatically lead to life-long addiction. These beliefs are particularly widespread with respect to opiates (heroin), but even here the power of these chemical substances to permanently influence behavior is exaggerated.

> **The "chemicalistic" fallacy**

As we can see from Table 6.1, drugs vary widely in their ability to influence behavior and produce physical dependence. But even more important, one-sided, "chemicalistic" interpretations of the effects of drugs on the human organism fail to take into account the important role of personality

Table 6.1. Major psychoactive drugs

Name	Slang Name(s)	Usual Adult Single Dose	Duration of Action (Hours)	Medical Uses (Present and Projected)	Risk of Potential for: Tolerance	Physical Dependence
Alcohol				None	Yes	Moderate
Whiskey, gin, etc.	Hard stuff, booze, cocktail	1-2 oz.	2-4			
Beer	Suds	12 oz.				
Wine		4 oz.				
Nicotine		1-2 cigarettes	1-2	None. Not recommended because even small quantities are poisonous.	Yes	Maybe
Cigarettes, cigars, snuff, tobacco	Fags, weed, coffin pegs					
Sedative-hypnotics			4-8	Tension, insomnia, neurosis	Yes	High
Alcohol						
Barbiturates	Sleeping pills, downers, goofballs					
Nembutal	Yellow jackets	50-100 mg				
Seconal	Reds					
Phenobarbital	Phennies			Epilepsy		
Chloral hydrate		250-500 mg				
Doriden		500 mg				
Miltown, Equanil		300 mg				
Quaalude, Sopor		500 mg				
Valium						
Stimulants			4-12	Narcolepsy, fatigue, sleepiness. No longer recommended for obesity.	Yes	Maybe
Amphetamines	Uppers, pep pills					
Benzedrine	Bennies	25-5 mg				
Dexedrine	Dexies			Hyperactive children		
Methedrine	Speed, meth					
Caffeine						
Cocaine	Coke, snow	1-2 snorts	2-4	Local anesthetic (now rarely prescribed)		
Ritalin		10 mg		Obesity		
Preludin		25 mg		Obesity		
Tenuate		25 mg				
Tepanil		25 mg				
Narcotics			4-6	Severe pain	Yes	High
Opiates						
Heroin	H, junk, shit, smack, horse	1 bag, balloon, or paper				
Morphine		15 mg				
Opium (paregoric)		12 pellets		Diarrhea		
Codeine		32-64 mg				
Synthetics						
Methadone		5-10 mg	12-24	Heroin addiction		
Demerol		50-100 mg	4-6			
Percodan		5 mg				

The effects of drugs upon the person are relative

and situational factors in drug use and the drug experience. As Peter Laurie states: "Drugs are used quite differently in different social situations; very often the situation and the expectations of the user have far more effect than the chemical."[56] Countless studies, for example, document that the effects of substances such as marijuana, LSD, heroin, and alcohol depend

Reasons for Use and Abuse	Short-term Effects of Average Use	Long-term Effects of Frequent or Heavy Use	Laws and Public Policy
Relaxation, getting high (euphoria), conformity, overavailability, advertising.	Central nervous system (CNS) depressant, drowsiness, decreased alertness and inhibitions, driving accidents.	Impaired coordination and judgment, drowsiness, stupor, permanent liver and brain damage, obesity, violence, addiction, death.	Fully available legally for use and sale, except for mild criminal penalties (usually not enforced) to those under 18 or 21. Powerful lobby, legally advertised with token exceptions. Large black market to avoid taxes. Not classified as drug.
Relaxation (stimulation), ritual, conformity, over-availability, advertising, boredom.	CNS stimulant, increased wakefulness. Also body poison and air pollutant.	Heart attack, stroke, lung cancer, bronchitis, emphysema, high mortality of newborn offspring, fire, pollution, death.	Fully available legally for use and sale, except for mild criminal penalties (usually not enforced) to those under 18 or 21. Powerful lobby, legally advertised with token exceptions. Large black market to avoid taxes. Not classified as drug.
Relaxation or sleep, over-prescription by physicians, getting high, drug-company promotion.	CNS depressant, sedation, drowsiness, sleep, decreased alertness and inhibitions	Impaired coordination and judgment, drowsiness to stupor, confusion, addiction, suicide.	Readily available in unlimited amounts by medical prescription, which can be obtained from more than one doctor and refilled 5 times in 6 months. Other manufacture, sale, and possession prohibited by federal and state "dangerous drug" laws. Large illicit traffic (black market). Moderate penalties.
Relief of fatigue or sleepiness, overprescription to physicians, getting high, drug-company promotion.	CNS stimulant, increased alertness (wakefulness) and decreased fatigue, reduced hunger, restlessness.	Sleeplessness, weight loss and malnutrition, irritability, delusions, and hallucinations (toxic psychosis).	Generally available by medical prescription. Advertised and promoted to doctors (except cocaine). Other distribution and possession barred by federal and state "dangerous drug" laws (except codeine, which is covered by "narcotic" laws). Medium black market. Moderate to severe penalties.
Relief of pain, cough, or diarrhea; elimination of withdrawal symptoms; getting high; wide distribution by organized crime and government officials in S.E. Asia, Turkey, and Mexico.	CNS depressant, sedation, drowsiness, analgesia, decreased alertness and inhibitions.	Constipation, decreased hunger and weight, temporary impotency or sterility, addiction, accidental death from overdose, social stigmatization and frequent criminality as a result of public policy (not a drug effect).	Available by special narcotics prescription from physicians (except heroin, which is not used medically in U.S.). Other production, sale, and possession banned by U.S. and state narcotic laws. Extensive illicit traffic. Severe penalties.

Source: Joel Fort, *American Drugstore*. Boston: Educational Associates, 1975.

upon the personal characteristics of the subject and the context or situation of drug use. Street users experience morphine as pleasurable; most patients in hospitals do not.[57] The importance of psychological and situational factors in drug use is also attested to by the frequent use of placebos in medical therapy and scientific research.[57] Alcohol, barbiturates, morphine, and

Table 6.1. Major psychoactive drugs (Continued)

Name	Slang Name(s)	Usual Adult Single Dose	Duration of Action (Hours)	Medical Uses (Present and Projected)	Risk of Potential for:	
					Tolerance	Physical Dependence
Psychedelics (hallucinogens)				Alcoholism, narcotic addiction, and emotional adjustment of dying persons.	Yes	No
LSD	Acid	150-250 micrograms	10-12			
Mescaline (peyote)	Cactus, mushrooms					
Psilocybin		350 mg	12-24			
STP, MDA		25 mcg	6-8			
DMT						
Scopolomine (belladonna)						
Tranquilizers				Schizophrenia, agitation, anxiety, vomiting.	No	No
Phenothiazines		500-600 mg				
Thorazine		2-5 mg	6-12			
Stelazine		20-60 mg				
Prolixin						
Librium			4-8	Tension		
Valium						
Antidepressants			12-24	Severe depression	No	No
Imipramines						
Elavil		50 mg				
Tofranil		50 mg				
MAO inhibitors						
Nardil		15 mg				
Lithium		600 mg				
Amphetamines (see above)						
Miscellaneous				None	Maybe	No
Inhalants		1-2 sniffs				
Glue, solvents			2			
Gasoline, aerosols			1			
Nitrous oxide	Gas	Variable	1			
Carbon dioxide (built up through rapid breathing)	Gas	Variable	4-6			
Amyl nitrite	Popper	1 ampule				
Over-the-counter pseudosedative and sleep drugs		1 pill				
Compoz						
Sleepeze						
Nutmeg	Spice	Variable	1-2			
Cannabis sativa				Glaucoma, asthma, depression, loss of appetite, high blood pressure, headache, alcoholism.	No	No
Marijuana	Pot, grass, weed	1 cigarette	2-4			
Hashish (charas)	Hash	1 cake or pipe	2-6			
Caffeine			2-4	Fatigue, sleeplessness, coma.	Yes	No
Coffee, tea	Java					
Cola drinks	Coke					
No-Doz, Tirend						
APC, Excedrin	Headache pills			Headache		

Drug use and addiction involves social and psychological processes

heroin are all capable of producing physical dependence, but as we have seen, most people who use these addictive drugs do not become addicts. As Goode points out, drug use and the effects of drugs upon the user's behavior involve many social and psychological as well as physiological processes.[58]

Reasons for Use and Abuse	Average Use Short-term Effects of	Long-term Effects of Frequent or Heavy Use	Laws and Public Policy
Mind expansion, perceptual changes, mystical experience, problem solving.	Intense visual and other sensory experience, rapid flow of thoughts, mood changes, anxiety or panic.	Hallucinations, delusions (acute psychosis), confusion, impaired judgment.	Unavailable legally except from U.S. government to a very few mental researchers and for use by Indians (peyote). Otherwise prohibited by federal and state "dangerous drug" laws. Medium illicit traffic. Moderate penalties.
Relaxation, relief of agitation; hallucinations or delusions; prescription by physicians.	Easing of anxiety or tensions, improved functioning, suppression of neurotic or psychotic symptoms.	Destruction of blood cells, jaundice (liver damage), hypertension, skin rash, blurred vision, decreased initiative (apathy) muscle stiffness, convulsions.	Readily available for indefinite periods by prescription. Advertised and promoted to doctors. Negligible black market.
Relief of depression (to feel normal), prescription by physicians	Improved mood and functioning, more energy.	Destruction of blood cells, jaundice (liver damage), hypertension, skin rash, blurred vision, decreased initiative (apathy) muscle stiffness, convulsions.	Readily available for indefinite periods by prescription. Advertised and promoted to doctors. Negligible black market.
Getting high, relaxation, substitute for other substances, overavailability	CNS depressant, drowsiness, impaired coordination and judgment. Over-the-counter drugs provide mainly a placebo effect as the combination used is almost inactive.	Liver or kidney damage, hallucinations, confusion, death.	Most are fully available to all ages. Some restrictions on airplane glue, nitrous oxide, and amyl nitrite. Not considered drugs. Not usually covered by criminal laws.
Relaxation, getting high, conformity, ready availability, reaction to distortions about its dangers.	Mixed CNS effects, increased appetite, decreased alertness and inhibitions, changed time perspective.	Acute (short-lived) panic or hallucinations, bronchitis.	Unavailable by medical prescription. Cultivation, sale, and possession prohibited by U.S. and state laws. Enormous black market; not much enforcement.
Increased alertness, relaxation (stimulation), conformity (custom), ready availability, work break, boredom, advertising.	CNS stimulant, increased wakefulness, reduction of fatigue.	Insomnia, restlessness, stomach irritation.	Fully available for use and sale to children and adults. No civil or criminal penalties. Not classified as drug.

The circumstances or context of drug use often has as much to say about the drug's long-term behavioral effects upon the user as the chemical substance itself. For example, Charles Winick's study of physicians addicted to narcotics revealed some interesting contrasts to street patterns of addiction. Physician addicts do not incur the availability and cost problems of

Alternative patterns of drug use and addiction

supporting their habit; they are able to self-administer high quality narcotics under sanitary conditions, and they guard against nutritional deficiencies. As a result, even with many years of narcotics use, their physical health is not affected. Moreover, as far as could be determined, they were able to function within a very demanding occupation.[59]

PSYCHOLOGICAL EXPLANATIONS

The above discussion illustrates the basic idea that contrary to the "chemicalistic" fallacy, the effect of drug use upon the human organism is *relative*. Physiological explanations of drug use and addiction fail to account for the role that social and psychological factors play in determining how a drug is used. They also do not specify what the individual experiences as a result of drug use or what the effects of drugs upon the person's behavior and general social functioning will be. Physiological theories are clearly limited in their ability to explain why people become involved with drugs in the first place and also why some but not all people persist in drug use to the point of addiction. Likewise, physiological explanations cannot account for the large number of behavioral effects and patterns of drug use found among drug users and addicts. Moreover, the physiological approach is unable to explain why some addicts return to drug or alcohol use after withdrawal or detoxification, when obviously at this point there can be no physiological basis for such behavior.

In contrast to the physiological explanations, psychologists and other social scientists have stressed the importance of investigating the people who use drugs rather than the drugs themselves. From this perspective, psychologists have attempted to explain addiction in terms of what drugs do *for* people rather than *to* them. What is it about people that attracts them to drug use, particularly excessive drug use and addiction? In attempting to answer such questions, psychologists have developed a numer of theories, the most popular of which are the *reinforcement* and *personality* theories.

Reinforcement Theory. This theory is based upon a fundamental principle of conditioned learning, namely that humans and other animals tend to continue in activities that are reinforced (i.e., they bring about pleasure) and will likewise tend to refrain from behaviors that bring about unpleasantness, pain, or punishment. In terms of this principle, psychologists emphasize that, for many individuals, the use of drugs and alcohol constitutes a very pleasant and rewarding activity because these substances may relieve depression, anxiety, tension, and boredom. Many people, for example, may develop a pattern of frequent and excessive drinking in order to lessen anxieties that result from many of life's stressful situations.

Consistent with reinforcement principles, Alfred Lindesmith developed an important theory of drug—particularly opiate—addiction. For Lindesmith, the development of physical dependence is a necessary precondition,

Physiological theories cannot explain why people begin to use drugs

What do drugs do for people?

The roles of pleasure and pain in habit formation

but is not in itself a sufficient explanation, for addiction. In order for addiction to actually occur, the person must first begin to experience withdrawal distress. In addition, the individual *must* be aware of or link this distress with the absence of the drug. It is only under this circumstance that the individual will become addicted and actively engage in the habitual use of drugs for the primary purpose of avoiding withdrawal. Thus, in Lindesmith's view, it is not the euphoric or pleasurable aspects of drug use that produce addiction; on the contrary, addiction ultimately results from the person's overwhelming need to avoid withdrawal distress.[60]

Addiction results from the fear of withdrawal

In spite of the appeal of reinforcement theories, they still have a number of deficiencies. For one thing, reinforcement theories ignore the important roles that group and sociological factors play in drug use and the development of addiction. Moreover, with respect to psychological factors in alcoholism, experiments at the Laboratory of Alcohol Research (NIAAA) have shown that, contrary to reinforcement theory, alcohol actually tends to increase rather than decrease stress, anxiety, and depression, at least among chronic drinkers. Thus, while people may initially turn to alcohol to relieve their anxieties and problems, once the stage of chronic drinking is reached, alcohol no longer serves this purpose.[61]

The limitations of reinforcement theories

Personality Theories. Psychological explanations have also stressed the importance of various personality factors and traits in an attempt to explain why some people become addicted to drugs and alcohol. Thus personality explanations stress that the possession of certain personality characteristics actually predisposes individuals to addiction. When combined, these traits make up what some psychologists term the addict or alcoholic personality type. Many researchers agree that both the addict and alcoholic personality types tend to share certain psychological similarities, especially those of high dependence needs and an extreme sense of personal inadequacy.

Do personality characteristics lead to addiction?

Laurie feels the addict is unable to handle anxiety, never feels "self-satisfaction," and is plagued with conflicts over sexuality and aggression.[62] From the standpoint of personality, alcoholics have frequently been described as emotionally immature, highly self-indulgent, sexually maladjusted, unable to tolerate frustration, and unable to relate to others.[63] Often psychologists and psychiatrists trace the origins of many of these traits to inconsistent and unstable family relationships and the child's inadequate socialization within the family. This leads to a lack of maturity, deep feelings of insecurity, and other personality maladjustments in later adult life.[64]

The origins of personality traits

Although in recent years personality theories have sparked a considerable amount of research into the etiology of drug addiction and alcoholism, these theories still remain inadequate on a number of counts. There has been some but nevertheless little agreement on the part of psychologists, psychiatrists, and others concerning the identity of the specific psychological traits that make up the so-called addict personality. Again, even though psycholo-

Critique of personality trait theory

gists would tend to assert that certain personality traits exist prior to and are a cause of drug addiction or alcoholism, it may very well be that such traits are actually a result of drug addiction or excessive drinking rather than their cause. Finally, personality theories of addiction encounter another problem, namely their inability to explain why many people, who also exhibit high dependence needs, chronic anxiety, strong feelings of personal insecurity, and so on, do not become drug addicts or alcoholics. Addicts and nonaddicts alike may sometimes manifest similar personality characteristics.[65]

Sociological theories stress the influence of group factors

SOCIOLOGICAL EXPLANATIONS

In contrast to psychological theories, sociological explanations stress the importance of examining group factors and the influence of the person's social environment in attempting to explain the phenomena of drug addiction and alcoholism. A number of theories, for example, attempt to analyze the specific social and social-psychological processes underlying individual addiction and alcoholism. In essence, these theories attempt to explain how and why certain people become involved in drug use and addiction. Other theories attempt to explain why rates of alcoholism and addiction vary among different groups and categories of people. In this section, we will focus upon an analysis of social learning theories and subcultural theories of addiction. Finally we will present a brief analysis of the sociocultural influence on alcoholism.

Drug use and addiction is learned behavior

Learning Theories. In general, sociological theories view drug use and addiction as products of *social learning* rather than as a result of personality traits or maladjustments. For example, Sutherland's theory of differential association, although originally developed to account for various forms of criminal behavior, can also explain many other forms of deviant and non-deviant social behavior, such as driving a car, robbing a bank, or using drugs.[66] The various points of Sutherland's theory were presented in some detail in the preceding chapter. In essence, Sutherland's theory would state that people *learn* drug use and addiction, and that this learning occurs in and through interaction with others who exhibit such behavior. In addition, Burgess and Akers point out in their social learning theory, which they term *differential association reinforcement*, that people are often introduced to and encouraged in drug and alcohol use by friends or others in the surrounding environment. In part, this process operates through a system of positive reinforcements (such as rewards) from others in the form of social status, praise, social approval, or comradeship.[67]

Most people are introduced to drugs by others

Theories such as these assign a great deal of importance to the person's environment and associations and to the influence these social factors play in the development of drug use and addiction. In the vast majority of cases, people become turned on to drugs by acquaintances, friends, or some other persons with whom they come into contact in their environment. This holds true even for such commonplace drugs as alcohol and nicotine. Many persons initially use these drugs for social and recreational purposes when in the company of others. In many instances the initial use of these substances is not really very pleasurable. Often people must *learn* to enjoy alcohol.[68]

Sociologist Howard Becker used a learning perspective in his well-known analysis on becoming a marijuana user. He pointed out that marijuana smoking tends to be a social and group-supported activity. Typically, people are initially exposed to marijuana use through their associations with others. In order to continue in marijuana use, the individual must first learn certain things from other users. According to Becker, "No one becomes a user without (1) learning to smoke the drug in a way which will produce real effects; (2) learning to recognize the effects and connect them with drug use (learning, in other words, to get high); and (3) learning to enjoy the sensations he perceives."[69] Without the example and guidance of other users, such learning would be extremely difficult.

Becking a marijuana user

Subcultural Theories. Consistent with the above learning theories, many sociologists view drug use and drug addiction as an outgrowth or product of a drug subculture. From this point of view, people become involved in drug use and addiction as a result of learning and social reinforcement processes, which occur through their participation with and gradual absorption into (i.e., socialization) the subculture. Sociologists have noted the presence (to one degree or another) of subcultural patterns of drug use for a number of substances, including LSD, marijuana, and some amphetamines, particularly methedrine.[70] The existence of a drug subculture is also apparent with regard to opiates, particularly heroin use. Criminologist Richard Quinney describes the subcultural aspects of drug use and addiction in the following terms:

The subcultural system of drug use

> Drug addiction involves participating in an elaborate subculture supported by group norms, which one writer has called a "survival system." This involves justifying the ideology for drug usage and the "reproductive" system: that addicted persons must continually recruit new members in order to sell them drugs to support their habit. There is also defensive communication, with its own argot for drugs, suppliers, and drug users, which must be learned by the initiates, and the "neighborhood warning system," in which addicts are protected by others. Supporting the habit requires a complex distribution network of the illegal drugs, a "circulatory" system that teaches addicts how to secure illegal drugs. Drugs are imported and wholesale distribution is made mostly by crime syndicates or other highly organized groups.[71]

The subculture itself maintains distinctive norms, values, beliefs, and ways of acting specific to drug use, which individuals come to learn and accept. Subcultures provide the person with opportunities to learn the techniques and skills for using drugs, ideologies and interpretations for drug use and the drug experience, and sets of rationalizations and social encouragement for continuing the use. The person also acquires knowledge of the drug distribution and supply network.[72]

ALCOHOLISM AND SOCIOCULTURAL FACTORS

Unlike many other drug addicts, alcoholics as a whole are not integrated within an organized alcoholic subculture. Nevertheless, sociologists have noted that group and social factors do play an important role in influencing rates of alcoholism among various groups and categories of people. Certain groups and societies, such as Americans (particularly Irish Americans) and the French, are characterized by a fairly high frequency of drinking and also have relatively high rates of alcoholism. Among the French, this is particularly true of northern France. Other groups, such as the Italians (both in Italy and Italian Americans), and the Jews—particularly the orthodox Jews, also have a high frequency of drinking, yet their rates of alcoholism are relatively low.[73]

One factor that would appear to be related to the incidence of excessive drinking and alcoholism would be the attitude of the group or society toward drinking. Certain groups and societies, such as the United States, France, and Ireland, tend to have ambivalent and conflicting attitudes toward alcohol use; other groups, such as Jews and Italians, hold positive and somewhat permissive attitudes toward drinking.[74]

Albert Ullman has also noted the importance that *integrated* drinking patterns play in low rates of alcoholism. According to Ullman, "in any group or society in which the drinking customs, values and sanctions—together with the attitudes of all segments of the group or society—are well established, known to and agreed upon by all, and are consistent with the rest of the culture, the rate of alcoholism will be low." Such conditions are more likely to be present among the Italians and orthodox Jews than among Irish Americans. Consistent with this view, Clinard enumerates various conditions that tend to be conducive to higher rates of alcoholism: "There is evidence that alcoholism is associated with culture where there is a conflict over its use, where children are not introduced to it early, where drinking is done outside of meals, and where it is drunk for personal reasons and not as a part of the ritual and ceremony or part of family living."[75] Under circumstances of *integrated* drinking patterns, drinking will be permitted yet integrated within and regulated by group customs, and excessive drinking and drunkenness will be subject to rather strong penalties.

It would seem that the incidence of alcoholism tends to be low when groups or societies have a positive attitude toward alcohol use, when alcohol

Group and social factors in alcoholism

Different groups have different attitudes toward alcohol

The integration of drinking behavior is associated with low rates of alcoholism

and its moderate use are viewed as acceptable, when the use of alcohol is well integrated with the group's institutional ways of living (its traditions, ceremonies, family life), and when there are taboos against excessive drinking and drunkenness. Under these conditions, there is less chance that people will express their conflicts and anxieties by excessive drinking since alcohol will not be viewed as an object of dependence or escape.[76] In addition to ethnic differentials, some evidence suggests that Ullman's formulations concerning cultural and normative influences on drinking are also useful in accounting for sex differences in alcoholism.[77]

The influence of sociological factors

RESPONSES TO DRUG ADDICTION AND ALCOHOLISM

Throughout this century there have been a number of social responses to the phenomena of drug addiction and alcoholism. With respect to drugs other than alcohol, public concern and public policy have focused largely upon narcotics use and narcotics addiction. In general public policy and societal reaction toward addiction have stressed a punitive and legally suppressive orientation.[78] Emphasis has been upon the development of laws that would restrict and ultimately eliminate narcotics traffic, while addicts as well as users have been defined and stereotyped primarily as criminals.[79] Alcoholics, although not widely labeled as criminals, have often been treated as social outcasts, being stereotyped as undependable, morally corrupt, and dishonest. In fact, as Strauss notes, up until the 1940s imprisonment or some other form of institutionalization constituted the only available method for dealing with alcoholics.[80]

The dominant reaction to addiction: Punitive and legally suppressive

A punitive and largely criminalistic method remains as a dominant approach in dealing with the drug addict today. On the other hand, there are indications (particularly during the last decade or so) that some authorities have begun to question the effectiveness of a legally suppressive approach for dealing with drug use and addiction.[81] Increasingly, addiction to alcohol or other drugs is being viewed as a sickness rather than as a crime or sign of immorality. Consistent with this view, there have been more calls for treatment and rehabilitation in the form of medical, psychiatric, or social therapy for addicts and alcoholics. It should be stressed, however, that although rehabilitative approaches are receiving more attention today, such efforts still represent only a minority point of view, particularly with respect to narcotics addiction.[82]

Rehabilitative approaches have received little attention

In the remaining sections of this chapter we will examine the nature, origins, and consequences of twentieth century governmental legislative policy on narcotics use and addiction. We will then briefly examine a number of recent alternative approaches, which employ a variety of techniques and methods useful for the treatment and rehabilitation of the addict or alcoholic.

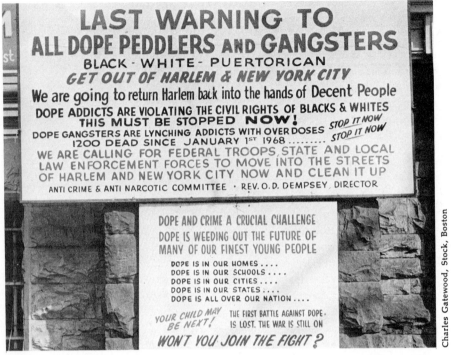

Charles Gatewood, Stock, Boston

Rather than deal with the reasons for drug and alcohol addiction, many people respond with hostile rejection of the addict.

The origins of the punitive approach to drug use

THE LEGISLATIVE RESPONSE: CRIMINALIZATION

Governmental control of addictive drugs began with the Harrison Act in 1914, which was basically a revenue measure limiting possession of opiates to particular registered parties. Responsibility for the act's enforcement was assigned to the Narcotics Division of the Treasury Department. This act instituted strict regulations of the use and sale of opiates and in essence criminalized their possession other than for "legitimate medical purposes."[83] In effect the act cut off over-the-counter supplies of opiates, but apparently the question as to whether a medical prescription constituted a "legitimate medical purpose" still remained. Regardless of the actual scope or intent of the act, officials of the Narcotics Division were opposed to the medical administration of opiates in the treatment of addiction and a series of criminal prosecutions of physicians was instituted. Also, the Supreme Court made several decisions that in effect prohibited opiate prescriptions. Drug use and addiction were becoming matters subject to governmental and legal regulation and control rather than to medical treatment.

The Narcotics Division, committed to an enlargement of its own power, organized an eventually successful effort to transfer control of narcotics out of the hands of physicians to law enforcement and federal authorities. The Narcotics Division engaged in a number of attempts to increase public fear and hostility toward drugs and drug users. Addicts were often branded as "worthless criminals" and "moral degenerates." The result has been a punitive rather than a rehabilitative and treatment-based policy toward addiction. In the years that followed, the Supreme Court (the Linder case) reversed its earlier rulings—actually upholding the medical approach to addiction—but by this time it was too late. Drug use and addiction had generally come to be viewed as police and penal matters, not as medical cases. In addition, faced with frequent prosecution and police harassment, most physicians ceased prescribing narcotics. These factors provided fertile ground for the rise and future growth of illicit narcotics traffic.[84]

The activities of the Federal Narcotics Division

Over the years, our punitive and legally suppressive drug policies have no doubt helped to curtail the growth of drug (particularly narcotics) use within our society, but in no way have they solved the drug problem. As we have previously seen, heroin use and addiction have grown tremendously over the last decade or more. Moreover, the development of restrictive opiate legislation has been largely responsible for the widespread growth of the current "street" addict population, which by necessity has become intimately linked to and dependent upon the criminal underworld.[85] In recent years there have been some indications of a shift from a punitive approach toward a rehabilitative and treatment-centered orientation to drug abuse on the part of the federal government.[86] Such indications would include the passage of the Narcotic Addict Rehabilitation Act, the formation of the National Commission on Marijuana and Drug Abuse, and the establishment of the National Institute on Drug Abuse. Nevertheless, as Reasons notes, "it appears that the criminal approach will remain the dominant method of handling the 'drug problem.' While 'treatment' and 'rehabilitation' receive more emphasis today than previously, the drug problem remains shaped largely by law enforcement personnel and societal conceptions of the user."[87]

The punitive approach has not solved the drug problem

THE CONSEQUENCES OF PUNITIVE POLICIES

The criminalization of addiction and the punitive handling of the drug offender have resulted in a number of consequences that paradoxically have added to the growth of drug use and related social problems. No doubt the most important consequence of the punitive approach has been "the creation of an addict subculture."[88] In the late nineteenth and early twentieth centuries, as we have previously noted, people could legally purchase narcotics; thus there was no need for addicts to unite. However, when drugs became illegal, addicts were faced with the necessity of coming together in order to purchase drugs from one another and to acquire knowledge regarding other

The creation of the drug subculture

illegal means of supply. The growth of this subculture brought about the development of group norms, beliefs, loyalties, and vigorous recruitment efforts aimed at perpetuating its existence. In fact, Goode links the substantial rise in narcotics addiction over the last decade or so directly to the recruitment powers of the addict subculture.[89]

Another important consequence of our punitive approach to addiction has been the appearance and growth of crime on the part of addicts.[89] Prior to the criminalization of opiate drug use, addicts could obtain narcotics easily and at a comparatively low cost. With the Harrison Act and other subsequent restrictive drug legislation, however, addicts were forced to resort to illegitimate (i.e., illegal) means of supply. As we have seen there is a significant relationship between addiction and crime, but the vast majority of addict crime is simply economically motivated. Continued addiction vastly increases the probability of the addict's arrest and imprisonment for some type of drug-related crime. In most cases, unfortunately, prisons provide merely a custodial and punitive environment where little in the way of treatment and rehabilitation is offered to deal with the addict's drug problems. In fact, rather than providing rehabilitation, some experts feel that prisons partly serve as subcultural breeding grounds for continued addiction.[90] Estimates indicate that as many as half of the inmates within our state and federal prisons have major drug or alcohol problems.[91]

By way of comparison, it is interesting to note that under the British system addiction is conceived largely as a medical rather than a law enforcement problem. The addict is viewed as a person with an illness rather than as a criminal. Until very recently British physicians were allowed to prescribe narcotic drugs under systems such as *heroin maintenance*, in which addicts could be maintained on a regularly prescribed minimum dose over an extended period of time. This system led to some abuses, however: A few doctors were found to be over-prescribing drugs. In the late 1960s the British government initiated a modified form of narcotic maintenance under a system of government-controlled and government-supervised clinics. Under this system, registered addicts can legally acquire a supply of narcotics at a moderate price. This system has not put an end to drug addiction; nevertheless, Great Britain's problem is relatively small compared to that of the United States. The system has helped prevent the rise of addict crime, lessened the spread of an addict subculture and, most important, avoided a punitive approach to addiction.

The third and final major consequence of our punitive and legally suppressive drug policy has been the growth of an extensive illegal drug market. We can see many parallels between today's period of antidrug legislation and our former period of Prohibition. In the long run, Prohibition failed; more important, Prohibition laws created many disastrous side effects. Most important of these was the development of a black market for alcoholic beverages. Similarly, our drug laws have given rise to a vast orga-

Restrictive legislation has resulted in more addict crime

The prison inmate is often an alcoholic or drug addict

The British approach to addiction

Prohibition has encouraged the growth of illegal sources of supply

nized crime industry which perpetuates itself by supplying goods that cannot be obtained through other channels. In turn, as we have seen, the high price of such illicit goods frequently forces addicts to become involved with other forms of crime.

The punitive and legally suppressive orientation toward drug and alcohol use and abuse has not worked. It has neither eliminated nor even really curtailed the use of these substances. In fact, as we have argued, this approach had probably had the opposite effect.

There has been an increased awareness of the necessity for alternative approaches to deal with the problems of drug addiction and alcoholism. In recent years, a number of public and private agencies, organizations, and programs have been formed, their purpose being to provide various forms of treatment for the relief or elimination of the individual's addiction.

AA AND OTHER PROGRAMS

There are a number of treatment programs available to the alcoholic today. Some programs specialize in providing one form of treatment, such as counseling, group therapy, or aversion therapy. Increasingly, however, it is common to find programs that offer a combination of treatments. Some of these latter programs, for example, provide for direct and simple detoxification yet combine this with other forms of medical and psychological treatment. *Antibuse* programs constitute another form of medically supervised treatment for alcoholism. Under these programs a person is first detoxified and then given regular doses of the drug antibuse (disulfiram). The individual taking antibuse will find that any further ingestion of even a tiny amount of alcohol will result in a series of very undesirable physical effects, such as severe headache, nausea, and vomiting. In general, antibuse programs and programs limited to providing detoxification treatment have not met with much success. Many individuals completing such programs eventually relapse into their former drinking patterns, since these methods provide only short-run physiological treatment. If treatment is to provide effective long-range results, broader and more inclusive programs of therapy, combining drug, medical, psychological, and social therapies must be utilized.

Antibuse and similar programs have not been highly successful

The agencies and organizations involved in alcoholic treatment are numerous. A partial list would include local voluntary alcoholism councils offering referral and "pretreatment" counseling, community mental health centers, detoxification centers, aversion therapy clinics, state and local hospitals, and private physicians. In addition, there are a host of government-sponsored alcoholism programs in training, research, education, and treatment funded through NIAAA.[92]

One of the most well-known and successful organizations dealing with the treatment of alcoholism is Alcoholics Anonymous (AA). This organization was created by two alcoholics in 1935. Since then AA has grown to an estimated 425,000 members in approximately 13,000 groups in the United States alone.[93] Alcoholics Anonymous is a voluntary organization whose basic goal is to have individuals remain sober through a system of fellowship, mutual assistance, and peer support. AA operates on the basis of group meetings and discussions and a helping network that is always available to each member in time of need. Members come together in group meetings in a spirit of cooperation and mutual respect to discuss their problems and receive support from others in their efforts to deal with alcohol. Although AA is nonsectarian, the program functions within a framework of strongly held religious principles. AA requires members to make an assessment of their own strengths and weaknesses, to recognize that in order to gain control over their lives and their drinking they must rely on a power superior to their own, and to realize that they must also be willing to make retribution to others they have previously harmed. The program focuses upon helping alcoholics redefine or relabel themselves in order to enhance their feelings of self-esteem and self-worth.[94]

Data proving the successfulness of AA treatment is lacking, although rough estimates place the recovery rate at 50 percent or more, at least among those who are sincerely motivated to do something about their problem. Although AA may not be suitable for all alcoholics, professionals often recommend it as part of a total treatment program.

The group meeting: A core aspect of the AA program

AA appears to be relatively successful

PROGRAMS DEALING WITH ALCOHOLISM AND ADDICTION

It is estimated that as many as ten million American workers have a serious drinking problem.[95] In 1947, Consolidated Edison of New York became the first company to develop a company detection and rehabilitation program. Since then, hundreds of companies have set up policies and programs designed to help alcoholic workers. Major efforts are now being put into the early detection of problem drinking. Early detection and treatment increase the likelihood of recovery; at this point, the workers may still be in good health, their families and community relationships may still be intact, and they may be more easily motivated to do something about the problem before it becomes more serious.[96] The following article discusses many of the recently enhanced efforts on the part of industry to deal with employee problem drinking and alcoholism. The article also discusses the increased concern of labor unions and insurance companies and their active involvement to detect and provide rehabilitative services to workers with drinking problems.

U.S. NEWS & WORLD REPORT READING——OBJECTIVES

1. To identify the various ways in which problem drinking constitutes an enormous financial burden to business and industry.

2. To list the various general measures that industry and labor have instituted to combat employee drinking problems.

3. To statistically document the effectiveness of industrial detection and rehabilitation programs.

What Industry Is Doing About 10 Million Alcoholic Workers

More than ever before, U.S. companies are trying to come to grips with one of their most perplexing problems—alcoholism.

All kinds of workers drink too much, from hourly laborers to highly paid officials in the executive suite.

Estimates of their numbers run as high as 10 million. They not only disrupt their own lives but also affect as many as 40 million family members and friends.

Absenteeism, low productivity, poor judgment, inefficiency in general—all these effects of problem drinking cost business and Government an estimated 10 billion dollars a year.

The first problem, and a difficult one, is to detect the employe who is imbibing too heavily.

John Lavino, Jr., director of health services for Kemper Insurance Companies, says it's time for employers to look further if they find themselves saying: "He's brilliant while he's here," or "She's the best worker I have when she isn't moody," or "I don't know what's happened to Bob, but he can't get along with people in the unit any more"—or if they find themselves shifting the work load from one employee to others.

It's not companies alone that are trying to single out and deal with drinkers. Labor unions, insurance companies and the liquor industry itself are joining the effort.

In the growing drive to combat the drinking problem:

- Individual companies, large and small, are stepping up efforts to detect alcoholic employees and encourage them to get treatment.
- Consortiums of firms are setting up programs, often in areas where there are not enough workers in any one company to justify a detection plan.
- In some cases, workers are encouraged to seek help through the anonymity of a group not identified with any one company.
- Medical treatment is being made available to alcoholics under many company insurance plans. Alcoholism is now treated not as a "crime" but, rather, as an illness.

Industrial measures to deal with employee drinking problems

Experts agree that singling out the problem drinker is far from easy. Dr. Alfred A. Smith, professor of psychiatry at New York Medical College says, after years of study, that "many heavy drinkers are not detected until alcoholism is well established."

OSTRICH APPROACH

Some employers have been reluctant to face the issue squarely, preferring to ignore alcoholism among employees in the early stages and then firing workers who become too far gone.

Says Dr. Smith: "There even seems to be a tacit understanding by management and supervisors that drinking is all right as long as you don't show it." He adds that many heavy drinkers build up a tolerance of alcohol that shows only when they have a serious physical breakdown, long after they have lost the capacity to work efficiently.

Corporate attitudes, however, are changing rapidly.

Kenneth Eaton, former deputy director of the National Institute on Alcohol Abuse and Alcoholism and now a consultant to many firms, contends that "industry has done more in the last five years than the previous 25 to come to grips with the problem of alcoholic workers. Ultimately, all large employers will take some organized approach to the problem."

CO-OPERATIVE SPIRIT

Among the large companies with alcoholic-detection programs are some of the nation's major distillers—for example, Hiram Walker, Seagram, Heublein and McCormick.

General Motors has more than 100 union-management committees on alcoholism functioning throughout the U.S. and Canada.

Some new industrial approaches to problem drinking

A recent study of employees in the program at GM's Oldsmobile division showed a 50 per cent decline in lost man-hours, a 30 per cent drop in sickness and accident benefits, 56 per cent fewer leaves of absence, 63 per cent fewer disciplinary actions, and an encouraging 82 per cent plunge in job-related accidents.

Some employers are using internal publications to remind workers that help is available, hopefully removing the stigma of alcoholism as a "dark secret" rather than as an illness that can be treated.

Kemper Insurance Companies offer a free booklet called "Detour Alcoholism Ahead" as a guide to identifying developing alcoholism. The booklet also lists sources of help for alcoholics and those concerned with their recovery.

A recent issue of *Monogram*, a publication of General Electric Company, carried both an article on the company's plan for combatting alcoholism and a first-person story by an employee who had been cured.

St. Regis Company's *Regis News* printed an article with the title, "Boozers Produce Costly Hangovers for Everyone."

In contrast to approaches such as these, other firms are pooling funds and setting up outside groups to work with problem drinkers. For small firms, this can save money and at the same time help the company avoid confrontation with workers while trying to help them.

One such consortium has been set up by several firms in the Philadelphia area. It works like this:

Employees of member firms can dial 24 hours a day the letters INFONOW, at work or from home. They receive preliminary psychiatric counseling. But the main pitch is to insist that the worker agree to further help.

A MATTER OF POLICY

One of the latest developments, though, is expansion of health insurance to cover treatment of alcoholics.

J. F. Follmann, Jr., former vice president of the Health Insurance Association of America, reports that 17 of the top health-insurance companies now will cover loss of income resulting from alcoholism if the illness is treated.

Mr. Follmann notes that such coverage has been made a requirement for group health-insurance contracts by a number of States, including Wisconsin, Minnesota, Illinois, Massachusetts, Washington, Connecticut, Louisiana, Mississippi and Michigan.

The AFL-CIO found in a recent study of 46 health and welfare-insurance plans that 37 provide some such benefits. Included were 17 of 18 Blue Cross-Blue Shield organizations and 6 of 12 unions that responded to the survey.

"While there are still some variations in coverage," the union study said, "the trend is overwhelmingly in the direction of recognition of alcoholism as a disease by those who provide insurance coverage."

Managements in many cases are getting full co-operation from unions. For one thing, teams of workers are being selected within companies to work with problem drinkers. These teams often are headed by self-admitted alcoholics who have been cured.

The concern of unions over alcoholism was summed up by Leo Perlis, director of the AFL-CIO's department of community services in the following words: "Unions, certainly, are concerned with their members not only as human beings but also as the producers of America's goods and services. In the long run, quality goods and services cannot be produced in quantity—if at all—by alcoholic managers or workers. Here, labor and management have a joint obligation not only to help a sick worker but to prevent a sick economy."

Evidence of the growing concern in unions over alcoholism

To help put words into action, the National Council on Alcoholism has set up a labor-management advisory committee. It is headed by James Roche, former chairman of General Motors, and George Meany, president of the AFL-CIO.

As for the liquor industry, the Distilled Spirits Council of the U.S., which represents most of the distillers, has been sponsoring seminars designed to educate employers on detection and treatment of drinkers. The Council has also been running an advertising campaign to encourage problem drinkers to seek help.

"None of this is a do-good, soft touch," says one who is close to the program. "It's to get results. Once a worker is found to have a drinking problem we expect him to accept help because his job is on the line."

This source adds:

"Often you can explain that alcohol is upsetting his job record, injuring his health, hurting his family and friends, and he goes right on drinking. But when you make it plain that he'll lose his job if he doesn't accept help—the message gets through."

CARROT AND STICK

Most companies with programs for dealing with problem drinkers insist that afflicted workers accept help as part of holding a job. In return, cured workers are not penalized in terms of job promotions or raises once they have overcome their drinking difficulties.

Yet, experts agree that despite all the progress much remains to be done, as shown by a study of 149 major firms with headquarters in New York City and branches throughout the world.

Many companies need to do much more about employee drinking

Of these firms only 51 deal directly on a regular basis with alcohol abuse. Of the 98 companies without programs, more than half indicated lack of interest or denied that they had a problem.

William C. Christian, who directed the study, says it "clearly indicates a need for greater effort to involve corporations in dealing with one of the nation's major health problems."

METHADONE MAINTENANCE

The rapid rise of methadone programs

Methadone is basically a synthetic narcotic that is widely used in the treatment of narcotics—specifically heroin—addiction. The first methadone program was developed in the early 1960s, and by 1977 thousands of narcotics addicts were receiving methadone in hundreds of clinics throughout the country.[97] Participation in methadone maintenance programs is typically voluntary, although in some instances individuals may be required to do so by a court. The clinics dispense methadone in a convenient oral form, and individuals, especially in the beginning of treatment, are required to come to the clinics daily. The system of daily reporting also aids in addict supervision and counseling, although it would appear that many clinics are not putting much effort into providing some of these valuable support services.[98] It is important to recognize that methadone maintenance in itself does not provide a remedy for addiction, but methadone does eliminate the threat of withdrawal while blocking the euphoria of heroin. The addict is thus in a better position to function more adequately within the context of work and community life.

Methadone maintenance programs have been the source of growing concern, debate, and controversy, particularly within recent years. Advocates of methadone maintenance stress that this approach represents a relatively effective way of dealing with heroin addiction, and that it drastically reduces the addict crime and death rates.[99] However, critics state that methadone maintenance simply trades one form of addiction for another and does not really come to terms with the fundamental reasons for the person's addiction. In some respects methadone maintenance has met with modest success. Nevertheless, methadone programs have encountered a number of problems that have reduced their effectiveness and lessened public support for their efforts. Methadone maintenance does not reach the majority of heroin addicts and it is likely that most addicts in the program eventually return to illicit drug use. Many clinics are understaffed and some addicts feel that maintenance programs are dehumanizing. Moreover, many community groups assert that methadone clinics endanger the safety of the surrounding neighborhood.[99]

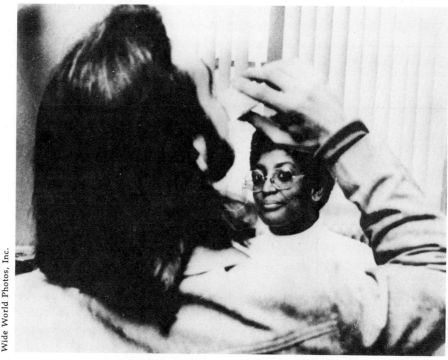

Wide World Photos, Inc.

A daily dose of methadone has enabled some addicts to kick their habit, but others claim it merely substitutes one addiction for another.

THERAPEUTIC COMMUNITIES

This alternative provides a form of drug treatment vastly different from methadone maintenance.[100] Therapeutic communities provide drug-free residential settings and are run mostly (if not entirely) by ex-addicts and others in the process of eliminating their habit. Synanon, the first of such communities, was founded in the late 1950s. Over the years a number of other programs and facilities, such as Daytop Village and Phoenix House, have been developed. Distinct from methadone maintenance, the basic purpose of therapeutic communities is to help the addict achieve total freedom from any drug dependence while assisting the person to resolve the fundamental reasons that precipitated addiction.[101]

Therapeutic communities often provide a controlled and highly structured environment for the addict. Addicts are given a series of daily work assignments and receive rewards and privileges for mature, responsible behavior. They are involved in continuous daily association with other addicts, from whom they receive encouragement, support, and criticism when necessary. The most important aspect of the therapeutic process is the

The therapeutic community: A drug-free residential setting

group meeting. During these sessions, residents openly express their attitudes and feelings toward themselves and other group members.

Compared to other approaches, therapeutic communities provide a highly structured and highly demanding treatment program. Many addicts do not prefer this type of approach; many others give it a try only to drop out during the earlier stages of treatment. The likelihood of success depends upon many factors. Those who are willing to invest a considerable period of time and are highly motivated to conquer their drug problems are most likely to profit substantially from this type of treatment.

Therapeutic communities place high demands upon the individual

SUMMARY

Drug and alcohol use is widespread throughout our society. Although many drugs and their use are socially approved and even encouraged within our society, the use of heroin and other substances termed "hard drugs" or "street drugs" meets with much social disapproval. Many people define our drug problem solely in terms of these latter disapproved substances. In reality, however, our drug problem is much broader, encompassing the use and abuse of many socially acceptable and legal substances.

In a strict scientific sense, a drug is a substance (other than food) that, by virtue of its chemical nature, affects the functioning or structure of living organisms. Social scientists use the more specific term *psychoactive drug,* which refers to substances that in some way affect the user's central nervous system. Psychoactive drugs are typically divided into three very general categories: stimulants, depressants, and hallucinogens. Drug abuse was defined as the excessive and/or compulsive use of a drug, to the degree that it harms the user's health or social functioning or results in harmful consequences to others. Thus any drug can be abused, although certain drugs—those capable of producing physical dependence (addiction)—run a high risk for abuse. The nature and consequences of the use and abuse of amphetamines, barbiturates, narcotics (heroin), and alcohol were examined, stressing in particular many of the personal, social, and economic costs of problem drinking and alcoholism.

Physiological and psychological theories for drug addiction and alcoholism were examined before giving attention to sociological explanations. Sociological explanations stress the importance of group factors and the influence of social environment on drug addiction and alcoholism. Many sociological theories, such as differential association and differential association reinforcement, view addiction and alcoholism as learned behaviors and attempt to explain these phenomena on the basis of social learning principles. Other sociological theories aim at explaining why rates of alcoholism and addiction vary among different groups and categories of people. Of particular importance here are the subcultural theories of addiction and theories that stress the importance that *integrated drinking patterns* have on low alcoholism rates.

In the present century there have been a number of societal responses to the phenomena of drug addiction and alcoholism. In general, governmental and public policies have stressed a punitive and legally suppressive orientation to these problems. Many drug addicts and users have been defined and stereotyped primarily as criminals; alcoholics, although not widely labeled as criminals, have often been treated as social outcasts, being stereotyped as undependable, morally corrupt, and dishonest. The criminalization of addiction and the punitive handling of the drug offender have resulted in a number of consequences, including the creation of an addict subculture, the growth of crime on the part of addicts, and the growth of an extensive illegal drug market.

In recent years there has been an increased awareness of the necessity for alternative approaches to deal with the problems of drug addiction and alcoholism. Treatment for alcoholism is provided through programs of counseling, group therapy, antibuse, or aversion therapy. AA and programs that combine drug, medical, psychological, and social therapies have been somewhat successful in the treatment of alcoholism. Methadone maintenance is another well-known approach to the treatment of narcotics (specifically heroin) addiction. Although this program has helped reduce addict crime and death rates, the maintenance system in itself is not really a remedy for addiction. In addition, recent evidence indicates that many methadone clinics are doing little to provide other important support services for the addict. Therapeutic communities provide a drug treatment alternative vastly different from methadone maintenance. These therapeutic communities provide a drug-free, residential setting for the treatment of addiction. This approach appears to be somewhat successful, but only for those who are highly motivated and willing to invest a considerable period of time and effort.

KEY TERMS

Alcoholics Anonymous
Drug abuse
Drug addiction
Alcoholism
Amphetamines
Antibuse programs
Chemicalistic fallacy
Barbiturates
Depressants
Differential association
Differential association reinforcement
Drug (scientifice definition)
Drug (social definition)
Drug subculture
Genetotrophic theory

Drug habituation
Hallucinogens
Harrison Act
Heroin maintenance
Learning theory
Methadone maintenance
Narcotics
Personality theory
Problem drinking
Psychoactive drugs
Reinforcement theory
Stimulants
Therapeutic communities
Tolerance
Withdrawal

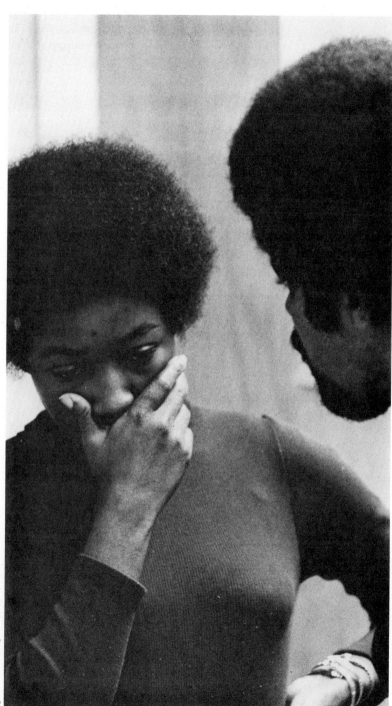

Eugene Luttenberg, Editorial Photocolor Archives

7

Family Problems

Chapter Objectives

1. To define the major functions of the family in American history and to examine recent changes.
2. To examine by essay the situation of the family as a place of violence for spouses and children.
3. To contrast in an essay three explanations for family violence.
4. To explain three responses to family violence.
5. To discuss, by essay, the extent and rate of divorce in America today.
6. To briefly describe five problems encountered by the children of divorce.
7. To examine in an essay three major explanations for divorce.
8. To briefly describe the sociologists' response to the problems of divorce and desertion.
9. To compare three alternatives to the established nuclear family.

INTRODUCTION

Divorce, desertion, and family violence are certainly not new, twentieth century phenomena. However, high rates of divorce and desertion and new attitudes toward family violence (once considered to be sound child-rearing and wife-handling methods) have prompted much concern about the fate of family life in America. Professional journals in the social sciences, newspapers, federal statistical data, and television documentaries have examined many of the problems associated with today's marriage and family life. Various titles of these professional and news articles, such as "Today's Marriages: Wrenching Experience or Key to Happiness?", "The American Family: An Embattled Institution," "The Death of the Family, Revisited," "The American Family, Can it Survive Today's Shocks?", "Battered Wives: An Emerging Social Problem," and "Violence in The Children's Room," reflect this concern about marriage and the family.

Many specialists in the field believe that this social institution, as it exists today in western society, has come upon perilous times. Many others see the family as being in a state of change. As we will later examine, many changes occurring in the family have been termed "problems" by some social scientists and "transitional readaptations," "acceptable developments," or "signs of adaptations" by others. Some have denied *any* fundamental changes in the family and base their positions on the continuity of demographic data.[1] They maintain that statistics for the past two decades have reflected America's commitment to marriage and family life. Yet, as we shall see, the divorce rate continues to climb and marriage rates have been dropping. Whether one views family problems as part of a movement toward a constructive reorganization of the American family, as a breakdown of society, or as a result of social change and new conditions, the fact remains that the family is undergoing many changes and, as a social institution, is experiencing many problems. In this chapter, we will focus on significant changes and problems encountered by what is considered to be the most important institution in society.

The family: An institution in a state of change

The family is considered the most important institution

CHANGING FUNCTIONS OF THE FAMILY

There is currently much concern in society about the many changes occurring in the family institution and about problems of family life because, among other things, the family is the most important agency of socialization. It is from family members, who first care for their needs, that children initially acquire the attitudes, beliefs, and cultural values.

The family is defined as a "socially sanctioned, relatively permanent grouping of people who are united by blood, marriage, or adoption ties, who generally live together and cooperate economically," and is mainly responsible for the early development of personality in the individual.[2] The family is also the first group to provide meaning and support to people. It is the first reference group, to which a child refers for attitudes, norms, values,

The family defined

and practices in evaluating his or her own behavior.[3] The individual's first interpretation of the physical and social world and the establishment of personal likes and dislikes are derived from the network of family relations. In fact, a child's experiences within the family structure are probably some of the most important series of contacts a person will ever have.

The family is the most important unit of socialization

Besides providing a strong influence during the socialization process, the family, according to most sociologists, has other important functions. As an institutionalized social structure, functions of the family vary over time and from one society to another. Many sociologists also believe that many traditional functions of the American family have been lost to other social institutions. The following are, however, among the more-or-less universal functions that are found throughout time and in all societies.[4]

Basic family functions

One universal function of the family is reproduction. This function has been viewed as a prerequisite for the survival of all societies. The family regulates the sexual drive. It also provides the means by which a person's social status is initially fixed. Changes in status (class, ethnic, religious) do occur during a family member's lifetime. However, much of the initial status acquired from the family is retained for life. An additional universal function of the family is the care, training, and protection of the young. Needs of young children, especially during their long period of dependence, must be administered to by their families. In addition, the family often functions as a protector for its members—especially the young, the elderly, and the infirm—against dangers from others, both inside and outside the clan, tribe, community, or society. Other functions include providing (1) recreation, (2) a basis for inheriting private property, and (3) an economic base for producing family services and goods.

In addition to having various functions, the family institution has various forms, according to such factors as kinship structure or family types, number of spouses or forms of marriage relationships, mate selection patterns, and authority patterns. These variations will be examined later in relation to social change. However, at this point it is important to make a distinction between the *conjugal* (*nuclear*) and the *consanguine* (*extended kinship*) family structures. With respect to kinship structure or family types, the family may be organized as a consanguine or conjugal unit. On a consanguine or extended kinship basis, the family consists of several generations of blood relations. The conjugal or nuclear unit consists of a husband, a wife, and their children. The nuclear family can, however, be part of an extended family that consists of all those people defined as kin.

The nuclear and extended families

According to Skolnick, the nuclear family—i.e., husband, wife, and children—is "universally found in every human society, past, present, and future."[4] Early in American history, when we were an agricultural society, the family performed many of the previously listed functions with only minimal amounts of help from other social institutions. With urbanization and industrialization (in addition to many other social changes), the father in the family ceased working on the farm, working instead away from home in the factories and mills of cities. Many mothers also started this kind of work, which meant that fewer items were made at home and more were made in industry. Thus, people began to consume more and more services and products. Other institutions began to take over functions that previously were the family's responsibility. Schools and churches took over education and religious training; the police became the protectors; the hospital, the health-care provider. Recreational functions also shifted away from the family.

The loss of family functions

In the earlier part of this century, some sociologists believed that the institution of the family was in a state of decline. Such factors as the mass migration to urban areas, the switch in the manufacturing emphasis from home to factory, and the growth of schools for very young children led to the belief that the family had outlived its usefulness. Many scholars at that time lamented the "passing" of the family. Later generations of scholars scoffed at these gloomy predictions of their predecessors. They were aware of the fact that the family had lost its functions of providing economic support, education, and health care. But its functions of nurturing and rearing children and offering refuge to adults from an impersonal and competitive society were more important than ever before.

Changes in family functions

In the 1940s and 1950s, there was little talk of family problems or decline. The marriage and remarriage rates increased, and the average age of people getting married decreased. Except for the war period, women were basically into homemaking careers at this time. The two decades prior to the early 1960s were the "middle-class society" years. Researchers state that during this period, the "keep-to-itself" life-style of the conjugal family meshed with a general mood of satisfaction with America as an affluent and bountiful society.[5]

Change began to occur again in the 1960s, and by the 1970s the family was again considered shaky. The media news and polls reflected national concern for the future of the family. The past decade reflected a "widespread sense of profound change in the values and assumptions of family life."[6] These changes, reflected in marital conflict and violence, parent-child conflict, and broken homes, have been recognized by many sociologists as family problems, and are considered by them to be social problems as well.

Polls reflect widespread concern for the family and its problems

Within the structure and processes of all families, there are stresses, tensions, and various degrees of conflict. These tensions may develop from sources outside the marital relationship or from the relationship itself. In many cases, couples and other family members, after quarreling or fighting, will resolve their respective differences. At times, positive results may develop from the resolution of conflict between family members. Many marriages, however, are continuously characterized by unresolved conflicts, and stresses remain as a more-or-less permanent characteristic of the marriage. These stresses are often manifested in violence. The role that violence plays in family life must be examined if we are to have a basic understanding of the many difficulties encountered by the American family.

A PLACE FOR VIOLENCE

Violence is part of American family life

Many people rightfully view the family as characterized by love and affection. It is also, however, characterized by violence. In many American families, violence is an everyday occurrence and a fundamental part of family life.[7] This fact may be somewhat difficult to believe, because many Americans have an idealized image of the family. Steinmetz and Straus, in their analysis of family violence, state that it takes some effort to view the family as a place where "conflict and physical violence are a regular part of the pattern of family life." It takes this effort because family attitudes, values, and rules of behavior all point in the opposite direction. There is, then, a discrepancy between the actual and the idealized pictures of the American family.[8] Although family violence is nothing new, sociologists have just began to examine this problem.[9] Before analyzing violence as it exists in the family, however, it is necessary to first define both conflict and violence and to discuss the relationship between them.

Conflict and violence

Conflict has been defined as a product of social interaction and as an effort to resolve a decision-making impasse. *Violence* has been defined as any behavior that threatens or causes physical damage to an object or person, and it can be the product of either an individual characteristic or a social interaction.[10] Whether conflict between family members is viewed as a normal, fundamental, and perhaps constructive part of social organization, or as a deviant, abnormal situation, social scientists consider conflict and violence to be part of the pattern of American family life. Conflict is seen by most people to be detrimental to groups, and many family members therefore protect the family's cohesiveness from tension and conflict.

Violence can but need not develop from conflict

Much of the time these feelings are merely covered up, not eliminated. This, in turn, can lead to uncontrollable conflict and tension. Many people stifle emotions that result from conflict, but when these "unpleasant" emotions finally surface, they "may cause unrepairable damage, since to show them is so against the Western middle class norm regarding marriage and the family."[11] Violent behavior can but need not develop from conflict. Violence may or may not characterize individuals who are otherwise involved in extensive conflict-ridden interaction.[12]

All people are trained for violence

Moral authorities and parents warn young children against violence. The behavior of adults, however, runs counter to that advice. Therefore, all people are trained for violence. Children learn that force is an effective means of stopping others' unpleasant behavior and that it, or its threat, affects others' calculations of profit and loss.[13] Children "can be persuaded to obey when faced with such consequences. The child experiences this directly, and watches it in others—the fright of his mother when his father

Burk Uzzle, Magnum Photos, Inc.

Violence is a part of many children's games and activities.

is furious, arguments and threats among neighbors, the battles with his
own siblings, and so on."[14]

SPOUSE ABUSE
Estimates of the extent of violence between husbands and wives and of
wife beating vary. A study in Chicago estimated that more police calls were
made for conflict between family members than for all criminal incidents
combined.[15] In significant numbers of divorce applications, spouses mention
overt violent behavior as a factor in their wanting a divorce. One study, in
fact, reports that 40 percent of the working-class couples requesting divorce
listed "physical abuse" as a major complaint.[16] Some sociologists believe
that many of the estimates of violence between spouses are low because
many incidents go unreported or because abuse is not listed as a major
cause of divorce.[17] In any event, the incidence of spouse abuse appears to
be more widespread than social scientists previously believed. Women are
usually on the "receiving end of the worst batterings" at home. When there
is a fight between a husband and wife, the wife, on the average, "comes
out the loser."[18]

**Women are usually on
the receiving end**

Husband abuse is one of the most unreported crimes

Men and women are equal victims of family violence

Violence in the family is an old tradition

Wives are not the only victims of family violence. Husband beating is considered by some sociologists to be one of the most unreported crimes. It has been estimated that each year at least 250,000 husbands in the United States are severely beaten by their wives.

A 1976 national survey of over 2,000 representative families indicates that about two million wives and an equal number of husbands commit one or more serious attacks on their spouses each year. Serious attacks range from kicks, punches, and bites to homicidal assaults with deadly weapons. Some sociologists see men and women as equal victims of family violence, since the homicides in husband-wife conflicts are fairly equally split between the sexes.[19]

CHILD ABUSE

Because families tend to be viewed as a center of love and gentleness, there is an equal tendency not to see actual violence levels in the family. Today parents are legally permitted to use physical punishment on their children. Research indicates that the majority of people in the United States believe it to be a moral obligation to use physical punishment to control their children, if other means fail.[20] It appears that society acknowledges physical punishment as violence only when it reaches extremes, such as severe injury or death.[21]

In previous periods of western history, children and wives appeared to have experienced more violence than they do today. Historical analysis of child abuse reveals, for example, that for many centuries, the maltreatment of children was justified by the belief that severe physical punishment was needed to "maintain discipline, to transmit educational ideas, to please certain gods, or to expel evil spirits."[22]

The rates of violence and abuse against children and wives are probably not as high today as they were in the past, but they are nonetheless high. For instance, studies of child abuse report that in America, many thousands of children are abused, brutally beaten, and killed by their parents each year.[23] Specific data on the number of abused wives and children are very difficult to obtain, and if available, are difficult to interpret because of variations in the definitions of events or because the populations studied may be unrepresentative of the general population. An example of this difficulty is found in David Gil's estimate of three million cases of varying degrees of child abuse every year. Steinmetz and Straus indicate that the problem with this type of estimate is that it depends on current definitions of abuse.[24] They state,

An ordinary spanking or slap by a parent would not be counted as abuse. But if the parties involved were husband and wife, then a spanking or slapping would be considered abuse by most Americans.

That has not always been the public attitude. Earlier in American history, it was considered quite appropriate for a husband to physically punish an erring wife. At some future time, we may also come to see what is now regarded as ordinary and permissible spanking of children as abuse. But whether we regard such acts as abuse or not, there is no question that they are violent acts.[25]

Gil has defined child abuse as follows: "physical abuse of children is the intentional, nonaccidental use of physical force, or intentional, non-accidental acts of omission, on the part of a parent or other caretaker inter-acting with a child in his care, aimed at hurting, injuring, or destroying the child."[26] This definition is unsatisfactory with respect to real-life situations, however, since it may not be possible to make a distinction between "in-tentional behavior" and "accidental behavior." It is quite difficult to prove that a child's injury is intentional rather than accidental, in spite of more sophisticated medical determination procedures.[27]

Child abuse defined

Research has shown that minimal levels of parental violence, such as hitting and spanking, are employed by at least 93 percent of American parents.[28] The physical abuse of children is neither a rare nor an unusual occurrence in American history. In fact, physical abuse of children appears to be endemic in our culture, because our norms of child rearing do not pre-clude the use of force toward children by their parents. It is actually en-couraged in subtle and not-so-subtle ways by many "professional experts" in child rearing, education, medicine, and the media.[29]

Physical abuse of chil-dren is endemic in American culture

Mothers tend to be more abusive than fathers to their children. This has been attributed to the fact that the major burden of child care responsi-bility falls on women. The birth of a child restricts the mother's mobility and freedom, both socially and occupationally. This, combined with the stressful demands of early child rearing, can, for many mothers, produce frustration, manifested in the tendency to be abusive to their children.

Mothers are more abusive than fathers

Research indicates that the most dangerous period for the abused child is from about 3 months to 3 years of age. A child is most vulnerable during this period and is "most defenseless and . . . least capable of meaningful social interaction." Three factors have been found to be related to the fre-quency of abuse among 3-month-old to 3-year-old children. First, unlike the older child, who may be able to absorb more physical punishment, the very young child lacks the durability to withstand violence. Second, frustration is created by the infant's inability to interact with the parent in a more socially meaningful manner. Third, the new child's birth often causes eco-nomic hardship for the parents.[30]

The very young child is more vulnerable to abuse

Sociologists have found that parents who are abusive to their children demand a much higher performance level from them than do parents who are not abusive. What is demanded is usually well beyond the children's capacity to understand, much less achieve. What typically occurs is that the parents "become angry because the child will not stop crying, eats poorly, [or] urinates after being told not to do so." The parents "feel righteous about the punishments they have inflicted on their children. They avoid facing the degree of injury they have caused, but they justify their behavior because they feel their children have been 'bad'."[31]

Child abuse is not just a problem of the poor

Gil's classic analysis of child abuse indicates that families in which abuse occurs are generally undereducated, disproportionately poor, and mainly headed by women. About 60 percent received public assistance. By no means, however, is child abuse a problem just of the lower socioeconomic levels. Middle- and upper-socioeconomic-level families also employ violence as a means of controlling their children.[32]

As we shall see in the first reading, recent studies have questioned the prior conclusions many social scientists made on the relationship between social class and physical punishment. These new studies caution against creating and using stereotypes with respect to social class. It is not that class differences do not exist, but that the differences are not great.[33]

Family violence, it should be noted, does not occur just between parent and child or man and wife, it also occurs between siblings. Because of the intimacy of a brother-sister relationship and because there is a potential for real rivalry for parental care and affection, there is a high potential for violence between two or more siblings.[34] Research also seems to indicate that children's aggressive tendencies are probably increased by parents who use physical punishment to control aggression in their children.[35]

ANALYZING FAMILY VIOLENCE

In the following reading, Suzanne Steinmetz and Murry Straus thoroughly examine several of the myths about violence in the family. In their analysis of the "sex myth"—that sexual drives are violence-producing mechanisms—the authors question the relationship between repression, sexual antagonism, segregation, and family violence. In their examination of the "catharsis myth"—that the expression of "normal" aggression between family members releases tension and reduces the likelihood of severe violence—the authors examine five factors that have accounted for the persistence of this myth in society. With an examination of "resource" and "frustration" factors, the article disproves the "class myth"—that intrafamily violence is mainly a low- or working-class phenomenon.

STEINMETZ AND STRAUS READING——OBJECTIVE

1. To examine in an essay three myths about violence in the family.

Some Myths About Violence in the Family
SUZANNE STEINMETZ AND MURRY STRAUS

The idealized picture of family life is a useful and perhaps even a necessary social myth. The utility of the myth results from the fact that the family is a tremendously important social institution. Therefore, elaborate precautions are taken to strengthen and support the family. In Western countries one of these supportive devices is the myth or ideology of familial love and gentleness. This ideology helps encourage people to marry and to stay married. It tends to maintain satisfaction with the family system despite the stresses and strains of family life. Thus, from the viewpoint of preserving the integrity of a critical social institution, such a mythology is highly useful.

At the same time, the semi-sacred nature of the family has prevented an objective analysis of the exact nature of intra-familial violence. To begin with there is the tendency we discussed above to deny or avoid consideration of the widespread occurrence of violence between family members in what are generally considered to be "normal families." This is the myth of family consensus and harmony. Another myth might be called the "psychopathology myth." This is the idea that husbands who hit their wives and parents who abuse their children are mentally ill. No doubt some are. But the studies of child abuse by R. J. Gelles and Sidney Wasserman indicate that such actions more often reflect the carrying out of a role model which the abusing parent or the violent husband learned from his parents and which is brought into play when social stresses become intolerable.

Although there are probably many other myths about violence in the family, we have selected the following as particularly important:

Important myths about family violence

(1) The class myth: intra-familial violence is primarily a lower or working class phenomena.
(2) The sex myth: sexual drives are violence-producing mechanisms.
(3) The catharsis myth: the expression of normal aggression between family members releases the tension and prevents severe violence.

Each of these is a myth because it oversimplifies the social context of the behavior. The conditions under which each myth and its opposite apply will be discussed.

THE CLASS MYTH

The evidence for concluding that working class and lower class families are more violent than middle class families is by no means clear. There are studies which show such differences. For example, George Levinger's study of divorce applicants found that 40 per cent of the working class wives indicated that "physical abuse" was a reason for seeking divorce, but only 23 per cent of the middle class wives reported this reason. Nevertheless, the almost one out of four middle class women reporting physical abuse hardly indicates a lack of violence in middle class families. A national sample survey conducted for the Violence Commission found that over one-fifth of the respondents approved of slapping a spouse under certain conditions. More directly relevant is the fact that there were no social class differences in this approval of slapping, nor in reports of having ever spanked a child. At the same time, almost twice as many low education respondents reported spanking *frequently* (42 per cent) than did high education respondents (22 per cent).

Despite the mixed evidence, and despite the fact that there is a great deal of violence in middle class families, we believe that research will eventually show that in the recent past intra-family violence has been more common as one goes down the socioeconomic status continuum. This is not because of the existence of a lower class "culture of violence" which encourages violent acts, and an opposite middle class culture which represses violence. Although such cultural elements are well documented, we see them as a response to more fundamental forces which affect families at all social levels. The class difference comes about because these structural factors impinge more frequently on the lower and working classes. In this introduction we will mention only two of these factors: the resources available to a family member, and the amount of frustration inherent in the familial and occupational roles.

THE RESOURCE FACTOR

We believe that the willingness and ability to use physical violence is a "resource." A family member can use this resource to compensate for lack of such other resources as money, knowledge, and respect. Thus, when the social system does not provide a family member with sufficient resources to maintain his or her position in the family, violence will tend to be used by those who can do so. Some indication of this is given in a study by John E. O'Brien, which concludes that "... there is considerable evidence that the husbands who ... displayed violent behavior were severely inadequate in work, earner, or family support roles." Although such lack of resources appropriate to a position which must be maintained is more likely to characterize lower class families than other strata, it is by no means confined to that stratum. A recession such as occurred in 1970–71, with high rates of unemployment among middle class occupational groups (e.g., aerospace engineers), would provide an opportunity to test this theory. In such a case, the resource theory of violence would predict that intra-family violence on the part of the husband would be greater among the unemployed than among a comparable middle class group who have not lost their jobs.

Such research remains to be done. But some indication that the predicted results might be found is suggested by a report of a British study. Statistics for Birmingham, England, showed a sharp rise in wife-beating during a six-month period when unemployment also rose sharply: "Frustrated, bored, unable to find a satisfying outlet for their energy, Britishers who are reduced to life on the dole meet adversity like men: they blame it on their wives. Then, pow!!!"

THE FRUSTRATION FACTOR

In a society such as ours, in which aggression is defined as a normal response to frustration, we can expect that the more frustrating the familial and occupational roles, the greater the amount of violence. Evidence for this is to be found in re-

Class differences are due to structural factors

Violence and "lack of resource"

search by McKinley, which shows that the lower the degree of self-direction a man has in his work, the greater the degree of aggressiveness in his relationship with his son. McKinley also found that the lower the job satisfaction, the higher the percentage using harsh punishment of children. This relationship held even when social class was controlled.

Severe dissatisfaction with one's job and being an educational dropout at one level or another were also found to contribute to a husband's use of physical violence on his wife. The frustration theory of violence would predict that with middle class educational expectations of at least one college degree, college dropouts may experience more frustration and job dissatisfaction, and thus resort to physical violence as a problem-solving device more often than do individuals who have completed the amount of education they desire.

The husband is not the only family member whose position may expose him to much frustration. The same principle applied to wives. But since the main avenue of achievement for women has been in familial rather than in occupational roles, we must look within the family for likely frustrating circumstances for women. An obvious one is the presence of a large number of children in the home. Another is a high degree of residential crowding. Both these factors have been found to be related to the use of physical punishment. As in the case of lack of resources, frustrations of this type are more common among the lower class. Since lower class wives are less likely to be provided with material means of carrying out family functions—few home appliances, little money for food— this would make her family role frustrating. As a result, intra-family violence is likely to be more common among the lower class.

On the basis of both the theoretical considerations and the empirical findings just described, we conclude that although intra-family violence is probably more common among lower class families, it is erroneous to see it as primarily a lower class or working class phenomenon. What we have called the "class myth" overlooks the basic structural conditions (such as lack of adequate resources and frustrating life experiences) which give rise to intra-family violence and which are present at all social levels, though to varying degrees. The class myth also overlooks the fact that differences *within* social classes are at least as important as sources of variation in violence, as are differences *between* classes. The class myth is an example of group stereotyping by social scientists. Granted that there is a theoretically important relationship between the use of violence and social classes, one cannot conclude from these relatively small differences (as many social scientists have done) that the use of violence in the family is characteristic or typical of the working or the lower class, but not of the middle class. Some kinds of intra-family violence are typical of *both* the middle and the working class (e.g., hitting children), even though the rate may be lower for middle class. Other kinds of intra-family violence are typical of *neither* class (e.g., physical fights between husband and wife), even though the rate is probably greater for the working class and especially the lower class.

THE SEX MYTH

Violence in sexual relations is directly related to violence in the family because the family is the main way in which sexual intercourse is made legitimate. That is not to say that sex is confined to the family—either in this age of supposed "sexual revolution" or probably in any other age or society. But at the same time, satisfaction of sexual needs is one of the major things which people seek through marriage. If, then, sex is a fundamental aspect of the family, and if sex and violence are related, there is something to be learned about violence in the family by looking at the linkage between sex and violence. In a certain sense, when we look at the connections between sex and violence, we are looking at a biological basis for violence within the family.

There is abundant evidence that sex and violence go together—at least in our society and in a number of others. At the extreme, sex and warfare have been associated in many ways, ranging from non-literate societies which view sex before a battle as a source of strength (or in some tribes, as a weakness) to the almost universally high frequency of rape by soldiers, often accompanied by subsequent genital mutilation and murder. In the fighting following the independence of the Congo in the early 1960's, rape was so common that the Catholic church is said to have given a special dispensation so that nuns could take contraceptive pills. Most recently, in the Pakistan civil war, rape and mutilation were an everyday occurrence. In Viet Nam, scattered reports suggest that rapes and sexual tortures have been widespread. Closer to home, we have the romantic view of the aggressive he-man who "takes his woman" as portrayed in westerns and James Bond type novels. In both cases, sex and gunfights are liberally intertwined.

Then there are the sadists and masochists, individuals who can only obtain sexual pleasure by inflicting or receiving violent acts. We could dismiss such people as pathological exceptions. But it seems better to consider sadism and masochism as simply extreme forms of a behavior which is widespread. Moreover, the sex act itself typically is accompanied at least by mild violence and often by biting and scratching.

Nevertheless, despite all of this and much other evidence which could be cited, we feel that there is little biological linkage between sex and violence. It is true that *in our society* and in many other societies, sex and violence are linked. But there are enough instances of societies in which this is not the case to raise doubts about the biological linkage. Consequently an intriguing issue is to determine the *social* conditions which produce the association between violence and sex.

THE REPRESSION THEORY

The most commonly offered explanation attributes the linkage between sex and violence to repressive sexual norms. Empirical evidence supporting this theory is difficult to establish. Societies which are high in restriction of extramarital intercourse are also societies which tend to be violent—particularly in emphasizing military glory, killing, torture, and mutilation of an enemy. But just how this carries over to violence in the sex act is not clear. Our interpretation hinges on the fact that sex is both restricted and defined as intrinsically evil. This combination sets in motion two powerful forces making sex violent in societies having such a sexual code. First, since sex is normally prohibited or restricted, engaging in sexual intercourse may imply license also to disregard other normally prohibited or restricted aspects of interpersonal relations. Consequently, aggressively inclined persons will tend to express their aggressiveness when they express their sexuality. Second, since sex is defined as evil and base, this cultural definition of sex may create a label or an expectancy which tends to be acted out.

By contrast, in societies such as Mangaia which impose minimal sex restrictions and in which sex is defined as something to be enjoyed by all from the time they are first capable until death, sex is nonviolent. Exactly the opposite of the two violence-producing mechanisms just listed seem to operate. First, since sex is a normal everyday activity, the normal standards for control of aggression apply. Second, since sex is defined as an act expressing the best in man, it is an occasion for altruistic behavior. Thus, Marshall says of the Mangaia: "My several informants generally agreed that the really important thing in sexual intercourse—for the married or for his unwed fellow—was to give pleasure to his partner; that her pleasure in orgasm was what gave the male partner a special thrill, separate from his own orgasm."

THE SEX ANTAGONISM AND SEGREGATION THEORY
Socially patterned antagonism between men and women is at the heart of a related theory to account for the association of sex and violence. This line of reasoning suggests the hypothesis that the higher the level of antagonism between men and women, the greater the tendency to use violence in sexual acts. However, if it is not to be tautological, such a theory must also contain related propositions which account for the sex role antagonism.

In societies such as our own, part of the explanation for antagonism between the sexes is probably traceable to the sexual restrictions and sexual denigration which were just discussed. The curse placed by God on all women when Eve sinned (Gen. 3: 16) is only the earliest example in our culture of the sexually restrictive ethic, the placing of the "blame" for sex on women, and the resulting negative definition of women—all of which tend to make women culturally legitimate objects of antagonism and aggression. The New Testament reveals much more antipathy to sex than the Old and contains many derogatory (and implicitly hostile) statements about women (I Cor. 7: 8–9 and 14: 34).

The present level of antagonism between sexes is probably at least as great as that indicated in these earlier examples. One can find numerous instances in novels and biographies and in everyday speech. For example, words indicating femaleness, especially in its sexual aspect (such as "bitch"), are used by men as terms of disparagement for other men; and terms for sexual intercourse, such as "screw," and "fuck," are used to indicate an aggressive or harmful act. On the female side, women tend to see men as exploiters and to teach their daughters that men are out to take advantage of them.

It would be a colossal example of ethnocentrism, however, to attribute antagonism between the sexes to the Western Judeo-Christian tradition because cultural definitions of women as evil are found in many societies. Obviously, more fundamental processes are at work, of which the Christian tradition is only one manifestation.

A clue to a possibly universal process giving rise to antagonism between the sexes may be found in the cross-cultural studies which interrelate sex role segregation, socialization practices, and sexual identity. Whiting, for example, concludes: "It would seem as if there were a never-ending circle. The separation

Sex as "evil" and "base" or "something to be enjoyed"

of the sexes leads to a conflict of identity in the boy children, to unconscious fear of being feminine, which leads to 'protest masculinity,' exaggeration of the differences between men and women, antagonism against and fear of women, male solidarity, and hence back to isolation of women and very young children."

Obviously the linkages between sex and violence are extremely complex and many other factors probably operate besides the degree of restrictiveness, the cultural definition of sexuality, and the antagonism between sexes. But even these factors are sufficient to indicate that it is incorrect to assume a direct connection between sexual drives and violence because such an assumption disregards the socio-cultural framework within which sexual relations are carried out. It is these social and cultural factors rather than sex drives *per se* which may give rise to the violent aspects of sexuality in so many societies.

THE CATHARSIS MYTH

The catharsis myth asserts that the expression of "normal" aggression between family members should not be bottled up. If normal aggression is allowed to be expressed, tension is released and the likelihood of severe violence is therefore thought to be reduced. This is a view with a long and distinguishd intellectual history. The term "catharsis" was used by Aristotle to refer to the purging of the passions or sufferings of spectators through vicarious participation in the suffering of a tragic hero. Freud's idea of "the liberation of affect" to enable the reexperiencing of blocked or inhibited emotions and Dollard *et al.*'s view that "the occurrence of any act of aggression is assumed to reduce the instigation of aggression" are modern versions of this tradition.

Applying this approach to the family, Bettelheim urges that children should learn about violence in order to learn how to handle it. Under the present rules (at least for the middle class), we forbid them to hit, yell, or swear at us or their playmates. Children must also refrain from destroying property or even their own toys. In this learning of self-control, however, Bettelheim holds that we have denied the child outlets for the instinct of human violence and have failed to teach them how to deal with their violent feelings.

Expression of violence leads to more violence

By contrast with assertions of this type, the empirical evidence bearing on the catharsis theory is almost overwhelmingly negative. Exposure to vicariously experienced violence has been shown to increase rather than decrease both aggressive fantasy and aggressive acts. Similarly, experiments in which children are given the opportunity to express violence and aggression show that the experimental children express more aggression after the purported cathartic experience than do the controls.

MYTHS AND STEREOTYPES

Like stereotypes, the myths we have just examined contain a kernel of truth but are oversimplifications. Thus, although there are probably differences between social classes in the frequency of intra-family violence, the class myth ignores the high level of intra-family violence present in other social strata. The sex myth, although based on historically accurate observation of the linkage between sex and violence, tends to assume that this linkage is biologically determined and fails to take into account the social and cultural factors which associate sex and violence in many societies. The catharsis myth seems to have the smallest kernel of truth at its core. An attempt to understand the reasons for the persistence of the latter myth in the face of devastating empirical and theoretical criticism suggested that its persistence may be due to factors such as the subtle justification it gives to the violent nature of American society and to the fact that violent episodes in a family can have the positive function of forcing a repressed conflict into the open for non-violent resolution.

Myths such as the ones we have just outlined, while they in some ways contribute to preserving the institution of family, also keep us from taking a hard and realistic look at the family and taking steps to change it in ways which might correct some of its problems.

EXPLANATIONS OF FAMILY VIOLENCE

There is a wide variety of explanations for violence in society and, in particular, in the family. Cultural theories focus on the approval of violence by a culture's value system and social norms. (Social norms are in this case guides that indicate the socially appropriate times for the use of violence.) Psychopathology theories explain violence in terms of abnormal psychological characteristics among people. Still others stress the idea that violence is a way of bringing about social change and, therefore, the workability of an institution or social unit. As we have seen in the reading on violence myths, some theories view violence as a means that can be used to attain wanted ends. That is, when other resources, such as love, respect, money or shared goals, are not available or are insufficient to achieve desired ends, violence tends to be employed.[36]

There are many explanations for family violence

In Steinmetz and Straus' article, several theories on violence were employed to disprove the myths.[37] In this section, we will briefly examine several of the more prominent theories that have been developed to explain violence in the family, particularly parental violence toward children. We will begin by examining the relationship between violence and culture, as well as the socialization process itself.

SOCIOCULTURAL EXPLANATION

The family as a social unit rests, to a certain degree, on the *threat* of force and violence as well as on their *use*. American culture, in subtle and not-so-subtle ways, encourages the use of a limited degree of physical force while rearing children in order to change nonsocial forms of behavior. The social norms of our culture dictate that parents are still primarily responsible for the training and socialization of their children. Cultural norms, therefore, provide for parents to have a degree of authority over their children. Part of this authority includes the right to punish them if they fail to conform to the norms of the family. Many people probably believe that the majority

Family violence is rooted in American culture

of Americans would support the punishment of parents who committed violent acts against their young children. The fact is, however, that according to a national opinion survey, the great majority of respondents were opposed to punishing these parents. Also, more than half of the respondents believed that abused children should be removed from the home "only as a last resort."[38] Corporal punishment, in other words, remains a strongly defended right traditionally rooted in our culture. When attempting to explain violence in the family (between parents and children and between spouses) it is important to consider such cultural dimensions.

Children learn violence through socialization

The behavior of abusive parents and spouses can also be explained by their prior socialization, during which they, themselves, were deprived of tenderness and love from their parents.[39] When children are socialized in a family that uses violence to solve problems, they are learning parental and marital roles centered on violence. When these children are themselves parents, they reenact the behavior learned in childhood, especially in stressful situations. Husbands who abuse their wives and parents who abuse their children have usually had, as role models, parents who used violence as a method of solving family problems. As Gelles states,

> The parent who recreates the pattern of abusive child rearing may be doing this because this is the means of child rearing he learned while growing up. It is the way he knows of responding to stress and bringing up his child.[40]

Social learning theory of violence: Aggression and violence are learned in numerous social settings

Social psychologists have formulated many of these ideas into what has been termed a *social learning theory*.[41] This theory focuses on the idea that violent or aggressive behavior is learned by children as they observe role models, imitate these models, and act out the roles. Therefore, what is important for determining whether children learn violent behavior is the extent to which role models are nonviolent or violent in nature. It is important to note that aggression and violence are not only learned through social interaction with others, they are also learned in other social settings that act as learning experiences, such as the presentation of violence in films and on television. Children *do* learn violent and aggressive responses from the behavior models on TV and in movies.

A problem with some of these approaches is that they tend to ignore a variety of psychological variables. Many psychological factors are considered to be relevant in the psychopathological approach.

PSYCHOPATHOLOGICAL EXPLANATIONS
Psychopathological explanations of violence in the family, particularly of child abuse, dominate the literature. This approach stresses that the parent who abuses a child is suffering from a psychological problem that must be

eliminated to prevent further abuse. The idea of mental illness pervades this approach. There is also the assumption that there are distinctive, psychopathic personality traits typical of the child abuser. The psychopathy is traced to the childhood of the abusive parents, when they themselves were abused.[42]

The psychopathological approach finds the disorder of abuse manifested in the child's relationships with the parents. A form of this is termed the "transference psychosis." The parents, in this state, act as children and view their own children as adults. They also *speak* of their children as though they were adults, calling them hostile and persecuting. They often see their own former guilt in their children. Gelles says that "as a result of the 'transference,' the parental distortion of reality is said to cause a misinterpretation of the infant child. The child is perceived as the psychotic portion of the parent whom the parent wishes to destroy. The child is projected as the cause of the parents' troubles and becomes a 'hostility sponge' for the parent."[43]

The cause of the psychopathy in abusive parents is the fact that they were reared in the same way, which is now recreated in the rearing of their own children. The psychopathology model of child abuse is said to be an elementary linear model in which "early childhood experience characterized by abuse creates psychological stress, which produces certain psychopathic states [which] . . . in turn cause abusive acts."[44]

One problem with the psychopathological explanation is that it tends to ignore social variables. In this theory, social, economic, and demographic factors are considered to be irrelevant. There are also other problems with this model. First, there is an inconsistency and a contradictory quality about the discussion of causes. Second, there is the inability to specifically determine those personality traits that characterize the pathology. Third, few studies have attempted to test this hypothesis. Fourth, the sampling techniques used to gather data were inadequate.[45]

SOCIAL AND ECONOMIC EXPLANATIONS

Social and economic factors also play an important role in explaining violence in the family. There is a wide variety of stress-producing social situations that generally seem to occur just prior to acts of spouse and child abuse. Data on unemployment strongly reflect, for example, that economic conditions produce and tend to increase frustration and stress levels that are then vented on children and wives. In an analysis of "battered children" (those who are bruised, drastically injured, and physically and psychologically malnourished), Raffali noted the presence of financial and marital difficulties among 90 percent of the most abusive families.[46] Gelles says that the birth of a child who is the product of an unwanted pregnancy is also a stress-producing social situation that occurs prior to violent and abusive acts.[47]

The idea of mental illness pervades this approach

The psychopathological explanation ignores social variables

Economic factors can play a role in family violence

OTHER EXPLANATIONS

Some social scientists believe that the root of the child abuse and violence problem is in the structure of society itself, and that such factors as child-rearing practices, parental socialization experiences, and values play only a supplementary role in abuse and merely "individualize what is essentially a social problem."[48] Other explanations focus on the lack in our society of the extended kinship network, which would monitor abusive parents and provide relief from children and spouses in times of stress. The developing equalitarian social structure has also been used to explain the violence and conflict in families.[49]

No one theory or approach can adequately explain all family violence. Each of the above theories or explanations emphasizes different factors in an attempt to account for abuse. There are, of course, many other explanations. When one is dealing with such a complex phenomenon, consisting of social, cultural, individual personality, economic, and other elements, no single explanation can account for all types of violence in the family.

RESPONSES TO FAMILY VIOLENCE

Responses to family violence are varied and are related to the theories that attempt to explain it. Responses have taken the form of individual counseling and therapeutic programs, behavior modification, and group and family counseling. In addition, there have been broader efforts to deal with both the legal dimensions and the environmental sources of the problem.

As noted earlier, the majority of Americans are opposed to punishing parents who abuse their children and are also not in favor of the removal of abused children from the home unless no other alternative is possible.[50] Similar attitudes exist when dealing with abused wives. These attitudes and the fact that child-care institutional facilities and shelters for abused spouses are inadequate have left thousands of children, wives, and even husbands in each state in need of protective services. This situation has finally led to the development of alternatives other than removal as a solution to abuse. These new responses reflect an attempt to treat rather than punish violent family members, in the hope of keeping families intact.

INDIVIDUAL CASEWORK TREATMENT

Much response to family violence takes the form of treating individual cases. A variety of materials is available that explores casework treatment for character-disordered parents of abused children. Basic treatment objectives are to work closely with clients and

> perform certain ego functions for them, such as setting limits on behavior, making realistic judgments for and with them, and helping them develop their own reality perception by pointing out distorted perceptions and consequences of their choices and acts.[51]

Treatment literature on abused children is sparse. When abused children are young and remain home, it is likely that the major direction of response to or "treatment for (rather than of) children is change in the malignant environment, either by removal from it or by changing it through treatment of the parents or removal of the abusive one." When abused children are older and are disturbed sufficiently to warrant direct treatment, three phases of treatment have been indicated. These are: (1) to help the child deal with reality and achieve stability in his or her environment; (2) to be firm and consistent when the child regresses and expresses hostility; and (3) to use psychotherapy when indicated.[52]

Three phases of treatment

Treatment literature on abused spouses is equally sparse. The abused spouse has traditionally been treated for abuse in the emergency rooms of hospitals and in physician's offices, in most cases returning home to the same conditions. Alternatives for the abused spouse, which will be discussed later, have just begun to be developed.

Problems with this approach have been cited by caseworkers and other professionals. There are four main disadvantages: first, there is often massive denial of abusive behavior and personal problems; second, there is often provocative behavior, such as hostility; third, there is often a preference for authority-based relationships and a fear of closeness; and fourth, there is little guilt over hostile, abusive behavior.[53]

Problems with the "individual" approach

BEHAVIOR MODIFICATION

Behavior modification techniques have also been considered as a response to violence in family members.[54] These techniques focus on the current behavior patterns and apply principles of operant conditioning to change behavior. Operant conditioning is based on B. F. Skinner's research, which stated that one can establish dependable behavior patterns in an individual through the use of rewards, which are given to the person each time a desired action is performed. The probability that the act will reoccur increases if the act is rewarded or reinforced each time it occurs. Removal of something unpleasant to the individual is also a form of reward. What all this means in terms of family violence is that undesirable behavior patterns, such as abuse, can be gradually eliminated by not rewarding the abuser.

Applying the principles of operant conditioning

GROUP METHODS

Response to family violence has also taken the form of group methods. Treating abusive parents and spouses with group therapy is considered by some social scientists to be preferable to other forms of treatment, especially if the abusive family members are isolated, socially unskilled, have problems of control over impulses, deny difficulties, and have authority problems.[55] We saw earlier that in many cases, abusive family members had been, themselves, subject to unreasonable demands made by their own parents. Therefore, it is theorized that abusive behavior patterns are trans-

Teaching "parenting"
techniques

mitted through the socialization process. Therapy groups attempt to teach "parenting" techniques to abusive parents who were exposed to violence as children, therefore breaking the cycle of child abuse. Through a variety of therapeutic methods, hospital, clinic, and community programs have not just taught abusive parents basic parenting methods. They have also offered alternative satisfactions and have impressed on patients the importance and necessity of getting help whenever they feel themselves becoming abusive.

Parents Anonymous

In 1970, the organization known as Parents Anonymous was founded. Similar to Alcoholics Anonymous, Parents Anonymous is organized around reliance on personal faith and insight and support gained from those with similar needs and experiences. Meetings are held by abusive parents to help one another deal with the abusive practices directed toward their children. The essential therapeutic element in Parents Anonymous is the provision of a meaningful reference group that is concerned with abstention from abuse. Unfortunately, only a small proportion of abusive parents is served by this effective community resource. Some of the reasons for this are that, in order for a parent to be helped by Parents Anonymous, he or she must first admit to being abusive and must be willing to try to change this behavior.

FAMILY THERAPY

We cannot understand
the individual's behavior
apart from the family

An additional response to problems of violent conflict between family members has been the examination and understanding of family interaction patterns and characteristics that have resulted in or promoted violence. The information that is gathered is then used to help family members control their violence. This mode of dealing with serious problems in family life is termed family therapy. Many therapists, researchers, and psychiatrists have advocated this response to family problems because it is based on the idea that individual family members and their behavior cannot be properly understood apart from their familial environments. Family therapy assumes that families are made up of "systems of behavior whose nature cannot be inferred from individual psychology or the larger society."[56] The behavior of each family member is contingent on the behavior of other members. Studies have shown, for example, that a family problem is related to the network of relationships between the members and is not caused solely by one member. This approach has implications for responses to child abuse. It may appear, for example, that the best means of dealing with child abuse is to remove the child from the household, and in some cases this may actually be the best short-term response. However, research has suggested that when the abused child is no longer present, another child in the family may become the target, or there may be an increase in violence between the husband and wife. Because of this possibility and the fact that family members can overtly or unconsciously reward and reinforce aggressive behavior, the family therapy approach is seen as an indispensible mode for handling marriage problems.[57]

DRUG THERAPY

Aggression-reducing drugs and other chemical agents have also been used to control violence in families. Such chemical responses are examined in greater detail in our analysis of mental health problems. At this point, however, it must be said that social factors have to be considered when attempting to use tranquilizing medications on aggressive family members. For example, research has shown that treating the aggressive member of a family with tranquilizing drugs, such as the phenothiazines, will tend to have little effect if *non*aggressive behavior is inconsistent with family interaction patterns; and in general, nonaggressive behavior *is* inconsistent with the interaction patterns of those families characterized by conflict. Use of tranquilizing drugs in such cases results in "family members provoking further aggressive behavior from the patient in order to restore the family 'system,' counteracting the effect of the drug."[58] The use of drugs to tranquilize aggressive family members has been effective where patterns of low conflict and low tension have been consistent with the effect of the drug. The short-term effect of these controlling drugs has been considered by many to be a successful mode of response. Others see the use of drugs in controlling violence as a "potential long-term threat" because they avoid dealing with underlying causal factors, focusing attention instead only on symptoms.[59]

Drug therapy: "Short-term success," "long-term threat"

ALTERNATIVE VALUE SYSTEMS

Some social scientists have responded to problems of family violence by suggesting that alternative value systems should be explored. For example, Whitehurst, in an analysis of alternative family structures and the reduction of violence, suggests that communes and group marriages may be the means for reducing the potential for family violence. He feels that these and other alternative family systems allow more individual autonomy and greater interpersonal openness than does the nuclear family. He rejects the hierarchical structure of traditional families; nevertheless, he questions his own analysis and indicates that future studies must be based on much more solid empirical evidence than is now available.[60]

Communal living as an alternative

SOCIAL CHANGE

Many social scientists believe that changes must be made at the societal level if we are to adequately respond to problems of violence in the American family. Therapy, counseling, and other educational treatment modes may be helpful and "desirable in their own right," but are not effective unless accompanied by fundamental social changes. Changes and reductions in the "frustrating life circumstances" that confront millions of people, especially the poor, will be required. Also advocated is a reduction in the cultural approval of violence and force.[61]

Changes must be made at the societal level

Dennis Stock, Magnum Photos, Inc.

The communal family can ease some of the pressures of parenting through sharing of child-rearing responsibilities.

Gil's series of responses

With respect to problems of child abuse, Gil advocates a series of responses aimed at different causal dimensions of violence. He advocates an attack on and elimination of major social conditions to which abuse is linked and additional measures that would approach the causes of child abuse indirectly. Since large families headed by women are overrepresented in abuse statistics, he calls for comprehensive family planning programs. To help prepare them for marriage and family life, adequate educational and counseling programs for both adolescents and adults are needed. Also proposed is a high quality neighborhood-based national health service, which would not only treat the acutely or chronically ill, but also provide for the promotion and maintenance of physical and mental health for area residents. There is also a need for establishing high quality community-based social services, which would reduce environmental stresses on family life and indirectly reduce the incidence of child abuse.[62]

Finally, in addition to the wide diversity of responses to family violence just examined, a national center on child abuse was instituted in 1974 in Denver, Colorado by the National Institute of Mental Health. Its purpose is to study the problem, establish a commission to deal with related legal issues, and help change current laws on child abuse. Also, the Mondale Law (Child Abuse Prevention and Treatment Act), passed in 1974 by Congress, is an important law dealing with the problem on a national level. The law assists communities and states in the organization and development of programs directed toward helping parents who abuse their children.

The Child Abuse Prevention and Treatment Act

SPOUSE SHELTERS

To deal more adequately with the problem of violence between husbands and wives, many American communities have provided community-based shelters for abused spouses (mainly women) to remove them from their abusive environment. These shelters offer immediate short-term relief and provide food, counseling, emotional support, and referral services. Many times, they also help people find new homes and jobs.

Spouse shelters

Many of the newly opened shelters and counseling centers are so busy that thousands of victims are turned away. Response to the problem of spouse abuse is further complicated by vague laws concerning family violence. According to a 1978 conference on domestic violence at Boston University, the responsibility for developing constructive programs on spouse abuse has "fallen through a bureaucratic crack between social welfare agencies and criminal prosecution departments. Overriding it all is the fact that the trouble occurs in the home—a family sanctuary protected by law and custom."[63]

Response to abuse confused by laws

Also at this conference, it was shown that much of the tragic violence between spouses is preventable because professionals often have prior warning of impending trouble. The following example was given: "In 50 percent of spouse-killing cases in Kansas City, Mo., . . . police have been called to the families' homes on disturbance calls at least five times before the homicide. In 85 percent of the cases, police had been summoned at least one prior time." Spouse victims, in many cases, do not know where to turn and police and court personnel "do not know what to do when family violence occurs."[64]

Tragic violence can be prevented

Among the suggestions offered by the Boston conference in response to the problem of family violence are: (1) train police and court personnel to deal better with abuse cases; (2) give police the power to enforce civil or family court temporary restraining orders; (3) establish additional shelters for the abused and counseling programs for both abused and abusers; and (4) develop more mediation procedures, speed up the legal process, and support legislation for researching the causes and cures for domestic violence.[65]

Some recommendations of the Boston University conference

With the growth of egalitarianism in our society, some people believe that there will be less violence between spouses. Whitehurst believes that, in the long run, this probably is true; however, in the short run, there will be

Less violence with sexual equality?

more violence. This will occur because one of America's dominant ideologies is still the idea of male superiority. Changes in employment and legal and economic rights that precipitate greater equality between men and women will result in strain and frustration for men attempting to retain their superior position. A generation of people living under egalitarian conditions and subscribing to egalitarian norms will have to pass before we see a reduction (if any) in violence between husbands and wives.[66]

DIVORCE AND DESERTION IN AMERICA

Many marriages are characterized by unresolved conflicts, i.e., stresses, tensions, and violence are a more-or-less permanent trait of the marriage. For many other couples, however, the stresses of continuing the marriage, whether accompanied by violence or not, are too great, and divorce or desertion becomes the only acceptable alternative.

THE EXTENT OF DIVORCE

In the United States, the marital system includes two people, each with highly individual values and needs, who live together. Obviously, these factors can create a high potential for stress, tension, conflict, violence, and voluntary departure. Marriage in America is a civil contract, and each state has specific conditions whereby the marriage may be dissolved. Divorces are obtained for reasons ranging from violation of marital obligation to mutual agreement.[67]

Divorce is viewed as an unfortunate event in most cultures

In most cultures, divorce is viewed as an unfortunate event for the people involved. It can also be viewed as an index of failure for the family system or as an escape valve, a "way out of the marriage itself."[68] Sociologist Powers does not view the high divorce rate in America as an index of failure or instability. She believes that it may reflect a more "mature outlook which says that the emotional basis for marriage is important and, therefore, people will not live in a union that's essentially unhappy for them and the children."[69]

Measuring the extent of divorce

In any event, several million Americans have been divorced during the past decade. The most common method of measuring the extent of divorce* is determining the number of divorces per year per 1,000 population.[70] As can be seen in Fig. 7.1, during the depression of the late 1920s and early 1930s, the divorce rate was 1.3 per 1,000 people. By 1940 it was 2.2, and it increased at the end of World War II to 4.3 in response to postwar readjustment demands. The divorce rate was high because many couples were separated during the war and were not able to maintain the marriage after

---

* Divorce rates have also been measured by the ratio of divorces granted in a given year to the number of marriages, and by the number of divorces per 1,000 married females 15 years old and older.

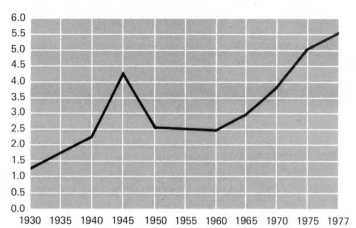

Fig. 7.1 Divorce rates per 1,000 population: 1930–1977. Source: Colonial times to 1957, Historical statistics of the United States, Series B-29, p. 22; 1957 to 1977, *Statistical Abstract of the United States: 1977*, p. 74.

the war. The rate was again 2.2 per 1,000 in 1960 and had climbed to 5.0 by 1977. During the year from January, 1977 to January, 1978 there were 1,087,000 divorces in the United States, yielding a divorce rate of 5.0. This indicates that, for every 1,000 people (including men, women, and children, married or not), five marriages ended in divorce or annulment. During that same year there were 2,178,000 marriages, yielding a marriage rate of 10.1 per 1,000, a drop from the 1950 marriage rate of 11.1.[71] In other words, we are approaching the point where one out of every two marriages ends in divorce.

In the past, a few countries have had higher divorce rates than the United States. Egypt's rates were higher from 1935 to 1954, and Japan's rates were higher from 1887 to 1919.[72] Today, however, America has the highest divorce rate in the world. This is true even for the elderly. The very early years of marriage produce the most strain on married couples, and the majority of divorces occur during this period. Estimates indicate that the number and rate of divorces will continue to rise and to set new records. It is also estimated that, by the year 2000, the figures will have doubled to about two million divorces a year.

America has the highest divorce rate in the world

VARIATIONS: DIVORCE, DESERTION, AND SEPARATION

The divorce rate in America varies with respect to many factors in society, for example, in relation to socioeconomic levels. Many people still believe that divorce occurs more frequently in the upper social strata. Research indicates, however, that the divorce rate in America is higher for the lower socioeconomic levels, although the difference is decreasing. This relation-

Divorce rates vary with social class

ship, according to sociologist Goode, holds true regardless of the index used for determining socioeconomic level (i.e., occupation, income, or education).

However, desertion and separation are more common forms of dissolving marriages among the lower social strata. Goode states,

Desertion and separation more common among the poor

> Unquestionably, the popular notion that it was the well-to-do who divorced was originally based on fact, for it was once only they who could afford it. Nevertheless, there was no reason to suppose that the marital stability of the lower strata was greater at any time in our history. The popular picture of lower-class family life as stable, warm, and inviting, with frequent exchange of kinship obligations and tightly knit against the outside world, was a literary stereotype, often used by authors who had never observed a lower-class family. Lower-class instability was probably expressed in separation and desertion when divorce was very difficult. These forms of dissolution continue to be more common among the lowest strata in our population.[73]

Desertion

Desertion occurs when the husband or wife leaves the family against the will of the other. Desertion by husbands, similar to divorce in many respects, places much economic strain on the wives and children because the husbands generally fail to support their abandoned families.[74] Many states legally require the deserting husband—but not the wife—to support the abandoned spouse and children. In contrast to past practices, courts have recently increased their efforts to track down deserting husbands in order to ease the taxpayers' economic burden of increasing public assistance costs.[75]

Desertion is no longer a male phenomenon

Desertion used to be almost always a male phenomenon. Today, the ratio of men to women deserters is almost even. Runaway relocation firms in the past handled 300 men for every woman. Recently, they have reported more tracings for women than for men. It is interesting to note the profile of women deserters. The majority are intelligent, concerned, and in their early 30s. They generally married at 19, produced one child during the first year of marriage and another in eighteen months, and most of them aspire to more than being a housewife.[76]

Desertion can be a bigger problem than divorce

Desertion involves many of the same problems of divorce; however, it can be more of a problem because of the complete unavailability of the deserting spouse. Unless the deserting spouse wants to be found, they tend to cover up their movements. According to Smart and Smart,

> The spouse left behind may have no idea why he was deserted and has no chance of receiving alimony or child support. Although divorced parents often do not try to explain to their children the reasons for the divorce, the deserted parent usually can give no explanation because he himself doesn't know what it is. The deserted spouse also cannot remarry until a divorce is secured.[77]

Eshleman states that the high rates of divorce and marital instability at lower socioeconomic levels have been attributed to lower income levels and greater frustration in meeting expenses.[78] In terms of economic rewards and job satisfaction, there appears to be "more socioeconomic dissatisfaction, and thus possibly more marital tension from that source, toward the lower social strata." Noneconomic relationships in terms of marriage and sexual adjustment are affected by economic status.

Goode believes that three class factors make it difficult, in terms of costs and desirability, for upper strata people to obtain a divorce. First, the kin and friends network in the upper strata is larger and more tightly knit, making the social consequences of divorce greater. Second, removal from family obligations in the upper strata is more difficult because of the complexities of long-range property investments and expenditures, such as annuities, houses, and insurance. Third, the wife's potential loss through divorce is greater at higher levels; therefore, she is not as willing to give up the marriage.[79]

Divorce rates in the United States vary also by geographic, demographic, and social factors. For example, with respect to geographic distribution, data indicate a general trend toward increase as one moves from the east coast to the west coast. Divorce rates are two, three, and even four times higher in the west than in the northeast. Geographic variations have been explained by the fact that, even though different factors will operate in different areas, it is believed that "divorce rates will be lower in culturally homogeneous, rather than heterogeneous, communities with primary face-to-face interactions in contrast to communities with anonymous and/or segmentalized relationships."[80] With respect to religion, we find that because of the Catholic church's stand against divorce, there tends to be a lower rate among Catholics than among Protestants. However, Catholic separation statistics are higher. The divorce rate tends to be the highest of all for couples who have no religious preference.

With respect to social characteristics in general, there are many background traits that are related to marriage dissolution rates. Many research studies summarized by Goode indicate that there is a greater tendency to divorce among people who: (1) come from an urban background; (2) marry when they are younger than 20 years old; (3) are acquainted with their future spouses for less than two years before marriage; (4) have no or only short engagement periods; (5) have parents who are unhappy in their own marriages; (6) do not attend church regularly or have different faiths; (7) have friends and relatives who disapprove of the marriage; (8) have backgrounds that are generally dissimilar; and (9) have disagreements on husband and wife role obligations.[81]

High divorce rates, with their high degrees of emotional stress and economic costs, have led many sociologists to label divorce as an American social problem. However, some sociologists have questioned its nature, asking if the problem is that "too many marriages end in divorce" or that

Noneconomic relationships are affected by economic status

Other factors related to variations in divorce rates

Religion and divorce

Some people are more prone to divorce

Divorce creates problems
for the individual and
society

"society makes divorce a wrenching, degrading experience."[82] In either case, divorce creates problems for the individual and for society in general. For men, women, and children of divorce, it can mean a difficult emotional and psychological readjustment and, as we shall shortly see, much economic difficulty. Economic pressures, especially on the women and children of divorce, at times necessitate receiving financial assistance from the community. Society, therefore, has the responsibility for supporting many broken families.

ONE-PARENT FAMILIES AND THE CHILDREN OF DIVORCE

Many problems and difficulties are experienced by one-parent families in America. One-parent families are those that, although originally intact, with parents married to each other, are now broken by divorce, desertion, separation, or death. Among the many difficulties that threaten after divorce is the drop in the standard of living. This holds true for the great majority of cases, and usually the drop is greater for the wife. Much of the time, single mothers have the problem of limited income and have to take time away from their children in order to earn a living. Even though divorced women are better able to economically care for themselves and their children now than in past decades, many—in particular older women—do not have the skills or training to obtain jobs that pay well.

A drop in living
standards

Those single mothers who do not work and remain home to take care of their children may enter the ranks of those on permanent welfare. Almost half of the families in which the husband is not present live under the poverty line. Many single mothers also count on child-support and alimony payments to provide for their children. Unfortunately, a high percentage of families that are supposed to receive recurrent, court-ordered payments actually receive little or no money.[83] Single parents—male or female—must also deal with the problems of maintaining discipline, educating their children, and promoting healthy emotional growth.

Children of divorce live
with mothers and fathers

Divorced men also experience financial difficulty because of added child-support payments, alimony, or because they, themselves, have sole custody of their children. Today, children of divorce live not only with their mothers but also with their fathers. Approximately one-half million children live with their divorced or separated fathers. Single fathers also need time to work and time to care for the children. The myth that single parents cannot raise healthy children increases the parent's anxiety and guilt. These feelings can then affect their ability to rear their children.[84]

Problems of adjustment

Children of divorce experience many difficulties, although in some cases the problems are not as severe as living in a tension-filled household often characterized by hatred and fighting. Before the divorce, many parents often fail to explain to the children why they are separating and what this will mean to the children's future with their parents.[85] After the divorce, some of the children's difficulties requiring adjustments include getting used to living with just one parent while only visiting the other. Some children believe that *they* are the cause for the divorce and feel rejected by the parents. This feeling is reinforced in cases where neither parent wants to assume custody.

As noted earlier, single parents, out of financial necessity, must often maintain full-time employment, which means that the children will often have only limited amounts of contact with and attention from their parent. Children of divorce, in many cases, must adjust to new and usually smaller living quarters, often without seeing many of their old friends. The majority of children must also eventually contend with their parent's dating other people. This can develop into problems around sharing the parent with others and having others live in the household. The children of divorced parents, in most instances, experience more problems and difficulties than do children from families that are not broken. However, it must be noted that, even though children from intact families usually make out much better economically, they are not always better adjusted or happier than children of single parents.

EXPLANATIONS: DIVORCE AND DESERTION

MOBILITY AND FAMILY FUNCTIONS

Our high divorce and desertion rates have been explained in various ways. Many social scientists have attributed them to mobility, the various stresses on the nuclear family system, and changes in family functions. Some social scientists believe that geographic and social mobility have weakened many of the nuclear family's ties to its kin. With the weakening of these ties, there is a loss of emotional support, financial advice, and various other forms of help that are important in maintaining a family and marriage. However, others such as Eugene Litwack believe that it is the least mobile people in the society—the poor—who are isolated from relatives. Kinship ties have changed with mobility but, according to Marvin Sussman, "middle-class nuclear families, regardless of geographical distance, tend to maintain an active, 'service network' with their relatives, giving and receiving advice, money, and help with young children."[86] In any event, in the nuclear family, spouses must rely heavily on each other for the satisfaction of emotional needs. Some sociologists believe that the affectional function of the family is the only remaining justification for the family as a societal institution. Ruben Hill states that, as our community contacts become increasingly formal and segmented, people turn more and more to the family as "the source of affectional security we all crave."[87]

The competitiveness, isolation, and mobility of our society place strains on family members, and their anxiety levels lead them to other family members for more emotional support. There is an insistent demand for

Mobility as a factor in divorce

affection from an institution that no longer has the traditional supporting structure. This demand leads to increased levels of anxiety and stress.

As examined earlier, many of the family's functions have been lost to other social institutions. The functions that many believe remain (i.e., reproduction, child care, and affection), are very much needed and are increasingly more difficult to provide. Many of the reasons given by couples for their desire to end their marriages reflect the difficulty some families have in meeting the affectional function. Spouses reported such complaints as mental cruelty, neglect, physical abuse, and problems in psychological and emotional interaction.[88]

Remaining family functions are increasingly difficult to provide

THE CHANGING ROLE OF WOMEN

The changing role of women has also been considered to be a factor in the breakup of some marriages. As we have seen in the analysis of sexism in this text, many women have taken jobs outside the home. This has occurred for both economic and emotional reasons. Many women, in addition to supplementing their spouses' incomes, are emotionally and intellectually unfulfilled in the roles of child-rearer, housekeeper, and supportive companion.

Woman's changing roles and marital breakups

Despite many barriers that continue to restrict women in their efforts toward economic and social equality, many wives have become economically independent from their husbands. This has, in turn, weakened traditional role relationships, as defined by the husbands. Equal opportunity for employment and the availability of jobs, which have provided many women with economic independence, have also added the burden of having two jobs—one at home and one at work. This often causes stress and resentment in the marriage, because traditional roles are being challenged. For other wives, economic independence means that it is easier to divorce their husbands and establish lives outside of marriage.

Traditional roles are being challenged

ROMANTICIZING MARRIAGE AND PARENTHOOD

Several social scientists have explained higher rates of divorce in terms of higher expectations for romantic love in marriage. In contrast to earlier periods in history, romantic love, not economics, is now considered to be the important factor in determining a marriage partner. Romantic love fades somewhat, or is even lost, when routines of marriage and family life begin. Job and household pressures, economic problems, and dirty dishes and diapers tend to push romantic feelings aside. Love is not really lost for the majority, however; the original romantic love merely shifts to a more mature, stronger, deeply fulfilling bond of affection. But many couples interpret the loss of romantic love as being symptomatic of a failed marriage. There are feelings of frustration and a loss of faith in the marriage itself.

Misinterpreting the loss of romantic love

In his analysis of parenthood, LeMasters addresses this "romantic complex" and other myths couples have about parenthood and the rearing of children. He states that parenthood is surrounded by folklore,* and that most men and women do not really know what being a parent means until they are parents themselves.[89] Some myths can be harmful and can increase stress between family members. For example, one folk belief is that "child rearing is fun." LeMasters states that, as every parent knows, rearing children "is probably the hardest and most thankless job in the world." Child rearing is hard, often nerve-racking work that involves a tremendous amount of responsibility. Yet many married couples in America still have a "romantic complex about child rearing and they tend to suffer from a process of disenchantment after they become parents."[90]

Child rearing is not all fun

Another myth is that it is easier to rear children today, because of modern medicine, appliances, and child psychology. Actually, mothers are in much more of a "rat race" today than in the past. LeMasters states,

It is not easier to rear children today

> Middle-class mothers, in particular, have become poorly paid cab drivers, racing from one place to another trying to get all of the children to their various appointments, helping to run the PTA, being a buddy to their husbands—plus holding a full- or part-time job in many instances.[91]

There are other myths, such as "there are no bad children, only bad parents," which makes parents the "bad guys." Another popular notion is that "love is enough to sustain good parental performance," which ignores the fact that love must also be guided by "knowledge and insight and . . . [be] tempered with self-control on the part of the parent" if it is to be effective. There is also the myth that "children improve a marriage," which reflects statistics confirming that children tend to stabilize marriage, but this is "not quite the same."[92]

LIBERAL DIVORCE LAWS

The increase in divorce also reflects more liberal divorce laws and a shift from the attitude that the marriage is more important than the individuals involved. Only a few decades ago, divorce was not considered as an alternative. In the past, many couples resigned themselves to an unhappy marriage because of social, economic, and family pressures or "because of the children." Today, there appears to be more concern for the happiness of the individual.

Divorce was not a likely alternative in the past

This does not mean that couples do not consider factors other than individual needs when contemplating a divorce. There are many factors that help to determine whether a couple decides on a divorce. What family and friends will think of them if they divorce influences the decision. The effect of the divorce on the children is still, in many cases, considered to be

Factors that help determine the decision to divorce

* By folklore or folk beliefs, LeMasters means "widely held beliefs which are not supported by facts."

an important factor for many. Whether the couple is financially able to meet the costs of divorce—i.e., if each can be self-sufficient and "make it alone"—is also a matter for consideration.[93] Even though there are many factors that couples must consider when contemplating dissolution of a marriage, divorce is still the most likely alternative when problems in a marriage make one or both partners dissatisfied.[94]

OTHER EXPLANATIONS

The isolated family

Other explanations of divorce tend to be more broad and general in nature. For example, some theories stress increasing urbanization and industrialization as causal factors.[95] Parsons has examined the American family and views it as "isolated." Mobility, as a product of industrialization, has weakened ties between extended family members. In the past, families tended to support each other in neighborhood communities. With urbanization, the neighborhood community has, to a great extent, broken apart. The result is that "many nuclear families have been forced to rely too exclusively on their own resources, and this has led in some instances to acute relational stress."[96]

In urban areas, there is also a greater probability of marrying someone who is socially, ethnically, or religiously different. People with dissimilar backgrounds tend to have higher rates of marital failure than those people whose backgrounds are homogeneous. There also tend to be fewer social and economic proscriptions against divorce in the city than in rural environments.

Four changes have created the dilemma

There is much debate in the academic community about the impact of urbanization, industrialization, and social change on the American family. Social scientists have recognized the facts that, in the past, the family was undermined by the loss of economic functions and that emotional functions were becoming increasingly important, since the family was the best institution for fostering child care and adult intimacy. Skolnick and Skolnick, in an analysis of domestic relations and social change, examined these changes in functions and stated that the conditions of life in America today *do* "undermine family ties and do generate exceptional needs for nurturant, intimate, and enduring relationships." The primary changes that have created this dilemma are (1) the loss of constraints and restrictions in work and marriage, (2) a general emotional and task overload, (3) contradictory social demands and values, and (4) demographic change.[97]

Constraints in Work and Marriage. With respect to the loss of constraints and restrictions, it can be noted that, in preindustrial societies, marriage and work were determined by tradition, hereditary status, and economic necessity, not by individual choice. Familial, community, and economic sanctions were imposed on families to ensure the continuity of marriages and their conformity to prescribed behavior. People have been liberated from such restrictions by modernization. Sociologists studying the family have noted that, whenever a traditional pattern of work and family is replaced by a modern pattern, it is "accompanied by an ideology of liberation."[98] Skolnick and Goode indicate that,

> Modernization promises freedom of opportunity to work that suits one's talents, freedom to marry for love and dissolve the marriage if it fails to provide happiness, and greater equality in the family between husband and wife, and between parents and children. The freedom of modern family life is bought at the price of fragility and instability in family ties.[99]

Emotional Overload. In regard to the second change, emotional and task overload, even sociologists who stress the vital societal functions played by the family today acknowledge that societies can put strain on families. Talcott Parsons, for example, states that,

> when the family and the home no longer functioned as an economic unit, women, children, and old people were placed in an ambiguous position outside the occupational world. For children, the shift to industrial work, and the removal of the father from the home, also meant that the mother became more of a central figure. Little boys could no longer observe and participate in father's work. This created a strain on both child and mother.[100]

Goode, a family sociologist, suggests that the family, through warmth and companionship, is supposed to compensate for the cold impersonal world.[101] Moore states, however, that family members have little on which to base their relationships after work, education, and other functions have been eliminated from the nuclear family.[102] The Skolnicks support this contention, pointing out that providing emotional security in a vacuum is difficult and that " 'togetherness' is harder to achieve by itself than as a by-product of joint effort."[103] Intimate relations, such as those occurring in families, "generate their own tensions and frustrations, which require some kind of outlet away from the home." The home can also be where "outside tensions are discharged explosively rather than being soothed away."[104]

Contradictory Demands and Demographic Change. The last two changes creating the dilemma confronting Americans today are contradictory demands and values and demographic change. With respect to the former, the ideology concerning today's conjugal family emphasizes the qualities of personal freedom, individualism, and sexual equality. The realities of the day-to-day life of the majority of Americans fails to fulfill these values. For all members of the family, there is the "contradiction between a moral-

Societies can create stress and strain on families

As the average lifespan increases, more couples are faced with the prospect of fifty, not twenty, years together.

The life span of marriage has increased from 20 to 50 years

ity stressing enjoyment and self-fulfillment and a morality of duty, responsibility, work, and self-denial."[105] With regard to the latter and final change, the Skolnicks note that it is difficult to comprehend how profoundly family life has been affected by such changes as the reduction of mortality rates and the use of contraceptive devices. As we have discussed in our analysis of sexism, women's childbearing and rearing patterns have shifted, leaving many years with no maternal responsibilities, which has in turn affected the makeup of the labor force. Earlier marriages and extended life spans have increased the duration of marriage from only about twenty years to more than fifty years. The Skolnicks state,

> The prospect of 50 years with the same person increases tensions in marriage and makes it more likely that dissatisfaction will lead to divorce. . . . in a rapidly changing society, the couple who seemed well-suited to each other in their early twenties may find themselves growing in different ways and at different rates later on.[105]

Levinger has also developed a general theory of divorce that focuses on the forces keeping marriages together and breaking them apart.[106] All marriages, for Levinger, contain forces that can make them fail or succeed. One such force is the "type of relationship" that exists between the married couple. The relationship may reflect mutually satisfying interests, and sexual fulfillment and may be a resource that sustains the marriage. On the other hand, the relationship may reflect the fact that they are growing apart from one another in terms of developing diverse interests and receiving less sexual and emotional fulfillment.

All marriages contain forces for failure or success

Another force consists of the presence or absence of "barriers to divorce." Social and cultural factors, such as religion, friends and relatives, moral position, and attitude toward children of the marriage, can act either as barriers or as facilitators of divorce. For example, if an individual's church, family, and friends do not condemn divorce and the person believes the children of the marriage will not be harmed by and may actually benefit from the divorce, that individual will be much more likely to divorce than a person whose church, family, and friends oppose the decision and act as barriers.

Barriers and alternatives enter into decisions

However, many couples stay married even though the quality of their relationship is poor and cultural and social barriers to divorce are not present. This behavior can be explained, in some cases, in terms of the attractiveness of "available alternatives." If an unhappily married spouse has the opportunity of finding an alternative sexual partner or of gaining economically or occupationally from the divorce, he or she will be more likely to divorce than those for whom the alternatives are not so pleasant.[107] Unfortunately, some marital relationships are so unbearable that *any* alternative is desirable.

RESPONSES: THE "DEATH" OF THE FAMILY

High rates of divorce and desertion have been explained in terms of the structure of the nuclear family. Some social scientists have responded to these problems by proclaiming that the nuclear family is either dying or already dead. The following points characterize this opinion. First, the nuclear family is the source of neurotic people, who do not become sufficiently autonomous to protect themselves against being "consumed by the mores, values, communication patterns, and expectations that are the hallmark of the family system prevalent in our society."[108] Second, the nuclear family is rigid and confining because of the limited role models provided by parents for their offspring. Third, it is considered to be the major cause of sexual conservatism. Fourth, it is a decadent institution with few, if any, redeeming features. Fifth, the nuclear family is the most important agent causing the breakdown of morality in American culture.

Is the nuclear family dead?

As we shall see, Crosby feels that the nuclear family is in a period of transition and readaptation rather than of decay. For some social scientists, however, both conservative and liberal, there is agreement about the "death"

The family is in a period of transition and readaptation

of the American family, but for different reasons. "Because the criterion of family success is 'adjustment' to the societal and cultural expectations" and "because the criterion of family success is the emotional wholeness and psychic authenticity of its members" are the liberal and conservative views, respectively. This second statement means that, in order for the family to be considered successful, its members must experience psychological and emotional well-being.[109]

The "demystification" of family life

Sociologists such as Crosby, stress the transition and readaptation of the family institution. The transition is "to an emphasis of human growth and authenticity of selfhood, while the adaptation is to a social functioning more congruent to a cultural milieu."[110] They believe that the strains and stresses on the family do not necessarily foretell its demise. What has occurred is a "demystification" of family life.[111] It is no longer perceived as the peaceful retreat from the harsh world. In other societies, marriage dissolution is not as disruptive to family functioning, because greater importance is placed on the responses of kinship groups and various "back-up institutions" that perform family functions. Skolnick states that America's need for such support systems outside of the family is reflected by the development of drop-in clinics, communes, and encounter groups.[112]

Some social scientists, such as David R. Mace, do not see the family and marriage as an obsolete, shopworn entity, but as a durable, flexible institution in transition. Many social scientists regard the nuclear family as universal "building blocks" of extended families. The instability of marriage and a loss in the sense of individuality are to be viewed as misfortunes and as legitimate causes for complaint and remediation. However, these and other problems can also be viewed as "incidental results of vast social changes to which neither our society in general nor our family system in particular have yet been able to accommodate themselves."[113] The family, in other words, is seen as the victim, not the cause, of the situation.

THE COMPANIONSHIP FAMILY

Companionship family: Nuclear patterns without a traditional orientation

For many social scientists, the way to respond to and deal with the traditional family and its problems is not to change the family's structure, for the cause of problems may not be the structure. It is possible that the cause of family problems, such as divorce and desertion, may be related to the ways in which family members perceive and interact with one another, not to the structure. Therefore, for Mace, the response to family problems is the "companionship family," which retains the nuclear pattern but not the traditional orientation. He states,

> The traditional nuclear family was essentially a power structure based on a system of authority and submission that was unable to foster creative relationships in an atmosphere of love and intimacy. The new companionship emphasis makes such creative relationships its central goal.[114]

This response is to affect change in the way people interact with one another. Malfunctioning nuclear families can function in a new mode by providing services that are necessary, "a new kind of training for relationships . . . programs for marriage enrichment and parent effectiveness."[115]

Many social scientists stress the need for pre- and postmarital counseling. Marital counseling can better prepare couples for the demands of family life and enable them to adjust their expectations of marriage. Others suggest that couples have family counseling before considering a divorce, as well.

Some sociologists believe that today's dominant family and marriage patterns often destroy attempts to form authentic relationships and individual identity. However, the family is not seen as the enemy, but as an institution that has to be made more flexible in an effort to develop people who can "possess greater capacities for loving and sharing."[116] Remmer's response, for example, is one that calls for a restructuring of society because of the high failure rate of the conventional family. Called for are solutions such as communes, cooperative families, and premarital education. The outright elimination of conventional marriage is not advocated; however, the "broadening of the selection of family structures," in order to alleviate the confining and constraining aspects of family life, is considered desirable.[117] In the following section, we will briefly examine some of these alternative family structures as responses to high rates of divorce and desertion.

The elimination of conventional marriage is not advocated

ALTERNATIVES TO THE NUCLEAR FAMILY

Before examining alternative family structures, however, it must be pointed out that high rates of divorce and desertion do not mean that Americans are dissatisfied with marriage. On the contrary, the great majority of people who divorce remarry. A major reason for this is that people have a great need for close, primary relationships, and marriage (to the right person) is a way of meeting this need. Research by Campbell has shown that married people are happier than single people and that, "if marriages aren't happy today, at least married people are." Even though there are many unhappy married people and satisfied single people, Campbell states that all of the married groups in his research, which included "men and women over 30 and under, with children and without—reported higher feelings about their lives than all of the unmarried groups—the single, divorced, or widowed." There is, then, a consistent link between marriages and satisfaction. However, Campbell questions which is cause and which is effect by noting that "marriage may make people happy, or perhaps happy people are more likely to marry."[118] However, many Americans are still unable to cope and are dissatisfied with the traditional family system. This dissatisfaction has been coupled with many encompassing changes in society. Thousands of people have therefore responded by seeking alternatives to the established

The majority of those who divorce remarry

There is a consistent link between marriages and satisfaction

nuclear pattern, many of which currently exist in the United States and which we will now briefly examine.

The commune is not a new concept

Communes and Group Marriage. One alternative to the nuclear family is the commune. This is not a new concept. From the time of Plato, utopians have visualized children being reared in various communal organizations. There are an estimated 3,000 or more communes in the United States to-day.[119] Some writers believe that they offer solutions to problems of modern monogamy. By creating something comparable to the extended family, they avoid many of the problems of confinement and the loneliness of monogamy. This form of social organization resembles the extended family in that family functions are shared. Their members believe they are fleeing from the "constriction, loneliness, materialism and the hypocrisy in straight society and the family life on which it is based."[120]

Rearing children through collective parenthood relieves pressure

It should be pointed out, however, that some communes have modified the communal family by working together during the day and returning to their individual families at night.[121] Norms vary from one commune to another. In many, members share the task of rearing children. Rearing children through collective parenthood can relieve pressure from individual parents and minimize the disruptive effects of desertion and divorce. A warm, concerned atmosphere can be obtained from this social structure when each parent takes some of the responsibilities for every child in the commune. Zablocki, a sociologist who has visited more than 100 communes says that the children do very well, and that it is natural for them to be brought up by many adults in extended families. However, in "spite of the talk of extended families, the extension in the new communes does not reach to a third generation. Indeed, the 'families' have a narrow age span, and it is possible that the children have never seen an adult over 30."[122]

In some communes, the members also share in sexual relations. Sexual sharing is viewed as "an answer to boredom and solves the problem of infidelity, or seeks to, by declaring extramarital experiences acceptable and admirable."[123]

Communes are not without problems

Communes are not, however, without problems. Albert Ellis found in his research that communes or "group marriages" tend to be unstable, although some have lasted for years. It is almost impossible to find four or more adults who can live in harmony and love. There are also difficulties of scheduling and coordinating lives and of the intrusion of jealousy and love conflicts.[124] There are also problems in sharing work and establishing leadership. A more serious problem, according to Hunt, is related to the fact that because most group marriages are based on a form of semiprimitive agrarian life, there is a reintroduction of patriarchalism. It is a problem "because such a life puts a premium on masculine muscle power and endurance and leaves the classic domestic and subservient roles to women." The emotional limitations are also serious, because "its ideal is sexual free-

While the nuclear family is undergoing
changes, it continues to be the choice of many.

Rick Smolan

dom, but the group marriages that most nearly achieve this have the least
cohesiveness and the shallowest interpersonal involvements."[125]

Philip Slater states that members of a commune generally create the
same type of society within which they themselves were reared. He states,

> It is ironic that young people who try to form communes almost al-
> ways create the same narrow, age-graded, class-homogeneous society
> in which they were formed. A community that does not have old
> people and children, white-collar and blue-collar, eccentric and con-
> ventional, and so on, is not a community at all, but the same kind of
> truncated and deformed monstrosity that most people inhabit today.[126]

Trial Marriage. Another alternative response to the established nuclear
family is trial marriage, or cohabitation. Living together without a marriage

license has become an increasingly common alternative for many young people in America. Many of these couples share their lives and derive much emotional satisfaction from the relationship. In the majority of cases, when the couples decide to have children, they get married. Margaret Mead addressed this very process in her proposal for a "two-step" marriage. The first step amounts to what would be a trial marriage, in which the couple would agree not to have any children. This would be a period of exploration and adjustment. If it progressed to a stable relationship, and the couple desired to have children, the second step could occur: a license would be obtained and a "parental marriage" would be made, allowing the couple to have a family. This type of contractual arrangement enables the couple to develop a reasonably secure relationship before having children.[127]

Swinging. Some couples have mutually agreed to exchange partners for extramarital sex. This is commonly known as "swinging." These couples desire to end the sexual exclusiveness of marriage. Swingers claim that it is not as destructive to a marriage as a long, drawn-out love affair, and they advocate a change of sexual partners as a way of making marriage more interesting. Participant research by Paulsons concluded that some marriages appeared to become more happy and stable because of this type of behavior.[128]

Serial Monogamy. The alternative of serial monogamy occurs when an individual continues on a cycle of marriage and divorce. The person may marry and divorce several times during a lifetime. This alternative is increasingly being followed, because divorce laws have become less severe and the social stigma of being divorced has become almost nonexistent.

Single Parent Families. The phenomenon of the "single parent family" has also been considered to be a response to the problems and dissatisfactions of conventional family life. For mother and child, the stigma of birth outside of marriage is no longer as strong as it was in the past. According to a recent article in *Time* on the future of the American family, "no longer fearful about complete ostracism from society, many single girls who become pregnant now choose to carry rather than abort their babies and to support them after birth without rushing pell-mell into what might be a disastrous marriage."[129]

However, the unwed mother who decides to keep, but is socially and economically unprepared to rear, her child is a matter of social concern for some people. Children who are illegitimate and poor are viewed by some Americans as "burdens to society." Complaints that federal programs such as Aid to Families with Dependent Children (AFDC) subsidize unmarried

Margin notes

"Two-step marriage"

Participant research

The stigma of birth outside of marriage is no longer so strong

"Burdens to society"

mothers and add to already high costs are frequently heard. Many people also stereotype unwed mothers as being promiscuous and morally corrupt.

Laws concerning illegitimacy discriminate against children of unwed mothers. Legal consequences vary, but in many states, unless a child's paternity is established within a few years after birth, while the father still is alive, the child cannot inherit the father's property. Some states grant more protection and rights to illegitimate children now than they have in the past. Recently, laws discriminating against illegitimate children have been ruled unconstitutional by the United States Supreme Court. This reflects a movement toward abolishing the stigma associated with illegitimacy. The court stated that children should not be discriminated against or punished because of their parents' behavior. Other benefits previously unobtainable to illegitimate children have also been made available through the Social Security Act.[130] The legal status of illegitimate children, then, appears to have improved substantially in the past decade, and all indications reflect a continuation of this trend.

The student should keep in mind that these alternatives do not mean that the nuclear family structure will fade away. Only about 5 percent of the people in the United States do not marry during their lifetimes. What will most likely occur during the next several decades is an increased tolerance among Americans for a broader range of alternative family and marriage structures.

The nuclear family will not fade away

SUMMARY

In this chapter we have focused on some of the significant changes and problems encountered by the American family. The history of the American family was examined, as were changes in family functions. The family, we have seen, is often a place of conflict and violence. Spouse and child abuse are widespread problems today. A broad variety of myths about family violence and several explanations of violence were examined. We also saw how responses to family violence have taken the forms of individual counseling, therapeutic programs, behavior modification, and group and family counseling.

Divorce and desertion were then analyzed, and the factors related to the divorce rate (i.e., socioeconomic, geographic, demographic, and social) were examined. The problems created by divorce for the individuals involved and for their children were examined. Major explanations for divorce and desertion were studied and were followed by responses to divorce and desertion. Included in the response section was an analysis of the death of the nuclear family, responses to that issue, and some alternatives to the traditional nuclear family system in America.

KEY TERMS

Behavior modification
Child abuse
Communes
Companionship family
Conflict
Desertion
Divorce
Drug therapy
Extended family
Family functions
Family therapy
Group method response

Individual treatment
Mobility
Nuclear family
One-parent family
Parents Anonymous
Psychopathological explanation
Serial monogamy
Single parent family
Sociocultural explanation
Spouse abuse
Swinging

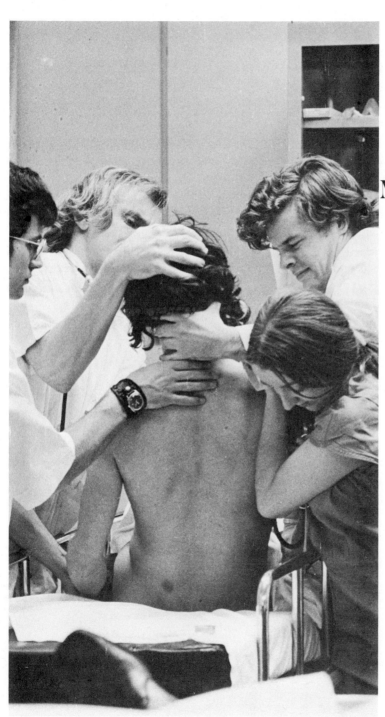

8
Physical and Mental Health

Chapter Objectives

1. To list the three dimensions of the health care crisis and to compare the first two.
2. To examine in an essay at least four aspects of our inadequate health care delivery system.
3. To compare the three explanations of the health care crisis.
4. To list, according to NCHSR, the five goals of a national health insurance policy and the seven basic policy questions that must be addressed in designing a national health insurance plan.
5. To define mental illness according to the medical model, including in your definition the distinction between psychoses and neuroses.
6. To examine in an essay the statement "Mental illness is a myth."
7. To document the prevalence and costs of mental illness and, in a brief essay, to examine three social factors related to its rates and treatment.
8. To select and compare two (including one sociological) explanations of mental illness.
9. To examine by essay three of the major treatments for mental illness.

DEFINING THE PROBLEM OF HEALTH CARE

America's health care professionals have unsurpassed scientific knowledge. Our medical technological advancements have enabled us to steadily increase the average life expectancy of our citizens. Americans spend billions of dollars each year on health care. Yet even with this vast amount of knowledge, equipment, and expenditures, many people lack even the most basic health care needs. It is because of this that we have what has been termed a "health crisis" in America. This problem exists because on one hand Americans believe that adequate health care is a basic human right—not a privilege—yet, on the other hand, the right to health care is denied to millions of Americans.

Many people lack basic health care

Not only is health care unavailable to millions, especially the poor, it is also inadequate for millions of others because of a wide variety of factors. For example, those Americans who have some form of health insurance find that its coverage is limited and that a prolonged illness can prove economically as well as physically catastrophic. Other conditions and situations contribute to the health care crisis in America. A significant percentage of our nation's hospitals do not meet basic standards of adequacy and safety. As a result of inadequate and unnecessary treatment and operations and the overprescription of drugs, thousands of people die each year. The costs of health care have soared in the past several years and run into the billions of dollars. Our nation's infant mortality rates are higher than those of a dozen other countries. Our death rates from cancer and heart disease are among the highest in the world.

Many conditions contribute to the health care crisis

In the first part of this chapter we will discuss health care in America and the various problems that contribute to the health care crisis. We will also explain the basis for the crisis and examine the variety of responses to health care problems. In the second part of this chapter we will examine the problems of mental illness, their explanations, and the various responses to these problems that have developed. We will begin the first part with an examination of health, health status, and the three dimensions of the health care crisis.

HEALTH AND HEALTH STATUS

Good health is one of the most important goals for most people in America. The World Health Organization defines health as a state of complete mental and physical well being. Many individuals believe good health to be freedom from disease and pain. Studies have shown that, while people can identify or describe healthy people, "our conception of health is questioned when an apparently healthy person dies unexpectedly."[1]

In many respects, the concepts of health and health status are difficult to define and measure. There is no universally accepted "index of health status," according to the Public Health Service, The Health Resources Administration, and the National Center for Health Statistics and Health

No universally accepted index of health status

Services Research.[2] These health agencies note that no one definition is adequate for the many different types of decisions that must be made about health programs and resources.

Indicators of health status

There is even more difficulty in categorizing groups of people with respect to their health status because measuring it is an elusive process.[3] In fact, the total death rates, life expectancy rates, and infant mortality rates are commonly used as indicators. According to various federal health agencies, a variety of measures are used because of the absence of a single well-accepted measure of health status. The following measures have also been used as indicators: self-perceived health status; the incidence and prevalence of selected diseases; the measures of disability. A note of caution is needed, however, in that interpretation of these measures is rarely straightforward. An example is given in an analysis of data on the nation's health:

> If . . . the number of diseases people report increases over time, it might be concluded that overall health status is deteriorating. However, improvements in the health care system might have resulted in more frequent physician contacts and identification of previously undiagnosed illnesses. It might also reflect changes in diagnostic procedures used by physicians or changes in levels of awareness or concern. None of these measures would necessarily reflect an actual change in health status, only a change in how it is measured.[4]

Three dimensions of the health care crisis

Keeping in mind the above factors, we can now examine the current health status of Americans. Since a wide variety of problems contribute to the health care crisis, we will examine health care by viewing: (1) the growing incidence of disease conditions; (2) the growing demands by the public for adequate health care services; and (3) the broad inadequacies in health care delivery.

THE GROWING INCIDENCE OF DISEASE CONDITIONS

The first dimension of the health care crisis to be examined is our nation's health status and the growing incidence of disease conditions. National evidence shows improvement in health in recent years. The death rate in 1976 was 8.9 deaths per 1,000 people and represents the lowest death rate ever to be recorded in America.[5] Death rates from heart and cerebrovascular disease are declining. In addition, four-fifths of our noninstitutionalized population were reported to be in good or excellent health.[6] However, in spite of these and many other improvements, much evidence exists that shows a growing incidence of disease conditions.

Many improvements, yet a growing incidence of disease conditions

For example, statistics reflect an increase in the incidence of cancer, venereal disease, emphysema, and a variety of other illnesses. An estimated 30 million people have some limitations of activity as a result of chronic diseases, which in many cases have a long-term impact on these people.[7] Chronic illnesses can change their life-style to the point where they cannot continue in major activities, such as working at their jobs or at home. They can also be limited in the kind or amount of major activity. Heart problems, arthritis, and orthopedic impairments were among the major causes of limited activity. With many of the conditions being very serious, about 10 million people report some form of heart disease.[8] More than 23 million Americans have hypertension, and over 18 million are suffering from arthritis.[9] Death rates for suicide, cancer, homicide, and alcoholism have increased.[10] More accidents take place than ever before in our history. Infant mortality and tuberculosis rates continue to be high for the poor and for other groups of disadvantaged people.[11] Even with the availability of immunizations, there are frequent epidemics of communicable diseases, such as the San Antonio, Texas diphtheria epidemic of 1970.[12] According to recent Public Health Service reports, over 30 percent of the children 1 to 4 years of age are not protected against measles, and almost 40 percent are unprotected against rubella. Over one-third of America's children are not protected against polio and about one-quarter are not protected against diphtheria-pertussis-tetanus.[13]

As stated previously, one measure of health is "self-perceived health status," and four-fifths of our population have reported themselves as being in good or excellent health. It should be pointed out, however, that significant differences in response patterns exist according to the age and income of the respondents. Among those people who are between 45 and 64 years of age, only "53 percent of those in families with incomes of less than $5,000" stated that they were in good or excellent health. Almost 40 percent of the people in families with an income of $15,000 or more stated they were in good or excellent rather than fair or poor health.[14] People who are poor, in other words, see themselves as being in worse health than those who are not poor.

Poverty and Health. Not only do the poor *see* themselves as being in fair or poor health, they *are* in poor health. Even with Medicaid and other programs, they do not have as much access to good medical care as do people in the middle and upper classes. The effects of poverty are very much evident in the general health and the distribution of disease in the lower classes. As we have seen in the chapter on poverty, there are high degrees of malnutrition and disease among the poor. Our nation has one of the highest infant mortality rates of the leading industrial nations, and the lower classes have rates of infant mortality higher than that of the rest of the nation. Poor people are hospitalized more frequently than they have been in the past—although many poor are *still* not admitted to hospitals because they do not have insurance, Medicare, or Medicaid—and when admitted they remain in the hospital longer than people in higher income

Major types of health problems

The poor see themselves as being in poor health

The poor are in poor health

levels.[15] Their longer periods of hospitalization are in all probability due to their having more serious health problems. Their not receiving any prior treatment or only episodic treatment from inadequate hospital emergency rooms or out-patient and health department clinics is also a factor.

As noted in the chapter on racism, the health condition of poor minority groups is such that they suffer a high incidence of illness and early death. Tuberculosis—rare today but considered to be a major disease at the turn of the century—occurs among blacks and other minorities at a rate four times higher than that among whites. More blacks than whites die from diseases that have been medically controlled. Blacks are still more than four times as likely to die from cancer, cardiovascular disease, and hypertension than whites.[16] The incidence of disease conditions is, then, more evident among people who are poor and among our nation's minority groups. Studies have shown that those aspects of our health care delivery system that are available to some of the poor are characterized by disorganization, depersonalization, and an inadequate emphasis on health counseling.[17]

Environment and Health. In many respects—even among the poor and our nation's minorities—many feared infectious diseases are controlled with immunizations, antibiotics, and sanitation. However, as is noted in Chapter 10, our high incidence of many serious illnesses is strongly related to conditions in our environment. Most forms of cancer have been traced to substances in the environment. Many of our neurological disorders and birth defects are a result of exposure to various drugs, lead, and pesticides. As one article in the environment chapter states, "twentieth-century noise and stress, overconsumption of food and drugs, and the existence of rural and urban slums that are environmental disaster areas all combine to threaten the health of Americans."[18] The poor, then, pay a heavy toll in terms of health for their environment. The costs that are incurred through our failure to keep our environment clean are prohibitive in terms of declining health, high medical costs, and death rates.

GROWING DEMAND FOR ADEQUATE HEALTH CARE
The second factor that helps us understand the health care crisis in America is the growing demand by the public for adequate health care services. Because of the increasing publicity given to health care problems by the mass media, the government, and others, many more Americans are becoming aware of the health care crisis. The public is more aware of the facts that the poor have significantly worse health and that they receive less and poorer health care than do the middle and upper classes. They are also more aware of the facts that personal resources are related to the quality of health care and that adequate levels of health care are still not available to people living in much of rural America, city ghettos, Indian reservations, and migratory communities. In any event, the poor and also the middle classes in America are now demanding the health care services that are available to

Minority groups and incidence of disease

Poor health is related to our polluted environment

Many more Americans are aware of the health crisis

the wealthy. They are also demanding a part in the planning and decision-making processes of health care services. There has, in other words, been a significant shift in attitudes toward health care. No longer is it considered to be a privilege, available only to people who are able to pay. Health care is now viewed as a basic right. While there is a long way to go in making it a reality, the federal government has established health care as a right through some of the health legislation of the 1970s. Health care is something to which every American has a just claim. Health is, according to Vice President Walter F. Mondale, "the first of all liberties."[19]

Health care now viewed as a basic right

INADEQUACIES IN HEALTH CARE DELIVERY
In addition to the growing incidence of disease conditions and the increased public demand for adequate health care, the health care crisis can be understood by the inadequacies in our health care delivery system.

The present structure of health care delivery in America is quite complex. It is an accumulation of old as well as new social health care patterns among physicians, other health personnel, and consumers, which has been implanted upon a densely populated, technologically complex industrial society.[20] The evolution of the present health care delivery system into its "firm entrenchment in the private practice, fee-for-service economic structure" is rooted in American history. These roots today nourish the remains of early styles of health care delivery. Nakagawa states that to date, "supporters of this historical pattern of health care have blocked the planning of health care services by their allegiances to the present costly and inefficient structure." Also, at this development stage, dominant health care professionals have not incorporated some of the major changes in social attitudes, such as consumer rights and the acceptance of large organizations as "legitimate structures for social and health services." The planning of health care services will be examined later, but first we will discuss the current "costly and inefficient" structure of health care delivery.[21]

Structure of health care delivery is complex

NATIONAL HEALTH EXPENDITURES

According to Joseph A. Califano, Jr., Secretary of the Department of Health, Education and Welfare (HEW), the major problem in America's health care industry is "runaway costs." Each year health care spending uses a greater share of our gross national product (GNP).[22] In 1950, the cost figures for health care in the United States totaled $12 billion, or 4.5 percent of the GNP. In 1976, the figures were $139.3 billion, or 8.6 percent of the GNP.[23] This represents an average annual increase rate of 9.9 percent for total health expenditures.[24] As can be seen in Fig. 8.1, expenditures for health care have more than tripled in the past twelve years. Half the increase is attributed to rising prices of medical services and goods; 40 percent is attributed to greater per capita health services utilization, improvements, and complexity. About 10 percent is due to population growth.[25] The estimated

The problem of "runaway costs"

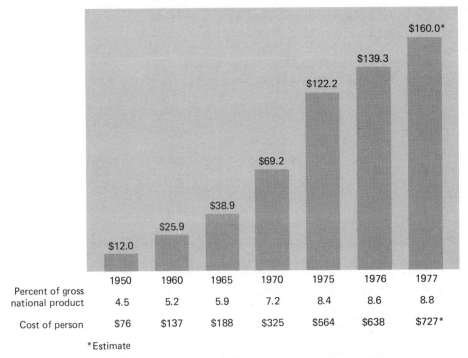

	1950	1960	1965	1970	1975	1976	1977
	$12.0	$25.9	$38.9	$69.2	$122.2	$139.3	$160.0*
Percent of gross national product	4.5	5.2	5.9	7.2	8.4	8.6	8.8
Cost of person	$76	$137	$188	$325	$564	$638	$727*

*Estimate

Fig. 8.1 National health expenditures (in billions): 1950–1977. Source: U.S. Census Bureau, *Statistical Abstract of the United States: 1977*, p. 94.

Health expenditures will soon double

figures for national health expenditures for 1977, as shown in Fig. 8.1, are even higher—$160 billion, or about $727 per person. Secretary Califano fears that these health expenditures will double in just a few short years.[26]

Increases for health care expenditures are, for many reasons, not uniform across the country. According to one federal study,

> the age distribution of a population influences the need for health services and the eligibility for Medicare and other age-related programs. Migration patterns have changed the age distribution in some areas. Price levels of hospital and professional services rose more steeply in some areas than in others. The supply of hospital beds and professional manpower varies from one area to another. This variation influences access and thus utilization levels which, along with prices, determines expenditures. Factors in an area's general economy are also significant. The level of personal income governs the ability to pay for care and influences the location of professionals, and industrialization is associated with the prevalence of health insurance coverage and use of insurance as a payment source for health care.[27]

HIGH COSTS OF HEALING: HOSPITALS

A major reason for the sharp rise in health costs is charges made by hospitals. A hospital stay that cost $16 per day in 1950 now costs over $160 per day. The average hospital stay in 1965 cost $311; today, it's almost $1300. By 1987 a hospital stay is predicted to cost $640 per day. At those rates, as Vice President Mondale stated, "it will soon be cheaper to fly to the French Riviera and lie in the sun than to stay overnight in an American hospital." If unchecked, total hospital costs could reach $220 billion per year by 1985.[28] A large portion of these costs are due to the acquisition of more expensive equipment and an increase in the number of hospital employees and staff in proportion to patient populations.[29] Higher prices for goods and services bought by hospitals and wage increases for hospital employees also account for a high percentage of these spiraling costs.

Average hospital costs

Some of the high costs are due to poor hospital management. Costs increase when hospitals in the same community are competing with one another for the latest, most technologically advanced—and expensive—equipment. Duplicated equipment and facilities mean higher health care prices for the consumer. Poor hospital management also contributes to the high health care costs by discouraging less costly outpatient treatment (where the patient does not stay overnight) for the many thousands of hospital procedures than can be effectively performed in this manner. Lack of hospital self-care facilities and preventive services also contribute to the high health care costs.

Poor hospital management

HIGH COSTS OF HEALING: DOCTORS

A recent newsmagazine article on America's doctors reports that the medical profession is in trouble and that the "attack on physicians" developed from a crisis in health care costs. An American Medical Association (AMA) poll reports that 3 out of 4 doctors consider medical costs their biggest problem. Health officials report, however, that it is "none other than doctors themselves who are at the core of the cost crisis." One special report notes that "working under conflicting pressures from hospital administrators, the public, drug companies, insurance carriers, and medical schools, it is the physician who makes the key decisions." He or she (although 91 percent of physicians are men) "is the one who sends the patient to the hospital, orders the tests and performs the procedures."[30]

Doctors are at the core of the cost crisis

According to HEW, physicians generate 70 percent of total costs, when one counts bills paid for hospitalization, surgery, drugs, and other medical procedures ordered by physicians. *Each* doctor, it is estimated by the government, generates over $200,000 in medical costs every year. This figure *excludes* the charges for the doctor's own services. A doctor's average income for 1978 is estimated at $75,000 a year. Many specialists, and in particular surgeons, earn more than $250,000 a year. Doctors, on the other hand, believe that their incomes are comparable to those of middle-level

Many specialists earn more than a quarter of a million dollars a year

business executives and are justified by the high costs of medical education, high malpractice insurance premiums, and long work days.[31]

HIGH COSTS OF HEALING: UNNECESSARY TREATMENT

There are two million unnecessary operations each year

Another factor contributing to the high costs of health care, and one that is directly injurious to the public's health, is the significant number of unnecessary treatments and operations. Congressional investigations report that more than 2 million unnecessary operations are performed each year in the United States. According to a series of articles appearing in the *New York Times*, studies indicate that, of the 14 million nonemergency operations performed each year, 2.4 million are unnecessary. In addition, some 11,900 people died during these unneeded operations.[32]

Overprescription of drugs

Many millions of dollars are also spent on the unnecessary overprescription of antibiotics and other drugs. The estimate for antibiotics *alone* is six billion doses consumed yearly. Some 22 percent of these doses are considered to be unnecessary and have resulted in over 10,000 fatal and near-fatal reactions. When other drugs are included the death rates are in the tens of thousands; the rates for reactions resulting in hospitalization are in the hundreds of thousands.[33]

Unnecessary surgery has been attributed to the large number of surgeons, whose livelihoods depend upon performing surgery, and to our fee-for-service economic structure, in which doctors are paid each time a patient is treated. Lower rates of surgery occur where there are proportionately fewer surgeons and where patients are not covered by fee-for-service insurance plans.[34]

Most surveys and research studies indicate that, in general, "overall quality of care in U.S. hospitals is good," and that "multidisciplinary teams at special centers such as intensive-care and burn units, chronic-pain clinics and rehabilitation institutions offer new hope to sufferers of the most devastating illnesses." Yet, other studies lead to charges of "unnecessary surgery and hospitalization, misuse of drugs and radiation treatments and instances of incompetence."[35] All of these factors affect the costs of health care and, of course, affect the overall quality of America's health care.

THE MALDISTRIBUTION OF HEALTH CARE PROFESSIONALS

Maldistribution: A serious problem with the medical profession

Another problem adding to the crisis in health care is the maldistribution of health care professionals. Karen Davis, head of Health Planning at HEW, has stated that the "number one problem with the medical profession is maldistribution. We've got the wrong kinds of doctors in the wrong place doing the wrong things."[36]

No longer a doctor shortage

In 1970, Roger Egeberg, Assistant Secretary of HEW, stressed the need for 50,000 new physicians in order to effectively deal with the doctor shortage.[37] No longer do we have this shortage of doctors or even hospital beds. Between the late 1960s and the mid-1970s, almost two dozen medical

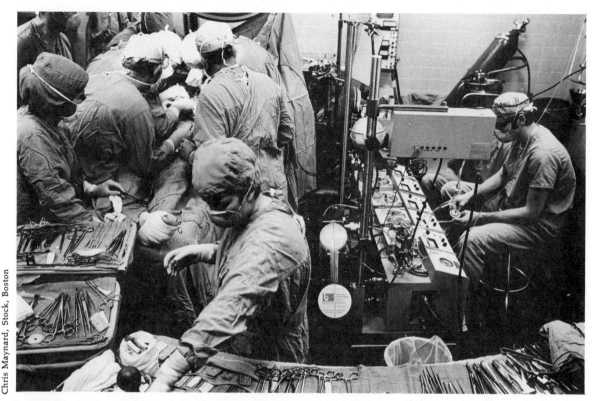

Chris Maynard, Stock, Boston

Increased technology has brought with it increased costs of hospitalization.

schools were created, and the number of students attending medical schools has increased significantly in the past few years. In the last five years, the number of doctors has increased by one-third. Estimates are that in 1980, the United States will have one doctor for about every 500 people. Some newsreports even indicate that, far from being worried about a doctor shortage, we are worried about a doctor *surplus*. Some health officials are concerned that in most sections of the United States we may soon have too many people treating patients, which could "further increase the country's total health budget and worsen the potential problem of unnecessary treatments."[38]

There have also been more protests that, while we have been increasing our own supply of physicians through the formation of new medical schools and increased admissions to all schools, we have also been encouraging an even more rapid entry of foreign medical graduates, "whose training for delivery of health services is widely questioned."[39] Federal reports indicate that in each of the last four years for which data are available, the number of foreign medical graduates admitted to this country exceeded the total number that graduated from American medical schools. This group of "undereducated physicians, often unlicensed, who have either not taken or have failed a licensing examination, and who have never passed a proficiency examination" has been labeled by leading medical journals as a "medical underground."[40]

A "medical underground"

Even with this increase in the number of physicians, a shortage does exist in terms of geographic distribution. In the mid-1970s, there were an estimated 196 physicians providing patient care for approximately every 100,000 people in large urban areas. Small nonurban counties, however, had a ratio of only 40 doctors for every 100,000 individuals.[41] Federal statistics show that the number of physicians per 100,000 population varied from 429 in the District of Columbia and 236 in New York to 85 in Alaska and 78 in South Dakota.[42] Almost half of all physicians live in only seven states. The

Population of doctors is low in many small communities

population of doctors is so low in many small communities that the physicians limit their practices and accept only the number of patients they feel they can serve. Patients who go to the large, out-patient departments of hospitals receive fragmented care after long waits. But the long waits and fragmented care are experienced by patients of private practitioners, as well.

Long waits and fragmented care

Irene Ramey states that "three and four-hour waiting periods in a reception room followed by five-minute visits are not uncommon. Under such conditions, it is to be expected that errors are made in diagnosis and treatment and that there is a lack of proper follow-up."[43]

Not only is there a geographic maldistribution of physicians, but also of other health professionals, such as speech pathologists and occupational and physical therapists. In one community, the ratio of these professionals can be 1 to 2,000 or 3,000 people; in another, the ratio can be as high as 1 to 147,000 people.[44]

The maldistribution problem exists also in the number of doctors who practice in various specialty areas. The selection of specialty training in residency is not based upon national need but is "based upon personal choice and upon the availability of residencies."[45] Today, only about one-seventh

Few physicians are in general practice

of America's physicians—not half as many as in 1950—are in general practice or primary care. Yet, some "90 percent of the problems that send patients to doctors do not require any specialty training." AMA statistics indicate that about 54,000 of the nation's 340,000 licensed physicians are in general practice, "258,361 in different specialties from aerospace medicine to allergies, 6,445 in teaching, 11,161 in administration and 7,944 in research." A recent article summarizes the problem, noting that "even as the overall supply of doctors increases, health officials worry that there are too many

Too many specialists

specialists, as well as too many doctors in affluent metropolitan areas—with not enough doctors interested in general practice and disease prevention or willing to practice in rural areas and inner cities where the need is greatest."[46]

HEALTH INSURANCE

The inadequacy and expense of voluntary health insurance is an additional problem contributing to the health care crisis in America. According to government figures, about four-fifths of our population is covered by private health insurance for hospital care and surgical services. This means that about 20 percent of our population is not covered by any health insurance. According to federal data:

> The proportion of people having such coverage increased with income, rising from 37 percent for the lowest income group (under $3,000) to more than 90 percent among families of $15,000 or more.[47]

Private studies have indicated that as low as 6 percent of Americans have no health insurance, a figure that is much lower than the government's estimate. One 18-month study claims that half of the 12.2 million people who lack insurance earn less than $10,000 a year, are "unemployed, under-employed, self-employed, or chronically ill, whom private companies won't insure."[48] The researchers claim that these people make too much to qualify for Medicaid but are too unhealthy or poor to obtain private coverage. Since this study was financed by a large drug company, Roche Laboratories, and recommended that the government "provide coverage just for the unpro-tected" rather than develop a new system for national health insurance, one might suspect that these private figures are low and that the government's figures are probably a more accurate estimate of the uninsured.

Millions of Americans are not covered by any health insurance

Those Americans who are covered by some type of health insurance usually find that it is inadequate and unreliable. Some 92 million people are insured by the large network of Blue Cross/Blue Shield plans, which "have a reassuring public image" but do not necessarily give adequate protection. As one recent article on coverage noted, Blue Shield is "supposed to take care of surgery, but it pays according to fixed rates that often cover less than 50 percent of actual fees."[49] Private insurance plans such as Blue Cross/Blue Shield, union plans, and commercial insurance companies pay only about one quarter of all health care expenses.[50] Also, these plans are primarily *group* insurance plans, which cover people who are members of particular unions or who work at a particular company or organization. This has meant a loss of coverage for many Americans when they are out of work through loss of job or lay-off. During the 1976 recession, 2.7 million workers and their families lost coverage for health insurance.[51]

Those who have health insurance find it inadequate

Many plans do not cover the costs of home care, doctor's office visits, and preventive health examination, but cover only parts of inpatient, medical, and surgical care. What this means for the average American is that a larger percentage of personal income must go to the increasing health and insur-ance costs. Even with insurance coverage, the great majority of policies do not protect against serious or long-term illnesses. As one popular magazine

Serious illness can be economically destructive

Problems of Medicaid

states, "One catastrophe, like cancer, severe burns or a massive coronary, would probably take every cent you own."[52] Almost half of the people who file for bankruptcy claim that it is because of medical debts.[53]

As far as *public* health insurance programs (such as Medicare and Medicaid) are concerned, many aged and poor have been helped by these programs but others have not. Many of the problems of Medicare and the aged have been discussed in the chapter on agism and will not be repeated here. With Medicaid, the following problems have been encountered:

1. Inadequate funding, which eliminates millions of poor from the programs.
2. Bureaucratic "red tape," which discourages and prevents many poor who are in need from receiving benefits.
3. Higher health care costs due to increased demands for health services.
4. Overcharges and fraudulent abuse by some hospitals, physicians, nursing homes, and others.

Needless to say, voluntary health insurance and government programs are inadequate in meeting the health care needs of the great majority of American families.

EXPLAINING THE HEALTH CARE CRISIS

LACK OF AN OVERALL SYSTEM

The health care crisis has been explained in a wide variety of ways. We will examine some of the more important explanations. First, one can view the crisis in health care by noting the lack of an overall system for providing health care. Health care delivery in the United States is not a nonsystem but a profusion of ununified systems, some of which are in conflict with one another. This can and does result in both overlaps and gaps in the comprehensiveness of various services and in discontinuity of care. Ms. Ramey states that each power group trys "to bring pressure to have its system instituted as 'the' one." She states also:

> Leadership by the Executive Branch of government in Washington is spasmodic and all too frequently is designed to appease whatever power group has the public ear at a given moment. Vast sums of money are appropriated for specific diseases rather than for an overall approach to the health of all citizens. The Department of Health, Education, and Welfare is reorganized every year or two. This, combined with turnover of department heads, prevents any long-term, continuing approach to anything .... actions (of Congress and the President) are focused on reelection rather than on serious, long-range planning and careful implementation of programs with continuous, objective evaluation.[54]

Unlike other industrialized societies, America does not have a comprehensive health delivery system. Most industrialized nations have a comprehensive national health insurance program. As noted above, we pay for health care through a profusion of private and governmentally sponsored programs designed, in most cases, for particular groups—i.e., the aged, the poor, union workers, group plans, etc. We also pay directly out of our own pockets for medical care. We operate under the fee-for-service method of remuneration. Physicians basically set the fees for the specific services delivered, which tends to place more emphasis upon the treatment rather than on preventive aspects of health care. Nations that have comprehensive health delivery systems have their physicians salaried and there is, therefore, a greater tendency to stress the preventive aspects of health care. Physicians tend to favor the fee-for-service method. It is "supposed to relate [to] the physician's regard to what work he does and to his degree of enthusiasm and competence." Some critics, however, view it as a "form of piecework remuneration rendered obsolete by fundamental changes in the character and cost of health services."[55] According to the Health Administration, the fee-for-service system in a marketplace that is less than totally free, combined with higher amounts of insurance for inpatient care, tends to:

1. encourage consumers and physicians to substitute hospital for ambulatory care, resulting in higher costs;

2. encourage providers to overprescribe or supply services that are marginally needed, if at all.

3. deter consumers from seeking relatively inexpensive care in the early stages of illness at the risk of requiring more expensive care later on.[56]

This first explanation for the health care crisis, then, stresses a fragmented health care system of independent provider units. Lack of effective planning and coordination results in a wide variety of problems, ranging from the maldistribution of resources and the lack of comprehensive care, with continuity, to the duplication of facilities and services and increased costs. As some sociologists have stated, "the present system of health care, based on the physician's fee-for-service and a combination of public and private insurance programs, has resulted in spiraling costs without providing adequate care, especially to underprivileged groups."[57]

THE MEDICAL-INDUSTRIAL COMPLEX
The second way in which the crisis in health care is explained is in terms of the "American health industry" or the "medical-industrial complex." The "American health industry" consists of doctors, medical schools, hospitals, health insurance companies, and drug companies. Health care is "no more the top priority of this 'industry' . . . than the production of safe, cheap, efficient, pollution-free transportation is a priority of the American automobile industry." This "health establishment" has been described as "both

Many other nations have comprehensive health delivery systems

Physicians tend to favor fee-for-service payment

efficient and systematic in extracting profits in terms of differences between income and expenditures."[58] In other words, the health care system is *not* a chaotic, uncoordinated, unplanned profusion of unified systems. It is dominated primarily by institutions, such as hospitals, research laboratories, and drug companies. There are various examples of the economic interplay that has emerged among the above parties.

Health care system dominated primarily by institutions

> University research centers do a multimillion dollar business in health research and masterminded a multimillion dollar budget in public funds. Profit-making hospitals, now public corporations listed on the stock exchange, take an unlimited flow of health insurance funds. There is no limit to their budgets since insurance companies set no rates on what hospitals may charge a third party. Pharmaceutical firms and drug outlets may charge all that traffic will bear.[59]

According to this second explanation, there are three major components to the health care system in our society—medical empires, the financing-planning complex, and the medical-industrial complex. They will be examined later in the reading by the Health Policy Advisory Center. For now, it is sufficient to say that the second explanation attributes the current crisis in health care to the power of organized medical-industrial empires, and to the fact that health is a multibillion dollar business of inextricably interlaced university research centers, government agencies, hospitals, and insurance companies.[60]

EXTERNAL FORCES

A third point of view explains the health care crisis not in terms of an ununified private medical system or a medical-industrial complex, but in terms of complex forces that are "outside the control of any medical establishment."[61] These forces—"the living patterns and habits of people beyond the control of medicine"—affect the birth- and death rates and the rates of cancer and heart problems. This point of view admits to some flaws in private medicine, but questions why, with so much dissatisfaction with the way in which our government is run, reformers want American medicine to be nationalized and bureaucratized. For Schwartz, the adoption and implementation of "revolutionary proposals" aimed at transforming American health care will mean higher costs while at the same time "providing less satisfaction and poorer treatment for millions."[62] Strong opposition to governmental efforts to regulate or finance health care is also reflected by the American Medical Association. Parrott, a former President of the AMA, is very much against liberal efforts to "create a more centralized and efficient health care system," and believes that "thousands of individual physicians working in an environment free of governmental interference have provided the strength and genius of American health care."[63]

Living patterns and habits affect health

The AMA

There are a variety of responses to the poor status of our nation's health, the growing demands for adequate health care, and the many different inadequacies in health care delivery. The most important response, and therefore the one that we will stress, is the demand for a national health insurance program. Before examining the issue of national health insurance and some of the more important federal acts and programs that have attempted but failed to reform the structure of our health care delivery system, we must address some very important questions related to health and its delivery.

RESPONDING TO THE HEALTH CARE CRISIS

Some of these questions are: What kind of health care delivery system will we have in the next several years? What will be its main objective? What kinds of services will be provided by this emerging system? First, we must move toward a health delivery system that stresses the prevention of disease. Second, the system must include *intensive* education as a basic function. Third, the system must pay attention to the social services and supports people need in order to play their social roles and control their lives.

LEVINE READING——OBJECTIVES

1. To list the three goals that must be a part of our health delivery system if we are to promote health and not merely treat illness.
2. By essay, explain the role public service workers can play in the expanding health delivery system.

Expanding the Scope of Health Care
SOL LEVINE

There is no longer any need to justify the judicious use of paraprofessionals to extend the capacity of the health delivery system. Even if there were no important new developments in the organization of health care, there would be obvious need to expand significantly the employment of public service workers in the health sector. However, in any deliberations about the future deployment of public service workers in the health delivery system, we can be much more informed in our thinking and more pertinent in our recommendations if we develop a clear image of the kind of health system which is evolving. What kind of health delivery system can we envision in the next few years? What will be the main goals and objectives and what types of services will be provided by the emerging health

Reprinted by permission from *Social Policy*, November–December 1975. This article was adapted from the preliminary and final reports of the 1975 National Conference on Social Welfare Task Force on "Social Components of Physical and Mental Health Services."

delivery system? If we can answer these questions, we can specify more appropriately the roles new public service workers will perform in the health system.

In this article I will focus on specific goals and functions which, in my judgment, must be encompassed by the delivery system if it is designed to *promote health* and not merely to treat illness. Our legitimate aspirations regarding the scope and functions of a health system have been so frustrated by our present mode of organizing, financing, and delivering health services that we have become embarrassed to delineate and project simple basic goals for the system lest we sound hortatory or platitudinous. Even some of the most sophisticated critics of the present health system have been mentally imbued and affected by the assumptions and criteria of the present system. When we speak of improving health services, who among us does not conjure in his/her mind the building of new hospitals, additional coronary care units, cobalt machines, dialysis, and other impressive forms of medical technology? They are important components of our medical armamentarium, to be sure, but how far do these take us in promoting health and preventing illness?

This is not to deny that we do, in fact, possess an impressive medical technology which can often spell the difference between health and sickness, even life and death. Moreover, the American people, for the most part, cherish and seek the technical care they can obtain. Indeed, one major task in the next few years will be to find ways of making the health technology we already possess readily available to the American population, particularly low-income people and minority groups in inner cities and in rural communities. While relatively few people complain about the technical level of care they receive from the health delivery system, harsh criticism and even indignation is often expressed about other aspects of the health system: the high cost of care, the unavailability of neighborhood physicians, the amount of time required to obtain care and the frustration involved, and dehumanization which patients and families experience as they try to cope with the inadequacy, complexity, and segmentalization of the health system. Dramatic testimony to the unsatisfactory state of our present mode of organizing health care is provided by the specter of tired and sometimes desperate patients pushing their way into crowded and overtaxed emergency rooms in an effort to obtain care which otherwise is not available.

Clearly, then, our elaborate technology should be made available to patients in a more humanized manner. This will require, among other things, that we move away from a delivery system which is hospital-centered, geared to the needs and practices of medical specialists, and organized to provide services for episodic illness. We should try to move toward a health delivery system which uses the hospital as a significant resource but which is mainly concerned with providing primary care on an ambulatory basis in neighborhoods and communities. It would seem that new public service workers could play a much more significant role in a health delivery system which emphasizes community-based primary care to recipients.

1. *The goals of the delivery system of the future should include to a much greater extent the promotion of health and the prevention of disease.*

Public service workers will be able to contribute even more significantly if the goals and functions of the health delivery system are changed. We must move away from a "medical repair system" which focuses upon episodic illness, and,

The goal of promoting health

Humanized technology

in large part, reflects the failures of our present system, to a health delivery system whose primary goals are the promotion of health and the prevention of disease. This would represent a most serious shift in our focus and emphasis. And if we are serious and deliberate in changing the goals and functions of our health system, there will be enormous opportunities for usefully employing new public service workers.

It will be necessary for us to develop and to use a definition of health which encompasses significant social components. Health will not be viewed as the mere absence of disease but as the ability of the individual to control her/his life and to perform crucial social roles such as worker, parent, spouse, and citizen. The health delivery system will then be assessed largely in terms of the degree to which it contributes to the ability of people to perform their social roles maximally and to control their lives to the fullest possible extent. The health goals would vary for each individual with the objective of having each person achieve the fullest level of health possible. What is to be emphasized is that each person could achieve a maximal level of health for him or herself, depending on age, physical condition, life circumstances, etc. A specific example can be used to illustrate the general principle. If, with the appropriate social supports and health care, an aged person has the capacity to participate in the community and to follow a pattern of living which she or he found enjoyable, it would violate the health goals we are espousing to place him or her in a nursing home. A health system which, in fact, placed such people in nursing homes where they could not fulfill their health potential—where they could not perform their social roles and control their lives—would be regarded as failing in its essential purpose.

2. *As the health-care delivery system shifts from one which is primarily a hospital-based "repair system" to one with great emphasis on providing primary care and promoting health, an additional major function may be assumed by the health system: intensive and comprehensive health education.*

Studies by epidemiologists, economists, medical sociologists, and other health investigators have demonstrated that the health status of a people is determined less by the traditional patient-care services which are dispensed to them than by social conditions in which they live and the health practices they follow—in short, by their style of life. There is little doubt that the things we eat, how much we smoke and drink, how we manage our automobiles, and the way we live—all of these play a tremendous role in affecting our health. The distinguished public health physician George James once remarked that if we encouraged people to give up cigarettes we could do more to improve the health of our people than all the skills and technology presently in the domain of medicine. The health system must include intensive and comprehensive health education as basic and essential functions. To do this adequately, it will be necessary to make use of the skills of the new public service workers.

We can expect some resistance to these new health goals and functions from a number of health professionals who regard themselves as specially trained people using complex and sophisticated skills to manage illness and pathology, not to interfere with people's personal habits or way of living. Some will argue that personal health habits are so deeply embedded in people's history and culture that they are very difficult, if not impossible, to modify. Others will contend that we have no right to tamper with people's way of life.

The promotion of health and the prevention of disease

Health education

We believe that humanistic values, concerns about costs, as well as our changing definition of health will cause health professionals and others involved in forging a new health system to address themselves finally to personal health styles. Many physicians, nurses, and other health professionals already take into account the personal and cultural life-styles of their patients. When interpreting pain and symptoms and in prescribing appropriate health regimens, health professionals have found it necessary to consider the personal characteristics, life-styles, and cultural backgrounds of their patients. It will be necessary for health personnel to expand their knowledge, skills, and understanding regarding psychological, social, and cultural factors as they begin to achieve the new goals of the health system: promoting health and fostering preventive care.

One prototype of the new form of health delivery may be found in the present Multiple Risk Factor Intervention Trial Centers (MRFIT) which attempt to prevent heart disease among patients who have a high risk of developing heart disease: adult males who are overweight, have high cholesterol levels, high hypertension, and who smoke are clearly very likely candidates for heart disease. The program attempts to use a wide range of methods to modify the behavior and style of life of these people. Accordingly, counseling is sometimes provided as well as various forms of group discussion or group therapy. In attempting to modify the health habits and life-styles of these adult males, physicians have found it necessary to enlist the aid of other personnel such as counselors, clinical psychologists, and social workers.

If programs like MRFIT were expanded on a much broader basis, it would clearly be necessary to make use of many new public service employees in the health delivery system. It would be desirable to develop new kinds of personnel who know a good deal about appropriate health habits, who can assess the kinds of problems people from different ethnic cultures, communities, and social-class backgrounds will encounter in modifying their health behavior and styles of life. Public service employees working in this field will not only have to know much about health care but a great deal about sociology, psychology, and health education. In addition, they will have to possess a range of specialized interpersonal skills, and they will have to be equipped to work with different kinds of groups in varying settings. Clearly new employees will have to acquire not only cognitive knowledge of social science disciplines but they will also have to possess interpersonal, clinical, and group work skills. Some of them may work in physicians' offices, others in clinics or health centers, and others may serve as outreach workers who visit the homes of patients and families.

It is important to add a clarifying note here. Some people may recoil from the idea of an aggressive health system dictating tastes and habits to people in matters of physical and mental health. While it is preferable to have individuals make their own choices, so long as their behavior is not harmful to others, it would be the responsibility of a health system to make a serious and sustained effort to inform the public: not merely to transmit information casually or mechanically but to get people's attention, to reach them psychologically, to provide them with realistic alternatives, and, when indicated, to help them implement their decision to change their health practices. Public health service workers and other health personnel will have to relate to recipients on a face-to-face basis and to consider their cultural values and preferences in order to find the most appropriate ways of informing them and helping them to change their practices. If an individual elects to pursue a mode of living which departs from the ideal prescriptions of the health workers, the latter, at least, have fulfilled their responsibility in having informed the patient.

3. *The emerging health delivery system will also have to pay attention to various kinds of social services and social supports which people need so that they may be able to perform their social roles and control their lives.*

A considerable start has already been made in this direction in some health delivery systems. Various social services are provided and there is awareness that the patient is a whole person who performs different social roles and is part of the social network which impinges upon her/his health status. Thus health professionals have learned to rely upon social workers to ascertain whether the social resources of a patient recovering from surgery are sufficient and appropriate to permit her/him to return home, or whether the job setting to which a cardiac patient is returning may be too stressful, or whether there is need to redesign family goals and responsibilities so that the physical recovery of a cardiac patient is not obstructed. In such cases, social services have been used as in instrument to achieve medical care of therapy objectives.

Unfortunately, the role of the social worker in medical settings has often been narrowly defined and his or her skills have often not come to the fore unless a patient is referred to social services by a physician. There have been a host of social needs which patients and families have had in managing illness which have been ignored or which have received little attention from the health delivery system. It is hoped that as the health delivery system develops new goals, these social dimensions will receive much more attention. For example, we have not given sufficient attention to the dying patient or to the problems of his or her spouse or kin or to the mother of a child with a newly diagnosed genetic illness or to the family of a patient who has undergone a serious surgical procedure. A dying patient may frequently be capable of performing fuller social roles for an appreciable and treasured piece of time if the health system were properly oriented and capable of providing appropriate services. But even more, the families of sick and dying patients are not capable of performing their own roles and living their lives to the fullest or maintaining a state of social health because of the disruptions which they encounter and the failure of the health system to provide appropriate social services and supports to them.

Navarro has argued that many patients come to the health delivery system for care rather than cure. This is understandable when we consider that health problems are increasingly chronic in nature and are amenable to palliation but not cure. Many of the people who come to the health system because of disability and dependence require social care and supports more than they require traditional medical service. How adequate are the available services for a blind person whose physical condition is not amenable to medical intervention or for a child with a serious physical or emotional handicap? The health delivery system has not done much for people who come to it with problems of living such as drinking, boredom, loneliness, or the lack of capability to function well at daily living or to utilize the existing sources of society. As the health delivery system as-

Social services and supports

sumes the goal of fostering health and helping people to perform their social roles, it will no longer be able to ignore these concerns, for these are the main business of a health system.

We will have to train public service employees to provide necessary social services and social supports to meet these problems. Many of the skills which will be necessary for the public service employees to obtain will resemble some of the skills which social workers presently possess. They will include making an inventory of patients, families, and community resources, counseling, life rearrangement, discussions and deliberations with employers as well as other diagnostic and interpersonal services.

To achieve the new goals of the health system it would also be necessary to expand various social support services which go beyond individual or group counseling or social services to sick patients on a one-to-one basis. The health system will have to develop and make use of a number of social support services such as child- and day-care services, foster homes, homemaker services, transportation services, income maintenance, etc. Clearly, an expanding number of positions will have to be filled by public service employees as we try to achieve health goals which have been articulated here.

However, it is necessary to realize that the new functions which will be assumed by the health delivery system and additional health workers may not automatically have impact or be effective in modifying the status and behavior of recipients. Our experience with health education efforts to date does not give cause for easy confidence. We have learned that health education methods may fail for all kinds of reasons. If the message which is conveyed by health personnel conflicts with existing values, beliefs, attitudes, or health practices of recipients, considerable resistance may be encountered. In these cases, recipients may fail to hear or attend to the message or they may forget or reinterpret it so that the objectives of health educators are frustrated.

On the other hand, we have learned a good deal about ways of overcoming various types of resistance. In addition, we have developed greater knowledge about what kinds of psychological conditions must obtain in order for health education methods to be effective. We have learned about the limits of mass media and the relative potential of face-to-face methods in varying contexts and settings. We have also learned how the characteristics of the educator, the message, and the recipients may all influence the success of the health education venture. What becomes readily apparent is that the new functions which the public health service workers will be asked to assume are in many ways much more complex and difficult to learn than some of the other skills which paraprofessionals have assumed in the health delivery system. They are qualitatively different from serving as a dental aide or an orthopedic assistant or a medical librarian assistant or even a mental health worker. The new skills which will be necessary for public health service workers to learn involve a combination of basic scientific knowledge such as psychology and sociology, clinical skills such as interviewing group work, and health education and various kinds of interpersonal and intergroup skills. Indeed, unlike many other tasks for which paraprofessionals have been trained in the past, the new roles assumed by the public health service workers may require specific personality characteristics which may be an important basis for recruitment and selection. It would appear that the task of developing appropriate selection criteria and training requirements will be much more difficult.

It will be necessary to develop very specific job descriptions of the roles the new public service workers will assume, the functions they will perform, and the services they will provide. Even today the actual roles and job requirements of the professional social worker and health educator, who to some extent will serve as models for the new public health service workers, though with some important modifications and refinements, are only vaguely appreciated or recognized by many other health workers such as physicians, nurses, and administrators. As a prior condition for the effective use of the new public service workers, it will be necessary to explicate and legitimate the services provided by the social worker and health educator and provide for their services under the new health insurance legislation. Furthermore, unless the specific tasks assumed by the new public service workers are explicated, legitimated, and covered by emerging health insurance legislation, our projection of a delivery system which will incorporate new functions and be staffed by public health service workers will be little more than a rationalistic exercise. One crucial question which must be addressed is how the new functions and activities outlined here will be related to and integrated with other parts of the health delivery sysem. How, for example, will these new functions be grafted onto an ongoing neighborhood health center or a health maintenance organization? If we are to incorporate a new definition of health with all of its social implications and to deal with the health styles and practices of recipients, should we consider new ways of organizing personnel and assigning responsibilities? Should we consider, for example, assigning the role of captain of the team to someone other than the physician since medical care will be but one, though an important component, in the promotion of health? Whatever changes we contemplate in the mode of organizing and deploying personnel, it is crucial that we give considerable forethought, planning, and evaluation to how the new functions are and will be incorporated into the existing health organization structures. If we do not plan carefully, there is good reason to believe that we may be creating new sources of confusion and frustration within the health delivery system.

Public service workers

Levine noted the importance of planning to avoid confusion and frustration in our health care delivery system. It appears, when reviewing past efforts in health care, that our government has not planned carefully.

The Hill-Burton Act of almost thirty-five years ago and the Regional Medical Program of the 1960s both attempted and failed to regionalize health care in America. The Comprehensive Health Planning (CHP) Act of 1966 subsidized state health planning agencies whose functions were "vaguely defined" and was an attempt at systemizing health care delivery. CHP has been "phased out," and we now have a new federal legislative effort to deal with the health care crisis, under the name of the National Health Planning and Resources Development Act of 1974. It appears, however, that we are no closer to health care systemization than we were

Attempts at systemizing health care have failed

in the 1960s. According to Somers, the problem of fragmentation "remains as the most conspicuous landmark of the delivery system."[64]

A major part of the government's health strategy in dealing with several aspects of the health care crisis, combined with efforts on the part of employers and providers, has been the alternative delivery system, or the health maintenance organization (HMO).

HEALTH MAINTENANCE ORGANIZATIONS

HMOs are designed for preventive health care and low costs

In 1970, HMOs were proclaimed by the government to be the "centerpiece" of our nation's health care strategy because they "represented a more efficient way of organizing and delivering health services."[65] HMOs are medical group practice programs that, for a fixed annual premium, provide comprehensive medical services and hospital care to their subscribers. They are designed to stress preventive health care services and to keep down the costs of health care.

HEW's white paper, "Toward A Comprehensive Health Strategy for the 1970s" concisely states the claims of HMOs. The paper states that HMOs

> simultaneously attack many of the problems comprising the health
> care crisis. They emphasize prevention and early care; they provide
> incentive for holding down costs and for increasing the productivity
> of resources; they offer opportunities for improving the quality of
> care; they provide a means for improving the geographic distribution
> of care; and by mobilizing private capital and managerial talent, they
> reduce the need for federal funds and direct controls. . . . Because
> HMO revenues are fixed, their incentives are to keep patients well,
> for they benefit from patient well days, not sickness. Their entire cost
> structure is geared to preventing illness and, failing that, to pro-
> moting prompt recovery through the least costly services consistent
> with maintaining quality.[66]

In 1973, Congress passed the Health Maintenance Organization Act, and authorized $375 million to help finance HMOs. Congress also made it mandatory for employers of 25 or more people to offer an HMO option as part of their employee health insurance plan.

HMOs' effectiveness questioned

Evidence exists supporting the view that HMOs have brought about reductions in overall medical costs. They also appear to have reversed traditional incentives "in the fee-for-service sector to do unnecessary surgery, prolong hospitalization, and construct unneeded facilities."[67] Other studies, however, question the contention that HMOs maintain and promote health.[68]

According to HEW, by 1980 HMOs were expected to be available to 90 percent of the population.[69] Today, there are about 200 HMOs in the country, serving about seven million people, which indicates that movement toward them has certainly not been as fast as HEW had expected.[70] The federal commitment to HMOs has somewhat diminished due to pressure from the AMA, which has traditionally been against the group practice of medicine.[71] A recent report by the Secretary of HEW to the President and Congress did not mention HMOs, which seems to further underscore their lack of support from the federal government.[72]

HMOs' future uncertain

NATIONAL HEALTH INSURANCE

The major, and to many sociologists the most important, response to the status of our nation's health, the growing demands for adequate health care, and the many different inadequacies in the present delivery system is the goal of a national health insurance program.

According to a Louis Harris poll, a majority of Americans favor a comprehensive national health insurance program that is supported by federal taxes. They also want the government, under national health insurance, to control hospital costs, physicians' fees, and other charges.[73]

Majority of Americans favor a national health insurance program

As we have noted earlier, many Americans are protected against many of the financial problems that are associated with ill health by a variety of

Senator Edward Kennedy of Massachusetts is one of the leading proponents of National Health Insurance.

Wide World Photos, Inc.

private and public health insurance programs. The coverage is, however, inadequate for millions. When examined carefully, federal studies indicate "many serious gaps in protection, both in terms of individuals with little or no health insurance coverage and in terms of services which are not covered."[74] It is because many people, some more than others, face the prospects of high financial risk from illness that a national health insurance plan has been under serious consideration by the government. According to the National Center for Health Services Research (NCHSR), the goals of a national health insurance policy include:

NCHSR: Goals of a
national health
insurance

1. assurance of access to medical care for all persons;
2. encouragement of access to early care;
3. control of rapidly rising health care costs;
4. assurance of quality care, and;
5. dispersion of the uneven and unexpected burdens of large expenses for medical care over the entire population so that the burden to each citizen is small.[75]

There is much debate as to which type of national health insurance plan will best meet most of the above goals. Rivlin believes that the argument today is between those forces (the incrementalists) who believe national health insurance objectives can be achieved by "patching up the existing system" and those forces (the big-change advocates) who believe "fee-for-service medicine and mixed public-private financing has to be replaced in its entirety." She states:

Incrementalists vs.
big-change advocates

> The incrementalists see a continuing role for private insurance companies and generally favor keeping both Federal spending and Federal regulation to a minimum. The big-change advocates see no workable substitute for having the Federal Government take over health financing and closely regulate the health-care industry.[76]

There are several basic policy questions that must be addressed in designing a national health insurance plan:

Basic policy questions
on national health
insurance

1. Who should be covered?
2. What types of services should be covered?
3. How much should consumers pay out of pocket for health care?
4. How should health care services be delivered?
5. How should national health insurance be financed?
6. How should providers of health care be reimbursed?
7. What type of administrative structure should be used to operate the program?

The following is a brief summary of some recent studies on national health insurance. The review suggests answers to some of the above policy questions and serves to highlight several of the many problems that are faced by those policymakers designing a program that will attempt to meet the earlier noted goals.[77]

The target population (Who should be covered by health insurance?). —To obtain universal coverage and equal access to health care for all individuals, national health insurance might expand existing programs, redefine eligibility, or establish a new program. Medicaid and Medicare programs limit enrollment now. Medicaid covers only welfare categories, and Medicare is limited to Social Security beneficiaries, railroad retirees, the disabled, and the very poor (others may buy at a substantial cost). The result is that of all poor people, 9.5 million (39 percent) are excluded from Medicaid, and probably several hundred thousand near poor and medically indigent elderly are without Medicare coverage. Thus current health programs do not achieve universal coverage of health care expenses. An estimated 18 million persons did not have any protection against health care expenses in 1978.

Scope of benefits (What should be covered?).—Private health insurance, Medicaid, and Medicare do not cover certain types of services, such as nursing home care, mental health services, optical services, and dental services, or do not cover them adequately. A comprehensive benefit package might be recommended to reduce the overall burden of medical care expenses on the patient and to equalize the burden across income groups.

Cost sharing by consumers (How much should consumers pay out of pocket?).—Cost sharing does deter persons from using physicians' services. However, low-income persons are more likely to cut back on their use of health services when they are faced with copayments, coinsurance, or deductibles than are high-income persons. If equal access to medical care is an objective of national health insurance, cost sharing should be tied to the level of income.

The complexities resulting from a health insurance program with income-related cost sharing might be enormous. Not only might there be higher administrative costs but it might be even harder for individuals to comply with the regulations of such a national health insurance plan than it currently is for them to comply with Medicare. Consumer supplementation of public health insurance might overcome the deterrent effect and undermine the objectives of equal access to medical care. Nevertheless, it can be argued that cost sharing, which is basically private financing of medical care, would allow tax revenues to be spent on other public goods that could not be accomplished through private financing.

Financing (How should national health insurance be financed?).—The most progressive methods for financing health insurance are through income taxes or taxes on payrolls and unearned income. In addition, the medical expense deduction benefits those in higher income tax brackets the most. The most regressive financing methods are premiums and out-of-pocket payments that are not income related. The regressivity of premiums, coinsurance, copayments, and deductibles can be altered by varying them with income. The income transfer of national health insurance may be quite substantial, and should be given explicit consideration by the policymaker.

Reimbursement (How should providers be reimbursed?).—Prospective reimbursement mechanisms have exhibited promise in controlling the rise in hospital costs. However, experience with and evaluation of additional reimbursement methods are needed to achieve more than marginal impact on hospital cost inflation. . . .

Administrative (How should national health insurance be administered?).—Theoretical and empirical literature on the advantages of Federal, State, and private administration of national health insurance is limited. The question still before us is whether there should be a significant Federal role in processing and auditing claims, either similar to the current role under Medicare or enlarged to take over the functions of the fiscal intermediaries [private health insurance companies].[78]

THE KEY TO QUALITY HEALTH CARE

The following article from the Health Policy Advisory Center is critical of liberal approaches to the health care crisis, which advocate governmental intervention as a means of achieving an efficient, equitable health care system. A national health insurance program is viewed as a tool by which the complex of powerful health care institutions in our society will grow in power and wealth. Equality of adequate health care, according to this report, can only be achieved by decentralizing the control of our health care system. This will enable all "who work in and use the system" to "share in establishing its priorities and goals." The Health Policy Advisory Center is a leader in forming a health consumers movement that has at its aim the "creation of community-controlled neighborhood health centers." This approach stresses the idea that "increasing the power of the individual consumer" is the "key to quality health care."[79]

HEALTH PAC READING——OBJECTIVE

1. Examine, by essay, three major reasons why the Health Policy Advisory Center believes that there is a health care "system" in America.

The Health Care Crisis

HEALTH POLICY AND ADVISORY CENTER

The health-care system seems so chaotic, so unplanned, so uncoordinated, that many people call it a nonsystem. To cure the health care crisis, they conclude, we must turn it into a system. Specifically, they argue, some form of national health insurance would provide financially shaky hospitals with a stable income. Doctors should be encouraged to form group practices to increase efficiency—the equivalent of corner grocers banding together to open a supermarket. And hospitals and medical schools should be linked together into regional networks which would be able efficiently and rationally to plan for the medical needs of an entire region. More money, more planning, more coordination—that is the standard prescription for the ailing American health system.

But careful examination of the structure of health care indicates that, in fact, there is a health care system; it is not totally chaotic and unplanned. It seems chaotic only if it is described in terms of private doctors. Years ago, the doctors did dominate and control health care; but now health care is dominated by institutions—hospitals, medical schools, research laboratories, drug companies, health insurance companies, health planning agencies, and many others. Many people don't even have a private doctor any more; the hospital clinic and emergency room have become their doctor. Less than 20 percent of the nation's health expenditures now go for private doctors; most of the rest goes to institutions. And, more than nine out of ten health workers these days are not doctors at all, but workers employed by health care institutions—nurses, dieticians, X-ray technicians, orderlies, laboratory technicians, etc. The health institutions are big and growing rapidly and as they grow they are becoming more and more interconnected to form a system.

There are three major components to the existing American health-care system: medical empires, the financing-planning complex and the health-care profiteers, especially the medical-industrial complex.

There is a health care system

MEDICAL EMPIRES

Medical empires are the primary units. They are privately controlled medical complexes, usually but not always organized with a medical school at the hub. From these centers, radiating out like spokes on a wheel, are a network of affiliations to smaller private hospitals, city hospitals, state mental hospitals, neighborhood health centers and subspecialty programs such as alcoholism, rehabilitation or prison health. To each of these affiliated programs, the medical center provides professional personnel in return for health rake-offs of the affiliated programs' resources. In fact, the benefits of such arrangements are often so highly weighted in favor of the medical center that *exploitation* is the only fair description of the relationship—thus the term "empires." These networks of medical centers with their far-reaching affiliations resemble a mother country's relationship to its colonies. This resemblance has been exacerbated by the fact

Reprinted by permission from *Prognosis Negative: Crisis in the Health Care System.* New York: Vantage, 1976.

that many of the affiliation relationships are with hospitals, neighborhood centers and special programs in poor communities, most often populated by blacks, Puerto Ricans, Chicanos, Asians or Appalachians.

Empires have their own priorities

The empires have their own priorities. Some of these are related to expansion and profit-making, others are related to research and teaching, and still others are concerned with control—influencing policy both locally and nationally. How much any of these priorities relate to patient care is the critical question. The answer is complicated and in many instances not yet fully understood. On balance, however, these priorities are the basis for the exploitative relationship between the medical center and its affiliates.

For example, take Einstein College of Medicine (a medical school) and Montefiore Hospital and Medical Center (a close ally). Together they have come to control most of the medical resources in the Bronx, an entire borough of New York City. Through affiliation contracts, Einstein/Montefiore monopolizes care at three out of the four city hospitals in the Bronx, the only state mental hospital in the borough, several neighborhood health centers, prison health services, several private voluntary hospitals and numerous nursing homes. Of the 6,670 beds in general care hospitals in the Bronx, 4,500 are controlled by Einstein/Montefiore; most doctors practicing in the Bronx are affiliated with Einstein/Montefiore.

What has this arrangement meant for patients? Perhaps—and this has not been proven—the technical-scientific management of hospitalized patients has improved. But the price for this questionable improvement—questionable both in terms of money and in terms of distorted priorities—is enormous:

> In sheer dollars, the affiliation of the city hospitals to Einstein/Montefiore has increased the money coming into those hospitals by over $37 million a year.

> In the outpatient departments of the affiliated hospitals, sub-specialty clinics have proliferated—in some cases to more than 100 in number. Patients have found their care fragmented, with no single doctor taking responsibility. On the one hand, the patient has no one to see for a common cold; on the other hand, when he or she has a more complicated illness, it takes a visit to three or four separate clinics before a diagnosis can be made, and even then a different doctor may supervise the patient's treatment each visit.

> In the inpatient services (i.e., hospitalized patients), all of the hospitals were converted through affiliations into teaching institutions. Patients frequently find themselves subjected to unnecessary and occasionally dangerous procedures. Liver biopsies (removal of tissue from the liver), for example, are performed primarily to teach interns how to do the procedure; Caesarean sections and hysterectomies are performed when their medical necessity is questionable at best, so that the residents can gain more experience in performing these operations.

> In research, the affiliations have brought more academic interest to the affiliated hospitals, but not necessarily more patient-oriented controls. In one such hospital, patients admitted for a routine tubal ligation (sterilization) were given medication prior to the operation and then had their ovaries

biopsied to determine the effect of the medication on the ovaries. The patients were not asked for their informed consent. Moreover, it turned out that no research proposal had been submitted, as required, to the hospital's research committee.

Besides elevating the medical center's priorities without regard for patient's priorities, medical empires tend to institutionalize the unequal relationship between the mother-medical center and the colony-affiliated hospital. This is done in overt ways, with the medical center extracting natural resources from the affiliated hospital. Patients with interesting or rare diseases are taken from the affiliated hospital and brought to the medical center, while patients with mundane medical problems are "dumped" by the medical center onto its affiliates. Likewise, talented medical teachers and researchers located in the affiliated hospitals are asked to spend unpaid teaching time at the medical center. This means that their talents are utilized by the medical center while their salary continues to be paid out of the affiliated hospital's budget. When the affiliated hospital, on the other hand, wants the expertise of a researcher at the medical center, it has to pay handsomely for a lecture or consultation.

In addition to such overt discrimination, there are more subtle ways in which inequalities within a medical empire are institutionalized. Patients being referred from the affiliated hospital to the medical center for some specialized procedure, such as cardiac catheterization or cobalt therapy, may end up on waiting lists for months. The scheduling priorities are explicit: Private patients come first, clinic patients from the medical center come second and the affiliated hospital's patients come third. Another example is the fact that pension programs and other fringe benefits for the professional personnel on the medical center's staff are significantly more generous than those for the affiliated hospital's staff. The list could go on and on.

Inequalities are institutionalized

Some people may minimize the importance of medical empires. "It hasn't happened here," they will say, "The county medical society is still the strongest force in town." While such an observation may be accurate in many rural and some suburban communities, the nationwide trend is very clear: In Cleveland, Case Western Reserve Medical School controls many of the medical resources. In Baltimore, it's Johns Hopkins Medical School; in Seattle, it's the University of Washington; in North Carolina, it's Duke University and the University of North Carolina. And everywhere the results are the same: The structure of health care is organized around the institutional priorities of the medical center and not the health-care needs of the patient. And that disparity of priorities is most accentuated when the individual is not an affluent private patient at the medical center but a poor or uninsured ward or clinic patient at one of its affiliated institutions.

THE FINANCING-PLANNING COMPLEX

The second main part of the health care system is the financing-planning complex. The most important part of this complex is the multibillion dollar Blue Cross operation, whose insurance plans cover 80 million people, four of every 10 Americans. Through the publicly funded Medicare and Medicaid programs,

Blue Cross

Blue Cross administers insurance benefits for an additional 32 million people. Altogether, Blue Cross disburses about half of all hospital revenues.

Because it is by far the nation's largest single health insurer, Blue Cross also plays a very important role in setting health policy: Its leaders sit on governmental advisory committees, advise congressional committees, and, together with representatives of the big private hospitals, set up and run area-wide comprehensive health planning agencies.

Blue Cross is closely allied with the big hospitals. It was set up during the Depression by financially starved hospitals to provide them a guaranteed income, and it continues to be dominated by the major hospitals. Nearly half of the members of the boards of directors of local Blue Cross plans (Blue Cross operates in 74 localities) are hospital representatives. Needless to say, hospitals and health consumers often have very different interests. Consumers want high-quality, low-cost, relevant health care; hospitals, on the other hand, are often more interested in institutional expansion and the prestige gained through the acquisition of well-known researchers, fancy medical equipment and new and larger buildings. This is why the hospital-dominated Blue Cross has consistently failed to support consumer concerns such as cost and quality control.

THE HEALTH-CARE PROFITEERS

The medical-industrial complex has always made an enormous profit

The third part of the health system are the health-care profiteers, especially the medical-industrial complex. An alliance exists between the providers of health care (doctors, hospitals, medical schools and the like) and the companies that make money from people's sickness (drug companies, hospital supply companies, hospital construction companies, commercial insurance companies, and even companies that provide medical services for profit—profit-making proprietary hospitals, chains of nursing homes for old people, laboratories, etc.). Health care is one of the biggest businesses around, and one of the fastest-growing.

The magnitude of the medical-industrial complex is hard to believe. For example, in 1969 drug companies (Abbott, Upjohn, Merck, etc.) had after-tax profits of about $600 million. The drug industry rated first, second, or third in profitability among all U.S. industries during the 1960's, causing Forbes Magazine, a financial journal, to call it "one of the biggest crap games in U.S. Industry."

Hospital supply companies (Becton-Dickinson, American Hospital Supply, etc.), which sell hospitals and doctors everything from sheets and towels and bedpans to surgical instruments, X-ray machines and heart-lung machines, had after-tax profits of $400 million in 1969. Proprietary (profit-making) hospitals and nursing homes earned nearly $200 million. (There are even nationwide chains of hospitals and nursing homes run by such businesses as Holiday Inns.)

The commercial insurance companies and the construction firms which build hospitals make additional millions, and, of course, the doctors themselves are still the highest paid people around. Even the banks are getting in on the act, with loans to hospitals both for building and for operating expenses. The patient at one of New York's prestigious hospitals, for example, finds that $3 a day of his hospital bill doesn't go for services at all; it goes to the banks for interest payments.

THE SYSTEM IN HEALTH

And not only do all of these empires, insurance people, financiers, businessmen and doctors make a lot of money from people's bad health, they do it with togetherness. Their mutual needs coincide: Prestigious medical empires require the manufacture of expensive equipment and the presence of large construction companies; and, of course, only large institutions can afford the expensive products of the medical equipment and drug manufacturers. And all of these groups require the stable, lenient financing of Blue Cross, Medicare and Medicaid and other medical insurers. Their growing interdependence is evident. Increasingly drug and medical equipment executives, banking and real estate/construction company executives sit on boards of trustees at academic medical centers. Meanwhile, hospital and medical school professionals moonlight as consultants to drug and hospital supply companies and sometimes sit on their boards of trustees.

The best thing about the health business is that the profits are sure (as long as you're not a patient or taxpayer, that is). Blue Cross, Medicare and Medicaid hand the doctors and hospitals a virtual blank check. The hospital, in effect, simply tells Blue Cross how much its expenses are, and Blue Cross pays the bill. In the boom years of the 1960's there was no cost control to speak of. The inflation in health-care costs that resulted has led to some belt-tightening more recently. But the accepted definition of a necessary health-care cost remains very generous.

In the health business profits are sure

Some costs of course may be necessary for better patient care. But they also may be "necessary" for the purchase of seldom-used and expensive equipment that is available in another hospital across the street; for plush offices and high salaries for doctors and hospital administrators; for expenses incurred in fighting off attempts by unions to organize hospital workers; or for hiring public relations firms to clean up the hospital's poor image in the community. The health industry and the doctors get rich; the consumer and the taxpayer pay the bill.

Even the so-called nonprofit hospitals get in on the fun. All that "nonprofit" means is that such hospitals don't have to pay out their excess income to stockholders. They also don't have to pay it back to their patients in the form of cheaper rates. Instead, they use it to grow; to buy more fancy (even if unnecessary) equipment, more plush offices, more public relations; to pay staff doctors even higher salaries; to buy up real estate, tear down poor people's housing, and build new pavilions for private patients.

There is, then, a health care *system*. Its components are, in addition to the doctors, the vast network of health care resources that make up the medical empires; the financing and planning complex of agencies dominated by Blue Cross; and the medical-industrial complex. But if American health care is provided by such a big, well-organized, interconnected, business-like system, why is it so poor? The answer is that *health care is not the aim of the health-care system.* The health-care system exists to serve its own ends. The aims of big medical centers are teaching and research. The hospitals and medical schools seek to expand their real estate and financial holdings. And everyone, from hospitals and doctors to drug companies and insurance companies, wants to make profits. Health care for patients is a means to these ends, but is not the sole end in

The health care system exists to serve its own ends

itself. And so the patient sees a system which is expensive, which is fragmented into dozens of specialties, which has no time to treat him in a dignified way, and which doesn't even take care of him very well.

1. Adapted and updated (1976) from "Your Health Care in Crisis," a Health/PAC special report. Reprinted in *Prognosis Negative: Crisis in the Health Care System*, David Kotckhuck (ed.), Vantage, 1976.

DEFINING THE PROBLEM OF MENTAL ILLNESS

In the United States today, mental health care of high quality and reasonable cost should be readily available to all who need it. This is not the case.

We are impressed with the progress that has been made in this direction. We are equally impressed by what has not occurred. The mental health services system which currently exists is still in a state of evolution. It combines public and private personnel, facilities, and financing without clearly established lines of responsibility or accountability.

For some Americans this system presents few problems. They are able to obtain the care they need.

For too many Americans this does not occur. Despite improvements in the system, there are millions who remain unserved, underserved, or inappropriately served.

—Because of where they live or because of financial barriers, far too many Americans have no access to mental health care.

—Because the services available to them are limited or not sufficiently responsive to their individual circumstances, far too many Americans do not receive the kind of care they need.

—Because of their age, sex, race, cultural background, or the nature of their disability, far too many Americans do not have access to personnel trained to respond to their special needs.

The President's Commission
on Mental Health, 1978

MENTAL HEALTH AND MENTAL ILLNESS

In the second part of this chapter we will examine the social problem of mental illness. Mental illness and the poor quality of mental health care are of great concern to many Americans. The way in which our society has responded to those individuals who have been termed mentally ill has often been—at best—unenlightened. Most of the time, however, society has responded with ignorance and brutality. We will begin our examination of mental illness and mental health care by first defining "mental health" and "mental illness."

There are many definitions of mental health because there is no agreement as to what constitutes good mental health. With the understanding that the borderline between mental health and mental illness is, at times, hazy, we can define mental health with the criteria of a mentally healthy personality developed by A. H. Maslow and B. Mittlemann. According to them, the mentally healthy personality exhibits the following qualities, although not all may be equally present, all the time, in all mentally healthy persons. They are:

The mentally healthy person

> an adequate feeling of security and realistic self-evaluation; attainable life goals based on realistic self-evaluation and adequate contact with the everyday world of reality; self consistency and the ability to profit from experience; a judicious degree of spontaneity and emotionally appropriate to the occasion; a judicious balance between in-group cooperativeness and maintenance of individuality; and appropriate physical desires gratified in appropriate ways.[80]

Mental illness has been defined as a "disease," or as a "way of behaving." It is an imprecise concept that is difficult to define and that has led to much controversy in the field of mental health. It is important to have a clear understanding of how the concept is defined because the way we respond to the problems of mental health depends upon the way it is defined. For example, if mental illness is defined as a disease, the mode of treatment would more than likely include drug therapy and perhaps even electroshock therapy or surgery. If it is defined in terms of sociostructural factors, then the response would include social and organizational changes. And if it is psychologically defined as deviance, the response may include psychotherapy. Let us examine some of the major definitions of mental illness.

Response to mental illness related to how it is defined

MEDICAL MODEL: MENTAL ILLNESS AS DISEASE

The most prevalent view of mental illness today is the medical model, which views mental illness as a disease that necessitates treatment as such. Just as a physical disease is a disturbance of a person's physical system, mental disorder is a disturbance of the person's psychological and personality system. The aim of the medical model of mental illness is to treat the "diseased" mind as one would treat any other part of the body, so it will return to its prior healthy state. Removal of or relief from those tensions, anxieties, and maladjustments that underlie the mental disorders and abnormal behavior will enable the mentally ill person to again function in society. According to this definition, mental illness is not a lack of interpersonal coping skills or a "label," as other definitions suggest, but is real, with emotional and physical causes as well as effects.

The medical model of mental illness has developed a classification system in which different types of mental disorders and illnesses are defined. This enables the medical practitioner to diagnose the symptom and begin treatment of the patient. This classification system, however, is not completely satisfactory. As we shall see later, many social scientists do not accept these categories as valid. Also, many health professionals themselves do not always agree on the diagnosis of a patient's mental disorder. According to the medical model, the major categories of mental illness or disorders are *neuroses* and *psychoses*. It should be noted that, when using the medical model, diagnosis of cases is not always precise. Each disorder category denotes only general descriptive characteristics, and professional diagnosis of specific cases may therefore reveal some inconsistency. It may also happen that specific persons manifest a variety of symptoms of more than one form of disorder.[81]

Neuroses. Neuroses are the less serious, more common forms of mental illness, which include excessive expressions of anxiety, unsuccessful or inadequate attempts to cope with fearful situations, or prolonged tension. Included in neurosis is behavior that can be seen in normal people but is "manifested in neurotics with greater frequency, intensity, or duration."[82] The types of neuroses are: *anxiety neurosis, obsessive-compulsive neurosis,* and *hysteria.*

Anxiety neurotics are generally fearful, worried, and tense. They have difficulty performing normal, daily functions and find it difficult to interact with others because of high degrees of anxiety. Sometimes the fears may be specific and unrealistic, as in *phobias* (fear of crowds, closed or high places, animals, or the dark). Obsessive-compulsive neurosis consists of obsessive thoughts and compulsion. According to Silverman, a psychologist, "an obsessive reaction is a persistent, habitual, involuntary thought that dominates the individual's thoughts."[83] The person is then blocked from productive behavior. A compulsion is an irrational act that results from obsessive thoughts, such as when an individual's inability to control thinking about germs manifests itself in excessive bathing. Hysteria

Aim of medical model: To treat a "diseased mind"

Medical model major categories: Neuroses and psychoses

Neuroses: Less serious forms of mental illness

Three neuroses: Anxiety, obsessive-compulsive, and hysteria

neurotics have symptoms that involve extreme forgetfulness, temporary paralysis, or inability to hear or see.[84]

Neuroses, then, are considered to be less serious forms of mental illness. Neurotic behavior involves low degrees of impaired functioning. Unlike the psychotic person, who is not oriented to social reality, the neurotic does not break from reality, but continues trying to fuction in the real world. Because neuroses are less impairing and distressful than psychoses, hospitalization is usually not necessary.

Psychoses. Psychoses are mental disorders that are more serious than neuroses because there is severe impairment of mental functioning and a break with reality. The distortion of reality is so extreme that people who are psychotic are unable to adequately function in society. Some psychoses have physical causes. They are termed *organic psychoses* and are caused by brain tumors, drug and alcohol intoxication, syphilis, metabolic disorders, senility, and brain injury. Unlike organic psychoses, *functional psychoses* do not have a physical basis, but seem to be caused by the individual's life situation and experiences and have a psychological basis.

Psychoses: More serious types of mental illness

Organic and functional psychoses

Before examining some of the major types of psychoses, it is important to note that neurotic people can also be incapacitated to the point where they are unable to function in the social environment. But neurotics are generally interested in, and try to cope with the environment, whereas psychotics do not in the same way seek to adjust to the society. Rather, as Silverman states, they adjust the world to themselves. In doing this, the psychotic "creates a personal world markedly different from the world that most of us agree upon. For this reason, we say that the psychotic has lost touch with reality."[85]

According to the medical model, *schizophrenia* is the most commonly diagnosed psychosis. It is estimated that at least 200,000 Americans are currently hospitalized with this disorder.[86] The following symptoms of this psychosis are not seen in all schizophrenics and are rarely observed in a single person. However, they do constitute "the entity known as schizophrenia," and are "hallucinations, delusions, disturbances of language and thought, gross inefficiency, and isolation from others."[87]

Schizophrenia

There are four types of traditional schizophrenic classifications. In *simple* schizophrenia, the person withdraws from reality and is passive and apathetic. A *hebephrenic* schizophrenic appears childish, foolish, and has bizarre thoughts and feelings; hallucinations are also common. In *catatonic* schizophrenia, the person's responses are characterized by attitude and behavior changes ranging from aggressive behavior to periods of muscular rigidity (the catatonic stupor). *Paranoid* schizophrenics are hostile and very suspicious of others; thinking is often disorganized, and illogical delusions predominate.[88]

Traditional classifications

Some social scientists have found these traditional classifications to be unsatisfactory* and have classified schizophrenia as being one of two types.[89] How a person is categorized depends upon what has happened in the personality adjustment before the diagnosis. Silverman states:

Process and reactive schizophrenia

> Process schizophrenia occurs in individuals whose personalities have undergone a progressive process of increasing severe maladaptive behavior. If the schizophrenic deterioration has been gradual the prognosis (prediction for recovery) is very poor. . . . reactive schizophrenia occurs in individuals whose schizophrenic behavior is triggered by a traumatic experience or by adolescence, but whose earlier personality and level of adjustment could be termed adequate. Thus, the reactive schizophrenic is one who suffers a sudden personality collapse.[90]

Manic depressive psychosis

Manic depressive psychosis is an affective disorder (it involves severe changes in mood) and the classic symptom is rapid mood swings, from excitement and elation to severe depression. At times, patients will exhibit either the manic symptoms or depressive reactions. Others will exhibit both stages or moods on a cyclical basis that varies in regularity and length. In the manic stage, people believe they have "got it made," and that there is no limit to what they can do. There is euphoria, elation, and much hyperactivity. People who are in this stage are difficult to deal with in that they are overactive, impulsive, extremely talkative, have a short attention span, and engage in unrealistic behavior. In the depressed stage, they experience much pessimism, melancholy, and self-depreciation. With strong feelings of despair and hopelessness, they may be driven to attempt suicide. This risk of suicide is one of the "most serious problems, for the depression will usually lift eventually, but the danger of self-harm warrants extreme caution while the depression lasts."[91]

SOCIAL MODEL: MENTAL ILLNESS AS MYTH AND DEVIANCE
The dominant view of mental illness is the medical model, which, as we have seen, uses a broad-based, general classification of mental illness. However, Thomas Szasz and Thomas Scheff have stated that psychiatrists do not agree on the symptoms and diagnosis of mental illness, which makes the medical model and its use of general classifications suspect. Unlike the medical model, which views symptoms as something to be diagnosed and

---

* First, since the symptoms of schizophrenia can be symptomatic of more than one classification, we cannot be certain that identification of symptoms will enable us to diagnose the disorder. Second, the traditional classes do not take into account that many patients undergo symptomatic alterations during the course of their illness.

classified, social models tend to view symptoms as "difficulties of living" with one's self and others, or as interpersonal behavior problems.

Szasz, a psychiatrist, believes that mental disorders are "problems in living" and are to be understood by examining the social conditions within which they have been created. Mental disorders are not physical diseases. For Szasz, mental disorders are viewed as deviations from social and legal norms, or as deviations from particular institutionalized social expectations. He believes that mental illness is a myth. It is not that the psychological problems labeled as mental illness do not exist, but that it is misleading to term them "illnesses." They should instead be considered as manifestations of unresolved living problems.[92]

Szasz: The myth of mental illness is deviation from norms and social expectations

Scheff defines mental illness as a type of learned behavior and as a result of labeling. When people violate socially and culturally defined conventions that are considered to be natural—a part of human nature—they are labeled as mentally ill. What causes certain behavior to become a mental disorder is that the society labels it as such. This idea implies that what is defined as mental illness will vary from one society to another.[93]

Scheff: Mental illness is learned behavior and a result of labeling

In social and psychological theory, it has become increasingly common to see mental disorder as representing certain varieties of social deviance. In terms of this social model, mental disorder involves deviation from the expectations of others. Mental disorder as deviance from norms focuses attention on the social definitions and on the degree of social tolerance accorded to certain types of nonconforming behaviors. Thus, behaviors felt to indicate mental disorder at one time or in one society may not be seen as reflective of mental disorder in another time or society. According to Thomas Scheff, mental disorders as deviance simply represent a form of "residual rule breaking." Each society sets up certain rules and typically applies various labels to people who violate certain social conventions. Thus we have the terms "drunkard," "thief," and "prostitute." The forms of deviance or norm violations left over ("residual"), for which a group has no specific labels, simply become packaged under the broad category of "mental disorder." Types of nonconformity labeled mental disorder often include excessive aggressiveness, types of speech felt to be incoherent or nonrational, withdrawal from interpersonal relations, compulsive actions, delusions, phobias, states of depression, and often simply a general awkwardness in interpersonal relations with others.[94]

Mental disorder: Deviation from expectations of others

There are other definitions of mental illness besides the medical and social models. Functional definitions, for example, stress that mental illness should be defined in terms of a person's ability to function in the community, at work, and at home. A person who can function well in society is mentally healthy; a person who does not function well is mentally ill. Statistical definitions of mental illness stress the point that any person who is different from the great majority is abnormal.

Other definitions of mental illness

MENTAL ILLNESS: PREVALENCE, COSTS, AND SOCIAL FACTORS

Mental illness: A major social problem

From the standpoint of prevalence and treatment, current statistics substantiate the fact that mental illness is a major social problem in America today. The 1978 President's Commission on Mental Health estimates that 15 percent of the population at any one time needs some type of mental health care.[95] Other estimates of the total number of Americans manifesting some type of mental illness are also high. According to federal data, there were over 6.7 million patient care episodes* in mental health facilities in 1975.[96] These figures exclude private psychiatric office practice and many other psychiatric service modes of all types.[97] Estimates of people receiving treatment from private psychiatrists range from 750,000 to 1,200,000 each year.[98]

Probably impossible to know the extent of mental illness

These figures are an inadequate index of mental illness in the United States today. In fact, it is probably impossible to know the actual extent of mental disorders in our society. Even if we were able to accurately determine how many Americans are being treated for mental disorders by their clergymen, physicians who are not psychiatrists, marriage counselors, mental health professionals, and others, the total would exclude many Americans who are mentally ill.

High costs of mental illness

Insofar as the costs of mental illness are concerned, the direct costs of mental illness were estimated at $1.7 billion per year in the later 1950s. In 1976 the cost of providing mental health services was about $17 billion, or about 12 percent of all health costs.[99]

* "Patient care episodes" is defined as the "number of residents in inpatient facilities or the number of persons on the rolls of outpatient facilities, plus the total additions to both types of facilities during the year."

The high cost of private, individualized psychiatric help has led to the growth of "crisis centers" and self-help "hot lines."

Since the statistics on mental illness provide only a rough estimate on its incidence and prevalence,* research on the relationship between incidence and prevalence of mental disorders and various social factors is a difficult process. Nevertheless, social scientists have noted a variety of relationships between social conditions and mental illness.

Mental illness: Social factors

For example, with repect to the relationship between social class and the incidence and prevalence of mental illness, studies by Faris and Dunham in Chicago, and Hollingshead and Redlich in New Haven, have found that the lower the socioeconomic class, the greater the likelihood of serious mental disorders. Hollingshead and Redlich developed a socioeconomic scale ranging from the highest class (I) to the lowest (V), which revealed that the prevalence and incidence of psychosis was significantly greater in class V. Other studies by Brill and Storrow, Hass, Albronda, Myers, and Rushing and Srole have supported these findings, and some revealed relationships between social class and the treatment of mental illness. It appears that the lower an individual's socioeconomic status, the more restricted the range of available therapies.[100]

Social class and mental illness

Other social factors related to rates and to treatment of mental illness are: a) *occupational status*—those in lower occupational categories have higher rates of first admissions to mental hospitals; b) *sex*—men have a slightly higher hospitalization rate and are generally more frequently treated for mental disorders than women; c) *race*—rates of mental illness are higher for blacks and Puerto Ricans. It should be noted that women have a higher rate of depressive disorders than men and there are higher rates of mental illness among married women then married men. Gove views the "role of married women" as related to mental illness and attributes this relationship to the: (1) low unstable status associated with the "wife's role" and its unencouraging and nonsupportive nature; (2) problems of combining "wife" and "career" roles; and (3) the fact that women's role expectations are diffused and ill defined—they have to be "everything to everybody."[101] Phyllis Chester has challenged findings on male-female admission rates to mental hospitals and believes that the rates for females are higher and reflect the restricted roles and secondary status of women in society.[102]

Other social factors related to mental illness

THE SOCIAL PROBLEM OF MENTAL ILLNESS

A variety of other social factors and conditions are related to the nature, incidence, prevalence, treatment, and care of the mentally ill in America. In the following reading many of these dimensions are examined. In this reading, the findings and assessment of the President's 1978 Commission

* Incidence is the proportion of new cases within a population in a given time frame. Prevalence is the number of cases at a particular point in time.

on Mental Health are examined. The report notes the progress and the problems of inadequate mental health care in America and examines the difficulties in defining our society's mental health problems.

PRESIDENT'S COMMISSION READING——OBJECTIVE

1. List eight major points made in the "Findings and Assessment" section of the President's 1978 Commission on Mental Health.

Findings and Assessment

Within the past quarter of a century a number of significant developments have shaped America's response to the needs of those with mental and emotional problems.

—Basic research in America and abroad following World War II contributed to the development of more effective psychoactive drugs and forms of psychotherapy, each of which made possible the release of thousands of patients from large mental institutions.

—The final report of the Joint Commission on Mental Illness and Health, published in 1961, placed strong emphasis on community-based services by calling for a reduction in size and, where appropriate, the closing of large State hospitals; the development of mental health services in local communities; and the upgrading of quality of care in remaining smaller State hospitals so that patients could be returned as quickly as possible to their communities.

—The Mental Retardation Facilities and Community Mental Health Centers Construction Act of 1963, plus subsequent amendments, provided the programmatic vehicle for establishing a network of publicly funded community mental health centers throughout the country.

Federal involvement

—Major investments by the Federal Government in training mental health professionals and a dramatic rise in the number and types of mental health personnel, including paraprofessionals, have resulted in a marked increase in mental health care providers in both the public and private sectors.

—Federal initiatives in health care financing programs, such as Medicare and Medicaid, and an expansion of benefits in social service programs have in some States enabled a larger number of people with mental disabilities to live in their own communities instead of State hospitals.

—A Joint Commission on the Mental Health of Children was established in 1965 to address the problems of inadequate mental health services for children and adolescents. Even though many of its recommendations were not acted upon, some resulted in additional services for children and adolescents.

—The civil rights and consumer movements have been the impetus for legislative and court activities which have accelerated the release of patients from large mental institutions.

—Reforms of State laws have led to changes in commitment procedures, and court decisions emphasizing patients' rights have set minimum standards for patient care in institutions.

Report to the President from the President's Commission on Mental Health, 1978.

Before these developments occurred, large, generally isolated, State mental hospitals were the mainstay of America's publicly funded mental health services system; approximately 75 percent of all the people who received care were residents of the institutions in which they received that care. Now three of every four persons receiving formal mental health care are outpatients in public and private settings. More inpatient care in public and private facilities is also available in local communities. While the number of people in State hospitals has declined from more than 550,000 in 1955 to less than 200,000 in 1975, State hospitals continue to provide a major portion of long-term care for those with chronic mental illness.

More outpatient care

An increase in the numbers and types of mental health personnel and in the range of services they provide has accompanied this shift in the location of mental health services.

The supply of psychiatrists, psychologists, psychiatric social workers, and psychiatric nurses has more than doubled. They have found employment not only in hospitals, clinics, and other mental health facilities, public and private, but also in such diverse settings as courts, correctional institutions, and schools.

Many other categories of professional and paraprofessional mental health workers now are involved in providing care. These include marriage, sex, and family therapists; counseling and guidance personnel; recreational, art, music, drama, dance, and vocational therapists; and alcoholism and drug abuse counselors. Paraprofessionals comprise almost half the patient care staff of mental health facilities.

Many people provide care

Beyond this, many people whose work is not primarily in the mental health area, such as primary care physicians, clergy, teachers, and public health nurses, are actively engaged in helping people with mental and emotional difficulties.

The dollars devoted to providing mental health services have also increased markedly. In the late 1950's the direct cost of mental illness was estimated to be $1.7 billion a year. By 1976 the direct costs of providing mental health services was about $17 billion, approximately 12 percent of all health costs. Over 50 percent of these expenditures were for services provided in nursing homes and public mental hospitals.

THE UNDERSERVED

Despite progress, many persons who should have benefited from these changes still receive inadequate care. This is especially true of people with chronic mental illness, of children, adolescents, and older Americans.

Many still receive inadequate care

Racial and ethnic minorities, the urban poor, and migrant and seasonal farmworkers continue to be underserved.

In rural America there are few facilities and few people trained to provide mental health care.

Changes in public attitudes have led to an awareness of the lack of appropriate services for many women and for such groups as Vietnam veterans, the deaf, and others with physical handicaps.

By concentrating on the difficulties these Americans experience in obtaining care, we can see more clearly the fundamental problems in planning, organizing, delivering, and financing mental health services throughout the mental health system.

The plight of the chronically mentally ill illustrates the difficulties that exist in developing comprehensive service systems in local communities. There are people who have severe mental disabilities which often persist throughout their lives. Some require a sheltered environment, some need a variety of services, and some need only periodic assistance. There are still other chronically disabled individuals who achieve a high level of independent functioning. As a group they are the individuals who are, have been, or in earlier times might have been residents of State mental hospitals and who were intended to benefit most from the shift to community-based care.

A basic premise of the movement toward community-based services was that care would be provided in halfway houses, family and group homes, private hospitals and offices, residential centers, foster care settings, and community mental health centers. Social and human services were to have been integrated with more formal mental health care, resulting in a complete range of services.

Inadequate community care

In the few communities that had this broad range of services, many patients made effective transitions from State hospitals to the community. The majority of communities, however, did not have the necessary services, were not given proper assistance to develop them, or enough time to prepare to receive returning patients.

Time and again we have learned—from testimony, from inquiries, and from the reports of special task panels—of people with chronic mental disabilities who have been released from hospitals but who do not have the basic necessities of life. They lack adequate food, clothing, or shelter. We have heard of woefully inadequate follow-up mental health and general medical care. And we have seen evidence that half the people released from large mental hospitals are being readmitted within a year of discharge. While not every individual can be treated within the community, many of the readmissions to State hospitals could have been avoided if comprehensive assistance had existed within their communities.

Because sufficient services and appropriate financial assistance are not available, many people with chronic mental illness have no choice but to live in poorly maintained boarding homes or cheap occupancy hotels and rooming houses. Because public and private health insurance programs provide insufficient outpatient benefits, many, both young and old, who could be cared for in community settings end up in nursing homes, which often are not equipped to serve patients with mental health needs.

These needs cannot be met unless we make basic changes in public policies and programs, particularly in how we plan, coordinate, and finance mental health care. There must be a much clearer delineation of responsibility and accountability for the care delivered to this population.

It makes little sense to speak about American society as pluralistic and culturally diverse, or to urge the development of mental health services that respect and respond to that diversity, unless we focus attention on the special status of the groups which account for the diversity, whether defined in terms of race, ethnicity, sex, age, or disability.

According to the 1975 Special Census, the population of America includes 22 million Black Americans and 12 million Hispanic Americans. There are 3 million Asian and Pacific Island Americans and 1 million American Indians and Alaska Natives. Appropriate services are not available to many of them, even though social, economic, and environmental factors render them particularly vulnerable to acute and prolonged psychological and emotional distress.

Too often, services which are available are not in accord with their cultural and linguistic traditions. The number of Asian and Pacific Island Americans utilizing mental health services increases dramatically when services take into account their cultural traditions and patterns. Language barriers prevent many Hispanic Americans from seeking care, and when they do seek it the absence of bilingual personnel can reduce the effectiveness of treatment. Government funded or operated programs often ignore existing cultural, social, and community supports in the American Indian community.

A frequent and vigorous complaint of minority people who need care is that they often feel abused, intimidated, and harassed by non-minority personnel. Like everyone else, minorities feel more comfortable and secure when care is provided by practitioners who come from similar backgrounds. Yet fewer than 2 percent of all psychiatrists in America are Black. The percentage of Hispanic American psychiatrists is even lower, and there are only 13 psychiatrists in the country who are American Indian. A recent survey by the American Psychological Association estimates that of all the doctoral-level health services providers in psychology, 0.9 percent are Black, 0.7 percent are Asian, 0.4 percent are Hispanic, and 0.1 percent are American Indian.

The special needs of minorities

Seasonal and migrant farmworkers and their families, many of whom belong to racial minorities, represent a population of approximately five million which has been almost completely excluded from mental health care. The constant mobility as they move from place to place in search of work frequently prevents them from obtaining any care, let alone continuity of care.

The common bond among these racial and ethnic minority groups is that all encompass people whose basic mental health needs have not been sufficiently understood by those involved in the planning and delivery of mental health services.

Just as there are special mental health needs that relate to cultural and racial diversity, there are special needs that relate to age.

Our laws and public policies affirm the principle that every American child should have the opportunity to realize his or her full potential. Appropriate mental health care can be essential for the realization of this potential.

As the Commission traveled throughout America, we saw and heard about too many children and adolescents who suffered from neglect, indifference, and abuse, and for whom appropriate mental health care was inadequate or nonexistent. Too many American children grow to adulthood with mental disabilities which could have been addressed more effectively earlier in their lives through appropriate prenatal, infant, and early child development care programs.

Troubled children and adolescents, particularly if they are from racial minorities, are too often placed in foster homes, special schools, mental and correctional institutions without adequate prior evaluation or subsequent follow-up. Good residential facilities specializing in the treatment of special problems are in short supply.

Children's needs

During the past two decades, many adolescents have struggled to adapt to rapid social changes and conflicting, often ambiguous, social values. There has been a dramatic increase in the use and misuse of psychoactive drugs, including alcohol, among young people and nearly a three-fold increase in the suicide rate of adolescents.

Services that reflect the unique needs of children and adolescents are frequently unavailable. Our existing mental health services system contains too few mental health professionals and other personnel trained to meet the special needs of children and adolescents. Even when identified, children's needs are too often isolated into distinct categories, each to be addressed separately by a different specialist. Shuttling children from service to service, each with its own label, adds to their confusion, increases their despair, and sets the pattern for adult disability.

At the other end of the age spectrum, the 23 million Americans over the age of sixty-five—one-third of whom are below the official poverty line—constitute another large segment of the population underserved by our current mental health care system.

The elderly's needs

The prevalence of mental illness and emotional distress is higher among those over age sixty-five than in the general population. Up to 25 percent of older persons have been estimated to have significant mental health problems. Yet only 4 percent of patients seen in public outpatient mental health clinics and 2 percent of those seen in private psychiatric care are elderly.

Part of the problem is attitudinal. Too often the elderly are told, and many believe, that adverse psychological symptoms are natural aspects of growing old. Senility is a term loosely applied to thousands of older Americans, yet as many as 20 to 30 percent of those so labeled have specific conditions that can be diagnosed, treated, and often reversed.

The elderly are subjected to multiple psychological stresses brought about by such things as social isolation, grief over loss of loved ones, and fears of illness and death. Yet there are almost no outreach efforts or in-home services in existing mental health programs to bring them into contact with the kinds of services they need. The personnel who are available to help them are often inadequately trained to address their special concerns. Instead, we confine our older citizens to nursing homes where good mental health care is seldom available.

Most of the problems we have described are expressed in terms of the needs of special segments of the population. They refer to individuals who do not receive adequate mental health care because of who they are.

Women's needs

This is also true for women. Many do not receive appropriate care from the mental health service system. The rapidly changing role of women has left many traditionally trained mental health practitioners ill-prepared to deal with the new problems that women face as a result. We know that women have expressed realistic concerns about the quality of their lives and their place in our society. Many report that the response of the mental health services system is often "treatment" aimed at encouraging them to accept the status quo and their "natural" position in life. We are concerned by the failure of mental health practitioners to recognize, understand, and empathize with the feelings of powerlessness, alienation, and frustration expressed by many women.

Other Americans do not receive adequate care because of where they are. While this is particularly true of those who live in rural America, it is also true of Americans who live in small towns and in the poorer sections of American cities.

Mental health personnel and facilities, particularly those in the private sector, are located primarily in the more affluent urban areas of the country. Americans who do not live in these areas do not have ready access to mental health services. They often must travel long distances even to receive emergency care, and neither specialized nor comprehensive services are available to them.

DEFINING MENTAL HEALTH PROBLEMS

Documenting the total number of people who have mental health problems, the kinds they have, how they are treated, and the associated financial costs is difficult, not only because opinions vary on how mental health and mental illness should be defined, but also because the available data are often inadequate or misleading. This difficulty is compounded by the subjective nature of many mental health problems. People fear mental illness and they often do not report it. Many problems are never treated and never recorded.

For the past few years the most commonly used estimate has been that, at any one time, 10 percent of the population needs some form of mental health services. This estimate has been used in national projections for the services and personnel needed to provide mental health care. There is new evidence that this figure may be nearer 15 percent of the population.

15 percent of the population needs some mental health services

While these figures depict the magnitude of this Nation's mental health problems, they tell us little about the specific nature of these problems. They also tell us little about the types of mental health services required to meet these problems.

We know that 6.7 million people, 3 percent of the American population, were seen in the specialized mental health sector in 1975. Approximately 1.5 million persons were hospitalized in the specialized mental health sector in 1975.

We also know that, of the estimated 2 million Americans who have been or would be diagnosed as schizophrenic, approximately 600,000 receive active treatment in any one year. Most current estimates state that about 1 percent of the population suffers from profound depressive disorders. There is new evidence that this figure may be higher. More than 1 million Americans have organic psychoses of toxic or neurologic origin or permanently disabling mental conditions of varying causes.

Because diagnostic criteria vary so widely, different surveys of general populations show that the overall prevalence of persistent, handicapping mental health problems among children aged three to fifteen ranges from 5 to 15 percent. These conditions include emotional disorders, the so-called conduct disorders, and impairments or delays in psychological development.

As many as 25 percent of the population are estimated to suffer from mild to moderate depression, anxiety, and other indicators of emotional disorder at any given time. The extent and composition of this group varies over time. Although most of these problems do not constitute mental disorders as conventionally diagnosed, many of these persons suffer intensely and seek assistance. By and large, such individuals cope with these stresses with the aid of family, friends, or professionals outside the mental health system. These individuals constitute a significant portion of primary health care practice in the United States.

25 percent suffers from mild or temporary emotional disorders

There are large numbers of Americans who suffer from serious emotional problems which are associated with other conditions or circumstances:

—Alcohol abuse is a major social, physical, and mental health problem with an annual cost to the Nation estimated at over $40 billion. Approximately 10 million Americans report recent alcohol-related problems, yet only 1 million are receiving treatment for alcoholism. While many are treated in mental hospitals, outpatient treatment of alcoholism has in recent years been increasingly independent of the mental illness treatment network.

—The non-medical use and misuse of psychoactive drugs is a complex phenomenon which is not well understood. It has social, legal, health, and mental health implications. Many with drug-related problems turn to mental health practitioners and facilities for assistance. As in the case of alcoholism, most treatment efforts are independent of the mental health service system.

—There were an estimated 200,000 cases of child abuse reported in America in 1976. Because many cases are never reported, the actual number is much larger. This is an enormous, poorly understood problem with serious mental health implications.

—By conservative estimates at least 2 million American children have severe learning disabilities which, if neglected, can have profound mental health consequences for the child and the family.

—There are 40 million physically handicapped Americans, many of whom suffer serious emotional consequences because of their disabilities.

—According to the President's Committee on Mental Retardation, one-third of the 6 million people who are mentally retarded suffer from multiple handicaps, which often include serious emotional difficulties.

Other damaging factors

America's mental health problems cannot be defined only in terms of disabling mental illnesses and identified psychiatric disorders. They must include the damage to mental health associated with unrelenting poverty and unemployment and the institutionalized discrimination that occurs on the basis of race, sex, class, age, and mental or physical handicaps. They must also include conditions that involve emotional and psychological distress which do not fit conventional categories of classification or service.

Our purpose in emphasizing this broad view of mental health is not to foster unrealistic expectations about what formal mental health services can or should accomplish. It is not to suggest those working in the mental health field can resolve far-reaching social issues. We are firmly convinced, however, that mental health services cannot adequately respond to the needs of the citizens of this country unless those involved in the planning, organization, and delivery of those services fully recognize the harmful effect that a variety of social, environmental, physical, psychological, and biological factors can have on the ability of individuals to function in society, develop a sense of their own worth, and maintain a strong and purposeful self-image.

EXPLAINING MENTAL ILLNESS

Previous centuries: Mentally ill possessed by the devil

What causes mental illness is a question people have asked since virtually the beginning of human existence. In previous centuries, it was believed that the mentally ill were possessed by the devil or by evil spirits or that they just had "bad blood." Today, there is a wide variety of theories that attempt to explain the problem of mental illness. Some stress genetic and biochemical factors. Others stress sociological and psychological factors. Since there are many types of mental illness, no single theory or cause of mental illness can best explain this serious social problem. We will examine some of the major theories.

GENETIC, BIOCHEMICAL, AND PSYCHOLOGICAL EXPLANATIONS

Some explanations of mental illness stress genetic or hereditary factors. Numerous studies have suggested that predispositions toward particular psychoses do appear to be genetically inherited. These predispositions "set the stage" for the disorder or illness. They do not, in themselves, cause the disorder. Thus, scientists have noted, genetic factors "must be considered with respect to environmental variables."[103] Based upon data from much research comparing identical and fraternal twins, many studies suggest that genetic variables are involved in schizophrenia.* Other available evidence suggests a genetic influence in manic-depressive psychosis.[104] However, much of the same research notes that nongenetic variables play an important role in mental illness, and that additional research is necessary first, to determine the exact nature of genetic involvement and second, to identify those inherited characteristics that may predispose a person to become psychotic.[105] Since no particular genetic structure has been clearly associated with schizophrenia, manic-depression, or other mental disorder, the hereditary or genetic theories are problematic. Scientists, however, continue to search for genetic factors that could demonstrate a genetic transmission of mental disorders.

Biochemical theories attribute mental illness to the presence or lack of chemicals in the bloodstream and brain of the mentally ill. Studies suggest that because there is too much of a chemical or chemicals present in an individual (serotonin, methylated idoleamines, or taraxein, for example), the person will exhibit mental disturbances and schizophrenic behavior patterns.[106] Some research indicates that the absence of particular enzymes, (for example, monoamine oxidase [MAO] or dopamine-B-Hydrolase [DBH]) or their presence in improper amounts may be implicated in schizophrenia.[107] Other studies have discredited some of the above by finding no significant differences in the levels of these substances and enzymes in schizophrenics as compared with nonschizophrenics.[108] One cannot, however, dismiss the effects of chemicals on contributing to or controlling mental illness. In relation to controlling psychotic behavior, many schizophrenic patients have benefited from the use of drug or chemotherapy. Many patients diagnosed as manic-depressive have responded well from the use of lithium carbonate. Certain chemicals are necessary for the occurrence of thoughts and other brain processes. Chemical changes, some of which may be produced by environmental factors, can cause behavior abnormalities and are thought to be related to depression.[109]

In addition to the genetic and biochemical explanations of mental illness, there are various psychological explanations, which have their basis

Genetic explanation: Predisposition to mental illness

Biochemical theories: Mental illness a chemical imbalance

---

* According to psychologists, the "heritability of schizophrenia . . . is studied by determining the percentage of twin pairs in which both twins develop schizophrenia; that is, a measure of concordance applied."

in learning and Freudian psychoanalytical theory. Learning theorists believe that, just as we learn other forms of behavior, we learn abnormal behavior. Abnormal behavior is learned through operant conditioning whereby behavior is positively reinforced. In other words, maladaptive behavior is learned by the mentally ill because it is rewarded by conditions within the environment.

Using a model of personality development, psychoanalytical theory explains mental illness in terms of early childhood development and its profound effect on adult functioning. It stresses the role of unconscious factors in governing human behavior—normal as well as abnormal. Freudian psychoanalysis tended to be limited and deterministic with respect to the concept of human nature. Later, followers of the psychoanalytic approach such as Horney, Fromm, and Sullivan emphasized the interpersonal and sociocultural dimensions of human behavior. The person was not to be viewed just as a biological machine. Social variables in shaping personality were to be taken into account. Maladaptive behavior was not just attributed to problems experienced during the stages of psychosocial and psychosexual development, but were also attributed to cultural and social forces.[110]

SOCIOLOGICAL EXPLANATIONS
Sociological explanations have also been developed in an attempt to account for mental illness and its various forms. We will examine the following major sociological explanations of mental illness: *social structure theory*, *anomie theory*, and *labeling theory*.

Social Structure and Anomie Theories. Social structure theory attributes mental illness to the structure of society itself. Mental illness is viewed as a product of an oppressive society, one characterized by high rates of social change, anonymity, complexity, and impersonality. Living in a highly competitive, individualistic society is viewed as being the basic cause of much mental illness. Social as well as economic inequalities within society have created much personal frustration and conflict, which precipitates mental illness. The society itself is "sick" and individual mental illness is symptomatic of this sickness. Mental illness, in other words, is linked to the organization of society itself.

Anomie, as we have seen in earlier chapters, involves a lack of integration between cultural goals and the opportunity for some people to use the "legitimate" means to attain those goals. Much emphasis is placed on the attainment of certain goals in our society, i.e., to have material possessions and be economically successful. Our society also prescribes particular "approved means" (good education, a high paying job) for the attainment of such goals. However, because of their position within the structure of society, some people (i.e., people in low socioeconomic positions, certain minority groups) have highly limited, or are virtually denied, access to the use of legitimate means for goal attainment. The pressures and frustrations

Abnormal behavior is learned

Mental illness rooted in early childhood development

Mental illness linked to organization of society

experienced by people in this situation are often of such severity that they actually induce the individual to retreat from society. When the person who is blocked in goal attainment gives up on both goals and means to goals, "retreatism" occurs. The mentally ill exemplify forms of retreatist escape. Anomie theory, then, explains mental illness in terms of people's responses to the pressures and frustrations of failure experienced in our society.[111] This theory fails to account for the many individuals who experience goal blockage and are not considered mentally ill and also for those who have not experienced goal blockage yet are among the ranks of the mentally ill.

Labeling Theory. An additional major sociological explanation of mental illness is termed labeling. Similar to the theory of anomie, this theory looks to the society within which we live, not within individuals themselves, for the causes of mental illness. Unlike the theory of anomie, however, labeling theory explains mental illness in terms of a label attached to people by others in society. In defining "mental illness," we noted that when people violate social conventions that are considered to be natural they are labeled as mentally ill. What causes certain behavior to become a mental disorder is that society labels it as such. Mental disorders are social roles assigned by others in society and are not conditions peculiar to individuals.

Labeling theorists believe their approach best explains chronic mental illnesses. People who are labeled as mentally ill learn the appropriate roles for being mentally ill. They then conform to the expectations of others, who define and treat them according to the traditional cultural definitions of madness. Later, their behavior becomes indistinguishable from the behavior of others labeled as mentally ill.

Critics of this approach question how much mentally ill people suffer from the social stigma of being labeled as "sick" and believe that the effects of labeling are exaggerated. They note that expectations and labeling may be a determinate of and have a long-term effect upon behavior; however, they will also indicate a cause and effect relationship whereby the behavior of people in the short run causes the expectations of, and also the labels from, others in society. Mental illness cannot be viewed simply as a lack of interpersonal coping skills or a label because it has emotional as well as physical causes and effects. Critics will also note that many societies label people much less than ours, yet mental illness occurs in all societies. In America, many people have recovered from their psychotic episodes, even after having been labeled as mentally ill.[112]

> Mental illness: Form of retreatist escape

> Mental illness as a label

> The critics: Mental illness not simply a label

RESPONSES TO MENTAL ILLNESS

INDIVIDUAL THERAPY

At the beginning of our analysis of the mental health problem, we stated that modes of treatment for the problems of mental health are related to how mental illness is defined. When explained in terms of a medical model, there is a tendency to respond to the problems of mental illness with the use of drugs (chemotherapy), electroshock (EST), surgery, and psychotherapy.

Chemotherapy. Chemotherapy is the use of drugs in the treatment of psychiatric patients. The following are some of the more common medications used by psychiatrists and physicians in mental hospitals and on an out-patient basis.

Drugs are used to treat schizophrenics and relieve depression

Major tranquilizers, such as chlorpromazine (Thorazine), haloperidol (Haldol), thiothixene (Navane), and fluphenazine (Prolixin), are *neuroleptic* or *antipsychotic agents* that are used at times to calm intensely overactive, excited patients, or to treat schizophrenics. Minor tranquilizers, such as chlordiazepoxide (Librium) or diazepam (Valium), are used widely for less severe agitation and anxiety. Other drugs, such as the antidepressants (Elavil, Triavil, Tofranil, Sinequan, and Norpramin), are used to relieve depression.[113] These and other medications are used to allow patients to become more accessible to therapists through the reduction and sometimes the relief of overt symptoms.

Drugs also used to control patients

Unfortunately, drugs are often used to control patients rather than to alleviate their symptoms. Drugs have helped many patients; for others, drugs only suppress or mask symptoms. We have also been able to greatly reduce the number of patients in mental hospitals with the use of chemotherapy, but as we will later examine, this has led to a variety of other problems.

Electroshock Therapy and Surgery. Electroshock therapy (EST) and surgery have been and still are used in the treatment of the mentally ill. EST is an electrical current to the patient's brain through electrodes attached to the head. In past years, estimates of the number of patients treated with EST have ranged from 50,000 to a quarter of a million. Because of the growing controversy with this form of treatment, it is not used as frequently today as it was in the past. Currently, it tends to be used in cases of severe depression and when all other forms of treatment have failed.

EST and psychosurgery are not used as frequently today

Psychosurgery is the surgical removal of parts of the brain. Because of its controversial nature, psychosurgery—especially the lobotomy (in which the frontal lobe nerves are severed)—is rarely used today in the treatment of mental illness.

Psychotherapy is also employed when mental illness is defined in terms of the medical model. However, psychotherapy is the major mode of response when mental illness is defined in terms of psychological factors.

Psychotherapy. A major treatment process of the mentally ill is individual psychotherapy and counseling. We will now briefly examine some of the current major approaches, which have a variety of useful dimensions in the healing of the mentally ill.

The goal of psychoanalytic therapy is to reform the character structure of the person. This is accomplished by making the unconscious conscious in the individual. Focusing upon reliving childhood experiences, past experiences are, according to Corey, "reconstructed, discussed, analyzed, and interpreted with the aim of personality reconstruction."[114] There occurs a "working through" of repressed conflicts that will enable the patient to experience a more gratifying life. Psychoanalytic therapy is considered to be a psychodynamic approach to counseling and psychotherapy in that it is based upon unconscious motivation, insight, and personality reconstruction.

Personality reconstruction

Existential-humanistic, client-centered, and *gestalt* therapies are the relationship-oriented or experiential therapies, which are based upon humanistic psychology. Existential therapy has as its goal to "expand self-awareness" and "increase choice potentials—that is, to become free and responsible" for the direction of your life.[115] The approach has clients experience their existence as "authentic" by becoming aware of their own existence and potentials and how they can open up and act on their potentials.

Theories based on humanistic psychology

Client-centered therapy is based on the idea that people have within themselves the capability to understand the factors in their lives that are causing their problems.[116] The patient or "client" also has the ability for constructive personal change and self-direction. Change is thought to occur if the therapist establishes a relationship with the client that is characterized by acceptance, warmth, and accurate empathic understanding. The goal of client-centered therapy is to provide an atmosphere where the client can engage in self-exploration in order to first, recognize blocks to growth and second, experience formerly distorted or denied aspects of self.

The basic aim of gestalt therapy is to challenge the patient to move to "self-support" from a position of "environmental support," to "make the patient not dependent upon others," according to Perls, "but to make the patient discover from the first moment that he can do many things, much more than he thinks he can do."[117] It focuses on the what and how of behavior and on past unfinished business that prevents current effective functioning.

Transactional analysis, behavior therapy, rational-emotive therapy, and *reality therapy* are termed behavior-oriented, rational-cognitive, and the "action" therapies. The basic therapeutic goal of transactional analysis (TA) is to help the person make new decisions about current behaviors and future direction.[118] It aims to have the individual "gain awareness of how freedom of choice has been restricted by following early decisions about his or her life position and to provide options to sterile and deterministic ways of living."[119]

Behavior-oriented "action" therapies

Behavior therapy is concerned with behavior change and the creation of new conditions of learning. The rationale is that all behavior, including maladaptive behavior, is learned. Corey states, "If neurosis is learned, it can be unlearned, and more effective behaviors can be acquired."[120] In behavior therapy the clients select the specific goals.

There is one important goal in rational-emotive therapy—the "minimization of the client's central self-defeating outlook and his acquiring a more realistic tolerant philosophy of life."[121] It is a teaching and learning process, whereby the person attains happiness by learning to think rationally.

The goal of reality therapy is to help the client achieve autonomy and to assist the client in defining life goals.[122] It involves learning to behave realistically and responsibly, and making value judgments about behavior, and deciding on a plan of action for change.

No common philosophy unifies these current approaches to psychotherapy and counseling. When working with their clients, most therapists do not restrict themselves to any one particular approach. Patients are basically helped to understand the nature of their problem or problems and, using this knowledge, attempts are made to work out solutions.

Most therapists do not restrict themselves to only one approach

GROUP AND FAMILY THERAPY

In addition to individual psychotherapy and counseling, other treatments in current use are group and family therapy. These treatment techniques are reflective of the importance of social factors in explaining mental illness. Group therapy is a treatment process that enables an individual to achieve various degrees of insight into personal problems and to feel more open through interaction with others. Obtaining support from others who have similar problems, experiences, and feelings will often facilitate the recognition that the problems may not be unique. Group therapy creates a community feeling and allows the person to share the experiences of others and to feel supported in working out solutions.

Groups are supportive of the individual

Sociologists and other mental health professionals have advocated family therapy in the treatment of mental illness because, in most cases, mental disorders cannot be understood apart from the familial and social environments. Family therapy assumes that families are behavior systems whose nature cannot be inferred from individual psychology. The behavior of an individual family member is viewed as being contingent upon the behavior of other members. In family therapy the patient and family members work together to achieve insight into their emotional conflicts and problems. Many mental disorders have their roots in the complex patterns of interpersonal family interactions. In many cases, communication problems and conflicts between family members have contributed to an individual's mental disorder. Without family therapy, it is difficult for these families to work out their problems. Family therapy attempts to change attitudes and improve interpersonal communication so that the goal of an improved emotional climate can be achieved and the patient helped.

Mental disorders cannot be understood apart from the family and social environment

Aim of family therapy: Improvement of communication and emotional climate

Some sociologists view many of the discussed responses as inadequate and harmful to those people in our society who are labeled as mentally ill.

Wide World Photos, Inc.

"One Flew Over the Cuckoo's Nest," with Jack Nicholson, dramatized some of the problems of patients in mental institutions.

They advocate changing the system through a process of reconstruction. Changes advocated range from educational programs geared toward removing the stigma of mental illness to closing all large state hospitals and, finally, to changing society itself. One major change for which many have fought is the deinstitutionalization of mental patients.

INSTITUTIONALIZATION

The mental health delivery system has been failing to adequately treat many Americans who suffer from mental disorders. In the past, as a response to mental illness, large numbers of the chronically mentally ill were confined in state hospitals. In 1946, there were almost 600,000 patients confined in 500 state institutions.[123] There were very few recoveries and some patients remained institutionalized for twenty to fifty years. The deplorable conditions, brutality, and nonexistent services that have been characterisic of these institutions are described in the next reading.

Confinement at state hospitals

THE PROBLEMS OF DEINSTITUTIONALIZATION

In the past fifteen years, a variety of clinical, social, economic, and political factors have led to a limitation in hospitalization. A reduction in the number of patients in public mental hospitals (deinstitutionalization) and a trend toward treating the chronically mentally disabled in the community, on an outpatient basis, resulted. Recently, there have been a variety of problems occurring with this process of deinstitutionalization. Test and Stein note two disturbing trends: first, a significant increase in the number of public hospital readmissions in which patients are caught in a "revolving door"— coming in and out—of mental hospitals; second, the increasingly poor quality of life experienced by the patients in the community. Patients are simply "moved from the back wards of the hospital to the back alleys of the community."[124] The various problems of deinstitutionalization are examined in the following reading, "No Place To Go," by Amitai Etzioni.

ETZIONI READING——OBJECTIVE

1. Examine, by essay, three of the problems that have occurred from deinstitutionalization.

No Place To Go

AMITAI ETZIONI

In the engineering of new technology—spacecraft, missiles, even toys—it is standard practice to move systematically from a theoretical concept to a small-scale model, subject it to testing and modification, and then build a few full-scale prototypes before mass production is authorized. In contrast, new social policies still tend, all too often, to go directly from concept to implementation. As a result, the spread of a new policy, which reflects the mood of the times, often resembles nothing so much as a fashion wave.

"Deinstitutionalization" is one of the trendiest new policies in recent years. Its concept is a simple one: state institutions—from mental hospitals to training schools for the retarded to reform schools for juvenile delinquents and correctional facilities for adult criminals and drug addicts—should be drastically cut back and their inmates given similar services "in the community." Everybody will be better off: the ex-inmates will be treated more humanely and have a better chance for rehabilitation, and the public will pay less for its care and get more for its money.

As an idea, deinstitutionalization became popular in the social reform climate of the 1960s, but from the start one of its strengths was its appeal to both liberals and conservatives. Deinstitutionalization was pioneered first in the late sixties

Deinstitutionalization

in California, where Governor Ronald Reagan welcomed it as a conservative strategy for cutting back on big government and big state budgets. By 1973 there were only about 7,000 patients left in California's mental hospitals (down from 22,000 in 1967). Meanwhile, on the other side of the country radical reformers began pursuing a similar policy concerning juvenile delinquents. As head of the Massachusetts Youth Services Department, Jerome Miller, an impassioned social-work-professor-turned-administrator, set about closing reform schools, his aim being "to tear down the system to the point where Heinrich Himmler and the SS couldn't put it back together again."

The idea caught on in other states. As of 1968, New York began releasing mental patients so fast that by 1974, there were 46,000 fewer patients in the state's mental hospitals than there had been a decade earlier. Indiana's 1973–74 biennial budget called for a cut of $2.4 million in institutional expenditures because of a planned transfer to community care. Jerome Miller moved on in 1973 to become head of the Illinois Department of Children and Family Services, where he ordered his staff to cut the number of children in treatment centers and other institutions by one third. By 1974, in the ten states where deinstitutionalization of juvenile delinquents was most advanced, 48 per cent of the delinquents were not in institutions.

The widespread acceptance of deinstitutionalization, however, raises important questions about it. What are the main forces propelling it? What are its merits, and the limits of its applicability?

To a large extent, the track record of deinstitutionalization is a disappointing and even frightening one, one that is becoming another example of reformers charging too blindly in one direction and ignoring the consequences of the charge. If we now realize that many people who are institutionalized should not be, the experience of releasing large numbers of them stands as a powerful argument for the existence of some, albeit drastically improved, institutions.

SQUALOR AND BRUTALITY

By far the strongest argument for deinstitutionalization is based on the deplorable conditions and non-existent services that are characteristic of many institutions. The facts are well known: for years the back wards of state mental hospitals have been full of oversedated zombies, warehoused and forgotten. Facilities for the retarded are so understaffed that basic custodial care, let alone education or training, is barely being provided. Prisons are grossly overcrowded and fail to rehabilitate; exposes have disclosed squalor and brutality right out of a Dickens novel in some state training schools for juvenile delinquents, which have gained a reputation as trade schools of crime.

Such conditions have existed for years, however, and they do not in and of themselves suggest deinstitutionalization as the obvious response. Rather, the policy has gained momentum lately due to the efforts of three vocal and energetic constituencies, each with its own rationale for promoting deinstitutionalization.

First are the civil libertarians, who in recent years have increasingly brought the low level and poor quality of services provided in state-run institutions to the attention of the courts. Their legal arguments center around such violations of rights as unjust imprisonment, deprivation of liberty without due process, and

Why deinstitutionalize?

cruel and unusual punishment—all, they say, are implicit in the involuntary confinement of persons in institutions that fail to provide decent living conditions or sufficient opportunities for rehabilitation or cure.

To cite only one of quite a few examples, in January 1976, following a series of hearings during which medical and health authorities as well as prisoners described the "snake-pit" conditions in Alabama prisons, U.S. District Court Judge Frank M. Johnson, Jr. ruled that prison life in Alabama amounted to "cruel and unusual punishment" and was therefore in violation of the Eighth Amendment. He then announced that the Court was prepared to close every prison in the state if officials did not correct the conditions that had caused what the judge characterized as "the rampant violence and jungle atmosphere."

Retarted and severely physically handicapped children have also been affected by court decisions. One line of litigation has pursued their equal right to a free public school education along with children of normal I.Q. And television exposure of conditions at the Willowbrook school, a large state facility for the retarded on Staten Island, led to a court-supervised agreement to transfer the institution's 2,000 inmates back to the communities they came from—either back to their parents, to foster homes, or to small community treatment facilities.

Much more encompassing in their critique of institutions than the civil libertarians are such social essayists as Paul Goodman, Erving Goffman, R.D. Laing, Thomas Szasz, Ivan Illich, and Jessica Mitford. Although each has his or her distinctive personal position, all can be characterized as influential "abolitionists"—that is, people inclined strongly toward the position that institutional inmates would be better off if institutions were abolished, rather than decreased in number and size and upgraded in services. Generally their arguments are based less on research than on personal observation, experience, and empathetic insight. They say that institutions are dehumanizing; that they foster crippling dependency; and perhaps worst of all, that they exaggerate the seriousness of the problem as a means of continually justifying the need for their existence. To Thomas Szasz, mental illness is a "myth." Jessica Mitford sees prisons and prison reform as a con game.

Finally, deinstitutionalization has found great favor among legislators and administrators because of its expected savings for taxpayers. Rep. Edward Koch calculated that at-home services now costing $12,000 to $13,000 a year for people in nursing homes would be lower, between $3,000 and $9,000 each a year. State governments have shown a great interest in deinstitutionalization, because care for residents in state institutions is typically paid entirely out of the state budget, while the cost of "community facilities"—halfway houses or boarding houses or foster care—are to varying degrees paid for by federal funds funneled through Medicare, Medicaid, or Supplemental [Social] Security Income (SSI).

A POOR FIT

To find alternative means of care

Follow-up on the fate of those released from institutions suggests that the fit between the rhetoric and the reality of deinstitutionalization is a poor one. To be effective, deinstitutionalization has to be a two-part policy: getting the inmates out of the institutions, *and* then finding alternative means of caring for them. The first half of the policy has been pursued with enthusiasm. For example, between 1969 and 1974 Wisconsin's mental hospital population dropped 84 per cent, North Carolina's 79 per cent, and Alaska's 78 per cent. Nationwide the decrease was 44 per cent. But there has been only token development of the community care needed to adequately service the huge numbers being discharged from mental hospitals (and from other institutions). As of late 1973, the National Institute of Mental Health counted only 209 psychiatric halfway houses in the entire country (as compared, for example, with the nation's 23,000 nursing homes).

Enormous numbers of mental patients have thus been released into communities they are not prepared to cope with and that are not prepared to cope with them. For many ex-mental patients the situation is sink or swim—either fend for onset without any support services (other than welfare) or be reinstitutionalized. A New York study found that 29 per cent of released mental patients returned to the asylum within six months, and about half returned eventually.

Sink or swim

OVERNIGHT CLOSINGS

Recent scandals involving the high cost and poor quality of nursing home care have prompted much interest in deinstitutionalizing elderly nursing home residents. There is ample evidence that many persons in nursing homes need neither round-the-clock supervision nor the kinds of highly skilled medical care that can best be provided in an institution. Home health agencies and day centers could in many instances provide the services the elderly require under more humane, less confining circumstances, with less potential for abusive practices, and at lower per-person cost—*if* such services existed.

In youth services, crash deinstitutionalization, involving the virtually overnight closings of large state training or reform schools in bureaucratic surprise attacks, has frequently meant that officials had to find alternative placement for large numbers of youngsters all at once. The trend has been to farm them out to myriad small projects under private-sector auspices. Hastily created and ill-supervised by state officials, many are in the hands of fast-buck artists, with scanty qualifications to run such programs. Thus, for instance, *Corrections* magazine reported that when Jerome Miller was in the midst of closing Massachusetts training schools right and left and needed places to park the kids, just about anyone could walk into his office with just about any innovative-sounding scheme and leave with a contract to provide "community care."

With so few community care programs of any kind, let alone ones of adequate quality, deinstitutionalized people returning to the community tend to be left with little or no care. Instead, for the majority of released inmates, most of whom are ex-mental patients or former residents of institutions for the retarded, "community care" means one of three things; living with relatives, isolated existence on one's own, or entering a boarding care or nursing home.

For quite a few former inmates who have been unnecessarily institutionalized, one of these options works, so for them, deinstitutionalization is a good policy. For others, all three options are at best deeply problematic. Return to a loving, accepting family is highly desirable, but many long-time inmates have no families. For others, mental patients and juvenile delinquents in particular, family tensions have played a major role in creating the problems that led to institutionalization in the first place. In still other cases, the family views caring for the former inmate as a burden that is accepted only reluctantly and resentfully. When the

Willowbrook school for the retarded was closed, New York state officials complained about how few parents would take their children back—or even give consent for foster care placement. The parents claimed that they had previously tried to care for their children at home and this had proved impossible, and that they did not believe that children with such serious handicaps could be adequately served or supervised in foster homes.

Ex-mental patients who live on their own frequently end up eking out a lonely existence in a welfare hotel in a deteriorating, high-crime neighborhood. (A New York study found that 25 per cent of welfare hotel residents were ex-mental patients.) Many spend their days in a daze, for the most part harmless but also helpless and hopeless.

For those ex-mental patients incapable of functioning wholly independently and who cannot rely on relatives, nursing and boarding care homes are virtually the only alternative. Cynthia Barnet and Philip Leaf, two University of Wisconsin graduate students, followed up the fate of patients released from Bryce State Hospital. Of 2,600 patients, 500 to 600 had ended up in nursing homes, with the number rising rapidly. Whether these facilities are an improvement over the back wards of state mental hospitals is questionable. Psychiatric services are very seldom available; overtranquilization is every bit as common as in state hospitals. Government care and safety standards are low, especially for boarding homes, yet most homes do not meet them. In releasing a Senate long-term care subcommittee report on the boarding home industry, Senator Frank Moss, the subcommittee's chairman, said, "Operators understand that the way to make a profit is to cut back on food, staff, bedding, and other vital services. Whatever is not spent becomes profit. To make matters worse, there is absolutely no accountability; no states require boarding home operators to file cost reports to show how money is being used."

We have looked at the consequences of deinstitutionalization for ex-inmates, but the policy has an impact, often negative, on the community as well. Parents worry about the one or two ex-inmates who may not be harmless, and about the "birds of prey" (muggers, drug-pushers) that ex-inmates attract. Fear—oftentimes uninformed and downright bigoted, but in other cases quite understandable—causes communities to oppose the construction of needed halfway houses and treatment centers. In the case of facilities for drug addicts and juvenile delinquents, security precautions can result in mini-fortresses, walled off from all community contact. Where attempts have been made to cut security precautions to a minimum to create a setting more conducive to effective treatment, behavior of those people who cannot be controlled—who, even if few, may be highly dangerous, or at least very abusive—has resulted in public outcry and political backlash.

RETHINKING THE APPROACH

As the defects of deinstitutionalization have become more evident, several of the states that pioneered the policy have had to retrench and rethink their approach. Thus, the current head of the Massachusetts Department of Youth Services has conceded that more "secure slots," in institutional settings, are required for "heavy offenders." In California, scandals in the for-profit boarding care industry that grew up to provide living arrangements for released mental patients sparked a state senate investigation whose final report was highly critical of

Many spend their days in a daze

Negative community impact

deinstitutionalization. Before Governor Reagan's term was out he had to abandon plans for further mental hospital closings, reopen two facilities, and increase the state budget for mental institutions.

Does this mean that deinstitutionalization has shown itself a failure and should be abandoned? No more than that such a simple solution should ever have been so uncritically adopted and so sweepingly applied. The lesson is that the social world is complicated above all because people have a variety of needs and capacities, which require accordingly a variety of responses: some people will continue to require institutionalization, some can have their needs met in halfway houses, and some can live at home.

Unfortunately, however, it must be conceded that our current ability to predict who will do well in a particular kind of institutional setting is far from outstanding. Psychiatrists have a difficult time advising judges as to which mental patients are potentially violent and hence dangerous to the community and may well require institutionalization. In California, a small but still alarming number of deinstitutionalized mental patients ran amok and killed people. One man murdered his wife and three of his five children before killing himself. In another case, a woman who was refused institutionalization beheaded her daughter and son. Another patient, who had protested being released, saying he could not cope on the outside, went on a spree and murdered 17 people.

A realistic modesty about the precision of our powers of prediction, however, is one of the best arguments against heavy reliance on involuntary commitment. But not holding large numbers of almost certainly harmless though perhaps marginally functional persons in institutions against their will is quite different from shipping them out whatever their wishes, or closing down so many institutions that, for those who really need it, access to such care is severely curtailed.

The current high rate and ill effects of revolving-door placements could be cut back by adopting policies that recognize from the start that a sizable group of those needing services will continue to require institutionalization, while a substantial majority of the rest will require extensive support services simply to stay on the outside and avoid being abused or exploited, let alone cope successfully with life's pressures. Above all, what we need most is to curb our enthusiasm for oversimplification and learn to live with, and respond to, the complexities of the world.

There is no simple approach

ALTERNATIVE COMMUNITY MODELS

Studies in many ways supportive of Etzioni have noted that one of the major health-care problems in this decade is that we do not have an effective means to care for and treat chronically disabled psychiatric patients. Test and Stein state that

> many innovative and intensive approaches, such as the dramatic shortening of patients' hospital stay and attempts to make use of community agencies for treatment, have not been effective in helping patients achieve a sustained community tenure with an adequate quality of life.[125]

Teaching patients coping skills

According to Test and Stein, the "training in community living" model offers hope for a solution to the serious deficiencies in other approaches. They believe that this approach, "by virtually eliminating hospitalization, intensively teaching patients the coping skills necessary to live in the community, and assertively keeping patients involved in treatment and insuring continuity of care, was clearly more effective than the progressive short-term hospitalization plus community aftercare which constitutes the present mode of treatment." The new model was also economicaly feasible to implement, and patient gains were not at the "expense of additional burden to the family or community."[126] Whether this approach will prove to be a beginning of more effective treatment for the chronically mentally ill remains to be seen.

SUMMARY

In the first part of this chapter, we have seen that in spite of our medical technology, knowledge, and annual expenditures of billions of dollars, many Americans lack basic health care. There is in fact a health care crisis. There is also a growing incidence of disease conditions. The public is demanding more adequate health care services, not as a privilege but as a right. Our health care delivery system is inadequate and expensive because of the high costs of hospitals, doctors, and treatment. Maldistribution of health care professionals and incomplete and expensive voluntary health insurance adds to the health care crisis in America.

This crisis has been explained as a product (1) of a segmented non-system that has led to overlaps and gaps in the comprehensiveness of care, (2) of the medical-industrial complex organized for profit, and (3) of the external living patterns and habits of Americans.

Responses to the health care crisis have taken many forms, such as various governmental programs and organizations. Others have advocated the use of HMOs as a way of dealing with the crisis. The major response to our nation's health care crisis has been the demand for a national health insurance program. However, other responses have also been called for, such as those advocated by the Health Policy Advisory Center.

In the second part of this chapter, we have seen that mental illness and inadequate mental health care are serious social problems in America. Mental illness has been defined as a disease, as "problems of living," as learned behavior, and as a result of labeling. Millions of Americans manifest some type of mental illness. Many social factors are related to the rates and treatment of mental illness. The President's Commission on Mental Health has reported the progress and problems of mental health and inadequate mental health care in America.

Mental illness has been explained in terms of genetic, biochemical, and psychological factors. It has also been attributed to the structure of society itself, as a way of responding to the pressures and frustrations of failure experienced in daily life, and in terms of a label attached to people by others in society.

Responses to the problem of mental illness and inadequate mental health care have ranged from chemotherapy and family, group, and psychotherapy to the institutionalization and deinstitutionalization of mental patients. A major response has been the call for community-based mental health centers and services.

KEY TERMS

American health industry
American Medical Association
Biochemical explanation
Chemotherapy
Community Mental Health Centers
   Program
Deinstitutionalization
Deviance
Electroshock therapy
Epidemiology
Family therapy
Fee-for-service payment
Functional disorder
Genetic explanation
Group therapy
Health care
Health care crisis
Health care delivery
Health insurance
Health maintenance organizations
Health status
Incidence
Institutionalization
Labeling

Medicaid
Medical-industrial complex
Medical model
Medicare
Mental disorder
Mental health
Mental illness
MRFIT
Myth of mental illness
National health insurance
National Institute of Mental Health
Neuroses
Organic psychoses
President's Commission on Mental
   Health
Prevalence
Psychoses
Psychosurgery
Psychotherapy
Residual rule breaking
Schizophrenia
Social factors
Social structure and anomie theories

9
Population

Chapter Objectives

1. To list some of the reasons why rapid and excessive population growth constitutes one of the most serious social problems of our time.

2. To briefly describe the history of world population growth, identifying the three periods that manifested dramatic increases in the human population and the major source of our current worldwide population explosion.

3. To define the following terms: crude birthrate, crude death rate, population growth rate.

4. To discuss in an essay the nature of exponential population growth and its consequences.

5. To describe in an essay some of the major problems resulting from vast population growth that face the industrialized nations and the less-developed countries.

6. To discuss the various reasons for the massive contemporary population growth within the world's less-developed nations, listing the factors that favor high rates of fertility.

7. To compare in an essay the patterns of birth-, death, and population growth rates exhibited by the developed and less-developed nations of the world.

8. To analyze the Malthusian theory of population growth, defining "positive checks" and "preventive checks," and listing various reasons why this theory did not hold true for the industrializing nations of the period.

9. To analyze in an essay the theory of demographic transition.

10. To list various arguments for and against the possibility that the less-developed nations will also experience a full demographic transition.

11. To discuss in a brief essay the nature of the family planning approach to fertility control, evaluating its effectiveness and identifying its major weaknesses and the obstacles that hamper its efforts.

12. To list a few of the smaller developing nations where both economic development and family planning have been influential in lowering fertility rates.

13. To briefly discuss some of the methods for fertility control besides family planning.

THE EXTENT AND CONSEQUENCES OF WORLD POPULATION GROWTH

It is interesting to note that when national and even worldwide opinion polls ask people to name the most important problem facing their societies today, people will most often reply "the high cost of living," "unemployment," "dissatisfaction with government," or "crime." The fact is, however, that rapid population growth constitutes one of the most serious social problems of our time.[1]

Population increase has already placed severe strains upon the supply of food and many natural resources within large numbers of nations throughout the world. Today, for example, over one-half of the world's population suffers from undernutrition or malnutrition and it is estimated that at least ten million people, mostly in the underdeveloped or less-developed countries, die of starvation each year.[2] The majority of survivors in these countries can rarely count on obtaining many of the fundamental necessities of life, such as basic health care, clothing, or education. In the more developed industrialized nations, starvation is by and large not a problem; still, population pressures have severely taxed the ability of such nations to provide adequate housing, transportation, medical services, and jobs for growing numbers of people.

Undernutrition and malnutrition: Daily facts of life for most people

At present, world population stands slightly over 4.2 billion and is growing by approximately 190,000 persons per day.[3] Such growing numbers necessitate greatly increased demands upon the world's food and energy supplies, and at least some people are beginning to realize that the earth does not have enough resources to support the many increased billions of people in the years to come. One thing is certain: Overpopulation, like the other major social problems we have discussed, will simply not go away of its own accord. Increased public recognition and large-scale active public involvement in the development of national and worldwide policies and programs to deal with the problem of unchecked population growth are needed. Unless such concerted action is forthcoming, it is likely that, in the long run, population growth will be stopped, but only as a result of unimagined human suffering, from worldwide environmental deterioration, famine, epidemics, and the like.

More people means increased demands on resources

THE HISTORY OF WORLD POPULATION GROWTH

Very little is known about human population increase prior to relatively modern times. The well-known demographer Kingsley Davis states that around 8000 B.C. the human population numbered only around five million. By 1750 A.D. there were approximately 791 million people, and within another 100 years the world's population had increased to 1.25 billion. At present, world population stands at slightly over 4.2 billion. At our current rate of growth, the Population Reference Bureau estimates that it will reach 6 billion 233 million by the year 2000 and will actually double its present

The growth of world population

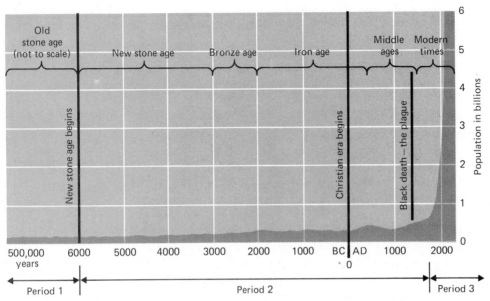

Fig. 9.1 World population growth in history. Source: "How Many People Have Ever Lived on Earth?" *The Population Bulletin*, 18 (Feb. 1962), p. 5.

number within only forty-one years. If population were to continue to grow at this rapid rate, we could project that within 200 years world population would reach approximately 124 billion people. But such vast numbers of people will never actually materialize since, in the absence of some direct form of human intervention to control population growth, world resources would be pushed beyond their limits and a rise in mortality would, by necessity, follow.[4]

Effects of the Agricultural and Industrial Revolutions

Throughout most of human existence, world population has tended to grow rather slowly. In fact, Davis identifies only three periods manifesting dramatic increases. The first occurred approximately 8000 B.C. and was associated with the Agricultural Revolution—i.e., the development of agricultural tools and animal husbandry. The development and spread of agriculture allowed people to establish more permanent areas of settlement and helped to ensure a larger and more stable food supply. The second major wave of population increase occurred around 1750 and continued through the nineteenth century and was associated with the arrival of the Industrial Revolution throughout much of Europe and North America. The Industrial Revolution brought mechanization to agriculture, and a vast growth in manufacturing, science, and engineering technology followed. All of this had the effect of increasing the general living standard through improved housing, clothing, and food supplies. Medical knowledge expanded and advances in sanitation technology were made during this

Consequences of exponential growth

period. The overall result was a dramatic decrease in the death rate as well as increased life expectancy, both of which escalated population growth throughout the world's industrialized nations during the eighteenth and nineteenth centuries.[5]

Prior to the twentieth century, therefore, most major instances of population growth were the result of technological advancements.[6] During the twentieth century a third major wave of population increase occurred, largely, however, within the economically underdeveloped, nonindustrialized African, Asian, and Latin American countries. The vast population growth within these areas was predominantly the result of a declining death rate and an increased life expectancy, which began to occur around the 1920s and has vastly accelerated since the post-World War II period—beginning around 1945.

Recent population growth

The specific reasons for the death rate decline and the resultant sharply increased population within these nations will be discussed later in this chapter. For now, we can point out that the vast population growth within these countries constitutes the main threat and thrust of our current population explosion. Thus, in contrast to the industrially developed nations of the world, such as the United States and most European countries (whose birthrates have shown an overall general decline since the turn of the century), the populations of the underdeveloped nations have swelled to almost three-fourths of the world's total population. Furthermore, in most of these countries, population growth shows little sign of abating.

The source of the current population problem

Perhaps the only glimmer of hope comes from statistics supplied by the Worldwatch Research Institute. These statistics indicate that there may be some signs of a slight slowdown in the growth of world population, partly as a result of a wider acceptance of birth control programs within some nations of western Europe, East Asia, and North America. The institute's projections indicate that world population may swell to approximately 5.5 billion by the year 2000 rather than to more than 6 billion, as projected by the Population Reference Bureau and the United Nations.[7] Even assuming the validity of the lower projection, which is obviously somewhat optimistic, this still does not signify the end of our population problem. In the long run, a slightly slower rate of population growth would still lead to an overpopulated world. In addition, most of the nations in which the use of birth control methods is growing or already widespread are at least fairly (and some highly) industrialized. As of the present, then, birth control has not had much impact upon the source of our current population explosion, the less-developed nations.[8] Finally, even the Worldwatch people admit that the possible slowdown of world population growth is partly the result of increased rates of starvation within some of the world's less-developed nations.[9]

Population growth may be slowing

As we have suggested earlier, one of the major difficulties in finding solutions to the problem of rapid population growth is the fact that so many people do not define the situation as problematic at all, while many others (often within the industrial nations) feel that it is not *their* problem.

Barriers to a solution of the problem

Ignorance and attitudes such as these present major obstacles to effective action against our population problem. If massive environmental deterioration, famine, and epidemics do eventually occur within many areas, they are bound to have profoundly detrimental effects upon our entire planet.

THE ELEMENTS OF POPULATION GROWTH

There are a number of factors that influence the size and growth of human populations. Chief among these are the birthrate and the death rate. Migration (the movement of people from one territory or country to another) can also affect the size of populations, although for most countries it plays a less influential role today than in previous historical periods. The *crude birthrate* is the annual number of births per thousand members of the population; the *crude death rate* is the annual number of deaths per thousand.[10] The difference between these rates yields another important demographic measure known as the *population growth rate*. For example, according to the Population Reference Bureau, Brazil has a crude birthrate of 36 per thousand and a crude death rate of 8 per thousand. This means that Brazil's population growth rate (birthrate minus death rate) equals 28 per thousand, or 2.8 percent. Thus, at the current rate, the population of Brazil is growing by an additional 2.8 percent more people each year. Again for example, the crude birth- and death rates for Mexico were 42 and 8 per thousand respectively, yielding an annual population growth rate of 3.4 percent.[11] These rates of growth may not sound very large but they actually are, because population growth is *exponential*, similar to the way in which compounded interest works. For example, a hypothetical population growing at an annual rate of 4 percent for 17 years will increase not by 68 percent (17 × 4) but will actually double in size—an increase of 100 percent during this period. Each year, in other words, the previous increase is added on to the population base figure, the *total* of which continues to grow at the same rate.

Exponential population growth has a number of important consequences of which the reader should be aware. First of all, it has a significant influence upon a population's *doubling time*. Thus, a population growing at 1 percent per year will double in sixty-nine years; one growing at 2 percent will double in thirty-five years; a third growing at 3 percent will double in twenty-three years; and still another growing at 3.5 percent will double in only twenty years.[12] Second, exponential population growth ensures that, given a steady high rate of growth, any population, even a small one, will ultimately experience a dramatic increase in size. Thus, a population of only 10 million growing at 3 percent annually will increase to 20 million in twenty-three years; to 40 million in forty-six years; to 80 million in sixty-nine years; and to 160 million in only ninety-two years. Third, as we shall see in more detail later, exponential population growth has particularly startling consequences for many of the less-developed, largely agrarian

Major demographic measures

Population growth is exponential

nations of the world. Many of these countries already have fairly large population bases, and the majority are characterized by high rates of population growth.[13] Finally, exponential growth also has important consequences for worldwide population growth. At present, world population stands at approximately 4.2 billion and has a growth rate of 1.7 percent per year, thus doubling every forty-one years.[14] At this rate, world population would increase to approximately 23 billion persons within only a century.

Obviously, population cannot continue to grow indefinitely at this rate. Thus the major and more realistic question for most demographers concerns the circumstances under which population growth will come to an end and the consequences of this growth in the interim.[15] Population growth can be slowed by a substantial decline in the birthrate, by a significant increase in the death rate, or by both of these factors operating simultaneously. In the future it seems likely that world population growth will be brought under control by a combination of these factors, although many demographers are of the opinion that sharp increases in mortality may play a more dominant role.[16] In the meantime, it is virtually certain that we will be living in a more crowded world. Therefore, the social, economic, political, and ecological consequences of overpopulation must be recognized and understood if we intend to take any type of effective action to deal with our present and future population problems.

As we have previously seen, the patterns of population growth and change among the industrialized nations of the world are quite different from those of the largely agrarian nations. The factors that affect population growth and its consequences and overpopulation within these areas also differ considerably. In the following sections, we will examine the dynamics and consequences of population change within both the developed and less-developed nations.

GROWTH IN THE DEVELOPED NATIONS

As we have previously pointed out, large-scale population growth initially occurred among the developed nations as a consequence of improved standards of living and of other technological advancements associated with the Industrial Revolution. Davis notes, for example, that northwestern Europeans (the leaders of the Industrial Revolution) comprised 18 percent of the world's population in 1650, but by 1920 they accounted for almost 35 percent of the total. However, during the present century, as we have noted, there has been a general reversal of this trend. The less-developed nations have shown marked increases in population growth, particularly in recent years, and the developed nations have exhibited substantial birthrate declines. Recent U.N. projections indicate that, of the present developed nations, the population of North America and all of Europe will comprise only 13 percent of the world's total by the year 2000.[17] The only notable turnabout in the general birthrate decline within a number of developed

How will population growth cease?

Population decline in the developed nations

nations (particularly Europe and the United States) was the post-World War II "baby boom" of the 1940s and 1950s. Since the peak of the "baby boom" in the mid-1950s, birthrates within the developed nations have resumed their long-term decline. Recently, in many cases, this decline has rapidly accelerated.

Current growth rates in the developed nations

Largely as a result of declining births, the annual growth rates of most industrial nations now stand at 1 percent or less. Today, for example, Japan is growing at 1.0 percent per year, the USSR is growing at 0.9 percent, and the industrialized countries of Oceania-Australia and New Zealand are growing at rates of 0.8 percent and 1.0 percent, respectively. Most notable, however, are the low growth rates on the European continent. The populations of eastern and southern European nations are increasing at an average rate of 0.7 percent and 0.8 percent, respectively, each year, while the average growth rate for countries within northern and western Europe stands at 0.1 percent per year. Certain European countries, such as the United Kingdom and Belgium have stopped growing; in other words, their rate of increase is now at 0.0 percent per year. Other European countries, such as East and West Germany and Luxembourg, now have *negative* growth rates, i.e., their populations are actually beginning to decline.[18]

The United States, like other industrial nations, also experienced a general decline in birthrates during the twentieth century. This pattern was temporarily interrupted during the "baby boom" of the 1940s and 1950s, with births reaching a peak of 3.8 children per woman in 1957. Since that

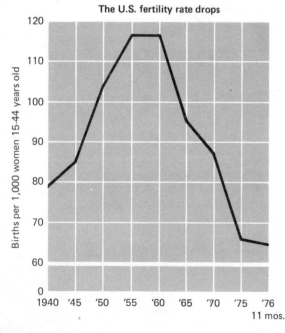

The U.S. fertility rate drops

Births per 1,000 women 15-44 years old

Fig. 9.2 The declining U.S. birthrate. Source: *Time*, Feb. 28, 1977.

time, birthrates have again shown a steady decline. By the early 1970s births fell to 2.1 children per woman, the number that demographers refer to as *replacement level fertility*. Replacement level is slightly over two children per woman, thus allowing for a certain amount of infant mortality and for women who do not bear children. At this point, in other words, children would be born in sufficient numbers to only replace (rather than to exceed) the number of parents. Thus in the long run, *zero population growth* would come about, since ultimately the ratio of births to deaths would balance out and our population would cease to grow.

Replacement level fertility

The attainment of replacement level fertility does not mean that population automatically or instantly stops growing. Today, the population of the United States stands at approximately 218.4 million, and the average woman is bearing only 1.8 children, a rate that is actually less than that necessary for replacement. Still, assuming this rate remains constant, our population will grow to around 260 million or so by the year 2000 before possibly stabilizing at approximately 270 million around the year 2025.[19] This continued growth results from the relatively young age structure of our population. The majority of the children born during the "baby boom" have now entered their own childbearing years. In fact, an additional 7 million people will enter young adulthood (20 to 34 years of age) between now and 1987.[20] Assuming that these large numbers of people limit themselves to just replacement level fertility, our population will still grow for many years before eventually reaching true zero population growth.

U.S. population still shows substantial growth

Of course, in spite of these projections, we cannot be sure that the United States will actually reach true zero population growth even in the long run. Immigration, for example, is also an important factor in determining long-term population growth rates. At present, some population organizations are concerned that our current high levels of both legal and illegal immigration will make it more difficult for us to achieve a stationary population in the future.[21] Perhaps more important, we cannot be sure that in the future women will still be willing to limit themselves to only one or two children. The current trends toward postponing marriage and deferring parenthood may also begin to shift, particularly if general economic conditions improve.[22] As the Commission on Population Growth and the American Future pointed out, even if we maintain replacement level fertility, population will still grow significantly in the years to come. The long-term effects of growth at replacement levels will be serious enough; however, if we exceed that level, we will be involved in rapid exponential population growth, the long-term effects of which would be disastrous to our environment and our way of life.[23]

Zero population growth may never occur

Do the developed industrialized nations, such as the United States, have population problems? What are some of the consequences of population growth within these nations? Even though birthrates within the industrialized nations have been declining throughout much of the twentieth century,

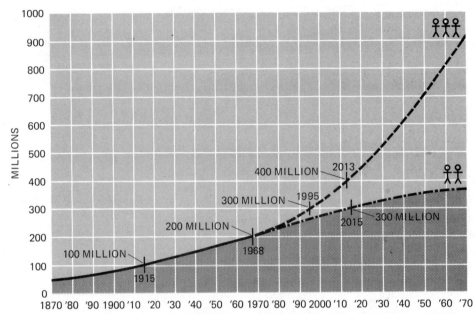

Fig. 9.3 U.S. population: 2- vs. 3-child family. The population of the United States passed the 100-million mark in 1915 and reached 200 million in 1968. If families average two children in the future, growth rates will slow, and the population will reach 300 million in the year 2015. At the 3-child rate, the population would reach 300 million in this century and 400 million in the year 2013. (Projections assume small future reductions in mortality, and assume future immigration at present levels.) Source: Prior to 1900—U.S. Census Bureau, *Historical Statistics of the United States, Colonial Times to 1957*, 1961. 1900 to 2020—U.S. Census Bureau, *Current Population Reports*, Series P-25. 2021 to 2050—unpublished Census Bureau projections. Beyond 2050—extrapolation.

Effects of population growth: The United States

the fact remains that many industrial nations are still experiencing population growth. Even excluding our high rates of immigration, the U.S. population, for example, will expand by over 40 million people by the turn of the century.

Even under nongrowth conditions, industrial nations as a whole place a great deal of pressure on resources and the environment. People within the United States, for example, enjoy relatively high standards of living; we are "heavy" into consumption of goods and services. Under conditions of population growth even higher demands are made upon both the physical environment and natural resources. An emergency shortage is already upon us due in part to a sharp increase in our per capita consumption of energy over the last two decades.[24] Also, water shortages are being experienced in the southwestern United States, and the Commission on Population Growth indicates that, as a result of our growing population and economic activity, we can expect water shortages to spread to northern and eastern states in the years to come.[25]

In the future it is even possible that food supply in the United States may become a problem. Recent statistics indicate that yields for most of our primary crops are either leveling off or actually declining.[26] Moreover, the water shortages may actually limit agricultural productivity of land already in use. Future population growth will most likely necessitate finding millions more acres of agricultural land, and high-quality farm land is already in rather short supply.[27]

Land, water, and food shortages

In addition to placing heavy strains upon resources, population growth within industrial nations has already had a number of detrimental effects upon the quality of our environment and our way of life. One of the major problems affecting environmental quality within industrial nations is pollution, which is generally more severe within highly developed industrialized societies like our own than in less-developed nations. In the words of the Commission on Population Growth and the American Future: "As the gross national product goes up, so does the production of pollutants."[28] Ultimately, this is because a high standard of living necessitates more industrial productivity of goods and services. In turn, this generates more industrial waste, more automotive pollution, and more pollution resulting from the disposal of personal wastes, all of which pollute our air, water, and land. Moreover, the need to support growing numbers of people at a high standard of living only tends to make the problem worse.

Industrial nations are heavy polluters

The quality of life and the environment within industrial nations is also affected by where people live. For example, the long-term trend toward urbanization that is characteristic of industrial societies has resulted in severe overcrowding, air and noise pollution, congestion, traffic tie-ups, and housing shortages within our urban areas. Many people attempt to escape these problems and their accompanying frustrations by moving to the suburbs. Ultimately, however, this proves to be no solution at all since the suburbs begin to develop more rapidly than the central cities.[29] In 1960, 33 percent of our population had already taken up residence in suburban areas, and by 1976 this figure increased to almost 40 percent.[30] Moreover, the Bureau of the Census reported that from 1970 to 1977, nonmetropolitan (largely rural) areas within the United States experienced a faster rate of population growth than metropolitan areas (the larger cities and their suburbs). Part of this nonmetropolitan growth can be attributed to an expansion of metropolitan development.[31] In the long run, many metropolitan areas, together with all the problems they foster, simply keep growing into a continuous belt of urban development, called a *megalopolis*. Few problems of living have been solved; many more have been created.

The megalopolis: A belt of overlapping metropolitan areas extending over a large territory

Ultimately, population growth involves many industrial nations, particularly the United States, in a vicious cycle of problems. On the one hand, there is the problem of how to fulfill the needs and demands of many more millions of Americans for food, water, housing, jobs, transportation, recreation, public services, and countless other commodities. On the other hand, the solution to this problem merely creates others in terms of social and

A vicious cycle of problems

environmental costs, in particular draining our own as well as worldwide resources. As we shall see, however, the need for these resources is actually far more urgent in the less-developed nations than in our own.

U.S. FERTILITY TRENDS

As we have pointed out, the U.S. birthrate has shown a steady decline since the 1957 "baby boom" peak. Assuming that our present low fertility rates remain stable, our population will continue to increase by many millions during the next half-century. Nevertheless, population stability and true zero population growth appear likely for the United States in the long range. The following article discusses these present and future trends and some of the underlying factors responsible for them. In addition, the article discusses many of the social, cultural, and personal consequences attendant to population stability.

TIME READING——OBJECTIVES

1. To statistically document contemporary trends in the American birthrate and our probable future pattern of population growth.
2. To write a brief essay identifying some of the underlying factors responsible for the current fertility decline in the United States.
3. To discuss in an essay some of the major cultural consequences that would more than likely occur in our society as a result of population stability.

Looking to the ZPGeneration

Worship Cupid, but Don't Be Stupid! advises a press release put out by Zero Population Growth, Inc. A Valentine received by some Americans last week, inscribed *Love . . . Carefully,* was equipped with a red condom. But few young couples in the U.S. today need antinatalist exhortations or equipment. Since 1957 the fertility rate has dropped from a peak of 3.76 children per woman to a record low of 1.75 last year. Though it may rise in the next 30 years, it is highly improbable that Americans in the foreseeable future will again engage in the great procreational spree of the postwar years. The baby boom has become a bust.

The nation is seemingly on its way to the long-debated goal of Zero Population Growth (ZPG), the theoretical point at which deaths and births balance out. If present fertility and mortality rates remain constant, the U.S. population may stabilize around the year 2025 at between 260 million and 270 million (up from 216 million today).

Americans nowadays are painfully aware that resources may be increasingly short and expensive in coming years. Inflation has already made the cost of

The fertility rate has been dropping since 1957

rearing a large family (now estimated at more than $250,000 for four children from cradle through college) all but prohibitive. The pleasure principle may be a factor too. Richard Brown, manager of population studies for a General Electric think tank in Washington, observes: "Children are competing with travel, the new house and professional standing. Once the checkbook is balanced and all other desires have been indulged, a couple will think of having a child—or, indeed, that child may have its place in the list of Wants & Goals."

The biggest, if least predictable, element in the fertility rate is the attitude of the American woman. As the economic, social and political status of women has improved, the desirability and mystique of motherhood has declined. Says Princeton's Charles Westoff, a world-renowned demographer: "There is a very pronounced change in the attitude of women toward marriage, childbearing and working, and all these attitudes seem to lead in one direction: they don't want three or four children." As Berkeley Demographer Judith Blake Davis puts it succinctly: "You won't find those sacrificial mothers any more."

Attitudes of American women: The major factor in fertility

Thus—if the U.S. is indeed headed for ZPG—people will for the first time in history be consciously forging their own destiny.

Not all sociologists, demographers and economists agree that a stable population is necessarily desirable. Some worry about the social and cultural implications of a markedly older population. By the year 2020 there will be almost twice as many people over 65 (43 million) as there are today, exerting immense new pressures on the Social Security, pension and Medicare systems. To Columbia

Arthur Tress, Magnum Photos, Inc.

Even in the United States today, couples with many children may be unable to make ends meet.

University Sociologist Amitai Etzioni, "ZPG spells a decadent society, à la France in the '30s, à la Berlin in the early '30s. This means a less innovative society, a society in which fewer people will have to attend, care, feed, house and pay for a larger number."

Most futurists, however, agree that a better life is in store for a stabilized population. Among those who believe in the beneficial effects is Demographer Westoff: "ZPG will reduce pressures on the environment and on resources. It will probably increase per capita income. It will reduce pressure on governmental services. And it will give society an opportunity to invest more in the quality than in the quantity of life."

Pressure on the environment *(margin note)*

LESS POLLUTION

Other experts point out that with fewer children, families will have more discretionary income to spend on the pursuit of pleasure—and for better health care and education. Air, water and noise pollution should be reduced. With a drop in the number of youths in their teens and twenties, the segment responsible for most crime today, the cities may be safer.

With an older and less adventurous population, demographers predict, there will be less pressure on the nation's congested beaches, lakes, waterways, hiking trails, ski slopes and wilderness areas—while sales of art supplies, mah-jongg, backgammon, books and endless varieties of electronic games should soar. The station wagon, the Patton tank of suburbia, may be replaced by smaller cars. The automakers expect to sell more of the handy vans that are already a part of the youth culture as well as more recreational vehicles: motor homes, campers, dune buggies, Jeeps, motorcycles and mopeds. Education may finally get better, as the teacher-student ratio improves. Says Economist Alan Sweezy of the California Institute of Technology: "I think ZPG is going to be a very good thing for higher education. There will be an end to overcrowding."

Some benefits of population stability *(margin note)*

There will be a continuing increase in the demand for adult education, with the emphasis on practical skills and crafts rather than abstract knowledge. Says Vincent Ficcaglia, an economist at the Cambridge-based Arthur D. Little think tank: "What is changing is the type of learning people want. It's much less formal: they don't want or they already have a liberal arts degree. What they do want is to acquire skills to satisfy their own creative urges or help them survive—plant-growing and plumbing, for instance." Colleges and universities will have to adjust swiftly to this developing educational market—even if tenured professors of medieval English have to be retrained to teach ceramics and auto repair.

Smaller families of course can live in smaller houses. Experts also foresee a greater demand for town houses, condominiums and apartments as suburbanites move back into the cities to take advantage of the cultural opportunities clustered in urban centers.

The move back to the city will intensify *(margin note)*

All Americans will be affected by the new lifescape:

Children tend to be physically and psychologically healthier when there are fewer of them in a family—and when they are wanted. The University of Michigan's Robert Zajonc, a psychologist who studies educational trends closely, already notes a marked rise in the IQs of the ZPGeneration now in primary school. Verbal and linguistic skills, he finds, increase in inverse proportion to the size of the family; smaller families, as he puts it, are "more adult-oriented than sibling-oriented." Education may revert in part from classroom to living room. Children may again receive wisdom from respected, caring elders.

Family size and its effects

The middle aged will, more than ever, tote society's Sisyphean boulder. They will not need to spend as much time and money on so many offspring, but they will increasingly have new dependents—the old. By 2020, it is estimated that only one out of three Americans will be a taxpayer, and that liened group should be more heavily composed of the middle aged. In contrast to the whiz-kid executive syndrome of the '70s—a direct result of the baby boom—the reins of power will revert to older hands. For the middle-age, middle-management sector, there will be fewer shots at the top, though there will be more titular promotions and merit raises to reward the faithful. On the positive side, lessened competition may result in heightened creativity. People may concentrate on doing what they know best, rather than aspiring to levels at which they may prove incompetent, or be bored, or both.

The elderly, as a much bigger and therefore more influential segment of the population, with longer life expectancy, will almost certainly insist on filling a more productive role in society than they occupy today. With a smaller work force, the mandatory retirement age within the next quarter-century will have to be advanced to 70. Indeed, many social critics have long argued that the nation is spinning off an incalculably valuable resource by relegating robust, creative people to senior citizens' ghettos. The graying of America will offer new opportunities for the retired. There is already a crying need in the U.S. for day-care centers and kindergartens where working couples may safely leave their children; they could ideally be—and may have to be—staffed by older people. Some futurists have suggested that the elderly may form a class of "professional parents" for children of working couples. Some demographers, including Australia-based Lincoln Day, have proposed that retired couples be given state subsidies to take over abandoned small farms, where they could help increase the food supply. A report on the future of agriculture, published last week, strongly advocated a revival of small farms, located near cities, that could provide food more cheaply than agribusiness can in the face of the enduring, expensive energy shortage. Many retired people could find new and rewarding lives as small-scale producers of food.

The role of the elderly will expand

One of the most heartening aspects of the new society, Stanford University Biologist Paul Ehrlich believes, is the speed with which it has come about. "It indicates that attitudes and customs are not so deeply ingrained that they cannot change rather quickly," he notes. "Ten years ago, we believed that the attitudes of women and the kinds of lives they lived would be something that had to change slowly, over decades. Actually there was a remarkably swift change between 1968 and 1970. It indicates that other attitudes we believe to be deeply held could also change quickly. Like the attitude that Americans must consume energy and other resources out of proportion to their needs."

Attitudes are often quick to change

Already, from Ithaca, N.Y., to Evanston, Ill., from Kalamazoo, Mich., to Livermore, Calif., empty elementary and now high schools are being converted to make room for shops, restaurants, arts workshops. Headstart programs, day-care centers, concert halls, studios, ballet schools, adult classes, seminars for unwed mothers, vocational training and housing for the elderly. Young doctors trained as pediatricians or gynecologists are increasingly transferring to the lamentably neglected area of public health. The transformation from growthmania to a less-is-more society will demand greater adjustments and some painful decisions. Nevertheless, demographers point out a controlled population will allow the U.S. to reorder its priorities and reassess its values before they are dictated by scarcity.

Not least, the joy of having children will be enhanced.

GROWTH IN THE LESS-DEVELOPED NATIONS

Prior to the twentieth century, birthrates and death rates within the economically and industrially less-developed nations of Africa, Asia, and Latin America remained at consistently high levels. Thus, although these areas contained relatively large (and also relatively young) populations, population growth did not occur to any appreciable degree. During the twentieth century, however, particularly after World War II, the populations within these areas began to expand dramatically. This vast growth within these nations, as we have previously pointed out, was largely the result of sharp and rapid declines in death rates (particularly in infant and child mortality) and increases in life expectancy. What caused the sudden, large-scale decline in mortality within these nations?

After World War II, medical and other scientific knowledge produced antibiotics, vaccines, insecticides, public health programs, and advanced medical techniques and procedures that were rapidly exported from the industrialized nations to the less-developed countries of the world through the efforts of various international health agencies. The result was "instant death control," to use Paul Ehrlich's phrase, which in turn had a profound effect upon population increase within these nations.[32] Kingsley Davis notes, for example, that Ceylon's death rate declined 40 percent in only three years (1945 to 1948), largely due to controlling malaria through the use of DDT. Moreover, as Davis notes, "nothing was required of the Ceylonese themselves . . . . the spectacular decline in the death rate came about through no basic economic development or change in (their) institutional structure." Ceylonese mortality was simply reduced for them by outside experts armed with modern medical technology. Similar patterns in death-rate reductions held true for virtually all the less-developed nations in the decades following World War II. One by one, diseases such as malaria, diphtheria, cholera, smallpox, and dysentery were virtually conquered wherever they existed by means of easily and rapidly acquired medical and scientific knowledge. The result was a massive decline in death rates (particularly infant and child mortality) within the less-developed nations—a faster and greater decline than the developed nations experienced during the Industrial Revolution.[33]

Massive population growth: A postwar phenomenon

Reasons for the massive mortality decline

Table 9.1. Population growth in specific nations: 1978

NATION	TOTAL (MILLIONS)	BIRTHRATE (PER THOUSAND)	DEATH RATE (PER THOUSAND)	POPULATION GROWTH RATE	NUMBER OF YEARS TO DOUBLE POPULATION
United States	218.4	15	9	0.6	116
Canada	23.6	16	7	0.9	77
United Kingdom	56.0	12	12	0.0	—
West Germany	61.3	10	12	−0.2	—
USSR	261.0	18	9	0.9	77
China	930.0	22	8	1.4	50
Indonesia	140.2	38	14	2.4	29
India	634.7	34	14	2.0	35
Pakistan	76.8	44	14	3.0	23
Nigeria	68.4	49	21	2.8	25
Brazil	115.4	36	8	2.8	25
Mexico	66.9	42	8	3.4	20
Japan	114.4	16	6	1.0	69
Italy	56.7	14	10	0.4	173
Ireland	3.2	22	10	1.1	63
France	53.4	14	10	0.3	231

Source: The Population Reference Bureau, *1978 World Population Data Sheet*, Washington, D.C. 1978.

A second and highly important contributing factor to the massive population growth within the less-developed nations of the world is the fact that, in spite of wholesale declines in death rates, birthrates within most of these nations have remained high. As a result of this combination, the annual rates of population growth of most African, Asian, and Latin American nations stand in excess of 2 percent. Even more ominous is the fact that approximately 40 percent of the population within the less-developed countries is now *younger than 15*.[34] It is likely, therefore, that these nations will exhibit vast population growth in the future.

High birthrates and low death rates mean population growth

The pattern of low death rates with continued high birthrates within less-developed nations stands in sharp contrast to that of the developed nations, whose birthrates have shown an overall general decline, following the earlier decline in death rates associated with the Industrial Revolution. Specific explanations for these fertility differentials will be developed later in this chapter. For now we can say that the current world population explosion can be attributed to the effect of high fertility combined with lowered mortality characteristically found within the world's less-developed nations.

Rapid and large-scale population growth has created many problems for the less-developed countries, perhaps the most serious of which is hunger. Estimates indicate that as many as one-half of the world's population is either chronically hungry, starving, or at least suffering serious dietary deficiencies (malnutrition). The vast majority of these people live within the less-developed countries, primarily in African, Asian, and, to a lesser extent, Latin American nations. The problems of hunger and malnutrition have serious consequences, particularly for infants and young children. Rates of infant mortality (infants younger than 1 year), often due to malnutrition and related diseases, stand at 157 per thousand births in Bolivia, 137 in Indonesia, 129 in India, 139 in Pakistan, 159 in Zambia, 160 in Uganda, and 157 in Nigeria.[35] Moreover, malnutrition in the form of protein deficiencies tends to hinder the development of bones and muscles and also frequently leads to irreversible mental retardation in infants and young children.[36]

Perhaps most tragic is that each year it is likely that more rather than fewer people within the less-developed nations face starvation and chronic malnutrition, despite the fact that many of these nations have actually increased their agricultural production and also receive food imports from the developed nations.[37] This growing problem results primarily from the fact that increased agricultural output simply cannot keep pace with population growth. Each year world population grows by an additional 80 million people, with the vast majority of this growth taking place within the less-developed nations.[38] India, for example, has experienced a general rise in food production over the last several years, yet population increase, which adds over a million people *each month* to the country's total population, has literally outstripped food gains.[39] Population growth is often fastest in very poor countries. Niger (in western Africa), for example, has a yearly per capita income level of only $160 yet a 2.7 percent yearly rate of population growth.[40]

Given current worldwide population projections, it is likely that food production will have to increase many times over in order to supply minimum nutritional needs for an additional two to three billion people by the year 2000. Not even considering the fact that most of the world's productive land is already being farmed, mass increases in agricultural productivity will also be very expensive, since fertilizers, oil, and farm machinery are costly. In fact, these costs are already too large for the pocketbooks of many less-developed nations. Thus in the long run, it is likely that growing numbers of people in the world will have to exist with hunger, malnutrition, disease, and starvation as facts of life.

Rapid population growth has also created severe problems for the economic development of many of the less-developed nations. In order for a country to experience economic development (i.e., a growth in the standard of living), a certain amount of the country's national income must be reinvested each year into new income-producing investments, such as new factories, machinery, and general technology. Davis notes that, given a stable population, a country must invest 3 to 5 percent of its national income each year in order to create a 1 percent growth in per capita income. However, if a country's population is increasing by 2.5 or 3 percent each year, an annual investment of up to 20 percent of national income is necessary in order to raise the economic standard of living.[41] The poorer nations of the world just cannot afford this level of investment. Thus, even though many less-developed countries are experiencing some economic expansion, most if not all of these gains must be used to satisfy the basic needs of more and more people while the general standard of living remains essentially unchanged. True economic growth is simply cancelled out by population growth since little, if any, national income is left over for investment into additional economic (i.e., new income-producing) development.

Population growth and socioeconomic development

For the individual, the lack of national economic development in the face of (and resulting from) rapid population growth frequently translates to a lifetime of poverty and chronic unemployment. Given the pressures of population growth upon their economies, the majority of the less-developed nations are struggling just to keep their growing numbers at a more-or-less subsistence level. In India, despite an 8 percent increase in per capita income during 1975, roughly half of the population still lives on an average income of $35 per year.[42] Over 40 percent of the vast Indian population is very poor even by Indian standards: The government has defined poverty as a monthly income of $8 or less per person.[43] Moreover, the population of India is projected to grow by an additional 400 million people in the next twenty years.

Lack of economic development means personal poverty

Population increase resulting from high birthrates has traditionally been greatest within the vast rural areas of less-developed Asian, African, and Latin American nations. There has been such a large build-up of this rural population that there is simply no use for their labor and the land cannot support their numbers. As a result, increasing numbers of the unemployed and destitute rural population have migrated to the cities in the hope of finding jobs. This pattern of rural-to-urban migration, combined with the city's own natural increase, has been responsible for a vast growth in urban population within the less-developed nations. In fact, in recent years urban population growth (in cities of over 100,000) within the less-developed nations has actually outpaced the rate of population growth as a whole.

Rural-to-urban migration

The phenomenon of urban population growth has often been noted in reference to cities that lie within the less-developed Asian and African

Latin American cities
are growing faster
than ever

nations, but it is often found within Latin American nations as well. Latin American cities are now growing at rates in excess of 4 percent per year, and projections indicate that by the year 2000, Latin American cities will contain as many as 500 million people (19 of the cities alone will contain approximately 250 million people).[44] In fact, some projections indicate that by as early as 1985, Mexico City may contain almost one-third of Mexico's entire population.[45]

In most cases, the shift of population to the cities offers little solution to the migrant's problems. The lack of economic development in the first place (at least relative to population growth) plus the daily crush of newcomers to the city means few jobs are available. If work is eventually found, the pay will probably be low because the rural migrant tends to be both unskilled and uneducated. It is more likely that most of these migrants will simply join the ranks of the huge unemployed or underemployed

The squatter population

shantytown squatter populations, which typically form in city parks, near rivers, on sidewalks, and on rooftops. The squatter populations of Hong Kong, Manila, and some Peruvian cities are well-known examples of this massive urban ghetto development, where poverty, disease, and lack of privacy and sanitation are daily facts of life. Moreover, the vast growth of these cities, resulting from rapid rural-to-urban migration and natural increase, also introduces a host of other urban problems, such as pollution, overcrowding, poor transportation, and massive housing shortages, all of which make it very difficult to improve urban living standards.[46]

In the previous sections of this chapter we have examined the patterns of population growth and the consequences of this growth for the developed and less-developed nations. However, we must again emphasize that large-scale population growth, regardless of where it occurs, brings many serious national and international consequences. As we have seen, most if not all nations have little to gain from continual large-scale population growth. On the contrary, overpopulation and the current population explosion pose many distinct hazards and threats to worldwide resources, our environment, and indeed the very quality of life for all upon our planet.

EXPLANATIONS FOR POPULATION GROWTH AND CHANGE

Periods of population
growth

Throughout most of human existence, world population has tended to grow rather slowly, with the exception of the period of the Agricultural Revolution (8000 B.C.). Then the world population remained fairly stable until the eighteenth and nineteenth centuries, during which time the European and North American populations began again to escalate. In the twentieth century, as birthrates fell within the industrialized nations, a third wave of population increase occurred within the less-developed nations of the world. As we have pointed out in some detail, it is the vast population growth within these countries that constitutes the main thrust and threat of our current population explosion. What makes populations increase, decrease, or remain stable?

THE MALTHUSIAN PRINCIPLE

Thomas Malthus (1766–1834), a central figure in early demographic studies, was the first to provide a major theoretical explanation for population growth and its consequences. Basic to Malthusian theory is the notion that populations have a tendency to increase at an exponential rate. Malthus noted, however, that throughout most of history, populations did not actually manifest any long-term periods of sustained explosive growth. Rather, periodic population growth would inevitably be followed by population decline. In his famous book, *Essay on the Principle of Population* (1798), Malthus developed an explanation for the growth and decline of human numbers based upon the relationship between the rate of population growth and the rate of growth in the food supply (i.e., the means of subsistence).[47]

Malthus: Exponential growth

In his theory, Malthus argued that populations have a tendency to grow at a geometric rate (2,4,8,16, . . .), whereas the means of subsistence (food supply and production) increases only arithmetically (1,2,3,4,5, . . .).[48] Malthus emphasized that given this faster rate of population growth, there would always be a certain degree of strain between population and the means of subsistence.[49] Ultimately, populations would grow to the point where they would exceed their means of support. At this point other factors, which Malthus termed *positive checks* (such as famine, disease, and war), would come into play. These factors would increase the death rate, thus reducing the population to a point once again compatible with the level of food production and supply.[50] In essence, Malthus emphasized that there was a close relationship among the availability of food, fertility, and mortality. Increase the availability of resources (food) and the standard of living increases, mortality decreases, and population grows. Given, however, the natural tendency of populations to increase geometrically, such growth would inevitably outstrip food supply and mortality would increase, thus bringing an end to population growth.

Population and the means of support

Needless to say, Malthus's ideas were not very popular or warmly received by his contemporaries. He wrote at a time that many have referred to as the "golden age" of the Industrial Revolution, an age characterized by increased standards of living, declining mortality, and a resultant growth in population. His pessimism ran in direct contradiction to the beliefs of others, who envisioned continued progress and future abundance. In effect, his theory posed a clear threat to the widespread optimism characteristic of the industrializing nations during this period. According to Malthus, population growth would inevitably lead to hunger, disease, and poverty for most of the human race. In his later writings, however, Malthus expressed the hope that a "death rate" solution to the problem of population increase could possibly be avoided through the application of what he termed *pre-*

Malthus had many critics

Positive and preventive checks

ventive checks (to reduce the birthrate), in the form of sexual abstinence, delayed marriage, and continence in marriage.[51]

In the long run, Malthus's pessimistic predictions did not hold true for the industrializing northern European and North American regions. Unfortunately, however, the recent population explosion occurring within the less-developed nations of the world is a clear reminder that the Malthusian principle cannot be easily dismissed. Around the year 1650, for example, growth rates were low enough that population doubled only once every 1200 years or so. Between 1650 and 1850, however, doubling time was cut to approximately 200 years. At current rates of growth, world population

Faster doubling times

will double within only 41 years! Our review of the present and future consequences of such dramatic growth for all nations of the world raises doubts as to whether, at least in the long run, we will be able to truly avoid the Malthusian prophecy.

DEMOGRAPHIC TRANSITION THEORY

As we have seen, Malthus was concerned with the consequences of large-scale population growth within the then-industrializing European and North American nations. Ultimately, his pessimistic predictions for these nations have not held true. First of all, he did not envision the truly massive increase in agricultural productivity that resulted from the growth of industrial technology. Gains in agricultural productivity (the means of subsistence) gave the industrialized nations the capacity to feed and maintain vastly increased numbers of people. Second and perhaps more important, Malthus did not forsee the eventual impact of industrialization upon fertility. Starting in the late nineteenth and continuing throughout the twentieth centuries, as we have previously noted, birthrates declined within the industrialized nations of the world, the only reversal being the 1945–1957 "baby boom."

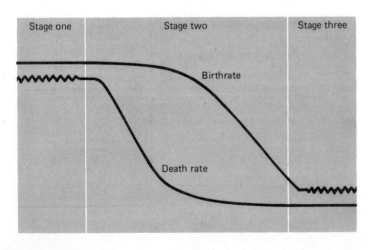

Fig. 9.4 The demographic transition. Stage one is characterized by a high birthrate and a high death rate, resulting in population stability. Stage two is marked by a sharp decline in the death rate while the birthrate remains relatively high. The result is rapid population growth. Stage three is characterized by low birth- and death rates, once again yielding population stability.

In 1945 Kingsley Davis developed the theory of *demographic transition* in order to more adequately account for the pattern of population change characteristically found within industrialized societies. According to this theory, a decline in a society's death rate will inevitably be followed by a *voluntary* decline in its birthrate. Moreover, various factors related to economic and industrial development itself are responsible for this sequence. In terms of the demographic transition, societies experiencing economic development pass through the following three basic stages of population growth:[52]

Stage one is characterized by high rates of both fertility and mortality. This stage is typically found within traditional, premodern societies. Since the high birth- and death rates are roughly equal, the rate of population growth is virtually nil. This stage was characteristic of European and American societies in the centuries prior to their industrialization.

Stage two is characterized by a decline in the death rate while birthrates remain high. This stage is typically found within the earlier periods of industrialization. The death rate declines as a result of advances in the standard of living and the growth of medical knowledge and technology. As a result of the widening gap between high birthrates and lowered death rates, population increases rapidly. This stage was characteristic of the industrializing nations during the eighteenth and nineteenth centuries.

Stage three is characterized by low rates of fertility and low death rates and is typical of today's highly industrialized societies. In this stage industrialization, economic development, and urbanization begin and continue to influence people's attitudes toward family size. Smaller families are preferred to large ones as couples begin to recognize that, given the high standards and costs of living, large families constitute a substantial economic liability rather than an economic asset, as was the case in preindustrial times. As a result, couples voluntarily have fewer children, the birthrate drops to a level approximating the low death rate, and the rate of population growth declines, more or less holding at a very low (and perhaps even negative) level. Eventually, contraceptive birth control methods also tend to become popular and widely used within the industrialized societies, since such devices ensure that the "small family ideal" is achieved and maintained. Couples prefer fewer children, and the eventual rise of a sophisticated birth control technology helps to guarantee low levels of unplanned fertility.[53]

DEMOGRAPHIC TRANSITION AND THE LESS-DEVELOPED NATIONS
Does the theory of the demographic transition also apply to the less-developed societies? Will these nations also experience a full demographic transition? Currently, demographers are divided on this issue; no one can really say for certain whether the less-developed nations will proceed through the entire process. As we pointed out earlier, present industrialized societies experienced a decline in death rates (and a resultant population growth) due to improvements in the standard of living and the growth of

Declining mortality yields declining fertility

The small family ideal

medical knowledge and technology. These changes and improvements occurred rather gradually, extending over many generations, and there was more than ample time for values and attitudes concerning family size to adapt to new living conditions.

However, the situation for the less-developed countries has been quite different. Prior to the twentieth century, death rates—particularly rates of infant mortality — within these nations were high, thus necessitating corresponding high levels of fertility. In recent years, as we have seen, the less-developed nations have experienced rapid declines in their death rates as a result of the large-scale importation of medical and scientific knowledge from the industrialized nations. This reduction in mortality was massive and sudden, providing virtually no time for readjustment in values and attitudes that have traditionally favored high fertility. Birthrates therefore continued to remain at traditionally high levels. Today high birthrates and low death rates remain characteristic of the majority of the underdeveloped regions of the world. The result has been vast population growth. Indonesia has a birthrate of 38 per thousand and a death rate of 14; Mexico, a birthrate of 42 and a death rate of 8; Kenya, a birthrate of 48 and a death rate of 15.[54] In general, the annual rate of population growth within the less-developed nations exceeds 2 percent, which means that their populations will double exponentially every 35 years or less.

But why has fertility within the less-developed nations continued to remain high? What factors have contributed to and encouraged their high birthrates? Answers to these questions require consideration of the traditions and values that for centuries have stressed the importance and desirability of large families. Until recent years, death rates (particularly of infants) were very high within the less-developed nations. Traditionally, large families have been encouraged to ensure that at least some of the children would survive into their adult years, take over the family land, and help the parents in their old age. Large families have also been traditionally viewed as an economic asset to the agricultural economies of these countries, each child representing an important source of labor for tilling the soil and harvesting crops.

At present, the large family may still serve these functions, to a certain degree, within some of the less-developed nations. Increasingly, however, large families and the cultural values that encourage high fertility are proving to be highly detrimental to the quality of life. Today, as a result of the introduction of modern medicine, the majority of children will live well into adulthood. Moreover, as we have seen, rapid population growth has already created some serious problems for the less-developed nations—hunger, malnutrition, disease, and starvation. In brief, many of the cultural values and traditions designed to ensure large families are simply lagging behind many of the modern medicines and technological innovations, which have drastically altered the patterns of population growth within the underdeveloped

The importation of knowledge vs. the impact of tradition

Prior benefits of large families

David Hurn, Magnum Photos, Inc.

The traditional ways often stand side-by-side with the latest technological advances in less-developed nations.

nations. Technological change has proceeded more quickly than a change in traditions and values.

    Many proponents of demographic transition theory feel that the less-developed nations will eventually experience a transition from high to low rates of fertility similar to the transition that has occurred within the world's developed nations. In fact, recent data indicate that a number of small and somewhat economically advanced less-developed nations, such as Chile, Costa Rica, Argentina, and Taiwan, are now experiencing lowered birth- and growth rates. Proponents of demographic transition have regarded this evidence as a sign that perhaps the other less-developed nations may likewise experience the transition to lowered fertility. Dudley Kirk notes, however, that before a country can experience a transition in fertility, it must first meet and surpass a "threshold" level of socioeconomic growth, particularly as this is related to educational advancement and increases in per capita income.[55] If this is the case, then a birthrate decline within the remaining less-developed nations will not occur unless they can reach a sufficient level of economic development. The problem with this is that

Technology vs. custom

The "threshold" of economic development

those nations with the highest birthrates are typically very poor and very overpopulated. And as we have seen, true economic development is most difficult for nations such as these, since overpopulation and high rates of population growth frequently cancel any economic gains.

Despite demographic transition, population could still grow

Moreover, as Ehrlich has pointed out, a considerable amount of time would no doubt be required for the world's less-developed nations to experience economic development, industrialization, and a full transition to low fertility rates. Thus, even if a demographic transition does occur, it may not happen quickly enough to avoid explosive population growth. In Ehrlich's view, therefore, the demographic transition provides neither short- nor long-range solutions to the world's population crisis.[56]

RESPONSES TO OVERPOPULATION

As we pointed out in the beginning of this chapter, world population in the present century is growing more rapidly than it has in any other period of recorded human history. Short of the admitted unlikely possibility of rapid and massive economic development, industrialization, and full transition to lowered fertility on a worldwide level, what can be and is being done to deal with the problem of population growth? Basically, population growth can be either reduced or stopped in two ways: by increasing our mortality rate or by decreasing fertility. For obvious reasons, no one is advocating programs to increase mortality; rather, methods to decrease fertility provide the only legitimate governmental course of action to reduce population growth. At present, governments have universally adopted a voluntary approach to fertility control, often in line with the development of family planning programs. Some population experts feel, however, that nothing short of compulsory and coercive programs of population control will be sufficient to avoid a future worldwide catastrophe.

Voluntary fertility control

FAMILY PLANNING: THE DEVELOPED NATIONS
Even though birthrates within the industrially developed countries have been declining for some time, most of these nations are still experiencing population growth. As we have seen, these nations have a number of population problems of their own. Moreover, given the fact that many of these countries (particularly the United States) consume far more than their proportionate share of world resources, it is in the interest of *all* nations that population increase within industrial countries be stopped or at least held to minimal levels.

Family planning: Helping people have the number of children they desire

Today, many of the world's industrialized nations actively support voluntary family planning. These programs operate on the basic notion that couples should be able to have the number of children they desire. Family planning is most typically a clinic-based approach to child bearing, in which trained professionals advise couples on the nature and use of contraceptive techniques. Emphasis is also placed upon the health and welfare of the family and its ability to economically provide for its members.

Family planning constitutes the major thrust of population policy in the United States, with planning services available nationwide. While family planning services have been available to and in fact utilized by many people within the general population, subsidized services within the United States "are officially available only to the needy." This policy stands in contrast to Canada and many European nations, where "free or subsidized services and supplies are available through national health or social security schemes to the general population."[57]

FERTILITY CONTROL: THE DEVELOPED NATIONS
The use of a variety of contraceptive birth control devices (with or without official family planning assistance) has also tended to become very popular in industrialized nations, particularly within recent decades. As in the United States, contraceptives are legal, widely accepted, and available in the vast majority of European nations. Dorothy Nortman has recently compiled data indicating, for example, that within the developed Asian (i.e., Japan and Australia), North American, and European nations surveyed, approximately two-thirds of the married women of reproductive age are using some form of contraceptive device. The figure for the United States stands at 70 percent.[58] Many of the European nations have shown far more initiative than the United States, however, in the development of sex education within school programs.

In addition to the more traditional forms of birth control devices, such as the "pill," the IUD, and condoms, recent evidence indicates that increasing numbers of individuals within the developed nations are also turning to abortion and sterilization for fertility control, and a growing number of nations now permit abortion on request within the first three months of pregnancy. In recent years the nations that have made abortion available on extremely liberal grounds include Great Britain, Finland, Austria, Canada, Denmark, Sweden, East and West Germany, The Netherlands, and the United States.[59] The United States Supreme Court in effect legalized abortion· in 1973, ruling that the "government must not interfere with the right of any woman to have an abortion in the first three months of her pregnancy if she so chooses."[60] In 1973, the number of legal abortions in the United States stood at 744,600. In 1976, this figure increased to over 1,115,000, including 300,000 that were financed through Medicaid.[61]

Today sterilization has also become legal or at least unregulated in every industrialized nation, with the exception of France, Italy, Turkey, and some parts of Canada. In Europe, the latest figures show that approximately five million people have chosen sterilization for fertility control. In the United States, the last remaining state regulations prohibiting sterilization were eliminated in 1972.[62] According to data supplied by the Associa-

Family planning: The major thrust of U.S. policy

Contraceptives are widely available in industrial societies

The liberalization of abortion

Sterilization is growing quickly

Table 9.2. Developing countries that support organized family planning programs to promote health and human rights (Category B) and also to reduce population growth (Category A): 1977

REGION AND COUNTRY	POPULATION IN 1976 (MILLIONS)	CATEGORY	REGION AND COUNTRY	POPULATION IN 1976 (MILLIONS)	CATEGORY
Africa			Nepal	12.9	A
Algeria	17.3	B	Pakistan	72	A
Benin, People's Republic of	3.2	B	Papua New Guinea	2.8	B
			Philippines	43.3	A
Botswana	0.7	A	Singapore	2.3	A
Egypt	38.0	A	Sri Lanka	13.8	A
Gambia	0.53	B	Taiwan	16.3	A
Ghana	9.6	A	Thailand	42.9	A
Kenya	13.8	A	Turkey	40.1	A
Lesotho	1	B	Viet Nam, Socialist Republic of	49	A
Liberia	1.7	B			
Mali	5.6	B	*Latin America*		
Mauritius	0.87	A	Barbados	0.24	A
Morocco	17.8	A	Bolivia	5.8	B
Nigeria	65	B	Brazil	111	B
Rhodesia	6.5	B	Chile	10.5	B
South Africa	25.7	B	Colombia	25.2	A
Sudan	18.3	B	Costa Rica	2.1	B
Tanzania	15.7	B	Cuba	9.5	B
Tunisia	5.7	A	Dominican Republic	5.1	A
Uganda	11.8	B	Ecuador	7.3	B
Zaire	25.2	B	El Salvador	4.3	A
Asia and Oceania			Guatemala	5.9	A
Afghanistan	19.6	B	Haiti	4.7	B
Bangladesh	81	A	Honduras	2.8	B
China, People's Republic of	845	A	Jamaica	2.1	A
			Mexico	61.8	A
Fiji	0.58	A	Nicaragua	2.3	B
Hong Kong	4.5	A	Panama	1.7	B
India	610	A	Paraguay	2.7	B
Indonesia	135	A	Peru	16.1	B
Iran	34	A	Puerto Rico	3.2	A
Iraq	11.5	B	Trinidad & Tobago	1.1	A
Korea, Republic of	35.7	A	Venezuela	12.3	B
Malaysia, Peninsular	10.9	A			

Table 9.2. *(Continued)*

Summary: Developing Countries

	CATEGORY A	CATEGORY B	BALANCE	TOTAL
Number of developing countries				
All regions	34	29	66	129
Africa	7	13	29	49
Asia	18	3	26	47
Latin America	9	13	11	33
Percent distribution of population by government position				
All regions	76	16	8	100
Africa	21	48	31	100
Asia	92	4	4	100
Latin America	36	62	2	100

Source: Dorothy Nortman and Ellen Hofstatter, *Population and Family Planning Programs*, Ninth edition. New York: The Population Council, 1978, Table 6.

tion for Voluntary Sterilization, approximately 9.5 million people in the United States had undergone sterilization by the end of 1976, and this figure is increasing by more than a million persons each year.[63] Also significant are the 1973 findings supplied by the National Survey of Family Growth, which indicated that in the United States one in four couples using contraception relied on sterilization as their method of fertility control. Moreover, among couples in which the woman was 30 or older, sterilization had become the leading birth control method.[64]

As noted earlier in this chapter, growth rates within most of the industrially developed nations now stand at 1 percent or less per year, largely as a result of declining births, and in a few cases these nations have either stopped growing or are experiencing negative growth rates. There is no question that family planning and the widespread availability of contraceptive methods have greatly facilitated this process. However, we must not lose sight of the fact that birthrates within the developed nations have been declining since roughly the turn of the century, well in advance of family planning programs and modern contraceptive techniques. As we have seen, factors related to industrialization, socioeconomic development, and urbanization have ultimately been responsible for declining fertility rates and for the small family ideal within these nations. The mere availability of contraceptives cannot account for their widespread acceptability and use. Rather, the rise of birth control technology within industrial nations helps ensure that desired low fertility levels are maintained. Given these present

Birthrate declines occurred before contraceptives

and long-term trends, it appears likely that birthrates within the developed nations will remain near or below replacement levels. But what about the less-developed nations, which now comprise almost three-fourths of the world's total population? How have their governments dealt with the problem of population growth, and to what degee have these efforts been successful?

FAMILY PLANNING AND FERTILITY CONTROL: THE LESS-DEVELOPED NATIONS

The first essential step to come to terms with the problem of population growth is to recognize that a problem does actually exist. However, at least until recently, the majority of the world's fastest growing countries either ignored or denied their problem of population growth. Nortman indicates that as of 1960, only two countries in the world, India and Pakistan, had given support to some form of organized family planning program. By the mid-1970s, this figure had increased to some thirty nations, and today sixty-three of the less-developed nations (comprising over 90 percent of the people in the developing world) support governmentally and/or privately sponsored family planning programs.[65] As in the industrialized nations, family planning programs in less-developed countries are typically clinic-based; contraceptives such as pills and IUDs are made available and people are advised of their nature and use. Increasingly, family planning programs have also incorporated information and services on sterilization and abortion in line with the legalization and liberalization of these fertility control measures by more and more governments.[66]

Family planning is new in the less-developed nations

Aside from the growth of governmental support for family planning, the most critical question is whether such programs in and of themselves can bring about or at least greatly facilitate a reduction in fertility and population growth rates within the world's less-developed nations. On this issue the evidence is not always so clear-cut, and demographic experts vary considerably in their opinions of the merits of the family planning approach to fertility reduction. Those who support family planning argue that in virtually all nations where these programs have been introduced fertility has decreased. Many of these experts view the problem of overpopulation largely as one of "excess," "unplanned," or "unwanted" fertility. Some are also of the opinion that many people, even those living in the poorest nations, can be brought to understand the undesirable personal and social consequences of large families. In general, family planners feel that "if governments make these [birth control] methods and the knowledge of their use readily and freely available to everyone, people would have fewer children."[67]

Do family planning programs work?

On the other hand, many opponents of family planning have amassed evidence indicating that family planning in and of itself has been largely unsuccessful in dealing with the problem of population growth, and that such programs alone will continue to have little impact upon fertility levels within the less-developed countries. Many of these experts argue that only under conditions of improved socioeconomic development, industrialization, and increases in the standard of living will a demographic transition to lower fertility rates occur within these regions. In essence, they argue that, given certain improvements in a society's socioeconomic conditions and a relatively equitable distribution of socioeconomic benefits, people in the underdeveloped nations will be motivated to reduce their fertility and birthrates will decline.[68]

National growth must be distributed more equally

In the less-developed countries, family planning programs face a number of obstacles that tend to impede their effectiveness. Demographers have pointed out that in order for family planning programs to effect declines in fertility several conditions must be fulfilled: (1) effective means of contraception must be available; (2) people must be aware of this fact; and (3) people must be willing to accept these methods. In many of the less-developed nations contraceptives are not widely accessible and/or many people are not aware that they can be obtained. This situation results pri-

Obstacles to family planning

Marilyn Silverstone, Magnum Photos, Inc.

In India, where overpopulation has reached a critical level, the government is actively involved in efforts to educate its citizens about contraception.

marily from the fact that sound family planning programs are very expensive, especially for these countries, and shortages of medical facilities and medical staffs make things worse. Moreover, in many less-developed nations, large numbers of people live in rural areas and villages, so for the most part, family planning information and services are geographically inaccessible. Even nations that have placed much effort into establishing governmental and/or private family planning programs, such as Mexico, India, and Colombia, have not experienced much success in surmounting this obstacle. In India alone, 80 percent of the population lives in rural villages.[69]

Finally, when contraceptives can be obtained and people have knowledge of this, there is still no guarantee that people will find contraceptives acceptable to their values, beliefs, and way of life. Many people within the less-developed nations tend to be somewhat skeptical and hesitant when it comes to technological innovation; still others find it difficult to believe that contraceptive devices can really prevent something so natural as childbirth. There is no question that factors such as these help explain, in part, the relative lack of contraceptive use found within under-developed areas. For example, Nortman indicates that, even though there has been a recent increase in contraceptive use within some of these countries, the percentage of married women of reproductive age using contraceptives exceeded 33 percent in only 9 out of 29 less-developed regions surveyed.[70]

Without doubt, the major weakness of the family planning approach to fertility control lies in the fact that these programs typically emphasize that people should have (and be encouraged to have) the number of children they desire. Unfortunately, that number is not always economically healthy for their society.[71] Moreover, as Nortman indicates, "regardless of the effect on fertility, all government support of family planning programs is justified *a priori* on the grounds of health and the inherent right of couples to choose the spacing and number of their children."[72] In a society where couples typically want only one or two children, family planning would likely be successful in holding population growth to the desired replacement levels. However, in the less-developed nations, the number of children couples desire, expect, and *actually do have* is usually around four.[73] Under these circumstances, even if contraceptives become more widely obtainable, population growth will remain a major problem.

In spite of these obstacles and weaknesses, family planners note that birthrates have shown at least a slight to moderate decline in two of the larger less-developed nations, India and China, as well as in a few of the smaller developing areas or nations, such as Colombia, Costa Rica, Chile, South Korea, Taiwan, and Hong Kong. India's involvement with family planning began in 1952, and recent evidence indicates that between 1969 and 1976 the percentage of married women of reproductive age using contraceptives increased from 7 or 8 percent to 18 or 20 percent.[74] Nevertheless, as we have seen, India still faces an extremely critical population problem. In recent decades, the birthrate there has shown only a slight decline,

Most women in less-developed nations do not use contraceptives

The major weakness of family planning

Some developing nations have experienced declining birthrates

from a traditional 40 or so per thousand to a present level of 34. Given India's continued high birthrate and young age structure, the nation's already massive population of 634 million is projected to increase to almost 1034 million by the year 2000 and to double within the next thirty-five years.

On the other hand, based upon the limited information available, it would appear that China might have made at least some progress in checking rates of fertility. In 1964 China's birthrate stood at 35.5; recent estimates now indicate that it falls somewhere between 14 and 37. In large part, this is because China's emphasis on population control goes far beyond that of virtually all other birth control programs. The Chinese family planning program stresses the importance of extensive contraceptive use, late marriage, spacing births, and a two-child-per-family norm.[75] According to Lester Brown, "The comprehensive Chinese effort focuses not only upon providing family planning services, including abortion, but also upon reshaping economic and social policies to encourage small families and upon an intensive public education campaign extolling the benefits of smaller families."[76] Even with a reduction in birthrates, however, China's enormous population of 930 million is still growing, according to the Population Reference Bureau, at an estimated rate of 1.4 percent per year, which yields a doubling time of only fifty years.[77]

The Chinese effort: Extensive family planning plus social and economic change aimed at improving the standard of living

Birthrates have also shown impressive declines within a number of the smaller developing countries previously mentioned. We must point out, however, that these places typically represent some of the more advanced of the world's less-developed nations. In many although not all cases, birthrates started to decline in these areas in advance of family planning programs, although the programs did serve to hasten declines that were already underway.

OTHER APPROACHES TO FERTILITY CONTROL

In general we must conclude that family planning has had some but nevertheless only a limited influence in promoting fertility decline within the world's less-developed nations. Family planning efforts have indeed grown within these countries; more and more governments have come out in support of them, and in some areas there have also been fairly significant increases in the use of contraception. Yet birthrates within these nations still remain high, averaging 36.4 per thousand, compared to 17.4 in the world's developed nations.[78] Family planning and the use of contraception have been key factors in facilitating fertility declines in the developed nations, where modernization and industrialization have long been influential in the formation of values and attitudes favoring low fertility and small families. However, in the less-developed nations, people still tend to value relatively large families. As a result, even where official family planning programs are available and the people know of them, it is not uncommon to find that the people turn to their use only *after* they have established large families.[79]

Differential birthrates

Given the fact that family planning programs have not been very successful in reducing fertility and population growth within the less-developed nations, what alternatives are available? In a few instances governments have devised systems of *incentives,* in the form of gifts or cash payments, to those who utilize contraceptives or consent to sterilization.[80] Davis, however, has urged the adoption of a national population policy, going far beyond mere family planning, that would ultimately bring about value, attitudinal, and normative change favoring small rather than large families. Such a policy would incorporate a number of social and economic measures and reforms, which in Davis' view would yield conditions favoring fertility decline. Such measures would include: economic advantages in taxes, education, and housing to single rather than married persons; increased education and equalization of employment opportunities for women; and the requirement that couples be able to demonstrate their "economic viability" before obtaining a marriage license. Davis feels that measures such as these would no doubt be adequate to elicit fertility reduction. If not, he recommends the adoption of several additional changes, such as eliminating the use of family names, relieving older children from the responsibility for their parents, and centering recreational activities around the place of work, not the home.[81]

Such measures could possibly effect declines in fertility, although at present, governments have tended to resist instituting measures of this type for the purpose of fertility control. It has been noted, however, that in the industrialized world and also in China, where rates of female employment are high and where social and economic policies and conditions are conducive to the equalization of women's rights and the expansion of their roles in society, birthrates and rates of population growth have declined.[82]

Beyond family planning and the use of the above incentives, some experts have also emphasized the importance of government's instituting some form of *compulsory* population control. In one way or another under this type of system, the freedom and rights of the individual with respect to childbearing would be considered secondary to the rights and welfare of the entire society. In line with this alternative, various compulsory measures aimed at restraining fertility have been suggested, including the development of a licensing system, whereby a woman would be allowed to have only a specific number of children, and the mandatory sterilization of an individual after the birth of a specific number of children. In theory, it would not be difficult to introduce a system of fertility control based on coercive measures. In practice, however, the threats to personal rights and freedoms posed by compulsory programs are evident. In India, massive public outrage against the government's recent crash (and often coercive) program of sterilization was the primary reason for the defeat of Indira Gandhi's Congress Party in the spring 1977 national elections.[83] At present, governments are highly resistant to imposing compulsory measures of birth control upon their populations, and most experts are of the opinion that such measures should be attempted only as a final recourse. If all other alternatives to fertility control fail, however, governments may feel compelled to restrict some of our personal freedoms in the interest of worldwide survival.

Currently, many population experts are increasingly of the opinion that the development of *comprehensive* population policies represent the only viable approach to dealing with the problem of overpopulation. Such policies would create programs designed to vastly expand the availability of contraception within the less-developed nations while at the same time actively encouraging large-scale social and economic change conducive to lowering fertility. These measures would include the expansion of health care, a rise in the level of literacy, equalization of rights for women, equable distribution of income, expansion of occupational opportunities, development of social security systems, and rural and agricultural development.[84]

Comprehensive population policies could be the answer

Policies such as these have yet to be actually implemented in the vast majority of the world's less-developed nations. Moreover, even if such policies are effective in reducing fertility, their implementation and impact would require a considerable amount of time. One thing is certain: time is running out, and the development of large-scale population policies will require an unprecedented level of international cooperation if global disasters are to be avoided.

Time is not on our side

TRYING TO STOP RUNAWAY POPULATION GROWTH

Today, as we have seen, world population is growing faster than in any other period in human history. Given present trends, world population is projected to increase by an additional two billion people within the next twenty years. The vast majority of this growth is occurring within the world's less-developed nations as a consequence of high fertility and rapidly declining mortality. Faced with the fact that family planning efforts alone have had only a limited influence in bringing about fertility reductions in developing nations, demographers and other experts are now urging governments to adopt comprehensive population polices aimed at promoting fertility decline. The following *Time* essay is based upon excerpts of a speech delivered by World Bank President Robert S. McNamara at the Massachusetts Institute of Technology. The essay discusses the historical and contemporary growth of world population and indicates some of the important steps that are needed in order to "defuse the population bomb."

TIME READING——OBJECTIVES

1. To statistically document the historical growth of world population.
2. To identify and discuss in an essay the various social and economic policy actions that governments can take to stimulate fertility decline.

How to Defuse the Population Bomb

Population growth has an important influence on our future

Except for thermonuclear war, population growth is the gravest issue the world faces over the decades immediately ahead. In many ways it is an even more dangerous and subtle threat than war, for it is less subject to rational safeguards, and less amenable to organized control. It is not in the exclusive control of a few governments, but rather in the hands of hundreds of millions of individual parents. The population threat must be faced—like the nuclear threat—for what it inevitably is: a central determinant of mankind's future, one requiring far more attention than it is presently receiving.

Last year the world's population passed 4 billion. Barring a holocaust brought on by man or nature, the world's population right now is the smallest it will ever be again. How did it reach 4 billion? For the first 99% of man's existence, surprisingly slowly. For the last 1% of history, in a great rush. By 1750, the total had reached only about 800 million. Then, as the Industrial Revolution gathered momentum, population growth began rapidly to accelerate. By 1900, it had doubled to 1.6 billion; by 1964, it had doubled again to 3.2 billion; and by the end of the century, it is projected to double again to about 6.3 billion. Given today's level of complacency in some quarters, and discouragement in others, the likely scenario is for a world stabilized at about 11 billion.

The sudden population surge has been a function of two opposite trends: the gradual slowing down of the growth rate in the developed nations, and the rapid acceleration of the rate in the developing countries. The experience of the developed countries gave rise to the theory of the demographic transition. It holds that societies tend to move through three distinct demographic stages: 1) high birth rates and high death rates, resulting in near stationary populations: 2) high birth rates but declining death rates, producing growing populations; and finally, 3) low birth rates and low death rates, re-establishing near stationary populations.

Stages of demographic transition

The fundamental question is: What, if anything, can rationally and humanely be done to accelerate the demographic transition in the developing world? Is that acceleration realistically possible? It is.

With the help of modern mass communications, which are both more pervasive and more influential than ever, an increasing number of governments in the developing world are committed to lowering fertility, and an even larger number to supporting family-planning programs. Family-planning services are essential, but can succeed only to the extent that a demand for lower fertility exists. That demand apparently does not now exist in sufficient strength in most of the developing countries. There are a number of policy actions that governments can take to help stimulate the demand. None of them is easy to implement. All of them require some reallocation of scarce resources. Some of them are politically sensitive. But governments must measure those costs against the immeasurably greater costs in store for societies that procrastinate while dangerous population pressures mount.

Family planning is in low demand in most developing countries

What, then, are those specific social and economic actions most likely to promote the desire for reduced fertility? The importance of enhancing the status of women is critical. The number of illiterate females is growing faster than illiterate males.

Of all the aspects of social development, the educational level appears most consistently associated with lower fertility. And an increase in the education of women tends to lower fertility to a greater extent than a similar increase in the education of men. In Latin America, for example, studies indicate that women who have completed primary school average about two children fewer than those who have not. Schooling tends to delay the age of marriage for girls, and thus reduces their total possible number of childbearing years. Further, education enables both men and women to learn about modern contraceptives and their use. It broadens their view of the opportunities and potential of life, inclines them to think more for themselves, and in addition, it reduces their suspicion of social change.

Infant and child mortality rates can be brought down relatively simply and inexpensively, if national health policies are carefully designed. The return in lowered fertility and healthier children and more equitably served families is clearly worth the effort. Malnourished mothers give birth to weak and unhealthy infants, and have problems nursing them. Such infants often die, and this leads to frequent pregnancies, which in turn diminish their occupational and economic status. This makes sons more desirable than daughters, and when only daughters are born, another pregnancy must ensue in order to try again for a son.

In addition, policies must be shaped that will assist the urban poor to increase their work productivity. In practice, this means a comprehensive program designed to increase earning opportunities in both the traditional and the modern sectors; provide equitable access to public utilities, transport, education and health services; and establish realistic housing policies.

Economic growth must be distributed more equitably. Typically, in most of the developing countries, the upper 20% of the population receives 55% of the national income, and the lowest 20% receive 5%. In the rural areas, this is reflected in the concentration of land ownership. According to a survey by the U.N.'s Food and Agriculture Organization, the wealthiest 20% of the land owners in most developing countries own between 50% and 60% of the cropland. The roughly 100 million small farms in the developing world—those less than 5 hectares—are concentrated on only 20% of the cropland. It is little wonder that national economic growth itself has had less than optimum effect on the fertility patterns of the vast mass of the population.

Excessive fertility is itself a serious obstacle to economic growth. But unless the benefits of growth are directed more equitably to the lower 40% of the income groups, where in fact fertility rates are likely to be the highest, then economic growth as such will not move the society forward at an optimum rate of progress. But through an increase in income, small-farm families will almost certainly experience a beneficial decline in their traditionally high fertility. For the income will give them access to better health and education and living standards, which in turn are likely to lead to smaller families.

A number of governments are moving in the direction of coercion. Some have introduced legal sanctions to raise the age of marriage. A few are considering direct legal limitations on family size and sanctions to enforce them. No government really wants to resort to this. But neither can any government afford

More education for women tends to lower fertility

The work output of the urban poor must be increased

Equitable distribution of wealth is crucial

Some governments have taken action to lower fertility

to let population pressure grow so large that social frustrations finally erupt into irrational violence and civil disintegration.

We know that eventually the world's population will have to stop growing. What is uncertain is how. And when. At what level. And with what result. We can avoid a world of 11 billion, and all the misery that such an impoverished and crowded planet would imply. Man is still young in cosmic terms. In the time perspective of the universe, he is recent, and tentative, and perhaps even experimental. He makes mistakes. And yet, if he is truly *sapiens*—thinking and wise—then surely there is promise for him.

SUMMARY

Rapid and excessive population growth constitutes one of the most serious social problems of our time. The growth of human numbers has already had many detrimental effects upon the quality of life within most nations and has placed severe strains upon the supply of food and many of the world's natural resources. Throughout most of human existence world population has tended to grow rather slowly. Prior to the twentieth century, population growth resulted from various technological advancements associated with the Agricultural and Industrial Revolutions. During this century, however, a third wave of population growth occurred within the world's less-developed African, Asian, and Latin American countries. The vast increase within these countries constitutes the main threat and thrust of the current population explosion.

Today, rates of population growth between the developed and less-developed nations reveal striking contrasts. Growth rates within most industrially developed nations now stand at 1 percent or less per year, with fertility rates near and occasionally below replacement level. Even so, most of these nations are still experiencing growth in absolute numbers. Population increase and the high standards of living characteristically found within the industrialized nations have produced a number of adverse consequences, including the deteriorating quality of life and excessive strains upon national and worldwide environmental resources.

Growth rates within the majority of less-developed nations now stand in excess of 2 percent per year, yielding a doubling time of 35 years or less. Many of these nations already have massive populations, yet exponential population growth and young age structures ensure that even the smaller less-developed nations will soon become overpopulated. Rapid and large-scale population growth within the less-developed nations resulted from the combined effects of high fertility and rapid declines in mortality and has created many serious problems, including hunger, malnutrition, disease, starvation, lack of economic development, and widespread poverty.

In addition to examining the scope and consequences of the population problem, two major explanations for population growth and change were also discussed in detail: the Malthusian theory and the theory of demographic transition. According to Malthus, the growth or decline of human populations could be accounted for by the availability of the means of subsistence. Increase the means of subsistence and population will increase. Inevitably, however, population growth will exceed these means, at which point famine, disease, and war will come into play, increasing mortality and thus holding population growth in check. According to demographic transition theory, economic development, industrialization, and urbanization ultimately combine to bring about lowered fertility and declining rates of population growth, because people increasingly come to recognize that large families constitute an economic liability rather than an asset. As a whole, the less-developed nations have not experienced a full transition to lowered fertility rates. In recent years, death rates within these countries have been drastically reduced as a result of the use of modern medical and other scientific knowledge. The reduction in mortality was massive and sudden, providing virtually no time for readjustment in values, norms, and attitudes, which currently favor high fertility.

Factors related to industrialization and the widespread availability, acceptance, and use of contraception and family planning have yielded low rates of population growth within the industrialized nations. Within the less-developed countries, major stress has been placed upon the development of a voluntary family planning approach to deal with population growth. In general, this approach has met with very limited success. At present, many experts are urging the development of comprehensive population policies for the less-developed nations. These policies would expand the availability of contraception while simultaneously encouraging large-scale social and economic changes conducive to lowering fertility.

KEY TERMS

Crude birthrate
Crude death rate
Demographic transition theory
Exponential growth
Family planning programs
Malthusian theory of population
   change

Megalopolis
Positive checks
Preventive checks
Replacement level fertility
Zero population growth

Florence Sharp

10
Environment

Chapter Objectives

1. To describe the balance of ecosystems that exist in nature.

2. To identify the major sources of water, land, and air pollution and to discuss their effects upon our health and well-being.

3. To statistically document the current and future dimensions of our declining resources, describing the nature and origins of our energy crisis, and to discuss alternatives to a coal-nuclear future.

4. To identify in an essay the advantages and disadvantages of the increased use of coal and nuclear power.

5. To evaluate the role of technology and technological change in the creation of many of our environmental problems.

6. To briefly describe the major findings of the *Limits To Growth* report regarding the effects of industrial and population growth upon our environment.

7. To identify the dominant attitudes and values within our society that have played a major role in generating our current environmental crisis.

8. To discuss by means of essay some of the steps that should be taken by the government in order to more effectively deal with our environmental problems.

9. To list various ways in which large-scale environmental education programs could be of assistance in improving the quality of our environment.

10. To describe in an essay some of the methods for reducing energy waste, now and in the future.

OUR ENVIRONMENT AND ITS PROBLEMS

If we were asked to conjure up pictures of an ideal environment or images of the true beauty of nature, many of us would no doubt focus upon some serene and scenic place where the air and sky were crystal clear, the waters were pure, and the forests were full of color and life. Perhaps this is how the environment should be, but there are signs all around telling us that our environment is undergoing large-scale deterioration. Our air, within rural as well as urban areas, has become highly polluted with varieties of toxic substances. Many of our rivers are becoming semisolid garbage cans. Some of our lakes are biologically dead as a result of the dumping and run-off of industrial and agricultural wastes. Our oceans have become disposal sites for sewage, radioactive wastes, and oil. More and more of our land has become dumping or burial grounds for the billions of tons of household, industrial, and agricultural wastes that we throw away each year, much of it nondegradable. The noise in many of our urban areas has increased to the point where it adds to our physical and emotional stress. To make matters far worse, we have been using up many of our environment's nonrenewable resources as if there were no tomorrow. The result is that we now face imminent and severe shortages of many fossil fuels, minerals, and other basic materials.

Signs of environmental deterioration

THE ECOSYSTEM AND HUMAN ACTIVITIES

Central to our understanding of environmental issues is the fact that the problems of environmental pollution, environmental degradation, and resource depletion that we will discuss are ultimately a direct result of people's conscious and deliberate attempts to change and exploit their habitat for their own ends. In this attempt we have actually interfered with and harmed many of nature's natural processes and cycles. As a consequence, the health, well-being and very existence of life upon our planet has been threatened.

People are disrupting nature's cycles

All living organisms depend upon the life support systems of land, air, water, and energy. In describing our environment, ecologists often use the term *biosphere,* referring to the thin band or layer of air, water, and soil in which virtually all living creatures exist and with which they are interdependent. Humans and all other life forms share in the biosphere and are supported by it.[1] *Ecosystems* are parts or subdivisions of the biosphere and "consist of communities of plants, animals, and microorganisms along with the air, water, soil or other substrate that supports them."[2] Ecosystems are virtually infinite in number, ranging from simple interdependent communities of microscopic life to far more complex forms, such as lakes, oceans, and forests. The largest and most complex interdependent ecosystem is the entire "global ecosystem," i.e., the biosphere itself.

Ecosystems and the biosphere

Regardless of the size or complexity of any particular ecosystem, the fact remains that all organisms within it tend to form a balanced and inter-

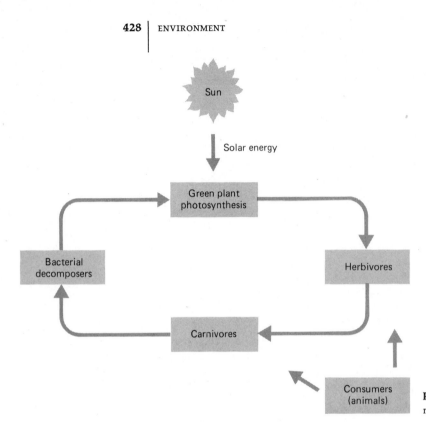

Fig. 10.1 Nutrition cycle: Environmental food chains.

Nature's "web of relationships"

dependent "web of relationships" with each other and with the environment around them. Each element or organism plays its own interlocking part through various types of energy cycles or exchanges within the system, the ultimate purpose of which is the maintenance and perpetuation of life.[3] The balance, circularity, and interdependence found within nature's ecosystems is well illustrated in the existence of *food chains*. The basic source of all energy is the sun. Green plants (producers) absorb energy from the sun and nutrients from the environment around them in order to produce food. Certain animals (consumers) feed on the plants and are in turn eaten by other consumer animals, including humans. All life forms eventually die, at which point their bodies are decomposed by bacteria. Ultimately, stored energies and nutrients are returned to the earth for reuse by the plants.

Food chains: Cycles of use and renewal

Other elements of nature, such as nitrogen, carbon, phosphorus, and water, also go through their own cycles of use and renewal.[4] The ecosystems that comprise our habitat or environment never achieve total and lasting balance, however; natural events, such as droughts, fires, or drastic changes in climate, can sometimes interfere with nature's cycles. Thus, a prolonged frost may kill off various green plants, which in turn may threaten the survival of the animals who normally feed off those plants.

Today, however, as we have noted above, most of our environmental problems are the direct result of human action. We have increasingly interfered with the stability and balance of our planet's ecosystems, disturbing many of nature's life-support cycles. In recent years, world population has been growing faster than in any other period of human history. That means more people than ever are placing increased strains upon a planet that has limited, not infinite, resources. Our technologies have given us the capacity to alter the earth's surface, yet in doing so we have often eliminated entire ecosystems, such as forests, rivers, lakes, and arable lands, only to replace them with highways, dams, industrial plants, etc. Likewise, the products and by-products of our technologies and our industrial production processes have been responsible for vast increases in environmental pollution. The Committee on Natural Resources of the National Academy of Sciences has described the role of human activities in causing the environmental crisis as follows:

Human activities and environmental problems

> Man is altering the balance of a relatively stable system by his pollution of the atmosphere with smoke, . . . alteration of the energy and water balance, . . . over-grazing, reduction of evapotranspiration, irrigation, drainage, . . . building of cities and highways; by his clearing forests and alterations of plant surface cover, changing the reflectivity of the earth's surface and soil structures; by his land-filling, construction of buildings and seawalls, and pollution, bringing about radical changes in the ecology of estuarine areas; by the changes he effects in the biologic balance, . . . the erection of dams and channel works; and by the increasing quantities of carbon dioxide an industrial society released to the atmosphere.[5]

Moreover, because of the interdependences found throughout nature's "web of life," human disturbance of ecological balances through manipulation and/or exploitation of our environment frequently leads to unintended and adverse consequences for many life forms, including our own. The often severe strains we have placed upon our planet's fixed resources have resulted in growing shortages of food, minerals, and fossil fuels, for which we are now only beginning to pay. The dumping of industrial wastes and scores of toxic chemicals into our rivers, lakes, and oceans has resulted in the destruction of countless forms of acquatic life. Many of these same toxic substances have also found their way into our own bodies as a result of complex food chain activities. We have also introduced more and more pollutants into our air, and the absorption and accumulation of these substances (many of which are toxic) into our bodies pose severe health problems, such as heart and various respiratory diseases.

We are increasingly disrupting ecological balances

As we shall discuss later in this chapter, environmental problems have resulted from a number of factors, including the growth of population,

Some sources of environmental problems

technology, and industrialization, as well as our own attitudes favoring neglect of and disregard for the environment around us. Before examining each of these factors in detail, it is important that we take a closer look at the scope of many of our current environmental problems, such as air and water pollution, our misuse of the natural landscape, the growing hazards of chemical and pesticide pollution, and finally, the serious problem of resource depletion.

ENVIRONMENTAL DETERIORATION

Air Pollution. Of all forms of pollution, people seem to be most aware of and concerned about the pollution of our atmosphere. This concern is more than justified. Estimates indicate, for example, that in recent years we have annually released into our air as much as 200 million tons of pollutants,

Types of air pollution | including nitrogen and sulfur oxides, carbon monoxide, particulate matter,

While the damage done to our air by these smokestacks is obvious, we are still uncovering their potential to cause disease in human beings.

Nicholas Sapieha, Stock, Boston

Table 10.1. Major sources of air pollution

| SOURCE | POLLUTANTS DEPOSITED ANNUALLY* | | | | |
	CARBON MONOXIDE	SULFUR OXIDES	HYDRO-CARBONS	PARTICU-LATES	NITROGEN OXIDES
Transportation	77.4	.8	11.7	1.3	10.7
Fuel combustion	1.2	26.3	1.4	6.6	12.4
Industrial processes	9.4	5.7	3.5	8.7	.7
Solid waste disposal	3.3	—	.9	.6	.2

Source: Environmental Protection Agency, as listed in *Statistical Abstract of the United States: 1977*, p. 205.

* In millions of tons.

and hydrocarbons. Approximately 35 to 40 percent of this dust, dirt, and poisonous gas (particularly carbon monoxide and hydrocarbons) comes from transportation sources, especially the automobile. Another 20 to 30 percent (consisting mostly of sulfur and nitrogen oxides) comes from stationary fuel combustion sources, such as homes and power plants, which burn fossil fuels to generate heat and power. An additional 15 to 20 percent or so (mostly in the form of sulfur oxides, particulate matter, and carbon monoxide) results from industrial manufacturing processes (see Table 10.1).

Air pollution adversely affects our well-being in many ways. Dust and dirt in the air make our throats burn and our eyes water. Nitrogen and sulfur oxide fumes cause coughing and make breathing more difficult. Carbon monoxide pollution impairs the flow of oxygen in our bodies, thus placing increased stress upon the coronary and central nervous systems. Given the presence of certain atmospheric conditions, such as temperature inversions, air pollution can have sudden and truly catastrophic effects. Thermal inversions occur when a layer of warm air traps a layer of cooler air underneath it, closer to the earth's surface. If that air is polluted, this condition can sicken and actually kill very large numbers of people. This occurred in London in 1952, killing approximately 4,000 people. A similar incident occurred in Donora, Pennsylvania in 1948, killing twenty people and sickening or severely affecting the health of 6,000 additional residents. Over the last twenty-five years or so other cities, such as New York and Birmingham, have repeatedly experienced dense pollution stagnation, resulting in increased rates of respiratory irritation, sickness, and death among area residents.[6]

Air pollution: Adverse effects

Disasters such as these are the clearest and most alarming signals of the threat that air pollution poses for us all. Increasingly, however, people are becoming more and more aware of the fact that long-term exposure to the levels of toxic substances in our everyday air poses a far greater and

Air pollution and human disease

more widespread menace to public health. Air pollution does far more than cause throat and eye irritation. Researchers have noted that air pollution has directly contributed to increased rates of emphysema, chronic bronchitis, chronic asthma, penumonia, lung cancer, and heart disease.[7]

As a result of passage of the 1970 Clean Air Act, which set standards and goals for industrial and automotive pollution reduction, progress has been made in cleaning up our atmosphere. Nevertheless, the air quality within most of our industrial regions and major urban areas is still below even those standards set by the act.[8] Moreover, as we shall see later in this chapter, there are whole "new breeds" of chemical pollutants being introduced into our atmosphere, which pose additional environmental and public health risks. Given the complexity of our ecosystems, we must come to the realization that simply cleaning up our environment on a piecemeal basis will not provide a long-term answer to our problems.

Water Pollution. People depend upon water as well as air for survival. In some areas water is becoming scarce and that which remains is becoming increasingly polluted and dangerous for human consumption. Each day many tons of pollutants, emanating from rural and municipal sewage systems, agriculture, and industry, pour into our rivers, lakes, and oceans. Contaminants include inadequately treated sewage, various solid wastes, sludge, oil, metals, minerals, synthetics, and thousands of chemical compounds, such as phosphates, nitrates, detergents, pesticides, and hydrocarbons.[9]

The growth of urban populations has added immensely to our municipal sewage disposal and water purification problems. In some cases it has become virtually impossible to adequately treat all the sewage that municipalities dump into nearby waters. Many of our urban water treatment facilities are finding it more difficult to chemically treat all the contaminants found within the drinking water coming from polluted lakes and rivers.[10] Industry is also a heavy polluter of our lakes, streams, and rivers. Industry needs water for manufacturing, but when the water is returned to its source, it is often contaminated with oil, solid wastes, lead, detergents, acids, and toxic chemicals.[11]

The Allied Chemical Corporation, to give one example, was fined $13.2 million in 1976 for discharging chemical wastes, including the pesticide kepone, into Virginia's James River.[12] Every day since 1968, the Reserve Mining Company of Silver Bay, Minnesota, has dumped 67,000 tons of taconite wastes, containing asbestos-like fibers, into Lake Superior. A 1976 court ruling ordered that the dumping be stopped as of July 1977; however, that court order was appealed.[13] The Mahoning River Valley at Youngstown, Ohio, is another site of vast river pollution. Each day, several local steel mills dump approximately 158 tons of grease, cyanide, oil, and metal particles into the Mahoning River.[14] In recent years, some of our

"New breeds" of chemical pollution

Some sources of water pollution

Sometimes it is impossible to treat all our municipal sewage

Examples of industrial pollution

Table 10.2. A look at pollution in U.S. Rivers

Some river segments officially rated as unswimmable in part for at least 50 per cent of the year because of pollution—

Big Sioux River in South Dakota

Catawba River in South Carolina

Cedar River in Iowa

Chattahoochee River in Georgia

Connecticut River in Connecticut

Des Moines River in Iowa

Grand River in Michigan

James River in Missouri

Jordan River in Utah

Mississippi River (Rock Island to Cairo, Ill.)

Missouri River (lower portion)

Monocacy River in Maryland

North Platte River in Wyoming

Red River in Louisiana

Rio Grande in New Mexico

Roanoke River in Virginia

Susquehanna River in Pennsylvania

Tar River in North Carolina

Yazoo River in Mississippi

Yellowstone River in Montana

Note: River segments are rated as too polluted for safe swimming when bacteria counts at sampling stations rise to levels considered hazardous to health. Typically, pollution is highest near cities, while headwaters, tributaries and other stretches may be swimmable.

Source: Environmental Protection Agency. Reprinted by permission from *U.S. News & World Report*, February 7, 1977, p. 46.

rivers have become so polluted that they have actually caught on fire—the Buffalo and Cuyahoga Rivers are two cases in point.

Many of our agricultural techniques that heavily employ inorganic phosphates and nitrates for the fertilization of farmlands have also been partly responsible for the deterioration of our lakes and rivers. As a result of irrigation and rainfall, these fertilizers eventually wind up in our water-

Agricultural practices frequently pollute our water

ways. When the algae die bacterial decomposition sets in, which drains the water of oxygen and ultimately brings about the destruction of large numbers of fish and other acquatic life. Lake Erie, which at one time was declared biologically dead, serves as a classic example of such nutrient pollution. In addition to fertilizer run-off, a significant amount of phosphates entering our waters comes from industrial wastes and municipal sewage.[15]

Our oceans have also become dumping grounds for many pollutants, such as chemicals, acids, sewage, gases, dirt, and millions of tons of junk, which enter the oceans from rivers or from our atmosphere. The amount of all pollutants (pesticides, fertilizers, sewage, oil) found within ocean waters has increased tremendously in recent years. A record five million tons of oil, for example, are now dumped into the oceans annually, and one-third of this dumping is done deliberately through the "flushing out" of oil tankers before reloading.[16] The pollution of our oceans has already resulted in massive ecological damage, the fouling of beaches, and the destruction of vast numbers of sea birds and acquatic life.

Contamination of lakes, streams, rivers, and oceans also creates many problems for our species. The mass destruction of acquatic life, for example, poses a direct threat to our own food resources. In addition, according to the Environmental Protection Agency (EPA), from 1961 to 1973 in the United States there were over 200 outbreaks of disease or poisonings caused by contaminated drinking waters. More than twenty people died and some 55,000 became ill. Furthermore, the EPA estimates that only one out of ten disease outbreaks ever comes to official attention.[17]

Land Degradation. The land surface of our planet serves as man's principal habitat, yet we have increasingly degraded, exploited, and polluted the land upon which we depend for survival. We misuse the land that is available to us in many ways. Each year we pour millions of tons of artificial fertilizers over our farm lands to increase crop yields. The use of these compounds has doubled at least a dozen times within the last twenty-five years.[18] These substances do temporarily increase farm yields, yet they also have some devastating ecological effects. As mentioned earlier, many of these substances eventually wind up in our waterways, causing extreme water pollution. In addition, the massive use of artificial fertilizers has the long-term effect of actually reducing the capacity of the soil to retain its own natural nitrogen content. Paul Ehrlich estimates that this dramatic increase in the use of artificial fertilizers has resulted in a "50% reduction of the original organic nitrogen content of Midwestern soils."[19]

We also overrun more and more of our remaining natural and cultivable land through the practice of strip-mining and by the construction of dams, highways, cities, and industrial parks, for example. John McHale estimates that, in the United States alone, the construction of highways and urbanization reduces the balance of our cultivable lands by over a million acres each year.[20]

Ocean pollution: Record levels

Some adverse effects of water pollution

Massive fertilization reduces soil quality

Effects of strip-mining and construction

The exploitation and degradation of our land is nowhere more clearly seen than in the mistreatment of another vast and immensely important ecosystem, our forests. Forests provide the ecological habitat for countless forms of animal and plant life. They also serve as natural reservoirs for water and purify the air by extracting carbon dioxide and replacing it with oxygen. Forests are thus vital for maintaining our local, regional, and even global ecological balance. Yet human activities, particularly the massive logging (cutting down) of forests, have resulted in the elimination of vast amounts of forest acreage. When the early colonists came to this country, the United States constituted one of the richest forest areas of the world, containing a minimum of 1000 million acres of forest.[21] Today, we are left with only a fraction of that area. As Raymond Dasmann states,

The decline of forest acreage

> Properly managed, forests can enrich human life in a variety of ways which are both material and psychological. Poorly managed, they can be a source for the disruption of the environment of an entire region. However, through the centuries we have seen a pattern repeated. The misuse of axe or saw, of fire or grazing, causes forest destruction. This leads to disruption of watersheds, to the erosion or loss of fertility of soils, to siltation and flooding in stream valleys, and to loss of the continued productivity of the land on which man must depend.[22]

As is all too often the case, human activities result in the destruction of forest ecosystems—deforestation. Eventually forest areas are replaced by barren or weed-covered wastelands.

We also exploit and degrade the land around us by dumping billions of tons of solid wastes, trash, and garbage upon it year after year. We discard 3.5 billion tons of solid wastes annually. Approximately 360 million tons come from households, municipalities, and industry; two billion tons are agricultural wastes; another 1.1 billion tons are mineral wastes.[23] Ehrlich describes the situation in the following terms:

Litter: 3.5 billion tons of solid wastes each year

> Each year in the United States we must dispose of some 55 billion cans, 26 billion bottles and jars, 65 billion metal and plastic bottle caps, and more than half a billion dollars worth of other packaging materials. Seven million automobiles are junked each year, and the amount of urban solid wastes (trash and garbage) collected annually is approximately 200 million tons. Every man, woman and child in the United States is, on the average, producing nearly a ton of refuse annually.[24]

Recently our disposal problems have become aggravated by the fact that more and more wastes are made of modern plastics and synthetic fibers that are ecologically nondegradable.[25] The current methods for disposing of

Solid wastes are often nondegradable

these wastes (primarily dumping and burning) are inadequate and hazardous to our environment. Burning (especially plastics and synthetics) increases air pollution; dumping grounds and junk yards are not only unsightly, they also pollute the environment around them and are often breeding grounds for disease.

These problems of environmental pollution and degradation have been a long time in the making. Everyone desires a healthy environment. Yet, as we have seen, many of our own values, attitudes, and practices have contributed significantly to the environmental crisis now upon us. Effective solutions to many of these problems demand that we, as individuals and as a society, begin to reevaluate our relationship to the environment and become willing to make basic changes in the ways we use its precious resources.

THE COST OF A HEALTHY ENVIRONMENT

As we have seen, pollution of our land, air, and water constitutes a serious threat to our environment as well as to our own well-being and survival. In recent years some gains have been made in eliminating some of the "visible" pollution around us: many of our rivers are not quite as filth-ridden, and our urban air is less smog-laden. The following *U.S. News & World Report* article points out, however, that we are just beginning to deal effectively with many of these long-term environmental problems. The costs involved in cleaning up the environment are indeed high, in terms of money and in terms of reductions in our consumption patterns and living standards. Yet the costs incurred through our failure to clean up the environment will be prohibitive: declining health, skyrocketing medical costs, loss of productivity, and even higher death rates. Moreover, as the article documents, people are only beginning to realize that we are becoming endangered by a whole new breed of pollution, namely *chemical* pollution. These pollutants typically take the form of natural and synthetic food additives, new pesticides and herbicides, many synthetic substances, and large numbers of chemical compounds manufactured each year. Not all these substances present direct threats to our environment or our personal well-being; however, their existence poses new concerns for our nation's health, both present and future.

U.S. NEWS & WORLD REPORT READING——OBJECTIVES

1. To identify the various costs of cleaning up and failing to clean up our environment.
2. To list several examples of occupational health hazards resulting from on-the-job exposure to contaminants.
3. To document by way of example and statistics the degree to which natural and synthetic chemical additives are present within our food.

A Clean America: Will People Pay the Price?

Rarely in its history has the U.S. faced a dilemma with such profound implications for the nation's future.

Evidence is mounting steadily that, unless Americans can clean up the environment in which they live, their health, mental well-being and life expectancy are at stake.

Yet the price to be paid for the cleaning up is staggering—in dollars, loss of convenience and perhaps the reduction of living standards.

A few steps have already been taken:

Less than a decade ago, the Buffalo River in New York was so polluted with waste oil that it caught fire. Today, after a massive cleanup job, game fish are returning.

The quality of the air has been visibly improved in Pittsburgh, once the smoky city of steel mills buried perpetually under a cloud of industrial contamination.

Marine life is coming back to Escambia Bay in Florida where only five years ago the oyster and shrimp industry had been virtually wiped out and rotting fish covered the water's surface for miles and miles.

ECOLOGICAL DEADLINE?

To move from scattered efforts to an all-out fight to improve the environment may cost more than many if not most Americans are willing to pay. But the need for decision is closing in. Subtle killers are emerging where the balance of nature has been knocked askew.

A pervasive industrial chemical called PCB floats invisibly through air and water. It is brought to the dinner table in fish and other foods. It is even present in mothers' milk. The substance has been found to cause cancer in laboratory animals.

A pesticide called Kepone, let loose from a small manufacturing plant on a Virginia river, threatens the entire ecology of Chesapeake Bay.

Fibers of asbestos, a known carcinogen, are finding their way into the lungs of factory workers and garage mechanics.

The twentieth-century technology that has generated today's affluence has also created pestilence as deadly as the epidemics of times past, though slower-acting. "All we've done is exchange bubonic plague for cancer," says Dr. William Lijinsky of the Frederick Cancer Research Center in Frederick, Md.

Historically, physicians have always looked to the environment for clues to the diseases at hand. Today, the leading causes of death are chronic diseases—disabling disorders such as heart disease, cancer, stroke and diabetes. The exact causes are unknown, but the environment is coming to be considered a major factor in virtually all.

The environment: A major factor in the etiology of many diseases

According to the World Health Organization, 70 to 90 per cent of all cancers in human beings can be traced to substances in the environment. Scientists also know that many birth defects and neurological disorders result from environmental conditions such as exposure to lead or to certain drugs and pesticides.

One of the most widely recognized environmental health hazards is smoking. Researchers link tobacco use to a variety of respiratory disorders and rate it high on the list of causes of lung cancer.

In addition, twentieth-century noise and stress, overconsumption of food and drugs and the existence of rural and urban slums that are environmental disaster areas all combine to threaten the health of Americans.

Just as nineteenth-century physicians looked to rivers filled with sewage and to stinking swamps for the causes of typhoid and yellow fever, today's physicians are looking for clues to modern diseases in a complex environment that has been shaped by the post-World War II chemical revolution.

TIME LAG

A factor that makes the environmentally caused diseases so hard to combat is time lag. A tendency toward high blood pressure, for example, begins in the first year of life. Most heart attacks occur after the age of 40. Cancers can have incubation periods of 20 to 40 years.

Many diseases take time to appear

Thus, a disease may reflect the environment of 30 years ago when the seeds of the ailment were sown. Similarly, today's environment may be producing diseases that will be predominant 30 years from now.

What many scientists and medical experts fear is this: The dramatic rise in the use of chemicals that began in the early '60s may result in an epidemic of chemical-related diseases, particularly cancer, in the next few decades. On the other hand, health officials point out that the rates for some cancers, such as cancer of the stomach, are going down.

Because it is too soon to know the impact of recent changes in the environment, the debate over a "time bomb" theory continues.

A direct cause-and-effect relationship between environment and disease has not been established in all cases. But certain diseases and certain kinds of environmental contamination are frequently associated:

- Workers in synthetic-rubber plants are found to have a higher-than-average incidence of leukemia, the cancerous blood disease.
- In homes where large amounts of the pesticide chlordane have been used to kill termites, children have developed aplastic anemia, a blood condition that is usually fatal.

PINPOINTING TROUBLE AREAS

A map can provide startling evidence of the association of pollution and the killer ailments.

Disease is not randomly distributed

New Jersey has the greatest concentration of chemical industries and the highest rate of cancer in America. In Ohio, people whose drinking water comes from Lake Erie or the Ohio River have an 8 per cent higher incidence of cancer than those living in other parts of the State. Both sources of water are heavily polluted.

Whenever man moves to clean up the world around him, however, he steps into the realm of trade-offs.

The cost of an extensive war on pollution is enormous—a minimum of 271 billion dollars over the next decade, according to estimates by the President's Council on Environmental Quality.

Just who would pay that bill, the private sector or the public through Government funds, is a growing issue. So far this country is depending largely on the private sector. But when huge, expensive plants are at stake, the cost of change could be too big for private companies to afford without massive Government support.

Environmental protection can cost heavily in direct outlays. Some businessmen complain that overzealous antipollution standards are a dangerous brake on the nation's economic growth. The reply of the Council on Environmental Quality is that cleanup costs will not hurt over-all productivity, economic growth or jobs in the long run.

In one sense, the cost of cleaning up the environment is passed on to the consumer. It is estimated that laws already on the books to help clean up the air will cost each homeowner in the U.S. more than $5 a month in added electricity charges by 1985.

But failure to clean up pollution costs money, too—in the form of declining health, skyrocketing medical costs and loss of time on the job.

And the hazards are not limited to industry. Health officials estimate that smoking-related diseases by themselves cost Americans 18 billion dollars a year or $10 a month for the average home-owner—though it is difficult to show the cost to health in terms of dollars because the impact is indirect and long-delayed.

At other times, failure to keep the environment clean quickly leads to direct economic losses. In Hopewell, Va., home of the ill-fated Kepone factory, property values have plummeted, and some former employees are still too sick from Kepone poisoning to go back to work. Fishermen along the James River and other places on the East Coast have suffered damage to their business.

Sorting out the dilemma of environmental protection on the one hand and economic growth on the other—the reality of jobs today versus the uncertainty of health tomorrow—will be a major task for the Carter Administration.

So far, Jimmy Carter is on record as a strong advocate of preventive health measures, including protection against harmful substances in the environment. At the same time, the President's concern with the state of the economy and the need to reduce unemployment suggests a businesslike approach to these issues.

The first public-health movement to improve the environment, called the "great sanitary awakening," began in England during the 1850s when the industrial revolution crowded people into cities, sewage ran through the streets, and cholera and typhoid were major problems. A result of the "awakening" was a dramatic decline in the common infectious diseases.

A TURNING POINT

In recent years, another awakening to the fact that a polluted environment is a source of disease came with the publication of Rachel Carson's "Silent Spring" in 1962 which sold millions of copies. Carson described how the widespread use of the pesticide DDT, which had contaminated fields and streams, posed a threat to living creatures, including man, all over the globe.

Scientists point out that the majority of synthetic compounds that have been added to the environment since the 1940s are benign. It is the significant minority, however, that is causing problems.

Roughly 1,000 new chemicals are produced every year. More than 12,000 compounds are already on the Government's toxic-substance list; 1,500 are sus-

Cleaning up the environment is costly but necessary

The proliferation of chemicals

pected of causing tumors; 30 compounds currently used in industry are known to cause cancer. Many products that support the nation's standard of living—from high-energy transformers to decaffeinated coffee to plastic seat covers—have been made from substances on the list.

Does eliminating these substances from the environment actually reduce disease? There is evidence that it does. A British study of cancer trends shows that since the reduction of air pollution in London in the last 25 years, lung-cancer rates in that city have begun to decline.

Now scientists worry that the world's most powerful industrialized nation is moving toward its deadline for choosing between today's comforts and tomorrow's survival. The choice is beginning to look as hard as any that America has had to make in its two centuries of freedom.

NEW BREED OF POLLUTANTS: THE DANGERS THEY CARRY

Pollution once was thought of as a highly visible enemy—obvious in filth-ridden rivers and stinging urban smog.

Now, just as progress is being made to clean up the most blatant offenses to the environment, scientists are uncovering whole new families of pollutants harmful to humans.

Pollution is becoming more invisible

These pollutants are less visible and, therefore, harder to track down and handle than their predecessors.

The roots of an environmental disaster often must be traced back laboriously to find the culprit spills, wastes or a law-abiding factory putting out a chemical compound thought to be harmless.

All this goes to the very foundations of today's industrial, urban society and to its components: high-speed transport, mechanized agriculture, modern food processing, the demand for "miracle" drugs—and people's desire to maintain stability and prosperity.

These rising complexities and the costs involved in fighting pollution's rapid spread are raising a hard question about the prospects of bringing it under control: At what point will the tide become irreversible?

Feeling grows among those who ponder that question that only a determined and early assault on pollution can keep it from becoming a disaster to American life and well-being in years ahead.

CONTAMINATION ON THE JOB

Each year thousands of workers die from on-the-job pollution

The National Institute for Occupational Safety and Health (NIOSH) estimates that 100,000 deaths from on-the-job pollution occur annually, with 390,000 new cases of illness reported each year.

Pollution that strikes at specific occupations has been getting attention from the public ever since an English surgeon, Sir Percival Pott, in 1775 noted that London chimney sweeps exposed to soot and coal tar had an increased incidence of scrotal cancer.

Yet even in this area, the war on pollution is running into new problems of costs and conflicting social needs.

The American Iron and Steel Institute, for instance, estimates that it will cost the industry 800 million dollars to clean up its coke ovens by 1983.

Industry sources also say that so far there is no technology available to meet this goal during the next decades. They fear the result could be the loss of tens of thousands of jobs as the ovens are shut down.

Already, Johns-Manville Corporation, the largest miner and miller of asbestos in the free world, has spent 50 million dollars during the last decade to reduce the asbestos hazard to its workers.

A wide variety of industries are running into the same problem of costs and possible job attrition. Says Dr. Joseph K. Wagoner of NIOSH in Cincinnati: "In every industrial setting, you can find some substance that is at least suspected of being mutagenic [causing changes in gene structure], if not carcinogenic [inducing cancer]."

A number of studies have shown that the constant exposure to contaminants in certain occupations results in an increased risk of disease:

- Coke-oven workers in the steel industry are 10 times more likely to get lung cancer than other steelworkers, according to a long-term study by epidemiologist Dr. J. W. Lloyd, formerly of NIOSH.   **Evidence of occupational pollution and its effects**
- Asbestos workers have a 1-in-5 chance of getting lung cancer, a 1-in-10 chance of getting a digestive-tract cancer and a 1-in-20 chance of getting mesothelioma, a rare cancer of the lining of the lung, according to investigations by Dr. I. J. Selikoff at the Mount Sinai School of Medicine.
- Workers who were exposed to vinyl chloride have a much greater risk of developing cancer of the liver, brain and lungs than the general population, according to studies by a team of NIOSH scientists. Their report was recently published in the annals of the *New York Academy of Sciences*.

Doctors point out that the risk of getting cancer is by no means the only danger in the workplace, but just one of the easiest diseases to keep track of because the Government requires reports on all cancer cases.

Employees in a Texas plant producing the pesticide leptophos, for example, have suffered crippling disorders of the central nervous system, including partial paralysis.

Lead poisoning remains a problem in mines, smelters and lead-battery factories. Almost half of the employees at a Salt Lake City lead smelter were treated in 1975 for symptoms such as nausea, abdominal cramps, irritability and tremors.

Historically, chronic lung disease goes with work in mines, foundries and sandblasting operations. NIOSH estimates that 25 percent of those exposed to silica dust for more than 30 years will have silicosis, a crippling respiratory disease.

Health researchers are collecting hundreds of case studies such as these in an effort to further protect workers with information on the factory environment and assessment of its hazards to the outside world.

Says Dr. Wagoner of NIOSH: "We are experiencing diseases today from hazards we didn't control yesterday. What we don't take care of today will be there for our children to handle tomorrow."

HOW POLLUTION MULTIPLIES
Beyond the factory walls, an even larger threat is unleashed when products of uncertain toxicity turn up on store counters.

Some new varieties of chemical pollution

. More of these are being found every month among the thousand or so new chemicals that are introduced and marketed in the U.S. annually.

It is among a relatively small number of the 30,000 compounds already in use, however, that some of the worst contamination is being uncovered.

Over the years, the major chemical companies have voluntarily kept thousands of compounds off the market following in-house testing.

Most plastics, food additives, industrial solvents and other synthetic substances that keep America booming appear to be harmless. A few are not, however, and they create this problem:

Up until now, the Government has been unable to find out the quantity or composition of new chemicals that are being used in manufacturing. This has made it almost impossible to warn industrial purchasers of the danger potential—and doubly hard to trace an environmental poisoning back to its source.

To remedy that deficiency, the Toxic Substances Control Act that became law in 1976 requires more rigorous testing and controls for use of new chemicals.

The major impetus for passage of the law came from PCB's, or polychlorinated biphenyls. This compound has been on the market for four decades—in electrical transformers, capacitors, and in paints, inks, paper, plastics, adhesives, sealants and hydraulic fluid.

In the early 1970s, because of growing concern about the compound, Monsanto Company, the principal U.S. manufacturer of the chemical, voluntarily restricted sales to "closed systems," where it would be less likely to escape into the environment.

Now the company has announced that it will stop making the chemical by October 31 of this year. And Congress has banned most PCB production and use after Jan. 1, 1978.

PCB's will be around for years to come

Despite the ban, PCB's will be around for a long time. Example: The World Trade Center in New York City has some 250,000 fluorescent-light fixtures, each with a PCB-filled capacitor to reduce the fire hazard. The chemical is harmless in this closed system.

It is in the junk yard where the real PCB contamination problems begin. The compound does not readily break down in nature, and is rapidly destroyed only by incineration at unusually high temperatures.

In the absence of that precaution, PCB's are leached from trash bags by rain-water runoff or evaporate when burned at moderate temperatures and are carried hundreds of miles into the air before falling to earth in rain or snow.

One researcher believes that there are 300,000 tons of PCB's in U.S. junk yards, and that 60,000 tons have already been dumped into U.S. waters.

Traces of this compound are found in nearly all human-tissue samples taken in industrialized countries. It is in mothers' milk and in the flesh of fish of many fresh-water lakes and streams. The chemical has shown up in penguin eggs in Antarctica and in animals captured in Greenland.

PCB contamination has caused the shutdown of commercial fishing in the Hudson River, and levels detected in some of the Great Lakes species have cut deeply into the commercial-fishing industry in those waters.

From laboratory tests as well as the tragic PCB poisoning of human beings in Japan in the late '60s, scientists know the compound can cause reproductive disorders, skin lesions, liver trouble, loss of hair and problems with metabolism. In laboratory animals, PCB's have caused cancer and mental retardation.

Some effects of PCB's upon the human body

According to Joseph Highland of the Environmental Defense Fund, the average breast-fed child is getting 10 times more PCB's through its mother's milk than is considered safe by the Food and Drug Administration.

PCB-contamination levels in the U.S. are generally far below those that have produced immediate health problems. As yet, however, doctors do not know what a low exposure rate over a long period of years might do to a human.

Another chemical—PBB's or polybrominated biphenyls—turned out to be the culprit in a disastrous farm poisoning in Michigan that began in 1973. The PBB's are structurally akin to PCB's, but are five times more toxic.

The chemical was accidentally mixed in feed for cattle, hogs and chickens, and thousands of animals were mysteriously wiped out before the cause was determined. More than 500 of the most heavily contaminated farms in Michigan were quarantined and unknown numbers of people were exposed. Researchers are still trying to ascertain what PBB exposure does to humans.

PESTICIDES—"A BACKLASH?"

Each day, nearly a billion pounds of chemicals are knowingly released into the environment—pesticides, herbicides and fungicides.

Thousands of tons of chemicals are released into our environment daily

These chemicals largely make possible America's unsurpassed farm productivity by killing insects, weeds and fungus growth. Without them, says a Dow Chemical Company spokesman, farm output would drop by a quarter and food prices would jump 50 per cent.

Only a few of the thousands of insecticides in use are even suspected of being hazardous to humans if properly applied. Most disintegrate rapidly in nature after doing their job.

Yet some may be exacting a price in human health. How big a price? It could take decades to find out.

The average American adult carries in his or her fat tissue more than one tenth of a gram of pesticide residue. The chemicals commonly show up in mothers' milk, and also are transferred through the placenta from mother to child before birth.

Once in the fat tissue, the residue tends to stay there, building up over the years. Traces of pesticides are commonly found in beef, fish and poultry—organisms that concentrate the chemicals the same way humans do.

So far, there have been almost no direct links between pesticides and chronic human disease. The hitch is that it will take 20 to 40 years, or longer, to get a definite answer.

Warning Signs. Widespread use of synthetic organic chemicals—modern pesticides—did not start until the late 1950s. If there is a direct link between some of these chemicals and, say, cancer, it should soon begin showing in cancer statistics.

William Lijinsky, a top researcher at the National Cancer Institute, believes that the more chemicals a person has in one's body, the more likelihood of contracting some kind of cancer. Even so, he feels that the use of DDT—banned in 1972—would be acceptable if it were applied sparingly. But, he claims, sparing use is not the American way.

The people who make pesticides take exception to this view, explaining that they spend hundreds of thousands of dollars training farmers and dealers how to use their products properly and safely. One company official said:

"Any farmer who sprays more than is absolutely necessary won't be farming long. He'll go bankrupt. Pesticides are very expensive."

To determine hazards to man, scientists look for early warning signs in other species. In the laboratory, the rat is most commonly used. On the basis of these rat tests, the Environmental Protection Agency has banned or suspended five of the most potent pesticides that were on the market—DDT, dieldrin, aldrin, heptachlor and chlordane. Mirex will join the list on June 30, 1978. Some 50,000 brand names are still in use, however, and EPA is laboriously re-examining all.

Chlorinated hydrocarbons are being carefully reexamined by the EPA

A whole family of these chemicals, called chlorinated hydrocarbons, are at the top of the list for thorough reassessment. Those compounds in which the agency is particularly interested include: Kepone, endrin, BHC, chlorobenzilate and chloroform. In suspending heptachlor and chlordane, Russell Train, former chief of the Environmental Protection Agency, said: "I have found that these compounds cause cancer in laboratory animals and that laboratory tests are reliable indications of the human cancer hazard."

Pesticide makers place a different light on this finding. From a Dow Chemical Company booklet: "Tumors in rodents that are subjected to large amounts of irritants over a major part of their lives is not surprising. . . . They do not prove that the amounts of such chemicals encountered in the human environment will or can produce cancer or birth defects in people or in other animals."

FOOD—THE HIDDEN TRAPS

The risk of food poisoning, ever present a half century ago, has been virtually eliminated. And much of the credit goes to widespread use of man-made chemicals over the last two decades.

This process begins in the field where plants are nurtured and protected by fertilizers and pesticides. In feed lots, cattle are given antibiotics to keep healthy and DES (diethylstilbestrol), an estrogen growth hormone, to help them gain weight. In processing plants, thousands of chemicals are added to food to improve appearance, enhance flavor and vitamin content, extend "shelf life" and protect the consumer from spoilage.

Many chronic diseases may be related to what we eat

The over-all result is an abundant, basically healthful supply of food. But questions are being raised over the long-term impact of a chemical-rich diet. Increasingly, physicians are looking at what Americans eat for clues to major chronic diseases.

Health scientists, for example, know that a diet high in salt and animal fats increases the risk of heart disease. Recent studies linked a high-fat diet to cancer of the breast, bowel and uterus.

One theory is that many chemicals found in food break down more easily in fat, so it is the two factors—the fat and the chemicals—working together that promote the degenerative process of chronic diseases.

Some physicians believe that the widespread use of refined sugar may be involved with diabetes. The incidence of this disease has jumped 50 per cent in the last decade. If complications of diabetes are added to the death toll, this disease emerges as the third major killer after heart disease and cancer.

The Doubts.   As scientists piece together the puzzle of diet and the rise of chronic diseases, what stands out is this: Synthetic substances are everywhere.

Artificial flavors such as strawberry and wintergreen are used instead of the real ingredients. Preservatives are added to keep meat from changing color, bread from becoming moldy, fats from getting rancid. Emulsifiers, stabilizers and thickeners make the cream thick and keep the oil and vinegar from separating in ready-mix salad dressing.

Colors—more than 90 per cent are synthetic—enter all kinds of food, from meats and wines to potato chips.

Many synthetic food additives may be hazardous to our health

According to the Food and Drug Administration, more than 2,100 natural and synthetic additives are used directly in food.

What concerns health officials such as Dr. David P. Rall of the National Institute of Environmental Health Sciences is that many chemicals used in food have not been adequately tested for links to cancer, genetic mutations, birth defects and behavior problems.

The Food and Drug Administration, in fact, announced in January that it plans to review, and in some cases retest, every food additive on the market to assure safety. These will all be single-chemical tests, however, and while one compound by itself may be harmless, when combined with other substances, it can give chronic disease a foothold.

Nitrites, added to goods to prevent botulism, are not hazardous if used alone. But when combined with the enzymes in the stomach, they form nitrosamines— shown in animal studies made by Dr. Lijinsky to be a powerful cancer-causing substance.

Some recent action by the FDA

More recently, FDA has banned cyclamates, a synthetic sweetener, and Red Dyes No. 2 and 4, artificial colors used in hundreds of foods from chocolate to shredded wheat. The agency is now making a second attempt at banning DES.

DES is a known carcinogen. Whether the low amounts found in beef present a health risk is under debate. A recent study sponsored by the Council for Agricultural Sciences and Technology found no evidence of a cancer hazard from the use of DES in livestock. The evidence on cyclamates and Red Dyes No. 2 and 4 is not yet considered conclusive by FDA. But since studies fail to prove that any one of these compounds is safe, the agency has taken them off the market.

The stakes are high. The food industry is the largest and fastest growing in the country. This year, sales will reach 200 billion dollars. Since 1960, the number of items on supermarket shelves has increased from 1,500 to 32,000. The use of chemicals in food has doubled in the last two decades to more than 1 billion pounds a year—or 5 pounds of chemicals for every man, woman and child. Says Dr. Rall:

"You can't get rid of every chemical in the food supply. First you have to identify those that pose the greatest harm, and then look at the relative task. We're just beginning."

FALLOUT FROM PILLS

The 7,000 pills swallowed every second in the U.S. are not normally classified as an environmental problem.

The fact is, however, that people are occasionally getting undesirable side effects from drugs—just as they can from polluted air, water and food. This is putting drugs under the same spotlight as smog, smoking, DDT and detergents.

Agreement is widespread that drugs save lives. They offer hope to the afflicted. Americans can choose from 1,800 different kinds of prescription drugs, as many as 20,000 combination drugs, and up to an estimated 500,000 over-the-counter remedies.

Penicillin, ushering in the era of antibiotics, has virtually eliminated death from bacterial infections; schizophrenics now can lead productive lives, thanks to drug therapy, and *l*-dopa has lifted the outlook for patients with Parkinson's disease.

But there is stark evidence that this age of miracle drugs has also created its own hazards. Perhaps as many as 30,000 deaths a year come from adverse drug reactions, according to one study, and some calculations range to more than 100,000. A nationwide Commission has been set up to monitor adverse drug reactions in the future.

Drugs: A new environmental problem

Side Effects. Drug error, the wrong drug at the wrong time to the wrong patient, is a common type of accident in hospitals. It is one of the three leading causes of malpractice claims, according to the U.S. Government's Malpractice Commission.

The past gives warning that drug-induced disease, even under top medical supervision, is a risk of modern life. Thalidomide, the drug that caused deformed limbs in babies, is a symbol of that risk. There are others:

Daughters of mothers who took DES during pregnancy carry a much higher risk of developing a rare cancer of the cervix and vagina.

Chloramphenicol, which is effective against serious typhoid infections, was prescribed to roughly 4 million patients during 1967 for a variety of conditions from acne to sore throats.

Following Senate hearings on the drug, the patients were made aware of the risk of the serious blood disease—aplastic anemia—that is associated with this antibiotic.

Aspirin and birth-control pills—two of the most widely taken drugs in the U.S.—have both been linked to serious health side effects in a small number of people.

Much of the anxiety and confusion over drug side effects stem from the fact that so little is really known about the long-term effects of most drugs.

Little is known about the long-term effects of most drugs

Even less is known about how chemicals in drugs interact with those in food, in the air and the workplace.

Dr. Robert L. DuPont, director of the National Institute on Drug Abuse, admits: "We haven't grasped the significance of so many new developments in drugs and the environment. We're still stroking our beards. We don't have a knowledge base and we don't have a plan."

CLEAN AIR VS. JOBS, ENERGY

Trouble is now developing in the fight against air pollution after years of steady gains.

Millions of Americans are breathing cleaner, less-hazardous air today as a result of a billion-dollar battle to reduce emissions from autos and factories.

That hard-won progress, however, is coming into collision with the nation's burgeoning energy and economic worries.

Basically, President Carter and Congress are having to ask this question: Should the nation continue the costly fight against air pollution—or should it concentrate its resources on producing more energy, more jobs and over-all economic growth?

Pollution vs. prosperity

Studying recent trends, environmentalists fear that their concerns are about to take a back seat to economic needs. Among the trends:

- Auto makers' emphasis has shifted from emission controls to conserving fuel and holding down car prices.
- To curb oil imports and save natural gas for homes, a rise in coal burning is planned. Critics say this will cause dirtier air around factories and generating facilities.
- The Environmental Protection Agency, because of local opposition and court setbacks, has virtually abandoned efforts to curb auto congestion in urban areas.

Better Air. Doubts about the air-pollution fight come at a time when Americans from Boston to Los Angeles are enjoying cleaner air.

Since the EPA first adopted national air-quality standards in 1970, air-pollution levels have steadily declined in major urban areas. The latest EPA analysis shows these major reductions in air pollution:

In 1974, some 24 million fewer people were exposed to unhealthy levels of particulates—smoke and dust that can cause breathing problems and respiratory illness—than in 1970. That's a 33 per cent decrease, with the biggest improvement occurring in the Northeast and Great Lakes regions.

The fight against pollution: Gains and losses

Levels of sulphur dioxide, which can irritate the upper respiratory tract, have decreased 30 per cent in urban areas. Most cities now meet federal health standards.

Pollution from carbon monoxide, which can affect the heart and brain, has decreased about 5 per cent a year because of improved emission controls on autos.

On the other side, the EPA cites these facts:

Studies indicate that some of the air-pollution problems are moving out of urban centers to rural areas, where the air is getting dirtier.

Auto makers say it is impossible to meet strict 1978 emission standards, and are building 1978 cars with 1977 controls in anticipation that Congress will relax the standards.

Many businesses being caught in ever-tightening cleanup schedules are balking at the huge expenditures required of them. They question the benefit of spending so much for what they say will be a marginal return in cleaning up the environment.

The EPA's Roger Strelow concludes: "Future gains in air quality are going to be much harder to achieve than the ones in the past."

DECLINING RESOURCES

Nonrenewable resources

The shortage of many natural resources (minerals, metals, and fossil fuels) constitutes a global, not simply a national, problem. Resources such as these are termed *nonrenewable*. They were deposited in the earth in limited quantities by geological events that occurred many millions of years ago. Once these resources are used, they are for all practical purposes destroyed.[26] The rate at which we have extracted nonrenewable resources from the earth has increased dramatically in recent years. According to McHale, "we now consume in various ways over 200 tons per capita as against approximately 50 tons per capita around the turn of the century."[27]

Industrial societies contribute to world resource depletion

The shortage of natural resources constitutes a particularly severe problem for industrialized societies, which are highly dependent upon these substances for the maintenance of high standards of living and productivity. Ironically, it is these very nations that have contributed in large part to the growing problem of resource depletion through their disproportionate and wasteful use of these materials. The United States, for example, accounts for approximately 6 percent of the world's population, yet we currently consume about 30 percent of the world's raw materials.[28] We consume about 60 percent of the world's natural gas, over 40 percent of the world's aluminum, 30 percent or more of the cobalt, copper, nickel, and petroleum, and 25 percent or more of the iron, lead, and zinc.[29] Moreover, in recent years, the United States has become dependent upon foreign sources for almost all of its basic raw materials, with the notable exception of bituminous coal. The developed nations comprise only about 30 percent of the world's population, yet these nations as a whole consume vast amounts of the world's resources.[30]

Given the fact that many of the world's resources are limited and nonrenewable, how long can supplies last? Researchers at the Massachusetts Institute of Technology recently conducted an extensive study, *Limits To Growth*, which indicated that many of the world's resources are in a state

Table 10.3. Time schedule for resource decline

	GEOLOGICAL TIME REQUIRED TO PRODUCE 1 TON (MILLIONS OF YEARS)	MAN'S REMOVAL RATE (MILLIONS OF TONS PER YEAR)
Petroleum	250	600
Coal	1,000	2,000
Iron	2,000	200
Lead	4,000	4

Source: John McHale, *World Facts and Trends,* Second edition. New York: Macmillan, 1972, p. 19.

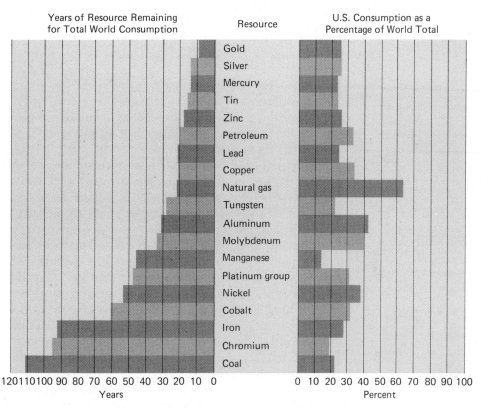

Years of Resource Remaining for Total World Consumption	Resource	U.S. Consumption as a Percentage of World Total

Fig. 10.2 Nonrenewable natural resources. Source: Donella H. Meadows et al., *Limits to Growth*, Second edition. New York: Universe Books, 1974.

of rapid decline. The study also projected that, given the persistence of present trends (i.e., the growth of population and per capita consumption), known supplies of many resources will be used up in the relatively near future. The researchers projected that known supplies of lead, copper, silver, zinc, and tin will be exhausted within twenty-one years or less. Aluminum will be consumed in thirty-one years; chromium and iron, in less than one hundred years, natural gas in about twenty-two years; and nickel, in fifty-three years.

How fast are resources declining?

As we shall see later in this chapter, many of the findings of the MIT researchers have been the subject of criticism and debate within certain circles of the scientific community. Given, however, the exponential growth of population and resource consumption, it is possible that the era of world resource abundance may soon be coming to an end. The situation of declining resources raises doubts as to whether, in the long run, industrialized nations will be able to maintain their relatively high standards of living.

The end of world resource abundance

Whether many of the less-developed nations will ever be able to raise their living standards to the level of those found within the industrialized world is also highly doubtful.[31]

Energy. The problem of resource depletion is most apparent in the area of energy. Since the turn of the century, the industrialized nations of the world have become increasingly dependent upon the use of fossil fuels (oil, coal, and natural gas) for the production of energy. As we mentioned above, however, these fuels are available in the earth in only limited quantities. The current energy crisis has resulted from the fact that in recent decades many nations of the world (particularly the industrialized nations) have placed such heavy demands upon these finite resources that they are rapidly approaching the point of exhaustion. Of all the conventional fossil fuels, coal remains the most plentiful; world supplies will probably last the next several centuries or longer. The situation is much more critical, however, for supplies of petroleum and natural gas. Geologist M. King Hubbert estimates that world supplies of these fossil fuels will be substantially depleted within approximately 100 years.[32] World production of oil is expected to peak around the year 1990 and then to steadily decline until the year 2050, at which point the total supply (an estimated two trillion barrels) will be exhausted.[33]

> **Coal: The most abundant fossil fuel**

Underlying the growing energy crisis is the fact that the industrialized nations (particularly the United States) have been consuming vast amounts of energy, often far beyond their legitimate requirements. Americans comprise only a few percent of the world's population, yet we use one-third of its energy.[34] In fact, we have the highest per capita energy consumption on earth. In gasoline alone we consume over seven million barrels of fuel each day, which is enough to send 1,591,579 automobiles from New York City to Los Angeles. Our own oil wells are not sufficient to handle even our gasoline needs. Our use of electricity is currently growing at the same rate as before the Arab embargo, and at this rate we can again expect large-scale blackouts in the early 1980s.[35]

> **The United States consumes one-third of world energy**

Some people may feel that our energy extravagance is justified by the need to maintain a high standard of living. But the fact is that each year we consume at least twice the amount of energy needed to maintain this standard, and our energy demands are climbing by a near-record 4 percent per year.[36] Much of our energy consumption is inefficient energy use and just plain waste: in our industrial manufacturing processes, in our methods of transportation (big cars remain as popular as ever), and in our commercial and household energy use. Given our present levels of energy consumption, it is estimated that the United States will exhaust virtually all of its own oil and natural gas resources within the next thirty to forty years.[37] Yet many Americans have simply managed to ignore or remain unconcerned about this frightening prospect. Recent nation-wide public

> **Much of our energy consumption is energy waste**

opinion surveys on national concerns have found that the energy problem ranked behind unemployment, crime, inflation, health care, education, and defense. Only 38 percent felt that energy problems are real. In addition, approximately one-half of those polled were actually unaware that the United States needs to import any part of the oil it uses.[38] All too often, when it comes to corporate profits or our own national comfort, concern for the environment and resources takes second place.

The crisis in energy has lead many authorities to begin reassessing alternative sources for future fuel production. Two alternative sources, coal and nuclear energy, have now been given top priority.[39] The employment of these energy sources, however, poses a number of hazards to both our health and our environment. Coal has the advantage of being in plentiful supply within the United States, and it eventually might also prove to be a relatively inexpensive energy source for utilities and industry. For these reasons alone, coal will play a major part in meeting our energy needs for the future. Nevertheless, coal is the dirtiest fuel available today. Increased coal production will necessitate intensified strip-mining activities, which have already ruined too much of our land. Burning coal also releases large amounts of sulfur dioxide and other pollutants into our atmosphere. Stricter federal regulations on the mining and burning of coal may ease the situation somewhat; still, it is a virtual certainty that increased reliance upon coal will result in more pollution and environmental deterioration.

Coal: Advantages and disadvantages

It is also clear that, in addition to coal, nuclear power will increasingly serve as a major source of energy in the near as well as long-range future. Nuclear power currently supplies about 3 percent of all our energy needs, and projections indicate that by 1985 our reliance upon nuclear energy will almost triple. Approximately 9 percent of our nation's current electrical

Nuclear power: A source of electricity

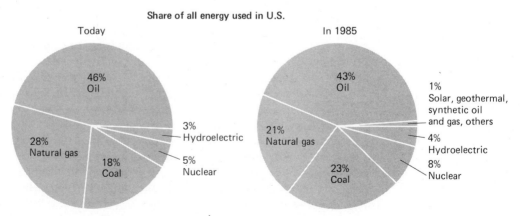

Share of all energy used in U.S.

Today — 46% Oil, 28% Natural gas, 18% Coal, 5% Nuclear, 3% Hydroelectric

In 1985 — 43% Oil, 21% Natural gas, 23% Coal, 1% Solar, geothermal, synthetic oil and gas, others; 4% Hydroelectric; 8% Nuclear

Fig. 10.3 The coming changes in fuels: In the years just ahead, Americans will depend less on natural gas and oil than they do today. Source: *U.S. News & World Report*, Feb. 21, 1977, p. 19.

Wide World Photos, Inc.

One major concern of nuclear energy opponents and proponents alike is the safe disposal of nuclear waste.

Nuclear power: Major issues

generating capacity is nuclear, and the Federal Energy Administration (FEA) projects that by 1985, 23 percent of our electricity will come from atomic sources.[40] Advocates of nuclear power feel that it has a number of advantages: it can supply an unlimited amount of energy; it is relatively inexpensive (compared to oil); and it creates less environmental pollution than the burning of coal.[41] In spite of advocates' claims, however, there is a continuing and heated controversy over the safety of nuclear power. Many argue that its potential risks to the environment and to human life itself far outweigh any potential benefits of its use in the production of energy.

Concern over the hazards of nuclear power is primarily focused upon two major issues: the safety of the nuclear reactors and the safe disposal of massive quantities of highly dangerous radioactive wastes. With regard to the reactors, there is always the danger of malfunctions, sabotage, or accidental damage to the reactor core itself as a result of fire, explosions, or natural disasters. Such a situation could discharge massive doses of radiation into the environment.[42]

An Atomic Energy Commission (AEC) bulletin published in 1964 reported eleven "critical accidents" that resulted in personnel's exposure to radiation and/or damage to the reactor. In 1966, a breeder reactor near Detroit experienced a "near miss" situation—it went beyond the "maximum credible accident" specifications established for that installation.[43] In 1975, the Brown's Ferry Reactor in Alabama caught fire: Seven of the twelve safety systems of the reactor were knocked out, but the remaining systems prevented a reactor meltdown. The 1979 near-meltdown at Three Mile Island proved that our present safeguards are not wholly effective, although the crisis was ultimately averted.[44] Supporters of nuclear power point out that, to date, despite occasional "mishaps," the safety record of conventional nuclear plants has been remarkable, and that the chance of a person's being fatally injured by a nuclear accident is five billion to one.[45] Opponents are anything but satisfied with the nuclear safety record. As far as they are concerned, it takes only one major nuclear disaster to wipe out thousands of lives.

Nuclear accidents

DISPOSING OF ATOMIC WASTE

As mentioned above, a second and potentially more serious problem of nuclear energy is how to dispose of ever increasing amounts of radioactive nuclear wastes, which consist largely of plutonium, spent uranium fuel rods, and massive amounts of unusable radioactive sludge. Each year thousands of tons of radioactive wastes are added to the nation's stockpile, and our present technological systems for their safe handling and disposal are highly inadequate. In future years, the storage problem is likely to become much more critical, as additional conventional reactors are built and as advanced breeder reactors (which produce massive amounts of plutonium) come into increased use. The following *Time* article discusses the growing crisis of atomic garbage and some of the new governmental proposals for dealing with this problem.

TIME READING——OBJECTIVES

1. To list the major varieties of nuclear "garbage."
2. To discuss in a brief essay the major difficulties involved in storing nuclear wastes.
3. To identify the typical methods currently being used most often for storing radioactive wastes.

The Atom's Global Garbage

In rural Cattaraugus County, 40 miles south of Buffalo, the West Valley nuclear reprocessing plant has been shut down since 1973, when the Getty Oil Co. ceased operations there. Meanwhile, the radioactive waste created by the plant is buried in landfill trenches. Some of the poisonous garbage periodically leaks into Cattaraugus Creek, which feeds into Lake Erie, the source of water for Buffalo and surrounding communities.

In France, a reprocessing plant at Cap de la Hague, near Cherbourg, stores its nuclear waste in giant steel tanks. But the tanks leak. The storage area has reached three times the acceptable levels of radiation. Traces of plutonium are being found along the Normandy coast, and crabs in the area have begun to show ulcerous sores.

At present there is no technology for the disposal of atomic garbage

Examples like these underscore one of the most frightening challenges of the atomic age: how to get rid of a rising flood of radioactive sludge that results from reprocessing uranium to extract plutonium, which is used to make atom bombs and as fuel for fast-breeder reactors. At the moment there is no technology for disposing of this deadly garbage. But the stockpiles of nuclear waste smoldering away in upstate New York are only part of the problem. In addition, each of the nation's 65 nuclear generating stations also produces waste in the form of spent uranium fuel rods, which are stored in dumping areas next to the plant. These storage areas have now begun to fill up, and the power stations have discovered that it is becoming difficult to find additional storage areas—a problem that could soon slow further development of nuclear energy or cause some power plants to shut down altogether.

Last week the Carter Administration took a long overdue step to deal with the nuclear waste from generating plants and proposed that the Government take over responsibility for storing the spent fuel. The companies would transfer the material to the Government on a voluntary basis and pay a storage fee. How many storage sites will be needed and where they will be located has not yet been decided. So far, the industry's inventory of spent fuel is 2,500 metric tons, and by 1985, when some 75 new nuclear generators will have come into production, the backlog will be nearly ten times that amount. Estimates put the inventory for the year 2000 at an awesome 190,000 metric tons.

The government's ideas on what to do about the problem

Though the program is expected to be self-supporting, the White House will probably have to seek congressional authorization to spend up to $100 million for construction of a storage facility. The Government favors eventually depositing the spent fuel on a more nearly permanent basis in geologic formations like salt beds. But studies to determine the feasibility of such storage methods will not be completed until the mid-1980s.

One aspect of the plan that is certain to draw the fire of antinuclear groups is the President's offer to have the U.S. store the atomic waste of foreign reactors that use American fuel. Spent uranium rods used in reactors can be reprocessed to yield plutonium, which could be used for military purposes. By holding the spent foreign fuel in the U.S., Washington hopes to curb the global proliferation of nuclear weapons.

The industry's reaction to the plan is generally good. Says Gordon Corey, vice chairman of Chicago's Commonwealth Edison, the nation's biggest user of nuclear power: "I'm pleased as punch with the program. It's high time." Until now, atomic-powered electric utilities have had to keep their spent fuel rods in water in large on-site storage tanks that resemble swimming pools. For a time, the U.S. also sealed a small amount of its waste in containers and dumped it into the ocean. That practice was stopped in 1970, but concern about it lingers on. Last week researchers using a specially equipped submarine began an examination of an underwater atomic dumping ground 50 miles off San Francisco. They were attracted by reports that the metal barrels have broken open and are allowing radioactive waste to spread across the ocean floor.

Growing public concern about the environmental impact of atomic waste is hurting some utilities. In California, which has two nuclear generators in operation, worried state legislators last year passed a law blocking the licensing of any additional facilities until the waste problem is solved. A recent Energy Research and Development Administration study reported that as many as 23 nuclear plants may have to shut down entirely by the mid-1980s if alternative storage room is not provided. The Administration hopes its plan will prevent these and other plants from shutting down. If such shutdowns were allowed to occur, the White House would have no hope of increasing nuclear production from its present level of 10% of the nation's electricity supply to the 1985 target of 20%.

Still, no expert in or out of Government regards the plan as anything like a permanent solution to the waste problem. Critics of nuclear power contend the program does not amount to a hill of isotopes; the only way to deal with the deadly waste, they argue, is to slow or even discontinue the development of atomic power. Says Environmentalist Barry Commoner: "All the program does is take a difficult problem off the backs of the utilities and put it on the back of the Government. It's dodging the issues. The real difficulty is that there are no adequate ways of dealing with the waste."

Commoner has a point. Unlike spent fuel rods, which are comparatively easy to handle, a great deal of the radioactive material is sludge and extremely difficult to contain. This highly poisonous witches' brew is left over in the reprocessing of spent fuel. Much of the present inventory has been produced by the Government's nuclear weapons buildup. The waste is stored in massive underground steel tanks like those near Richland, Wash., Aiken, S.C., and Idaho Falls. It totals 75 million gals., enough to fill a supertanker to overflowing. Because of its intense radioactivity, however, the waste regularly eats through thick concrete and steel tanks and seeps into the ground. The last major spill occurred at Richland in 1973 when 115,000 gals. spilled undetected into the ground, significantly raising the radioactive level in the area. One way to resolve the problem would be to solidify this sludge, package it in concrete or glass and bury it deep in the earth. But as yet no technology for doing this exists, and estimates of the cost of developing one range from $2 billion to $20 billion.

The ultimate nuclear headache, however, is disposing of the reactors themselves. By 2000, there will be roughly 300 nuclear facilities around the U.S., and at least 15 of them will have become obsolete and dangerous to operate. Short of welding shut the entrances and placing the facilities under guard forever, the only

Possible cutbacks in nuclear power plant construction

The ultimate problem: The disposal of reactors themselves

solution is to dismantle them and bury the pieces. The difficulty of the task is now being underscored in the desolate Santa Susana Mountains, 40 miles northwest of Los Angeles, where a small Government-built experimental generator is being torn down.

Workmen, using remote-control cutting torches and closed-circuit television, are slicing up the reactor a piece at a time. The slabs are then hoisted by a crane into an 8,000-gal. water tank, and will eventually be transported in sealed containers to a burial site in the Nevada desert. The task will take another year to complete and will cost about $8 million. To pull down an average-size commercial reactor today could conceivably cost as much as $100 million, and that cost is likely to soar in the years ahead.

Nuclear wastes: An international problem

Like the U.S., Europe and Japan are also struggling with the nuclear-waste problem and have yet to devise a way to resolve the issue. In Britain, for example, a reprocessing facility at Windscale on the Irish Sea is now the focus of a highly publicized government inquiry, following a still unexplained storage-tank leak last March. France's La Hague reprocessing plant has been a center of controversy almost from the time it was built in 1961. Critics charge that the aging plant is a catastrophe waiting to happen. Many areas of the plant that were once serviceable have become so radioactive that workers must wear heavy, protective suits. Moreover, the contamination is spreading throughout the facility, and breakdowns have increased dramatically. As for safety, signs inside the plant warn: IF THERE IS A CRITICAL REACTION YOUR BEST PROTECTION IS TO FLEE.

West Germany and Japan both have their hands full trying to dispose of the mounting stockpile of spent fuel at their reactors. The Bonn government, for instance, rapidly accelerated its nuclear electrification program after the 1973 Arab oil boycott, and now has 13 atomic power plants. But the whole program has fallen into a state of semiparalysis as a result of political opposition and a barrage of court injunctions from environmentalists.

Washington's belated recognition of the U.S.'s leadership responsibility in nuclear-waste management is a small but significant step. But it must be followed up with a continuing vigorous effort to resolve the menacing threat of nuclear waste to the safety and well-being of whole populations. Otherwise the full dawning of the atomic age could be postponed indefinitely, with grave consequences for a world already facing the threat of energy shortages.

Alternative energy sources

As we have seen, both government and industry are now placing major emphasis upon coal and the development of nuclear power as "ultimate solutions" to our growing energy problems. Some, but unfortunately not enough, stress is being given to the importance of conserving energy and altering our wasteful patterns of energy use. Moreover, neither government nor industry has made much progress in developing new technologies that would hasten the development of environmentally less hazardous energy sources, for example, synthetic fuels and geothermal and solar energy. Coal is a plentiful yet still finite resource. Nuclear plants produce only electricity; nuclear power alone will not eliminate our dependence upon fossil fuels.[46]

Do the benefits of nuclear power outweigh its potential hazards to our environment and personal safety? This question needs to be raised with respect to many of our other "solutions" to environmental problems.

EXPLANATIONS FOR ENVIRONMENTAL PROBLEMS

In the previous sections of this chapter we have examined in some depth the state of the environment. In general, as we have seen, our environment is showing progressive signs of large-scale deterioration. We have repeatedly noted that many of the problems of environmental pollution and degradation and resource depletion are the result of human actions. Humans have increasingly interfered with and damaged the balance of our environmental ecosystem. How and in what specific ways has this happened? What are the specific causes of the environmental crisis? These problems have resulted from a number of factors, including technology, the growth of population, and industrialization as well as our own values and attitudes favoring neglect of and disregard for the environment around us.

The environmental crisis: Contributing factors

TECHNOLOGICAL CHANGE
In the 1950s, an intensive pesticide program was launched to exterminate the spruce budworm that was then destroying much of the forest acreage near New Brunswick, Canada. The pesticide used was DDT, a "broad-spectrum pesticide," meaning that it is highly lethal to many animal species, not only to budworms.[47] Unfortunately, the pesticide run-off into the nearby Mirimichi River was also responsible for the destruction of over 90 percent of the river's vast salmon population.[48]

The effects of pesticides

In 1962, Rachel Carson's classic book *Silent Spring* brought the Mirimichi River and other similar tragic incidents to nationwide attention. The book clearly described many of the grave ecological dangers associated with the careless widespread use of new chemical technologies, particularly pesticides such as DDT and other chlorinated hydrocarbons. These substances are capable of killing numerous species of animal life, and their concentrations can be accumulated in lower-order species and eventually carried through food chains to meat- and fish-eating organisms.[49] Although her book was criticized by some scientists, Ms. Carson accomplished her primary purpose—to bring to public attention many of the unknown dangers of pesticide use.

Pesticides and food chains

Rachel Carson and other environmentalists are not against technology itself, but they oppose applications of technology that result in more environmental damage than environmental good. Ecologist Barry Commoner, for example, believes that much of our environmental deterioration can be directly linked to the rise of "new productive technologies" rather than to increased affluence or population growth. In his words, new "productive technologies with intense impacts on the environment have displaced less destructive ones."[50] According to Commoner, these technologies and their

Environmental deterioration and new technologies

improper application have resulted in a near 2000 percent increase in pollution in the United States since World War II.[51] As Commoner notes,

> Soap powder has been displaced by synthetic detergents; natural fibers (cotton and wool) have been displaced by synthetic ones; ... railroad freight has been displaced by truck freight; returnable bottles have been displaced by non-returnable ones. On the road, the low-powered automobile engines of the 1920's and 1930's have been displaced by high-powered ones. On the farm ... fertilizer has displaced land. Older methods of insect control have been displaced by synthetic insecticides, such as DDT. ... Range-feeding of livestock has been displaced by feedlots.[52]

Technologies can benefit our standard of living but can cause environmental harm

The employment of these technologies often benefits our standard of living but also involves substantial environmental costs. Feedlots produce heavy deposits of animal wastes, thus contributing to high nitrate levels within surface waters. The excessive use of pesticides involves threats to the well-being of many animal species, including humans. The manufacture and use of synthetic detergents creates far more environmental pollution than does soap. Synthetic fibers require much heat and energy to produce and are also ecologically nondegradable. Automobiles give us comfort and luxury, but they also consume large amounts of fuel and are a major source of environmental pollution.[53] Many environmentalists feel, however, that technology itself is not at fault; rather, the narrow misapplication of technology, without knowledge and/or concern for its potential ecologically disruptive side-effects, is the heart of our current environmental crisis.

ECONOMIC AND POPULATION GROWTH

As we have seen above, technology, in particular the all too rapid, narrow, and careless application of technological innovations as an answer to certain problems, can have many unforeseen negative ecological results. While some environmentalists see technology as the major source of environmental problems, many others are primarily concerned about the detrimental consequences of industrialization and/or population growth.[54] It should be obvious from earlier discussions (above and in Chapter 9) that the problems of environmental pollution and resource depletion are closely linked to the growth of both industrialization and population.

Population and industrial growth: Environmental effects

In 1970, a group of European scientific scholars known as the Club of Rome sponsored a large-scale intensive study conducted at the Massachusetts Institute of Technology. This study focused on the future, worldwide consequences of our current patterns of population and industrial growth, agricultural production, resource depletion, and pollution. The researchers were particularly interested in assessing the future consequences of population and industrial growth upon human societies and the global eco-

Some future consequences of growth

system. Using a series of sophisticated computer models, the research group was able to make a number of projections about the quality of future human life. The results of this research were published in the book *Limts To Growth* (1974). The general finding was that, given current rates of exponential growth in production, resource depletion, population, and pollution, we will likely experience a decline and in fact a collapse of "population and industrial growth . . . within the next century at the latest."[55] In other words, given current growth patterns, our global ecosystems will be unable to support large numbers of people as well as industrial growth by the year 2100. The MIT researchers concluded that the only way to avoid such a catastrophe is to impose certain limits on global population and economic growth.

As we mentioned, the MIT research focused on the creation of a number of computer models showing the consequences of various growth factors, for one another and for the global ecosystem. In the "world model standard run," the researchers simply assumed that twentieth century growth trends would continue, with "no major change" in the future. In this case, world resources would become depleted and eventually exhausted, the industrial economy would collapse, and population death rates would surge.

The "world model standard run"

The researchers went on to develop a number of alternative computer models in order to avoid this situation. Suppose resources and energy were unlimited? In this case, population would grow and industrialization would increase dramatically, but environmental pollution would eventually engulf the global ecosystem and a massive surge in death rates would occur. But suppose we find technological solutions to the pollution problem? Here, pollution does not become problematic, but population and industrialization continue to grow, placing massive pressures upon the supply of arable lands. Food consumption declines, death rates increase significantly, and "collapse comes about this time primarily from food shortage."[56] Thus, regardless of the model employed, the MIT projections indicate that *growth itself* inevitably leads to social, economic, and environmental collapse. The MIT researchers suggested that the only way of avoiding these situations would be to develop policies for curtailing and stabilizing current population and industrialization levels. Stability and equilibrium of population and production is necessary to avoid global catastrophe.

Alternatives to collapse

The *Limits To Growth* report has been criticized on several counts. Some feel that the researchers give little credit to the capabilities of future technology to deal with environmental problems; others argue for the likelihood that new supplies of resources will be discovered at a rate far outpacing population growth. Still others feel that any attempt to reduce the entire global ecosystem to elementary computer models is both naive and simplistic. The MIT report has also been a source of deep concern for many who recognize basic predicaments in the report's findings. If it is

Criticisms of *Limits To Growth*

in fact necessary to limit economic growth in order to avoid global catastrophe, what about the fate of the world's less-developed nations, which need to industrialize in order to improve their standards of living? Also, are the industrial nations willing to reduce their standards of living out of concern for the environment and the larger world community? One may find fault with some of the report's findings, but it is difficult to question its basic principle. We live in a world of fixed resources and intricately balanced ecosystems, and there are limits to the strains we can place upon our environment.

ATTITUDES AND VALUES

In addition to these factors, many of our environmental problems must be understood in relation to, and as a consequence of, some of the major attitudes and values characteristically found within our society. One such attitude can best be called an *exploitive* view of nature, which is joined to and reinforced by a traditional belief that nature's resources are simply unlimited. Our exploitive attitude is perhaps most clearly evident in our attempts to use the environment for our own selfish interests. All too often we think of the environment in terms of commodities—how much wood, oil, and metal can be extracted from it, or how much we can use it for the disposal of garbage and other wastes. Little do we realize that we cannot separate ourselves from the environment. We too are part of nature; we are dependent upon it and also have responsibility for it.

To a certain degree, these attitudes are an outgrowth of religious teachings that placed people at the center of the universe, second in importance to God. In this view, the environment's primary purpose was to serve people, to be used by us for utilitarian motives. The early colonists and their succeeding generations were steeped in these beliefs. Moreover, these people found a world of apparently unlimited resources. Nature's goods seemed free for the taking, and somewhere there would always be more. These attitudes and beliefs laid the foundation for environmental degradation and exploitation. Today, even though some people have come to realize that we must redefine our relationship to the environment, there is little doubt that an expansionist, exploitive ideology still persists and is the root of many contemporary environmental problems.

Finally, many of our environmental ills can be traced directly to a number of major American values, most notably the importance we assign to economic growth and material consumption. Today, as in the past, much of our economic enterprise is centered around the importance of growth and expansion: the larger our productive apparatus and the more we produce, the better. Economic growth and expansion were, no doubt, at one time absolutely essential for the development of our industrial economy, but now the dominant value has become growth for the sake of growth. The

Our exploitive view of nature

The origins of our attitudes

Our values create problems

amount of goods we produce is truly massive: millions of bottles, automobiles, televisions, appliances, and electronic gadgets. In most cases production has increased far beyond the point of meeting our basic needs.

Unfortunately, we all too often gauge the quality of life in terms of the gross national product (GNP). The value that Americans assign to economic growth is closely related to, and in many ways largely a consequence of, the value we assign to material wealth and the possession and consumption of goods. For many people, the desire for material possessions now exceeds the one-time excessive goal of two automobiles and two televisions per family: today, we have moved closer to the point of one television, stereo, and vehicle for *each* individual household member.

There is little question, as sociologist Jonathan Turner astutely points out, that we have become deeply involved in a vicious cycle of "consumption-production," each supporting and reciprocally influencing the other.[57] Thus our values of materialism and consumption have played a major role in the development of a massive productive apparatus. Once in existence, however, this apparatus has a vested interest in stimulating as much consumption as possible through advertising, through making things "bigger and better," and through building into products various degrees of "planned obsolescence." This "consumption-production" cycle has generated many of our most serious environmental problems. Large-scale production reduces many important resources, including energy, and industrial manufacturing processes are a prime source of environmental pollution (see Table 10.1). At the same time, massive consumption results in increased problems of waste disposal, evidenced by the fact that each year Americans use the environment as the dumping ground for a minimum of 3.5 billion tons of solid wastes.

For many, the solution to these various environmental ills lies in the increased development and use of technology. But, as Turner points out, the mere faith in and application of science and technology is simply not enough to meet the challenges posed by our current environmental problems. As Turner notes,

> The ecological crisis is thus much more than a technological problem; its solution may require some changes in basic values and institutions. Generating the technology is the least of the difficulties in meeting current ecological problems. In fact, to continue to wait on a technological breakthrough is probably unnecessary because, as the President's Council on Environmental Quality noted in 1971, the knowledge to solve many ecological problems is currently available. The technology ethic, then, poses a curious dilemma: It will assist in the solution of ecological problems, but, at the same time, blind faith in its powers diverts attention away from the real source of the problem, the basic structure of American society.[58]

Corporations help us to create consumer desires, making us feel that we should or must have all kinds of products

Effects of the "consumption-production" cycle

Faith in technology is not enough

Solutions for many of our environmental problems certainly involve but nevertheless go far beyond the sphere of technology. As we have seen, truly worthwhile solutions will also entail value, attitudinal, and institutional change. Such change will necessarily call for substantial economic costs, now and in the future. Thus the more important question is whether we, as individuals and as a society, are willing to pay the price for a sound and healthy environment.

RESPONSES TO PROBLEMS

Early environmental concern

During the nineteenth and early twentieth centuries, environmental concern focused primarily around the general conservationist movement goals of protecting the wilderness, improving and beautifying the land, and expanding the national park system. In spite of the fact that many conservationist laws were passed at the federal and state levels, these regulations by and large did little to improve environmental quality.

THE ENVIRONMENTAL MOVEMENT

The post-World War II decades marked a period of accelerated industrial, economic, technological, and population growth for the United States. This growth, however, also placed increased stress upon many of our environment's resources and contributed to higher rates of pollution. Concern for the deteriorating quality of our environment gave rise to a renewed growth of the environmental movement in the 1960s and early 1970s.

Effects of the environmental movement: New legislation

Ultimately, this movement was responsible for the enactment, early in this decade, of a number of laws and regulations that aimed at alleviating problems and improving environmental quality. Such legislation included, for example, the National Environmental Protection Act of 1970 (which created the Environmental Protection Agency (EPA) and the Council on Environmental Quality), the Clean Air Act of 1970, and the Federal Water Pollution Control Act (FWPCA) of 1972. At the federal level, the EPA was given major responsibility for environmental quality. Since then, many of these earlier acts have been extended and/or amended, and additional pieces of environmental legislation have been enacted, including the Safe Drinking Water Act of 1974, the Toxic Substances Control Act of 1976, and the Surface Mining Control and Reclamation Act of 1977.

Some progress has been made in dealing with environmental problems

As a result of increased federal, state, and local governmental concern and involvement, some progress has been made in the effort to remedy a number of our most blatant environmental ills. In general, for example, we are breathing cleaner air today than in 1970, partly because of regulations requiring the installation of industrial and automotive pollution control devices. Pollution levels within some of our nation's rivers have also been reduced, as a result of increased federal regulations limiting the discharge of industrial wastes. In the effort to clean up the nations' waterways,

United Press International

Famous personages, like Robert Redford, have lent their names and time to efforts to clean up and preserve our environment.

the federal government is allocating approximately $18 billion in grants to a number of cities for the expansion of their municipal sewage treatment processes. It is also possible that some of the soil damage caused by strip-mining practices may be curtailed in the future, as a result of the passage of the Safe Mining Control and Reclamation Act of 1977, which requires mining operators to restore excavated lands to their original soil contours and conditions.

LIMITED PROGRESS
Yet in spite of this legislation it is apparent, as discussed earlier in this chapter, that only limited progress has been made in surmounting many of these environmental problems. Latest EPA findings indicate, for example, that "a majority of Americans breathe air that is considered harmful to their

health, despite evidence that in general the air is cleaner than it used to be."[59] The results of national EPA surveys showed that 606 counties within the United States failed to meet federal standards for smog, 424 failed to meet standards for particulate matter, 190 did not meet standards for carbon monoxide, and 108 did not meet sulfur dioxide standards.[60] The Carter Administration's insistence on the expanded use of coal as a short- and possibly long-run solution to dwindling oil and natural gas supplies also poses potential environmental hazards to both our air and land. Despite the Surface Mining Control and Reclamation Act, many environmentalists are very concerned that increased use of coal will inevitably bring about greater degradation of our land through strip-mining.

Based upon EPA findings, the Council on Environmental Quality reported in 1977 that ground water (which is the source of drinking water for approximately one-half of our population) "has been contaminated locally in all parts of the nation and regionally in some heavily populated and industrialized areas."[61] Contaminants include heavy metals, radioactive wastes, organic compounds, and so on. Cities also have a long way to go in cleaning up their water supplies. As of mid-1977, only about 30 percent of the nation's 13,000 municipal treatment plants provided secondary water treatment. EPA data also indicate that during 1976, 18 states listed pesticide contamination and 35 states listed heavy metal contamination among their major water pollution problems.[62] As mentioned earlier in this chapter, agricultural run-off and industrial and municipal discharge are the primary sources of such contamination.

Why haven't we made more progress in solving our environmental problems? In some cases, our slow progress on the environmental front can be traced directly to the actions (or lack of action) of governmental regulatory agencies themselves.[63] It is one thing to pass a law giving an agency "broad powers," but the actual implementation, regulation, and enforcement of these laws is something else. In some cases, environmental laws have not been effectively enforced; in others, enforcement agencies have been unwilling to levy sanctions upon the polluter, and when sanctions are applied, they are frequently in the form of minor fines. In still other instances, official deadlines for municipal and industrial waste treatment or disposal and pollution abatement may be set far (perhaps too far) in the future. If these deadlines are not met, extensions permitting the perpetuation of environmentally harmful practices may be granted by environmental agencies or by other federal or state authorities.

For example, as a result of a 1977 EPA ruling, the Atlantic Ocean will continue to serve as a dumping ground for east coast sludge and industrial wastes until December 31, 1981. Also, automobile manufacturers have been given a series of extensions for reducing auto emissions. Originally specified in the Clean Air Act of 1970, the deadline was 1975, but it has now been postponed to 1980 for unburned hydrocarbons and to 1981 for carbon monoxide. Likewise, as mentioned earlier, a recent federal district court

Insufficient government action

decision allowed the Reserve Mining Company of Silver Bay, Minnesota to continue dumping asbestos-like taconite wastes into Lake Superior until April 15, 1980.[64]

But the government cannot be held solely accountable for all of our environmental problems. Our corporate industry is also a prime offender. Our economy is structured around the importance of continuous growth, and corporations have strong vested interests in maximizing production, expansion, and profit. As we have seen above, corporations have played a key role in generating a massive "production-consumption" cycle that in itself has given rise to many of our environmental problems. Corporations have also done a first-rate job in actively lobbying against antipollution laws, which may require the installation of expensive pollution control devices or prohibit companies from using a nearby waterway as a free dumping ground for their wastes. In one way or another, environmental legislation adds to manufacturing costs and therefore ultimately reduces corporate profits.

Finally, as noted in some detail earlier, we cannot ignore the fact that individuals are also prime contributors to most of our environmental ills. *People* pollute and waste energy and other resources. Our exploitive view of nature and the importance we assign to economic growth and the possession and consumption of material goods combine to favor neglect of and disregard for the environment around us. If the "buck must stop," it *should* certainly stop with many of us.

People also pollute

OTHER APPROACHES: PRESENT AND FUTURE

Governmental Action. As we have noted, the government has in recent years become more involved in dealing with many ecological problems. However, if environmental problems are to be handled in a truly effective manner, increased governmental action is necessary. For one thing, stricter enforcement of legislation presently on the books is needed. In many instances, environmental pollution laws are not effectively enforced, while in other cases only minimum civil penalties (small fines, for example) are imposed. This situation needs to be changed. Environmental laws should not be disregarded by business and industry, and far stiffer economic sanctions (perhaps even criminal penalties) should be levied against violators. If industrial polluters were faced with heavy fines that by law could not be passed on to the public in the form of higher prices, many would take steps to rapidly curb or eliminate their pollution. Moreover, systems of tax writeoffs or credits to business and industry might be very effectively used by government to promote additional research into methods of pollution reduction. Tax breaks could also be given to companies as incentives for installing pollution control devices.[65]

More government action is needed

The government could also provide legislation and monies for the expansion of mass transit systems and the development of nationwide recycling programs. Most environmental experts view the automobile as an

The need for mass transit and nationwide recycling

Table 10.4. The bill for cleaning up America: $271 billion

Estimates of pollution-control costs in U.S. over next 10 years

	BILLIONS OF DOLLARS
To fight air pollution	$143
Private spending:	
On auto pollution	$ 56
On industrial pollution	$ 49
On utilities pollution	$ 32
Government spending: On pollution from public buildings, incinerators, and other government facilities	$ 6
To fight water pollution	$116
Private spending:	
On industrial pollution	$ 59
On utilities pollution	$ 13
Government spending: On waste-treatment plants and sewers	$ 44
To fight noise pollution	$ 4
To fight solid wastes, radiation, other forms of pollution	$ 8
Total cost	$271

Note: Costs in 1976 dollars to discount effects of inflation.

Source: Council on Environmental Quality. Reprinted from *U.S. News & World Report*, February 7, 1977, p. 43.

ecological disaster—it pollutes, consumes resources, and wastes energy. Improvements in and expansion of mass transit systems are badly needed to lessen people's dependence upon the automobile as a basic source of transportation. Large-scale recycling programs could also be of tremendous aid in resource conservation. The Council on Environmental Quality estimates that each year we discard billions of tons of mineral wastes alone. Reuse of the metals found within these wastes would aid in resource and energy conservation.[66] Moreover, as we will mention shortly, recycling processes are also applicable to many of the other products and goods we use.

Finally, more governmental funding is needed for research into solutions for many environmental problems. This is a particularly urgent need in such areas as the development of alternative energy sources, research into the nature and effects of chemical and toxic substance pollution, and the improvement of technologies for solid waste disposal.

Education. As we mentioned earlier, people are more aware of environmental problems today than in the past. Nevertheless, there is a desperate need for large-scale environmentally oriented education programs in our schools and through the mass media. Most people need basic information concerning our environment's problems, the causes of these problems, and what can be done about them. As we have noted earlier, many people do not know or believe that an energy crisis exists, and many others are not aware that the United States must import oil to meet its energy needs. Environmental education would help inform people of the hazards of pollution and resource depletion and the various alternative solutions for dealing with these problems. With regard to conserving resources, for example, many people know that cans, bottles, and paper can be recycled, but few are aware that virtually *all* our products—cars, clothing—could be recycled if originally manufactured with that end in mind. Even much of our municipal waste could be treated and recycled as agricultural fertilizer. Recycling saves energy, cuts pollution, and conserves natural resources. Thus the present and future potential benefits of recycling processes are enormous, and people should be informed of this alternative.

People are often unaware of the environmental consequences of their actions, particularly regarding resource and energy waste. They need to know more about how they waste resources and energy and how to eliminate this waste. The automobile, for example, is a prime source of energy waste in our society. People need more information on the advantages of smaller cars over the larger "gas guzzling" automobiles, and they also need more knowledge about the benefits of expanded mass transportation systems. Compared to the automobile, mass transit is quieter, less nerve-racking, safer, usually quicker, less expensive, less polluting, and more energy-saving.

In these and many other ways, environmental education could help people gain more knowledge and understanding of the issues. It is hoped that such education would also aid in the growth of values and attitudes favoring conservation of resources and greater respect for our environment.

Energy. As we have seen above, the problem of resource depletion is most apparent in the area of energy. Supplies of fossil fuels, especially oil and natural gas, are dwindling, yet the national and global demand for energy increases each year. Projections indicate, for example, that the U.S. demand

---

Marginal notes:

Some areas for additional research

The importance of environmental education

Learning about energy waste and ways to minimize it

Energy: Resources
decline and demands
grow

for electrical power alone will climb by over 4 percent per year during the period 1980 to 85, and that world demand for energy will double within two or three decades.[67] Faced with declining energy resources and rising energy costs, the United States has recently intensified its efforts to find new domestic fossil fuel sources in order to reduce our dependence upon foreign imports. Several major American oil companies, for example, have recently been given Supreme Court approval to commence large-scale drilling operations for oil and gas in the Atlantic Ocean off the coast of New Jersey.[68] Aside from the obvious environmental hazards accompanying such activities, many people feel that these and similar efforts represent a rather short-sighted response, since more emphasis is placed upon relieving the symptoms than on dealing with the causes or sources of our energy problems.

One major reason for our growing energy crisis is the simple matter of our energy extravagance and waste. As we mentioned earlier, Americans use approximately one-third of the world's energy, yet we waste as much as one-half of that amount. Vast amounts of energy are wasted in our transportation methods, our industrial manufacturing processes, and our personal and household uses. In fact, most of the fuel energy used to make electricity is wasted at the power plant.[69] What can be done to reduce energy waste? First of all, the technology for waste elimination could be developed rather easily—and in some cases already exists—if both industry and consumers are willing to pay for it. Second, and perhaps more im-

Steps to conserve
energy and eliminate
gross waste

portant, a serious commitment from the people to conserve energy in their day-to-day activities would have a significant impact. Driving slower, using mass transit, buying fewer "labor-saving" gadgets, insulating homes, lowering thermostats—all these and more would help alleviate the present crisis. Again, this calls for a willingness to make certain adjustments in our lifestyles and standards of living.

In the years to come, the long-term response on the part of government and industry will favor an increased reliance upon coal and nuclear power to meet our nation's energy needs. But as discussed above, the employment of these energy sources involves a number of present and future health and environmental hazards. In the coming years, technological innovations may be able to reduce some of these risks. For example, we may eventually be able to devise safer methods for the disposal of radioactive wastes. Nevertheless, risks will still be present.

Alternatives to the
coal-nuclear future

Are there any alternatives to a coal-nuclear future? Many argue that alternatives are needed and in fact exist. Along these lines, policies and programs aimed at conserving energy and reducing energy waste are of utmost importance. Energy conservation *now* would lessen our dependence on coal and avoid some of the environmental hazards attendant to the increased future use of this energy source. In addition, energy conservation yields other important environmental benefits, such as reduced pollution and conservation of other natural resources. Moreover, by slowing our rate of energy depletion, conservation will also give us more time for, and flexibility in, the development of environmentally clean, safe, and renewable (or virtually inexhaustible) energy sources, particularly solar and geothermal energy.

It is unfortunate that over the last two or three decades very little federal funding has been allocated for research into solar and geothermal technology. However, there have recently been some significant increases in the federal solar research and development budget.[70] Solar energy is an unlimited and virtually pollution-free source that is best suited to dry, sunny climates. However, many problems related to construction of solar energy operating and storage systems must be dealt with before solar energy can be put to large-scale use. In the future, it is clear that renewable rather than nonrenewable (fossil fuel) sources will, by necessity, play a major role in meeting U.S. and world energy needs. It is also vital that

Peter Menzel, Stock, Boston

A commitment to environmental quality is essential to the continuation of natural food chains.

strategies for dealing with current as well as future energy needs and problems be proposed and selected primarily upon the basis of environmental merits and concerns.

A serious commitment to environmental quality is essential now and in the future

Solutions to environmental problems require not only an awareness of what the problems are and the reasons for their existence but also a commitment on the part of our society's institutions and people to do something about them. Such a commitment will necessarily require a willingness on our part to reevaluate our relationship to the environment and make certain changes in values, attitudes, and ways of living, which have ultimately caused most of our problems. Some people, especially those in our corporate structure, will have objections to almost any type of remedial change that entails sacrifice on their part. But, as we have seen, we are already paying, and paying heavily, for our attitudes and behaviors that favor exploitation and neglect of our habitat. Fortunately, more and more people are becoming aware of the seriousness of our environmental problems. They are also coming to realize that human life and well-being depend in large measure upon a strong and continuing commitment to environmental quality. Are we willing to pay the price for a sound and healthy environment? Can we afford not to?

SUMMARY

There are signs all around us indicating that our environment is undergoing large-scale change and deterioration. Much of this deterioration is a direct consequence of human actions. Increasingly, we have abused and exploited our environment, to the point where we have destroyed or harmed many of its ecosystems, which are necessary for our well-being and survival.

Many of our environmental problems are essentially pollution problems. We have released into our atmosphere millions of tons of pollutants, especially carbon monoxide, sulfur and nitrogen oxides, hydrocarbons, and just plain dust and dirt. Our rivers, lakes, and oceans have become disposal sites for wide varieties of agricultural, industrial, and municipal pollutants, such as inadequately treated sewage, solid and radioactive wastes, oil, metals, and thousands of chemical compounds. Finally, our land has been degraded and exploited by our actions. We have reduced soil quality through the massive use of artificial fertilizers. Large-scale strip-mining and logging have eliminated vast amounts of cultivable and forested lands, respectively. We litter the land by dumping billions of tons of solid wastes on it each year.

Declining natural resources (minerals, metals, and fossil fuels) also constitute a major and growing environmental problem. The problem of resource depletion is particularly apparent in the area of energy. In recent decades, many nations (particularly industrialized nations) have placed such heavy demands upon finite fossil fuel resources, such as oil and natural gas, that these fuels are rapidly approaching the point of exhaustion. Coal and nuclear power will likely serve as alternative energy sources in the future; however, increased reliance upon these energy sources poses a number of potential hazards to both health and the environment.

Environmental problems have resulted from a number of factors, including technology, the growth of population, and industrialization as well as our own values and attitudes favoring neglect of and disregard for the environment around us. In assessing the role of technology, many environmentalists point out that the application of technologies often involves a series of environmental "trade-offs"—i.e., their application often benefits our standard of living, yet it also results in much environmental harm. Other environmentalists and scientific scholars link many of our problems of pollution and resource depletion to the growth of industrialization and population. The *Limits To Growth* report concluded, for example, that unless population and industrial growth are curtailed and stabilized, we will experience global ecological catastrophies. Finally, though by no means least important, our attitudes and values favoring an exploitive view of nature, economic growth, and material consumption are also at the root of many of our environmental problems. Attitudes and values such as these have helped lay the foundation for a massive "consumption-production" cycle, which in turn generates environmental pollution, resource depletion, and waste disposal problems.

The environmental movement in the 1960s and early 1970s was responsible for government legislation aimed at alleviating environmental problems. As a result of this legislation some limited progress has been made in surmounting many of our environmental ills. In order to effectively deal with our problems, other approaches and alternatives need to be explored. In terms of governmental action, more legislation and stricter enforcement of existing legislation is needed. There is also a need for more governmental support for the development of mass transit systems and the establishment of nationwide recycling programs. Increased governmental funding for basic environmental research is also necessary. There is a desperate need for large-scale environmentally oriented educational programs in our schools and through the mass media. Finally, much more emphasis needs to be placed upon the reduction of energy waste in our society. Technology may be of some assistance here, but a serious public commitment to energy conservation is equally, if not more, important. In the years to come, coal and nuclear power will likely play an expanded role in meeting our nation's energy needs. As we have seen, there are environmental risks as well as benefits associated with these energy sources. But there are also other alternatives, such as programs aimed at energy conservation and the development of renewable energy sources, such as solar and geothermal power.

KEY TERMS

Biosphere

Deforestation

Ecology

Ecosystem

Food chain

Fossil fuels

Nondegradable wastes

Nonrenewable resources

Renewable resources

Thermal inversion

Notes

CHAPTER 1

1. H.J. Gans, "The Poor Pay All," *Social Policy*. New York: Social Policy Corporation, 1971, Jul.–Aug.; see also H.S. Becker, "Whose Side Are We On?" *Social Problems*, 14,3(Winter 1967).

2. R.K. Merton and R. Nisbet, *Contemporary Social Problems*, Fourth edition 1976. New York: Harcourt Brace Jovanovich, pp. 9–11, 24–27.

3. D. Hebding and L. Glick, *Introduction to Sociology*. Reading, Mass.: Addison-Wesley, 1976, pp. 5, 22–23, 26, 229–31, 304–07, 325–29, 397.

4. R.K. Merton, *Social Theory and Social Structure*. New York: The Free Press, 1965, pp. 132, 139–57.

5. W.F. Ogburn, *Social Change with Respect to Culture and Original Nature*, Revised edition, New York: Viking Press, 1950.

6. R. Bierstedt, *The Social Order*. New York: McGraw-Hill, 1963, p. 12.

7. A.W. Gouldner, "Anti-Minotaur: The Myth of a Value-Free Sociology," *Social Problems*, 9(1962).

8. G.P. Berreman, "Speech to Council," *Newsletter of the American Anthropological Association*, 12(Jan. 1971), p. 19.

9. R.A. Dentler, *Major Social Problems*. Chicago: Rand-McNally, 1972, pp. 9–10.

10. W.I. Thomas and F. Znaniecki, *The Polish Peasant in Europe and America*. New York: Alfred A. Knopf, 1927.

11. R.J. Antonio and G. Ritzer, *Social Problems, Values and Interests in Conflict*. Boston: Allyn & Bacon, 1975, pp. 4–5.

12. P.B. Horton and G.R. Leslie, *The Sociology of Social Problems*. New York: Appleton-Century-Crofts, 1965, pp. 32, 34.

13. E.H. Johnson, *Social Problems of Urban Man*. Homewood, Ill.: Dorsey Press, 1973, pp. 38, 48.

14. E.W. Burgess, "Social Problems and Social Processes," in *Human Behavior and Social Processes*, ed. A.M. Rose. Boston: Houghton Mifflin, 1962, pp. 385–86.

15. R.L. Akers, *Deviant Behavior, A Social Learning Approach.* Belmont, Cal.: Wadsworth, 1973, pp. 7, 17.
16. E.H. Sutherland and D.R. Cressey, *Criminology.* Philadelphia: J.B. Lippincott, 1970, p. 75.
17. H.S. Becker, *Outsiders: Studies in the Sociology of Deviance.* New York: The Free Press, 1973.
18. D.S. Eitzen, *Social Structures and Social Problems in America.* Boston: Allyn & Bacon, 1974, p. 11.
19. R. Quinney, *The Social Reality of Crime.* Boston: Little, Brown, 1970, pp. 9–10.
20. L.A. Coser, ed., *Georg Simmel.* Englewood Cliffs, N.J.: Prentice-Hall, 1965, p. 19.
21. L.A. Coser and B. Rosenberg, *Sociological Theory: A Book of Readings.* New York: Macmillan, 1957, p. 171.
22. G.V. Vold, *Theoretical Criminology.* New York: Oxford University Press, 1958, p. 204.
23. H.M. Hodges, Jr., *Conflict and Consensus, An Introduction To Sociology.* New York: Harper & Row, 1971, p. 220.
24. R.K. Merton and R. Nisbet, *Contemporary Social Problems*, Third edition. New York: Harcourt Brace Jovanovich, 1971, pp. 9–14.
25. R.M. Williams, Jr., *American Society*, Third edition. New York: Alfred A. Knopf, 1970, pp. 454–58, 462–64.

CHAPTER 2

1. S. Lens, *Poverty: Yesterday and Today.* New York: Crowell, 1973, pp. 8–9, 13, 126, 141, 176. This provides a good history of poverty in America, on which some of this historical section was based.
2. R. Hunter, *Poverty.* New York: Macmillan, 1907.
3. J.K. Galbraith, *The Affluent Society.* London: Penguin Books, 1962.
4. M. Harrington, *The Other America.* New York: Penguin Books, 1976.
5. E. May, *The Wasted Americans.* New York: Signet, 1965.
6. U.S. Bureau of the Census, "Money, Income and Poverty Status of Families and Persons in the United States: 1975 and 1974 Revisions," (Advance Report) *Current Population Reports*, Series P-60, No. 103, Washington, D.C., 1976, pp. 1, 3, 45.
7. J.B. Williamson and K.M. Hyer, "The Measurement and Meaning of Poverty," *Social Problems*, 22,5(Jun. 1975):652–63.
8. R.D. Friedman, *Poverty: Definition and Perspective.* Washington, D.C.: American Enterprise Institute, 1965.
9. D. Matza and H. Miller, "Poverty and Proletariat," in R.K. Merton and R. Nisbet, *Contemporary Social Problems*, New York: Harcourt Brace Jovanovich, 1976, pp. 644, 646.
10. J. Huber, "Political Implications of Poverty Definitions," in *The Sociology of American Poverty*, eds., J. Huber and P. Chalfant. Cambridge, Mass.: Schenkman, 1974.
11. P. Townsend, "Poverty as Relative Deprivation: Resources and Style of Living," in *Poverty, Inequality and Class Structure*, ed. D. Wedderburn. London: Cambridge University Press, 1974.
12. V.R. Fuchs, "Redefining Poverty and Redistributing Income," *The Public Interest*, 8(Summer 1967): 88–95.
13. N.Y. Glazer and C.F. Creedon, *Children and Poverty: Some Sociological and Psychological Perspectives.* Chicago: Rand-McNally, 1970.
14. S.F. Stouffer *et al.*, *The American Soldier.* Princeton: Princeton University Press, 1949, p. 250.

15. U.S. Bureau of the Census, *Statistical Abstract of the United States: 1976, 1977,* 97th and 98th editions. Washington, D.C., 1976, 1977, Table 496, pp. 289, 291, 316. See also Budget of the U.S. Government, 1977.

16. S.M. Miller and F. Riesmann, *Social Class and Social Policy.* New York: Basic Books, 1968, pp. 3–4.

17. H.P. Miller, "The Dimensions of Poverty," in *Poverty as a Public Issue,* ed. B.B. Seligman. New York: The Free Press, 1965.

18. A.B. Hollingshead and F.C. Redlich, *Social Class and Mental Illness: A Community Study.* New York: John Wiley, 1958.

19. L.W. Warner, M. Meaker, and K. Eells, *Social Class in America: A Manual of Procedure for the Measurement of Social Status.* Chicago: Science Research Associates, 1949.

20. S.M. Miller and P. Roby, *The Future of Inequality.* New York: Basic Books, 1970.

21. W. Sage, "Violence in the Children's Room," *Human Behavior,* Jul. 1975.

22. U.S. Department of Health, Education and Welfare, "The Condition of Education: A Statistical Report on the Condition of Education in the United States: 1976," Washington, D.C., p. 59.

23. U.S. Senate Subcommittee Report on Labor and Public Welfare, "Migrant and Seasonal Farmworker Powerlessness, Part Two," Washington, D.C., 1970.

24. Senate Select Committee Report on Nutrition and Human Needs, E.A. Schaefer, M.D., Washington, D.C., 1970.

25. The National Advisory Council on Economic Opportunity, Second Annual Report, "Continuity and Change in Antipoverty Programs," Washington, D.C., Mar. 1969.

26. Senate Select Committee Report on Nutrition, H.P. Chase, Washington, D.C., 1971.

27. P.W. Perry, "The Night of Ageism," *Mental Hygiene,* Summer 1974. See also *The Washington Post,* Apr. 27, 1974.

28. D. Hebding and L. Glick, *Introduction to Sociology.* Reading, Mass.: Addison-Wesley, 1976, pp. 226–27.

29. R.D. Fave, "The Culture of Poverty Revisited: A Strategy for Research," *Social Problems,* 21,5(Jun. 1974).

30. O. Lewis, "The Culture of Poverty," in *Explosive Forces in Latin America,* ed. J.J. Tepaske and S.N. Fisher. Columbus, Oh.: Ohio State University Press, 1964.

31. D.P. Moynihan, ed., *On Understanding Poverty.* New York: Basic Books, 1969.

32. F.L. Fernbach, "Policies Affecting Income Distribution," in *Poverty in America,* ed. M.S. Gordon. San Francisco: Chandler, 1965.

33. J.H. Turner, *American Society: Problems of Structure.* New York: Harper & Row, 1976.

34. A. Etzioni, *Social Problems.* Englewood Cliffs, N.J.: Prentice-Hall, 1976, pp. 9, 14–15, 28–29, 31–32.

35. B. Coward, J. Feagin, and J.A. Williams, Jr., "The Culture of Poverty Debate: Some Additional Data," *Social Problems,* 21,5(Jun. 1974):621–34.

36. E. Liebow, *Tally's Corner.* Boston: Little, Brown, 1967.

37. C. Valentine, *Culture and Poverty.* Chicago: University of Chicago Press, 1968, pp. 114–20.

38. H. Rodman, "The Lower-class Value Stretch," *Social Forces,* 42(Dec. 1963):205–15.

39. H.J. Gans, *People and Plans: Essays on Urban Problems and Solutions.* New York: Basic Books, 1968, pp. 321–46.

40. *Op. cit.,* Moynihan: "Culture and Class in the Study of Poverty: An Approach to Anti-poverty Research," by H.J. Gans.

41. K. Marx, "Relative Surplus Population and Capital Accumulation," in *Poverty, Economics and Society,* ed. H. Ginsburg. Boston: Little, Brown, 1972.

42. D. Caplovitz, *The Poor Pay More: Consumer Practices of Low Income Families*. New York: The Free Press, 1963.

43. J.H. Skolnick and E. Currie, *Crisis in American Institutions*. Boston: Little, Brown, 1973, views of W. Waller, p. 3.

44. H.J. Gans, "The Poor Pay All," *Social Policy*. New York: Social Policy Corporation, Jul.–Aug., 1971.

45. *Op. cit.*, Miller and Roby.

46. L. Rainwater, *What Money Buys*. New York: Basic Books, 1974.

47. *Op. cit.*, Etzioni, pp. 15–20. This gives a more complete analysis of these approaches.

48. J. Turner and C. Starnes, *Inequality: Privilege and Poverty in America*. Pacific Palisades, Cal.: Goodyear, 1976, pp. 121–22, 125–27, 129–30, 138–39.

49. J.R. Feagin, *Subordinating the Poor: Welfare and American Beliefs*, Englewood Cliffs, N.J.: Prentice-Hall, 1975, pp. 2, 22, 34–35, 37, 95, 98, 101, 104, 106–07, 109.

50. R. Hofstadter *Social Darwinism in American Thought*. Boston: Beacon Press, 1962.

51. R.H. Bremner, *From the Depths*. New York: New York University Press, 1956.

52. C.W. Weinberger, "The Reform of Welfare: A National Necessity," *The Journal of The Institute for Socioeconomic Studies*, 1,1(Summer 1976):9–12, 14–15.

53. *Op. cit., Statistical Abstract: 1976.*

54. U.S. Bureau of the Census, "Characteristics of Households Purchasing Food Stamps," *Current Population Reports*, Series P-23, No. 61, Washington, D.C., Jul. 1976, p. 5. See also, *National Journal*, 8,8(Feb. 1976).

55. U.S. Social Security Bulletin, Jan. and Sep. 1976.

56. W. Chapman, Washington Post Service, *The Philadelphia Enquirer*, May 3, 1977.

CHAPTER 3

1. L. Wirth, "The Problem of Minority Groups," in *The Science of Man in the World Crisis*, ed. R. Linton. New York: Columbia University Press, 1945, pp. 347–72.

2. U.S. Bureau of the Census, *Statistical Abstract of the United States: 1976*, Ninety-seventh edition, Washington, D.C., 1976.

3. H.M. Golden, "Black Ageism," *Social Policy*, 7,3(Nov.-Dec. 1976):41.

4. K. Amundsen, *The Silenced Majoriy: Women and American Democracy*. Englewood Cliffs, N.J.: Prentice-Hall, 1971, p. 45.

5. B.B. Solomon, "Is It Sex, Race, or Class?" *Social Work*, 21,6(Nov. 1976); *op. cit.*, Amundsen.

6. G.E. Simpson and J.M. Yinger, *Racial and Cultural Minorities*. New York: Harper & Row, 1958.

7. G.W. Allport, *The Nature of Prejudice*. Reading, Mass.: Addison-Wesley, 1954.

8. *Op. cit.*, Simpson and Yinger, and Allport. See also D. Hebding and L. Glick, *Introduction to Sociology*. Reading, Mass.: Addison-Wesley, 1976, pp. 268–300.

9. P.L. Kasschau, "Age and Race Discrimination Reported by Middle-Aged and Older Persons," *Social Forces*, 55,3(Mar. 1977):728–42.

10. U.S. Bureau of the Census, "A Statistical Portrait of Women in the United States," *Current Population Reports*, Special Studies, Series P-23, No. 58, Apr. 1976, p. 1.

11. S. Feldman, *The Rights of Women*. Rochelle Park, N.J.: Hayden, 1974, pp. 53–54.

12. *Ibid.*, pp. 73–75.

13. B. Payne and F. Whittington, "Older Women: An Examination of Popular Stereotypes and Research Evidence," *Social Problems*, 23,4(Apr. 1976):488–504.

14. *Op. cit.*, Hebding and Glick, p. 94.

15. M. Mead, *Sex and Temperament in Three Primitive Societies*. New York: William Morrow, 1935; *op. cit.*, Hebding and Glick, p. 94.
16. *Op. cit.*, Mead.
17. *Op. cit.*, Feldman, p. 78.
18. K. Lamott, "Why Men and Women Think Differently," *Horizon*, 19,3(May 1977):44.
19. A. Montague, *The Natural Superiority of Women*, Revised edition. New York: Macmillan, 1968.
20. *Op. cit.*, Feldman, pp. 78–79.
21. *Ibid.*, p. 89.
22. *Ibid.*, pp. 41–44. The figures from the Chase Manhattan Bank were $257.53 for 1972; figures were adjusted for 1978.
23. Department of Labor Statistics, Washington, D.C., Dec., 1976. Also *Newsweek*, Dec. 6, 1976, p. 68.
24. *Op. cit.*, *Statistical Abstract: 1976*, p. 355 and "Statistical Portrait of Women." See also U.S. Department of Labor, Manpower Report to the President, Washington, D.C., Mar. 1973, p. 128ff.
25. *Op. cit.*, *Statistical Abstract: 1976*, and *Newsweek*, Dec. 6, 1976.
26. B. Deckard, *The Women's Movement: Political, Socioeconomic, and Psychological Issues*. New York: Harper & Row, 1975, p. 81.
27. *Op. cit.*, *Statistical Abstract: 1976*, p. 124, and *1977*, p. 452. The actual years of schooling are 12.4 years for men and 12.3 years for women.
28. *Ibid.*, 1976.
29. *Op. cit.*, Amundsen, pp. 33–34.
30. *Op. cit.*, *Newsweek*, p. 68.
31. *Op. cit.*, Deckard, pp. 88–89.
32. *Ibid.*, p. 86.
33. *Op. cit.*, *Newsweek*, pp. 68–70.
34. *Op. cit.*, "Statistical Portrait of Women," pp. 1, 21.
35. M.N. Ozawa, "Women and Work," *Social Work*, 21,6(Nov. 1976).
36. J.W. Vander Zanden, *American Minority Relations*, Second edition. New York: Ronald Press, 1966, pp. 48–49.
37. *Ibid.*
38. *Op. cit.*, *Statistical Abstract: 1976*, p. 405.
39. *Ibid.*, p. 373.
40. *Ibid.*
41. *Op. cit.*, Amundsen, p. 45.
42. *Op. cit.*, *Statistical Abstract: 1976*, p. 361. See also U.S. Bureau of the Census, "The Social and Economic Status of the Black Population in the United States," *Current Population Reports*, Special Studies, Series P-23, No. 54, 1974, p. 64.
43. W. Brink and L. Harris, *The Negro Revolution in America*. New York: Simon & Schuster, 1964, pp. 48–62.
44. *Ibid.*
45. *Op. cit.*, *Statistical Abstract: 1976*, p. 124.
46. *Op. cit.*, "The Social and Economic Status of the Black Population in the United States," p. 3.
47. *Op. cit.*, *Statistical Abstract: 1976*. See also "Birth Expectations and Fertility: June 1972," *Current Population Reports*, Series P-20, No. 248, Washington, D.C., 1973.
48. A. Pinckney, *Black Americans*, Second edition. Englewood Cliffs, N.J.: Prentice-Hall, 1975.
49. D.D. Enos *et al.*, "Blacks, Chicanos, and the Health Care System," in *Understanding Social Problems*. New York: Praeger Publishers, 1976, pp. 242–43.

50. *Ibid.*

51. L. Duberman, *Social Inequality: Class and Caste in America.* Philadelphia: J.B. Lippincott, 1976, p. 244.

52. *Op. cit.*, Pinckney, pp. 35–36.

53. *Op. cit.*, Duberman, p. 254.

54. *Op. cit.*, Hebding and Glick, p. 279.

55. *Op. cit.*, Vander Zanden, p. 70.

56. *Ibid.*

57. C. Joffe, "Sex Role Socialization and the Nursery School: As the Twig is Bent," *The Journal of Marriage and the Family*, National Council on Family Relations, Aug. 1971.

58. R. Linton, *The Study of Man.* New York: Appleton-Century-Crofts, 1936, renewed copyright 1964, pp. 113–19.

59. *Op. cit.*, Deckard, pp. 27–28.

60. A.S. Rossi, "Sex Equality: The Beginnings of Ideology," in *Confronting the Issues: Sex Roles, Marriage, and the Family*, ed. K.C.W. Kammeyer. Boston: Allyn & Bacon, 1975, pp. 364–76.

61. L.A. Serbin and K.D. O'Leary, "How Nursery Schools Teach Girls to Shut Up," *Psychology Today*, 1975.

62. C. Anderson, *Sex and Caste in America.* Englewood Cliffs, N.J.: Prentice-Hall, 1971.

63. *Op. cit.*, Deckard, p. 38.

64. M. Komarovsky, "Functional Analysis of Sex Roles," in *Sourcebook in Marriage and the Family*, ed. M.B. Sussman. Boston: Houghton Mifflin, 1968, p. 261.

65. *Op. cit.*, Deckard, pp. 33–34.

66. *Op. cit.*, Feldman, p. 36.

67. *Op. cit.*, Vander Zanden.

68. R. Wright, *Black Boy.* New York: Signet, 1945, pp. 161–62.

69. *Op. cit.*, Hebding and Glick, p. 279.

70. P. Van den Berghe, *Race and Racism.* New York: John Wiley, 1967.

71. O.C. Cox, *Caste, Class, and Race.* New York: Doubleday, 1948, pp. 322, 475.

72. E. Reed, *Problems of Women's Liberation.* New York: Pathfinder Press, 1969.

73. *Op. cit.*, Deckard, pp. 417–18.

74. *Ibid.*

75. *Ibid.* See also H. Blumer, "Race Prejudice as a Sense of Group Position," in *Race Relations*, eds. J. Masuka and P. Valien. Chapel Hill, N.C.: University of North Carolina Press, 1961, pp. 215–27.

76. *Ibid.*

77. *Op. cit.*, Vander Zanden, p. 104.

78. *Ibid.*, pp. 108–09.

79. *Ibid.*, pp. 80–81.

80. A.D. Grimshaw, "Urban Racial Violence in the United States," *American Journal of Sociology*, 64(1960):114–15.

81. *Op. cit.*, Vander Zanden.

82. *Op. cit.*, Hebding and Glick, p. 282.

83. *Ibid.* p. 280.

84. *Op. cit.*, Deckard, pp. 419–20.

85. A. Koedt, E. Levine, and A. Rapone, eds., "Politics of the Ego: A Manifesto for New York Radical Feminists," in *Radical Feminism.* New York: Quadrangle, 1973, pp. 379–80.

86. S. Firestone, *The Dialectic of Sex.* New York: Bantam Books, 1970.

87. *Op. cit.*, Koedt *et al.*

88. *Op. cit.*, Deckard, pp. 426–28.

89. R. Daniels and H.H.L. Kitano, *American Racism: Exploration of the Nature of Prejudice.* Englewood Cliffs, N.J.: Prentice-Hall, 1970, pp. 16–17.

90. *Op. cit.*, Vander Zanden, p. 381. See also 1972 edition, pp. 377–408.

91. *Op. cit.*, Vander Zanden, 1972 edition, p. 403.

92. P.I. Rose, *They and We.* New York: Random House, 1974.

93. *Op. cit.*, Vander Zanden, 1972 edition, pp. 422–45.

94. *Ibid.*

95. *Ibid.*

96. K. Lewin, *Resolving Social Conflicts.* New York: Harper & Row, 1949, pp. 186–200.

97. *Op. cit.*, Vander Zanden, pp. 422–45.

98. *Op. cit.*, Vander Zanden, Third edition, p. 307.

99. *Op. cit.*, Deckard, pp. 243–44.

100. J.R. Howard, *The Cutting Edge: Social Movements and Change In America*, Philadelphia: J.B. Lippincott, 1974, p. 140; *op. cit.*, Deckard, pp. 234, 252.

101. *Op. cit.*, Howard, p. 140

102 E. Flexner, *Century of Struggle.* New York: Atheneum, 1971, p. 75.

103. *Op. cit.*, Deckard, pp. 269, 276, 284.

104. *Ibid.*, pp. 301–03, 320–21.

105. B. Friedan, *The Feminine Mystique.* New York: Dell, 1963.

106. U.S. Department of Labor, Employment Standards Administration, Women's Bureau, *A Working Woman's Guide To Her Job Rights*, Leaflet No. 55, Revised 1975, p. 4.

107. *Ibid.*

108. W.H. Chafe, "Feminism in the 1970's," *Dissent*, Fall 1974.

109. *Ibid.*

110. *Ibid.*

111. *Ibid.*

112. *Ibid.*

113. J. Hole and E. Levine, *Rebirth of Feminism.* New York: Quadrangle, 1971, p. 440.

114. *Op. cit..* Deckard, p. 344.

115. *Ibid.*

116. *Op. cit.*, Howard.

117. *Op. cit.*, Chafe.

118. *Ibid.*

119. The Equal Rights Amendment, 1977.

120. M.I. Miller and H. Linker, "Equal Rights Amendment Campaigns in California and Utah," *Society*, 11(May-Jun. 1974):40–53.

121. *Op. cit.*, Deckard, p. 392.

122. L.C. Wohl, "The Sweetheart of the Silent Majority," *Ms*, 2,9(Mar. 1974).

123. *Op. cit.*, Chafe.

124. W.F. Cheek, *Black Resistance Before the Civil War.* Beverly Hills, Cal.: Glencoe Press, 1970; *op. cit.*, Van den Berghe.

125. *Op. cit.*, Van den Berghe, p. 81.

126. *Op. cit.*, Cheek, pp. 1, 19.

127. *Op. cit.*, Van den Berghe, pp. 82–83.

128. *Ibid.*; *op. cit.*, Cheek, p. 10.

129. *Op. cit.*, Vander Zanden, pp. 340–41.

130. *Op. cit.*, Van den Berghe, p. 84.

131. *Ibid.*

132. *Op. cit.*, Vander Zanden, p. 348.

133. *Op. cit.*, Van den Berghe, pp. 91–92.

134. *Op. cit.*, Howard, pp. 23, 25.

135. *Ibid.*
136. *Op. cit.*, Vander Zanden, pp. 262–63. See also J.H. Lave, "The Changing Character of the Negro Protest," *The Annals of the American Academy of Political and Social Science*, 357(1965):119–26.
137. M.L. King, Jr., "Behind the Selma March," *Saturday Review of Literature*, Apr. 3, 1965, p. 16.
138. *Op. cit.*, Van den Berghe, p. 93.
139. *Op. cit.*, Vander Zanden, pp. 171–76.
140. R. Dynes and E.L. Quantelli, "Looting in American Cities: A New Explanation," *Transaction*, May 1968, p. 14; *op. cit.*, Vander Zanden.
141. T.M. Tomlinson, "The Redevelopment of a Riot Ideology Among Urban Negroes," *American Behavioral Scientist*, 2(1968):27–31; *op. cit.*, Vander Zanden.
142. F. Fanon, *The Wretched of the Earth*. New York: Grove Press, 1966, p. 73; *op. cit.*, Vander Zanden.
142. W.J. Wilson, *Power, Racism, and Privilege*. New York: Macmillan, 1973.

CHAPTER 4

1. "The Graying of America," *Newsweek*, Feb. 28, 1977, pp. 56–57.
2. P.L. Kasschau, "Age and Race Discrimination Reported by Middle-Aged and Older Persons," *Social Forces*, 3(Mar. 1977):728–42.
3. R.C. Atchley, *The Social Forces in Later Life: An Introduction To Social Gerontology*. Belmont, Cal.: Wadsworth, 1972, pp. 7–8.
4. *Ibid.*
5. *Ibid.*, p. 9.
6. U.S. Bureau of the Census, *Statistical Abstract of the United States: 1977*, Washington, D.C., 1977.
7. U.S. Bureau of the Census, "Social and Economic Characteristics of the Older Population: 1974," *Current Population Reports*, Special Studies, Series P-23, No. 57, Nov. 1975, p. 3.
8. *Op. cit.*, Atchley, pp. 12–13.
9. B. Payne and F. Whittington, "Older Women: An Examination of Popular Stereotypes and Research Evidence," *Social Problems*, 23,4(Apr. 1976):488–504.
10. *Ibid.*
11. *Ibid.*
12. *Op. cit.*, Kasschau. See also P.L. Kasschau, "Perceived Discrimination in a Sample of Aerospace Employees," *The Gerontologist*, 16(Apr. 1976):166–73.
13. *Op. cit.*, Atchley, p. 37.
14. *Ibid.*, pp. 100, 107–08.
15. *Ibid.*
16. *Ibid.*
17. *Op. cit.*, *Statistical Abstract: 1977*, Tables 665 and 745, pp. 451, 460.
18. *Op. cit.*, "Social and Economic Characteristics of the Older Population: 1974," p. 26.
19. *Op. cit.*, *Statistical Abstract: 1977*, p. 303.
20. *Op. cit.*, Atchley, p. 193.
21. *Op. cit.*, "The Graying of America," pp. 56–57.
22. *Ibid.*
23. *Op. cit.*, Atchley, p. 143.
24. U.S. Senate, Special Report to the Special Committee on Aging, J.H. Schultz, "Pension Aspects of the Economics of Aging: Present and Future Roles of Private Pensions," Jan. 1970.
25. *Op. cit.*, Atchley, pp. 113–14.

26. *Ibid.*
27. National Center for Health Statistics, Vital and Health Statistics, Series 10, No. 32, p. 46.
28. *Op. cit.,* "Social and Economic Characteristics of the Older Population: 1974," p. 45.
29. *Op. cit.,* Vital and Health Statistics.
30. *Op. cit.,* Atchley, pp. 100, 107–08.
31. *Op. cit.,* "Social and Economic Characteristics of the Older Population: 1974."
32. *Op. cit.,* Atchley, pp. 123–27.
33. *Ibid.*
34. *Ibid.*
35. *Ibid.*
36. G.F. Streib, "Are the Aged a Minority Group?" in *Applied Sociology,* eds. A.W. Gouldner and S.M. Miller. New York: The Free Press of Glencoe, 1965.
37. *Op. cit.,* Atchley, p. 37.
38. A. Rose, "The Subculture of the Aging: A Framework for Research in Social Gerontology," in *Older People and Their Social World,* eds. A. Rose and W. Peterson. Philadelphia: F.A. Davis, 1965, pp. 3–16.
39. *Op. cit.,* Atchley, pp. 31–32, 34–36, 38.
40. *Ibid.*
41. *Ibid.*
42. R.J. Havighurst, "Successful Aging," in *Process of Aging,* Volume 1, eds. R. Williams *et al.* New York: Atherton Press, 1963, pp. 299–320.
43. B. Neugarten, *Personality in Middle and Late Life.* New York: Atherton Press, 1964; R.C. Atchley, "Retirement and Leisure Participation: Continuity or Crisis," *The Gerontologist,* II, Part 1 (1971):29–32; *Op. cit.,* Atchley, pp. 35–36.
44. *Op. cit.,* Atchley, *The Social Forces in Later Life,* p. 39.
45. F. Cottrell, *Aging and The Aged.* Dubuque, Iowa: Wm. C. Brown, 1974, p. 63.
46. E. Bowles, "Older Persons as Providers of Services: Three Federal Programs," *Social Policy,* Nov.-Dec. 1976, p. 81.
47. *Op. cit.,* Cottrell, pp. 63–64.
48. *Ibid.*
49. *Ibid.,* p. 65; *op. cit.,* Atchley, *Social Forces in Later Life,* p. 329.
50. *Op. cit.,* Atchley, *The Social Forces in Later Life,* pp. 329–30.
51. 1971 White House Conference on Aging, Government and Non-Government Organization, Recommendations for Action, Washington, D.C., 1972.
52. 1971 White House Conference on Aging, Report to Delegates from the Conference Sections and Special Concerns Sessions, Nov. 1971.
53. *Op. cit.,* Cottrell, pp. 65–66.
54. A.M. Rose, "The Subculture of the Aging: A Framework for Research in Social Gerontology," in *Aging in America: Readings in Social Gerontology,* eds. C.S. Kart and B.B. Manard. New York: Alfred Publishing, 1976, pp. 42–60.
55. *Op. cit.,* Atchley, *The Social Forces in Later Life,* pp. 245, 254.
56. *Op. cit.,* Bowles, pp. 80–81.
57. *Ibid.*
58. "Foster Grandparents Get High Ratings in Five Studies," *Aging,* Dec. 1968, pp. 14–15.
59. F. Reissman, " 'The Helper' Therapy Principle," *Social Work,* 10,2(Apr. 1965); *op. cit.,* Bowles, p. 88.
60. "Growing Old Happy," *Newsweek,* Feb. 28, 1977, p. 57.
61. *Ibid.*
62. *Op. cit.,* Cottrell, p. 28.
63. *Senior Citizen News,* Oct. 1977, p. 4.

64. *Op. cit.*, Cottrell, p. 28.

65. *Op. cit.*, Atchley, *The Social Forces in Later Life*, p. 260.

66. *Ibid.*

67. E.F. and F.D. Shelley, "A Retirement Index," *Social Policy*, Nov.–Dec. 1976, pp. 52–54.

68. *Ibid.*

69. "What Congress is Hearing About Retirement," *U.S. News and World Report*, W.A. Harriman testimony, Oct. 3, 1977, p. 30.

70. *Ibid.*, M. Biaggi testimony, p. 30.

71. *Ibid.*, G.F. Jankowski testimony, p. 31.

72. *Ibid.*, G.A. Skoglund testimony, p. 31.

CHAPTER 5

1. D. Hebding and L. Glick, *Introduction to Sociology*. Reading, Mass.: Addison-Wesley, 1976, p. 304.

2. J.Q. Wilson, "Crime and Punishment: 1776–1976 (Bicentennial Essay)," *Time*, Apr. 26, 1976, pp. 82–84. See also "Too Much Law?" *Newsweek*, Jan. 10, 1977, pp. 42–47.

3. *Op. cit.*, Hebding and Glick, pp. 305–06.

4. *Ibid.*, pp. 310–11.

5. E.H. Sutherland and D.R. Cressey, *Criminology*, Ninth edition. Philadelphia: J.B. Lippincott, 1974, p. 8.

6. *Op. cit.*, Hebding and Glick, p. 314.

7. *Ibid.*

8. A.M. Platt, *The Child Savers*. Chicago: University of Chicago Press, 1969, pp. 73–80 and A.L. Mauss, *Social Problems as Social Movements*. Philadelphia: J.B. Lippincott, 1975, pp. 128–38.

9. *Op. cit.*, Hebding and Glick, pp. 314–15.

10. *Ibid.*, pp. 306–08. See also H.A. Block and G. Geis, *Man, Crime, and Society*, Second edition. New York: Random House, 1970, pp. 73–74.

11. *Op. cit.*, Hebding and Glick, pp. 306–09; Block and Geis, pp. 74–75; Sutherland and Cressey, pp. 15–16.

12. A. Hopkins, "On the Sociology of Criminal Law," *Social Problems*, 22,5(Jun. 1975):609–19.

13. A.B. Smith and H. Pollack, "Crimes Without Victims," *Saturday Review*, Dec. 4, 1971.

14. J.K. Moreland *et al.*, *Social Problems in the United States*, New York: Ronald Press, 1975, pp. 63–64.

15. L. Olson, "LEAA and Crime: 1968–75," *Nation's Cities*, 13,12(Dec. 1975):20–26.

16. *Op. cit.*, Moreland *et al.*, pp. 63–64.

17. The President's Commission on Law Enforcement and Administration of Justice Report, "The Challenge of Crime in a Free Society," Washington, D.C., 1967. Further references to this Commission are based on the 1968 edition of *The Challenge of Crime in a Free Society*. New York: E.P. Dutton, 1968.

18. *Ibid.*, pp. 38, 55.

19. *Ibid.*, pp. 160–61.

20. G. Gallup, "The Dimensions of Crime in the United States," *The Gallup Opinion Index*, Report #124, Oct. 1975, pp. 6–17. See also G. Gallop, "Most Important National Problem," *The Gallup Opinion Index*, Report #148, Nov. 1977, p. 4 and G. Gallup, "Public Becoming Less Concerned Over Crime," *Gallup Poll Release*, Dec. 18, 1977.

21. *Op. cit.*, *Gallup Poll Release*.

22. "The Elderly: Prisoners of Fear," *Time*, Nov. 29, 1976, pp. 21–22.

23. "Way of Life of Old People Curbed by Fear and Crime," *The New York Times*, Apr. 12, 1976, pp. 1, 22.

24. FBI: *Uniform Crime Reports 1977*, Oct. 1978.

25. *Ibid.*, p. 35.

26. *Ibid.*, pp. 35–36, 147–148.

27. *Op. cit.*, Sutherland and Cressey, pp. 27–30. See also E.H. Johnson, *Crime, Correction, and Society*. Third edition. Homewood, Ill.: Dorsey Press, 1974, pp. 60–62.

28. *Ibid.*, p. 4.

29. National Center for Juvenile Justice, (Preliminary Report), *Juvenile Court Statistics 1975*, pp. iv, v.

30. *Ibid.*, pp. 3–5, 10, 12. See also National Center for Juvenile Justice, (Preliminary Report), *Juvenile Court Statistics 1974*, pp. 3–5.

31. *U.S. News & World Report*, June 7, 1976.

32. M. Garrett and J.F. Short, Jr., "Social Class and Delinquency: Predictions and Outcomes of Police-Juvenile Encounters," *Social Problems*, 22,3(Feb. 1975):368–83; *op. cit.*, Sutherland and Cressey, p. 26.

33. *Uniform Crime Reports 1977*, p. 169.

34. *Ibid.*, p. 182.

35. J. Treaster, "Violence of Youth Gangs is Found at a New High," *The New York Times*, May 1, 1976, p. 21.

36. *Ibid.*, pp. 171, 175, 177, 183.

37. *Ibid.*, p. 184.

38. U.S. Bureau of the Census, *Statistical Abstract of the United States: 1977*, Washington, D.C., p. 25.

39. E.H. Sutherland, *White Collar Crime*. New York: Dryden Press, 1949.

40. W.C. Reckless, *The Crime Problem*, Third edition. New York: Appleton-Century-Crofts, 1961, pp. 31–32.

41. *Op. cit.*, "The Challenge of Crime in a Free Society," p. 97.

42. *Ibid.*, pp. 135–37.

43. *Ibid.*, pp. 98–99.

44. U.S. Department of Justice, National Criminal Justice Information and Statistics Service, Law Enforcement Assistance Administration (LEAA) Reports, "Crime in the Nation's Five Largest Cities," Washington, D.C., 1974, and "Victimization Surveys in Thirteen American Cities," Washington, D.C., 1975. See also J.B. Cordrey, "Crime Rates, Victims, Offenders: A Victimization Study," *Journal of Police Science and Administration*, 3,1(1975):100–10 and G. Gallup, "One Household in Five Hit by Crime in Last 12 Months," *Gallup Poll Release*, Dec. 22, 1977.

45. C. Beccaria, *An Essay on Crimes and Punishments*. London: Almon, 1767.

46. *Op. cit.*, Reckless, p. 233.

47. C. Lombroso, *Crime, Its Causes and Remedies*, trans. H.P. Horton. Boston: Little, Brown, 1912.

48. *Op. cit.*, Sutherland and Cressey, p. 53.

49. W.H. Sheldon, *Varieties of Delinquent Youth: An Introduction to Constitutional Psychiatry*. New York: Harper & Brothers, 1949. See also E. Kretschmer, *Physique and Character*, trans. W.J.H. Sprott. New York: Harcourt Brace, 1925; *op. cit.*, Reckless, pp. 277–83.

50. *Op. cit.*, Sutherland and Cressey, p. 117.

51. *Op. cit.*, Hebding and Glick, p. 323.

52. *Op. cit.*, Sutherland and Cressey, p. 155.

53. *Op. cit.*, Hebding and Glick, p. 309.

54. E. Durkheim, *The Rules of Sociological Method*, trans. S.A. Solovay and J.H. Mueller. New York: The Free Press, 1964, pp. 64–75.

55. *Op. cit.*, Sutherland and Cressey, p. 56.
56. H.S. Becker, *Outsiders: Studies in the Sociology of Deviance.* New York: The Free Press, 1963, pp. 9, 34, 37–39.
57. *Ibid.*
58. *Op. cit.*, Hebding and Glick, p. 324.
59. *Ibid.*, pp. 325–26.
60. *Op. cit.*, Sutherland and Cressey, pp. 75–77.
61. *Ibid.*, pp. 76–77.
62. *Ibid.*, pp. 40–47; *op. cit.*, Sutherland.
63. R. Akers, *Deviant Behavior: A Social Learning Approach.* Belmont, Cal.: Wadsworth, 1973, pp. 177–81.
64. *Op. cit.*, Johnson, p. 159.
65. *Op. cit.*, Akers, pp. 182–83.
66. M.L. DeFleur and R. Quinney, "A Reformulation of Sutherland's Association Theory and a Strategy for Empirical Verification," *Journal of Research in Crime and Delinquency*, 3(Jan. 1966):1–22.
67. *Op. cit.*, Akers, pp. 45–61.
68. D.R. Cressey, "Application and Verification of the Differential Association Theory," *Journal of Criminal Law, Criminology, and Police Science*, 43,1(1952):43–52; *op. cit.*, Reckless, p. 306.
69. T. Hirschi, *Causes of Delinquency.* Berkeley, Cal.: University of California Press, 1969.
70. E. Durkheim, *Suicide*, Book II, trans. J.A. Spaulding and G. Simpson. Glencoe, Ill.: Free Press, 1951.
71. R.K. Merton, *Social Theory and Social Structure.* New York: The Free Press, 1965, pp. 132, 139–57; *op. cit.*, Hebding and Glick, p. 326.
72. *Op. cit.*, Hebding and Glick, pp. 326–28.
73. *Ibid.*, pp. 327–28.
74. *Ibid.*, pp. 328–29.
75. A.K. Cohen, *Delinquent Boys.* New York: The Free Press, 1955.
76. *Op. cit.*, Hebding and Glick, pp. 329–31.
77. G. Sykes and D. Matza, "Techniques of Neutralization: A Theory of Delinquency," *American Sociological Review*, 22(Dec. 1957):664–70.
78. R.A. Cloward and L.E. Ohlin, *Delinquency and Opportunity.* New York: The Free Press, 1960.
79. *Op. cit.*, Akers, pp. 14–15; Sutherland and Cressey, p. 104; Hebding and Glick, p. 331.
80. R. Korn and L. McCorkle, *Criminology and Penology.* New York: Holt, Rinehart & Winston, 1966, pp. 374–98.
81. *Ibid.*, pp. 403–05; *op. cit.*, Beccaria.
82. *Op. cit.*, Korn and McCorkle, pp. 411–12.
83. *Ibid.*, pp. 410–14.
84. *Ibid.*, pp. 413–14.
85. U.S. Department of Justice, LEAA, National Advisory Commission on Criminal Justice Standards and Goals, *Corrections*, Washington, D.C., 1973, p. 43.
86. U.S. Department of Justice, LEAA, National Criminal Justice Information and Statistics Service Report, "Prisoners in State and Federal Institutions on December 31, 1976," No. SD-NPS-PSF-6A, Mar. 1977.
87. U.S. Department of Justice, LEAA, National Criminal Justice Information and Statistics Service, *Source Book of Criminal Justice Statistics: 1976*, Feb. 1977, pp. 244–45.
88. *Ibid.*, pp. 632–33.
89. T. Sellin, "Homicides in Retentionist and Abolitionist States," in *Capital Punishment*, ed. T. Sellin. New York: Harper & Row, 1967, pp. 135–38. See also T. Sellin, *The Death Penalty.* Philadelphia: American Law Institute, 1959, pp. 34–57.

90. *Op. cit., Source Book of Criminal Justice Statistics: 1976*, p. 689.
91. U.S. Department of Justice, LEAA, National Criminal Justice Information and Statistics Service Report, "Prisoners in State and Federal Institutions on December 31, 1975," No. SD-NPS-PSF-3, Feb. 1977, p. 1.
92. U.S. Department of Justice, LEAA, News Release, Apr. 4, 1977.
93. *Op. cit., Uniform Crime Reports: 1977*, p. 35.
94. Federal Bureau of Investigation, *Uniform Crime Reports: 1975*, Washington, D.C., Aug. 1976, p. 46.
95. *Op. cit., Source Book of Criminal Justice Statistics: 1976*, p. 249.
96. *Op. cit.*, Sutherland and Cressey, p. 575.
97. *Op. cit.*, Block and Geis, pp. 469–71.
98. *Op. cit., Corrections*, p. 312.
99. *Op. cit., Source Book of Criminal Justice Statistics: 1976*, p. 668.
100. *Op. cit.*, Sutherland and Cressey, pp. 461–71.
101. *Op. cit., Uniform Crime Reports: 1975*, p. 44.
102. *Op. cit.*, Sutherland and Cressey, p. 584.
103. *Op. cit., Corrections*, p. 391.
104. *Ibid.*, p. 394.
105. *Op. cit., Uniform Crime Reports: 1975*, p. 46.
106. *Op. cit., Source Book of Criminal Justice Statistics: 1976*, pp. 748–49.
107. *Op. cit., Corrections*, p. 597.
108. *Ibid.*, p. 600.
109. R. Martinson, "What Works?—Questions and Answers About Prison Reform," *The Public Interest*, Spring 1974.
110. "Coming: Tougher Approach to Juvenile Justice," *U.S. News & World Report*, Jun. 7, 1976, pp. 65–67; "Capital Punishment," *The Gallup Opinion Index*, Report #132, Jul. 1976.
111. "Reviving the Death Penalty," *Newsweek*, Jul. 12, 1976, pp. 14–15.

CHAPTER 6

1. J. Fort, *The Pleasure Seekers: The Drug Crisis, Youth, and Society*. Indianapolis: Bobbs-Merrill, 1969; J. Fort and C. Cory, *American Drugstore*. Boston: Educational Associates, 1975, pp. 4–6; "The Methadone Jones," *Newsweek*, Feb. 7, 1977, p. 29.
2. "RX for Drug Prices?" *Newsweek*, Jun. 7, 1976, pp. 75–76.
3. *Op. cit.*, Fort and Cory, p. 6. See also "A Revolution in Drinking Reshapes the Liquor Industry," *Newsweek*, Mar. 21, 1977, pp. 71–73.
4. *Op. cit.*, Fort and Cory, p. 4.
5. *Ibid.*
6. *Ibid.*, pp. 6–7, 17–21.
7. The National Commission on Marihuana and Drug Abuse, Second Report, "Drug Use in America: Problem in Perspective," Washington, D.C., 1973, pp. 12, 13, 42.
8. *Ibid.* See also J.A. Clausen, "Drug Use," in *Contemporary Social Problems*, Fourth edition, eds. R.K. Merton and R. Nisbet. New York: Harcourt Brace Jovanovich, 1976, p. 144.
9. *Op. cit.*, "Drug Use in America: Problem in Perspective," p. 42.
10. *Ibid.*, p. 9.
11. E. Goode, *Drugs in American Society*. New York: Alfred A. Knopf, 1972, p. 18.
12. *Op. cit.*, "Drug Use in America: Problem in Perspective," p. 10.
13. *Op. cit.*, Fort and Cory, p. 40, and Goode, Chapters 2, 4, 5.
14. *Op. cit.*, Fort and Cory, p. 4.
15. *Ibid.*
16. *Ibid.*

17. *Ibid.*, pp. 39, 41; M.B. Clinard, *Sociology of Deviant Behavior*, Fourth edition. New York: Holt, Rinehart & Winston, 1974, p. 390.
18. *Ibid.*, Fort and Cory, p. 18, and Clinard, p. 390.
19. *Op. cit.*, Goode, pp. 136–37.
20. *Ibid.*
21. *Op. cit.*, "Drug Use in America:" p. 79.
22. "Drug Abuse Update," *U.S. News & World Report*, Jan. 17, 1977, p. 69.
23. "Customsmen Increase Seizure of Narcotics and Drugs by 40%," *The New York Times*, Jan. 2, 1977, p. 10.
24. *Op. cit.*, Goode, p. 152.
25. *Op. cit.*, Fort and Cory, pp. 40–41.
26. *Ibid.*, p. 41.
27. A.L. Mauss, *Social Problems as Social Movements*. Philadelphia: J.B. Lippincott, 1975, p. 247; *op. cit.*, Goode, pp. 126, 153, 160, and "Drug Use in America:" p. 194.
28. *Op. cit.*, "Drug Abuse Update," p. 69.
29. *Op. cit.*, "Drug Use in America:" pp. 43, 145.
30. The Domestic Council Drug Abuse Task Force, *White Paper on Drug Abuse*, Washington, D.C., 1975, p. 23.
31. *Op. cit.*, Goode, pp. 188–89.
32. *Ibid.*, p. 190.
33. *Op. cit.*, Mauss, pp. 243–45.
34. *Op. cit.*, Goode, pp. 159–60, 196.
35. "Bagging Heroin/B," *Time*, Oct. 25, 1976, p. 75. See also "The Mexican Connection," *Newsweek*, Mar. 15, 1976, pp. 28–30.
36. *Op. cit.*, "The Methadone Jones," p. 29.
37. *Op. cit.*, "Drug Use in America:" pp. 69, 80, 144.
38. *Op. cit.*, Fort and Cory, p. 38.
39. *Ibid.*, p. 30.
40. U.S. Department of Health, Education and Welfare, National Institute on Alcohol Abuse and Alcoholism, *Alcohol and Alcoholism*, Washington, D.C., 1972, pp. 4–7. See also "Alcohol and Sex," *Newsweek*, Mar. 1, 1976, p. 59.
41. N. Kessel and H. Walton, *Alcoholism*. Baltimore: Penguin Books, 1976, p. 16.
42. *Op. cit.*, Merton and Nisbet: "Alcoholism and Problem Drinking," by R. Straus, p. 193.
43. *Op. cit.*, Kessel and Walton, pp. 92–106.
44. Estimates based upon "Drinkers at 38-Year Record Level Due to Changing Habits of Women," *Gallup Poll Release*, Feb. 13, 1977, which shows the percentage of persons 18 and older who use alcoholic beverages and the number of people 18 and older in the U.S. population. Data from U.S. Bureau of the Census, "Population Estimates and Projections," *Current Population Reports*, Series P-25, No. 721, Jul. 1, 1977. See also U.S. Department of Health, Education and Welfare, National Institute on Alcohol Abuse and Alcoholism, *Alcoholism and Its Treatment*, Washington, D.C., 1972, p. 2; *op. cit.*, *Alcohol and Alcoholism*, pp. 8–9.
45. U.S. Department of Health, Education and Welfare, National Institute on Alcohol Abuse and Alcoholism, Second Report to Congress, "Alcohol and Health," Washington, D.C., 1977, p. 37.
46. *Ibid.*, pp. 37–43. See also "What Industry is Doing About 10 Million Alcoholic Workers," *U.S. News & World Report*, Jan. 21, 1976, pp. 66–67.
47. *Op. cit.*, "Alcohol and Health," p. 7 and "Drinkers at 38-Year Record Level."
48. Information on the various sociocultural correlates of drinking and problem drinking presented in this section are drawn in part from *Alcohol and Alcoholism*, pp. 9–10, 15–16, and "Alcohol and Health," pp. 7–14.

49. G. Gallup, "Parental Alcohol Abuse Affects One Out of Five Teens," Mar. 15, 1978.

50. "Study Finds Drinking—Often to Excess—Now Starts At Earlier Age," *The New York Times*, Mar. 27, 1977, p. 38.

51. C. Becker and S. Kronus, "Sex and Drinking Patterns: An Old Relationship Revisited in a New Way," *Social Problems*, Apr. 1977, pp. 482–97.

52. "Women Alcoholics," *Newsweek*, Nov. 15, 1976, pp. 73–74.

53. R.J. Williams, *Alcoholism: The Nutritional Approach*. Austin, Tex.: University of Texas Press, 1959.

54. *Op. cit.*, *Alcohol and Alcoholism*, p. 13.

55. *Op. cit.*, Goode, p. 3.

56. P. Laurie, *Drugs*. Baltimore: Penguin Books, 1970, p. 13.

57. *Op. cit.*, Goode, pp. 7, 8.

58. *Ibid.*, pp. 3–8, 27–30.

59. C. Winick, "Physician Narcotic Addicts," *Social Problems*, 9(1961):174–86.

60. *Op. cit.*, Goode, p. 174. See also A. Lindesmith, *Addiction and Opiates*. Chicago: Aldine, 1968, and R. Akers, *Deviant Behavior: A Social Learning Approach*. Belmont, Cal.: Wadsworth, 1973, p. 89.

61. *Op. cit.*, *Alcohol and Alcoholism*, p. 15.

62. *Op. cit.*, Laurie, pp. 36–41.

63. *Op. cit.*, Kessel and Walton, pp. 56–68, and *Alcohol and Alcoholism*, p. 15.

64. *Op. cit.*, *Alcohol and Alcoholism*, p. 15.

65. *Op. cit.*, Clinard, p. 217.

66. E.H. Sutherland and D. Cressey, *Criminology*, Ninth edition. Philadelphia: J.B. Lippincott, 1974, pp. 75–77.

67. *Op. cit.*, Akers, pp. 49–57, 84–85.

68. *Ibid.*, pp. 123, 133.

69. H.S. Becker, *Outsiders: Studies in the Sociology of Deviance*. New York: The Free Press, 1963, pp. 46–58. See also H.S. Becker, "Becoming a Marihuana User," in R. O'Brien, C. Schrag, and W. Martin, *Readings in General Sociology*, Fourth edition. New York: Houghton Mifflin, pp. 280–85.

70. *Op. cit.*, Goode, pp. 81, 112, 135, 167–79.

71. R. Quinney, *Criminology*. Boston: Little, Brown, 1975, p. 128.

72. *Ibid.*, p. 128; *op. cit.*, Akers, pp. 81–85.

73. *Op. cit.*, *Alcohol and Alcoholism*, p. 15; Kessel and Walton, p. 45; Straus, pp. 200–01; Clinard, p. 469.

74. *Op. cit.*, Clinard, p. 468.

75. *Ibid.*, p. 470. See also A.D. Ullman, "Sociocultural Backgrounds of Alcoholism," *The Annals of the American Academy of Political and Social Science*, 315(1958): 48–54.

76. *Op. cit.*, Kessel and Walton, pp. 46, 52.

77. A. Ullman, "Sex Differences in the First Drinking Experience," *Quarterly Journal of Studies on Alcohol*, 18(1957):229–39.

78. D. Hebding and L. Glick, *Introduction to Sociology*. Reading, Mass.: Addison-Wesley, 1976, p. 315.

79. *Ibid.*, pp. 315–16.

80. *Op. cit.*, Straus, p. 212.

81. C.E. Reasons, "The Addict as Criminal," *Crime and Delinquency*, 21,1(Jan. 1975): 19–21, 24–27.

82. *Ibid.*

83. *Op. cit.*, Clausen, p. 168.

84. *Ibid.*; *op. cit.*, Goode, pp. 191–93, and Akers, p. 106.

85. *Op. cit.*, Goode, p. 194.
86. R.J. Weiner, "Shifting Perspectives in Drug Abuse Policy," *Crime and Delinquency*, 22,3(Jul. 1976):347–58.
87. *Op. cit.*, Reasons, p. 27.
88. *Op. cit.*, Goode, p. 195.
89. *Ibid.*, pp. 195–96.
90. *Ibid.*, p. 199.
91. R.A. Roffman and C. Froland, "Drug and Alcohol Dependencies in Prisons: A Review of the Response," *Crime and Delinquency*, 22,3(Jul. 1976):359–66.
92. *Op. cit.*, Alcohol and Alcoholism, pp. 27–35.
93. U.S. Department of Health, Education and Welfare, National Institute on Alcohol Abuse and Alcoholism, "Facts About Alcohol and Alcoholism," Publication #(ADM)76-31, Washington, D.C., 1976, pp. 29–30.
94. H.M. Trice and P.M. Roman, "Delabeling, Relabeling, and Alcoholics Anonymous," in *Deviance: Action, Reaction, Interaction*, eds. F. Scarpitti and P.T. McFarlane. Reading, Mass.: Addison-Wesley, 1975, pp. 268–76.
95. *Op. cit.*, "What Industry is Doing About 10 Million Alcoholic Workers," p. 66.
96. *Op. cit.*, Alcohol and Alcoholism, p. 28.
97. *Op. cit.*, "The Methadone Jones."
98. "The Methadone Mess," *Time*, May 24, 1976, p. 47.
99. *Op. cit.*, "The Methadone Jones."
100. *Op. cit.*, Fort and Cory, pp. 51–52.
101. *Op. cit.*, Goode, pp. 223–25.

CHAPTER 7

1. R.S. Pickett, "The American Family: An Embattled Institution," *The Humanist*, May–Jun., 1975.
2. D. Hebding and L. Glick, *Introduction to Sociology*. Reading, Mass.: Addison-Wesley, 1976, p. 139.
3. F. Elkin and G. Handel, *The Child and Society: The Process of Socialization*. New York: Random House, 1972, p. 105.
4. A. and J. Skolnick, *Family in Transition*. Boston: Little, Brown, 1971.
5. A. and J. Skolnick, *Intimacy, Family, and Society*. Boston: Little, Brown, 1974, pp. 1–2.
6. *Ibid.*
7. W.J. Goode, "Force and Violence in the Family," *The Journal of Marriage and the Family*, 33(Nov. 1971):624–36; G.R. Bach and P. Wyden, *Intimate Enemy*. New York: William Morrow, 1968, pp. 17–33; J. Sprey, "On the Management of Conflict in Families," *The Journal of Marriage and the Family*, 33(Nov. 1971):722–32.
8. S. Steinmetz and M.A. Straus, *Violence in the Family*. New York: Dodd, Mead, 1974, p. 6.
9. J.E. O'Brien, "Violence in Divorce-Prone Families," *The Journal of Marriage and the Family*, 33(Nov. 1971):692–98.
10. *Op. cit.*, O'Brien.
11. L.A. Coser, "Some Social Functions of Violence," in *Patterns of Violence, The Annals of the American Academy of Political and Social Science*, 364(Mar. 1966). See also L.A. Coser, "The Functions of Conflict," in *Sociological Theory: A Book of Readings*, eds. L.A. Coser and B. Rosenberg. New York: Macmillan, 1957, pp. 218–19.
12. *Op. cit.*, O'Brien.
13. *Op. cit.*, Goode.

14. *Ibid.*
15. R.I. Parnas, "The Police Response to the Domestic Disturbance," *Wisconsin Law Review*, 914(Fall):914–60.
16. *Op. cit.*, O'Brien.
17. *Op. cit.*, Steinmetz and Straus, p. 46.
18. *Time*, Mar. 2, 1978, p. 69.
19. *Ibid.*
20. R. Stark and J. McEvoy, "Middle Class Violence," *Psychology Today*, Nov. 4, 1970, pp. 52–65.
21. *Op. cit.*, Steinmetz and Straus, p. 47.
22. *Ibid.*: "A History of Child Abuse and Infanticide," by S.X. Radbill, pp. 173–79.
23. *Ibid.*: "Child Abuse as Psychopathology: A Sociological Critique and Reformulation," by R.J. Gelles.
24. D.G. Gil, *Violence Against Children*. Boston: Harvard University Press, 1970.
25. *Op. cit.*, Steinmetz and Straus, p. 142.
26. *Op. cit.*, Gil.
27. *Ibid.*
28. *Op. cit.*, Stark and McEvoy.
29. *Op. cit.*, Gil.
30. *Op. cit.*, Gelles, pp. 196–97.
31. *Op. cit.*, Goode, p. 40.
32. *Op. cit.*, Gil.
33. *Op. cit.*, Steinmetz and Straus: "Social Class Differences in Parent's Use of Physical Punishment," by H.S. Erlanger, pp. 150–66.
34. *Ibid.*: "Some Causes of Jealousy in Young Children," by M. Sewell, p. 82.
35. *Ibid.*, p. 3.
36. *Op. cit.*, Goode.
37. *Op. cit.*, Steinmetz and Straus.
38. *Op. cit.*, Gil.
39. *Op. cit.*, Goode.
40. *Op. cit.*, Gelles, p. 199.
41. A. Bandura and R.H. Walters, *Social Learning and Personality Development*. New York: Holt, Rinehart & Winston, 1963.
42. *Op. cit.*, Gelles.
43. *Ibid.* See also R. Galdston, "Observations of Children Who Have Been Physically Abused by Their Parents," *American Journal of Psychiatry*, 122,4(1965):440–43; B.F. Steel and C.B. Pollack, "A Psychiatric Study of Parents Who Abuse Infants and Small Children," in *The Battered Child*, eds. R.E. Heffer and C.H. Kempe. Chicago: University of Chicago Press, 1968, pp. 103–47; S. Wasserman, "The Abused Parent of the Abused Child," *Children*, 14(Sep.–Oct. 1967):175–79.
44. *Op. cit.*, Gelles.
45. *Ibid.*
46. H.C. Raffali, "The Battered Child: An Overview of a Medical, Legal, and Social Problem," in *Deviance: Action, Reaction, Interaction*, eds. F.R. Scarpitti and P.T. McFarlane. Reading, Mass.: Addison-Wesley, 1975.
47. *Op. cit.*, Gelles.
48. *Op. cit.*, Erlanger.
49. *Op. cit.*, Steinmetz and Straus: "Violence in Husband-Wife Interaction," by R.N. Whitehurst, pp. 75–82.
50. *Op. cit.*, Gil.
51. *Op. cit.*, Steinmetz and Straus: "Treatment of Child Abuse," by S.R. Zalba, pp. 212–22.

52. *Ibid.*
53. *Ibid.:* "Training Parents to Control an Aggressive Child," by G.R. Patterson, J.A. Cobb, and R.S. Ray, pp. 308–14.
54. *Ibid.*
55. *Ibid.:* Zalba.
56. *Op. cit.,* Skolnick and Skolnick: "A Review of the Family Therapy Field," by J. Haley, pp. 60–71.
57. *Op. cit.,* Steinmetz and Straus, p. 120.
58. *Ibid.:* "Family Interaction Patterns, Drug Treatment, and Change in Social Aggression," by M. Cohen *et al.,* pp. 120–26.
59. *Ibid.,* p. 49.
60. *Ibid.:* Whitehurst, p. 315.
61. *Ibid.,* p. 146.
62. D.G. Gil, "A Conceptual Model of Child Abuse and its Implications for Social Policy," *Violence Against Children, The Journal of Marriage and the Family,* 33(Nov. 1971):644–48.
63. *The Christian Science Monitor,* Apr. 6, 1978, p. 17.
64. *Ibid.*
65. *Ibid.*
66. *Op. cit.,* Steinmetz and Straus: Whitehurst, pp. 75–82.
67. R.F. Winch, *The Modern Family,* Third edition. New York: Holt, Rinehart & Winston, 1971, pp. 574–75.
68. J.R. Eshleman, *The Family: An Introduction.* Boston: Allyn & Bacon, 1974, pp. 618–19.
69. *U.S. News and World Report,* Oct. 27, 1975, pp. 153–55.
70. *Op. cit.,* Eshleman, pp. 618–19.
71. U.S. Census Bureau, *Statistical Abstract of the United States: 1977,* Washington, D.C., 1978, p. 74. See also *Monthly Vital Statistics,* Apr. 18, 1978.
72. *Op. cit.,* Eshleman.
73. W.J. Goode, "Family Disorganization," in *Contemporary Social Problems,* eds. R.K. Merton and R. Nisbet. Harcourt Brace Jovanovich, 1976, pp. 532–34, 537–38.
74. M.S. and L. Smart, *Families: Developing Relationships.* New York: Macmillan, 1976, pp. 427–28.
75. *Ibid.*
76. *Ibid.*
77. *Ibid.*
78. *Op. cit.,* Eshleman, p. 630.
79. *Op. cit.,* Merton and Nisbet: Goode, pp. 533–34.
80. *Op. cit.,* Eshleman, pp. 625–26.
81. *Op. cit.,* Merton and Nisbet: Goode, pp. 537–38.
82. D.E. Poplin, *Social Problems.* Glenview, Ill.: Scott, Foresman, 1978, p. 395.
83. *Op. cit.,* Skolnick and Skolnick.
84. J.K. Burgess, "The Single-Parent Family: A Social and Sociological Problem," *Family Coordinator,* 49(1970):136–44.
85. P. Bohannon, *Divorce and After.* Garden City, N.Y.: Doubleday, 1970.
86. B.R. Fetterolf, *Society Today.* New York: CRM/Random House, 1978, p. 346.
87. *Op. cit.,* Hebding and Glick, p. 146.
88. G. Levinger, "Sources of Marital Dissatisfaction Among Applicants for Divorce," in *Families In Crisis,* eds. P.H. and L.N. Glasser. New York: Harper & Row, 1970, pp. 126–32.
89. E.E. Le Masters, *Parents in Modern America: A Sociological Analysis.* Homewood, Ill.: Dorsey Press, 1970, pp. 18–20, 23, 25–29.
90. *Ibid.*

91. *Ibid.*
92. *Ibid.*
93. *Op. cit.*, Smart and Smart, pp. 427–28.
94. *Ibid.*
95. E.W. Burgess and H.J. Locke, *The Family: From Institution to Companionship.* New York: American Book, 1945.
96. D.R. Mace, "In Defense of the Nuclear Family," *The Humanist*, May–Jun., 1975.
97. *Op. cit.*, Skolnick and Skolnick, pp. 11–16.
98. *Ibid.* See also W.J. Goode, *World Revolution and Family Patterns.* New York: The Free Press, 1963.
99. *Op. cit.*, Skolnick and Skolnick, p. 12.
100. T. Parsons, *Essays in Sociological Theory: Pure and Applied.* Cambridge, Mass.: Harvard University Press, 1958.
101. *Op. cit.*, Goode, *World Revolution and Family Patterns.*
102. B.M. Moore, Jr., "Thoughts on the Future of the Family," in *Political Power and Social Theory*, Cambridge, Mass.: Harvard University Press, 1958.
103. *Op. cit.*, Skolnick and Skolnick, pp. 13–14, 16–17.
104. *Ibid.*
105. *Ibid.*
106. G. Levinger, "Marital Cohesiveness and Dissolution: An Integrative Review," *The Journal of Marriage and the Family*, Feb. 27, 1976.
107. *Ibid.*
108. J.F. Crosby, "The Death of the Family Revisited," *The Humanist*, May–Jun., 1975.
109. *Ibid.*
110. *Ibid.*
111. *Op. cit.*, Skolnick and Skolnick.
112. *Ibid.*
113. *Op. cit.*, Mace.
114. *Ibid.*
115. *Ibid.*
116. *Op. cit.*, Pickett.
117. *Ibid.*
118. A. Campbell, "The American Way of Mating," *Psychology Today*, May, 1975.
119. *Op. cit.*, Hebding and Glick, pp. 147–48.
120. M. Hunt, "The Future of Marriage," in *Conflict and Consensus*, ed. H.M. Hodges, Jr. New York: Harper & Row, 1973, pp. 264–74.
121. *Op. cit.*, Hebding and Glick.
122. *Ibid.*
123. *Op. cit.*, Hunt.
124. A. Ellis, "Group Marriages: A Possible Alternative?" in *The Family in Search of a Future*, ed. H.A. Otto. New York: Appleton-Century-Crofts, 1970.
125. *Op. cit.*, Hunt.
126. *Op. cit.*, Hebding and Glick, p. 148.
127. M. Mead, "Marriage in Two Steps," *Redbook*, Jul. 1966.
128. C. and R. Palson, "Swinging in Wedlock," *Society*, 9,4(1972).
129. *Op. cit.*, Hebding and Glick, p. 149.
130. U.S. Supreme Court, *Levy* vs. *Louisiana*, 1964.

CHAPTER 8

1. U.S. Department of Health, Education, and Welfare, *Health, United States: 1976–1977*, Washington, D.C., No. (HRA) 77-1231, pp. 47, 217.
2. *Ibid.*

3. *Ibid.*
4. *Ibid.*
5. U.S. Bureau of the Census, *Statistical Abstract of the United States: 1977*, Washington, D.C., 1977, p. 55.
6. *Op. cit., Health, United States.*
7. U.S. Department of Health, Education, and Welfare, "Parameters of Health in the United States," in A.D. Schwartz and C.S. Kart, *Dominant Issues in Medical Sociology.* Reading, Mass.: Addison-Wesley, pp. 378–93.
8. *Ibid.*
9. *Op. cit., Health, United States*, pp. v–vi.
10. K. Davis, "U.S. Health Care: The Road Ahead," in *How Can Health Care of United States Citizens Best Be Improved?* Senate Document No. 95-39, Washington, D.C., 1977, p. 13.
11. *Op. cit.*, "Parameters of Health," p. 381.
12. I. Ramey, "The Crisis in Health Care: Fact or Fiction?" in *Health Care Dimensions*, ed. M. Levinger. Philadelphia: F.A. Davis, 1974, pp. 17–18.
13. *Op. cit., Health, United States*, p. v.
14. *Ibid.*
15. *Ibid.*
16. *Ibid.*, p. vi.
17. M. Herman, "The Poor, Their Medical Needs and the Health Services Available to Them," *Annals of The American Academy of Political and Social Science*, Jan. 1972.
18. *U.S. News & World Report*, Feb. 7, 1977, p. 40.
19. *The Nation's Health*, American Public Health Association, Jul. 1977, p. 1.
20. *Op. cit.*, Levinger: "The Social Organization of Health Care and The Myth of Free Choice," by H. Nakagawa, pp. 80–81.
21. *Ibid.*
22. J.A. Califano, remarks made at 1977 meeting of the American Medical Assn., San Francisco.
23. *Op. cit., Statistical Abstract: 1977*, Table No. 134, p. 94.
24. *Op. cit., Health, United States*, p. vii.
25. *Ibid.*, p. 55.
26. "America's Doctors: A Profession in Trouble." *U.S. News & World Report*, Oct. 17, 1977, pp. 50–58.
27. *Op. cit., Health, United States*, pp. 56–57.
28. *Op. cit., The Nation's Health*, p. 1, and *Statistical Abstracts: 1977*, p. 194.
29. *Op. cit., Health, United States*, p. 55.
30. *Op. cit.*, "America's Doctors: A Profession in Trouble."
31. *Ibid.*
32. *The New York Times*, Jan. 27–29, 1976, p. 1 ff.
33. *Ibid.*
34. *Ibid.*
35. *Op. cit.*, "America's Doctors: A Profession in Trouble."
36. *Ibid.*
37. *U.S. News & World Report*, Feb. 23, 1970, pp. 68–73.
38. *Ibid.; op. cit., Health, United States*, p. vii.
39. *Op. cit., How Can the Health Care Be Improved?*: "Health and Health Policy," by H.M. Somers, p. 3.
40. R.J. Weiss *et al.*, "Foreign Medical Graduates and the Underground," *New England Journal of Medicine*, 290(Jun. 20, 1974):1408–13. See also T.D. Dublin, "Foreign Physicians: Their Impact on U.S. Health Care," *Science*, 187:(Aug. 2, 1974): 407–14, and R.J. Weiss *et al.*, "The Effect of Improving Physicians—Return

to a Pre-Flexerian Standard," *New England Journal of Medicine*, 290(Jun. 27, 1974):1453–57.

41. *Op. cit.*, "Parameters of Health," p. 384.
42. *Op. cit.*, *Health, United States*, p. vii. Statistics are for 1974 and apply to the number of active nonfederal physicians.
43. *Op. cit.*, Ramey, p. 20.
44. *Ibid.*
45. *Ibid.*
46. *Op. cit.*, "America's Doctors: A Profession in Trouble."
47. *Op. cit.*, *Health, United States*, pp. 363–64.
48. Pracon Inc., study financed by Roche Laboratories, *Medical World News*, Dec. 9, 1978, pp. 113–14.
49. T. Cohen and M. Miner, "Health Insurance: How Much Do You Need?" *Harper's Bazaar*, Aug. 1971, p. 87.
50. *Op. cit.*, *Health, United States*, p. 363.
51. R. Margolis, "National Health Insurance—The Dream Whose Time Has Come?" *The New York Times Magazine*, Jan. 9, 1977.
52. *Op. cit.*, Cohen and Miner.
53. *Op. cit.*, Margolis.
54. *Op. cit.*, Ramey, p. 22.
55. E. Johnson, *Social Problems of Urban Man*, Homewood, Ill.: Dorsey, 1973, pp. 450–60.
56. *Op. cit.*, *Health, United States*.
57. J. Williamson *et al.*, eds., *Social Problem, The Contemporary Rebates*. Boston: Little, Brown, pp. 424–25.
58. *Op. cit.*, Johnson.
59. *Op. cit.*, Nakagawa, p. 85. See also B. and J. Ehrenrich, *The American Health Empire: Power, Profits and Politics*. New York: Random House, 1970.
60. *Op. cit.*, Nakagawa.
61. *Op. cit.*, Johnson, p. 451. See also H. Schwartz, "Health Care in America: A Heretical Analysis," *Saturday Review*, Vol. 54, 1971, pp. 14–17, 55.
62. *Op. cit.*, Schwartz.
63. *Op. cit.*, Williamson.
64. *Op. cit.*, Somers, pp. 3–4.
65. *Ibid.*
66. U.S. Department of Health, Education, and Welfare, *Toward a Comprehensive Health Policy for the 1970's: A White Paper*, Washington, D.C., 1971, pp. 31–32.
67. P. Star, "The Undelivered Health Care System," *The Public Interest*, Winter 1976, pp. 67–81.
68. *Op. cit.*, Schwartz: "The HMO: Background Considerations," by D. Mechanic, pp. 499–507.
69. *Op. cit.*, White Paper, p. 37.
70. *Op. cit.*, Star, and Somers, p. 4.
71. *Op. cit.*, Williamson, p. 424.
72. *Op. cit.*, *Health, United States*.
73. *Medical World News*, Jan. 23, 1978, p. 14.
74. *Op. cit.*, *Health, United States*, p. 111.
75. *Ibid.*
76. *Op cit.*, Williamson: "Agreed: Here Comes National Health Insurance," by A. Rivlin, p. 428.
77. For a complete analysis of this report, see *Health, United States*, pp. 111–25.
78. *Ibid.*
79. *Op. cit.*, Williamson, p. 425.

80. A.H. Maslow and B. Mittlemann, *Principles of Abnormal Psychology*. New York: Harper & Row, 1951, pp. 14–15.

81. D. Hebding and L. Glick, *Introduction to Sociology*, Reading, Mass.: Addison-Wesley, 1976, p. 318.

82. A.H. Buss, *Psychology Behavior In Perspective*. New York: John Wiley, 1978, p. 411.

83. R.E. Silverman, *Psychology*, Brief edition. New York: Appleton-Century-Crofts, 1972, p. 336.

84. *Op. cit.*, Buss, p. 412.

85. *Op. cit.*, Silverman, p. 340.

86. *Op. cit.*, Buss, p. 413.

87. U.S. Department of Health, Education and Welfare, Public Health Service, Alcohol, Drug Abuse and Mental Health Administration, *Schizophrenia Bulletin*, Vol. 1, No. 13, Washington, D.C., Summer 1975, p. 7.

88. R. Silverman, *Psychology*, Second edition. Englewood Cliffs, N.J.: Prentice-Hall, pp. 472–74.

89. *Ibid.*

90. *Ibid.*

91. *Op. cit.*, Buss, p. 407.

92. T.S. Szasz, "The Myth of Mental Illness," *The American Psychologist*, Feb. 15, 1960, pp. 113–18. See also T.J. Scheff, ed., *Mental Illness and Social Process*. New York: Harper & Row, 1967, pp. 242–54, and Thomas Szasz, *The Myth of Mental Illness: The Foundations of a Theory of Personal Conduct*. New York: Harper & Row, 1961.

93. T. Scheff, *Being Mentally Ill: Sociological Theory*. Chicago: Aldine, 1966. See also T. Scheff, "The Role of the Mentally Ill and the Dynamics of Mental Disorder," *Sociometry*, 1963, pp. 436–53.

94. *Op. cit.*, Hebding and Glick, p. 318. See also T.J. Scheff, "The Labeling Theory of Mental Illness," *American Sociological Review*, June 1974.

95. "Report of the President's Commission on Mental Illness," Vol. 1, Washington, D.C., 1978, pp. 1–78.

96. *Op. cit.*, *Statistical Abstract: 1977*, Table No. 167, p. 108.

97. *Ibid.*

98. U.S. Department of Health, Education and Welfare, National Institute of Mental Health, *Utilization of Mental Health Facilities: 1971*, Washington, D.C., 1971.

99. *Op. cit.*, The President's Commission Report, p. 4.

100. R.E.L. Faris and H.W. Dunham, *Mental Disorders in Urban Areas*. Chicago: University of Chicago Press, 1938; A.B. Hollingshead and F.C. Redlich, *Social Class and Mental Illness: A Community Study*. New York: John Wiley, 1958; N.Q. Brill and H.A. Storrow, "Social Class and Psychiatric Treatment," *Archives of General Psychiatry*, 3(1960):340–44; K. Hass, "The Middle-Class Professional and the Lower-Class Patient," *Mental Hygiene*, 47(1963):408–10; H.F. Albronda *et al.*, "Social Class and Psychotherapy," *Archives of General Psychiatry*, 10(1964): 276–83; J.K. Myers *et al.*, *A Decade Later: A Follow-up of Social Class and Mental Illness*. New York: John Wiley, 1968; W. Rushing, "Two Patterns in the Relationship Between Social Class and Mental Hospitalization," *American Sociological Review*, Vol. 34, Aug. 1969, pp. 533–41; L. Srole *et al.*, *Mental Health in the Metropolis: The Midtown Manhattan Study*, Revised edition. New York: Harper & Row, 1975.

101. W.R. Gove, "The Relationship Between Sex Roles, Marital Status and Mental Illness," *Social Forces*, Sep. 1972.

102. P. Chester, *Women and Madness*. New York: Avon, 1972.

103. *Op. cit.*, Silverman, p. 552.

104. D. Rosenthal, *Genetics of Psycho-Pathology*. New York: McGraw-Hill, 1971.

105. *Op. cit.*, Silverman.

106. G. Heath *et al.*, "Behavior Changes in Nonpsychotic Volunteers Following the Administration of Taraxein, The Substance Extracted from Serum of Schizophrenic Patients," *American Journal of Psychiatry*, 114(1958):917–20. See also T. Millon, *Modern Psychopathology: A Biosocial Approach to Maladaptive Learning and Functioning*. Philadelphia: Saunders, 1969, p. 154.

107. *Op. cit.*, Silverman, p. 553.

108. R.J. Wyatt, "Dopamine B-Hydroxylase Activity in Brains of Chronic Schizophrenic Patients," *Science*, 187, pp. 368–70, 1975.

109. J. Weiss *et al.*, "Neurotransmitters and Helplessness: A Chemical Bridge to Depression?" *Psychology Today*, Vol. 8, No. 7 (Dec. 1974), pp. 59–62.

110. G. Corey, *Theory and Practice of Counseling and Psychotherapy*. Belmont, Cal.: Wadsworth, 1977, pp. 10–18.

111. R.K. Merton, *Social Theory and Social Structure*. New York: The Free Press, 1965.

112. W.R. Gove, "Societal Reactions as an Explanation of Mental Illness: An Evaluation," *American Sociological Review*, 35, Oct. 1970, pp. 873–83.

113. R. and N. Cain, "A Compendium of Psychiatric Drugs, Parts I and II," *Drug Therapy*, Jan. and Feb. 1975.

114. *Op. cit.*, Corey, pp. 23–24. This section on psychotherapy is largely based upon the analysis of these therapies by Corey.

115. R. May, ed., *Existential Psychology*. New York: Random House, 1961.

116. C. Rogers, *Client Centered Therapy*. Boston: Houghton Mifflin, 1951.

117. F. Perls, *Gestalt Therapy Verbatim*. Moab, Ut.: Real People Press, 1969.

118. E. Berne, *Transactional Analysis in Psychotherapy*. New York: Grove Press, 1961.

119. *Op. cit.*, Corey, p. 100.

120. *Ibid.*, p. 121.

121. A. Ellis, "Rational Emotive Therapy," in *Current Psychotherapies*, ed. R. Corsini. Itasca, Ill.: Peacock, 1973.

122. W. Glasser, *Reality Therapy*. New York: Harper & Row, 1965.

123. A.L. Crawford and B.B. Buchanan, *Psychiatric Nursing*. Philadelphia: F.A. Davis, 1974, p. 13.

124. M.A. Test and L.I. Stein, "A Commentary Approach to the Chronically Disabled Patient," *Social Policy*, May–Jun. 1977, pp. 8–16.

125. *Ibid.*

126. *Ibid.*

CHAPTER 9

1. "What People Around the World Say," *U. S. News & World Report*, Jan. 24, 1977, p. 66.

2. P. Ehrlich, *The Population Bomb*. New York: Ballantine Books, 1971, p. 3.

3. Population Reference Bureau, "World Population Data Sheet: 1978," Washington, D.C., 1978, and "World Population Reaches 4 Billion," *The New York Times*, Mar. 29, 1976, p. 25. See also "World Population Prospects As Assessed in 1973," New York: United Nations Population Studies #60, 1977.

4. K. Davis, "The World's Population Crisis," in *Contemporary Social Problems*, Fourth edition, eds. R.K. Merton and R. Nisbet. New York: Harcourt Brace Jovanovich, 1976, pp. 267–68; op. cit., "World Population Data Sheet: 1978."

5. *Op. cit.*, Merton and Nisbet; Davis, pp. 268, 270.

6. *Ibid.*, p. 269. See also D. Heer, *Population and Society*, Second edition. Englewood Cliffs, N. J.: Prentice-Hall, 1975, pp. 6–11.

7. "Population Implosion," *Newsweek*, Dec. 6, 1976, p. 58. See also "Reduction in

World Birth Rate Attributed to Control Programs," *The New York Times*, Apr. 29, 1976, p. 35, and "Population Implosion?" *Saturday Review*, Jun. 26, 1976, pp. 50–51.

8. "Profile of a World Overflowing With People," *U. S. News & World Report*, Mar. 28, 1977, pp. 54–55.

9. "World Population Trends," *Science*, 194,4266(Nov. 12, 1976):704. See also "The Slowing Growth of World Population," *Science News*, 110,20(Nov. 13, 1976): 316–17; "The Growth of Population is Slowing Down," *The New York Times*, Nov. 21, 1976, p. 8; *op. cit.*, "Population Implosion," *Newsweek*, p. 58.

10. J. Matras, *Populations and Societies*. Englewood Cliffs, N. J.: Prentice-Hall, 1973, p. 22.

11. *Op. cit.*, "World Population Data Sheet: 1978."

12. "Timeclock of Doubling Populations," *The Unesco Courier*, May 1974, pp. 8–9.

13. *United Nations Demographic Yearbook: 1975*. New York: United Nations, 1976, pp. 139–40, 153–57.

14. *Op. cit.*, "World Population Data Sheet: 1978."

15. *Op. cit.*, Merton and Nisbet: Davis, p. 267.

16. *Op. cit.*, Ehrlich, pp. 16–17.

17. *Op. cit.*, "Profile of a World Overflowing with People," and Merton and Nisbet: Davis, p. 269.

18. *Op. cit.*, "World Population Data Sheet: 1978."

19. *Ibid.* See also "Looking to the ZPGeneration," *Time*, Feb. 28, 1977, pp. 71–72; "Profile of an Aging America," *U.S. News & World Report*, Aug. 8, 1977, p. 54; National Center for Health Statistics, "Monthly Vital Statistics Report," Washington, D.C., Mar., Apr., and May 1978; U.S. Bureau of the Census, "Population Profile of the U.S.: 1977," *Current Population Reports*, Series P-20, No. 324, Apr. 1978, pp. 1, 3; and "Projections of the Population of the U.S.: 1977–2050," *Current Population Reports*, Series P-25, No. 704, Jul. 1977.

20. "What Shifts in Population will Mean for Industry," *U. S. News & World Report*, May 30, 1977, pp. 60–62.

21. "Planning for How Many People?" *Bio Science*, 26,7(Jul. 1976):427, and "Illegal Immigration Swells Population," *The New York Times*, Aug. 10, 1977, p. 30.

22. "The Nation's Youth—Impact Near Its Peak," *U. S. News & World Report*, Aug. 15, 1977, pp. 50–51. See also "New Look at America Today—Evidence of Major Change," *U. S. News & World Report*, May 16, 1977, pp. 64–65.

23. Report of the Commission on Population Growth and the American Future, "Population and the American Future," New York: The New American Library, Signet, 1972.

24. *Op. cit.*, Merton and Nisbet: Davis, p. 282.

25. *Op. cit.*, *Population and the American Future*, pp. 60–64.

26. "Doubts Are Growing That U.S. Can Keep Feeding the World," *U. S. News & World Report*, Nov. 8, 1976, pp. 83–84.

27. *Ibid.*; *op. cit.*, *Population and the American Future*, pp. 65–66.

28. *Op. cit.*, *Population and the American Future*, p. 66.

29. *Op. cit.*, Merton and Nisbet: Davis, p. 282.

30. *Op. cit.*, "New Look at America Today—Evidence of Major Change," pp. 64–65, and "Profile of a World Overflowing," pp. 54–55.

31. *Op. cit.*, "Population Profile of the U.S.: 1977," pp. 1, 26, 32.

32. *Op. cit.*, Ehrlich, p. 15.

33. *Op. cit.*, Merton and Nisbet: Davis, pp. 271–72.

34. *Op. cit.*, "World Population Prospects As Assessed in 1973," p. 24.

35. *Op. cit.*, "World Population Data Sheet: 1978."

36. J. Mayer, "The Dimensions of Human Hunger," *Scientific American*, 235,4(Sep. 1976):40–49.
37. "Food: A Battle Won, Not the War," *The New York Times*, Jan. 30, 1977, p. 19.
38. *Op. cit.*, Mayer, p. 46.
39. "The Elephant Turns Frisky," *Time*, Feb. 7, 1977, p. 55; *op. cit.*, "World Population Data Sheet: 1978."
40. *Op. cit.*, "World Population Data Sheet: 1978."
41. *Op. cit.*, Merton and Nisbet: Davis, p. 273.
42. "The Price India Pays for Indira Gandhi's 'Reforms'," *U. S. News & World Report*, Jan. 24, 1977, pp. 37–40.
43. *Op. cit.*, "The Elephant Turns Frisky," p. 55.
44. F.C. Turner, "The Rush to the Cities in Latin America," *Science*, 192,4243(Jun. 4, 1976):955–61.
45. M. Alisky, "Mexico's Population Pressures," *Current History*, 72,425(Mar. 1977): 106–34.
46. *Op. cit.*, Merton and Nisbet: Davis, pp. 279–80.
47. T. Malthus, *Essay on the Principle of Population*, ed. A. Flew. Baltimore; Penguin Books, 1971 (originally published 1798).
48. *Op. cit.*, Heer, p. 19.
49. *Op. cit.*, Matras, p. 13.
50. *Op. cit.*, Heer, p. 19.
51. *Op. cit.*, Matras, p. 13.
52. *Ibid.*, pp. 24–26; *op. cit.*, Heer, p. 13.
53. C.F. Westoff, "The Decline of Unplanned Births in the United States," *Science*, 191,4222(Jan. 9, 1976). See also "Nation Found Near Point of No Unwanted Births," *The New York Times*, Jan. 3, 1976, pp. 1, 15.
54. *Op. cit.*, "World Population Data Sheet: 1978."
55. D. Kirk, "A New Demographic Transition," in *Rapid Population Growth: Consequences and Policy Implications*, Study Committee for the National Academy of Sciences. Baltimore: Johns Hopkins University Press, 1971, pp. 123–47.
56. *Op. cit.*, Ehrlich, p. 8. See also P. Ehrlich and J. Holdren, "Avoiding the Problem," *Saturday Review*, Mar. 6, 1971, p. 56.
57. D. Nortman, "Changing Contraceptive Patterns: A Global Perspective," *Population Bulletin*, Population Reference Bureau, 32,3(Aug. 1977):6.
58. *Ibid.*, pp. 12–13. See also "Study Finds Sterilization Gains Fastest of Birth-Curb Methods," *The New York Times*, May 5, 1976, p. 22.
59. *Op. cit.*, "Changing Contraceptive Patterns: A Global Perspective," pp. 24–25.
60. "The Supreme Court Ignites A Fiery Abortion Debate," *Time*, Jul. 4, 1977, pp. 6–8.
61. "The High Court's Abortion Rulings: What They Mean," *U.S. News & World Report*, Jul. 4, 1977, p. 66.
62. "Birth Control: More People Are Turning to Sterilization," *The New York Times*, May 22, 1977, p. 7.
63. *Op. cit.*, "Changing Contraceptive Patterns: A Global Perspective," p. 17.
64. *Op. cit.*, "Study Finds Sterilization Gains Fastest" and "Birth Control: More People Are Turning." See also "More on Vasectomies," *Newsweek*, Jan. 12, 1976, p. 64.
65. *Op. cit.*, "Changing Contraceptive Patterns: A Global Perspective," p. 4.
66. *Ibid.*; *op. cit.*, "The Growth of Population is Slowing Down," p. 8.
67. A.J. Dyck, "Alternative Views of Moral Priorities in Population Policy," *Bio Science*, 24,4(Apr. 1977):272–76; *op. cit.*, "Population Implosion," *Newsweek*, p. 58, and Merton and Nisbet: Davis, p. 295.
68. *Op. cit.*, Dyck, pp. 273–74.
69. "Population Rise Eases in Colombia," *The New York Times*, Apr. 11, 1976, p. 23;

op. cit., "The Price India Pays for Indira Gandhi's 'Reforms'," pp. 37–40, and Alisky, pp. 106–34.

70. *Op. cit.,* "Changing Contraceptive Patterns: A Global Perspective," p. 10.
71. *Op. cit.,* Merton and Nisbet: Davis, p. 294.
72. *Op. cit.,* "Changing Contraceptive Patterns: A Global Perspective," p. 4.
73. *Ibid.,* p. 18.
74. *Ibid.,* p. 11.
75. *Ibid.,* p. 28.
76. *Op. cit.,* "The Growth of Population is Slowing Down," p. 8.
77. *Op. cit.,* "World Population Data Sheet: 1978."
78. *Op. cit.,* "Changing Contraceptive Patterns: A Global Perspective," p. 32.
79. *Op. cit.,* "Birth Control: More People Are Turning," p. 7.
80. *Op. cit.,* "The Price India Pays," pp. 37–40.
81. *Op. cit.,* Merton and Nisbet: Davis, p. 299.
82. *Op. cit.,* "Changing Contraceptive Patterns: A Global Perspective," p. 29, "World Population Trends," p. 704, and "The Growth of Population is Slowing Down," p. 8.
83. *Op. cit.,* "Birth Control: More People Are Turning," p. 7. See also "The Issue That Inflamed India," *Time,* Apr. 4, 1977, pp. 38–39, and "India After Indira," *Newsweek,* Apr. 4, 1977, pp. 32–42.
84. *Op. cit.,* "Changing Contraceptive Patterns: A Global Perspective," p. 34, "World Population Trends," p. 704, and Dyck, p. 276.

CHAPTER 10

1. R.F. Dasmann, *Environmental Conservation,* Fourth edition. New York: John Wiley, 1976, p. 6.
2. *Ibid.*
3. J. McHale, *The Ecological Context.* New York: George Braziller, 1970, p. 35.
4. *Ibid.,* pp. 49–59.
5. R. and L.T. Rienow, *Moment in the Sun.* New York: Dial Press, 1967, pp. 38–39.
6. U.S. Environmental Protection Agency, *Pollution and Your Health,* Washington, D.C., Office of Public Affairs, May 6, 1976, pp. 4–5.
7. P.R. and A.H. Ehrlich, *Population, Resources, Environment,* Second edition. San Francisco: W.H. Freeman, 1972, pp. 146–56; *op. cit.,* Dasmann, p. 374.
8. "Cleaning the Air," *Time,* Jul. 11, 1977, p. 80.
9. *Op. cit., Pollution and Your Health,* p. 9.
10. *Op. cit.,* Ehrlich and Ehrlich, p. 157.
11. *Ibid.,* p. 157.
12. "$13 Million Reminder," *Time,* Oct. 18, 1976, p. 83.
13. "Deadline for Reserve," *Time,* Jul. 26, 1976, p. 56.
14. "Safe Water or Jobs? A Classic Confrontation," *U.S. News & World Report,* Feb. 7, 1977, p. 47.
15. *Op. cit.,* Ehrlich and Ehrlich, p. 230, and Dasmann, p. 140.
16. "Oil is Pouring on Troubled Waters," *Time,* Jan. 10, 1977, p. 45.
17. *Op. cit., Pollution and Your Health,* p. 8.
18. *Op. cit.,* Ehrlich and Ehrlich, p. 229.
19. *Ibid.,* pp. 229–30.
20. J. McHale, *World Facts and Trends,* Second edition. New York: Macmillan, 1972, p. 19.
21. *Op. cit.,* Dasmann, p. 164.
22. *Ibid.,* p. 162.
23. *Op. cit.,* McHale, *World Facts and Trends,* p. 22.
24. *Op. cit.,* Ehrlich and Ehrlich, p. 159.

25. B. Commoner, *The Closing Circle*. New York: Bantam Books, 1971, p. 162.
26. *Ibid.*, p. 118; *op. cit.*, Dasmann, p. 9.
27. *Op. cit.*, McHale, *World Facts and Trends*, p. 19.
28. *Op. cit.*, Ehrlich and Ehrlich, p. 72.
29. D.H. Meadows *et al.*, *The Limits to Growth*, Second edition. New York: Universe Books, 1974, pp. 56–59.
30. *Op. cit.*, Ehrlich and Ehrlich, p. 72.
31. *Ibid.*, pp. 72–73.
32. *Ibid.*, p. 64.
33. "We Should Have Started Yesterday," *U.S. News & World Report*, Oct. 4, 1976, p. 39.
34. "Energy: Emerging Issue in Presidential Campaign," *U.S. News & World Report*, Oct. 4, 1976, p. 38.
35. *Ibid.*, p. 37.
36. "How the Energy Shortage Will Change Life in America," *U.S. News & World Report*, Feb. 14, 1977, p. 22. See also "$1 Trillion—The Cost of Meeting U.S. Energy Needs," *U.S. News & World Report*, May 2, 1977, p. 19.
37. "Opening the Debate," *Time*, Apr. 25, 1977, p. 28.
38. "Why Carter's Energy Program is Bogged Down in Congress," *U.S. News & World Report*, Oct. 10, 1977, p. 76.
39. "Winter's Legacy: Step-Up in Search For Fuel Supplies," *U.S. News & World Report*, Feb. 21, 1977, p. 19.
40. *Ibid.*, p. 20.
41. "How Safe is Nuclear Power," *Newsweek*, Apr. 12, 1976, p. 70.
42. *Op. cit.*, Dasmann, p. 330.
43. *Op. cit.*, Ehrlich and Ehrlich, p. 173.
44. "In the World of Nuclear Power: Crisis," *Life*, Vol. 2, May 1979, p. 22.
45. *Ibid.*, p. 70. See also "A 5 Billion-to-1 Disaster," *Newsweek*, Apr. 12, 1976, p. 74.
46. *Op. cit.*, Ehrlich and Ehrlich, p. 68.
47. *Op. cit.*, Dasmann, p. 368.
48. *Op. cit.*, Rienow and Rienow, p. 32.
49. *Op. cit.*, Dasmann, p. 370.
50. *Op. cit.*, Commoner, p. 175.
51. *Ibid.*, p. 136.
52. *Ibid.*, p. 142.
53. *Ibid.*, pp. 146–69. See also Commoner, "The Ecological Facts of Life," in *The Ecological Conscience*, ed. R. Disch. Englewood Cliffs, N.J.: Prentice-Hall, 1970, pp. 2–16.
54. *Op. cit.*, Ehrlich and Ehrlich. See also P. Ehrlich and J.P. Holdren, "Impact of Population Growth," *Science*, 171(Mar. 26, 1971):1212–15.
55. *Op. cit.*, Meadows *et al.*, p. 126.
56. *Ibid.*, pp. 124–40. See also K. Davis, "The World's Population Crisis," in *Contemporary Social Problems*, Fourth edition, eds. R.K. Merton and R. Nisbet. New York: Harcourt Brace Jovanovich, 1976, pp. 284–88.
57. J. Turner, *American Society: Problems of Structure*, Second edition. New York: Harper & Row, 1976, pp. 257, 259–61.
58. *Ibid.*, pp. 260–61.
59. "EPA: Air In Cities Is Hazardous," *The Philadelphia Inquirer*, Feb. 24, 1978, p. 1-A.
60. *Ibid.*, p. 2-A.
61. Council on Environmental Quality, "Eighth Annual Report of the Council on Environmental Quality," Washington, D.C., Dec. 1977, p. 3.
62. *Ibid.*, pp. 199, 235.
63. *Op. cit.*, Turner, pp. 270–71, 277–78.

64. *Op. cit.*, "Eighth Annual Report of the Council on Environmental Quality," pp. 18–19, 22, 42.

65. *Op. cit.*, Turner, pp. 269–75.

66. *Op. cit.*, "Eighth Annual Report of the Council on Environmental Quality," p. 300.

67. *Op. cit.*, "Winter's Legacy: Step-Up in Search For Fuel Supplies," p. 20, and "Eighth Annual Report of the Council on Environmental Quality," p. 273.

68. "Drilling Ahead in the Atlantic," *Time*, Mar. 6, 1978, p. 61.

69. *Op. cit.*, "Eighth Annual Report of the Council on Environmental Quality," p. 276.

70. *Ibid.*, pp. 273–76, 281.

Glossary

Absolute poverty line A poverty line based on family budget needs for minimum subsistence.

Acceptance A. A response to agism whereby the aged accept domination by youth and the middle-aged in order to survive in society. B. A minority group response to prejudice and discrimination in which the minority group members accommodate themselves to their subordinate or disadvantaged status.

Activity theory A theory of aging stating that middle- and old-age norms are the same; therefore the elderly are to be evaluated in terms of a middle-aged measure of success.

Aggressive action A response to prejudice and discrimination in which minority group members strike out against their subordinate status.

Aggressive rejection A response pattern of minority groups characterized by rejection of the dominant group's negative image of the minority members.

Agism The system of social, economic, political, and psychological pressures that supress groups because they exhibit biologically determined characteristic of old age.

Aid for Families with Dependent Children (AFDC) One of the largest public assistance programs created by the Social Security Act Amendments.

Alcoholics Anonymous A voluntary organization whose basic goal is to have its members remain sober through a system of fellowship, mutual assistance, and peer support.

Alcoholism The state of true physical and psychological dependence upon alcohol.

American Medical Association The largest professional organization of American physicians.

American underclass *(TIME)* America's poor population.

American Woman Suffrage Association (AWSA) A moderate woman's association founded in 1869 by Julia Ward and Lucy Stone that focused only on suffrage.

Amphetamines Synthetic stimulants, including a wide range of substances such as methedrine (speed), dexedrine, and benzedrine.

Anomic suicide Self-destruction resulting from the inability to cope with an abrupt breakdown or weakening of the norms of the group or society.

Anomie *(Merton)* A lack of integration between culturally prescribed goals and the availability of legitimate or institutionalized means (norms) for goal attainment.

Antibuse programs Medically supervised treatment for alcoholism in which a person is given regular doses of the drug antibuse, which induces very undesirable physical effects if alcohol is ingested.

Assimilation A response pattern of minority groups in which the members of the minority group want to become culturally and socially fused with the dominant group.

Barbiturates Depressant drugs, including such commonly used substances as phenobarbital, nembutal, and seconal.

Behavior modification Response to violence and aggression in family members that focuses upon the person's current behavior patterns and applies principles of operant conditioning to change behavior.

Biochemical explanation A theory that attributes mental illness to the presence or absence of chemicals in the bloodstream and brain of the mentally ill.

Biosphere The thin layer of air, water, and soil on our planet in which virtually all living creatures exist and with which they are interdependent.

Categoric risk The differential probability for a person who commits a crime to be arrested and ultimately imprisoned.

Chemicalistic fallacy *(Goode)* "The view that drug A causes behavior X, or that what we see as behavior and effects associated with a given drug are solely a function of the biochemical properties of that drug."

Child abuse *(Gil)* The intentional use of violence toward, or the intentional neglect of, children on the part of parents or other caretakers.

Children Savers The nineteenth-century American social movement that helped pave the way for many revisions in the juvenile justice and corrections system.

Children of divorce The children living in one parent families that were broken by divorce.

Civil law The body of legal regulations dealing with noncriminal offenses, which are handled by civil rather than criminal courts.

Civil Works Administration (CWA) Federal agency organized in the 1930s to develop programs and projects for improving our nation's roads, schools, parks, and public buildings.

Classical school of criminology An eighteenth-century school of thought stressing that, since human behavior is essentially rational and pleasure-oriented, punishments for criminal acts should be severe enough to outweigh any pleasures derived from the commission of such acts.

Communes An alternative to the nuclear family in

which a group of people live together and share family functions.

Community mental health centers The major governmental vehicle for providing comprehensive mental health services in local communities.

Competition The basic form of social interaction, according to conflict theorists.

Competition explanations The view that prejudice develops when two or more groups compete for scarce resources, material possessions, or power.

Conflict A product of social interaction and an effort that is directed toward resolving a decision-making impasse.

Conflict perspective An approach to poverty stressing that the social, economic, and political structure of America deprives the poor from a decent living standard.

Conflict subculture A social subdivision characterized by delinquent youths who engage in acts of violence (gang fighting).

Conflict theory The theoretical approach stressing the idea that social problems are a product of value conflicts within society—conflicts that in turn reflect basic inequalities in the distribution of power, wealth, and status.

Conformity Behavior that is in accordance with social norms and fulfills the expectations of others.

Consensus approach An approach to poverty that views the creation by the poor of a consensus behavior pattern, which is at odds with the dominate culture, to be the major ongoing cause of poverty.

Continuity theory A theory of aging based on the idea that experiences people have in life create particular predispositions that are, if possible, maintained.

Crime Behaviors that violate specific types of norms, which we call laws.

Criminal subculture The social subdivision comprised of delinquent youths and adult criminals.

Crude birthrate The annual number of births per thousand members of the population.

Crude death rate The annual number of deaths per thousand members of the population.

Culture The way of life of a society.

Culture lag The time lag between the adoption of an innovation and the establishment of cultural adjustments made necessary by the innovation.

Culture of poverty perspective A perspective of poverty stressing the idea that the different social strata manifest cultures distinctive of those various strata.

Deforestation The destruction of forest ecosystems.

Deinstitutionalization Reducing the number of patients in public mental hospitals and treating them, instead, in the community on an outpatient basis.

Delinquent subculture *(Cohen)* A subculture of working-class boys who manifest a "delinquent response," described as malicious, nonutilitarian, and negativistic.

Demographic transition theory A theory that examines the impact of industrial and economic development upon population growth. According to this theory, a decline in a society's death rate will inevitably be followed by a voluntary decline in its birthrate, a sequence for which various factors related to technological development itself are responsible.

Dependence A pattern of behavior in which one is physically or financially dependent on others. Many aged fear this role after being self-sufficient and independent for so long.

Depressants Those psychoactive substances that decrease or depress the functioning of the central nervous system.

Desertion The permanent departure from the family of either husband or wife, against the other's will.

Deviance Behavior that does not conform to norms or does not meet with the expectations of a group or society.

Deviance theory The theory that explains social problems in terms of people's behavior deviating from the norms of society.

Differential association *(Sutherland)* A learning perspective theory emphasizing that deviant behavior is learned in the course of associations with others.

Differential association reinforcement A reformulation of differential association linking it with many of the modern concepts found within operant conditioning or reinforcement theory.

Disability The restriction of any major physical activity, often as the result of chronic illness.

Discrimination An act or actual response whereby members of a particular group are accorded negative treatment on the basis of a certain characteristic or combination of traits, such as sex or race.

Disengagement An inevitable process within which an aged person reduces the number of new interper-

sonal relationships and makes changes in the remaining relationships.

Divorce Dissolution of a marriage by law.

Drug *(Scientific definition)* Any substance other than food that, by its chemical nature, affects the structure and functioning of the living organism.

Drug *(Social definition)* Any substance that has been arbitrarily defined as a drug by certain segments of society.

Drug abuse The excessive and/or compulsive use of a drug to the degree that it is harmful to the health or social functioning of the user or results in harmful consequences to others.

Drug addiction The development of physical dependence upon a drug.

Drug habituation The state of psychological dependence on a drug.

Drug subculture Subgroups maintaining sets of distinctive norms, values, beliefs, and actions specific to and favoring drug use.

Drug therapy A response to family violence in which certain chemical agents are used to control an individual's aggression.

Ecology The study of the interrelationships between living organisms and their environment.

Economic explanation A theory for prejudice based upon the belief that some people economically gain by it.

Ecosystem A subdivision of the biosphere encompassing a community of plants, animals, and microorganisms and the air, water, soil and other systems that support that community.

Ectomorphs *(Sheldon)* Those persons with body types described as tall and thin.

Electroshock treatment Passing an electric current through the brains of psychiatric patients to aid their return to "normality."

Endomorphs *(Sheldon)* Those persons with body types described as predominantly soft, round, and heavy set.

Equal Rights Amendment (ERA) A proposed amendment to the U.S. constitution. Its major focus is the removal of all employment inequities.

Evaluator A role in which the sociologist employs knowledge and research skills to determine the adequacy of specific programs for treating various social problems.

Evasive avoidance A response pattern of minority

groups in which they avoid situations that have a high probability of exposure to prejudice and discrimination.

Exponential growth A geometric progression in population growth (2, 4, 8, 16, 32, 64 . . .).

Extended family A family consisting of several generations of blood relatives.

External social control Those mechanisms operating outside the individual that serve to ensure conformity to group norms and others' expectations.

Family A socially sanctioned, relatively permanent grouping of people who are united by blood, marriage, or adoption ties, and who generally live together and cooperate economically.

Family functions Major family functions are: (1) socialization; (2) reproduction; (3) the care, training and protection of the young; (4) recreation; (5) provision of a basis for the economic inheritance of private property; and (6) economic production of family services and goods.

Family planning programs Organizations or projects that assist couples in the voluntary limitation of family size.

Family therapy A response to family violence based upon the idea that individual family members and their behavior cannot be understood apart from their familial environment.

Fatalistic explanations (*Feagin*) An explanation of poverty in which factors such as bad luck and illness are stressed.

Federal Emergency Relief Administration (FERA) Federal organization established in the 1930s to deal with our nation's poverty.

Fee-for-service payment A method of remuneration in which the physician receives a set fee for each specific service delivered.

Felonies More serious types of crime, such as criminal homicide, aggravated assault, and robbery.

Food chain The cyclical transfer of energy and nutrition within nature's ecosystems.

Food stamps Stamps provided by the federal government's Department of Agriculture to help the poor purchase food.

Fossil fuels Fuels (oil, coal, and natural gas) that are burned to produce energy.

Foster Grandparent Program (FGP) A program established to meet the needs of the aged in which the elderly care for children with special needs in hospitals, correctional homes, and day care centers.

Functional approach An approach to poverty that views poverty as a form of deviance, and the behavior of the poor as the reverse of what is adaptive in society.

Functionalist theory The theory that views society as a mosaic of interrelated parts or units existing for the most part in a state of harmony and cooperation. Social problems are viewed as dysfunctional for the society—they represent disruptions of the stability and order typically found within social systems.

Genetic explanation An explanation of mental illness suggesting that predispositions toward particular psychoses appear to be genetically inherited.

Genetotrophic theory The theory that alcoholism comes about through an hereditary flaw, which necessitates an exceptionally high need for a number of basic vitamins.

Geriatric Of or relating to the aged or aging.

The Great Depression The worst depression in America's history (1929).

Group method A response to violence whereby abusive parents and spouses are treated by group therapy.

Group therapy A treatment process that enables a person to achieve various degrees of insight into his or her problems and to feel more open through interaction with others.

Guaranteed annual income Referred to as a negative income tax, the guaranteed income would set an income floor for all individuals and families.

Hallucinogens Psychoactive substances that cause mild to intense distortions of visual and auditory functions. Their effects can vary considerably among users.

Harrison Act The first restrictive narcotic legislation, passed in 1914, which prohibited the sale and use of opiate substances.

Health (*World Health Organization*) A state of complete mental and physical well-being.

Health care The services necessary to maintain a state of complete mental and physical well-being.

Health care crisis The crisis in health care can be defined in terms of: (1) the growing incidence of disease conditions; (2) the growing demands by the public for adequate health care services; and (3) the broad inadequacies in health care delivery.

Health care delivery A complex accumulation of old and new social health care patterns among physicians, other health personnel, and consumers that is currently operating against our densely populated and technologically complex industrial society.

Health insurance Insurance that covers the costs of hospital care and medical and surgical services.

Health maintenance organization (HMO) Medical group-practice programs that, for a fixed annual premium, provide comprehensive medical services and hospital care to their subscribers.

Health status The following measures have been used as indicators of health status: (1) self-perceived health status; (2) the incidence and prevalence of selected diseases; and (3) measures of disability.

Heroin maintenance A British approach to narcotics addiction in which addicts are maintained on a regularly prescribed minimum dose for an extended period of time.

Heterogeneous society A society containing many different types of groups and categories of people.

Individual casework A response to family violence in which individual cases are treated.

Individualism An ideology that accounted for the slow development of humanitarian reform in the late 1800s.

Individualist explanation (*Feagin*) An explanation of poverty that places responsibility for it on the poor themselves.

Industrialization and urbanization Historians and sociologists note that with the growth of urban areas and industry, poverty in America became much more widespread and worse.

Innovation (*Merton*) The rejection of legitimate means to achieve culturally approved goals in favor of illegitimate means.

Institutionalization Treating large numbers of the chronically mentally ill in state mental hospitals.

Integration A response pattern of minority groups characterized by the minority's rejection of the idea that they are inferior. They instead attempt to integrate with members of the dominant group.

Internal social control That control developed within the person by internalizing the society's values and norms during the process of socialization.

Juvenile delinquency Illegal acts committed by people younger than eighteen years of age.

Labeling theory The theory that analyzes the social definitions of deviance along with the social reactions to, and the consequences for, those persons identified as deviant.

Labeling theory (*Scheff*) A theory that explains mental illness in terms of a label attached to people by others in society.

Laws A codified system of formalized norms or standards.

Learning perspective The perspective that sees deviant behavior as a product of learning from one's interactions with others.

Learning theory A theory that sees drug use and addiction as products of social learning.

Malthusian theory of population change This theory states that populations grow at a geometric rate (2, 4, 8, 16, . . .), whereas the means of subsistence (food) increases only arithmetically. Therefore populations ultimately exceed their food supplies and death rates rise.

Material culture The material things people create and use.

Medicaid A federal health program designed to lessen the financial burden of health care for the poor.

Medicare A federal nationwide health insurance program designed to lessen the financial burden of health care for the aged.

Medical-industrial complex The political and economic interplay between doctors, medical schools, hospitals, and health insurance and drug companies.

Medical models A model of mental illness defining it as a disease or as a behavior.

Mental health A state of mental well-being.

Mental illness A. (*Medical model*) A disorder or disease that necessitates treatment as such. B. (*Szasz*) Deviation from norms and social expectations. C. (*Scheff*) A type of learned behavior and a result of labeling.

Mesomorphs (*Sheldon*) Those persons with body types described as muscular and athletic. Sheldon claimed that mesomorphic persons were most likely to engage in criminal and delinquent behavior.

Methadone maintenance A program for the treatment of heroin addiction in which addicts are maintained on regular doses of the synthetic narcotic methadone.

Minority group (*Williams, Jr.*) Any culturally or physically distinctive and self-conscious social aggregate with hereditary membership and a high degree of endogamy that is subject to political, economic, or social discrimination by a dominant segment of a surrounding political society.

Minority group theory An explanation of agism stating that, because the aged share the common biological characteristics of old age, they experience prejudice, and other inequities.

Misdemeanors Less serious types of crime, such as petty theft and vagrancy.

Multiple Risk Factor Intervention Trial Centers (MRFIT) A new form of health delivery, which attempts to prevent heart disease among patients who have a high risk of developing heart disease. The program attempts to use a wide range of methods to modify the behavior and life-styles of these people.

"Myth" of mental illness (*Szasz*) Mental disorders are considered to be manifestations of unresolved living problems.

Narcotics Depressant drugs, in the form of opiates, such as opium and morphine, as well as synthetic narcotics, such as methadone and demerol.

National American Woman Suffrage Association (NAWSA) Women's organization that resulted from the merging of the NWSA and AWSA in 1890. Its goal was to obtain the right to vote.

National Center for Health Services Research (NCHSR) The federal research organization that has noted the following goals of a national health insurance policy: (1) assurance of access to medical care for all persons; (2) encouragement of access to early care; (3) control of rapidly rising health care costs; (4) assurance of quality care; and (5) dispersion of the uneven and unexpected burdens of large expenses for medical care over the entire population so that the burden to each citizen is small.

National health insurance A comprehensive national health insurance system with universal and mandatory coverage.

National Organization of Women (NOW) Founded in 1966, a moderate women's organization within the Women's Liberation Movement.

National Welfare Rights Organization (NWRO) An organization formed to protect the rights of welfare recipients.

National Women Suffrage Association (NWSA) Founded in 1869 by Susan B. Anthony and Eliza-

beth Stanton, this organization of women attempted to gain a wide variety of rights for women by applying pressure to the government.

Neuroses The less serious, more common forms of mental illness, which consist of excessive expressions of anxiety, unsuccessful or inadequate attempts to cope with fear, or outcomes of prolonged tension.

Neutrality A characteristic of the scientific method requiring that the researcher refrain from making personal value judgments as to the morality of the values or beliefs being studied.

New Deal Franklin D. Roosevelt's massive efforts to deal with the nation's widespread poverty of the 1930s.

Nondegradable wastes Discarded items made of modern plastics and synthetic fibers, which are largely immune to biological decomposition.

Nonmaterial culture That part of culture consisting of such elements as norms, customs, values, and beliefs.

Nonrenewable resources Resources such as minerals, metals, and fossil fuels, which were deposited in the earth in limited quantities by geological events that occurred millions of years ago.

Nontransferability The situation in which retirement credits cannot be transferred from one pension plan to another.

Norms Standards of expected behavior.

Nuclear family A family consisting of a wife and husband plus their children.

Objectivity The ability and willingness to study the subject matter of a given field without prejudice.

Old age (*Califano*) When only 4 percent of Americans were 65 or over (1900), 65 years of age was clearly old. Today, "the advance of health and life expectancies may make 65 a benchmark more arbitrary than reliable."

Old-Age, Survivors, Disability, and Health Insurance (OASDHI) Federal program that provides cash benefits to disabled or retired insured workers.

Older American's Volunteer Programs (OAVP) Federal programs that have been designed to provide meaningful work roles for the elderly.

One parent families Those families that were originally intact, with parent married to each other, that are now broken by divorce, desertion, separation, or death.

Opportunity structure perspective A perspective emphasizing the notion that deviant behavior often results from the lack of or denial to legitimate opportunities to reach societal goals.

Organic psychoses Psychoses that have physical causes, such as brain tumors.

Organized skepticism The standard of the scientific method requiring that all research and conclusions be subject to critical evaluation and verification by professional peers.

Parents Anonymous A response to family violence organized around the reliance on personal faith as well as insight and support gained by others with similar needs and experiences.

Parole The release of an offender from a correctional institution after part of the sentence has been served, with the condition that the offender remain under the custody and supervision of the institution (or another approved agency) until granted a final discharge.

Passing A response pattern of minority group members in which, because of expediency or self-hatred, an individual withdraws from the minority group and, if able, passes as a member of the dominant group.

Pension A sum of money paid on a regular basis to a person who has retired from the paid work force.

Personality explanations Explanations of prejudice stressing the idea that certain personality types are prone to prejudice.

Personality theory A theoretical explanation for drug and alcohol addiction stressing the notion that certain personality characteristics actually predispose individuals to addiction.

Positive checks *(Malthus)* Factors such as famine, disease, and war that limit population size by increasing the death rate.

Poverty The lack of money or material possessions.

Poverty cycle *(Moynihan)* The idea that low income results in poverty, which creates a cultural environment that then supresses motivation, aspirations, and a capacity to achieve.

Poverty traits *(Lewis)* The 70 traits that are characteristic of the culture of poverty.

Precision A standard of the scientific method, which demands that the scientist be as exact as possible when carrying out scientific research.

Preferences *(Fave)* The values of the poor resemble those of the middle class in terms of preferences. The level of preference indicates those values that a person prefers to realize.

Prejudice A rigid emotional attitude, belief, or predisposition to respond in a certain way toward a group of people.

President's Commission on Mental Health A commission appointed by President Carter in 1977 to examine the progress and the problems of inadequate mental health care in America.

Preventive checks *(Malthus)* Factors such as sexual abstinence, delayed marriage, and continence in marriage that limit population size by reducing the birthrate.

Probation The suspension of a sentence (conditional upon good behavior) followed by a certain period of community supervision.

Problem drinking The repeated use of alcohol that (1) exceeds customary dietary use and social customs, (2) causes physical health problems, (3) interferes with interpersonal relations, and (4) disrupts the fulfillment of economic, familial, or community obligations.

The Progressive Era A period of time at the end of the nineteenth century when various writers and intellectuals attempted to improve the plight of the poor.

Psychoactive drugs Those chemical substances that affect the user's central nervous system and thus influence mood, mind, perceptions, and emotions.

Psychological explanations Explanations of mental illness that have their basis in learning theory and Freudian psychoanalytical theory.

Psychopathological explanation An explanation of family violence stressing that the family member who abuses another family member is suffering from a psychological problem that must be eliminated to prevent further abuse. The idea of mental illness pervades this approach.

Psychoses Mental disorders that are more serious than neuroses in that there is severe impairment of mental functioning and a break with reality.

Psychosurgery The surgical removal of parts of the brain in the treatment of psychiatric patients.

Psychotherapy A major treatment process of the mentally ill in which patients are helped to understand the nature of their problem(s) and, using this knowledge, attempts are made to work out solutions.

Public service workers *(Levine)* Paraprofessionals used to extend the capacity of the health delivery system.

Racism A system of social, economic, political, and psychological activities and pressures that suppresses groups because they exhibit certain biologically determined racial characteristics.

Radical feminist One who believes that sexism's function is mainly psychological and economic.

Reinforcement theory A theoretical explanation for drug and alcohol addiction, based upon conditioned learning principles, stating that humans and other animals tend to continue in activities that cause pleasure (are positively reinforced) and will likewise tend to refrain from behaviors that cause unpleasantness, pain, or punishment.

Relative poverty line *(Fuch)* A poverty line equal to 50 percent of the median family income.

Renewable resources Resources available throughout nature in plentiful quantities that are capable of growth and/or self-replacement as long as they are not subject to rapid and excessive consumption.

Replacement level fertility The point where children are born in numbers sufficient only to replace rather than exceed the number of parents.

Residual rule breaking *(Scheff)* Forms of deviance or norm violations left over.

Retired Senior Volunteer Program (RSVP) A program in which aged volunteers provide activities for housing project and nursing home residents, shut-ins, and post-stroke victims.

Retirement The institutionalized separation of people from their occupational roles at a set age.

Retirement role The role played by an elderly person who is separated from his or her occupational role and is no longer a part of the paid labor force.

Retreatist subculture A deviant subculture involved in the consumption of drugs.

Retribution-deterrence The response to crime based on the notion that a wrongdoer should be punished in order to compensate for criminal acts. Moreover, punishment, if rationally utilized and imposed, would act to deter crime.

Revolving door The process whereby patients are continually entering and leaving mental hospitals.

Right to work The option of continuing to work beyond the age of 65.

Scapegoat theory A theory of prejudice in which minority groups become the targets, or scapegoats, for hostility. A scapegoat is a group, person, or thing that is forced to bear the blame for the misfortunes of others.

Schizophrenia The most commonly diagnosed psychoses in which the person exhibits the following symptoms: hallucinations, delusions, disturbances of language and thought, gross inefficiency, and isolation from others. These symptoms are not seen in all schizophrenics, and they are rarely all observed in a single person.

Scientific method A method of study in which a body of organized, factual, and verifiable data is obtained.

Segregation *(Allport)* An institutionalized form of discrimination, enforced legally or by common custom.

Self-fulfilling prophecy Believing a condition to be true when it is not can create the very condition not originally present.

Senior Companion Program (SCP) A program established to meet the needs of the aged, which uses the services of poor older people as a way of providing services to other aged in need.

Serial monogamy An alternative to the nuclear family pattern in which a person continues on a cycle of marriage and divorce.

Sexism A system of social, economic, political, and psychological activities and pressures that supresses groups because they exhibit certain biologically determined sexual characteristics.

Silent system A system of imprisonment also known as the "Auburn system," under which prisoners were not allowed to speak to, or even glance at, one another.

Single parent family An unwed mother or father with at least one child.

Situationalist perspective A perspective of poverty that views patterns of behavior among the poor and explains their behavior as a way of adapting to the environment.

Slavery Hereditary condition of being considered as someone's property and held in servitude without pay.

Social change Any change in the structure or social relationships of the society.

Social control The external and internal mechanisms a society uses for establishing conformity to its norms and expectations.

Social critic A role in which the sociologist presents opinions and knowledge in order to assess the adequacy of current philosophies and policies concerning major social problems. In this role some sociologists also become actively involved in the enactment of new policies and reform measures.

Social Darwinism The doctrine of social thinkers, such as Herbert Spencer and William Summner, that stressed the inevitability of poverty and the idea that society would be better off if the poor and disabled were not helped by private and/or governmental means.

Social disorganization A condition in which many of society's institutionalized norms and rules become ineffective guides for behavior. This situation is often a result of social change.

Social disorganization theory The approach that views social problems as products of social change, which necessitates adjusting and/or adapting to the new social conditions.

Social factors The relationships between social conditions (social class and occupational status, for example) and mental illness.

Social gerontology A field of study that deals with the nonphysical aspects of becoming old.

Social norms Standards of expected behavior.

Social organization A situation in which social norms, rules, and reciprocal expectations serve as effective guides for behavior.

Social problem A social situation that significant numbers of people consider to be undesirable and in need of remedy through group action.

Social problem (*Objective aspects*) Actual conditions (i.e., a rate of crime or incidence of drug abuse) that conflict with and have an adverse effect upon group needs, values, or standards of living.

Social problem (*Subjective aspects*) Peoples' awareness and definition of conditions as undesirable and in need of change.

Social reactions perspective The perspective emphasizing that deviance is really defined by social reactions to human behavior.

Socialist feminist One who believes that women's

oppression stems from the class system.

Socialization The process by which a person acquires the attitudes, beliefs, and values of his or her culture.

Social Security The major source of income for the great majority of America's aged.

Social structure and anomie theories Explanations of mental illness that link the social order of society with mental disability.

Society A relatively independent and self-perpetuating human group that occupies a particular territory and develops and shares a particular culture.

Sociocultural explanation An explanation of prejudice and violence based upon the belief that human attitudes and behavior are, to a great extent, patterned by culture and are part of its folkways and mores.

Sociology The scientific study of human interactions and their products or consequences.

Solitary system A system of imprisonment in the early nineteenth century under which each prisoner lived and worked in solitary confinement throughout the entire sentence.

Spouse abuse The intentional and nonaccidental uses of physical force or acts of omission on the part of a husband or wife that are aimed at hurting, injuring, or destroying the spouse.

Spouse shelters Community-based shelters for abused spouses (mainly women).

Stimulants Those psychoactive substances that increase the functioning of the central nervous system.

Structural explanations (*Feagin*) Explanations of poverty in which social and economic forces are blamed.

Subcultural theory The theory that explains criminal behavior on the basis of values and norms that are deviant from, and in conflict with, those of the general society.

Subcultures Groups or categories of people within society that maintain a number of distinctive values and norms distinguishing them from the wider culture.

Submissive acceptance A response pattern of minority groups characterized by their acceptance of the subordinate status imposed upon them by those in power.

Supplemental Security Income (SSI) A program established by the federal government in 1974 to help the aged, blind, and the permanently and totally disabled.

Swinging Marriage partners mutually agreeing to exchange partners for extramarital sex.

Techniques of neutralization Rationalizations developed within a delinquent subculture that permit its members to neutralize (justify) their delinquent acts.

Theory A tentative explanation of the causes of certain phenomena, such as crime, mental illness, and population growth.

Therapeutic communities Drug-free residential settings for the treatment of addiction, run mostly (if not entirely) by ex-addicts and others in the process of eliminating their drug habit.

Thermal inversion An atmospheric condition that occurs when a layer of warm air traps a layer of cooler, sometimes highly polluted air closer to the earth's surface.

Tolerance *(Fave)* The minimal level of acceptability.

Tolerance to drugs The situation in which the user requires more and more of a drug in order to get the same desired effect.

Trial marriage Living together without a marriage license.

Value conflict A situation in which certain values are incompatible.

Value-free study The quality of making observations, conducting research, and drawing conclusions in a detached and objective manner.

Value stretch perspective A perspective of poverty that views the poor as having a range of values that is wider than that of the nonpoor.

Verification process The checking of research findings by an audience of competent peers.

Vertical mobility A change of position showing a significant movement up or down in the stratification system.

Vested interest explanations The view that the dominant group (or groups) has a vested interest in another group's subordination. Prejudice becomes an instrument for defending this privilege and advantage.

Victimization studies Studies that attempt to measure the scope of crime by relying upon reports from actual victims rather than upon official law enforcement statistics.

Violence Any behavior that threatens or causes physical damage to an object or person. It can either be the product of an individual characteristic or of social interaction.

War on Poverty President Johnson's poverty program of the 1960s, which stressed providing greater opportunities to the poor.

Welfare abuses The many abuses on the part of the welfare bureaus themselves with which the poor have had to contend.

Welfare myths The many myths about the welfare poor, such as the belief that most people on welfare are readily employable.

Welfare reforms The many reforms of the late 1960s and early 1970s that eliminated welfare abuse on the part of welfare bureaus.

White House Conferences Federal responses to the problems of the aged in America.

Withdrawal A process resulting from the cessation of drug use once the body has become physically dependent on that substance.

Women's Liberation Movement A social movement of American women, which seeks to contend with the basic causes of sexual inequality. The movement has established two major goals: (1) equal job opportunity and equal pay for equal work; and (2) the Equal Rights Amendment to the U.S. Constitution.

Zero population growth A situation in which the ratio of births to deaths is balanced and population ceases to grow.

Index

Index